Mathematics and Its Applications in Science and Engineering

Mathematics and Its Applications in Science and Engineering

Editors

Araceli Queiruga-Dios
Maria Jesus Santos
Fatih Yilmaz
Deolinda M. L. Dias Rasteiro
Jesús Martín Vaquero
Víctor Gayoso Martínez

MDPI • Basel • Beijing • Wuhan • Barcelona • Belgrade • Manchester • Tokyo • Cluj • Tianjin

Editors
Araceli Queiruga-Dios
Department of Applied
Mathematics, School of
Industrial Engineering,
University of Salamanca,
Salamanca, Spain

Maria Jesus Santos
Department of Applied
Physics, Science Faculty,
University of Salamanca,
Salamanca, Spain

Fatih Yilmaz
Department of Mathematics,
Ankara Hacı Bayram
Veli University,
Çankaya/Ankara, Turkey

Deolinda M. L. Dias Rasteiro
Department of Mathematics
and Physics, Coimbra
Polytechnic—ISEC,
Coimbra, Portugal

Jesús Martín Vaquero
Department of Applied
Mathematics, Institute of
Fundamental Physics
and Mathematics,
Universidad de Salamanca,
Salamanca, Spain

Víctor Gayoso Martínez
Data Research &
Computation Group
(DRACO), Centro
Universitario de Tecnología y
Arte Digital (U-Tad),
Las Rozas de Madrid,
Madrid, Spain

Editorial Office
MDPI
St. Alban-Anlage 66
4052 Basel, Switzerland

This is a reprint of articles from the Special Issue published online in the open access journal *Mathematics* (ISSN 2227-7390) (available at: https://www.mdpi.com/journal/mathematics/special_issues/Mathematics_and_Its_Applications_in_Science_and_Engineering).

For citation purposes, cite each article independently as indicated on the article page online and as indicated below:

LastName, A.A.; LastName, B.B.; LastName, C.C. Article Title. *Journal Name* **Year**, *Volume Number*, Page Range.

ISBN 978-3-0365-5581-2 (Hbk)
ISBN 978-3-0365-5582-9 (PDF)

© 2022 by the authors. Articles in this book are Open Access and distributed under the Creative Commons Attribution (CC BY) license, which allows users to download, copy and build upon published articles, as long as the author and publisher are properly credited, which ensures maximum dissemination and a wider impact of our publications.

The book as a whole is distributed by MDPI under the terms and conditions of the Creative Commons license CC BY-NC-ND.

Contents

About the Editors vii

Preface to "Mathematics and Its Applications in Science and Engineering" ix

Araceli Queiruga-Dios, María Jesus Santos Sánchez, Fatih Yilmaz, Deolinda M. L. Dias Rasteiro, Jesús Martín-Vaquero and Víctor Gayoso Martínez
Mathematics and Its Applications in Science and Engineering
Reprinted from: *Mathematics* **2022**, *10*, 3412, doi:10.3390/math10193412 1

Norberto Urbina-Brito, María-Eusebia Guerrero-Sánchez, Guillermo Valencia-Palomo, Omar Hernández-González, Francisco-Ronay López-Estrada and José Antonio Hoyo-Montaño
A Predictive Control Strategy for Aerial Payload Transportation with an Unmanned Aerial Vehicle
Reprinted from: *Mathematics* **2021**, *9*, 1822, doi:10.3390/math9151822 3

Iskandar Waini, Anuar Ishak and Ioan Pop
Flow towards a Stagnation Region of a Curved Surface in a Hybrid Nanofluid with Buoyancy Effects
Reprinted from: *Mathematics* **2021**, *9*, 2330, doi:10.3390/math9182330 19

Mücahit AKBIYIK, Jeta ALO
On Third-Order Bronze Fibonacci Numbers
Reprinted from: *Mathematics* **2021**, *9*, 2606, doi:10.3390/math9202606 33

Ferhat Kürüz, Ali Dağdeviren and Paula Catarino
On Leonardo Pisano Hybrinomials
Reprinted from: *Mathematics* **2021**, *9*, 2923, doi:10.3390/math9222923 47

Nur Syazana Anuar, Norfifah Bachok and Ioan Pop
Influence of MHD Hybrid Ferrofluid Flow on Exponentially Stretching/Shrinking Surface with Heat Source/Sink under Stagnation Point Region
Reprinted from: *Mathematics* **2021**, *9*, 2932, doi:10.3390/math9222932 57

Natalia C. Roşca, Alin V. Roşca, Emad H. Aly and Ioan Pop
Flow and Heat Transfer Past a Stretching/Shrinking Sheet Using Modified Buongiorno Nanoliquid Model
Reprinted from: *Mathematics* **2021**, *9*, 3047, doi:10.3390/math9233047 71

Kohilavani Naganthran, Roslinda Nazar, Zailan Siri and Ishak Hashim
Entropy Analysis and Melting Heat Transfer in the Carreau Thin Hybrid Nanofluid Film Flow
Reprinted from: *Mathematics* **2021**, *9*, 3092, doi:10.3390/math9233092 83

Vicente Díaz-González, Alejandro Rojas-Palma and Marcos Carrasco-Benavides
How Does Irrigation Affect Crop Growth? A Mathematical Modeling Approach
Reprinted from: *Mathematics* **2022**, *10*, 151, doi:10.3390/math10010151 103

Lili Nemec Zlatolas, Luka Hrgarek, Tatjana Welzer and Marko Hölbl
Models of Privacy and Disclosure on Social Networking Sites: A Systematic Literature Review
Reprinted from: *Mathematics* **2022**, *10*, 146, doi:10.3390/math10010146 123

Lloyd Ling, Sai Hin Lai, Zulkifli Yusop, Ren Jie Chin and Joan Lucille Ling
Formulation of Parsimonious Urban Flash Flood Predictive Model with Inferential Statistics
Reprinted from: *Mathematics* **2022**, *10*, 175, doi:10.3390/math10020175 161

Andreas Tataris and Tristan van Leeuwen
A Regularised Total Least Squares Approach for 1D Inverse Scattering
Reprinted from: *Mathematics* **2022**, *10*, 216, doi:10.3390/math10020216 . . . . **179**

Tan Yi Liang, Nor Farhani Zakaria, Shahrir Rizal Kasjoo, Safizan Shaari, Muammar Mohamad Isa, Mohd Khairuddin Md Arshad, Arun Kumar Singh and Sharizal Ahmad Sobri
Hybrid Statistical and Numerical Analysis in Structural Optimization of Silicon-Based RF Detector in 5G Network
Reprinted from: *Mathematics* **2022**, *10*, 326, doi:10.3390/math10030326 . . . . **203**

María Teresa López-Díaz and Marta Peña
Improving Calculus Curriculum in Engineering Degrees: Implementation of Technological Applications
Reprinted from: *Mathematics* **2022**, *10*, 341, doi:10.3390/math10030341 . . . . **219**

Ola Hassan; Nahla Zakzouk; Ahmed Abdelsalam
Novel Photovoltaic Empirical Mathematical Model Based on Function Representation of Captured Figures from Commercial Panels Datasheet
Reprinted from: *Mathematics* **2022**, *10*, 476, doi:10.3390/math10030476 . . . . **239**

Antonios Charalambopoulos, Theodore Gortsas and Demosthenes Polyzos
On Representing Strain Gradient Elastic Solutions of Boundary Value Problems by Encompassing the Classical Elastic Solution
Reprinted from: *Mathematics* **2022**, *10*, 1152, doi:10.3390/math10071152 . . . . **269**

Anuar R. Giménez, Jesús Martín-Vaquero and Manuel Rodríguez-Martín
Analysis of Industrial Engineering Students' Perception after a Multiple Integrals-Based Activity with a Fourth-Year Student
Reprinted from: *Mathematics* **2022**, *10*, 1764, doi:10.3390/math10101764 . . . . **291**

Zhiqing Dang, Zhaopeng Dai, Yang Yu, Long Zhang, Ang Su, Zhihang You and Hongwei Gao
Team Control Problem in Virtual Ellipsoid and Its Numerical Simulations
Reprinted from: *Mathematics* **2022**, *10*, 1970, doi:10.3390/math10121970 . . . . **307**

Bo Li, Qi Zhang, Xue Li, Xiao-Ting He and Jun-Yi Sun
A Refined Closed-Form Solution for the Large Deflections of Alekseev-Type Annular Membranes Subjected to Uniformly Distributed Transverse Loads: Simultaneous Improvement of Out-of-Plane Equilibrium Equation and Geometric Equation
Reprinted from: *Mathematics* **2022**, *10*, 2121, doi:10.3390/math10122121 . . . . **327**

Jesús de-Prado-Gil, Osama Zaid, Covadonga Palencia and Rebeca Martínez-García
Prediction of Splitting Tensile Strength of Self-Compacting Recycled Aggregate Concrete Using Novel Deep Learning Methods
Reprinted from: *Mathematics* **2022**, *10*, 2245, doi:10.3390/math10132245 . . . . **359**

About the Editors

Araceli Queiruga-Dios

Araceli Queiruga-Dios is a graduate in Physics from the University of Salamanca (Spain), where she also obtained her PhD in Mathematics in 2006. She teaches mathematics in the Department of Applied Mathematics at the High School of Industrial Engineering of the University of Salamanca. She has participated in several research projects. She is author of several research papers and contributions to workshops and conferences. Her major fields of study include cryptography (secret, public and protocols), image processing, number theory, and the applications of mathematics to education.

Maria Jesus Santos

María Jesús Santos Sánchez holds a PhD in Physical Sciences from the Universidad de Salamanca. She is a full-time Lecturer in the Department of Applied Physics of the Faculty of Sciences at the Universidad de Salamanca—USAL (Spain). She is a member of the research group Energy Optimization, Thermodynamic and Statistical Physics. She is currently also the Vice-Dean for International Relations of the Faculty of Science USAL, member of the editorial committee of Ediciones Universidad de Salamanca, and President of the local committee of the Royal Spanish Physical Society, in Salamanca. Her current research interests include solar thermal plant optimization and physics teaching innovation. In recent years, she has participated in several projects for innovation and teacher improvement as well as European projects on teaching. The results have been published in magazines, in the form of several book chapters on educational innovation, as well as in three books. Researcher ID: E-2912-2016, Google Scholar: https://scholar.google.es/citations?user=348pp7UAAAAJ&hl=es.

Fatih Yilmaz

Fatih Yılmaz is Associate Professor of Mathematics and Vice Dean of the Faculty of Arts and Science at the Ankara Hacı Bayram Veli University in Turkey. He obtained his PhD in mathematics from Selçuk University, Turkey. His research works have been published in prestigious journals and have focused on matrix theory, graph theory, number theory, linear algebra, and combinatorics. He has published more than 40 papers and given talks at many international conferences. Additionally, he serves on the editorial board of numerous journals (such as Mathematics (MDPI), Axioms (MDPI), Entropy (MDPI), Turkish Journal of Mathematics and Computer Science) and was a partner in three projects supported by the EU.

Deolinda M. L. Dias Rasteiro

Deolinda M. L. Dias Rasteiro, Coordinator Professor, was born in Angola in 1968 but has lived in Portugal since 1974. She graduated in mathematics from the University of Coimbra in 1992 and obtained a Master in Statistics and Operations Research from the University of Lisbon in 1997 and PhD in Mathematics in Network Optimization in 2006 from the University of Aveiro. She is a Coordinator Professor at ISEC, where she served as Vice President from 2006 to 2010. She teaches Statistical Methods in the degree courses of Mechanical Engineering and Informatics, Applied Mathematics and Decision Support Methods in the master's courses in Electrical Engineering, Biomedical Engineering, and Physical Asset Management. She is currently chair of the Mathematics Special Interest Group at SEFI and co-responsible for the Mathematics Group at SPEE (Portuguese Society for Engineering Education). She has co-authored more than 60 articles in the fields of applied mathematics and education, and researching new methods to introduce mathematics to students has been her priority in recent years. She was responsible for Erasmus+ Rules_Math at IPC/ISEC, where she is also currently responsible for the Erasmus+ project: MATH-DIGGER (MATHematics DiGital Escape Rooms).

Jesús Martín Vaquero

Jesús Martín-Vaquero is Full Professor in the Department of Applied Mathematics at the University of Salamanca, Spain. He completed his BSc degree in Mathematics in the University of Salamanca (2002) and PhD (2012) in University Rey Juan Carlos (Madrid). He is co-author of over 40 papers and numerous contributions to workshops and conferences. He has also participated in numerous European, national, and regional funding projects and has also obtained some mobility grants for stays at the Universities of Milwaukee, Minnesota, Cambridge, Simon Fraser, and Salerno. He is editor of several different journals and has participated as invited editor for several special issues. His current research interests include the development of efficient numerical methods for solving nonlinear PDEs, approximation theory, and mathematical education based on projects and competencies.

Víctor Gayoso Martínez

Víctor Gayoso Martínez was born in Madrid (Spain) in 1975. He graduated in Telecommunication Engineering from the Polytechnic University of Madrid in 2002 and received his PhD degree from the same university in 2010. Since 1998, he has worked on topics related to mathematics, cryptography, smart cards, and Java technology in private companies (Telefónica), public research organizations (Spanish National Research Council, CSIC), and universities (Universidad Francisco de Vitoria and U-tad). He has published more than 25 articles in international journals and has participated in more than 45 international conferences. He currently teaches at Centro Universitario de Tecnología y Arte Digital (U-tad). He is co-author of two books on elliptic curve cryptography and cybersecurity.

Preface to "Mathematics and Its Applications in Science and Engineering"

Mathematics, which is applied in science and engineering problems, is seen as one of the most important languages and tools to address daily situations. This book contains several applications of mathematics that were presented at the II ICMASE conference (International Conference on Mathematics and its Applications in Science and Engineering) held in Salamanca (Spain) organized by the Universidad de Salamanca and the Ankara Hacı Bayram Veli Üniversitesi (Turky).

The researchers contributing to this book have extensive experience in mathematical courses and the application of mathematics in different countries.

This book is dedicated to professionals, researchers, as well as PhD and master's degree students. It covers several research topics from numerical linear algebra to approximation theory, geometry and its applications, and more. Each contribution was written by a different author or team of authors. The references also naturally supply a source of additional information about the subject of the chapter.

Araceli Queiruga-Dios, Maria Jesus Santos, Fatih Yilmaz, Deolinda M. L. Dias Rasteiro, Jesús Martín Vaquero, and Víctor Gayoso Martínez

Editors

Editorial

Mathematics and Its Applications in Science and Engineering

Araceli Queiruga-Dios [1,*], María Jesus Santos Sánchez [2], Fatih Yilmaz [3], Deolinda M. L. Dias Rasteiro [4], Jesús Martín-Vaquero [5] and Víctor Gayoso Martínez [6]

1. Department of Applied Mathematics, Higher Technical School of Industrial Engineering, Universidad de Salamanca, 37700 Béjar, Salamanca, Spain
2. Department of Applied Physics, Science Faculty, University of Salamanca, Plaza. de la Merced s/n, 37008 Salamanca, Spain
3. Department of Mathematics, Ankara Hacı Bayram Veli University, Ankara 06570, Turkey
4. Department of Mathematics and Physics, Coimbra Polytechnic—ISEC, 3045-093 Coimbra, Portugal
5. Department of Applied Mathematics, Institute of Fundamental Physics and Mathematics, Universidad de Salamanca, 37008 Salamanca, Spain
6. Data Research & Computation Group (DRACO), Centro Universitario de Tecnología y Arte Digital (U-Tad), Las Rozas de Madrid, 28290 Madrid, Spain
* Correspondence: queirugadios@usal.es

This book contains the successful submissions [1–19] of those invited to participate in a Special Issue of *Mathematics* on "Mathematics and Its Applications in Science and Engineering". These submissions were presented at the II. International Conference on Mathematics and its Applications in Science and Engineering (ICMASE), organized by the Universidad de Salamanca (Spain), which took place 1–2 July 2021.

These papers are related to new and innovative proposals for the use of mathematics in science and engineering, as well as in non-mathematical contexts; and applications of mathematics in tasks such as the use of differential equations to model structures, the shape of a machine or the growth of a population, or to ensure information security through cryptographic protocols.

Nowadays, *Mathematics* provides useful tools for engineering students, teachers, and professionals. It contains state-of-the-art research, which is of particular importance, as mathematical education has been changing and acquiring a different role in undergraduate and graduate degrees in recent years. The goal of this book, apart from its scientific contribution, is to integrate different methodologies for mathematical education.

Our call for submissions received the following response:

Submissions (40);
Publications (19);
Rejections (21);
Article types: Research Articles (19).

Published submissions are related to mathematical modelling in science and engineering applications; optimisation and control in engineering applications, complex systems modelling, stochastic models in physics and engineering, numerical methods for science and engineering applications; mathematics in engineering and scientific studies, good practices in motivating students to learn mathematics during university studies, assessing mathematics using applications and projects, and teaching and assessment methodologies in science and engineering, among other topics.

We found the selection and editorial process for the papers for this book very inspiring and rewarding. We would like to thank the editorial staff and reviewers for their efforts and help during the process.

Conflicts of Interest: The authors declare no conflict of interest.

Citation: Queiruga-Dios, A.; Santos Sánchez, M.J.; Yilmaz, F.; Dias Rasteiro, D.M.L.; Martín-Vaquero, J.; Gayoso Martínez, V. Mathematics and Its Applications in Science and Engineering. *Mathematics* **2022**, *10*, 3412. https://doi.org/10.3390/math10193412

Received: 18 July 2022
Accepted: 13 September 2022
Published: 20 September 2022

Publisher's Note: MDPI stays neutral with regard to jurisdictional claims in published maps and institutional affiliations.

Copyright: © 2022 by the authors. Licensee MDPI, Basel, Switzerland. This article is an open access article distributed under the terms and conditions of the Creative Commons Attribution (CC BY) license (https://creativecommons.org/licenses/by/4.0/).

References

1. Urbina-Brito, N.; Guerrero-Sánchez, M.; Valencia-Palomo, G.; Hernández-González, O.; López-Estrada, F.; Hoyo-Montaño, J. A Predictive Control Strategy for Aerial Payload Transportation with an Unmanned Aerial Vehicle. *Mathematics* **2021**, *9*, 1822. [CrossRef]
2. Waini, I.; Ishak, A.; Pop, I. Flow towards a Stagnation Region of a Curved Surface in a Hybrid Nanofluid with Buoyancy Effects. *Mathematics* **2021**, *9*, 2330. [CrossRef]
3. Akbiyik, M.; Alo, J. On Third-Order Bronze Fibonacci Numbers. *Mathematics* **2021**, *9*, 2606. [CrossRef]
4. Kürüz, F.; Dağdeviren, A.; Catarino, P. On Leonardo Pisano Hybrinomials. *Mathematics* **2021**, *9*, 2923. [CrossRef]
5. Anuar, N.; Bachok, N.; Pop, I. Influence of MHD Hybrid Ferrofluid Flow on Exponentially Stretching/Shrinking Surface with Heat Source/Sink under Stagnation Point Region. *Mathematics* **2021**, *9*, 2932. [CrossRef]
6. Roşca, N.; Roşca, A.; Aly, E.; Pop, I. Flow and Heat Transfer Past a Stretching/Shrinking Sheet Using Modified Buongiorno Nanoliquid Model. *Mathematics* **2021**, *9*, 3047. [CrossRef]
7. Naganthran, K.; Nazar, R.; Siri, Z.; Hashim, I. Entropy Analysis and Melting Heat Transfer in the Carreau Thin Hybrid Nanofluid Film Flow. *Mathematics* **2021**, *9*, 3092. [CrossRef]
8. Díaz-González, V.; Rojas-Palma, A.; Carrasco-Benavides, M. How Does Irrigation Affect Crop Growth? A Mathematical Modeling Approach. *Mathematics* **2022**, *10*, 151. [CrossRef]
9. Nemec Zlatolas, L.; Hrgarek, L.; Welzer, T.; Hölbl, M. Models of Privacy and Disclosure on Social Networking Sites: A Systematic Literature Review. *Mathematics* **2022**, *10*, 146. [CrossRef]
10. Ling, L.; Lai, S.; Yusop, Z.; Chin, R.; Ling, J. Formulation of Parsimonious Urban Flash Flood Predictive Model with Inferential Statistics. *Mathematics* **2022**, *10*, 175. [CrossRef]
11. Tataris, A.; van Leeuwen, T. A Regularised Total Least Squares Approach for 1D Inverse Scattering. *Mathematics* **2022**, *10*, 216. [CrossRef]
12. Yi Liang, T.; Zakaria, N.; Kasjoo, S.; Shaari, S.; Isa, M.; Arshad, M.; Singh, A.; Sobri, S. Hybrid Statistical and Numerical Analysis in Structural Optimization of Silicon-Based RF Detector in 5G Network. *Mathematics* **2022**, *10*, 326. [CrossRef]
13. López-Díaz, M.; Peña, M. Improving Calculus Curriculum in Engineering Degrees: Implementation of Technological Applications. *Mathematics* **2022**, *10*, 341. [CrossRef]
14. Hassan, O.; Zakzouk, N.; Abdelsalam, A. Novel Photovoltaic Empirical Mathematical Model Based on Function Representation of Captured Figures from Commercial Panels Datasheet. *Mathematics* **2022**, *10*, 476. [CrossRef]
15. Charalambopoulos, A.; Gortsas, T.; Polyzos, D. On Representing Strain Gradient Elastic Solutions of Boundary Value Problems by Encompassing the Classical Elastic Solution. *Mathematics* **2022**, *10*, 1152. [CrossRef]
16. Giménez, A.; Martín-Vaquero, J.; Rodríguez-Martín, M. Analysis of Industrial Engineering Students' Perception after a Multiple Integrals-Based Activity with a Fourth-Year Student. *Mathematics* **2022**, *10*, 1764. [CrossRef]
17. Dang, Z.; Dai, Z.; Yu, Y.; Zhang, L.; Su, A.; You, Z.; Gao, H. Team Control Problem in Virtual Ellipsoid and Its Numerical Simulations. *Mathematics* **2022**, *10*, 1970. [CrossRef]
18. Li, B.; Zhang, Q.; Li, X.; He, X.; Sun, J. A Refined Closed-Form Solution for the Large Deflections of Alekseev-Type Annular Membranes Subjected to Uniformly Distributed Transverse Loads: Simultaneous Improvement of Out-of-Plane Equilibrium Equation and Geometric Equation. *Mathematics* **2022**, *10*, 2121. [CrossRef]
19. De-Prado-Gil, J.; Zaid, O.; Palencia, C.; Martínez-García, R. Prediction of Splitting Tensile Strength of Self-Compacting Recycled Aggregate Concrete Using Novel Deep Learning Methods. *Mathematics* **2022**, *10*, 2245. [CrossRef]

Article

A Predictive Control Strategy for Aerial Payload Transportation with an Unmanned Aerial Vehicle

Norberto Urbina-Brito [1], María-Eusebia Guerrero-Sánchez [2], Guillermo Valencia-Palomo [1,*], Omar Hernández-González [2], Francisco-Ronay López-Estrada [3] and José Antonio Hoyo-Montaño [1]

1. Tecnológico Nacional de México-IT Hermosillo, Hermosillo, Ave. Tecnológico S/N, Hermosillo 83170, Mexico; D18331192@hermosillo.tecnm.mx (N.U.-B.); jose.hoyom@hermosillo.tecnm.mx (J.A.H.-M.)
2. Cátedras Conacyt-Tecnológico Nacional de México-IT Hermosillo, Ave. Tec. S/N, Hermosillo 83170, Mexico; maria.guerreros@hermosillo.tecnm.mx (M.-E.G.-S.); omar.hernandezg@hermosillo.tecnm.mx (O.H.-G.)
3. TURIX-Dynamics Diagnosis and Control Group, Tecnológico Nacional de México-IT Tuxtla Gutiérrez, Carr. Panam. km 1080, A.P. 599, Tuxtla Gutierrez 29050, Mexico; frlopez@ittg.edu.mx
* Correspondence: gvalencia@hermosillo.tecnm.mx; Tel.: +52-662-260-6500 (ext. 230)

Abstract: This paper presents the results of a model-based predictive control (MPC) design for a quadrotor aerial vehicle with a suspended load. Unlike previous works, the controller takes into account the hanging payload dynamics, the dynamics in three-dimensional space, and the vehicle rotation, achieving a good balance between fast stabilization times and small swing angles. The mathematical model is based on the Euler–Lagrange formulation and considers the dynamics of the vehicle, the cable, and the load. Then, the mathematical model is represented as an input-affine system to obtain the linear model for the control design. A constrained MPC strategy was designed and compared with an unconstrained MPC and an algorithm from the literature for the case of study. The constraints to be considered include the limits on the swing angles and the quadrotor position. The constrained control algorithm was constructed to stabilize the aerial vehicle. It aims to track a trajectory reference while attenuating the load swing, considering a maximum swing range of $\pm 10°$. Numerical simulations were carried out to validate the control strategy.

Keywords: unmanned aerial vehicle; predictive control; optimal control; suspended load; constraints

1. Introduction

In recent years, the development of aerial robotics has been rapid via both scientific and commercial research, since the use of these autonomous systems is now not restricted to the military field. The versatility of unmanned aerial vehicles (UAVs), together with recent technological advances, has allowed the development of new devices that have a higher degree of autonomy; hence, they considered for different types of applications, mainly in those where the user's safety may be compromised or where the areas of interest are difficult to access. The transport of a load suspended by a cable is one of the most common activities with unmanned aerial vehicles. The modeling and design of control strategies for these systems is a topic that has attracted the attention of researchers in recent decades; this is because there is a variety of tasks where fast and efficient handling of a load is required, which leads to aggressive movements that generate oscillations in the load that when not controlled can cause accidents. The works focused on the use of UAVs for payload transport are relatively recent [1].

There are several devices reported in the literature that are used to attach a load to such a vehicle. For example, in [2,3] a clamp-type mechanical device with only one degree of freedom that keeps the load attached to the structure of the UAV was used. In [4] the use of a manipulator with a robotic arm was mentioned. In these configurations, the load is closer to the vehicle's center of gravity, which causes increases in weight and rotational inertia that affect the maneuverability of the vehicle in flight. Another approach, which is widely used in transportation, consists of suspending the payload through a rope or cable connected directly to the vehicle's structure, allowing fast and agile movements. This approach adds degrees of freedom to the system, and a swinging motion of the payload that acts as a pendulum that can transmit oscillations through the cable and negatively affect the operations and stability of the vehicle in flight [5].

In the literature, different control strategies have been proposed to address the general problem of transporting a payload suspended by a cable from a UAV. For example, in [6] the effect of dynamic load disturbances introduced by instantaneously increased load mass and how those affect UAVs under PID flight control was studied. Ref. [7] introduced the use of dynamic programming to generate an optimal trajectory and adaptive control for maneuvering without swinging effects. Ref. [8] presented a nonlinear dynamic model and two IDA-PBC control algorithms for a quadrotor with a cable-suspended payload that explicitly incorporate total energy-shaping; however, the vehicle travels only in the x–z plane and then in the y–z plane to achieve control in three-dimensional space. Additionally, ref. [9] proposed a mathematical model of the interconnected multi-body system using Kane's equations and a tracking controller based on the backstepping technique. Ref. [10] considered a hierarchical scheme combining energy-based control (translational dynamics) and a nonlinear state feedback controller based on a linear matrix inequality (rotational dynamics) to solve the problem of transporting a cable-suspended payload by a UAV. Meanwhile, in [11] two novel nonlinear control algorithms for controlling a quadcopter's position and attenuating the swing angle of the payload were designed. The controllers take advantage of the natural coupling existing between the horizontal quadcopter movement and the payload oscillation; however, the vehicle only travels in one plane at a time. Ref. [12] shows a nonlinear control approach with an elaborately constructed integral term for an aerial transportation systems. This method achieves satisfactory anti-swing and positioning performance and reduces steady errors during real flight. A model of a quadrotor with a suspended payload was derived in [13]. The hierarchical control structure of inner-loop attitude and outer-loop position using PID was adopted in the design of trajectory tracking of the quadrotor transporting a payload. Ref. [14] presents a quadrotor with the payload connected to the vehicle through a cable. The payload swing is rejected by using a nonlinear controller based on a system model derived using the Euler–Lagrange equations. However, the payload is considered a disturbance. Ref. [15] presents a model and a proportional-derivative control of a quadrotor with payload uncertainties; the payload is also considered a disturbance. A mathematical model of the payload and quadrotor was presented in [16] through the Euler–Lagrange formulation. In addition, a robust sliding mode control was designed for the transitional movements to cope with both disturbances such as wind, and payload swings. Ref. [17] proposes an adaptive control technique to control the velocity of a volumetric payload with unknown mass, which is transported by a quadrotor in the presence of rotor down-wash.

Optimal control techniques have also been applied. For example, ref. [18] developed an iterative linear quadratic regulator (iLQR) optimal strategy of a mathematical model for a quadrotor with a cable-suspended heavy rigid body. The algorithm considers an anti-swinging load in a transporting task; however, the stabilization times are very long compared to the results of works found in the literature and to those obtained in the present article. Reference [19] explores a trajectory planning method based on predictive control for a quadrotor with a suspended payload. The authors contemplated the anti-swing and obstacle avoidance in the flight path. However, this research did not consider the rotational dynamics of the vehicle and treated the quadrotor as a three-dimensional overhead crane. Moreover, ref. [20] presented a linear quadratic Gaussian control method for a quadrotor transporting an unknown suspended load: the load parameters were unknown, and the load state was not available. This paper also did not consider the rotational dynamics of the vehicle. Reference [21] presents a cascade control strategy with anti-disturbance functionality and a predictive optimal function to control the rotation of a quadrotor carrying unknown payloads. However, the translational control was not realized and the payload was considered a disturbance.

The primary mission of aerial transportation is to maintain the hanging load within the desired operating and safety limits. Therefore, the prime aim is to design control algorithms that ensure minimal swing angles without sacrificing response times. However, some works listed above presented swing angles between ±12° and ±35°, or in order to achieve small angles, they employed very conservative control laws, resulting in long settling times—e.g., [18,22]. Thus, motivated by the previous works—where the authors dealt with the hanging payload transportation problem by (i) considering the payload as a disturbance; (ii) including the payload dynamics, but considering only a longitudinal translation of the UAV; (iii) considering three-dimensional dynamics but neglecting the rotation of the vehicle; or (iv) reducing the payload swing by sacrificing performance—in this paper, we offer an alternative approach to stabilize a quadrotor transporting a payload by using a predictive control strategy. Here, the quadrotor-payload system model includes the hanging payload dynamics, and the predictive controller considers both the system's translation dynamics in three-dimensional space and the vehicle's rotation. Constraints on the load swing angles are to keep the vehicle transporting a load within the desired operating and safety limits. Considering constraints on the quadrotor positioning in x and y allows one to avoid overshoot in the transient responses of this positioning and thus to evade further oscillations of the load angles. Predictive control was chosen for its inherent ability to handle constraints on the system's output, which are applied to restrict the maximum swing angle of the load, guaranteeing the safe flight of the aircraft. An additional contribution of this work is the linear model representation of the quadrotor-payload system used in the design of the model-based predictive control (MPC) strategy; although a modest contribution on its own, it is valuable within the controller design methodology. Moreover, as evidenced in the results section, this strategy achieves a good balance between fast stabilization times and small swing angles.

The article is organized as follows: Section 2 describes the nonlinear model of the quadrotor with the suspended load; in the same section, the linearized model used for the controller design is presented. Section 3 introduces the theoretical basis of the predictive controller. Section 4 shows the numerical results obtained. Section 5 presents the conclusions and future work. Finally, due to the many of variables used, the nomenclature is summarized in Appendix A.

2. Dynamic Model

This section aims to present the dynamic model that describes the complete system, including the coupling problem between the load suspended by means of a cable and the aerial vehicle as an integral problem and not as a disturbance. For this purpose, the following assumptions are made:

(a) The multi-rotor fuselage is considered rigid and symmetrical.
(b) The cable that connects to the load is attached to the center of mass of the air vehicle.
(c) The cable is considered rigid, inelastic, and massless. Its length is constant and is known.
(d) The payload is considered to be a point-mass.
(e) Aerodynamic effects on the load are neglected.

Consider a quadcopter type multirotor vehicle evolving in three dimensions, capable of carrying a suspended payload by means of a cable as shown in Figure 1. The inertial coordinate system fixed to ground is represented by $\{O\}$ and the body-fixed frame is defined by $\{B\}$.

The generalized coordinates of the model can be written as:

$$q = \begin{bmatrix} \xi & \eta & \mu \end{bmatrix}^T \in \mathbb{R}^8 \tag{1}$$

where $\zeta = \begin{bmatrix} x & y & z \end{bmatrix}^T \in \mathbb{R}^3$ represents linear positions and $\eta = \begin{bmatrix} \psi & \theta & \phi \end{bmatrix}^T \in \mathbb{R}^3$ represents angular positions of the vehicle. $\mu = \begin{bmatrix} \alpha & \beta \end{bmatrix}^T \in \mathbb{R}^2$ represents the oscillation angles of the suspended load. l is the length of the cable, d is the distance between the motors and the center of mass, the gravitational acceleration constant is represented by g, the mass of the quadrotor is defined by M, and the payload is m. The vector of control inputs is represented by $u = \begin{bmatrix} u_1 & \tau \end{bmatrix}^T \in \mathbb{R}^4$, where $u_1 = f_{P1} + f_{P2} + f_{P3} + f_{P4}$ is the total propulsive force and $\tau = \begin{bmatrix} \tau_\psi & \tau_\theta & \tau_\phi \end{bmatrix}^T$ are the input torques.

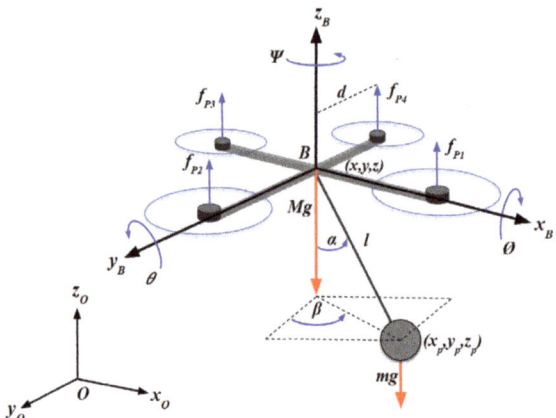

Figure 1. Three-dimensional quadrotor with a cable-suspended payload.

2.1. Euler–Lagrange Methodology

The Euler–Lagrange equations of motion represent an adequate and convenient analytical method to obtain the dynamic model of the system. Their mathematical structure allows one to analyze and study in detail all the physical phenomena of the plant quadrotor-payload, since the dynamic nature of the system is highly nonlinear, underactuated, and multivariable, and the subsystems are strongly coupled.

The Euler–Lagrange formulation is based on the energy of the system; therefore, the kinetic energy has to be calculated as the potential energy to obtain the Lagrangian of the system. The total kinetic energy $T_{QSP}(\dot{q})$ of the plant is represented by the following expression:

$$T_{QSP}(\dot{q}) = \underbrace{\frac{1}{2}M\dot{\zeta}^T\dot{\zeta} + \frac{1}{2}\dot{\eta}^T J \dot{\eta}}_{Quadrotor} + \underbrace{\frac{1}{2}m\dot{\zeta}_p^T\dot{\zeta}_p + \frac{1}{2}I_p(\dot{\alpha}^2 + \dot{\beta}^2)}_{Payload} \quad (2)$$

where J is the inertia matrix and I_p contains the mass moments of inertia of the payload. The positions relative to the center of the load in Cartesian coordinates are described by:

$$\zeta_p = \zeta + lr, \quad (3)$$

where $\zeta_p = \begin{bmatrix} x_p & y_p & z_p \end{bmatrix}^T$ and $r = \begin{bmatrix} s_\alpha c_\beta & s_\alpha s_\beta & -c_\alpha \end{bmatrix}^T$, to simplify the presentation, we have used the short notation $s_\alpha = sin(\alpha)$ and $c_\alpha = cos(\alpha)$. The potential energy is due to the position or the configuration of the body with respect to a reference frame, so the total potential energy is described by:

$$V(q) = Mgz + mg(z - lc_\alpha) \quad (4)$$

The Lagrangian L, which is what we are interested in calculating, is obtained by subtracting the kinetic energy T_{QSP} from the potential energy $V(q)$, as shown in the following expression:

$$L = \frac{1}{2}M\dot{\xi}^T\dot{\xi} + \frac{1}{2}\dot{\eta}^T J\dot{\eta} + \frac{1}{2}m\dot{\xi}_p^T\dot{\xi}_p + \frac{1}{2}I_p(\dot{\alpha}^2 + \dot{\beta}^2) - Mgz - mg(z - lc_\alpha) \quad (5)$$

By applying the Euler–Lagrange formulation,

$$\frac{d}{dt}\left(\frac{\partial L}{\partial \dot{q}}\right) - \left(\frac{\partial L}{\partial q}\right) = Bu, \quad (6)$$

we obtain the non-linear model of the quadrotor system with a suspended load by means of a cable represented by the following equations:

$$\ddot{x} = u_1((s_\phi s_\psi + c_\phi c_\psi s_\theta) - (mlc_\alpha\ddot{\alpha} + lms_\alpha\dot{\alpha}^2))/(m+M); \quad (7)$$

$$\ddot{y} = u_1((c_\phi s_\theta s_\psi - c_\psi s_\phi) - (mlc_\beta\ddot{\beta} + lms_\beta\dot{\beta}^2))/(m+M); \quad (8)$$

$$\ddot{z} = (u_1(c_\theta c_\phi) - (m+M)g - ml(s_\alpha c_\beta\ddot{\alpha} - ml(s_\beta c_\alpha\ddot{\beta} - ml\dot{\beta}^2 c_\alpha - ml\dot{\beta}^2 c_\beta + 2Mls_\beta s_\alpha\dot{\alpha}\dot{\beta})))/(m+M); \quad (9)$$

$$\ddot{\psi} = (\tau_\psi - \ddot{\theta}(I_y I_z c_\theta s_\phi c_\phi c_\theta s_\phi c_\phi) + I_x\dot{\phi}s_\theta - \dot{\psi}(I_x\dot{\theta}s_\theta c_\theta + I_y(-\dot{\theta}s_\theta c_\theta s_\phi^2 + \dot{\phi}c_\theta^2 s_\phi c_\phi) - I_z(\dot{\theta}s_\theta c_\theta c_\phi^2 + \dot{\phi}s_\phi c_\phi c_\theta^2)$$
$$-\dot{\theta}(I_x\dot{\psi}s_\theta c_\theta - I_y(\dot{\theta}s_\theta s_\phi c_\phi + \dot{\phi}c_\theta s_\phi^2 - \dot{\phi}c_\theta c_\phi^2 + \dot{\psi}s_\theta c_\theta s_\phi^2) + I_z(\dot{\phi}c_\theta s_\phi^2 - \dot{\phi}c_\theta c_\phi^2 - \dot{\psi}s_\theta c_\theta c_\phi^2 + \dot{\theta}s_\theta s_\phi c_\phi))$$
$$+ \dot{\phi}(I_x\dot{\theta}c_\theta - I_y\dot{\psi}c_\theta^2 s_\phi c_\phi + I_z\dot{\psi}c_\theta^2 s_\phi c_\phi))/(I_x s_\theta^2 + I_y c_\theta^2 s_\phi^2 + I_z c_\theta^2 c_\phi^2); \quad (10)$$

$$\ddot{\theta} = (\tau_\theta - \ddot{\psi}(I_y c_\theta s_\phi c_\phi - I_z c_\theta s_\phi c_\phi) - \dot{\psi}(-I_x\dot{\psi}s_\theta c_\theta + I_y\dot{\psi}s_\theta c_\theta s_\phi + I_z\dot{\psi}s_\theta c_\theta(c_\phi)^2) + \dot{\theta}(I_y\dot{\phi}s_\phi c_\phi - I_z\dot{\phi}s_\phi c_\phi)$$
$$-\dot{\phi}(I_x\dot{\psi}c_\theta + I_y(-\dot{\theta}s_\phi c_\phi + \dot{\phi}c_\theta c_\phi^2 - \dot{\psi}c_\theta s_\phi^2) + I_z(\dot{\psi}c_\theta s_\phi^2 - \dot{\psi}c_\theta c_\phi^2) + \dot{\theta}s_\phi c_\phi) + \dot{\theta}(I_y\dot{\phi}s_\phi c_\phi - I_z\dot{\phi}s_\phi c_\phi))/(I_y c_\phi^2 + I_z s_\phi^2); \quad (11)$$

$$\ddot{\phi} = (\tau_\phi + \ddot{\psi}I_x s_\theta + \dot{\psi}(I_y\dot{\psi}c_\theta^2 s_\phi c_\phi - I_z\dot{\psi}s_\phi c_\phi c_\theta^2 - \dot{\theta}(-I_x\dot{\psi}c_\theta + I_y(\dot{\theta}s_\phi c_\phi + \dot{\phi}c_\theta s_\phi^2 - \dot{\phi}c_\theta c_\phi^2) - I_z(\dot{\psi}c_\theta s_\phi^2 - \dot{\psi}c_\theta c_\phi^2 + \dot{\theta}s_\phi c_\phi))))/(I_x); \quad (12)$$

$$\ddot{\alpha} = (-mlc_\alpha\ddot{x} - mlc_\beta s_\alpha\ddot{z} - ml^2 c_\alpha c_\beta s_\alpha s_\beta\ddot{\beta} - gmls_\alpha c_\beta + ml^2\dot{\alpha}^2 c_\alpha s_\alpha - ml^2 c_\beta^2 s_\alpha c_\alpha\dot{\alpha}^2$$
$$+ 2ml^2 s_\alpha^2 c_\beta s_\beta\dot{\alpha}\dot{\beta} - ml^2 c_\beta^2 s_\alpha c_\alpha\dot{\beta}^2)/(ml^2(c_\alpha^2 + c_\beta^2 c_\alpha^2) + I_p); \quad (13)$$

$$\ddot{\beta} = (-mlc_\beta\ddot{y} - mlc_\alpha s_\beta\ddot{z} - ml^2 c_\alpha c_\beta s_\alpha s_\beta\ddot{\alpha} - gmls_\beta c_\alpha + ml^2\dot{\beta}^2 c_\beta s_\alpha - ml^2 c_\alpha^2 s_\beta c_\beta\dot{\beta}^2$$
$$+ 2ml^2 s_\beta^2 c_\alpha s_\alpha\dot{\alpha}\dot{\beta} - ml^2 c_\alpha^2 s_\beta c_\beta\dot{\alpha}^2)/(ml^2(c_\beta^2 + c_\beta^2 c_\alpha^2) + I_p). \quad (14)$$

In the previous expressions, I_x, I_y, and I_z represented the inertias of the quadrotor, and I_p represented the inertia of the suspended load.

2.2. Linear Model

In this subsection, the equations of motion of the quadrotor with a suspended load are linearized around the equilibrium points considering the state vector $\chi = [x\ \dot{x}\ y\ \dot{y}\ z\ \dot{z}\ \psi\ \dot{\psi}\ \theta\ \dot{\theta}\ \phi\ \dot{\phi}\ \alpha\ \dot{\alpha}\ \beta\ \dot{\beta}]^T$ and the output vector $y_c = [x\ y\ z\ \psi\ \theta\ \phi\ \alpha\ \beta]^T$. In order to determine them, the system is considered to be fixed in an equilibrium coordinate; i.e., the UAV is in a hover position. There is also an assumption of smooth movements, so the rotation and swing angles are relatively small. The translational and rotational system of the quadrotor with suspended load is linearized around the equilibrium point:

$$\chi_{eq} = [x_{eq}\ 0\ y_{eq}\ 0\ z_{eq}\ 0\ 0\ 0\ 0\ 0\ 0\ 0\ 0\ 0\ 0\ 0]^T, \quad (15)$$

and for control inputs:

$$u_{eq} = [(m+M)g\ 0\ 0\ 0]^T. \quad (16)$$

Then, equations can be represented in state space as follows:

$$\dot{\chi} = A_c \chi + B_c u$$
$$y_c = C_c \chi \tag{17}$$

By means of the Taylor series expansion and evaluating the equilibrium point, the linear model (17) is obtained with:

$$A_c = \begin{bmatrix} 0 & 1 & 0 & 0 & 0 & 0 & 0 & 0 & 0 & 0 & 0 & 0 & 0 & 0 & 0 & 0 \\ 0 & 0 & 0 & 0 & 0 & 0 & 0 & 0 & a_{2,9} & 0 & 0 & 0 & a_{2,13} & 0 & 0 & 0 \\ 0 & 0 & 0 & 1 & 0 & 0 & 0 & 0 & 0 & 0 & 0 & 0 & 0 & 0 & 0 & 0 \\ 0 & 0 & 0 & 0 & 0 & 0 & 0 & 0 & 0 & 0 & a_{4,11} & 0 & 0 & 0 & a_{4,15} & 0 \\ 0 & 0 & 0 & 0 & 0 & 1 & 0 & 0 & 0 & 0 & 0 & 0 & 0 & 0 & 0 & 0 \\ 0 & 0 & 0 & 0 & 0 & 0 & 0 & 0 & 0 & 0 & 0 & 0 & 0 & 0 & 0 & 0 \\ 0 & 0 & 0 & 0 & 0 & 0 & 0 & 1 & 0 & 0 & 0 & 0 & 0 & 0 & 0 & 0 \\ 0 & 0 & 0 & 0 & 0 & 0 & 0 & 0 & 0 & 0 & 0 & 0 & 0 & 0 & 0 & 0 \\ 0 & 0 & 0 & 0 & 0 & 0 & 0 & 0 & 0 & 1 & 0 & 0 & 0 & 0 & 0 & 0 \\ 0 & 0 & 0 & 0 & 0 & 0 & 0 & 0 & 0 & 0 & 0 & 0 & 0 & 0 & 0 & 0 \\ 0 & 0 & 0 & 0 & 0 & 0 & 0 & 0 & 0 & 0 & 0 & 1 & 0 & 0 & 0 & 0 \\ 0 & 0 & 0 & 0 & 0 & 0 & 0 & 0 & 0 & 0 & 0 & 0 & 0 & 0 & 0 & 0 \\ 0 & 0 & 0 & 0 & 0 & 0 & 0 & 0 & 0 & 0 & 0 & 0 & 0 & 1 & 0 & 0 \\ 0 & 0 & 0 & 0 & 0 & 0 & 0 & 0 & a_{14,9} & 0 & 0 & 0 & a_{14,13} & 0 & 0 & 0 \\ 0 & 0 & 0 & 0 & 0 & 0 & 0 & 0 & 0 & 0 & 0 & 0 & 0 & 0 & 0 & 1 \\ 0 & 0 & 0 & 0 & 0 & 0 & 0 & 0 & 0 & 0 & a_{16,11} & 0 & 0 & 0 & a_{16,15} & 0 \end{bmatrix}; \tag{18}$$

$$B_c = \begin{bmatrix} 0 & 0 & 0 & 0 & 0 & \frac{1}{M+m} & 0 & 0 & 0 & 0 & 0 & 0 & 0 & 0 & 0 & 0 \\ 0 & 0 & 0 & 0 & 0 & 0 & 0 & \frac{1}{I_z} & 0 & 0 & 0 & 0 & 0 & 0 & 0 & 0 \\ 0 & 0 & 0 & 0 & 0 & 0 & 0 & 0 & 0 & \frac{1}{I_y} & 0 & 0 & 0 & 0 & 0 & 0 \\ 0 & 0 & 0 & 0 & 0 & 0 & 0 & 0 & 0 & 0 & 0 & \frac{1}{I_x} & 0 & 0 & 0 & 0 \end{bmatrix}^T; \tag{19}$$

$$C_c = \begin{bmatrix} 1 & 0 & 0 & 0 & 0 & 0 & 0 & 0 & 0 & 0 & 0 & 0 & 0 & 0 & 0 \\ 0 & 0 & 1 & 0 & 0 & 0 & 0 & 0 & 0 & 0 & 0 & 0 & 0 & 0 & 0 \\ 0 & 0 & 0 & 0 & 1 & 0 & 0 & 0 & 0 & 0 & 0 & 0 & 0 & 0 & 0 \\ 0 & 0 & 0 & 0 & 0 & 0 & 1 & 0 & 0 & 0 & 0 & 0 & 0 & 0 & 0 \\ 0 & 0 & 0 & 0 & 0 & 0 & 0 & 0 & 1 & 0 & 0 & 0 & 0 & 0 & 0 \\ 0 & 0 & 0 & 0 & 0 & 0 & 0 & 0 & 0 & 0 & 1 & 0 & 0 & 0 & 0 \\ 0 & 0 & 0 & 0 & 0 & 0 & 0 & 0 & 0 & 0 & 0 & 0 & 1 & 0 & 0 \\ 0 & 0 & 0 & 0 & 0 & 0 & 0 & 0 & 0 & 0 & 0 & 0 & 0 & 0 & 1 & 0 \end{bmatrix}; \tag{20}$$

where $a_{2,9} = g(2l^2m^2 + Ml^2m + I_pm + I_pM)/(M+m)(ml^2 + I_p)$; $a_{4,11} = -g(2l^2m^2 + Ml^2m + I_pm + I_pM/(M+m)(ml^2 + I_p)$, $a_{2,13} = a_{4,15} = gl^2m^2(2l^2m^2 + Ml^2m + I_pm + I_pM)/(M+m)^2/(ml^2+I_p)^2$; $a_{14,9} = -glm(2l^2m^2 + Ml^2m + I_pm + I_pM)/(M+m)(ml^2 + I_p)^2 = a_{14,13} = a_{16,11}$; $a_{16,15} = -glm(2l^2m^2 + Ml^2m + I_pm + I_pM)/(M+m)(ml^2 + I_p)^2$.

3. Model-Based Predictive Control

Predictive control makes explicit use of a model of the plant to predict the output of the process in future instants, and based on the minimization of a cost function, a strategy is proposed to obtain the optimal control signal. The minimization of the cost function can be obtained explicitly if the model is linear and there are no constraints; otherwise, an iterative optimization method must be used.

3.1. State Space Model and Input Increments

The behavior of the plant considering the system in discrete-time without disturbances and without measurement errors with n states, l outputs, and m inputs can be described by the following model in state space:

$$\begin{aligned} x_{k+1} &= A_d x_k + B_d u_k \\ y_k &= C_d x_k \end{aligned} \quad (21)$$

where $x_{k+1} \equiv x(k+1)$, $x_k \in \mathbb{R}^n$ represents the sate vector, $y_k \in \mathbb{R}^l$ the output vector, $u_k \in \mathbb{R}^m$ the input vector, and k the time-step. For convenience, the increment in the control signal is considered an input variable as follows:

$$\Delta u_k = u_k - u_{k-1} \quad (22)$$

resulting in an augmented plant model:

$$\begin{aligned} \zeta_{k+1} &= A_\zeta \zeta_k + B_\zeta \Delta u_k \\ y_k &= C_\zeta \zeta_k \end{aligned} \quad (23)$$

where

$$\zeta_{k+1} = \begin{bmatrix} x_{k+1} \\ u_k \end{bmatrix}; \quad A_\zeta = \begin{bmatrix} A_d & B_d \\ 0 & I \end{bmatrix}; \quad B_\zeta = \begin{bmatrix} B_d \\ I \end{bmatrix}; \quad C_\zeta = \begin{bmatrix} C_d & 0 \end{bmatrix}.$$

3.2. Predictions

The future evolution of the states can be calculated by iterating over the model (23):

$$\underbrace{\begin{bmatrix} \zeta_{k+1} \\ \zeta_{k+2} \\ \zeta_{k+3} \\ \vdots \\ \zeta_{k+n_y} \end{bmatrix}}_{\overrightarrow{\zeta}_k} = \underbrace{\begin{bmatrix} A_\zeta \\ A_\zeta^2 \\ A_\zeta^3 \\ \vdots \\ A_\zeta^{n_y} \end{bmatrix}}_{P_{\zeta\zeta}} \zeta_k + \underbrace{\begin{bmatrix} B_\zeta & 0 & \cdots & 0 \\ A_\zeta B_\zeta & B_\zeta & \cdots & 0 \\ A_\zeta^2 B_\zeta & A_\zeta B_\zeta & \cdots & B_\zeta \\ \vdots & \vdots & \ddots & \vdots \\ A_\zeta^{n_y-1} B_\zeta & A_\zeta^{n_y-2} B_\zeta & \cdots & A_\zeta^{n_y-n_u} B_\zeta \end{bmatrix}}_{P_{\zeta\Delta u}} \underbrace{\begin{bmatrix} \Delta u_k \\ \Delta u_{k+1} \\ \vdots \\ \Delta u_{k+n_u-1} \end{bmatrix}}_{\overrightarrow{\Delta u}_{k-1}} \quad (24)$$

where the arrow notation denotes prediction and is defined as $\overrightarrow{x}_k = \begin{bmatrix} x_{k+1}^T & x_{k+2}^T & \cdots \end{bmatrix}^T$. n_y is the prediction horizon and n_u the control horizon—it is generally chosen by $n_u \leq n_y$. The state predictions can be obtained by extracting them from the augmented states:

$$\overrightarrow{x}_k = \underbrace{diag(\begin{bmatrix} I & 0 \end{bmatrix})}_{P_{x\zeta}} \overrightarrow{\zeta}_k. \quad (25)$$

By substituting the state prediction into the output equation, the output predictions can be obtained:

$$\overrightarrow{y}_k = P_{y\zeta} \zeta_k + P_{y\Delta u} \overrightarrow{\Delta u}_{k-1}, \quad (26)$$

where $P_{y\zeta} = diag(C) P_{\zeta\zeta}$ and $P_{y\Delta u} = diag(C) P_{\zeta\Delta u}$.

Finally, the input predictions are

$$\vec{u}_{k-1} = \underbrace{\begin{bmatrix} I & 0 & \cdots & 0 \\ I & I & \cdots & 0 \\ \vdots & \vdots & \ddots & \vdots \\ I & I & \cdots & I \end{bmatrix}}_{P_{u\Delta u}} \vec{\Delta u}_{k-1} + \underbrace{col\left(\begin{bmatrix} 0 & I \end{bmatrix}\right)}_{P_{u\zeta}} \zeta_k. \qquad (27)$$

Our paper adopts an independent model approach to prediction [23,24]. Then, by defining $\hat{y}_k$ as the output vector of the independent model (given by simulating model (21) in parallel with the plant), the model's residual estimate is $\hat{d}_k = y_k - \hat{y}_k$ and it is assumed to be constant over the prediction horizon. This value is subtracted from the reference to compensate for disturbances or model mismatches.

3.3. Cost Function

The most common cost function for obtaining the control law consists of penalizing the squared errors multiplied by a weight, that is, penalizing the difference between the reference minus the squared output plus the control effort multiplied by a weight, along a prediction and control horizon. The general expression of this function is:

$$J_{MPC} = \sum_{i=1}^{n_y} (y_{k+i} - \hat{r})^T Q (y_{k+i} - \hat{r}) + \sum_{i=0}^{n_u-1} \Delta u_{k+i}^T R \Delta u_{k+i} \qquad (28)$$

Q and R are tuning parameters that impact future behavior and $\hat{r}$ is the setpoint. By substituting the model of the predictions within the objective function by differentiating and setting it to zero, the optimal control sequence is obtained:

$$\vec{\Delta u}_{k-1}^* = -\left(P_{y\Delta u}^T diag(Q) P_{y\Delta u} + diag(R)\right)^{-1} P_{y\Delta u}^T diag(Q) \left(P_{y\zeta} \zeta_k - \vec{\hat{r}}\right) \qquad (29)$$

where $*$ denotes optimality. Additionally, the control input u_k is formed by adding to the previous input u_{k-1}, the first element of $\vec{\Delta u}_{k-1}^*$—that is, Δu_{k-1}^*.

3.4. The Constrained MPC Algorithm

Constraints help to keep the process within desired operating limits or conditions. Constraints have to be fulfilled for all the prediction horizon:

$$diag(A_x) \vec{x}_k \leq col(b_x); \quad diag(A_y) \vec{y}_k \leq col(b_y);$$
$$diag(A_u) \vec{u}_{k-1} \leq col(b_u); \quad diag(A_{\Delta u}) \vec{\Delta u}_{k-1} \leq col(b_{\Delta u}). \qquad (30)$$

where $A_x, A_y, A_u, A_{\Delta u} = [I, -I]^T$ and $b_x, b_y, b_u, b_{\Delta u}$ are vectors that contain the maximum and minimum values allowed in the form $[max \ min]^T$.

The cost function (28) and constraints (30) can be expressed in terms of the desicion variable $\vec{\Delta u}_{k-1}$, and the following quadratic programming optimization problem is obtained:

$$\vec{\Delta u}_{k-1}^* = \arg\min_{\vec{\Delta u}_{k-1}} \left\{ \frac{1}{2} \vec{\Delta u}_{k-1}^T \left(P_{y\Delta u}^T diag(Q) P_{y\Delta u} + diag(R)\right) \vec{\Delta u}_{k-1} + \left(P_{y\Delta u} diag(Q)(P_{y\zeta}\zeta_k - \vec{\hat{r}}_k)\right)^T \vec{\Delta u}_{k-1} \right\} \qquad (31)$$

$$\text{s.t.} \quad \underbrace{\begin{bmatrix} diag(A_x) P_{x\zeta} P_{\zeta\Delta u} \\ diag(A_y) P_{\zeta\Delta u} \\ diag(A_u) P_{u\Delta u} \\ diag(A_{\Delta u}) \end{bmatrix}}_{M_a} \vec{\Delta u}_{k-1} \leq \underbrace{\begin{bmatrix} col(b_x) \\ col(b_y) \\ col(b_u) \\ col(b_{\Delta u}) \end{bmatrix} - \begin{bmatrix} diag(A_x) P_{x\zeta} P_{\zeta\zeta} \\ diag(A_y) P_{y\zeta} \\ diag(A_u) P_{u\zeta} \\ 0 \end{bmatrix}}_{q_a(\zeta_k)} \qquad (32)$$

and the control law is:

$$u_k = u_{k-1} + \Delta u_k^*, \quad (33)$$

where Δu_k^* is the first element of $\underline{\Delta u}_{k-1}^*$.

3.5. MPC for a Quadrotor with a Suspended Load

This subsection presents the design and configuration with to implement the predictive control algorithm for a quadrotor carrying a suspended load. We start from a continuous state space model representation (17) to obtain a discretized and augmented version of the system (23) represented by the matrices $A_\zeta \in \mathbb{R}^{20 \times 20}$, $B_\zeta \in \mathbb{R}^{20 \times 4}$ and $C_\zeta \in \mathbb{R}^{8 \times 20}$ that are used to calculate the prediction matrices $P_{\zeta\zeta}, P_{\zeta\Delta u}, P_{y\zeta}, P_{y\Delta u}, P_{x,\zeta}, P_{u,\Delta u}, P_{u,\zeta}$ to form the unconstrained control law (29) and the optimization problem (31) and (32) for the constrained case. To solve the optimization problem, Matlab's *quadprog* function was used. It is worth mentioning that for this particular process, only constraints on the positions of the quadrotor x, y, and z, and on the oscillation angles of the suspended load α and β were considered.

The physical parameters of the suspended-load quadrotor system are presented in Table 1 and were taken from [8]. Predictive control tuning parameters are the prediction n_y and control n_u horizons, and the weights Q and R. To select the horizons, the tuning guidelines provided by [25] were used. In general, for stable open-loop models, the literature suggests that n_y should be larger than the settling time plus n_u. For unstable open-loop models, as this is the case, large values of n_y are preferred, and then the value is detuned until the system achieves the desired robustness. Here, intermediate values of n_y result in an adequate performance. The control horizon n_u was chosen to be as small as possible to get the required behavior while minimizing computational load (although a higher value of n_u should improve performance if the processing capabilities allow it). Finally, Q and R were heuristically adjusted—a compromise between response time and input rate (aggressiveness). Alternatively, a global search could be done to achieve better performance, as suggested by [26]. The tuning parameters of the predictive controller are presented in Table 2.

Table 1. System parameters.

Parameter	Value	Units
M	0.4	m
m	0.03	m
d	0.1	m
l	0.35	m
g	9.8	m/s^2
I_x	1.77×10^{-3}	kgm^2
I_y	1.77×10^{-3}	kgm^2
I_z	3.54×10^{-3}	kgm^2
I_p	1.00×10^{-6}	kgm^2

Table 2. Controller parameters.

Parameter	Value	Units
T_s	0.1	s
n_y	10	–
n_u	3	–
Q	I	–
R	$0.00001 \times I$	–

4. Numerical Simulations and Results

This section presents the numerical results of the simulations performed to validate the achievement of the designed MPC controller. The main goal was to bring the quadcopter to the desired reference position while the suspended load oscillation was restricted to a maximum swing of $\pm 10° = \pm 0.175$ rad. For the model's linearization, the values of $M, m,$ and g were constant and are defined in Table 1. The values of x_{eq}, y_{eq}, z_{eq} were zero, which is an arbitrary point in three-dimensional space located well above the ground.

4.1. MPC Performance

In transport operations with multirotors, rapid handling of loads is required, which can be dangerous because the load can generate unwanted oscillations that can vary the flight conditions—the process must be kept within limits. In this particular process, the use of constraints for positions x and y of the vehicle and in the oscillation angles of the load were considered to avoid overshoots that can cause damage to the transported payload and guarantee safety in operations. The results that correspond to the constrained predictive controller are presented in Figure 2.

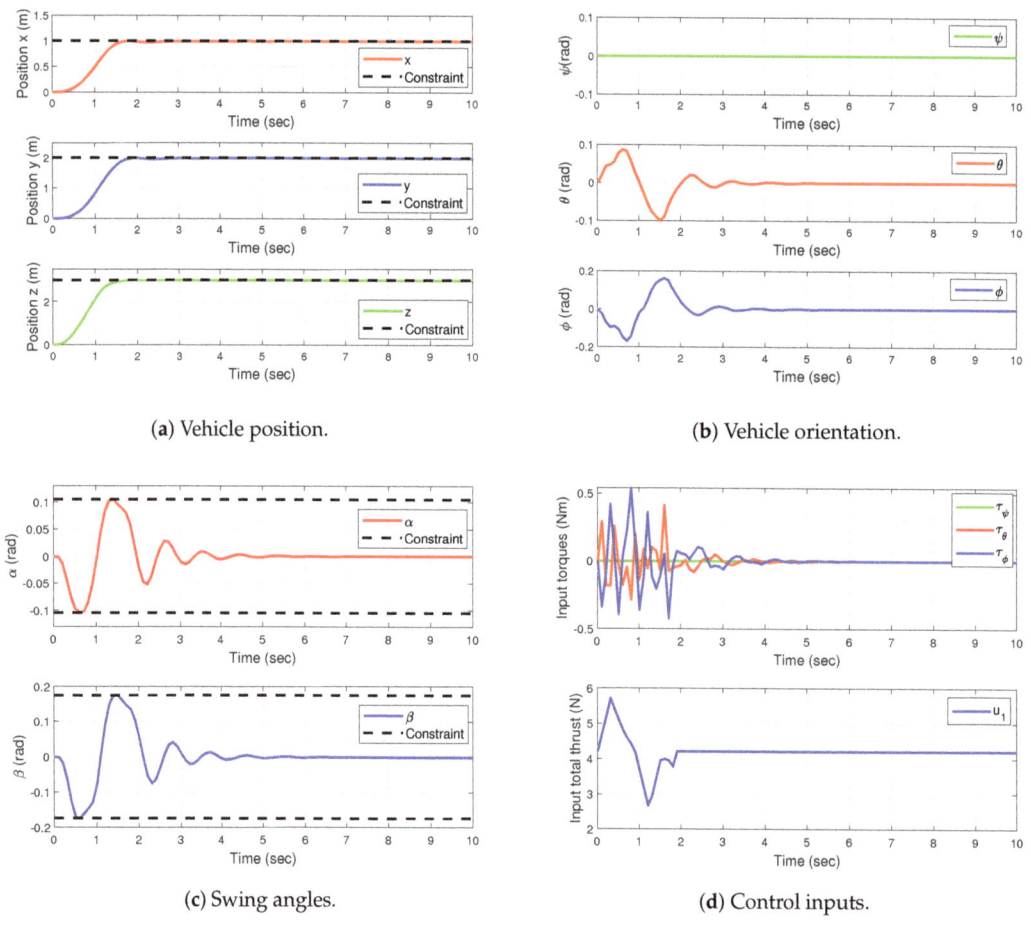

Figure 2. Results for the proposed predictive controller.

Figure 2a displays the positions x, y, and z of the quadrotor with their respective constraints $0 \leq x \leq 1, 0 \leq y \leq 2$, and $0 \leq z \leq 3$. The signals responded quickly to reach the reference in no longer than 3 s. The controller kept each constrained position x and y at its reference value without any overshoots in the transient responses to avoid further oscillations of the load angles.

In Figure 2b the attitude of the quadrotor is shown. No constraint was applied; however, lower values in θ and ϕ angles occurred in comparison to the unconstrained predictive control.

Figure 2c presents the swing angles of the suspended load with their respective constraints, for $-0.1047 \leq \alpha \leq 0.1047$ and $-0.1745 \leq \beta \leq 0.1745$. As can be seen, the predictive controller kept the oscillation within the established values, demonstrating good performance.

Figure 2d shows the variations of the control inputs in the quadrotor, which ensured that the oscillations of the suspended load did not exceed the values established in the constraints and that the air vehicle could stabilize quickly. In the bottom plot of this figure, we can see the force u_1 in the z axis that stabilized at $(m+M)g$ maintain hovering, and in the top plot the control torques τ_ψ, τ_θ, and τ_ϕ.

In summary, numerical simulations have been presented that demonstrate good performance by the predictive controller when considering the constraints to attenuate the oscillations of the suspended load. It is possible to place the quadrotor at a desired position while the oscillations of the load do not exceed the proposed limits. Next, the results of not considering the constraints are shown, for comparative purposes.

4.2. Comparative Results

In Figure 3, a direct comparison of the performance of the proposed MPC algorithm with respect to a nonlinear controller based on the feedback linearization proposed in Equation (16) of [22] has been added. The control law in [22] was chosen because it manages to achieve small swing angles of the payload.

For a better understanding of the figures, know that the subscript "c" means the constrained MPC controller and the subscript "l" the algorithm in [22]. In order to contrast the results with a more aggressive strategy, we also added the unconstrained MPC control law, which is referred to with the subscript "u". The performance responses of all controllers are displayed in Figure 3. In Figure 3c we can observe the swing angles. It is clear that [22] achieved smaller maximum angles, but the oscillation times for α and β were longer than in the MPC strategy. Moreover, by analyzing Figure 3a, it is possible to appreciate better performance in the vehicle position response of the proposed constrained MPC controller with respect to [22], because the settling time of the vehicle position obtained from control law u_l was larger than that obtained with the MPC law. In summary, ref. [22] achieveed small swing angles of the payload but at the cost of poor performance in the vehicle positioning and settling time of the payload swing. In contrast, this proposal produced shorter settling times for the payload and vehicle positioning while still meeting the constraints imposed on the payload swing angles.

In order to quantify the comparisons, Table 3 summarizes the results of the proposed controller and those of the algorithm in [22] with respect to performance measures and oscillation angles. We computed for α and β, the setting time (Ts) and the maximum swing (MS). The superior performance of the proposed scheme over the one in [22] is evidenced by the running-time cost J_{MPC}.

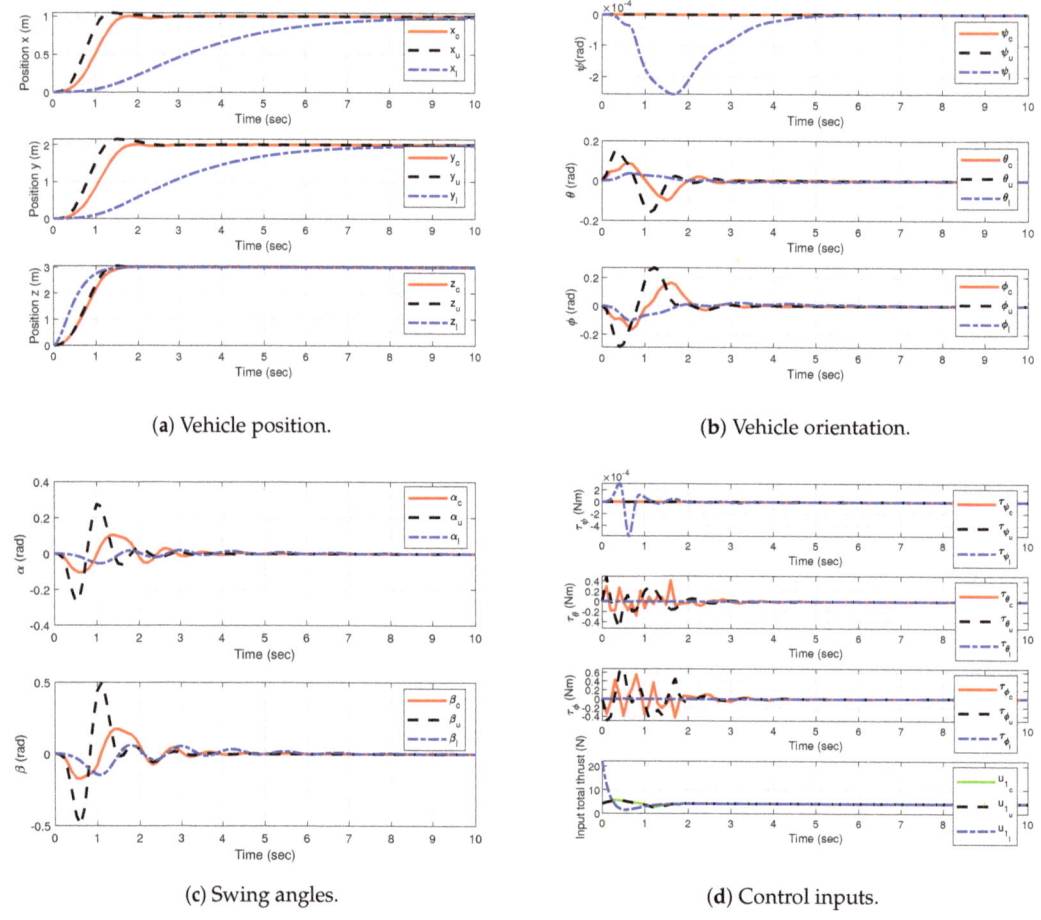

Figure 3. Comparison results for the proposed MPC with the controller of [22].

Table 3. Performances of the proposed control and the controller in [22].

Controller	Cost J_{MPC}	Swing Angle	Ts (s)	MS (Rad)
u_c	624.8	α	3.5	0.1
		β	3.5	0.175
u_u	985.1	α	3.5	0.28
		β	3.5	0.5
u_l	1997.3	α	7.2	0.05
		β	7.2	0.15

5. Conclusions

This work presents the formulation of a model-based predictive controller meant to solve the problem of transporting a payload suspended by a cable from a multi-rotor-type unmanned aerial vehicle. This strategy considers the three-dimensional translation and rotation of the aerial vehicle, and the payload dynamics. The dynamic model was obtained by formulating a Euler–Lagrange in a global approach that mathematically describes the relationship of the vehicle, the load, and the cable. Next, an affine representation of the input of the model was derived to obtain a linear model for the MPC design. It is worth mentioning that the steps carried out to obtain the linear model of the quadrotor-payload are specific for this system, and the linear model was used as a prediction model for the control strategy. Finally, we evaluated the dynamic model of the UAV with a suspended load, and the proposed controller, using a numerical simulation software. The simulations showed excellent performance by the MPC in comparison to a nonlinear controller based on feedback linearization from the literature. Therefore, the proposed controller demonstrated its ability to precisely control the multi-rotor and achieve rapid attenuation of the oscillation of the suspended load while keeping it within the limits of the constraints. Future work will include considering a flexible cable in the mathematical model and an MPC with variable constraints.

Author Contributions: Conceptualization, G.V.-P. and M.-E.G.-S.; methodology, N.U.-B. and O.H.-G.; software, F.-R.L.-E. and J.A.H.-M.; validation, N.U.-B. and O.H.-G.; writing—original draft preparation, G.V.-P. and M.-E.G.-S.; writing—review and editing, N.U.-B., O.H.-G., F.-R.L.-E. and J.A.H.-M. All authors have read and agreed to the published version of the manuscript.

Funding: This research was funded by Tecnológico Nacional de México grant number 9992.21-P.

Institutional Review Board Statement: Not applicable.

Informed Consent Statement: Not applicable.

Conflicts of Interest: The authors declare no conflict of interest.

Appendix A. Nomenclature

Tables A1 and A2 show the lists of variables used in the mathematical model and controller derivations.

Table A1. Mathematical model variables.

Variable	Description
O: x_O, y_O, z_O	Inertial frame
B: x_B, y_B, z_B	Body-fixed frame for quadrotor
ζ: x, y, z	Quadrotor linear positions
η: ψ, θ, ϕ	Quadrotor angular positions (yaw, pitch, roll)
μ: α, β	Oscillations angles of the payload
ζ_p: x_p, y_p, z_p	Payload position
q	Generalized coordinates vector
r	Unit vector of vehicle center of mass to payload
l	Cable length
d	Distance from motors to center of mass
M, m	Quadrotor and payload masses
g	Gravitational acceleration constant
u: u_1, τ	Control inputs
u_1	Total propulsive force
f_{Pi}	Propulsion force provided by the motor i
τ: $\tau_\psi, \tau_\theta, \tau_\phi$	Input torques
L	Lagrangian
T_{QSP}, V_q	Total kinetic and potential energy
I_x, I_y, I_z	Moments of inertia in x, y and z
I_p	Moment of inertia of the suspended payload
χ	State vector
χ_{eq}, u_{eq}	Equilibrium state and input vectors
y_c	Output vector
A_c, B_c, C_c	Continuous-time model matrices

Table A2. Predictive control variables.

Variable	Description
A_d, B_d, C_d	Discrete-time model matrices
ζ	Augmented state
$A_\zeta, B_\zeta, C_\zeta$	Augmented model matrices
x_k, u_k, y_k	Discrete state, input and output vectors
Δu_k	Increment in control signal
n_y, n_u	Prediction and control horizons
$P_{\zeta\zeta}, P_{\zeta\Delta u}$	Augmented state prediction matrices
$P_{y\zeta}, P_{y\Delta u}$	Output prediction matrices
$P_{x\zeta}$	State prediction matrix
$P_{u\Delta u}, P_{u\zeta}$	Input prediction matrices
$\vec{x}$	Column vector of prediction of x
Q, R	State and input penalty matrices
$\hat{y}_k$	Independent model output
$\hat{d}$	Model residual estimate
J_{MPC}	Cost function
x^*	Optimal value of x.
$\hat{r}$	Setpoint
$col(A_i)$	Block column vector of A_i matrices
$diag(A_i)$	Block diagonal matrix of A_i matrices
max, min	Maximum and minimum bound of a variable
T_s	Sampling time
$M_a, q_a(\zeta_k)$	Constraints matrices

References

1. Bernard, M.; Kondak, K. Generic slung load transportation system using small size helicopters. In Proceedings of the 2009 IEEE International Conference on Robotics and Automation, Kobe, Japan, 12–17 May 2009; pp. 3258–3264.
2. Ghadiok, V.; Goldin, J.; Ren, W. Autonomous indoor aerial gripping using a quadrotor. In Proceedings of the 2011 IEEE/RSJ International Conference on Intelligent Robots and Systems, San Francisco, CA, USA, 25–30 September 2011; pp. 4645–4651.
3. Mellinger, D.; Lindsey, Q.; Shomin, M.; Kumar, V. Design, modeling, estimation and control for aerial grasping and manipulation. In Proceedings of the 2011 IEEE/RSJ International Conference on Intelligent Robots and Systems, San Francisco, CA, USA, 25–30 September 2011; pp. 2668–2673.
4. Baizid, K.; Giglio, G.; Pierri, F.; Trujillo, M.A.; Antonelli, G.; Caccavale, F.; Viguria, A.; Chiaverini, S.; Ollero, A. Experiments on behavioral coordinated control of an unmanned aerial vehicle manipulator system. In Proceedings of the 2015 IEEE International Conference on Robotics and Automation (ICRA), Seattle, WA, USA, 26–30 May 2015; pp. 4680–4685.
5. Cruz, P.J.; Oishi, M.; Fierro, R. Lift of a cable-suspended load by a quadrotor: A hybrid system approach. In Proceedings of the 2015 American Control Conference (ACC), Chicago, IL, USA, 1–3 July 2015; pp. 1887–1892.
6. Pounds, P.E.; Bersak, D.R.; Dollar, A.M. Stability of small-scale UAV helicopters and quadrotors with added payload mass under PID control. *Auton. Robot.* **2012**, *33*, 129–142. [CrossRef]
7. Palunko, I.; Cruz, P.; Fierro, R. Agile load transportation: Safe and efficient load manipulation with aerial robots. *IEEE Robot. Autom. Mag.* **2012**, *19*, 69–79. [CrossRef]
8. Guerrero-Sánchez, M.E.; Mercado-Ravell, D.A.; Lozano, R.; García-Beltrán, C.D. Swing-attenuation for a quadrotor transporting a cable-suspended payload. *ISA Trans.* **2017**, *68*, 433–449. [CrossRef] [PubMed]
9. Klausen, K.; Fossen, T.I.; Johansen, T.A. Nonlinear control with swing damping of a multirotor UAV with suspended load. *J. Intell. Robot. Syst.* **2017**, *88*, 379–394. [CrossRef]
10. Guerrero-Sánchez, M.E.; Hernández-González, O.; Lozano, R.; García-Beltrán, C.D.; Valencia-Palomo, G.; López-Estrada, F.R. Energy-Based Control and LMI-Based Control for a Quadrotor Transporting a Payload. *Mathematics* **2019**, *7*, 1090. [CrossRef]
11. Guerrero-Sánchez, M.; Lozano, R.; Castillo, P.; Hernández-González, O.; García-Beltrán, C.; Valencia-Palomo, G. Nonlinear control strategies for a UAV carrying a load with swing attenuation. *Appl. Math. Model.* **2021**, *91*, 709–722. [CrossRef]
12. Liang, X.; Lin, H.; Zhang, P.; Wu, S.; Sun, N.; Fang, Y. A Nonlinear Control Approach for Aerial Transportation Systems with Improved Antiswing and Positioning Performance. *IEEE Trans. Autom. Sci. Eng.* **2020**. [CrossRef]
13. Ren, Z.; Hu, C.; Wu, H.; Sun, B.; Guo, Y. Obstacle Avoidance-based Control System Design of UAV with Suspended Payload. In Proceedings of the 2020 39th Chinese Control Conference (CCC), Shenyang, China, 27–29 July 2020; pp. 6839–6844.

14. Pizetta, I.H.B.; Brandão, A.S.; Sarcinelli-Filho, M. Load Transportation by Quadrotors in Crowded Workspaces. *IEEE Access* **2020**, *8*, 223941–223951. [CrossRef]
15. Pratama, G.N.P.; Masngut, I.; Cahyadi, A.I.; Herdjunanto, S. Robustness of PD control for transporting quadrotor with payload uncertainties. In Proceedings of the 2017 3rd International Conference on Science and Technology-Computer (ICST), Yogyakarta, Indonesia, 11–12 July 2017; pp. 11–15.
16. Rezaei Lori, A.A.; Danesh, M.; Amiri, P.; Ashkoofaraz, S.Y.; Azargoon, M.A. Transportation of an Unknown Cable-Suspended Payload by a Quadrotor in Windy Environment under Aerodynamics Effects. In Proceedings of the 2021 7th International Conference on Control, Instrumentation and Automation (ICCIA), Tabriz, Iran, 23–24 February 2021; pp. 1–6.
17. Lv, Z.; Li, S.; Wu, Y.; Wang, Q.G. Adaptive Control for a Quadrotor Transporting a Cable-suspended Payload with Unknown Mass in the Presence of Rotor Downwash. *IEEE Trans. Veh. Technol.* **2021**. [CrossRef]
18. Alothman, Y.; Gu, D. Quadrotor transporting cable-suspended load using iterative Linear Quadratic regulator (iLQR) optimal control. In Proceedings of the 2016 8th Computer Science and Electronic Engineering (CEEC), Colchester, UK, 28–30 September 2016; pp. 168–173.
19. Sun, B.; Chaofang, H.; Cao, L.; Wang, N.; Zhou, Y. Trajectory Planning of Quadrotor UAV with Suspended Payload Based on Predictive Control. In Proceedings of the 2018 37th Chinese Control Conference (CCC), Wuhan, China, 25–27 July 2018; pp. 10049–10054.
20. Erasmus, A.; Jordaan, H. Linear Quadratic Gaussian Control of a Quadrotor with an Unknown Suspended Payload. In Proceedings of the 2020 International SAUPEC/RobMech/PRASA Conference, Cape Town, South Africa, 29–31 January 2020; pp. 1–6.
21. Wang, Y.; Cai, H.; Zhang, J.; Li, X. Disturbance Attenuation Predictive Optimal Control for Quad-Rotor Transporting Unknown Varying Payload. *IEEE Access* **2020**, *8*, 44671–44686. [CrossRef]
22. Pizetta, I.H.B.; Brandão, A.S.; Sarcinelli-Filho, M. Modelling and control of a PVTOL quadrotor carrying a suspended load. In Proceedings of the 2015 International Conference on Unmanned Aircraft Systems (ICUAS), Denver, CO, USA, 9–12 June 2015; pp. 444–450.
23. Valencia-Palomo, G.; Rossiter, J.A. Auto-tuned predictive control based on minimal plant information. *IFAC Proc. Vol.* **2009**, *42*, 554–559. [CrossRef]
24. Rossiter, J. *A First Course in Predictive Control*; CRC Press: Boca Raton, FL, USA, 2018.
25. Garriga, J.L.; Soroush, M. Model predictive control tuning methods: A review. *Ind. Eng. Chem. Res.* **2010**, *49*, 3505–3515. [CrossRef]
26. Gutiérrez-Urquídez, R.; Valencia-Palomo, G.; Rodríguez-Elias, O.M.; Trujillo, L. Systematic selection of tuning parameters for efficient predictive controllers using a multiobjective evolutionary algorithm. *Appl. Soft Comput.* **2015**, *31*, 326–338. [CrossRef]

Article

Flow towards a Stagnation Region of a Curved Surface in a Hybrid Nanofluid with Buoyancy Effects

Iskandar Waini [1,2], Anuar Ishak [2,*] and Ioan Pop [3]

[1] Fakulti Teknologi Kejuruteraan Mekanikal dan Pembuatan, Universiti Teknikal Malaysia Melaka, Hang Tuah Jaya, Durian Tunggal 76100, Melaka, Malaysia; iskandarwaini@utem.edu.my
[2] Department of Mathematical Sciences, Faculty of Science and Technology, Universiti Kebangsaan Malaysia, UKM Bangi 43600, Selangor, Malaysia
[3] Department of Mathematics, Babeș-Bolyai University, 400084 Cluj-Napoca, Romania; ipop@math.ubbcluj.ro
* Correspondence: anuar_mi@ukm.edu.my

Abstract: This paper examines the impact of hybrid nanoparticles on the stagnation point flow towards a curved surface. Silica (SiO_2) and alumina (Al_2O_3) nanoparticles are added into water to form SiO_2-Al_2O_3/water hybrid nanofluid. Both buoyancy-opposing and -assisting flows are considered. The governing partial differential equations are reduced to a set of ordinary differential equations, before being coded in MATLAB software to obtain the numerical solutions. Findings show that the solutions are not unique, where two solutions are obtained, for both buoyancy-assisting and -opposing flow cases. The local Nusselt number increases in the presence of the hybrid nanoparticles. The temporal stability analysis shows that only one of the solutions is stable over time.

Keywords: curved surface; hybrid nanofluid; mixed convection; heat transfer; stability analysis; stagnation point

1. Introduction

The phenomenon of the flow on a stagnation region commonly occurs in aerodynamic industries and engineering applications. To name a few, such applications are polymer extrusion, drawing of plastic sheets, and wire drawing. In some situations, the flow is stagnated by a solid wall, while in other cases a free stagnation point or line exists interior to the fluid domain. Historically, Hiemenz [1] was the first researcher to consider the boundary layer flow toward a stagnation point on a rigid surface. Moreover, the axisymmetric flow was considered by Homann [2], whereas the oblique flow was studied by Chiam [3]. Furthermore, Merkin [4] studied a similar problem by considering the mixed convection flow. He discovered that the solution is not unique for the opposing flow case. However, Ishak et al. [5] exposed that the dual solutions occur for both opposing and assisting flows. Several studies on the stagnation point flow subjected to various flow and physical conditions have been considered by the researchers for the past few years. For instance, the magnetohydrodynamic and the double stratification effects were examined by Khashi'ie et al. [6]. The unsteady flow was studied by Dholey [7] and Fang et al. [8]. The stagnation point viscoelastic fluid flow was examined by Mahapatra and Sidui [9]. Moreover, Weidman [10] investigated the porous medium effects, while the thermophoretic and Brownian diffusions were reported by Kumar et al. [11].

In 1995, Choi and Eastman [12] introduced the nanofluid, which is a mixture of the base fluid and a single type of nanoparticles, to enhance the thermal conductivity. The advantages of nanofluids in a rectangular enclosure have been reported by Khanafer et al. [13], Tiwari and Das [14], and Oztop and Abu-Nada [15]. Several researchers have published papers on nanofluids with various physical aspects, for example, magnetic field [16], viscous dissipation and chemical reaction [17], activation energy [18], Dufour and Soret [19],

magnetic dipole [20], and velocity slip [21]. For additional references, the experimental study on the nanoparticle's viscosity behavior can be found in refs. [22,23].

Recently, some studies have found that advanced nanofluid consists of another type of nanoparticle dispersed into the regular nanofluid could improve its thermal properties, and this mixture is termed as 'hybrid nanofluid'. Hybrid nanofluid is used to signal a promising increase in the thermal performance of working fluids since this technology has resulted in a significant change in the design of thermal and cooling systems. As a result of the addition of more types of nanostructures, a fluid with better thermal conductivity is created. Furthermore, hybrid nanofluids are used in several applications, for example, in the vehicle brake fluid, domestic refrigerator, solar water heating, transformer, and heat exchanger [24]. The earlier experimental works that using the hybrid nanoparticles were reported by Turcu et al. [25] and Jana et al. [26]. Moreover, Suresh et al. [27] conducted experimental works using Al_2O_3-Cu hybrid nanoparticles to study the enhancement of the fluid thermal conductivity. Moreover, the significance of the combination of Al_2O_3 and other nanoparticles was reported by Singh and Sarkar [28] and Farhana et al. [29]. The numerical studies on the hybrid nanofluid flow were studied by Takabi and Salehi [30]. In recent years, hybrid nanofluid was attracting the researcher's attention to study the flow and thermal behavior, numerically. For instance, the flow in the mini-channel heat sink was done by Kumar and Sarkar [31]. Meanwhile, the flow between two parallel plates with the squeezing effect was reported by Salehi et al. [32] and Muhammad et al. [33]. Apart from that, Waini et al. [34] and Khan et al. [35] considered the flow towards a shrinking surface. For further reading, the review papers on hybrid nanofluid can be found in Refs. [36–40].

It seems that Sajid et al. [41] were the first who studied the flow over a curved surface. They found that less drag force is required to move the fluid on a curved surface rather than that on a flat surface. Later, Sajid et al. [42] extended their work by considering a micropolar fluid. Since then, many researchers have continued the study of the flow and heat transfer induced by a curved surface under different conditions. For example, Abbas et al. [43] studied the curved stretching surface under the effect of the magnetic field in a viscous fluid, then later, they extended the problem with heat generation and thermal radiation effects in a nanofluid flow as reported in Abbas et al. [44]. Similarly, Hayat et al. [45], Imtiaz et al. [46], and Saba et al. [47] also reported the flow over a curved stretching surface in a nanofluid. Furthermore, Sanni et al. [48] and Hayat et al. [49] considered the nonlinear stretching velocity of the curved surface, while Okechi et al. [50] reported on the exponentially stretching curved surface. The unsteady flow was reported by Saleh et al. [51]. Naveed et al. [52] examined the dual solutions in hydromagnetic viscous fluid flow past a shrinking curved surface. Meanwhile, Khan et al. [53] explored the hybrid nanofluid flow with mixed convection. Based on the paper by Khan et al. [53], this paper aims to investigate the stagnation point flow of a hybrid nanofluid towards a curved surface containing Al_2O_3-SiO_2 nanoparticles with buoyancy effects. It should be mentioned that the condition of the surface temperature was assumed constant in Khan et al. [53]. In contrast to [53], the present paper considers the prescribed surface temperature case. Additionally, this paper examines the temporal stability of the numerical solutions.

2. Basic Equations

Consider the flow configuration model as shown in Figure 1. Here, the curved surface with radius R is measured about the curvilinear coordinates (r, s) where r is normal to tangent vector at any point on the sheet and s is the arc length coordinate along the flow direction, so that large values of R correspond to small curvature (slightly curved surface).

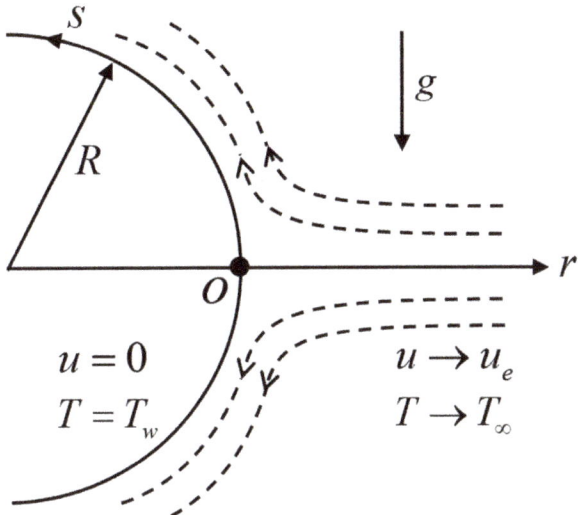

Figure 1. Flow configuration model of a curved surface.

According to Sajid et al. [41], the pressure is not constant across the boundary layer. Therefore, the pressure gradient in the case of a curved surface cannot be neglected. Here, it is supposed that $u_e(s) = as$ with $a > 0$ and $T_w(s) = T_\infty + T_0(s/L)$ where T_∞ is the constant ambient temperature, while T_0 and L, respectively, are the reference temperature and length. The prescribed surface temperature is employed to allow the similarity reduction of the equations. Considering hybrid nanofluid flow, a few assumptions are considered for the physical model. The hybrid nanofluid is assumed to be stable. Thus, the effect of nanoparticle aggregation and sedimentation is omitted. The nanoparticles are assumed to have a uniform size with a spherical shape. It is assumed that both the base fluid and nanoparticles are in a thermal equilibrium state, and they flow at the same velocity. Accordingly, under these assumptions along with the boundary layer approximations, the governing equations of hybrid nanofluid are [41,53]:

$$\frac{\partial}{\partial r}[(R+r)v] + R\frac{\partial u}{\partial s} = 0 \tag{1}$$

$$\frac{u^2}{R+r} = \frac{1}{\rho_{hnf}}\frac{\partial p}{\partial r} \tag{2}$$

$$v\frac{\partial u}{\partial r} + \frac{R}{R+r}u\frac{\partial u}{\partial s} + \frac{uv}{R+r} = -\frac{1}{\rho_{hnf}}\frac{R}{R+r}\frac{\partial p}{\partial s} + \frac{\mu_{hnf}}{\rho_{hnf}}\left(\frac{\partial^2 u}{\partial r^2} + \frac{1}{R+r}\frac{\partial u}{\partial r} - \frac{u}{(R+r)^2}\right) + \frac{(\rho\beta)_{hnf}}{\rho_{hnf}}(T-T_\infty)g \tag{3}$$

$$v\frac{\partial T}{\partial r} + \frac{R}{R+r}u\frac{\partial T}{\partial s} = \frac{k_{hnf}}{(\rho C_p)_{hnf}}\left(\frac{\partial^2 T}{\partial r^2} + \frac{1}{R+r}\frac{\partial T}{\partial r}\right) \tag{4}$$

subject to:

$$\begin{array}{ll} u = v = 0,\ T = T_w(s) & \text{at}\quad r = 0 \\ u \to u_e(s),\ \frac{\partial u}{\partial r} \to 0,\ T \to T_\infty & \text{as}\quad r \to \infty \end{array} \tag{5}$$

where v and u are the velocity components along r- and s- directions. Moreover, g and p are the acceleration caused by the gravity and the pressure, respectively, while the temperature is given by T. Furthermore, the thermophysical properties can be referred to in Tables 1 and 2 [30,53]. Please note that φ_1 (Al$_2$O$_3$) and φ_2 (SiO$_2$) are the nanoparticles volume fractions where $\varphi_{hnf} = \varphi_1 + \varphi_2$, and the subscripts $n1$ and $n2$ are corresponded to their solid components, while the subscripts hnf and f signify the hybrid nanofluid and base fluid, respectively.

Table 1. Thermophysical properties of nanoparticles and water.

Properties	Base Fluid	Nanoparticles	
	Water	Al_2O_3	SiO_2
ρ (kg/m^3)	997.1	3970	2200
C_p (J/kgK)	4179	765	745
k (W/mK)	0.613	40	1.4
$\beta \times 10^{-5}$ (1/K)	21	0.85	42.7
Prandtl number, Pr	6.2		

Table 2. Thermophysical properties of hybrid nanofluid.

Properties	Correlations
Dynamic viscosity	$\mu_{hnf} = \dfrac{\mu_f}{(1-\varphi_{hnf})^{2.5}}$
Density	$\rho_{hnf} = (1-\varphi_{hnf})\rho_f + \varphi_1 \rho_{n1} + \varphi_2 \rho_{n2}$
Heat capacity	$(\rho C_p)_{hnf} = (1-\varphi_{hnf})(\rho C_p)_f + \varphi_1 (\rho C_p)_{n1} + \varphi_2 (\rho C_p)_{n2}$
Thermal conductivity	$\dfrac{k_{hnf}}{k_f} = \dfrac{\frac{\varphi_1 k_{n1}+\varphi_2 k_{n2}}{\varphi_{hnf}} + 2k_f + 2(\varphi_1 k_{n1}+\varphi_2 k_{n2}) - 2\varphi_{hnf} k_f}{\frac{\varphi_1 k_{n1}+\varphi_2 k_{n2}}{\varphi_{hnf}} + 2k_f - (\varphi_1 k_{n1}+\varphi_2 k_{n2}) + \varphi_{hnf} k_f}$
Thermal expansion	$(\rho\beta)_{hnf} = (1-\varphi_{hnf})(\rho\beta)_f + \varphi_1 (\rho\beta)_{n1} + \varphi_2 (\rho\beta)_{n2}$

3. Similarity Transformations

Consider the similarity variables as in Sajid et al. [41]:

$$u = asf'(\eta), \quad v = -\frac{R}{R+r}\sqrt{a\nu_f}f(\eta), \quad p = \rho_f a^2 s^2 P(\eta), \quad \theta(\eta) = \frac{T-T_\infty}{T_w - T_\infty}, \quad \eta = r\sqrt{\frac{a}{\nu_f}} \quad (6)$$

where ($'$) signifies the differentiation with respect to η. Using Equation (6), the continuity equation, i.e., Equation (1) is identically fulfilled. Now, inserting Equation (6) in Equations (2) and (3), one obtains:

$$P' = \frac{\rho_{hnf}}{\rho_f}\frac{1}{K+\eta}f'^2 \quad (7)$$

$$\frac{\rho_f}{\rho_{hnf}}\frac{2K}{K+\eta}P = \frac{\mu_{hnf}/\mu_f}{\rho_{hnf}/\rho_f}\left(f''' + \frac{1}{K+\eta}f'' - \frac{1}{(K+\eta)^2}f'\right) + \frac{K}{(K+\eta)^2}ff' - \frac{K}{K+\eta}f'^2$$
$$+ \frac{K}{K+\eta}ff'' + \frac{(\rho\beta)_{hnf}/(\rho\beta)_f}{\rho_{hnf}/\rho_f}\lambda\theta \quad (8)$$

Then, the pressure P term in these equations is eliminated to obtain the following equation:

$$\frac{\mu_{hnf}/\mu_f}{\rho_{hnf}/\rho_f}\left(f^{iv} + \frac{2}{K+\eta}f''' - \frac{1}{(K+\eta)^2}f'' + \frac{1}{(K+\eta)^3}f'\right) + \frac{K}{K+\eta}\left(ff''' - f'f''\right) \quad (9)$$

Similarly, using Equation (6), Equation (4) is transformed to:

$$\frac{1}{\Pr}\frac{k_{hnf}/k_f}{(\rho C_p)_{hnf}/(\rho C_p)_f}\left(\theta'' + \frac{1}{K+\eta}\theta'\right) + \frac{K}{K+\eta}(f\theta' - f'\theta) = 0 \quad (10)$$

subject to:
$$f(0) = 0, \quad f'(0) = 0, \quad \theta(0) = 1$$
$$f'(\infty) = 1, \quad f''(\infty) = 0, \quad \theta(\infty) = 0 \quad (11)$$

where $K = R\sqrt{a/\nu_f}$ (=constant) specifies the curvature parameter, ν_f represents the fluid kinematic viscosity, and $Pr = \mu_f(C_p)_f/k_f$ represents the Prandtl number. Moreover, $\lambda = g\beta_f T_0/a^2 L = Gr_s/Re_s^2$ (=constant) represents the mixed convection or the buoyancy parameter, with $Gr_s = g\beta_f(T_w - T_\infty)s^3/\nu_f^2$ corresponds to the local Grashof number and $Re_s = u_e s/\nu_f$ stands for the local Reynolds number. Please note that $\lambda < 0$ signifies the opposing and $\lambda > 0$ signifies the assisting flows, while the forced convection flow (no buoyancy effects) is given by $\lambda = 0$.

The coefficient of the skin friction C_f and the local Nusselt number Nu_s are given as:

$$C_f = \frac{1}{\rho_f u_e^2}\mu_{hnf}\left(\frac{\partial u}{\partial r} - \frac{u}{R+r}\right)_{r=0}, \quad Nu_s = -\frac{s}{k_f(T_w - T_\infty)}k_{hnf}\left(\frac{\partial T}{\partial r}\right)_{r=0} \quad (12)$$

Using Equations (6) and (12), one gets:

$$Re_s^{1/2}C_f = \frac{\mu_{hnf}}{\mu_f}f''(0), \quad Re_s^{-1/2}Nu_s = -\frac{k_{hnf}}{k_f}\theta'(0) \quad (13)$$

Please note that by taking $\varphi_{hnf} = 0$ (regular fluid) and $K \to \infty$ (vertical plane surface), the problem reduces to the problem of Lok et al. [54] without the micropolar effects. Thus, the numerical values of $f''(0)$ and $-\theta'(0)$ can be validated with those obtained by them.

4. Stability Analysis

The temporal stability of the dual solutions as time evolves is studied. This analysis was first introduced by Merkin [55] and then followed by Weidman et al. [56]. First, consider the new variables as follows:

$$u = as\frac{\partial f}{\partial \eta}(\eta, \tau), \quad v = -\frac{R}{R+r}\sqrt{a\nu_f}f(\eta, \tau), \quad p = \rho_f a^2 s^2 P(\eta, \tau),$$
$$\theta(\eta, \tau) = \frac{T - T_w}{T_w - T_\infty}, \quad \eta = r\sqrt{\frac{a}{\nu_f}}, \quad \tau = at \quad (14)$$

Now, the unsteady form of Equations (3) and (4) are employed, while Equation (1) remains unchanged. On using (14), one obtains:

$$\frac{\mu_{hnf}/\mu_f}{\rho_{hnf}/\rho_f}\left(\frac{\partial^4 f}{\partial \eta^4} + \frac{2}{K+\eta}\frac{\partial^3 f}{\partial \eta^3} - \frac{1}{(K+\eta)^2}\frac{\partial^2 f}{\partial \eta^2} + \frac{1}{(K+\eta)^3}\frac{\partial f}{\partial \eta}\right) + \frac{K}{K+\eta}\left(f\frac{\partial^3 f}{\partial \eta^3} - \frac{\partial f}{\partial \eta}\frac{\partial^2 f}{\partial \eta^2}\right)$$
$$+ \frac{K}{(K+\eta)^2}\left(f\frac{\partial^2 f}{\partial \eta^2} - \left(\frac{\partial f}{\partial \eta}\right)^2\right) - \frac{K}{(K+\eta)^3}f\frac{\partial f}{\partial \eta} + \frac{(\rho\beta)_{hnf}/(\rho\beta)_f}{\rho_{hnf}/\rho_f}\lambda\left(\frac{\partial \theta}{\partial \eta} + \frac{1}{K+\eta}\theta\right) \quad (15)$$
$$- \frac{1}{K+\eta}\frac{\partial^2 f}{\partial \eta \partial \tau} - \frac{\partial^3 f}{\partial \eta^2 \partial \tau} = 0$$

$$\frac{1}{Pr}\frac{k_{hnf}/k_f}{(\rho C_p)_{hnf}/(\rho C_p)_f}\left(\frac{\partial^2 \theta}{\partial \eta^2} + \frac{1}{K+\eta}\frac{\partial \theta}{\partial \eta}\right) + \frac{K}{K+\eta}\left(f\frac{\partial \theta}{\partial \eta} - \frac{\partial f}{\partial \eta}\theta\right) - \frac{\partial \theta}{\partial \tau} = 0 \quad (16)$$

subject to:
$$f(0, \tau) = 0, \quad \frac{\partial f}{\partial \eta}(0, \tau) = 0, \quad \theta(0, \tau) = 1$$
$$\frac{\partial f}{\partial \eta}(\infty, \tau) = 1, \quad \frac{\partial^2 f}{\partial \eta^2}(\infty, \tau) = 0, \quad \theta(\infty, \tau) = 0 \quad (17)$$

Then, consider the following perturbation functions [56]:

$$f(\eta, \tau) = f_0(\eta) + e^{-\gamma \tau}F(\eta), \quad \theta(\eta, \tau) = \theta_0(\eta) + e^{-\gamma \tau}G(\eta) \quad (18)$$

Here, Equation (18) is used to apply a small disturbance on the steady solution $f = f_0(\eta)$ and $\theta = \theta_0(\eta)$ of Equations (9)–(11). The functions $F(\eta)$ and $G(\eta)$ in Equation

(18) are relatively small compared to $f_0(\eta)$ and $\theta_0(\eta)$. The sign (positive or negative) of the eigenvalue γ determines the stability of the solutions. By employing Equation (18), Equations (15)–(17) become:

$$\frac{\mu_{hnf}/\mu_f}{\rho_{hnf}/\rho_f}\left(F^{iv} + \frac{2}{K+\eta}F''' - \frac{1}{(K+\eta)^2}F'' + \frac{1}{(K+\eta)^3}F'\right) + \frac{K}{K+\eta}\left(f_0F''' + f_0'''F - f_0'F'' - f_0''F'\right)$$
$$+ \frac{K}{(K+\eta)^2}\left(f_0F'' + f_0''F - 2f_0'F'\right) - \frac{K}{(K+\eta)^3}\left(f_0F' + f_0'F\right) \qquad (19)$$
$$+ \frac{(\rho\beta)_{hnf}/(\rho\beta)_f}{\rho_{hnf}/\rho_f}\lambda\left(G' + \frac{1}{K+\eta}G\right) + \frac{\gamma}{K+\eta}F' + \gamma F'' = 0$$

$$\frac{1}{\Pr}\frac{k_{hnf}/k_f}{(\rho C_p)_{hnf}/(\rho C_p)_f}\left(G'' + \frac{1}{K+\eta}G'\right) + \frac{K}{K+\eta}\left(f_0G' + \theta_0'F - f_0'G - \theta_0F'\right) + \gamma G = 0 \qquad (20)$$

subject to:
$$F(0) = 0, \quad F'(0) = 0, \quad G(0) = 0$$
$$F'(\infty) = 0, \quad F''(\infty) = 0, G(\infty) = 0 \qquad (21)$$

To obtain γ of Equations (19) and (20), the new boundary condition $F''(0) = 1$ is included in Equation (21) to replace $F''(\infty) = 0$.

5. Results and Discussion

Equations (9)–(11) are solved numerically by using the bvp4c function in MATLAB software (Matlab_R2014b, MathWorks, Singapore). As described in Shampine et al. [57], the aforesaid solver occupies a finite difference method that employs the 3-stage Lobatto IIIa formula. The selection of the initial guess and the boundary layer thickness, η_∞ is important to achieve the convergence of the numerical solution. This convergence issue is also influenced by the value of the physical parameters considered. The effects of several physical parameters on the flow and the thermal fields are investigated.

The values of $f''(0)$ and $-\theta'(0)$ for various λ when $\varphi_{hnf} = 0$ (regular fluid), $\Pr = 0.7$ and $K \to \infty$ (plane surface) are compared with Lok et al. [54]. It is found that the results are comparable for each λ considered, as shown in Table 3. Moreover, the decreasing trend is observed in the first solution of $f''(0)$ and $-\theta'(0)$ for smaller values of λ. Furthermore, Table 4 provides the values of $Re_s^{1/2}C_f$ and $Re_s^{-1/2}Nu_s$ when $\Pr = 6.2$ and $K = 10^3$ for numerous values of φ_{hnf} and λ. The consequence of rising φ_{hnf} exaggerates the values of $Re_s^{1/2}C_f$ and $Re_s^{-1/2}Nu_s$ for both branch solutions. Moreover, the values of $Re_s^{1/2}C_f$ are reduced as λ decreases for both branch solutions. Meanwhile, the values of $Re_s^{-1/2}Nu_s$ for the first solution are decreased with the decrease in λ, but they are increased for the second solution.

Table 3. Values of $f''(0)$ and $-\theta'(0)$ when $\varphi_{hnf} = 0$ (regular fluid), $\Pr = 0.7$ and $K \to \infty$ for different λ.

λ	Lok Et Al. [54]		Present Results	
	$f''(0)$	$-\theta'(0)$	$f''(0)$	$-\theta'(0)$
−1.0	0.691693	0.633269	0.691661	0.633247
			(−0.285049)	(−0.222165)
−1.5	0.371788	0.578230	0.371754	0.578206
	(−0.527666)	(−0.004360)	(−0.527651)	(−0.004347)
−2.0	−0.039513	0.486576	−0.039572	0.486540
	(−0.578523)	(0.198572)	(−0.578476)	(0.198599)

Results in "( )" are the lower branch (second) solutions.

Table 4. Values of $Re_s^{1/2}C_f$ and $Re_s^{-1/2}Nu_s$ when $K = 10^3$ and $\Pr = 6.2$ for different physical parameters.

φ_{hnf}	λ	$Re_s^{1/2}C_f$		$Re_s^{-1/2}Nu_s$	
		First Solution	Second Solution	First Solution	Second Solution
2%	1	1.609474	0.652232	1.708511	2.232347
4%		1.684045	0.691249	1.759909	2.317150
6%		1.761695	0.731805	1.811141	2.401796
2%	−1	0.969496	−0.380839	1.530307	−1.239090
	−2	0.594987	−0.642901	1.403953	−0.295385
	−3	0.131804	−0.707488	1.208754	0.282748

Furthermore, the variations of $Re_x^{1/2}C_f$ and $Re_x^{-1/2}Nu_x$ against λ when $\Pr = 6.2$ and $K = 10^3$ for various φ_{hnf} are presented in Figures 2 and 3. The enhancement in the values of $Re_x^{1/2}C_f$ and $Re_x^{-1/2}Nu_x$ are observed with a high percentage of the hybrid nanoparticle compositions. Moreover, the dual solutions are obtained for both opposing ($\lambda < 0$) and assisting ($\lambda > 0$) flows where the turning point of the solutions occurs in the opposing region ($\lambda < 0$). It is noticed that the critical values are $\lambda_c = -3.6169, -3.6219, -3.6270$ for $\varphi_{hnf} = 2\%, 4\%, 6\%$, respectively. Additionally, it is observed that the second solution of $Re_x^{1/2}C_f$ and $Re_x^{-1/2}Nu_x$ are undefined for non-buoyant case ($\lambda = 0$). From Figure 3, there exists an asymptotic line at $\lambda = 0$ where the second solutions of $Re_x^{-1/2}Nu_x$ show that the values of $Re_x^{-1/2}Nu_x \to +\infty$ as $\lambda \to 0^+$ and $Re_x^{-1/2}Nu_x \to -\infty$ as $\lambda \to 0^-$.

Moreover, Figures 4 and 5 display the profiles of $f'(\eta)$ and $\theta(\eta)$ when $\varphi_{hnf} = 2\%, \Pr = 6.2$, and $K = 10^3$ for various values of λ. It is noticed that the profiles of the first and the second solutions are merged towards some values of λ. Additionally, a negative value ($\theta(\eta) < 0$) for the second solution of $\theta(\eta)$ is observed when $\lambda = 1$ and its gradient is greater than that of the first solution. Next, Figures 6 and 7 show the consequence of φ_{hnf} on $f'(\eta)$ and $\theta(\eta)$ when $\lambda = -1, \Pr = 6.2$, and $K = 10^3$. It is seen that both branch solutions of $f'(\eta)$ show the decreasing pattern, whereas both branch solutions of $\theta(\eta)$ increases for a higher percentage of φ_{hnf}.

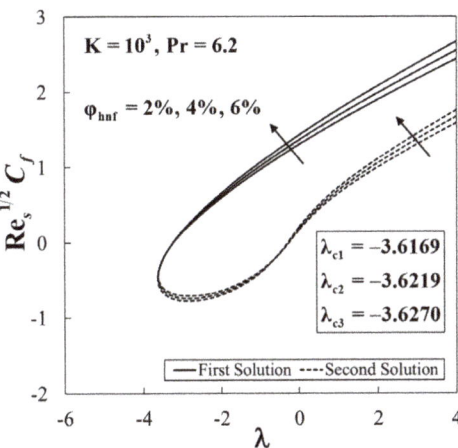

Figure 2. Variation of the skin friction coefficient $Re_s^{1/2}C_f$ against the mixed convection parameter λ for different values of φ_{hnf}.

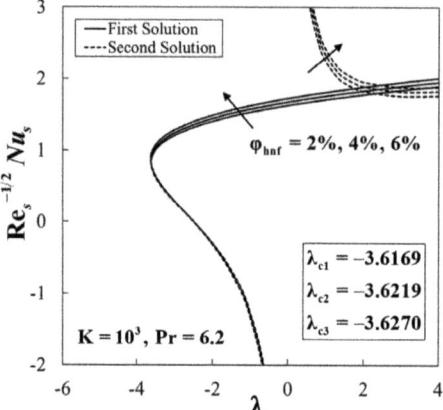

Figure 3. Variation of the local Nusselt number $Re_s^{-1/2} Nu_s$ against the mixed convection parameter λ for different values of φ_{hnf}.

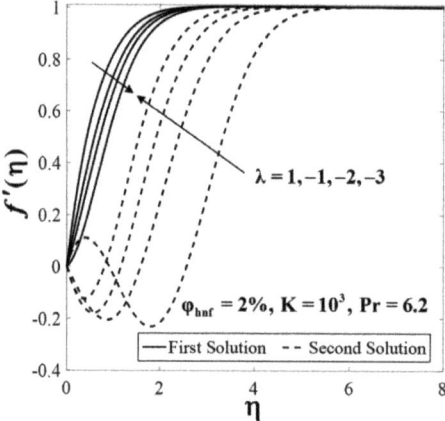

Figure 4. Velocity profiles $f'(\eta)$ for different values of λ.

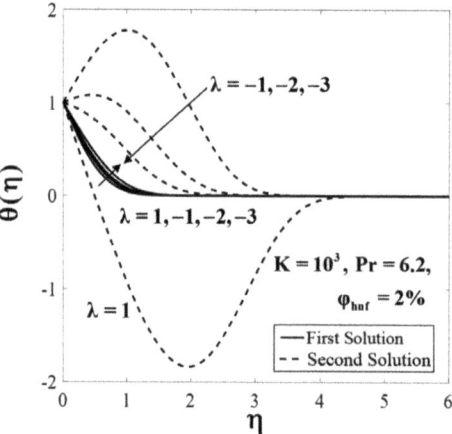

Figure 5. Temperature profiles $\theta(\eta)$ for different values of λ.

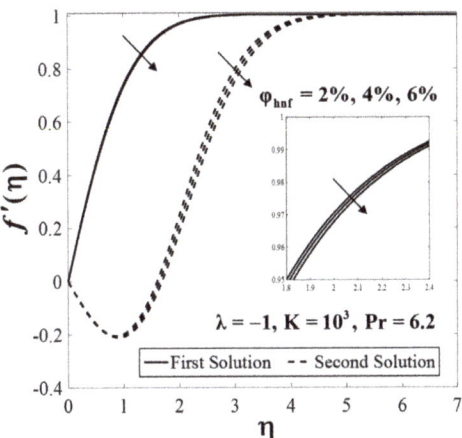

Figure 6. Velocity profiles $f'(\eta)$ for different values of φ_{hnf}.

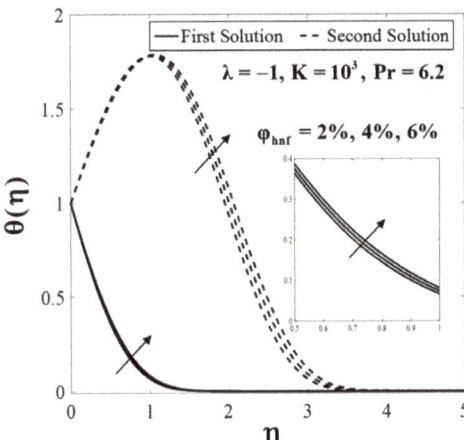

Figure 7. Temperature profiles $\theta(\eta)$ for different values of φ_{hnf}.

Furthermore, the dimensionless stream function is plotted to show the flow patterns. In this respect, the streamlines of the first and the second solutions for the opposing flow ($\lambda = -2$) when $\varphi_{hnf} = 2\%$, $K = 10^3$, and $Pr = 6.2$ are shown in Figures 8 and 9, respectively. The flow patterns for the first solution show that the fluid is moving away from the slot ($x = 0$) and acts as the normal stagnation point flow. Meanwhile, the flow is split into two regions for the second solution, i.e., upper and lower regions. The upper region has similar pattern with that of the first solution, whereas reverse flow is observed in the lower region.

The variations of the smallest eigenvalues γ against the mixed convection parameter λ when $\varphi_{hnf} = 2\%$, $Pr = 6.2$, and $K = 10^3$ are described in Figure 10. For the positive value of γ, it is noted that $e^{-\gamma\tau} \to 0$ as time evolves ($\tau \to \infty$). In the meantime, for the negative value of γ, $e^{-\gamma\tau} \to \infty$. These behaviors show that the first solution is physically reliable and stable over time.

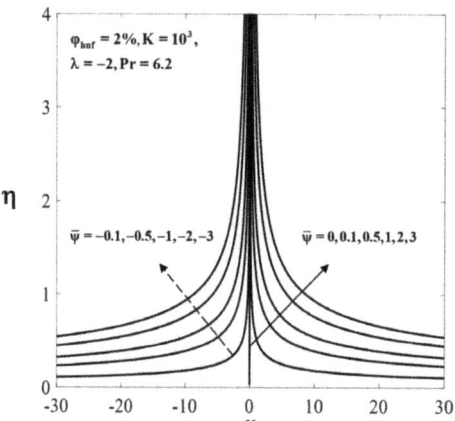

Figure 8. Streamlines for the first solution.

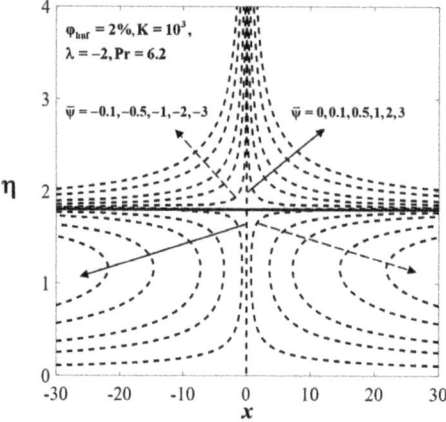

Figure 9. Streamlines for the second solution.

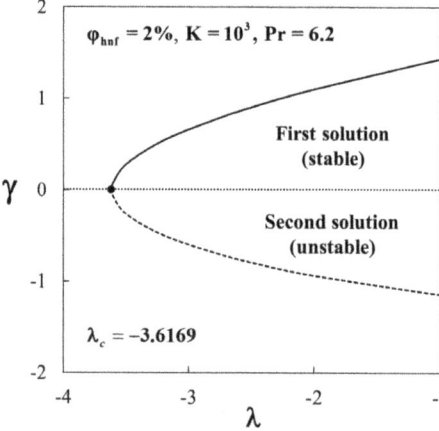

Figure 10. Variation of the smallest eigenvalues γ against the mixed convection parameter λ.

6. Conclusions

In the present paper, the stagnation point flow towards a curved surface containing Al_2O_3-SiO_2 hybrid nanoparticles with buoyancy effects was accomplished. Findings revealed that dual solutions appeared for both assisting ($\lambda > 0$) and opposing ($\lambda < 0$) flows. The dual solutions were found for $\lambda > \lambda_c$ and no solution for $\lambda < \lambda_c$, while the solutions bifurcated at $\lambda = \lambda_c$. It was found that the critical values occur in the opposing flow region ($\lambda < 0$). The domain of the mixed convection parameter λ where the dual solutions are in existence increases as the percentage of φ_{hnf} is increased. Moreover, the higher percentage of φ_{hnf} gave rise to the heat transfer rate and the skin friction coefficient. Lastly, it was found that the first solution is stable and physically reliable as time evolves, while the second solution is not.

Author Contributions: Conceptualization, I.P.; funding acquisition, A.I.; methodology, I.W.; Project administration, A.I.; supervision, A.I. and I.P.; validation, I.P.; writing—original draft, I.W.; writing—review and editing, A.I., I.P. All authors have read and agreed to the published version of the manuscript.

Funding: This research was funded by Universiti Kebangsaan Malaysia (Project Code: DIP-2020-001).

Acknowledgments: The financial supports received from the Universiti Kebangsaan Malaysia (Project Code: DIP-2020-001) and the Universiti Teknikal Malaysia Melaka are gratefully acknowledged.

Conflicts of Interest: The authors declare no conflict of interest.

References

1. Hiemenz, K. Die Grenzschicht an einem in den gleichförmigen Flüssigkeitsstrom eingetauchten geraden Kreiszylinder. *Dinglers Polytech. J.* **1911**, *326*, 321–410.
2. Homann, F. Der Einfluß grober Zähigkeit bei der Strömung um den Zylinder und um die Kugel. *Z. für Angew. Math. und Mech.* **1936**, *16*, 153–164. [CrossRef]
3. Chiam, T.C. Stagnation-point flow towards a stretching plate. *J. Phys. Soc. Jpn.* **1994**, *63*, 2443–2444. [CrossRef]
4. Merkin, J.H. Mixed convection boundary layer flow on a vertical surface in a saturated porous medium. *J. Eng. Math.* **1980**, *14*, 301–313. [CrossRef]
5. Ishak, A.; Nazar, R.; Arifin, N.M.; Pop, I. Dual solutions in mixed convection flow near a stagnation point on a vertical porous plate. *Int. J. Therm. Sci.* **2008**, *47*, 417–422. [CrossRef]
6. Khashi'ie, N.S.; Arifin, N.M.; Rashidi, M.M.; Hafidzuddin, E.H.; Wahi, N. Magnetohydrodynamics (MHD) stagnation point flow past a shrinking/stretching surface with double stratification effect in a porous medium. *J. Therm. Anal. Calorim.* **2019**, *8*, 1–14. [CrossRef]
7. Dholey, S. An unsteady separated stagnation-point flow towards a rigid flat plate. *J. Fluids Eng.* **2019**, *141*, 021202. [CrossRef]
8. Fang, T.; Wang, F.; Gao, B. Unsteady magnetohydrodynamic stagnation point flow—closed-form analytical solutions. *Appl. Math. Mech.* **2019**, *40*, 449–464. [CrossRef]
9. Mahapatra, T.R.; Sidui, S. Non-axisymmetric Homann stagnation-point flow of a viscoelastic fluid towards a fixed plate. *Eur. J. Mech. B/Fluids* **2020**, *79*, 38–43. [CrossRef]
10. Weidman, P. Non-axisymmetric stagnation-point flow in a fluid saturated porous medium. *J. Porous Media* **2020**, *23*, 563–572. [CrossRef]
11. Kumar, B.; Seth, G.S.; Nandkeolyar, R. Quadratic multiple regression model and spectral relaxation approach to analyse stagnation point nanofluid flow with second-order slip. *Proc. Inst. Mech. Eng. Part E J. Process. Mech. Eng.* **2020**, *234*, 3–14. [CrossRef]
12. Choi, S.U.S.; Eastman, J.A. Enhancing thermal conductivity of fluids with nanoparticles. *Proc. 1995 ASME Int. Mech. Eng. Congr. Expo. FED 231/MD* **1995**, *66*, 99–105.
13. Khanafer, K.; Vafai, K.; Lightstone, M. Buoyancy-driven heat transfer enhancement in a two-dimensional enclosure utilizing nanofluids. *Int. J. Heat Mass Transf.* **2003**, *46*, 3639–3653. [CrossRef]
14. Tiwari, R.K.; Das, M.K. Heat transfer augmentation in a two-sided lid-driven differentially heated square cavity utilizing nanofluids. *Int. J. Heat Mass Transf.* **2007**, *50*, 2002–2018. [CrossRef]
15. Oztop, H.F.; Abu-Nada, E. Numerical study of natural convection in partially heated rectangular enclosures filled with nanofluids. *Int. J. Heat Fluid Flow* **2008**, *29*, 1326–1336. [CrossRef]
16. Hamad, M.A.A. Analytical solution of natural convection flow of a nanofluid over a linearly stretching sheet in the presence of magnetic field. *Int. Commun. Heat Mass Transf.* **2011**, *38*, 487–492. [CrossRef]
17. Kameswaran, P.K.; Narayana, M.; Sibanda, P.; Murthy, P.V.S.N. Hydromagnetic nanofluid flow due to a stretching or shrinking sheet with viscous dissipation and chemical reaction effects. *Int. J. Heat Mass Transf.* **2012**, *55*, 7587–7595. [CrossRef]

18. Khan, U.; Zaib, A.; Khan, I.; Nisar, K.S. Activation energy on MHD flow of titanium alloy (Ti6Al4V) nanoparticle along with a cross flow and streamwise direction with binary chemical reaction and non-linear radiation: Dual solutions. *J. Mater. Res. Technol.* **2020**, *9*, 188–199. [CrossRef]
19. Waini, I.; Ishak, A.; Pop, I. Dufour and Soret effects on Al_2O_3-water nanofluid flow over a moving thin needle: Tiwari and Das model. *Int. J. Numer. Methods Heat Fluid Flow* **2021**, *31*, 766–782. [CrossRef]
20. Majeed, A.; Zeeshan, A.; Hayat, T. Analysis of magnetic properties of nanoparticles due to applied magnetic dipole in aqueous medium with momentum slip condition. *Neural Comput. Appl.* **2019**, *31*, 189–197. [CrossRef]
21. Ghosh, S.; Mukhopadhyay, S. Stability analysis for model-based study of nanofluid flow over an exponentially shrinking permeable sheet in presence of slip. *Neural Comput. Appl.* **2020**, *32*, 7201–7211. [CrossRef]
22. Olayiwola, S.O.; Dejam, M. Experimental study on the viscosity behavior of silica nanofluids with different ions of electrolytes. *Ind. Eng. Chem. Res.* **2020**, *59*, 3575–3583. [CrossRef]
23. Bollineni, P.K.; Dordzie, G.; Olayiwola, S.O.; Dejam, M. An experimental investigation of the viscosity behavior of solutions of nanoparticles, surfactants, and electrolytes. *Phys. Fluids* **2021**, *33*, 026601. [CrossRef]
24. Sidik, N.A.C.; Adamu, I.M.; Jamil, M.M.; Kefayati, G.H.R.; Mamat, R.; Najafi, G. Recent progress on hybrid nanofluids in heat transfer applications: A comprehensive review. *Int. Commun. Heat Mass Transf.* **2016**, *78*, 68–79. [CrossRef]
25. Turcu, R.; Darabont, A.; Nan, A.; Aldea, N.; Macovei, D.; Bica, D.; Vekas, L.; Pana, O.; Soran, M.L.; Koos, A.A.; et al. New polypyrrole-multiwall carbon nanotubes hybrid materials. *J. Optoelectron. Adv. Mater.* **2006**, *8*, 643–647.
26. Jana, S.; Salehi-Khojin, A.; Zhong, W.H. Enhancement of fluid thermal conductivity by the addition of single and hybrid nano-additives. *Thermochim. Acta* **2007**, *462*, 45–55. [CrossRef]
27. Suresh, S.; Venkitaraj, K.P.; Selvakumar, P.; Chandrasekar, M. Synthesis of Al_2O_3-Cu/water hybrid nanofluids using two step method and its thermo physical properties. *Colloids Surf. A Physicochem. Eng. Asp.* **2011**, *388*, 41–48. [CrossRef]
28. Singh, S.K.; Sarkar, J. Energy, exergy and economic assessments of shell and tube condenser using hybrid nanofluid as coolant. *Int. Commun. Heat Mass Transf.* **2018**, *98*, 41–48. [CrossRef]
29. Farhana, K.; Kadirgama, K.; Rahman, M.M.; Noor, M.M.; Ramasamy, D.; Samykano, M.; Najafi, G.; Sidik, N.A.C.; Tarlochan, F. Significance of alumina in nanofluid technology: An overview. *J. Therm. Anal. Calorim.* **2019**, *138*, 1107–1126. [CrossRef]
30. Takabi, B.; Salehi, S. Augmentation of the heat transfer performance of a sinusoidal corrugated enclosure by employing hybrid nanofluid. *Adv. Mech. Eng.* **2014**, *6*, 147059. [CrossRef]
31. Kumar, V.; Sarkar, J. Particle ratio optimization of Al_2O_3-MWCNT hybrid nanofluid in minichannel heat sink for best hydrothermal performance. *Appl. Therm. Eng.* **2020**, *165*, 114546. [CrossRef]
32. Salehi, S.; Nori, A.; Hosseinzadeh, K.; Ganji, D.D. Hydrothermal analysis of MHD squeezing mixture fluid suspended by hybrid nanoparticles between two parallel plates. *Case Stud. Therm. Eng.* **2020**, *21*, 100650. [CrossRef]
33. Muhammad, K.; Hayat, T.; Alsaedi, A.; Ahmad, B. Melting heat transfer in squeezing flow of basefluid (water), nanofluid (CNTs + water) and hybrid nanofluid (CNTs + CuO + water). *J. Therm. Anal. Calorim.* **2021**, *143*, 1157–1174. [CrossRef]
34. Waini, I.; Ishak, A.; Pop, I. Hybrid nanofluid flow over a permeable non-isothermal shrinking surface. *Mathematics* **2021**, *9*, 538. [CrossRef]
35. Khan, U.; Waini, I.; Ishak, A.; Pop, I. Unsteady hybrid nanofluid flow over a radially permeable shrinking/stretching surface. *J. Mol. Liq.* **2021**, *331*, 115742. [CrossRef]
36. Sarkar, J.; Ghosh, P.; Adil, A. A review on hybrid nanofluids: Recent research, development and applications. *Renew. Sustain. Energy Rev.* **2015**, *43*, 164–177. [CrossRef]
37. Babu, J.A.R.; Kumar, K.K.; Rao, S.S. State-of-art review on hybrid nanofluids. *Renew. Sustain. Energy Rev.* **2017**, *77*, 551–565. [CrossRef]
38. Sajid, M.U.; Ali, H.M. Thermal conductivity of hybrid nanofluids: A critical review. *Int. J. Heat Mass Transf.* **2018**, *126*, 211–234. [CrossRef]
39. Huminic, G.; Huminic, A. Entropy generation of nanofluid and hybrid nanofluid flow in thermal systems: A review. *J. Mol. Liq.* **2020**, *302*, 112533. [CrossRef]
40. Yang, L.; Ji, W.; Mao, M.; Huang, J. An updated review on the properties, fabrication and application of hybrid-nanofluids along with their environmental effects. *J. Clean. Prod.* **2020**, *257*, 120408. [CrossRef]
41. Sajid, M.; Ali, N.; Javed, T.; Abbas, Z. Stretching a curved surface in a viscous fluid. *Chin. Phys. Lett.* **2010**, *27*, 024703. [CrossRef]
42. Sajid, M.; Ali, N.; Abbas, Z.; Javed, T. Flow of a micropolar fluid over a curved stretching surface. *J. Eng. Phys. Thermophys.* **2011**, *84*, 864–871. [CrossRef]
43. Abbas, Z.; Naveed, M.; Sajid, M. Heat transfer analysis for stretching flow over a curved surface with magnetic field. *J. Eng. Thermophys.* **2013**, *22*, 337–345. [CrossRef]
44. Abbas, Z.; Naveed, M.; Sajid, M. Hydromagnetic slip flow of nanofluid over a curved stretching surface with heat generation and thermal radiation. *J. Mol. Liq.* **2016**, *215*, 756–762. [CrossRef]
45. Hayat, T.; Kiran, A.; Imtiaz, M.; Alsaedi, A. Hydromagnetic mixed convection flow of copper and silver water nanofluids due to a curved stretching sheet. *Results Phys.* **2016**, *6*, 904–910. [CrossRef]
46. Imtiaz, M.; Hayat, T.; Alsaedi, A. Convective flow of ferrofluid due to a curved stretching surface with homogeneous-heterogeneous reactions. *Powder Technol.* **2017**, *310*, 154–162. [CrossRef]

47. Saba, F.; Ahmed, N.; Hussain, S.; Khan, U.; Mohyud-Din, S.; Darus, M. Thermal analysis of nanofluid flow over a curved stretching surface suspended by carbon nanotubes with internal heat generation. *Appl. Sci.* **2018**, *8*, 395. [CrossRef]
48. Sanni, K.M.; Asghar, S.; Jalil, M.; Okechi, N.F. Flow of viscous fluid along a nonlinearly stretching curved surface. *Results Phys.* **2017**, *7*, 1–4. [CrossRef]
49. Hayat, T.; Saif, R.S.; Ellahi, R.; Muhammad, T.; Ahmad, B. Numerical study of boundary-layer flow due to a nonlinear curved stretching sheet with convective heat and mass conditions. *Results Phys.* **2017**, *7*, 2601–2606. [CrossRef]
50. Okechi, N.F.; Jalil, M.; Asghar, S. Flow of viscous fluid along an exponentially stretching curved surface. *Results Phys.* **2017**, *7*, 2851–2854. [CrossRef]
51. Saleh, S.H.M.; Arifin, N.M.; Nazar, R.; Pop, I. Unsteady micropolar fluid over a permeable curved stretching shrinking surface. *Math. Probl. Eng.* **2017**, *2017*, 3085249. [CrossRef]
52. Naveed, M.; Abbas, Z.; Sajid, M.; Hasnain, J. Dual solutions in hydromagnetic viscous fluid flow past a shrinking curved surface. *Arab. J. Sci. Eng.* **2018**, *43*, 1189–1194. [CrossRef]
53. Khan, M.R.; Pan, K.; Khan, A.U.; Nadeem, S. Dual solutions for mixed convection flow of $SiO_2 - Al_2O_3$/water hybrid nanofluid near the stagnation point over a curved surface. *Phys. A Stat. Mech. its Appl.* **2020**, *547*, 123959. [CrossRef]
54. Lok, Y.Y.; Amin, N.; Campean, D.; Pop, I. Steady mixed convection flow of a micropolar fluid near the stagnation point on a vertical surface. *Int. J. Numer. Methods Heat Fluid Flow* **2005**, *15*, 654–670. [CrossRef]
55. Merkin, J.H. On dual solutions occurring in mixed convection in a porous medium. *J. Eng. Math.* **1986**, *20*, 171–179. [CrossRef]
56. Weidman, P.D.; Kubitschek, D.G.; Davis, A.M.J. The effect of transpiration on self-similar boundary layer flow over moving surfaces. *Int. J. Eng. Sci.* **2006**, *44*, 730–737. [CrossRef]
57. Shampine, L.F.; Gladwell, I.; Thompson, S. *Solving ODEs with MATLAB*; Cambridge University Press: Cambridge, UK, 2003.

mathematics

Article

On Third-Order Bronze Fibonacci Numbers

Mücahit Akbiyik * and Jeta Alo

Department of Mathematics, Beykent University, Istanbul 34520, Turkey; jeta@beykent.edu.tr
* Correspondence: mucahitakbiyik@beykent.edu.tr

Abstract: In this study, we firstly obtain De Moivre-type identities for the second-order Bronze Fibonacci sequences. Next, we construct and define the third-order Bronze Fibonacci, third-order Bronze Lucas and modified third-order Bronze Fibonacci sequences. Then, we define the generalized third-order Bronze Fibonacci sequence and calculate the De Moivre-type identities for these sequences. Moreover, we find the generating functions, Binet's formulas, Cassini's identities and matrix representations of these sequences and examine some interesting identities related to the third-order Bronze Fibonacci sequences. Finally, we present an encryption and decryption application that uses our obtained results and we present an illustrative example.

Keywords: De Moivre-type identity; third-order Bronze Fibonacci numbers; Binet's formula; Affine-Hill chipher

Citation: Akbiyik, M.; Alo, J. On Third-Order Bronze Fibonacci Numbers. *Mathematics* **2021**, *9*, 2606. https://doi.org/10.3390/math9202606

Academic Editors: Araceli Queiruga-Dios, Abdelmejid Bayad, Maria Jesus Santos, Fatih Yilmaz, Deolinda M. L. Dias Rasteiro, Jesús Martín Vaquero and Víctor Gayoso Martínez

Received: 29 July 2021
Accepted: 11 October 2021
Published: 16 October 2021

Publisher's Note: MDPI stays neutral with regard to jurisdictional claims in published maps and institutional affiliations.

Copyright: © 2021 by the authors. Licensee MDPI, Basel, Switzerland. This article is an open access article distributed under the terms and conditions of the Creative Commons Attribution (CC BY) license (https://creativecommons.org/licenses/by/4.0/).

1. Introduction

In the literature, the roots of the equation $x^2 - x - 1 = 0$ are given as

$$\alpha_1 = (1 + \sqrt{5})/2,$$

$$\alpha_2 = (1 - \sqrt{5})/2,$$

and the following relation is satisfied

$$\left(\frac{1 \pm \sqrt{5}}{2}\right)^n = \frac{L_n \pm \sqrt{5} F_n}{2}, \qquad (1)$$

where L_n denotes the n-th Lucas number and F_n denotes the n-th Fibonacci number. Relation (1) is the *De Moivre-type identity* for Fibonacci numbers [1]. Lin, in [2,3], gave the De Moivre-type identities for the tribonacci and the tetranacci numbers by using the equation $x^3 - x^2 - x - 1 = 0$ and the equation $x^4 - x^3 - x^2 - x - 1 = 0$, respectively. Moreover, the authors in [4] obtained the De Moivre-type identities for the second- and third-order Pell numbers by using the roots of characteristic equations $x^2 - 2x - 1 = 0$ and $x^3 - 2x^2 - x - 1 = 0$, respectively. They presented a way to construct the second-order Pell and Pell–Lucas numbers and the third-order Pell and Pell–Lucas numbers. Additionally, in [5], the author studied the generalized third-order Pell numbers. In [6], the authors gave the De Moivre-type identities for the second-order and third-order Jacobsthal numbers.

The second-order Bronze Fibonacci sequence or short Bronze Fibonacci sequence is given by the linear recurrence equation $B_{n+1} = 3B_n + B_{n-1}$ with initial conditions $B_0 = 0$ and $B_1 = 1$; it is also called the 3-Fibonacci Sequence and is defined as the sequence A006190 in the OEIS [7]. In [8], Kartal extended the Bronze Fibonacci numbers to the Gaussian Bronze Fibonacci numbers and obtained Binet's formula and generating functions for these numbers. In [9], the author introduced $(l, 1, p + 2q, q)$ numbers, $(l, 1, p + 2q, q)$ quaternions, $(l, 1, p + 2q, q)$ symbol elements. In [10], the authors presented a special class of elements in the algebras obtained by the Cayley Dickson process, called l-elements or $(l, 1, 0, 1)$ numbers. They gave some properties of these sequences.

It is also known that Fibonacci Numbers are used in encryption theory. In [11], a class of square Fibonacci $(p+1) \times (p+1)$-matrices, which are based on the Fibonacci p numbers $p = 0, 1, 2, 3, ...$, with a determinant equal to ± 1, was considered. The author defined a Fibonacci coding/decoding method from the Fibonacci matrices which leads to a generalization of the Cassini formula. In [12], the authors present a new method of coding/decoding algorithms using Fibonacci Q matrices. In addition to this, the authors of [13] introduced two new coding/decoding algorithms using Fibonacci Q matrices and R matrices. In [12,13], the used methods are based on the blocked message matrices. In [14], the authors present an application in cryptography and applications of some quaternion elements. In [15], the authors presented a public key cryptosystem using an Affine-Hill chipher with a generalized Fibonacci (multinacci) matrix with large power k, denoted by Q_λ^k, as a key.

In this paper, we give the De Moivre-type identities for the second-order Bronze Fibonacci and the third-order Bronze Fibonacci numbers derived from the characteristic equations $x^2 - 3x - 1 = 0$ and $x^3 - 3x^2 - x - 1 = 0$, respectively. Thus, we define the generalized third-order Bronze Fibonacci numbers, third-order Fibonacci numbers, third-order Bronze Lucas numbers and modified third-order Bronze Fibonacci numbers. We present the generating functions, Binet's formulas, Cassini's identity, matrix representation of third-order Bronze Fibonacci sequences and some interesting identities related to these sequences. Finally, we develop an encryption and decryption algorithm using an Affine-Hill chipher with the third-order Bronze Fibonacci matrix as a key. At the end of paper, we give a numerical example of an encryption and decryption algorithm.

2. De Moivre-Type Identity for the Second- and Third-Order Bronze Fibonacci Numbers

In this section, we firstly obtain De Moivre-type identities for the second-order Bronze Fibonacci numbers. Next, we present a method for constructing the third-order Bronze Fibonacci numbers. We define the third-order Fibonacci numbers, third-order Bronze Lucas numbers, modified third-order Bronze Fibonacci numbers and generalized third-order Bronze Fibonacci numbers. We establish De Moivre-type identities for the third-order Bronze Fibonacci numbers.

The roots of the equation $x^2 - 3x - 1 = 0$ are

$$\alpha_{1,2} = \frac{3 \pm \sqrt{13}}{2}. \tag{2}$$

The De Moivre-type identity for the second-order Bronze Fibonacci numbers can be found as:

$$\left(\frac{3 \pm \sqrt{13}}{2}\right)^n = \frac{B_n^L \pm \sqrt{13} B_n^F}{2}, \tag{3}$$

where B_n^L represents the Bronze Lucas numbers, which form a Bronze Fibonacci sequence with the initial conditions $B_0^L = 2$ and $B_1^L = 3$, and B_n^F represents Bronze Fibonacci numbers with the initial conditions $B_0^F = 0$ and $B_1^F = 1$.

The third-order Bronze Fibonacci numbers are related to the roots of the equation

$$x^3 - 3x^2 - x - 1 = 0. \tag{4}$$

The three roots of this equation are

$$\alpha_1 = 1 + U + V,$$

$$\alpha_2 = 1 - \frac{1}{2}(U+V) + i\frac{\sqrt{3}}{2}(U-V),$$

$$\alpha_3 = 1 - \frac{1}{2}(U+V) - i\frac{\sqrt{3}}{2}(U-V),$$

where $U = \sqrt[3]{2 + \sqrt{4 - \frac{64}{27}}}$, $V = \sqrt[3]{2 - \sqrt{4 - \frac{64}{27}}}$, $UV = \frac{4}{3}$, and $U^3 + V^3 = 4$. Thus, the powers of the root α_1 can be calculated as follows:

$$\alpha_1^2 = \frac{11}{3} + 2(U+V) + 1(U^2+V^2),$$

$$\alpha_1^3 = \frac{39}{3} + 7(U+V) + 3(U^2+V^2),$$

$$\alpha_1^4 = \frac{131}{3} + 24(U+V) + 10(U^2+V^2),$$

$$\alpha_1^5 = \frac{443}{3} + 81(U+V) + 34(U^2+V^2),$$

$$\alpha_1^6 = \frac{1499}{3} + 274(U+V) + 115(U^2+V^2).$$

The coefficients of the above equations construct three third-order Bronze Fibonacci sequences, which are denoted by $\{\mathfrak{B}_n^{\mathcal{L}}\}$, $\{\mathfrak{B}_n^{\mathfrak{M}}\}$ and $\{\mathfrak{B}_n^{\mathfrak{F}}\}$, respectively.

1. $\{\mathfrak{B}_n^{\mathcal{L}}\}$ is a third-order Bronze Lucas sequence with the recurrence relation $\mathfrak{B}_n^{\mathcal{L}} = 3\mathfrak{B}_{n-1}^{\mathcal{L}} + \mathfrak{B}_{n-2}^{\mathcal{L}} + \mathfrak{B}_{n-3}^{\mathcal{L}}$ for $n \geq 3$ and $\mathfrak{B}_0^{\mathcal{L}} = 3, \mathfrak{B}_1^{\mathcal{L}} = 3, \mathfrak{B}_2^{\mathcal{L}} = 11$.
2. $\{\mathfrak{B}_n^{\mathfrak{M}}\}$ is a modified third-order Bronze Fibonacci sequence with the recurrence relation $\mathfrak{B}_n^{\mathfrak{M}} = 3\mathfrak{B}_{n-1}^{\mathfrak{M}} + \mathfrak{B}_{n-2}^{\mathfrak{M}} + \mathfrak{B}_{n-3}^{\mathfrak{M}}$ for $n \geq 3$ and $\mathfrak{B}_0^{\mathfrak{M}} = 1, \mathfrak{B}_1^{\mathfrak{M}} = 2$ and $\mathfrak{B}_2^{\mathfrak{M}} = 7$. Additionally, this sequence is also called Bisection of Tribonacci Numbers in OEIS with the code A099463, [7].
3. $\{\mathfrak{B}_n^{\mathfrak{F}}\}$ is a third-order Bronze Fibonacci sequence with the recurrence relation $\mathfrak{B}_n^{\mathfrak{F}} = 3\mathfrak{B}_{n-1}^{\mathfrak{F}} + \mathfrak{B}_{n-2}^{\mathfrak{F}} + \mathfrak{B}_{n-3}^{\mathfrak{F}}$ for $n \geq 3$ and $\mathfrak{B}_0^{\mathfrak{F}} = 1, \mathfrak{B}_1^{\mathfrak{F}} = 3$ and $\mathfrak{B}_2^{\mathfrak{F}} = 10$. The sequence is also a sum of even indexed terms of Tribonacci Numbers in OEIS with the code A113300 in [7].

The first eleven terms of the above sequences are presented in the Table 1.

Table 1. The third-order Bronze Fibonacci numbers.

N	0	1	2	3	4	5	6	7	8	9	10
$\mathfrak{B}_n^{\mathcal{L}}$	3	3	11	39	131	443	1499	5071	17,155	58,035	196,331
$\mathfrak{B}_n^{\mathfrak{M}}$	1	2	7	24	81	274	927	3136	10,609	35,890	121,415
$\mathfrak{B}_n^{\mathfrak{F}}$	1	3	10	34	115	389	1316	4452	15,061	50,951	172,366

Now, by using these three special third-order Bronze Fibonacci sequences we define a generalized third-order Bronze Fibonacci sequence as follows:

The sequence $\{\mathfrak{B}_n^{\mathfrak{G}}\}$ with the recurrence relation $\mathfrak{B}_n^{\mathfrak{G}} = 3\mathfrak{B}_{n-1}^{\mathfrak{G}} + \mathfrak{B}_{n-2}^{\mathfrak{G}} + \mathfrak{B}_{n-3}^{\mathfrak{G}}$ for $n \geq 3$, where $\mathfrak{B}_0^{\mathfrak{G}}, \mathfrak{B}_1^{\mathfrak{G}}, \mathfrak{B}_2^{\mathfrak{G}}$ are any arbitrary numbers not all being zero, is called a generalized third-order Bronze Fibonacci sequence.

By using the sequences $\{\mathfrak{B}_n^{\mathcal{L}}\}$, $\{\mathfrak{B}_n^{\mathfrak{M}}\}$, and $\{\mathfrak{B}_n^{\mathfrak{F}}\}$, and applying induction over n, we find

$$\alpha_1^n = \frac{1}{3}\mathfrak{B}_n^{\mathcal{L}} + \mathfrak{B}_{n-1}^{\mathfrak{M}}(U+V) + \mathfrak{B}_{n-2}^{\mathfrak{F}}(U^2+V^2). \tag{5}$$

Similarly, we obtain

$$\begin{aligned}\alpha_2^n = &\frac{1}{3}\mathfrak{B}_n^{\mathcal{L}} - \frac{1}{2}\mathfrak{B}_{n-1}^{\mathfrak{M}}(U+V) - \frac{1}{2}\mathfrak{B}_{n-2}^{\mathfrak{F}}(U^2+V^2) \\ &+ \frac{\sqrt{3}i}{2}\mathfrak{B}_{n-1}^{\mathfrak{M}}(U-V) + \frac{\sqrt{3}i}{2}\mathfrak{B}_{n-2}^{\mathfrak{F}}(U^2-V^2),\end{aligned} \tag{6}$$

and

$$\alpha_3^n = \frac{1}{3}\mathfrak{B}_n^{\mathfrak{L}} - \frac{1}{2}\mathfrak{B}_{n-1}^{\mathfrak{M}}(U+V) - \frac{1}{2}\mathfrak{B}_{n-2}^{\mathfrak{F}}(U^2+V^2)$$
$$- \frac{\sqrt{3}i}{2}\mathfrak{B}_{n-1}^{\mathfrak{M}}(U-V) - \frac{\sqrt{3}i}{2}\mathfrak{B}_{n-2}^{\mathfrak{F}}(U^2-V^2). \tag{7}$$

So, we have α_1^n, α_2^n and α_3^n in terms of $\mathfrak{B}_n^{\mathfrak{L}}$, $\mathfrak{B}_n^{\mathfrak{M}}$, and $\mathfrak{B}_n^{\mathfrak{F}}$. Consequently, Equations (5)–(7) are called De Moivre-type identities for the third-order Bronze Fibonacci numbers.

3. Generating Function and Binet's Formula for the Third-Order Bronze Fibonacci Numbers

In this section, we obtain the generating functions and Binet's formulas for the third-order Bronze Fibonacci sequences.

Theorem 1. *The generating function for the generalized third-order Bronze Fibonacci sequence $\{\mathfrak{B}_n^{\mathfrak{G}}\}$ is given by*

$$\mathfrak{B}^{\mathfrak{G}}(x) = \frac{\mathfrak{B}_0^{\mathfrak{G}} + (\mathfrak{B}_1^{\mathfrak{G}} - 3\mathfrak{B}_0^{\mathfrak{G}})x - (\mathfrak{B}_2^{\mathfrak{G}} - 3\mathfrak{B}_1^{\mathfrak{G}} + \mathfrak{B}_0^{\mathfrak{G}})x^2}{1 - 3x - x^2 - x^3}, \tag{8}$$

where $\mathfrak{B}^{\mathfrak{G}}(x) = \sum_{n=0}^{\infty} \mathfrak{B}_n^{\mathfrak{G}} x^n$.

Proof. Let $\mathfrak{B}^{\mathfrak{G}}(x) = \sum_{n=0}^{\infty} \mathfrak{B}_n^{\mathfrak{G}} x^n$. By using the recurrence relation, we find

$$\mathfrak{B}^{\mathfrak{G}}(x) = \sum_{n=3}^{\infty} \mathfrak{B}_n^{\mathfrak{G}} x^n + \mathfrak{B}_2^{\mathfrak{G}} x^2 + \mathfrak{B}_1^{\mathfrak{G}} x + \mathfrak{B}_0^{\mathfrak{G}}$$
$$= 3\sum_{n=3}^{\infty} \mathfrak{B}^{\mathfrak{G}}_{n-1} x^n + \sum_{n=3}^{\infty} \mathfrak{B}^{\mathfrak{G}}_{n-2} x^n + \sum_{n=3}^{\infty} \mathfrak{B}^{\mathfrak{G}}_{n-3} x^n + \mathfrak{B}^{\mathfrak{G}}_2 x^2 + \mathfrak{B}^{\mathfrak{G}}_1 x + \mathfrak{B}^{\mathfrak{G}}_0 \tag{9}$$
$$= 3x(\mathfrak{B}^{\mathfrak{G}}(x) - \mathfrak{B}_0^{\mathfrak{G}} - \mathfrak{B}_1^{\mathfrak{G}} x) + x^2(\mathfrak{B}^{\mathfrak{G}}(x) - \mathfrak{B}_0^{\mathfrak{G}}) + x^3 \mathfrak{B}^{\mathfrak{G}}(x) + \mathfrak{B}_2^{\mathfrak{G}} x^2 + \mathfrak{B}_1^{\mathfrak{G}} x + \mathfrak{B}_0^{\mathfrak{G}}$$

and $\mathfrak{B}^{\mathfrak{G}}(x)(1 - 3x - x^2 - x^3) = \mathfrak{B}_0^{\mathfrak{G}} + (\mathfrak{B}_1^{\mathfrak{G}} - 3\mathfrak{B}_0^{\mathfrak{G}})x + (\mathfrak{B}_2^{\mathfrak{G}} - 3\mathfrak{B}_1^{\mathfrak{G}} - \mathfrak{B}_0^{\mathfrak{G}})x^2$. □

Corollary 1. *The generating functions for the sequences $\{\mathfrak{B}_n^{\mathfrak{L}}\}$, $\{\mathfrak{B}_n^{\mathfrak{M}}\}$ and $\{\mathfrak{B}_n^{\mathfrak{F}}\}$ can be calculated as follows*

$$\mathfrak{B}^{\mathfrak{L}}(x) = \frac{-x^2 - 6x + 3}{1 - 3x - x^2 - x^3}, \tag{10}$$

where $\mathfrak{B}^{\mathfrak{L}}(x) = \sum_{n=0}^{\infty} \mathfrak{B}_n^{\mathfrak{L}} x^n$,

$$\mathfrak{B}^{\mathfrak{M}}(x) = \frac{1-x}{1 - 3x - x^2 - x^3}, \tag{11}$$

where $\mathfrak{B}^{\mathfrak{M}}(x) = \sum_{n=0}^{\infty} \mathfrak{B}_n^{\mathfrak{M}} x^n$ and

$$\mathfrak{B}^{\mathfrak{F}}(x) = \frac{1}{1 - 3x - x^2 - x^3}, \tag{12}$$

where $\mathfrak{B}^{\mathfrak{F}}(x) = \sum_{n=0}^{\infty} \mathfrak{B}_n^{\mathfrak{F}} x^n$.

Theorem 2. *Binet's formula for the generalized third-order Bronze Fibonacci numbers is given by:*

$$\mathfrak{B}_n^{\mathfrak{G}} = \frac{\mathfrak{B}_0^{\mathfrak{G}} \alpha_2 \alpha_3 - \mathfrak{B}_1^{\mathfrak{G}}(\alpha_2 + \alpha_3) + \mathfrak{B}_2^{\mathfrak{G}}}{(\alpha_2 - \alpha_1)(\alpha_3 - \alpha_1)} \alpha_1^n + \frac{-\mathfrak{B}_0^{\mathfrak{G}} \alpha_1 \alpha_3 + \mathfrak{B}_1^{\mathfrak{G}}(\alpha_1 + \alpha_3) - \mathfrak{B}_2^{\mathfrak{G}}}{(\alpha_3 - \alpha_2)(\alpha_2 - \alpha_1)} \alpha_2^n$$
$$+ \frac{\mathfrak{B}_0^{\mathfrak{G}} \alpha_1 \alpha_2 - \mathfrak{B}_1^{\mathfrak{G}}(\alpha_1 + \alpha_2) + \mathfrak{B}_2^{\mathfrak{G}}}{(\alpha_3 - \alpha_2)(\alpha_3 - \alpha_1)} \alpha_3^n. \tag{13}$$

Proof. We seek for constants d_1, d_2 and d_3 such that

$$\mathfrak{B}_n^{\mathfrak{G}} = d_1 \alpha_1^n + d_2 \alpha_2^n + d_3 \alpha_3^n.$$

These are found by solving the system of linear equations for $n = 0$, $n = 1$ and $n = 2$

$$d_1 \alpha_1^0 + d_2 \alpha_2^0 + d_3 \alpha_3^0 = \mathfrak{B}_0^{\mathfrak{G}}$$
$$d_1 \alpha_1^1 + d_2 \alpha_2^1 + d_3 \alpha_3^1 = \mathfrak{B}_1^{\mathfrak{G}}$$
$$d_1 \alpha_1^2 + d_2 \alpha_2^2 + d_3 \alpha_3^2 = \mathfrak{B}_2^{\mathfrak{G}}.$$

$\square$

Corollary 2. *Binet's formulas for the sequences $\{\mathfrak{B}_n^{\mathfrak{L}}\}$, $\{\mathfrak{B}_n^{\mathfrak{M}}\}$, and $\{\mathfrak{B}_n^{\mathfrak{F}}\}$ can be calculated as:*
$$\mathfrak{B}_n^{\mathfrak{L}} = \frac{3\alpha_2 \alpha_3 - 3(\alpha_2 + \alpha_3) + 11}{(\alpha_2 - \alpha_1)(\alpha_3 - \alpha_1)} \alpha_1^n + \frac{-3\alpha_1 \alpha_3 + 3(\alpha_1 + \alpha_3) - 11}{(\alpha_3 - \alpha_2)(\alpha_2 - \alpha_1)} \alpha_2^n + \frac{3\alpha_1 \alpha_2 - 3(\alpha_1 + \alpha_2) + 11}{(\alpha_3 - \alpha_2)(\alpha_3 - \alpha_1)} \alpha_3^n \text{ or after making the necessary arrangements}$$

$$\mathfrak{B}_n^{\mathfrak{L}} = \alpha_1^n + \alpha_2^n + \alpha_3^n, \tag{14}$$

$$\mathfrak{B}_n^{\mathfrak{M}} = \frac{\alpha_2 \alpha_3 - 2(\alpha_2 + \alpha_3) + 7}{(\alpha_2 - \alpha_1)(\alpha_3 - \alpha_1)} \alpha_1^n + \frac{-\alpha_1 \alpha_3 + 2(\alpha_1 + \alpha_3) - 7}{(\alpha_3 - \alpha_2)(\alpha_2 - \alpha_1)} \alpha_2^n$$
$$+ \frac{\alpha_1 \alpha_2 - 2(\alpha_1 + \alpha_2) + 7}{(\alpha_3 - \alpha_2)(\alpha_3 - \alpha_1)} \alpha_3^n, \tag{15}$$

$$\mathfrak{B}_n^{\mathfrak{F}} = \frac{\alpha_2 \alpha_3 - 3(\alpha_2 + \alpha_3) + 10}{(\alpha_2 - \alpha_1)(\alpha_3 - \alpha_1)} \alpha_1^n + \frac{-\alpha_1 \alpha_3 + 3(\alpha_1 + \alpha_3) - 10}{(\alpha_3 - \alpha_2)(\alpha_2 - \alpha_1)} \alpha_2^n$$
$$+ \frac{\alpha_1 \alpha_2 - 3(\alpha_1 + \alpha_2) + 10}{(\alpha_3 - \alpha_2)(\alpha_3 - \alpha_1)} \alpha_3^n. \tag{16}$$

4. Some Properties of $\{\mathfrak{B}_n^{\mathfrak{G}}\}$, $\{\mathfrak{B}_n^{\mathfrak{L}}\}$, $\{\mathfrak{B}_n^{\mathfrak{M}}\}$ and $\{\mathfrak{B}_n^{\mathfrak{F}}\}$

In this section, we give some properties of the third-order Bronze Fibonacci sequences such as some equalities and linear sums.

Using the definitions of three third-order Bronze Fibonacci sequences, the following results can be derived easily:

- $\mathfrak{B}^{\mathfrak{M}}_{n+1} = \mathfrak{B}^{\mathfrak{F}}_{n+1} - \mathfrak{B}^{\mathfrak{F}}_n$;
- $\mathfrak{B}^{\mathfrak{M}}_{n+3} = 2\mathfrak{B}^{\mathfrak{F}}_{n+2} + \mathfrak{B}^{\mathfrak{F}}_{n+1} + \mathfrak{B}^{\mathfrak{F}}_n$;
- $\mathfrak{B}^{\mathfrak{L}}_{n+2} = 2\mathfrak{B}^{\mathfrak{M}}_{n+2} - \mathfrak{B}^{\mathfrak{M}}_{n+1} - \mathfrak{B}^{\mathfrak{M}}_n$;
- $\mathfrak{B}^{\mathfrak{L}}_{n+3} = \mathfrak{B}^{\mathfrak{F}}_{n+3} + \mathfrak{B}^{\mathfrak{F}}_{n+1} + 2\mathfrak{B}^{\mathfrak{F}}_n$;
- $\mathfrak{B}^{\mathfrak{F}}_{n+3} - \mathfrak{B}^{\mathfrak{F}}_{n+1} = \mathfrak{B}^{\mathfrak{M}}_{n+3} + \mathfrak{B}^{\mathfrak{M}}_{n+2}$;
- $\mathfrak{B}^{\mathfrak{L}}_{n+4} = 10\mathfrak{B}^{\mathfrak{L}}_{n+2} + 4\mathfrak{B}^{\mathfrak{L}}_{n+1} + 4\mathfrak{B}^{\mathfrak{L}}_n$;
- $33\mathfrak{B}^{\mathfrak{L}}_{n+4} = -247\mathfrak{B}^{\mathfrak{L}}_{n+3} + 134\mathfrak{B}^{\mathfrak{L}}_{n+1} + 106\mathfrak{B}^{\mathfrak{L}}_n$;
- $\mathfrak{B}^{\mathfrak{L}}_{n+4} = 4\mathfrak{B}^{\mathfrak{L}}_{n+3} - 2\mathfrak{B}^{\mathfrak{L}}_{n+2} - \mathfrak{B}^{\mathfrak{L}}_n$;
- $\mathfrak{B}^{\mathfrak{M}}_{n+4} = 10\mathfrak{B}^{\mathfrak{M}}_{n+2} + 4\mathfrak{B}^{\mathfrak{M}}_{n+1} + 3\mathfrak{B}^{\mathfrak{M}}_n$;
- $\mathfrak{B}^{\mathfrak{F}}_{n+4} = 3\mathfrak{B}^{\mathfrak{F}}_{n+2} + 4\mathfrak{B}^{\mathfrak{F}}_{n+1} + 10\mathfrak{B}^{\mathfrak{F}}_n$;
- $\sum_{k=0}^{n} \mathfrak{B}^{\mathfrak{M}}_k = \mathfrak{B}^{\mathfrak{F}}_n$.

Theorem 3. *Linear sums for the generalized third-order Bronze Fibonacci numbers are given as follows:*

$$\sum_{k=0}^{n} \mathcal{B}^{\mathfrak{G}}_{k} = \frac{1}{4}(\mathcal{B}^{\mathfrak{G}}_{n+3} - 2\mathcal{B}^{\mathfrak{G}}_{n+2} - 3\mathcal{B}^{\mathfrak{G}}_{n+1} - \mathcal{B}^{\mathfrak{G}}_{2} + 2\mathcal{B}^{\mathfrak{G}}_{1} + 3\mathcal{B}^{\mathfrak{G}}_{0}), \quad (17)$$

$$\sum_{k=0}^{n} \mathcal{B}^{\mathfrak{G}}_{2k+1} = \frac{1}{4}(\mathcal{B}^{\mathfrak{G}}_{2n+4} - 3\mathcal{B}^{\mathfrak{G}}_{2n+3} - \mathcal{B}^{\mathfrak{G}}_{2} + 3\mathcal{B}^{\mathfrak{G}}_{1}), \quad (18)$$

$$\sum_{k=0}^{n} \mathcal{B}^{\mathfrak{G}}_{2k} = \frac{1}{4}(\mathcal{B}^{\mathfrak{G}}_{2n+3} - 3\mathcal{B}^{\mathfrak{G}}_{2n+2} - \mathcal{B}^{\mathfrak{G}}_{1} + 3\mathcal{B}^{\mathfrak{G}}_{0}). \quad (19)$$

Proof. From the linear recurrence relation of $\mathcal{B}^{\mathfrak{G}}_{n+3}$, we have:

$$\mathcal{B}^{\mathfrak{G}}_{n} = \mathcal{B}^{\mathfrak{G}}_{n+3} - 3\mathcal{B}^{\mathfrak{G}}_{n+2} - \mathcal{B}^{\mathfrak{G}}_{n+1},$$

or

$$\mathcal{B}^{\mathfrak{G}}_{0} = \mathcal{B}^{\mathfrak{G}}_{3} - 3\mathcal{B}^{\mathfrak{G}}_{2} - \mathcal{B}^{\mathfrak{G}}_{1},$$
$$\mathcal{B}^{\mathfrak{G}}_{1} = \mathcal{B}^{\mathfrak{G}}_{4} - 3\mathcal{B}^{\mathfrak{G}}_{3} - \mathcal{B}^{\mathfrak{G}}_{2},$$
$$\mathcal{B}^{\mathfrak{G}}_{2} = \mathcal{B}^{\mathfrak{G}}_{5} - 3\mathcal{B}^{\mathfrak{G}}_{4} - \mathcal{B}^{\mathfrak{G}}_{3},$$
$$\ldots$$
$$\mathcal{B}^{\mathfrak{G}}_{n-2} = \mathcal{B}^{\mathfrak{G}}_{n+1} - 3\mathcal{B}^{\mathfrak{G}}_{n} - \mathcal{B}^{\mathfrak{G}}_{n-1},$$
$$\mathcal{B}^{\mathfrak{G}}_{n-1} = \mathcal{B}^{\mathfrak{G}}_{n+2} - 3\mathcal{B}^{\mathfrak{G}}_{n+1} - \mathcal{B}^{\mathfrak{G}}_{n},$$
$$\mathcal{B}^{\mathfrak{G}}_{n} = \mathcal{B}^{\mathfrak{G}}_{n+3} - 3\mathcal{B}^{\mathfrak{G}}_{n+2} - \mathcal{B}^{\mathfrak{G}}_{n+1}.$$

Summing the left and the right sides of these equations, we obtain:

$$\sum_{k=0}^{n} \mathcal{B}^{\mathfrak{G}}_{k} = \sum_{k=3}^{n+3} \mathcal{B}^{\mathfrak{G}}_{k} - 3\sum_{k=2}^{n+2} \mathcal{B}^{\mathfrak{G}}_{k} - \sum_{k=1}^{n+1} \mathcal{B}^{\mathfrak{G}}_{k},$$

$$\sum_{k=0}^{n} \mathcal{B}^{\mathfrak{G}}_{k} = (\mathcal{B}^{\mathfrak{G}}_{n+1} + \mathcal{B}^{\mathfrak{G}}_{n+2} + \mathcal{B}^{\mathfrak{G}}_{n+3} + \sum_{k=0}^{n} \mathcal{B}^{\mathfrak{G}}_{k} - \mathcal{B}^{\mathfrak{G}}_{2} - \mathcal{B}^{\mathfrak{G}}_{1} - \mathcal{B}^{\mathfrak{G}}_{0}),$$

$$- 3(\mathcal{B}^{\mathfrak{G}}_{n+1} + \mathcal{B}^{\mathfrak{G}}_{n+2} + \sum_{k=0}^{n} \mathcal{B}^{\mathfrak{G}}_{k} - \mathcal{B}^{\mathfrak{G}}_{1} - \mathcal{B}^{\mathfrak{G}}_{0}),$$

$$- (\mathcal{B}^{\mathfrak{G}}_{n+1} + \sum_{k=0}^{n} \mathcal{B}^{\mathfrak{G}}_{k} - \mathcal{B}^{\mathfrak{G}}_{0}).$$

By solving this equation, we obtain

$$\sum_{k=0}^{n} \mathcal{B}^{\mathfrak{G}}_{k} = \frac{1}{4}(\mathcal{B}^{\mathfrak{G}}_{n+3} - 2\mathcal{B}^{\mathfrak{G}}_{n+2} - 3\mathcal{B}^{\mathfrak{G}}_{n+1} - \mathcal{B}^{\mathfrak{G}}_{2} + 2\mathcal{B}^{\mathfrak{G}}_{1} + 3\mathcal{B}^{\mathfrak{G}}_{0}).$$

In the similar way, by using the linear recurrence equation, we find:

$$\mathcal{B}^{\mathfrak{G}}_{1} = \mathcal{B}^{\mathfrak{G}}_{4} - 3\mathcal{B}^{\mathfrak{G}}_{3} - \mathcal{B}^{\mathfrak{G}}_{2},$$
$$\mathcal{B}^{\mathfrak{G}}_{3} = \mathcal{B}^{\mathfrak{G}}_{6} - 3\mathcal{B}^{\mathfrak{G}}_{5} - \mathcal{B}^{\mathfrak{G}}_{4},$$
$$\mathcal{B}^{\mathfrak{G}}_{5} = \mathcal{B}^{\mathfrak{G}}_{8} - 3\mathcal{B}^{\mathfrak{G}}_{7} - \mathcal{B}^{\mathfrak{G}}_{6},$$
$$\ldots$$
$$\mathcal{B}^{\mathfrak{G}}_{2n-1} = \mathcal{B}^{\mathfrak{G}}_{2n+2} - 3\mathcal{B}^{\mathfrak{G}}_{2n+1} - \mathcal{B}^{\mathfrak{G}}_{2n},$$

$$\mathfrak{B}^{\mathfrak{G}}{}_{2n+1} = \mathfrak{B}^{\mathfrak{G}}{}_{2n+4} - 3\mathfrak{B}^{\mathfrak{G}}{}_{2n+3} - \mathfrak{B}^{\mathfrak{G}}{}_{2n+2},$$

and by summing side by side, we obtain

$$\sum_{k=0}^{n} \mathfrak{B}^{\mathfrak{G}}{}_{2k+1} = (\mathfrak{B}^{\mathfrak{G}}{}_{2n+2} + \mathfrak{B}^{\mathfrak{G}}{}_{2n+4} + \sum_{k=0}^{n} \mathfrak{B}^{\mathfrak{G}}{}_{2k} - \mathfrak{B}^{\mathfrak{G}}{}_{0} - \mathfrak{B}^{\mathfrak{G}}{}_{2})$$

$$- 3(\sum_{k=0}^{n} \mathfrak{B}^{\mathfrak{G}}{}_{2k+1} - \mathfrak{B}^{\mathfrak{G}}{}_{2n+3} - \mathfrak{B}^{\mathfrak{G}}{}_{1})$$

$$- (\sum_{k=0}^{n} \mathfrak{B}^{\mathfrak{G}}{}_{2k} + \mathfrak{B}^{\mathfrak{G}}{}_{2n+2} - \mathfrak{B}^{\mathfrak{G}}{}_{0})$$

then, solving this equation we obtain:

$$\sum_{k=0}^{n} \mathfrak{B}^{\mathfrak{G}}{}_{2k+1} = \frac{1}{4}(\mathfrak{B}^{\mathfrak{G}}{}_{2n+4} - 3\mathfrak{B}^{\mathfrak{G}}{}_{2n+3} - \mathfrak{B}^{\mathfrak{G}}{}_{2} + 3\mathfrak{B}^{\mathfrak{G}}{}_{1}).$$

Similarly, for even indexes, we have

$$\mathfrak{B}^{\mathfrak{G}}{}_{0} = \mathfrak{B}^{\mathfrak{G}}{}_{3} - 3\mathfrak{B}^{\mathfrak{G}}{}_{2} - \mathfrak{B}^{\mathfrak{G}}{}_{1},$$

$$\mathfrak{B}^{\mathfrak{G}}{}_{2} = \mathfrak{B}^{\mathfrak{G}}{}_{5} - 3\mathfrak{B}^{\mathfrak{G}}{}_{4} - \mathfrak{B}^{\mathfrak{G}}{}_{3},$$

$$\mathfrak{B}^{\mathfrak{G}}{}_{4} = \mathfrak{B}^{\mathfrak{G}}{}_{7} - 3\mathfrak{B}^{\mathfrak{G}}{}_{6} - \mathfrak{B}^{\mathfrak{G}}{}_{5},$$

$$\ldots$$

$$\mathfrak{B}^{\mathfrak{G}}{}_{2n-2} = \mathfrak{B}^{\mathfrak{G}}{}_{2n+1} - 3\mathfrak{B}^{\mathfrak{G}}{}_{2n} - \mathfrak{B}^{\mathfrak{G}}{}_{2n-1},$$

$$\mathfrak{B}^{\mathfrak{G}}{}_{2n} = \mathfrak{B}^{\mathfrak{G}}{}_{2n+3} - 3\mathfrak{B}^{\mathfrak{G}}{}_{2n+2} - \mathfrak{B}^{\mathfrak{G}}{}_{2n+1},$$

and $\sum_{k=0}^{n} \mathfrak{B}^{\mathfrak{G}}{}_{2k} = (\mathfrak{B}^{\mathfrak{G}}{}_{2n+3} + \sum_{k=0}^{n} \mathfrak{B}^{\mathfrak{G}}{}_{2k+1} - \mathfrak{B}^{\mathfrak{G}}{}_{1}) - 3(\sum_{k=0}^{n} \mathfrak{B}^{\mathfrak{G}}{}_{2k} + \mathfrak{B}^{\mathfrak{G}}{}_{2n+2} - \mathfrak{B}^{\mathfrak{G}}{}_{0}) - \sum_{k=0}^{n} \mathfrak{B}^{\mathfrak{G}}{}_{2k+1}$; then, the result is obtained by solving this equation

$$\sum_{k=0}^{n} \mathfrak{B}^{\mathfrak{G}}{}_{2k} = \frac{1}{4}(\mathfrak{B}^{\mathfrak{G}}{}_{2n+3} - 3\mathfrak{B}^{\mathfrak{G}}{}_{2n+2} - \mathfrak{B}^{\mathfrak{G}}{}_{1} + 3\mathfrak{B}^{\mathfrak{G}}{}_{0}).$$

□

Corollary 3. *Linear sums for the third-order Bronze Lucas sequence* $\{\mathfrak{B}^{\mathfrak{L}}_{n}\}$ *are:*

$$\sum_{k=0}^{n} \mathfrak{B}^{\mathfrak{L}}{}_{k} = \frac{1}{4}(\mathfrak{B}^{\mathfrak{L}}{}_{n+3} - 2\mathfrak{B}^{\mathfrak{L}}{}_{n+2} - 3\mathfrak{B}^{\mathfrak{L}}{}_{n+1} + 4), \tag{20}$$

$$\sum_{k=0}^{n} \mathfrak{B}^{\mathfrak{L}}{}_{2k+1} = \frac{1}{4}(\mathfrak{B}^{\mathfrak{L}}{}_{2n+4} - 3\mathfrak{B}^{\mathfrak{L}}{}_{2n+3} - 2), \tag{21}$$

$$\sum_{k=0}^{n} \mathfrak{B}^{\mathfrak{L}}{}_{2k} = \frac{1}{4}(\mathfrak{B}^{\mathfrak{L}}{}_{2n+3} - 3\mathfrak{B}^{\mathfrak{L}}{}_{2n+2} + 6). \tag{22}$$

Corollary 4. *Linear sums for the modified third-order Bronze Fibonacci sequence* $\{\mathfrak{B}^{\mathfrak{M}}_{n}\}$ *are:*

$$\sum_{k=0}^{n} \mathfrak{B}^{\mathfrak{M}}{}_{k} = \frac{1}{4}(\mathfrak{B}^{\mathfrak{M}}{}_{n+3} - 2\mathfrak{B}^{\mathfrak{M}}{}_{n+2} - 3\mathfrak{B}^{\mathfrak{M}}{}_{n+1}), \tag{23}$$

$$\sum_{k=0}^{n} \mathfrak{B}^{\mathfrak{M}}{}_{2k+1} = \frac{1}{4}(\mathfrak{B}^{\mathfrak{M}}{}_{2n+4} - 3\mathfrak{B}^{\mathfrak{M}}{}_{2n+3} - 1), \tag{24}$$

$$\sum_{k=0}^{n} \mathfrak{B}^{\mathfrak{M}}{}_{2k} = \frac{1}{4}(\mathfrak{B}^{\mathfrak{M}}{}_{2n+3} - 3\mathfrak{B}^{\mathfrak{M}}{}_{2n+2} + 1). \tag{25}$$

Corollary 5. *Linear sums for the third-order Bronze Fibonacci sequence* $\{\mathfrak{B}_n^{\mathfrak{F}}\}$ *are:*

$$\sum_{k=0}^{n} \mathfrak{B}^{\mathfrak{F}}{}_{k} = \frac{1}{4}(\mathfrak{B}^{\mathfrak{F}}{}_{n+3} - 2\mathfrak{B}^{\mathfrak{F}}{}_{n+2} - 3\mathfrak{B}^{\mathfrak{F}}{}_{n+1} - 1), \tag{26}$$

$$\sum_{k=0}^{n} \mathfrak{B}^{\mathfrak{F}}{}_{2k+1} = \frac{1}{4}(\mathfrak{B}^{\mathfrak{F}}{}_{2n+4} - 3\mathfrak{B}^{\mathfrak{F}}{}_{2n+3} - 1), \tag{27}$$

$$\sum_{k=0}^{n} \mathfrak{B}^{\mathfrak{F}}{}_{2k} = \frac{1}{4}(\mathfrak{B}^{\mathfrak{F}}{}_{2n+3} - 3\mathfrak{B}^{\mathfrak{F}}{}_{2n+2}). \tag{28}$$

5. Cassini's Identity for the Bronze Fibonacci Numbers

In this section, we obtain the well known Cassini identity, sometimes called Simson's formulas, for the third-order Bronze Fibonacci sequences.

Theorem 4. *Cassini's identity for the generalized third-order Bronze Fibonacci numbers is given by*

$$\begin{vmatrix} \mathfrak{B}^{\mathfrak{G}}_{n+4} & \mathfrak{B}^{\mathfrak{G}}_{n+3} & \mathfrak{B}^{\mathfrak{G}}_{n+2} \\ \mathfrak{B}^{\mathfrak{G}}_{n+3} & \mathfrak{B}^{\mathfrak{G}}_{n+2} & \mathfrak{B}^{\mathfrak{G}}_{n+1} \\ \mathfrak{B}^{\mathfrak{G}}_{n+2} & \mathfrak{B}^{\mathfrak{G}}_{n+1} & \mathfrak{B}^{\mathfrak{G}}_{n} \end{vmatrix} = \begin{vmatrix} \mathfrak{B}^{\mathfrak{G}}_{4} & \mathfrak{B}^{\mathfrak{G}}_{3} & \mathfrak{B}^{\mathfrak{G}}_{2} \\ \mathfrak{B}^{\mathfrak{G}}_{3} & \mathfrak{B}^{\mathfrak{G}}_{2} & \mathfrak{B}^{\mathfrak{G}}_{1} \\ \mathfrak{B}^{\mathfrak{G}}_{2} & \mathfrak{B}^{\mathfrak{G}}_{1} & \mathfrak{B}^{\mathfrak{G}}_{0} \end{vmatrix} \tag{29}$$

Proof. By using the induction method, for $n = 1$

$$\begin{vmatrix} \mathfrak{B}^{\mathfrak{G}}_{5} & \mathfrak{B}^{\mathfrak{G}}_{4} & \mathfrak{B}^{\mathfrak{G}}_{3} \\ \mathfrak{B}^{\mathfrak{G}}_{4} & \mathfrak{B}^{\mathfrak{G}}_{3} & \mathfrak{B}^{\mathfrak{G}}_{2} \\ \mathfrak{B}^{\mathfrak{G}}_{3} & \mathfrak{B}^{\mathfrak{G}}_{2} & \mathfrak{B}^{\mathfrak{G}}_{1} \end{vmatrix} = \begin{vmatrix} 3\mathfrak{B}^{\mathfrak{G}}_{4} + \mathfrak{B}^{\mathfrak{G}}_{3} + \mathfrak{B}^{\mathfrak{G}}_{2} & \mathfrak{B}^{\mathfrak{G}}_{4} & \mathfrak{B}^{\mathfrak{G}}_{3} \\ 3\mathfrak{B}^{\mathfrak{G}}_{3} + \mathfrak{B}^{\mathfrak{G}}_{2} + \mathfrak{B}^{\mathfrak{G}}_{1} & \mathfrak{B}^{\mathfrak{G}}_{3} & \mathfrak{B}^{\mathfrak{G}}_{2} \\ 3\mathfrak{B}^{\mathfrak{G}}_{2} + \mathfrak{B}^{\mathfrak{G}}_{1} + \mathfrak{B}^{\mathfrak{G}}_{0} & \mathfrak{B}^{\mathfrak{G}}_{2} & \mathfrak{B}^{\mathfrak{G}}_{1} \end{vmatrix}$$

$$= \begin{vmatrix} \mathfrak{B}^{\mathfrak{G}}_{2} & \mathfrak{B}^{\mathfrak{G}}_{4} & \mathfrak{B}^{\mathfrak{G}}_{3} \\ \mathfrak{B}^{\mathfrak{G}}_{1} & \mathfrak{B}^{\mathfrak{G}}_{3} & \mathfrak{B}^{\mathfrak{G}}_{2} \\ \mathfrak{B}^{\mathfrak{G}}_{0} & \mathfrak{B}^{\mathfrak{G}}_{2} & \mathfrak{B}^{\mathfrak{G}}_{1} \end{vmatrix} = \begin{vmatrix} \mathfrak{B}^{\mathfrak{G}}_{4} & \mathfrak{B}^{\mathfrak{G}}_{3} & \mathfrak{B}^{\mathfrak{G}}_{2} \\ \mathfrak{B}^{\mathfrak{G}}_{3} & \mathfrak{B}^{\mathfrak{G}}_{2} & \mathfrak{B}^{\mathfrak{G}}_{1} \\ \mathfrak{B}^{\mathfrak{G}}_{2} & \mathfrak{B}^{\mathfrak{G}}_{1} & \mathfrak{B}^{\mathfrak{G}}_{0} \end{vmatrix}$$

Let us assume that this identity is true for $n = k$

$$\begin{vmatrix} \mathfrak{B}^{\mathfrak{G}}_{k+4} & \mathfrak{B}^{\mathfrak{G}}_{k+3} & \mathfrak{B}^{\mathfrak{G}}_{k+2} \\ \mathfrak{B}^{\mathfrak{G}}_{k+3} & \mathfrak{B}^{\mathfrak{G}}_{k+2} & \mathfrak{B}^{\mathfrak{G}}_{k+1} \\ \mathfrak{B}^{\mathfrak{G}}_{k+2} & \mathfrak{B}^{\mathfrak{G}}_{k+1} & \mathfrak{B}^{\mathfrak{G}}_{k} \end{vmatrix} = \begin{vmatrix} \mathfrak{B}^{\mathfrak{G}}_{4} & \mathfrak{B}^{\mathfrak{G}}_{3} & \mathfrak{B}^{\mathfrak{G}}_{2} \\ \mathfrak{B}^{\mathfrak{G}}_{3} & \mathfrak{B}^{\mathfrak{G}}_{2} & \mathfrak{B}^{\mathfrak{G}}_{1} \\ \mathfrak{B}^{\mathfrak{G}}_{2} & \mathfrak{B}^{\mathfrak{G}}_{1} & \mathfrak{B}^{\mathfrak{G}}_{0} \end{vmatrix}$$

then, by using the recurrence relation and properties of determinants, we find that (29) is satisfied for $n = k + 1$. □

From this theorem, we give the following corollary:

Corollary 6. *Cassini's identities for the third-ordered Bronze Fibonacci sequences* $\{\mathfrak{B}_n^{\mathfrak{L}}\}$, $\{\mathfrak{B}_n^{\mathfrak{M}}\}$, *and* $\{\mathfrak{B}_n^{\mathfrak{F}}\}$ *are given by*

$$\begin{vmatrix} \mathfrak{B}^{\mathfrak{L}}_{n+4} & \mathfrak{B}^{\mathfrak{L}}_{n+3} & \mathfrak{B}^{\mathfrak{L}}_{n+2} \\ \mathfrak{B}^{\mathfrak{L}}_{n+3} & \mathfrak{B}^{\mathfrak{L}}_{n+2} & \mathfrak{B}^{\mathfrak{L}}_{n+1} \\ \mathfrak{B}^{\mathfrak{L}}_{n+2} & \mathfrak{B}^{\mathfrak{L}}_{n+1} & \mathfrak{B}^{\mathfrak{L}}_{n} \end{vmatrix} = \begin{vmatrix} 131 & 39 & 11 \\ 39 & 11 & 3 \\ 11 & 3 & 3 \end{vmatrix} = -176, \tag{30}$$

$$\begin{vmatrix} \mathfrak{B}^{\mathfrak{M}}_{n+4} & \mathfrak{B}^{\mathfrak{M}}_{n+3} & \mathfrak{B}^{\mathfrak{M}}_{n+2} \\ \mathfrak{B}^{\mathfrak{M}}_{n+3} & \mathfrak{B}^{\mathfrak{M}}_{n+2} & \mathfrak{B}^{\mathfrak{M}}_{n+1} \\ \mathfrak{B}^{\mathfrak{M}}_{n+2} & \mathfrak{B}^{\mathfrak{M}}_{n+1} & \mathfrak{B}^{\mathfrak{M}}_{n} \end{vmatrix} = \begin{vmatrix} 81 & 24 & 7 \\ 24 & 7 & 2 \\ 7 & 2 & 1 \end{vmatrix} = -4, \tag{31}$$

$$\begin{vmatrix} \mathfrak{B}^{\mathfrak{F}}_{n+4} & \mathfrak{B}^{\mathfrak{F}}_{n+3} & \mathfrak{B}^{\mathfrak{F}}_{n+2} \\ \mathfrak{B}^{\mathfrak{F}}_{n+3} & \mathfrak{B}^{\mathfrak{F}}_{n+2} & \mathfrak{B}^{\mathfrak{F}}_{n+1} \\ \mathfrak{B}^{\mathfrak{F}}_{n+2} & \mathfrak{B}^{\mathfrak{F}}_{n+1} & \mathfrak{B}^{\mathfrak{F}}_{n} \end{vmatrix} = \begin{vmatrix} 115 & 34 & 10 \\ 34 & 10 & 3 \\ 10 & 3 & 1 \end{vmatrix} = -1, \tag{32}$$

respectively.

6. Matrix Representation of the Third-Order Bronze Fibonacci Numbers

In this section, we give the matrix representation of the the generalized third-order Bronze Fibonacci sequence. Additionally, we derive some properties of this sequence.

The Matrix representation of the generalized third-order Bronze Fibonacci sequence is given by

$$\begin{bmatrix} \mathfrak{B}^{\mathfrak{G}}_{n+3} \\ \mathfrak{B}^{\mathfrak{G}}_{n+2} \\ \mathfrak{B}^{\mathfrak{G}}_{n+1} \end{bmatrix} = \begin{bmatrix} 3 & 1 & 1 \\ 1 & 0 & 0 \\ 0 & 1 & 0 \end{bmatrix} \begin{bmatrix} \mathfrak{B}^{\mathfrak{G}}_{n+2} \\ \mathfrak{B}^{\mathfrak{G}}_{n+1} \\ \mathfrak{B}^{\mathfrak{G}}_{n} \end{bmatrix}. \tag{33}$$

By induction over n, we find

$$\begin{bmatrix} \mathfrak{B}^{\mathfrak{G}}_{n+2} \\ \mathfrak{B}^{\mathfrak{G}}_{n+1} \\ \mathfrak{B}^{\mathfrak{G}}_{n} \end{bmatrix} = \begin{bmatrix} 3 & 1 & 1 \\ 1 & 0 & 0 \\ 0 & 1 & 0 \end{bmatrix}^n \begin{bmatrix} \mathfrak{B}^{\mathfrak{G}}_{2} \\ \mathfrak{B}^{\mathfrak{G}}_{1} \\ \mathfrak{B}^{\mathfrak{G}}_{0} \end{bmatrix}.$$

Now, let us define a matrix **B** by

$$\mathbf{B} = \begin{bmatrix} 3 & 1 & 1 \\ 1 & 0 & 0 \\ 0 & 1 & 0 \end{bmatrix}. \tag{34}$$

Theorem 5. *For $n \geq 4$,*

$$\mathbf{B}^n = \begin{bmatrix} \mathfrak{B}^{\mathfrak{F}}_{n} & \mathfrak{B}^{\mathfrak{F}}_{n-1} + \mathfrak{B}^{\mathfrak{F}}_{n-2} & \mathfrak{B}^{\mathfrak{F}}_{n-1} \\ \mathfrak{B}^{\mathfrak{F}}_{n-1} & \mathfrak{B}^{\mathfrak{F}}_{n-2} + \mathfrak{B}^{\mathfrak{F}}_{n-3} & \mathfrak{B}^{\mathfrak{F}}_{n-2} \\ \mathfrak{B}^{\mathfrak{F}}_{n-2} & \mathfrak{B}^{\mathfrak{F}}_{n-3} + \mathfrak{B}^{\mathfrak{F}}_{n-4} & \mathfrak{B}^{\mathfrak{F}}_{n-3} \end{bmatrix} \tag{35}$$

and $\det \mathbf{B}^n = 1$.

Proof. For $n = 4$, we have

$$\mathbf{B}^4 = \begin{bmatrix} 115 & 44 & 34 \\ 34 & 13 & 10 \\ 10 & 4 & 3 \end{bmatrix} = \begin{bmatrix} \mathfrak{B}^{\mathfrak{F}}_{4} & \mathfrak{B}^{\mathfrak{F}}_{3} + \mathfrak{B}^{\mathfrak{F}}_{2} & \mathfrak{B}^{\mathfrak{F}}_{3} \\ \mathfrak{B}^{\mathfrak{F}}_{3} & \mathfrak{B}^{\mathfrak{F}}_{2} + \mathfrak{B}^{\mathfrak{F}}_{1} & \mathfrak{B}^{\mathfrak{F}}_{2} \\ \mathfrak{B}^{\mathfrak{F}}_{2} & \mathfrak{B}^{\mathfrak{F}}_{1} + \mathfrak{B}^{\mathfrak{F}}_{0} & \mathfrak{B}^{\mathfrak{F}}_{1} \end{bmatrix}.$$

Suppose that for $n = k$

$$\mathbf{B}^k = \begin{bmatrix} \mathfrak{B}^{\mathfrak{F}}_{k} & \mathfrak{B}^{\mathfrak{F}}_{k-1} + \mathfrak{B}^{\mathfrak{F}}_{k-2} & \mathfrak{B}^{\mathfrak{F}}_{k-1} \\ \mathfrak{B}^{\mathfrak{F}}_{k-1} & \mathfrak{B}^{\mathfrak{F}}_{k-2} + \mathfrak{B}^{\mathfrak{F}}_{k-3} & \mathfrak{B}^{\mathfrak{F}}_{k-2} \\ \mathfrak{B}^{\mathfrak{F}}_{k-2} & \mathfrak{B}^{\mathfrak{F}}_{k-3} + \mathfrak{B}^{\mathfrak{F}}_{k-4} & \mathfrak{B}^{\mathfrak{F}}_{k-3} \end{bmatrix}$$

then,

$$\mathbf{B}^{k+1} = \mathbf{B}^k \mathbf{B} = \begin{bmatrix} \mathfrak{B}^{\mathfrak{F}}_{k} & \mathfrak{B}^{\mathfrak{F}}_{k-1} + \mathfrak{B}^{\mathfrak{F}}_{k-2} & \mathfrak{B}^{\mathfrak{F}}_{k-1} \\ \mathfrak{B}^{\mathfrak{F}}_{k-1} & \mathfrak{B}^{\mathfrak{F}}_{k-2} + \mathfrak{B}^{\mathfrak{F}}_{k-3} & \mathfrak{B}^{\mathfrak{F}}_{k-2} \\ \mathfrak{B}^{\mathfrak{F}}_{k-2} & \mathfrak{B}^{\mathfrak{F}}_{k-3} + \mathfrak{B}^{\mathfrak{F}}_{k-4} & \mathfrak{B}^{\mathfrak{F}}_{k-3} \end{bmatrix} \begin{bmatrix} 3 & 1 & 1 \\ 1 & 0 & 0 \\ 0 & 1 & 0 \end{bmatrix}$$

and

$$\mathbf{B}^{k+1} = \begin{bmatrix} \mathfrak{B}^{\mathfrak{F}}_{k+1} & \mathfrak{B}^{\mathfrak{F}}_{k} + \mathfrak{B}^{\mathfrak{F}}_{k-1} & \mathfrak{B}^{\mathfrak{F}}_{k} \\ \mathfrak{B}^{\mathfrak{F}}_{k} & \mathfrak{B}^{\mathfrak{F}}_{k-1} + \mathfrak{B}^{\mathfrak{F}}_{k-2} & \mathfrak{B}^{\mathfrak{F}}_{k-1} \\ \mathfrak{B}^{\mathfrak{F}}_{k-1} & \mathfrak{B}^{\mathfrak{F}}_{k-2} + \mathfrak{B}^{\mathfrak{F}}_{k-3} & \mathfrak{B}^{\mathfrak{F}}_{k-2} \end{bmatrix}$$

which proves the theorem. Similarly, by using the properties of determinants and induction over n, we find that $\det \mathbf{B}^n = 1$. □

For $n \geq 4$, let us define a matrix

$$Y_n = \begin{bmatrix} \mathfrak{B}^{\mathfrak{G}}_{n} & \mathfrak{B}^{\mathfrak{G}}_{n-1} + \mathfrak{B}^{\mathfrak{G}}_{n-2} & \mathfrak{B}^{\mathfrak{G}}_{n-1} \\ \mathfrak{B}^{\mathfrak{G}}_{n-1} & \mathfrak{B}^{\mathfrak{G}}_{n-2} + \mathfrak{B}^{\mathfrak{G}}_{n-3} & \mathfrak{B}^{\mathfrak{G}}_{n-2} \\ \mathfrak{B}^{\mathfrak{G}}_{n-2} & \mathfrak{B}^{\mathfrak{G}}_{n-3} + \mathfrak{B}^{\mathfrak{G}}_{n-4} & \mathfrak{B}^{\mathfrak{G}}_{n-3} \end{bmatrix}. \qquad (36)$$

Theorem 6. *For $n, m \geq 4$*
1. $Y_n = \mathbf{B}^{n-4} Y_4$.
2. $Y_4 \mathbf{B}^n = \mathbf{B}^n Y_4$.
3. $Y_{n+m} = Y_n \mathbf{B}^m$.

Proof.
1. Since $\mathbf{B} Y_n = Y_{n+1}$, it can be easily shown by induction that $Y_n = \mathbf{B}^{n-4} Y_4$.
2. Using the definition of Y_n and induction, we find $Y_4 \mathbf{B}^n = \mathbf{B}^n Y_4$.
3. From 1 and 2, it follows that $Y_{n+m} = \mathbf{B}^{n+m-4} Y_4 = \mathbf{B}^{n-4} \mathbf{B}^m Y_4 = \mathbf{B}^{n-4} Y_4 \mathbf{B}^m = Y_n \mathbf{B}^m$.
□

Theorem 7. *For $n, m \geq 4$, we have*

$$\mathfrak{B}^{\mathfrak{G}}_{n+m} = \mathfrak{B}^{\mathfrak{G}}_{n} \mathfrak{B}^{\mathfrak{F}}_{m} + \mathfrak{B}^{\mathfrak{G}}_{n-1}(\mathfrak{B}^{\mathfrak{F}}_{m-1} + \mathfrak{B}^{\mathfrak{F}}_{m-2}) + \mathfrak{B}^{\mathfrak{G}}_{n-2} \mathfrak{B}^{\mathfrak{F}}_{m-1}. \qquad (37)$$

Proof. From the above theorem, we have $Y_{n+m} = Y_n \mathbf{B}^m$, or

$$\begin{bmatrix} \mathfrak{B}^{\mathfrak{G}}_{n+m} & \mathfrak{B}^{\mathfrak{G}}_{n+m-1} + \mathfrak{B}^{\mathfrak{G}}_{n+m-2} & \mathfrak{B}^{\mathfrak{G}}_{n+m-1} \\ \mathfrak{B}^{\mathfrak{G}}_{n+m-1} & \mathfrak{B}^{\mathfrak{G}}_{n+m-2} + \mathfrak{B}^{\mathfrak{G}}_{n+m-3} & \mathfrak{B}^{\mathfrak{G}}_{n+m-2} \\ \mathfrak{B}^{\mathfrak{G}}_{n+m-2} & \mathfrak{B}^{\mathfrak{G}}_{n+m-3} + \mathfrak{B}^{\mathfrak{G}}_{n+m-4} & \mathfrak{B}^{\mathfrak{G}}_{n+m-3} \end{bmatrix} = \\ \begin{bmatrix} \mathfrak{B}^{\mathfrak{G}}_{n} & \mathfrak{B}^{\mathfrak{G}}_{n-1} + \mathfrak{B}^{\mathfrak{G}}_{n-2} & \mathfrak{B}^{\mathfrak{G}}_{n-1} \\ \mathfrak{B}^{\mathfrak{G}}_{n-1} & \mathfrak{B}^{\mathfrak{G}}_{n-2} + \mathfrak{B}^{\mathfrak{G}}_{n-3} & \mathfrak{B}^{\mathfrak{G}}_{n-2} \\ \mathfrak{B}^{\mathfrak{G}}_{n-2} & \mathfrak{B}^{\mathfrak{G}}_{n-3} + \mathfrak{B}^{\mathfrak{G}}_{n-4} & \mathfrak{B}^{\mathfrak{G}}_{n-3} \end{bmatrix} \begin{bmatrix} \mathfrak{B}^{\mathfrak{F}}_{m} & \mathfrak{B}^{\mathfrak{F}}_{m-1} + \mathfrak{B}^{\mathfrak{F}}_{m-2} & \mathfrak{B}^{\mathfrak{F}}_{m-1} \\ \mathfrak{B}^{\mathfrak{F}}_{m-1} & \mathfrak{B}^{\mathfrak{F}}_{m-2} + \mathfrak{B}^{\mathfrak{F}}_{m-3} & \mathfrak{B}^{\mathfrak{F}}_{m-2} \\ \mathfrak{B}^{\mathfrak{F}}_{m-2} & \mathfrak{B}^{\mathfrak{F}}_{m-3} + \mathfrak{B}^{\mathfrak{F}}_{m-4} & \mathfrak{B}^{\mathfrak{F}}_{m-3} \end{bmatrix}. \qquad (38)$$

Since the $\mathfrak{B}^{\mathfrak{G}}_{n+m}$ entry is the product of the first row of the Y_n and the first column of $\mathbf{B}^n$, the result follows. □

Corollary 7. *For the third-ordered Bronze Fibonacci sequences $\{\mathfrak{B}^{\mathfrak{L}}_{n}\}$, $\{\mathfrak{B}^{\mathfrak{M}}_{n}\}$, and $\{\mathfrak{B}^{\mathfrak{F}}_{n}\}$, we have*

$$\mathfrak{B}^{\mathfrak{L}}_{n+m} = \mathfrak{B}^{\mathfrak{L}}_{n} \mathfrak{B}^{\mathfrak{F}}_{m} + \mathfrak{B}^{\mathfrak{L}}_{n-1}(\mathfrak{B}^{\mathfrak{F}}_{m-1} + \mathfrak{B}^{\mathfrak{F}}_{m-2}) + \mathfrak{B}^{\mathfrak{L}}_{n-2} \mathfrak{B}^{\mathfrak{F}}_{m-1}, \qquad (39)$$

$$\mathfrak{B}^{\mathfrak{M}}_{n+m} = \mathfrak{B}^{\mathfrak{M}}_{n} \mathfrak{B}^{\mathfrak{F}}_{m} + \mathfrak{B}^{\mathfrak{M}}_{n-1}(\mathfrak{B}^{\mathfrak{F}}_{m-1} + \mathfrak{B}^{\mathfrak{F}}_{m-2}) + \mathfrak{B}^{\mathfrak{M}}_{n-2} \mathfrak{B}^{\mathfrak{F}}_{m-1}, \qquad (40)$$

$$\mathfrak{B}^{\mathfrak{F}}_{n+m} = \mathfrak{B}^{\mathfrak{F}}_{n} \mathfrak{B}^{\mathfrak{F}}_{m} + \mathfrak{B}^{\mathfrak{F}}_{n-1}(\mathfrak{B}^{\mathfrak{F}}_{m-1} + \mathfrak{B}^{\mathfrak{F}}_{m-2}) + \mathfrak{B}^{\mathfrak{F}}_{n-2} \mathfrak{B}^{\mathfrak{F}}_{m-1}, \qquad (41)$$

respectively.

7. Application: Encryption and Decryption via Third-Order Bronze Fibonacci Numbers

In this section, as a useful application of all obtained results, we give a third-order Bronze Fibonacci encryption and decryption algorithm. In this algorithm, we use the

Affine-Hill chipher method for encryption using a third-order Bronze Fibonacci matrix as a key. First of all, let us list the notations which we use in the encryption and decryption algorithms:

- p is the number of the characters which the sender and receiver use. We chose p to be a prime.
- $\phi(p)$ is the image of the number p under the Euler Phi function. It is known that if p is prime then $\phi(p) = p - 1$.
- D is the private key of the receiver.
- P_1 is any primitive root of p.
- $P_2 = P_1^D \mod p$.
- (p, P_1, P_2) is the public key.
- ε is a positive integer which satisfies $1 < \varepsilon < \phi(p)$. The prime p provides a large key space for the selection of ε. This strengthens the security of the system.
- $\lambda = P_2^\varepsilon \mod p$.
- $\mathbf{T} = [\mathfrak{B}^{\mathfrak{F}}_\lambda \ \mathfrak{B}^{\mathfrak{F}}_{\lambda+1} \ \mathfrak{B}^{\mathfrak{F}}_{\lambda+2}] \mod p$ is the 1×3 shifting vector.
- $\mathbf{M} = [m_1 m_2 ... m_n]$ is the plain text and $\mathbf{E} = [e_1 e_2 ... e_n]$ is the cipher text. Note that if the plain text has not suitable length in Step 6 of encryption algorithm, zero will be added until it can be divided by 3 with no remainder.
- $\mathbf{M}_i$ is ith vector of type 1×3 obtained using the character table after dividing the plain text into 3-length parts.
- $\mathbf{E}_i$ is ith vector of type 1×3 obtained using the character table after dividing the cipher text $\mathbf{E}$ into 3-length parts.

Note that the prime number p and the large value of λ increase the security of three digital signatures $\lambda, k, \mathbf{T}$. This makes it difficult to break the system.

Encryption Algorithm:

- **Step 1:** The sender chooses a secret number ε where $1 < \varepsilon < \phi(p)$.
- **Step 2:** The sender calculates the signature $k = P_1^\varepsilon \mod p$.
- **Step 3:** The sender calculates $\lambda = P_2^\varepsilon \mod p$.
- **Step 4:** The sender constructs $\mathbf{B}^\lambda$.
- **Step 5:** The sender constructs $\mathbf{T}$.
- **Step 6:** The sender calculates $\mathbf{E}_i = \mathbf{M}_i \mathbf{B}^\lambda + \mathbf{T} \mod p$ for $1 \leq i \leq \frac{n}{3}$.
- **Step 7:** The sender sends the cipher text $E = [e_1 e_2 ... e_n]$ and the signature k.

Decryption Algorithm:

- **Step 1:** The receiver calculates $\lambda = k^D \mod p$.
- **Step 2:** The receiver calculates $\mathbf{B}^\lambda$ and $\mathbf{B}^{-\lambda}$.
- **Step 3:** The receiver calculates the shifting vector $\mathbf{S}$.
- **Step 4:** The receiver calculates $\mathbf{M}_i = (\mathbf{E}_i - \mathbf{T})\mathbf{B}^{-\lambda} \mod p$ for $1 \leq i \leq \frac{n}{3}$.
- **Step 5:** The receiver constructs the plain text $\mathbf{M} = [m_1 m_2 ... m_n]$.

Example 1. *Let $p = 29$ and consider 29—characters with the numerical values 1–26, 27, 28 and 29 are assigned for the alphabets A–Z, ., 0 and blank space, respectively. Consider that the plain text is "STAY AT HOME", private key is $D = 13$ and $P_1 = 11$. Then, we calculate $P_2 = 21$. So, the public key is (29,11,21).*

Encryption Algorithm:

- *Step 1: We choose $\varepsilon = 17$ where $1 < \varepsilon < 28$.*
- *Step 2: The signature $k = 3$.*
- *Step 3: $\lambda = 19$.*
- *Step 4: Since $\lambda = 19$ then $\mathbf{B}^{19} = \begin{bmatrix} 12 & 10 & 27 \\ 27 & 18 & 1 \\ 1 & 24 & 17 \end{bmatrix} \mod 29$, from Equation (35).*
- *Step 5: The shifting vector $\mathbf{T} = [\mathfrak{B}^{\mathfrak{F}}_{19} \ \mathfrak{B}^{\mathfrak{F}}_{20} \ \mathfrak{B}^{\mathfrak{F}}_{21}] = [12 \ 6 \ 28] \mod 29$. We can also use the Binet Formula (16) here to calculate the shifting vector $\mathbf{T}$.*

- **Step 6:**

$$E_1 = M_1 B^\lambda + T \mod 29$$
$$= [19\ 20\ 1] \begin{bmatrix} 12 & 10 & 27 \\ 27 & 18 & 1 \\ 1 & 24 & 17 \end{bmatrix} + [12\ 6\ 28] \mod 29$$
$$= [27\ 0\ 27] = [.\ .],$$
$$E_2 = M_2 B^\lambda + T \mod 29$$
$$= [25\ 29\ 1] \begin{bmatrix} 12 & 10 & 27 \\ 27 & 18 & 1 \\ 1 & 24 & 17 \end{bmatrix} + [12\ 6\ 28] \mod 29$$
$$= [23\ 19\ 24] = [WSX],$$
$$E_3 = M_3 B^\lambda + T \mod 29$$
$$= [20\ 29\ 8] \begin{bmatrix} 12 & 10 & 27 \\ 27 & 18 & 1 \\ 1 & 24 & 17 \end{bmatrix} + [12\ 6\ 28] \mod 29$$
$$= [28\ 21\ 8] = [0UH],$$
$$E_4 = M_4 B^\lambda + T \mod 29$$
$$= [15\ 13\ 5] \begin{bmatrix} 12 & 10 & 27 \\ 27 & 18 & 1 \\ 1 & 24 & 17 \end{bmatrix} + [12\ 6\ 28] \mod 29$$
$$= [26\ 17\ 9] = [ZQI].$$

- **Step 7:** We send the receiving (cipher) text $E = [.\ .WSX0UHZQI]$ and the signature $k = 3$.

  Decryption Algorithm:

- **Step 1:** $\lambda = 3^{13} \mod 29 = 19$.

- **Step 2:** Since $\lambda = 19$ then $B^{19} = \begin{bmatrix} 12 & 28 & 27 \\ 27 & 18 & 1 \\ 1 & 24 & 17 \end{bmatrix} \mod 29$,

  and $B^{-19} = \begin{bmatrix} 12 & 8 & 18 \\ 20 & 10 & 12 \\ 12 & 11 & 23 \end{bmatrix} \mod 29$,

- **Step 3:** We calculate the shifting vector $T = [12\ 6\ 28]$.

- **Step 4:** We calculate all $\mathbf{M}_i$, $i = 1, 2, 3, 4$ as follows:

$$\begin{aligned}
\mathbf{M}_1 &= (\mathbf{E}_1 - \mathbf{T})\mathbf{B}^{-19} \mod 29 \\
&= ([13\ 21\ 25] - [12\ 6\ 28]) \begin{bmatrix} 12 & 8 & 18 \\ 20 & 10 & 12 \\ 12 & 11 & 23 \end{bmatrix} \mod 29 \\
&= [19\ 20\ 1] = [STA], \\
\mathbf{M}_2 &= (\mathbf{E}_2 - \mathbf{T})\mathbf{B}^{-19} \mod 29 \\
&= ([23\ 19\ 24] - [12\ 6\ 28]) \begin{bmatrix} 12 & 8 & 18 \\ 20 & 10 & 12 \\ 12 & 11 & 23 \end{bmatrix} \mod 29 \\
&= [25\ 29\ 1] = [Y\ A], \\
\mathbf{M}_3 &= (\mathbf{E}_3 - \mathbf{T})\mathbf{B}^{-19} \mod 29 \\
&= ([23\ 19\ 24] - [12\ 6\ 28]) \begin{bmatrix} 12 & 8 & 18 \\ 20 & 10 & 12 \\ 12 & 11 & 23 \end{bmatrix} \mod 29 \\
&= [20\ 29\ 8] = [T\ H], \\
\mathbf{M}_4 &= (\mathbf{E}_4 - \mathbf{T})\mathbf{B}^{-19} \mod 29 \\
&= ([26\ 17\ 9] - [12\ 6\ 28]) \begin{bmatrix} 12 & 8 & 18 \\ 20 & 10 & 12 \\ 12 & 11 & 23 \end{bmatrix} \mod 29 \\
&= [15\ 13\ 5] = [OME].
\end{aligned}$$

- **Step 5:** The sending (plain) text $\mathbf{M} = [STAY\ AT\ HOME]$.

8. Conclusions

In this paper, we define some third-order Bronze Fibonacci sequences. Additionally, we present the De Moivre-type identities for the second- and third-order Bronze Fibonacci numbers. In addition to this, we obtain the generating functions, Binet's Formulas, Cassini's identity, and matrix representation of these sequences and some interesting identities related to the third-order Bronze Fibonacci sequences. Finally, we develop a new third-order Bronze Fibonacci encryption and decryption algorithm in encryption theory.

Author Contributions: Conceptualization, M.A. and J.A.; methodology, M.A. and J.A.; software, M.A. and J.A.; validation, M.A. and J.A.; formal analysis, M.A. and J.A.; investigation, M.A. and J.A.; resources, M.A. and J.A.; data curation, M.A. and J.A.; writing—original draft preparation, M.A. and J.A.; writing—review and editing, M.A. and J.A.; visualization, M.A. and J.A.; supervision, M.A. and J.A.; project administration, M.A. and J.A. All authors have read and agreed to the published version of the manuscript.

Funding: This research received no external funding.

Institutional Review Board Statement: Not applicable.

Informed Consent Statement: Not applicable.

Data Availability Statement: Not applicable.

Acknowledgments: The authors appreciate the anonymous referees for their careful corrections and valuable comments on the paper.

Conflicts of Interest: The authors declare no conflict of interest.

References

1. Basin, S.L. Elementary problems and solutions. *Fibonacci Q.* **1963**, *1*, 77.
2. Lin, P.-Y. De Moivre-Type Identities for the Tribonacci Numbers. *Fibonacci Q.* **1988**, *26*, 131–134.
3. Lin, P.-Y. De Moivre-Type Identities for the Tetranacci Numbers. In *Applications of Fibonacci Numbers*; Bergum, G.E., Philippou, A.N., Horadam, A.F., Eds.; Springer: Dordrecht, The Netherlands, 1991.
4. Yamaç Akbıyık, S.; Akbıyık, M. De Moivre-Type Identities for the Pell Numbers. *Turk. J. Math. Comput. Sci.* **2021**, *13*, 63–67.
5. Soykan, Y. On Generalized Third-Order Pell Numbers. *Asian J. Adv. Res. Rep.* **2019**, *6*, 1–18. [CrossRef]
6. Akbıyık, M.; Yamaç Akbıyık, S. De Moivre-type identities for the Jacobsthal numbers. *Notes Number Theory Discrete Math.* **2021**, *27*, 95–103. [CrossRef]
7. Sloane, N.J.A. The On-Line Encyclopedia of Integer Sequences. Available online: http://oeis.org/ (accessed on 28 July 2021).
8. Kartal, M.Y. Gaussian Bronze Fibonacci Numbers. *EJONS Int. J. Math. Eng. Nat. Sci.* **2020**, *13*. [CrossRef]
9. Savin, D. Special numbers, special quaternions and special symbol elements. *Model. Theor. Soc. Syst.* **2019**, 417–430. [CrossRef]
10. Flaut, C.; Savin, D. Some remarks regarding l-elements defined in algebras obtained by the Cayley-Dickson process. *Chaos Solitons Fractals* **2019**, *118*, 112–116. [CrossRef]
11. Stakhov, A.P. Fibonacci matrices, a generalization of the "Cassini formula", and a new coding theory. *Chaos Solitons Fractals* **2006**, *30*, 56–66. [CrossRef]
12. Taş, N.; Uçar, S.; Özgür, N.Y.; Kaymak, Ö.Ö. A new coding/decoding algorithm using Fibonacci numbers, Discrete Mathematics. *Algorithms Appl.* **2018**, *10*, 1850028.
13. Uçar, S.; Taş, N.; Özgür, N.Y. A new Application to coding Theory via Fibonacci numbers. *Math. Sci. Appl. Notes* **2019**, *7*, 62–70. [CrossRef]
14. Flaut, C.; Savin, D.; Zaharia, G. Properties and applications of some special integer number sequences. *Math. Methods Appl. Sci.* **2021**, *44*, 7442–7454. [CrossRef]
15. Prasad, K.; Mahato, H. Cryptography using generalized Fibonacci matrices with Affine-Hill cipher. *J. Discret. Math. Sci. Cryptogr.* **2021**. [CrossRef]

Article
On Leonardo Pisano Hybrinomials

Ferhat Kürüz [1,*,†], Ali Dağdeviren [2,†] and Paula Catarino [3,†]

1. Department of Computer Engineering, Istanbul Gelisim University, Istanbul 34310, Turkey
2. Department of Weight and Balance, Turkish Aviation Academy, Istanbul 34149, Turkey; m.a.dagdeviren@gmail.com
3. Department of Mathematics, University of Trás-os-Montes and Alto Douro, Quinta de Prados, 5001-801 Vila Real, Portugal; pcatarino23@gmail.com
* Correspondence: fkuruz@gelisim.edu.tr
† These authors contributed equally to this work.

Abstract: A generalization of complex, dual, and hyperbolic numbers has recently been defined as hybrid numbers. In this study, using the Leonardo Pisano numbers and hybrid numbers we investigate Leonardo Pisano polynomials and hybrinomials. Furthermore, we also describe the basic algebraic properties and some identities of the Leonardo Pisano polynomials and hybrinomials.

Keywords: hybrid numbers; Leonardo Pisano numbers; hybrinomials

1. Introduction

Fibonacci numbers, for $n \geq 2$, are given by the recurrence relation $F_n = F_{n-1} + F_{n-2}$ with the initial conditions $F_0 = 0, F_1 = 1$. There are many works regarding Fibonacci numbers, such as [1–3]. Furthermore, they have also been studied on different number systems such as quaternions and hybrid numbers [4,5].

When the literature is examined, it is seen that Leonardo Pisano numbers are only called Leonardo numbers. However, the name Leonardo in these studies refers to Leonardo Pisano, who is also called Fibonacci, from the Latin Filius Bonacci. It is well known that Leonardo commonly stands for Leonardo Da Vinci, so in this study to avoid confusion we prefer to use the name "Leonardo Pisano".

Leonardo Pisano numbers have recently been studied in detail by Catarino and Borges in [6] and they have demonstrated some properties of this sequence. For $n \geq 2$, Leonardo Pisano numbers are defined by the following recurrence relation

$$Le_n = Le_{n-1} + Le_{n-2} + 1 \tag{1}$$

where the initial conditions are $Le_0 = Le_1 = 1$. Moreover, another recurrence relation for Leonardo Pisano's numbers is

$$Le_{n+1} = 2Le_n - Le_{n-2}. \tag{2}$$

The relationship between Leonardo Pisano numbers and Fibonacci numbers can be given as

$$Le_n = 2F_{n+1} - 1. \tag{3}$$

Binet's formula and the characteristic equation of Leonardo Pisano numbers are

$$Le_n = \frac{2\alpha^{n+1} - 2\beta^{n+1} - \alpha + \beta}{\alpha - \beta} \quad \text{and} \quad \lambda^3 - 2\lambda^2 + 1 = 0 \tag{4}$$

respectively. Cassini's, Catalan and d'Ocagne's identities were defined in [6]. In [7] generalized Leonardo Pisano numbers have been defined. In [8], incomplete Leonardo Pisano numbers and matrix representation of Leonardo Pisano numbers have also been given. Additionally, in [9] the authors give some important properties of Leonardo Pisano numbers and in [10] hybrid Leonardo Pisano numbers are defined.

Hybrid numbers are a generalization of the complex, dual and hyperbolic numbers. A hybrid number can be denoted by $w = r_0 + r_1 \mathbf{i} + r_2 \varepsilon + r_3 \mathbf{h}$, where r_0, r_1, r_2, r_3 are real numbers [11]. Hybrid numbers, $\mathbb{K}$, are defined as

$$\mathbb{K} = \left\{ w = r_0 + r_1 \mathbf{i} + r_2 \varepsilon + r_3 \mathbf{h} : r_0, r_1, r_2, r_3 \in \mathbb{R}, \begin{array}{l} \mathbf{i}^2 = -1, \varepsilon^2 = 0, \mathbf{h}^2 = 1 \\ \mathbf{ih} = -\mathbf{hi} = \varepsilon + \mathbf{i} \end{array} \right\}. \quad (5)$$

Equality, addition and multiplication are defined by

(i) $w_1 = w_2 \iff r_0 = s_0, r_1 = s_1, r_2 = s_2, r_3 = s_3$,
(ii) $w_1 + w_2 = (r_0 + s_0) + (r_1 + s_1)\mathbf{i} + (r_2 + s_2)\varepsilon + (r_3 + s_3)\mathbf{h}$,
(iii) $w_1 \cdot w_2 = (r_0 + r_1\mathbf{i} + r_2\varepsilon + r_3\mathbf{h}).(s_0 + s_1\mathbf{i} + s_2\varepsilon + s_3\mathbf{h})$
$= (r_0 s_0 - r_1 s_1 + r_2 s_1 - r_1 s_2 + r_3 s_3) + (r_0 s_2 + r_1 s_0 + r_1 s_3 - r_3 s_1)\mathbf{i}$
$+ (r_0 s_2 + r_2 s_0 - r_2 s_3 + r_3 s_2 + r_1 s_3 - r_3 s_1)\varepsilon + (r_0 s_3 + r_3 s_0 + r_1 s_2 + r_2 s_1)\mathbf{h}$,

for hybrid numbers $w_1 = r_0 + r_1\mathbf{i} + r_2\varepsilon + r_3\mathbf{h}$ and $w_2 = s_0 + s_1\mathbf{i} + s_2\varepsilon + s_3\mathbf{h}$. More details on hybrid numbers can be found in [11].

Fibonacci polynomials were first studied by Bicknell [12]. Since then, many authors have published works on the subject of Fibonacci-type polynomials [13–17]. These types of polynomials have some considerable applications in number theory, geometry and algebra. Moreover, hybrinomial sequences have become an increasing area of attention. For instance, the authors studied Fibonacci and Lucas hybrinomials [18], Petroudi and Pirouz studied Van der Laan hybrinomials [19] and Petroudi et al. studied Narayana polynomials and Narayana hybrinomial sequences [20]. Moreover, Horadam hybrinomials were studied by Kızılateş in [21].

In this work, in Section 2, we define the Leonardo Pisano polynomials and hybrinomials. Then, in Section 3, we present some identities of Leonardo Pisano polynomial and hybrinomial sequences such as Catalan-like identities and summing formulas.

2. Leonardo Pisano Polynomials and Hybrinomials

In this section, we introduce Leonardo Pisano polynomials and hybrinomials.

Definition 1. *For a non-negative integer n, Leonardo Pisano polynomials $Le_n(x)$ are defined by*

$$Le_n(x) = \begin{cases} 1 & , n = 0, 1 \\ x + 2 & , n = 2 \\ 2x Le_{n-1}(x) - Le_{n-3}(x) & , n \geq 3 \end{cases}.$$

The first few Leonardo Pisano polynomials are $1, 1, x + 2, 2x^2 + 4x - 1, 4x^3 + 8x^2 - 2x - 1, 8x^4 + 16x^3 - 4x^2 - 3x - 2, 16x^5 + 32x^4 - 8x^3 - 8x^2 - 8x + 1$. Using Leonardo Pisano polynomials, we can define Leonardo Pisano hybrinomials.

Definition 2. *The nth Leonardo Pisano hybrinomial is defined as follows:*

$$Le_n^{[H]}(x) = Le_n(x) + \mathbf{i} Le_{n+1}(x) + \varepsilon Le_{n+2}(x) + \mathbf{h} Le_{n+3}(x). \quad (6)$$

The first four Leonardo Pisano hybrinomials are

$$Le_0^{[H]}(x) = 1 + \mathbf{i} + \boldsymbol{\varepsilon}(x+2) + \mathbf{h}(2x^2 + 4x - 1) \qquad (7)$$

$$Le_1^{[H]}(x) = 1 + \mathbf{i}(x+2) + \boldsymbol{\varepsilon}(2x^2 + 4x - 1) + \mathbf{h}(4x^3 + 8x^2 - 2x - 1) \qquad (8)$$

$$Le_2^{[H]}(x) = (x+2) + \mathbf{i}(2x^2 + 4x - 1) + \boldsymbol{\varepsilon}(4x^3 + 8x^2 - 2x - 1)$$
$$+ \mathbf{h}(8x^4 + 16x^3 - 4x^2 - 3x - 2) \qquad (9)$$

$$Le_3^{[H]}(x) = (2x^2 + 4x - 1) + \mathbf{i}(4x^3 + 8x^2 - 2x - 1) + \boldsymbol{\varepsilon}(8x^4 + 16x^3 - 4x^2 - 3x - 2)$$
$$+ \mathbf{h}(16x^5 + 32x^4 - 8x^3 - 8x^2 - 8x + 1). \qquad (10)$$

If we put $x = 1$, then we obtain

$$Le_0^{[H]}(x) = 1 + \mathbf{i} + 3\boldsymbol{\varepsilon} + 5\mathbf{h} = LeH_0$$
$$Le_1^{[H]}(x) = 1 + 3\mathbf{i} + 5\boldsymbol{\varepsilon} + 9\mathbf{h} = LeH_1$$
$$Le_2^{[H]}(x) = 3 + 5\mathbf{i} + 9\boldsymbol{\varepsilon} + 15\mathbf{h} = LeH_2$$
$$Le_3^{[H]}(x) = 5 + 9\mathbf{i} + 15\boldsymbol{\varepsilon} + 25\mathbf{h} = LeH_3$$

where LeH_n stand for Leonardo Pisano hybrid numbers. Therefore, it can be easily seen that Leonardo Pisano hybrinomials are a generalization of Leonardo Pisano hybrid numbers.

We can define the character of Leonardo Pisano hybrinomials by making use of the character of hybrid numbers that Özdemir defined in his article.

Definition 3. *The character of Leonardo Pisano hybrinomials is*

$$C(Le_n^{[H]}(x)) = Le_n^2(x) + Le_{n+1}^2(x) - 2Le_{n+1}(x)Le_{n+2}(x) - Le_{n+3}^2(x).$$

Using the character of the Leonardo Pisano hybrinomials, we can set the norm.

Theorem 1. *The norm of the Leonardo Pisano hybrinomials $Le_n^{[H]}(x)$ is given by*

$$\|Le_n^{[H]}(x)\| = \sqrt{|Le_{n+1}^2(x) - 2Le_{n+1}(x)Le_{n+2}(x) - 4x^2 Le_{n+2}^2(x) + 4xLe_{n+2}(x)Le_n(x)|}.$$

Proof. From the character of Leonardo Pisano hybrinomials which is given above,

$$\|Le_n^{[H]}(x)\|^2$$
$$= |Le_n^2(x) + Le_{n+1}^2(x) - 2Le_{n+1}(x)Le_{n+2}(x) - Le_{n+3}^2(x)|$$
$$= |Le_n^2(x) + Le_{n+1}^2(x) - 2Le_{n+1}(x)Le_{n+2}(x) - (2xLe_{n+2}(x) - Le_n(x))^2|$$
$$= |Le_{n+1}^2(x) - 2Le_{n+1}(x)Le_{n+2}(x) - 4x^2 Le_{n+2}^2(x) + 4xLe_{n+2}(x)Le_n(x)|.$$

□

In the following theorem using the matrix representation of hybrid numbers:

$$M(a + b\mathbf{i} + c\boldsymbol{\varepsilon} + d\mathbf{h}) = \begin{bmatrix} a + c & b - c + d \\ c - b + d & a - c \end{bmatrix},$$

we give the matrix representation for Leonardo Pisano hybrinomials.

Theorem 2. *Every Leonardo Pisano hybrinomials can be written in the following matrix form, for $Le_m^{[H]}(x)$*

$$M(Le_m^{[H]}(x)) = \begin{bmatrix} Le_m(x) + Le_{m+2}(x) & Le_{m+1}(x) - Le_{m+2}(x) + Le_{m+3}(x) \\ Le_{m+2}(x) + Le_{m+3}(x) - Le_{m+1}(x) & Le_m(x) - Le_{m+2}(x) \end{bmatrix}.$$

Proof. Using the matrix equivalent of hybrid units $1, \mathbf{i}, \boldsymbol{\varepsilon}$ and $\mathbf{h}$, we have

$$Le_m^{[H]}(x) = Le_m(x) + \mathbf{i}Le_{m+1}(x) + \boldsymbol{\varepsilon}Le_{m+2}(x) + \mathbf{h}Le_{m+3}(x)$$

$$M(Le_m^{[H]}(x)) = Le_m(x)\begin{bmatrix} 1 & 0 \\ 0 & 1 \end{bmatrix} + Le_{m+1}(x)\begin{bmatrix} 0 & 1 \\ -1 & 0 \end{bmatrix} + Le_{m+2}(x)\begin{bmatrix} 1 & -1 \\ 1 & -1 \end{bmatrix}$$

$$+ Le_{m+3}(x)\begin{bmatrix} 0 & 1 \\ 1 & 0 \end{bmatrix}$$

then we can write

$$M(Le_m^{[H]}(x)) = \begin{bmatrix} Le_m(x) + Le_{m+2}(x) & Le_{m+1}(x) - Le_{m+2}(x) + Le_{m+3}(x) \\ Le_{m+2}(x) + Le_{m+3}(x) - Le_{m+1}(x) & Le_m(x) - Le_{m+2}(x) \end{bmatrix}$$

□

Lemma 1. *Let $Le_n^{[H]}(x)$ be the nth Leonardo Pisano hybrinomial. The recurrence relation of $Le_n^{[H]}(x)$ is*

$$Le_n^{[H]}(x) = 2xLe_{n-1}^{[H]}(x) - Le_{n-3}^{[H]}(x).$$

Proof. Using equation (6);

$$Le_n^{[H]}(x) = Le_n(x) + \mathbf{i}Le_{n+1}(x) + \boldsymbol{\varepsilon}Le_{n+2}(x) + \mathbf{h}Le_{n+3}(x)$$
$$= 2xLe_{n-1}(x) - Le_{n-3}(x) + \mathbf{i}\{2xLe_n(x) - Le_{n-2}(x)\}$$
$$+ \boldsymbol{\varepsilon}\{2xLe_{n+1}(x) - Le_{n-1}(x)\} + \mathbf{h}\{2xLe_{n+2}(x) - Le_n(x)\}$$
$$= 2xLe_{n-1}^{[H]}(x) - Le_{n-3}^{[H]}(x).$$

□

Theorem 3. *Let $Le_n(x)$ be the nth Leonardo Pisano polynomial. The generating function of $Le_n(x)$ is defined as*

$$g_{Le_n(x)}(\lambda) = \sum_{n=0}^{\infty} Le_n(x)\lambda^n = \frac{1 + (1-2x)\lambda + (2-x)\lambda^2}{1 - 2x\lambda + \lambda^3}.$$

Proof. Assume that the generating function of Leonardo Pisano polynomial series $\{Le_n(x)\}$ is,

$$g_{Le_n(x)}(\lambda) = \sum_{n=0}^{\infty} Le_n(x)\lambda^n = Le_0(x) + Le_1(x)\lambda + Le_2(x)\lambda^2 + \cdots \quad (11)$$

Using this form, we obtain

$$-2x\lambda g_{Le_n(x)}(\lambda) = -2x\lambda Le_0(x) - 2x\lambda^2 Le_1(x) - 2x\lambda^3 Le_2(x) - \cdots, \quad (12)$$

$$\lambda^3 g_{Le_n(x)}(\lambda) = \lambda^3 Le_0(x) + \lambda^4 Le_1(x) + \lambda^5 Le_2(x) + \cdots. \quad (13)$$

If we sum these Equations (11)–(13) side by side, then we obtain

$$[1 - 2x\lambda + \lambda^3]g_{Le_n(x)}(\lambda) = Le_0(x) + Le_1(x)\lambda + Le_2(x)\lambda^2 - 2xLe_0(x)\lambda - 2xLe_1(x)\lambda^2$$
$$= Le_0(x) + \lambda(Le_1(x) - 2xLe_0(x)) + \lambda^2(Le_2(x) - 2xLe_1(x)) \quad (14)$$
$$= 1 + (1 - 2x)\lambda + (2 - x)\lambda^2$$

Then the proof is completed. □

Corollary 1. Let $Le_n^{[H]}(x)$ be the nth Leonardo Pisano hybrinomial. The generating function of $Le_n^{[H]}(x)$ is

$$G_{Le_n^{[H]}(x)}(\lambda) = \frac{Le_0^{[H]}(x) + \lambda[Le_1^{[H]}(x) - 2xLe_0^{[H]}(x)] + \lambda^2[Le_2^{[H]}(x) - 2xLe_1^{[H]}(x)]}{1 - 2x\lambda^2 + \lambda^3}.$$

Theorem 4. Let $Le_n(x)$ be the nth Leonardo Pisano polynomial. The Binet-like formula for the sequence $\{Le_n(x)\}$ is

$$Le_n(x) = A\alpha^n + B\beta^n + C\gamma^n$$

where α, β and γ are the roots of the characteristic equation $\lambda^3 - 2x\lambda^2 + 1 = 0$ and A, B, C are as follows:

$$A = \frac{\alpha^2 + (2-x)\alpha + (x+2)}{(\alpha - \beta)(\alpha - \gamma)}, \tag{15}$$

$$B = \frac{\beta^2 + (2-x)\beta + (x+2)}{(\beta - \alpha)(\beta - \gamma)}, \tag{16}$$

$$C = \frac{\gamma^2 + (2-x)\gamma + (x+2)}{(\gamma - \alpha)(\gamma - \beta)}. \tag{17}$$

Proof. Let $f(\lambda) = \lambda^3 - 2x\lambda^2 + 1 = 0$ be the characteristic equation of the recurrence relation $Le_n(x) = 2xLe_{n-1}(x) - Le_{n-3}(x)$. It is obvious that $f(\lambda)$ should have three distinct roots α, β and γ. Then, $\frac{1}{\alpha}, \frac{1}{\beta}$ and $\frac{1}{\gamma}$ are the roots of the equation

$$f(\lambda) = \lambda^3 - 2x\lambda^2 + 1 = 0 \tag{18}$$

$$f\left(\frac{1}{\lambda}\right) = \frac{1}{\lambda^3} - \frac{2x}{\lambda^2} + 1 = \frac{\lambda^3 - 2x\lambda + 1}{\lambda^3} = 0 \tag{19}$$

Since $\lambda^3 \neq 0$, then $h(\lambda) = \lambda^3 - 2x\lambda + 1$.

From the generating function of Leonardo Pisano polynomials and from the sum of geometric series, we have

$$g_{Le_n(x)}(\lambda) = \frac{1 + (1-2x)\lambda + (2-x)\lambda^2}{1 - 2x\lambda + \lambda^3} = \frac{A}{1-\alpha\lambda} + \frac{B}{1-\beta\lambda} + \frac{C}{1-\gamma\lambda}$$

$$= A\sum_{n=0}^{\infty}(\alpha\lambda)^n + B\sum_{n=0}^{\infty}(\beta\lambda)^n + C\sum_{n=0}^{\infty}(\gamma\lambda)^n \tag{20}$$

$$= \frac{A(1-\beta\alpha)(1-\gamma\lambda) + B(1-\alpha\lambda)(1-\gamma\lambda) + C(1-\alpha\lambda)(1-\beta\lambda)}{(1-\alpha\lambda)(1-\beta\lambda)(1-\gamma\lambda)}.$$

Then we have the following equality

$$1 + (1-2x)\lambda + (2-x)\lambda^2 = A(1-\beta\alpha)(1-\gamma\lambda) + B(1-\alpha\lambda)(1-\gamma\lambda) + C(1-\alpha\lambda)(1-\beta\lambda).$$

If we substitute λ by $\frac{1}{\alpha}$, we obtain

$$1 + (1-2x)\frac{1}{\alpha} + (2-x)\frac{1}{\alpha^2} = A\left(1 - \frac{\beta}{\alpha}\right)\left(1 - \frac{\gamma}{\alpha}\right) \tag{21}$$

$$\alpha^2 + (1-2x)\alpha + (2-x) = A(\alpha - \beta)(\alpha - \gamma) \tag{22}$$

then it is easy to obtain

$$A = \frac{\alpha^2 + (1-2x)\alpha + (2-x)}{(\alpha - \beta)(\alpha - \gamma)}. \tag{23}$$

In the same way, we can obtain B and C as follows:

$$B = \frac{\beta^2 + (1-2x)\beta + (2-x)}{(\beta-\alpha)(\beta-\gamma)}, \quad C = \frac{\gamma^2 + (1-2x)\gamma + (2-x)}{(\gamma-\alpha)(\gamma-\beta)}.$$

If we substitute A, B, C into (20), we obtain the following equation

$$g_{Le_n(x)}(\lambda) = A\sum_{n=0}^{\infty}(\alpha\lambda)^n + B\sum_{n=0}^{\infty}(\beta\lambda)^n + C\sum_{n=0}^{\infty}(\gamma\lambda)^n$$

$$= \sum_{n=0}^{\infty}[A\alpha^n + B\beta^n + C\gamma^n]\lambda^n$$

Consequently, we get

$$Le_n(x) = A\alpha^n + B\beta^n + C\gamma^n. \tag{24}$$

□

Theorem 5. *The Binet-like formula for the Leonardo Pisano hybrinomial sequence is*

$$Le_n^{[H]}(x) = A\underline{\alpha}\alpha^n + B\underline{\beta}\beta^n + C\underline{\gamma}\gamma^n$$

where $\underline{\alpha} = 1 + \alpha \mathbf{i} + \alpha^2 \varepsilon + \alpha^3 \mathbf{h}$, $\underline{\beta} = 1 + \beta \mathbf{i} + \beta^2 \varepsilon + \beta^3 \mathbf{h}$ *and* $\underline{\gamma} = 1 + \gamma \mathbf{i} + \gamma^2 \varepsilon + \gamma^3 \mathbf{h}$.
Additionally, A, B and C are as in (17).

Proof. We have $Le_n^{[H]}(x) = Le_n(x) + iLe_{n+1}(x) + \varepsilon Le_{n+2}(x) + \mathbf{h} Le_{n+3}(x)$ from (6) and $Le_n(x) = A\alpha^n + B\beta^n + C\gamma^n$ from the previous theorem.

$$Le_n^{[H]}(x) = (A\alpha^n + B\beta^n + C\gamma^n) + (A\alpha^{n+1} + B\beta^{n+1} + C\gamma^{n+1})\mathbf{i}$$
$$+ (A\alpha^{n+2} + B\beta^{n+2} + C\gamma^{n+2})\varepsilon + (A\alpha^{n+3} + B\beta^{n+3} + C\gamma^{n+3})\mathbf{h}$$
$$= A\underline{\alpha}\alpha^n + B\underline{\beta}\beta^n + C\underline{\gamma}\gamma^n.$$

□

3. Some Identities for Leonardo Pisano Polynomial and Hybrinomial Sequences

In this section we state some identities, such as Cassini-like, d'Ocagne-like identities, where Leonardo Pisano polynomials and hybrinomials are involved.

Theorem 6 (Sum identities). *Let $n \geq 1$ be an integer, $\{Le_k(x)\}$ is the Leonardo Pisano polynomial sequence and $\{Le_k^{[H]}(x)\}$ is the Leonardo Pisano hybrinomial sequence, respectively. Then*

i. $\displaystyle\sum_{k=0}^{n} Le_k(x) = \frac{1}{2-2x}\Big(4 - 3x + Le_{n-1}(x) + Le_n(x) - Le_{n+1}(x)\Big),$

ii. $\displaystyle\sum_{k=0}^{n} Le_k^{[H]}(x) = \frac{1}{2-2x}\Big(Le_0^{[H]}(x) + Le_1^{[H]}(x) + Le_2^{[H]}(x) - 2xLe_0^{[H]}(x)$
$\qquad - 2xLe_1^{[H]}(x) + Le_{n-1}^{[H]}(x) + Le_n^{[H]}(x) - Le_{n+1}^{[H]}(x)\Big).$

Proof.
i. From the definition of Leonardo Pisano polynomial sequence

$$Le_n(x) = 2xLe_{n-1}(x) - Le_{n-3}(x)$$

we have the following equations

$$Le_3(x) = 2xLe_2(x) - Le_0(x)$$
$$Le_4(x) = 2xLe_3(x) - Le_1(x)$$
$$Le_5(x) = 2xLe_4(x) - Le_2(x)$$
$$\vdots \qquad \vdots$$
$$Le_n(x) = 2xLe_{n-1}(x) - Le_{n-3}(x).$$

when we sum up these equations side by side we get

$$\sum_{k=3}^{n} Le_k(x) = 2x \sum_{k=2}^{n-1} Le_k(x) - \sum_{k=0}^{n-3} Le_k(x) \tag{25}$$

In order to equalize the indexes, we add $P_1 = Le_0(x) + Le_1(x) + Le_2(x)$, $P_2 = 2x(Le_0(x) + Le_1(x) + Le_n(x))$, and $P_3 = -(Le_{n-2}(x) + Le_{n-1}(x) + Le_n(x))$ to both sides. Therefore we can write

$$P_2 + P_3 + \sum_{k=0}^{n} Le_k(x) = P_1 + 2x \sum_{k=0}^{n} Le_k(x) - \sum_{k=0}^{n} Le_k(x) \tag{26}$$

Eventually, we obtain the desired result.

ii. The proof can be demonstrated the same way. □

We can verify the previous theorem with the following example.

Example 1. *The sum of the first four Leonardo Pisano polynomials $Le_0 = 1$, $Le_1 = 1$, $Le_2 = x + 2$, $Le_3 = 2x^2 + 4x - 1$ is $2x^2 + 5x + 3$. Indeed, we can verify this result using the previous theorem as follows:*

$$\sum_{k=0}^{3} Le_k(x) = \frac{4 - 3x + x + 2 + 2x^2 + 4x - 1 - 4x^3 - 8x^2 + 2x + 1}{2 - 2x}$$
$$= \frac{-4x^3 - 6x^2 + 4x + 6}{2 - 2x} = 2x^2 + 5x + 3.$$

Theorem 7 (Catalan-like Identities). *Let n and r be two non-negative integers and $n \geq r$.*

i. *The Catalan-like identity for Leonardo Pisano polynomials is*

$$Le_{n+r}(x)Le_{n-r}(x) - Le_n^2(x) = AB\alpha^{n-r}\beta^{n-r}(\alpha^r - \beta^r)^2$$
$$+ AC\alpha^{n-r}\gamma^{n-r}(\alpha^r - \gamma^r)^2$$
$$+ BC\beta^{n-r}\gamma^{n-r}(\beta^r - \gamma^r)^2.$$

ii. *The Catalan-like identity for Leonardo Pisano hybrinomials is*

$$Le_{n+r}^{[H]}(x)Le_{n-r}^{[H]}(x) - (Le_n^{[H]}(x))^2 = A^2\alpha^{2n}\underline{\alpha}^2 + B^2\beta^{2n}\underline{\beta}^2 + C^2\gamma^{2n}\underline{\gamma}^2$$
$$+ AB\alpha^{n-r}\beta^{n-r}(\alpha^{2r}\underline{\alpha\beta} + \beta^{2r}\underline{\beta\alpha})$$
$$+ AC\alpha^{n-r}\gamma^{n-r}(\alpha^{2r}\underline{\alpha\gamma} + \gamma^{2r}\underline{\gamma\alpha})$$
$$+ BC\beta^{n-r}\gamma^{n-r}(\beta^{2r}\underline{\beta\gamma} + \gamma^{2r}\underline{\gamma\beta}).$$

Proof. Proofs can be easily seen if the Binet-like formula is used for Leonardo Pisano polynomials and Leonardo Pisano hybrinomials. □

Corollary 2 (Cassini-like identities). *Let n be a positive integer.*

i. *The Cassini-like identity for Leonardo Pisano polynomials is*

$$Le_{n+1}(x)Le_{n-1}(x) - Le_n^2(x) = AB\alpha^{n-1}\beta^{n-1}(\alpha-\beta)^2 \\ + AC\alpha^{n-1}\gamma^{n-1}(\alpha-\gamma)^2 \\ + BC\beta^{n-1}\gamma^{n-1}(\beta-\gamma)^2.$$

ii. *The Cassini-like identity for Leonardo Pisano hybrinomials is*

$$Le_{n+1}^{[H]}(x)Le_{n-1}^{[H]}(x) - (Le_n^{[H]}(x))^2 = A^2\alpha^{2n}\underline{\alpha}^2 + B^2\beta^{2n}\underline{\beta}^2 + C^2\gamma^{2n}\underline{\gamma}^2 \\ + AB\alpha^{n-1}\beta^{n-1}(\alpha^2\underline{\alpha\beta} + \beta^2\underline{\beta\alpha}) \\ + AC\alpha^{n-1}\gamma^{n-1}(\alpha^2\underline{\alpha\gamma} + \gamma^2\underline{\gamma\alpha}) \\ + BC\beta^{n-1}\gamma^{n-1}(\beta^2\underline{\beta\gamma} + \gamma^2\underline{\gamma\beta}).$$

Theorem 8 (d'Ocagne-like identities). *Let m and n be two non-negative integers.*

i. *The d'Ocagne-like identity for Leonardo Pisano polynomials is*

$$Le_m(x)Le_{n+1}(x) - Le_{m+1}(x)Le_n(x) = AB(\alpha-\beta)(\alpha^n\beta^m - \alpha^m\beta^n) \\ + AC(\alpha-\gamma)(\alpha^n\gamma^m - \alpha^m\gamma^n) \\ + BC(\beta-\gamma)(\beta^n\gamma^m - \beta^m\gamma^n).$$

ii. *The d'Ocagne-like identity for Leonardo Pisano hybrinomials is*

$$Le_m^{[H]}(x)Le_{n+1}^{[H]}(x) - Le_{m+1}^{[H]}(x)Le_n^{[H]}(x) = AB(\alpha-\beta)(\alpha^n\beta^m\underline{\alpha\beta} - \alpha^m\beta^n\underline{\beta\alpha}) \\ + AC(\alpha-\gamma)(\alpha^n\gamma^m\underline{\alpha\gamma} - \alpha^m\gamma^n\underline{\gamma\alpha}) \\ + BC(\beta-\gamma)(\beta^n\gamma^m\underline{\beta\gamma} - \beta^m\gamma^n\underline{\gamma\beta}).$$

Proof. i. Let us use the Binet-like formula for Leonardo Pisano polynomials.

$$Le_m(x)Le_{n+1}(x) - Le_{m+1}(x)Le_n(x) \\ = AB\alpha^m\beta^n(\beta-\alpha) + AC\alpha^m\gamma^n(\gamma-\alpha) + AB\alpha^n\beta^m(\alpha-\beta) + BC\beta^m\gamma^n(\gamma-\beta) \\ + AC\alpha^n\gamma^m(\alpha-\gamma) + BC\beta^n\gamma^m(\beta-\gamma) \\ = AB(\alpha-\beta)(\alpha^n\beta^m - \alpha^m\beta^n) + AC(\alpha-\gamma)(\alpha^n\gamma^m - \alpha^m\gamma^n) \\ + BC(\beta-\gamma)(\beta^n\gamma^m - \beta^m\gamma^n).$$

ii. This can be proven similarly to (i) using the Binet-like formula for Leonardo Pisano hybrinomials. □

Author Contributions: Conceptualization, F.K., A.D. and P.C.; methodology, F.K., A.D. and P.C.; software, F.K. and A.D.; validation, F.K., A.D. and P.C.; formal analysis, F.K. and A.D.; investigation, F.K., A.D. and P.C.; resources, F.K., A.D. and P.C.; data curation, F.K., A.D. and P.C.; writing—original draft preparation, F.K. and A.D.; writing—review and editing, F.K., A.D. and P.C.; visualization, F.K. and A.D.; supervision, P.C.; project administration, P.C. All authors have read and agreed to the published version of the manuscript.

Funding: This research was partially funded by Portuguese Funds through FCT—FUNDAÇÃO PARA A CIÊNCIA E A TECNOLOGIA, within the Projects UIDB/00013/2020, UIDP/00013/2020 and UIDB/00194/2020.

Acknowledgments: The last author is a member of the Research Centre CMAT-UTAD (Polo of Research Centre CMAT—Centre of Mathematics of University of Minho) and also a collaborating member of the Research Centre CIDTFF—Research Centre on Didactics and Technology in the Education of Trainers of University of Aveiro.

Conflicts of Interest: The authors declare no conflict of interest.

References

1. Koshy, T. *Fibonacci and Lucas Numbers with Applications*; John Wiley and Sons: Hoboken, NJ, USA, 2019.
2. Horadam, A.F. A generalized Fibonacci sequence. *Am. Math. Mon.* **1961**, *68*, 455–459. [CrossRef]
3. Horadam, A.F. Basic properties of a certain generalized sequence of numbers. *Fibonacci Q.* **1965**, *3*, 161–176.
4. Halici, S. On Fibonacci quaternions. *Adv. Appl. Clifford Algebras* **2012**, *22*, 321–327. [CrossRef]
5. Dağdeviren, A.; Kürüz, F. On The Horadam Hybrid Quaternions. *arXiv* **2020**, arXiv:2012.08277.
6. Catarino, P.; Borges A. On Leonardo numbers. *Acta Math. Univ. Comenianae* **2019**, *89*, 75–86.
7. Shannon, A.G. A note on generalized Leonardo numbers. *Notes Number Theory Discrete Math.* **2019**, *25*, 97–101. [CrossRef]
8. Catarino, P.; Borges, A. A note on incomplete Leonardo numbers. *Integers* **2020**, *20*, 1–7.
9. Alp, Y.; Koçer, E.G. Some properties of Leonardo numbers. *Konuralp J. Math.* **2021**, *9*, 183–189.
10. Alp, Y.; Koçer, E.G. Hybrid Leonardo numbers. *Chaos Solitons Fractals* **2021**, *150*, 111–128. [CrossRef]
11. Özdemir, M. Introduction to hybrid numbers. *Adv. Appl. Clifford Algebras* **2018**, *28*, 1–32. [CrossRef]
12. Bicknell, M. A primer for the Fibonacci numbers VII. *Fibonacci Q.* **1970**, *8*, 407–420.
13. Horzum, T.; Kocer, E.G. On some properties of Horadam polynomials. *Int. Math. Forum* **2009**, *25*, 1243–1252.
14. Hoggatt, V.E., Jr.; Bicknell, M. Roots of Fibonacci polynomials. *Fibonacci Q.* **1973**, *11*, 271–274.
15. Catarino, P. The h(x)-Fibonacci quaternion polynomials: Some combinatorial properties. *Adv. Appl. Clifford Algebras* **2016**, *26*, 71–79. [CrossRef]
16. Özkan, E.; Altun, İ. Generalized Lucas polynomials and relationships between the Fibonacci polynomials and Lucas polynomials. *Commun. Algebra* **2019**, *47*, 4020–4030. [CrossRef]
17. Liana, M.; Szynal-Liana, A.; Wloch, I. On Pell hybrinomials. *Miskolc Math. Notes* **2019**, *20*, 1051–1062. [CrossRef]
18. Szynal-Liana, A.; Włoch, I. Introduction to Fibonacci and Lucas hybrinomials. *Complex Var. Elliptic Equ.* **2020**, *65*, 1736–1747. [CrossRef]
19. Petroudi, S.H.J.; Pirouz, M. On Some Properties and Identities of Van Der Laan Hybrinomail Sequence, Preprint. In Proceedings of the 5th International Conference on Combinatorics, Cryptography, Computer Science and Computing, Tehran, Iran, 17–18 November 2021.
20. Petroudi, S.H.J.; Pirouz, M.; Ozkoc, A. The Narayana Polynomial and Narayana Hybrinomial Sequences. *Konuralp J. Math.* **2021** *9*, 90–99.
21. Kizilateş, C. A Note on Horadam Hybrinomials. *Preprints* **2020**. [CrossRef]

Article

Influence of MHD Hybrid Ferrofluid Flow on Exponentially Stretching/Shrinking Surface with Heat Source/Sink under Stagnation Point Region

Nur Syazana Anuar [1,*], Norfifah Bachok [2,3] and Ioan Pop [4]

1 Faculty of Computer and Mathematical Sciences, Universiti Teknologi MARA, Shah Alam 40450, Selangor, Malaysia
2 Department of Mathematics & Statistics, Faculty of Science, Universiti Putra Malaysia, Serdang 43400, Selangor, Malaysia; norfifah@upm.edu.my
3 Institute for Mathematical Research, Universiti Putra Malaysia, Serdang 43400, Selangor, Malaysia
4 Department of Mathematics, Babes-Bolyai University, 400084 Cluj-Napoca, Romania; ipop@math.ubbcluj.ro
* Correspondence: nursyazana931@tmsk.uitm.edu.my

Abstract: The numerical investigations of hybrid ferrofluid flow with magnetohydrodynamic (MHD) and heat source/sink effects are examined in this research. The sheet is assumed to stretch or shrink exponentially near the stagnation region. Two dissimilar magnetic nanoparticles, namely cobalt ferrite, $CoFe_2O_4$ and magnetite, Fe_3O_4, are considered with water as a based fluid. Utilizing the suitable similarity transformation, the governing equations are reduced to an ordinary differential equation (ODE). The converted ODEs are numerically solved with the aid of bvp4c solver from Matlab. The influences of varied parameters on velocity profile, skin friction coefficient, temperature profile and local Nusselt number are demonstrated graphically. The analysis evident the occurrence of non-unique solution for a shrinking sheet and it is confirmed from the analysis of stability that only the first solution is the stable solution. It is also found that for a stronger heat source, heat absorption is likely to happen at the sheet. Further, hybrid ferrofluid intensifies the heat transfer rate compared to ferrofluid. Moreover, the boundary layer separation is bound to happen faster with an increment of magnetic parameter, while it delays when $CoFe_2O_4$ nanoparticle volume fraction increases.

Keywords: hybrid ferrofluid; dual solution; exponentially stretching/shrinking; stability analysis; heat source/sink

Citation: Anuar, N.S.; Bachok, N.; Pop, I. Influence of MHD Hybrid Ferrofluid Flow on Exponentially Stretching/Shrinking Surface with Heat Source/Sink under Stagnation Point Region. *Mathematics* **2021**, *9*, 2932. https://doi.org/10.3390/math9222932

Academic Editors: Araceli Queiruga-Dios, Maria Jesus Santos, Fatih Yilmaz, Deolinda M. L. Dias Rasteiro, Jesús Martín Vaquero and Víctor Gayoso Martínez

Received: 23 September 2021
Accepted: 21 October 2021
Published: 17 November 2021

Publisher's Note: MDPI stays neutral with regard to jurisdictional claims in published maps and institutional affiliations.

Copyright: © 2021 by the authors. Licensee MDPI, Basel, Switzerland. This article is an open access article distributed under the terms and conditions of the Creative Commons Attribution (CC BY) license (https://creativecommons.org/licenses/by/4.0/).

1. Introduction

Ferrofluids or magnetic colloids are made by disseminating magnetic nanoparticles like cobalt ferrite $CoFe_2O_4$, hematite Fe_2O_3, magnetite Fe_3O_4 and many other nanometer-sized particles containing iron in the base fluid [1]; as a result, these particles have a dipolar interaction energy and magnetic moment in the base fluid. Ferrofluids have various biomedicine and engineering applications specifically in drug delivery [2], chemical activity monitoring in the human brain in real-time, destruction of tumors and toxin elimination from the body [3], rotary seals in computer hard drives and other rotating shaft motors [4]. For these reasons, many researchers [5–8] have focused their investigation on ferrofluids. Usually, nanofluid comprises only one nanoparticle whereas the hybrid nanofluid comprises two distinct nanoparticles disseminated in a base fluid [9]. Through the combination of two dissimilar nanomaterials, hybrid nanofluids are created to improve their thermal and rheological properties [10]. Suresh et al. [11] presented an experimental investigation using a two-step method (thermomechanical method) to synthesize hybrid (Al_2O_3-Cu/water) nanofluid. The outcomes demonstrated that the prepared hybrid nanofluid for a concentration of 2% nanoparticle volume fraction increase its thermal conductivity by 12.11%. In another experimental investigation, Madhesh and

Kalaiselvam [12] examined the properties of Cu-TiO$_2$/water nanofluid in a cooling system, while Esfe et al. [13] scrutinized the thermal conductivity of the hybrid (Ag-MgO) nanofluid and discovered that its conductivity rises with augmentation of nanoparticles concentration. Chu et al. [14] examined the thermal performance and flow characteristics of hybridized nanofluid (MWCNT-Fe$_3$O$_2$/water) in a cavity. The flow features of hybrid ferrofluids (Fe$_3$O$_4$–CoFe$_2$O$_4$) with water–ethylene glycol mixture (50–50%) as a based fluid in the thin film flow were investigated by Kumar et al. [15] and they revealed that hybrid ferrofluid offers a higher rate of heat transfer than that of ferrofluid. Researchers from all over the world have been drawn to hybrid nanofluids because of their exceptional heat augmentation behavior, which gives fine control over heat transfer in numerous industries. Due to that, several experimental and theoretical investigations on hybrid nanofluid have been published widely such as in references [16–18]. Therefore, the aim of developing hybrid ferrofluid is therefore to manage heat transfer efficiently in the flow field.

It seems that magnetohydrodynamic (MHD), heat source (generation) and heat sink (absorption) effects are crucial in monitoring the heat transfer in the production of quality products as it depends on the heat monitoring factor. This is also mainly due to the reason that MHD terms extremely appeared in various engineering and industrial processes like MHD generator, cancer therapy, MHD power generation, nuclear reactor, etc. [19]. The influences of heat source and sink are also important in cooling problems associated with nuclear reactions, combustion processes, and magnetized utilization in neurobiology to learn brain function [20]. In view of the increasing importance of MHD and heat source/sink, a lot of work has been carried out to investigate these effects in boundary layer flow. For instance, the simultaneous impact of MHD, heat source/sink and suction instigated by a shrinking sheet can be observed in the work of Bhattacharyya [21] and observed that increasing heat sink parameters cause the heat transfer to enhance. Further, Gorla et al. [22] explored the same effects in a hybrid nanofluid-filled porous cavity. Recently, Armaghani et al. [23] scrutinized the generation/absorption of heat and MHD in their investigation of hybrid nanofluid in an L-shaped cavity. They deduced that using the highest number of sink power results in the best heat transfer. Furthermore, the studies on MHD flow and heat source/sink by means of various physical configurations have been conducted by Jamaludin et al. [24] and Reddy et al. [25].

Nowadays, the existence of non-unique solutions has gained the attention of modern researchers. In some boundary layer flow problems, non-unique solutions have generally been found for linear shrinking sheet cases. For instance, non-unique solutions have been observed by Wang [26], Bachok et al. [27], Kamal et al. [28] and Anuar and Bachok [29], among others for the stagnation flow problem. Meanwhile, Bhattacharyya and Vajravelu [30], Bachok et al. [31] and Anuar et al. [32] have observed the occurrence of non-unique solutions in their investigation of stagnation flow when the sheet is shrunk exponentially. They conclude that the domain of similarity solution to existing is larger for the stagnation flow in the exponential case rather than in the linear case. However, there also exist some situations where non-unique solutions happen to exist for both cases, i.e., stretching and shrinking (see for instance the research carried out by Lund et al. [33] and Waini et al. [34]). With regards to the existence of more than one solution, a stability analysis on the solutions obtained has been performed by some researchers. This kind of analysis is important in order to avoid any misleading interpretation of flow. Some important investigations concerning the stability analysis on the solutions of boundary layer flow problem were made by Merkin [35], Weidman et al. [36], Harris et al. [37] and more recently by Anuar et al. [38], Mustafa et al. [39] and Aladdin et al. [40,41], among others. It has been observed that the second solution has always been unstable and therefore unobtainable in practice, while the other solution is stable.

Owing to the nonlinearity of equations that describe most engineering and science phenomena, many authors used numerical methods such as finite element methods [22,23], shooting method [6,15,30] and bvp4c solver [18,24,34,40] to solve the governing equations. For the present problem, in solving the system of nonlinear equations, Matlab bvp4c built-in code is employed. The Matlab bvp4c solver is a residual control-based adaptive mesh solver. The algorithm is based on the Runge–Kutta improved formulas that have interpolation capability [42]. It has been used successfully by many researchers to solve boundary value problems from different models in science and engineering. This method was found to be robust and consistent, showing superiority over the shooting method.

The goal of this investigation is to scrutinize the heat generation/absorption of MHD hybrid ferrofluid ($CoFe_2O_4$–Fe_3O_4/water) flow instigated by an exponentially deformable sheet. In the light of the previous literature survey, it is worthy to mention that no attempt has been made on this kind of flow problem yet. Here, the similarity variable is used to convert the governing equations into an ODE which later be solved numerically using bvp4c (Matlab's built-in function). The computed results for relevant parameters concerning local Nusselt number and skin friction coefficient, together with temperature profile and velocity profile, are visualized graphically and elaborated in detail. Further, the occurrence of two solutions motivates us to identify the stable and unstable solutions by performing the stability analysis. In addition, this theoretical study would help engineers who are experimentally working on hybrid ferrofluids, and the findings are expected to reduce the cost of future experiments.

2. Problem Formulation

2.1. Mathematical Framework

The two-dimensional and steady flow of MHD hybrid ferrofluid past a deformable sheet are investigated and portrayed in Figure 1. The x-axis is selected along the direction of the horizontal surface while y-axis is perpendicular to it. The surface of the sheet is shrunk or stretched with exponential velocity $u_w(x) = a\exp(x/L)$ given that a and L are the positive constant and characteristic length, respectively. As shown in Figure 1, magnetic B and heat generation/absorption $Q(x)$ are applied parallel to the y-axis and will be defined later. Distant from the horizontal surface, the flow is kept at constant temperature T_∞ and free stream velocity $u_e(x) = b\exp(x/L)$; here b is the positive constant. Further, the surface temperature is assumed to vary as prescribed exponential function and denoted by $T_w = T_\infty + T_0 \exp\left(\frac{x}{2L}\right)$ where T_0 is the rate at which the temperature rises along the sheet is measured.

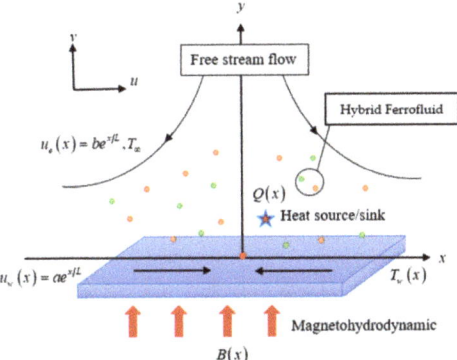

Figure 1. Flow model of shrinking sheet and its coordinate system.

Following the mathematical formulation and idea proposed by Kumar et al. [15], Wang [26] and Kamal et al. [28], the governing partial differential equations are denoted as:

$$\frac{\partial u}{\partial x} + \frac{\partial v}{\partial y} = 0 \qquad (1)$$

$$u\frac{\partial u}{\partial x} + v\frac{\partial u}{\partial y} = u_e\frac{du_e}{dx} + \frac{\mu_{hf}}{\rho_{hf}}\frac{\partial^2 u}{\partial y^2} - \frac{\sigma_{hf}}{\rho_{hf}}B^2(u - u_e) \qquad (2)$$

$$u\frac{\partial T}{\partial x} + v\frac{\partial T}{\partial y} = \frac{k_{hf}}{(\rho C_p)_{hf}}\frac{\partial^2 T}{\partial y^2} + \frac{Q(x)}{(\rho C_p)_{hf}}(T - T_\infty) \qquad (3)$$

(u, v) in the above equation indicates the velocity component in the (x, y) direction and T refers to the fluid's temperature. Further, μ denotes the dynamic viscosity, ρ refers to the density, σ and k are the electrical and thermal conductivity, respectively, and C_p is the specific heat where the subscript $'hf'$ signifies the hybrid ferrofluid.

The relevant boundary conditions are given as (Bachok et al. [27]):

$$T = T_w(x), \quad v = 0, \quad u = u_w(x) \quad \text{at} \quad y = 0; \quad T \to T_\infty, \quad u \to u_e(x) \quad \text{as} \quad y \to \infty \qquad (4)$$

2.2. Correlation Used for Hybrid Ferrofluid

The thermophysical properties for the hybrid ferrofluid are employed from the work of Takabi and Salehi [9] and Gorla et al. [22] (see Table 1). The first and second nanoparticles are denoted by subscripts "1" and "2" in the table. Further, φ is the summation of the volume concentration of two dissimilar kinds of nanoparticles, i.e., $\varphi = \varphi_1 + \varphi_2$.

Table 1. Thermophysical traits of hybrid ferrofluid.

Properties	Hybrid Ferrofluid
Density	$\rho_{hf} = (1 - \varphi)\rho_f + \varphi_1\rho_1 + \varphi_2\rho_2$
Thermal conductivity	$\frac{k_{hf}}{k_f} = \frac{((\varphi_1 k_1 + \varphi_2 k_2)/\varphi) + 2k_f + 2(\varphi_1 k_1 + \varphi_2 k_2) - 2\varphi k_f}{((\varphi_1 k_1 + \varphi_2 k_2)/\varphi) + 2k_f - (\varphi_1 k_1 + \varphi_2 k_2) + \varphi k_f}$
Heat capacity	$(\rho C_p)_{hf} = (1 - \varphi)(\rho C_p)_f + \varphi_1(\rho C_p)_1 + \varphi_2(\rho C_p)_2$
Dynamic viscosity	$\mu_{hf} = \mu_f/(1 - \varphi)^{2.5}$
Electrical conductivity	$\frac{\sigma_{hf}}{\sigma_f} = 1 + \frac{3(((\varphi_1\sigma_1 + \varphi_2\sigma_2)/\sigma_f) - \varphi)}{(((\varphi_1\sigma_1 + \varphi_2\sigma_2)/(\varphi\sigma_f)) + 2) - (((\varphi_1\sigma_1 + \varphi_2\sigma_2)/\sigma_f) - \varphi)}$

It should be emphasized that the desired hybrid ferrofluid is formed by suspending 1% of Iron Oxide (Fe_3O_4) nanoparticle into the base fluid (water). Then, Cobalt Iron Oxide ($CoFe_2O_4$) nanoparticle is added into the Fe_3O_4/water nanofluid and eventually formed a hybrid ferrofluid. In addition, the volume fraction of $CoFe_2O_4$ nanoparticles is fluctuated from 0 to 2%. Therefore, in this study, the first nanoparticle is denoted by Fe_3O_4 while the second nanoparticle refers to $CoFe_2O_4$. The physical characteristics of the base fluid and the nanosized particles are shown in Table 2 (Abbas and Sheikh [7], Oztop and Abu-Nada [43], Sheikholeslami et al. [44], Tlili et al. [45]).

Table 2. Thermophysical properties of nanoparticle and base fluid.

	Physical Properties			
	$C_p (J \cdot kg^{-1} \cdot K^{-1})$	$\rho (kg \cdot m^{-3})$	$k (W \cdot m^{-1} \cdot K^{-1})$	$\sigma (S \cdot m^{-1})$
water, H_2O	4179	997.1	0.613	0.05
Magnetic nanoparticles				
Magnetite, Fe_3O_4	670	5180	9.7	0.74×10^6
Cobalt Ferrite, $CoFe_2O_4$	700	4907	3.7	1.1×10^7
Non-magnetic nanoparticles				
Copper, Cu	385	8933	401	5.96×10^7
Titania, TiO_2	686.2	4250	8.9538	1×10^{-12}
Alumina, Al_2O_3	765	3970	40	1×10^{-10}

2.3. Similarity Solutions

The similarity transformations take the following form (Bhattacharyya and Vajravelu [30]):

$$\eta = y\left(\frac{b}{2\nu_f L}\right)^{1/2} \exp\left(\frac{x}{2L}\right), \quad \theta(\eta) = \frac{T - T_\infty}{T_w(x) - T_\infty}, \quad \psi = \left(2\nu_f L b\right)^{1/2} \exp\left(\frac{x}{2L}\right) f(\eta) \quad (5)$$

where ν_f, η and ψ are the kinematic viscosity, similarity variable and stream function, while f and θ is the dimensionless functions. Next, we defined $u = \partial\psi/\partial y$ and $v = -\partial\psi/\partial x$. Accordingly, Equation (1) is automatically satisfied.

We take $Q(x) = \frac{Q_0}{2L}\exp(x/L)$ and $B = B_0\exp(\frac{x}{2L})$ where Q_0 denotes the heat source/sink coefficient and B_0 is the constant magnetic field in order for the similarity solutions to exist. Variables (5) are substituted into the governing Equations (2) and (3) to produce the following ODEs:

$$\frac{\mu_{hf}/\mu_f}{\rho_{hf}/\rho_f} f''' - 2f'^2 + f f'' - \frac{\sigma_{hf}/\sigma_f}{\rho_{hf}/\rho_f} M(f' - 1) + 2 = 0 \quad (6)$$

$$\frac{1}{\Pr} \frac{k_{hf}/k_f}{(\rho C_p)_{hf}/(\rho C_p)_f} \theta'' + f\theta' - f'\theta + \frac{1}{(\rho C_p)_{hf}/(\rho C_p)_f} \beta\theta = 0 \quad (7)$$

in which prime denotes the differentiation with respect to η. Further, $\Pr = \nu_f (\rho C_p)_f / k_f$ and $M = \frac{2\sigma_f B_0^2 L}{b\rho_f}$ refer to the Prandtl number and magnetic field parameter, while $\beta = \frac{Q_0}{b(\rho C_p)_f}$ denotes the heat source/sink parameter where $\beta > 0$ stands for heat generation (source) and $\beta < 0$ refers to heat absorption (sink).

Subsequently, Equation (4) becomes:

$$\theta(0) = 1, \quad f'(0) = \lambda, \quad f(0) = 0; \quad \theta(\eta) \to 0, \quad f'(\eta) \to 1 \quad \text{as} \quad \eta \to \infty \quad (8)$$

Here, $\lambda = a/b$ is the stretching/shrinking parameter given that $\lambda < 0$ and $\lambda > 0$ denote the sheet is shrunk and stretch, respectively, $\lambda = 0$ refers to a static sheet.

2.4. Physical Quantities

The skin friction C_f and Nusselt number Nu_x are the physical quantities of interest in this research and can be described as:

$$C_f = \frac{\mu_{hf}\left(\frac{\partial u}{\partial y}\right)_{y=0}}{\rho_f u_e^2}, \quad Nu_x = -\frac{2L k_{hf}\left(\frac{\partial T}{\partial y}\right)_{y=0}}{k_f (T_w - T_\infty)} \quad (9)$$

By implementing the variables (5) into Equation (9), we have:

$$C_f \text{Re}_x^{1/2} = \frac{\mu_{hf}}{\mu_f} f''(0), \quad Nu_x \text{Re}_x^{-1/2} = -\frac{k_{hf}}{k_f} \theta'(0) \quad (10)$$

where $\text{Re}_x = 2L u_e / \nu_f$ is the Reynolds number.

3. Stability Analysis of Solutions

The present investigation admits more than one solution for some range of governing parameters. As a result, a stability analysis is required. The first step is to consider the current problem as an unsteady problem as suggested by Merkin [35]. Therefore, Equation (1) remains the same while the unsteady governing equations is rewritten as:

$$\frac{\partial u}{\partial t} + u\frac{\partial u}{\partial x} + v\frac{\partial u}{\partial y} = u_e \frac{du_e}{dx} + \frac{\mu_{hf}}{\rho_{hf}}\frac{\partial^2 u}{\partial y^2} - \frac{\sigma_{hf}}{\rho_{hf}} B^2 (u - u_e) \quad (11)$$

$$\frac{\partial T}{\partial t} + u\frac{\partial T}{\partial x} + v\frac{\partial T}{\partial y} = \frac{k_{hf}}{(\rho C_p)_{hf}}\frac{\partial^2 T}{\partial y^2} + \frac{Q(x)}{(\rho C_p)_{hf}}(T - T_\infty) \quad (12)$$

subjected to the conditions (4). Next, a new dimensionless time variable τ is introduced:

$$\tau = \frac{b}{2L} t \exp\left(\frac{x}{L}\right) \quad (13)$$

while the new dimensionless transformation can be rewritten as:

$$\eta = y\left(\frac{b}{2\nu_f L}\right)^{1/2} \exp\left(\frac{x}{2L}\right), \quad \psi = \left(2\nu_f L b\right)^{1/2} \exp\left(\frac{x}{2L}\right) f(\eta,\tau), \quad \theta(\eta,\tau) = \frac{T-T_\infty}{T_w(x)-T_\infty} \quad (14)$$

When the variables (13) and (14) are substituted into Equations (11) and (12), the obtained equations are:

$$\frac{\mu_{hf}/\mu_f}{\rho_{hf}/\rho_f}\frac{\partial^3 f}{\partial \eta^3} - 2\left(\frac{\partial f}{\partial \eta}\right)^2 + f\frac{\partial^2 f}{\partial \eta^2} + 2 - \frac{\sigma_{hf}/\sigma_f}{\rho_{hf}/\rho_f} M\left(\frac{\partial f}{\partial \eta} - 1\right) - \frac{\partial^2 f}{\partial \eta \partial \tau} + 2\tau\left(\frac{\partial f}{\partial \tau}\frac{\partial^2 f}{\partial \eta^2} - \frac{\partial f}{\partial \eta}\frac{\partial^2 f}{\partial \eta \partial \tau}\right) = 0 \quad (15)$$

$$\frac{1}{\Pr}\frac{k_{hf}/k_f}{(\rho C_p)_{hf}/(\rho C_p)_f}\frac{\partial^2 \theta}{\partial \eta^2} - \theta\frac{\partial f}{\partial \eta} + f\frac{\partial \theta}{\partial \eta} + \frac{\beta}{(\rho C_p)_{hf}/(\rho C_p)_f}\theta - \frac{\partial \theta}{\partial \tau} - 2\tau\left(\frac{\partial f}{\partial \eta}\frac{\partial \theta}{\partial \tau} - \frac{\partial f}{\partial \tau}\frac{\partial \theta}{\partial \eta}\right) = 0 \quad (16)$$

and the transform conditions are:

$$f(0,\tau) + 2\tau\frac{\partial f}{\partial \tau}(0,\tau) = 0, \quad \theta(0,\tau) = 1, \quad \frac{\partial f}{\partial \eta}(0,\tau) = \lambda,$$
$$\theta(\eta,\tau) \to 0, \quad \frac{\partial f}{\partial \eta}(\eta,\tau) \to 1 \quad \text{as} \quad \eta \to \infty \quad (17)$$

Afterwards, we write [36]:

$$f(\eta,\tau) = f_0(\eta) + e^{-\gamma\tau} F(\eta,\tau), \quad \theta(\eta,\tau) = \theta_0(\eta) + e^{-\gamma\tau} H(\eta,\tau), \quad (18)$$

for the purpose to specify the stability of the steady flow solution of $\theta(\eta) = \theta_0(\eta)$ and $f(\eta) = f_0(\eta)$. From the above equation, $F(\eta,\tau)$ and $H(\eta,\tau)$ are relatively smaller than $f_0(\eta)$ and $\theta_0(\eta)$, while γ is the smallest eigenvalues parameter. Substitute Equation (18) into Equations (15)–(17) and setting $\tau = 0$, we have $H(\eta) = H_0(\eta)$ and $F(\eta) = F_0(\eta)$. Therefore, the final linearized equations take the following form:

$$\frac{\mu_{hf}/\mu_f}{\rho_{hf}/\rho_f} F_0''' - 4f_0' F_0' + f_0 F_0'' + f_0'' F_0 - \frac{\sigma_{hf}/\sigma_f}{\rho_{hf}/\rho_f} M F_0' + \gamma F_0' = 0 \quad (19)$$

$$\frac{1}{\Pr}\frac{k_{hf}/k_f}{(\rho C_p)_{hf}/(\rho C_p)_f} H_0'' + f_0 H_0' + F_0 \theta_0' - F_0' \theta_0 - H_0 f_0' + \frac{\beta}{(\rho C_p)_{hf}/(\rho C_p)_f} H_0 + \gamma H_0 = 0 \quad (20)$$

associated with conditions:

$$H_0(0) = 0, \quad F_0'(0) = 0, \quad F_0(0) = 0; \quad H_0(\eta) \to 0, \quad F_0'(\eta) \to 0 \quad \text{as} \quad \eta \to \infty \quad (21)$$

To solve the above-linearized equations, we need to relax a boundary condition of $F_0'(\eta) \to 0$ when $\eta \to \infty$ and replace it with a new boundary condition $F_0''(0) = 1$ as advocated by Harris et al. [37]. This set of linearized equations will eventually display an infinite set of eigenvalues $\gamma_1 < \gamma_2 < \ldots < \gamma_n$.

4. Results and Discussion

With the help of Matlab's in-built function (i.e., bvp4c solver), the self-similar ODEs (6) and (7) associated with its conditions (8) are solved numerically. In this section, the Prandtl number is fixed to 6.2 which denotes water [43], and the nanoparticle volume fraction (φ_1, φ_2) is varied from 0 to 0.2. Further, we take $\beta = -0.2, -0.4, -0.6$ (for a heat sink),

$\beta = 0$ (without heat source/sink), $\beta = 0.2$, 0.4, 0.6 (for the heat source) and magnetic parameter $M = 0.1$, 0.2, 0.3.

4.1. Validation of Results

To validate the present model, we computed the outcomes as in Tables 3 and 4 for the skin friction coefficient $C_f \text{Re}_x^{1/2}$ and local Nusselt number $Nu_x \text{Re}_x^{-1/2}$ when $\lambda = -0.5, 0, 0.5$. The results of our numerical calculation are in a good harmony with the results obtained from the work of Bachok et al. [31] when M and β are set to zero. Therefore, we are assured that the present code is true and this problem can be solved using the bvp4c solver.

Table 3. Comparison values of $C_f \text{Re}_x^{1/2}$ for some values of λ when $\varphi_1 = 0.1$, $\varphi_2 = 0$ and $M = 0$.

	Cu-Water		Al$_2$O$_3$-Water		TiO$_2$-Water	
λ	Bachok et al. [31]	Present	Bachok et al. [31]	Present	Bachok et al. [31]	Present
-0.5	3.2381	3.238160	2.7531	2.753091	2.7827	2.782709
0	2.5794	2.579342	2.1929	2.192963	2.2166	2.216555
0.5	1.4682	1.468240	1.2483	1.248302	1.2618	1.261731

Table 4. Comparison values of $Nu_x \text{Re}_x^{-1/2}$ for some values of λ when $\varphi_1 = 0.1$, $\varphi_2 = 0$ and $\beta = 0$.

	Cu-Water		Al$_2$O$_3$-Water		TiO$_2$-Water	
λ	Bachok et al. [31]	Present	Bachok et al. [31]	Present	Bachok et al. [31]	Present
-0.5	3.2381	3.238160	2.7531	2.753091	2.7827	2.782709
0	2.5794	2.579342	2.1929	2.192963	2.2166	2.216555
0.5	1.4682	1.468240	1.2483	1.248302	1.2618	1.261731

4.2. Interpretation of Results

In Figures 2 and 3, numerical results for various nanoparticle volume fraction φ_1 and φ_2 for shrinking sheet ($\lambda = -1.2$) are plotted for velocity $f'(\eta)$ and temperature $\theta(\eta)$ profiles. Both figures are exemplified for 3 sets of nanoparticle volume fraction, i.e., $\varphi_1 = \varphi_2 = 0$ (Set 1), $\varphi_1 = 0.01$, $\varphi_2 = 0$ (Set 2) and $\varphi_1 = \varphi_2 = 0.01$ (Set 3). Here, set 1 indicates the regular fluid, while sets 2 and 3 refer to ferrofluid (Fe$_3$O$_4$/water) and hybrid ferrofluid (CoFe$_2$O$_4$–Fe$_3$O$_4$/water), respectively. From these graphical results, the second and first solutions are displayed through the dashed line and solid line, respectively. From the figures, we observed that set 3 shows a thinner boundary layer thickness (momentum and thermal) for the first and second solutions than sets 1 and 2. The disparities of skin friction coefficient $C_f \text{Re}_x^{1/2}$ and local Nusselt number $Nu_x \text{Re}_x^{-1/2}$ against stretching/shrinking parameter λ for some values of CoFe$_2$O$_4$ nanoparticle volume fraction φ_2 are portrayed in Figures 4 and 5. It is observed from Equation (10) that $C_f \text{Re}_x^{1/2}$ and $Nu_x \text{Re}_x^{-1/2}$ are directly associated with the dimensionless velocity gradient $f''(0)$ and temperature gradient $-\theta'(0)$ at the wall, respectively. It is seen that these physical quantities of interest ($C_f \text{Re}_x^{1/2}$ and $Nu_x \text{Re}_x^{-1/2}$) enhance with an upsurge in the volume fraction of CoFe$_2$O$_4$ nanoparticle φ_2 for the first solution. However, we observed that the values of $C_f \text{Re}_x^{1/2}$ and $Nu_x \text{Re}_x^{-1/2}$ decrease when stretching/shrinking parameter λ near its critical value λ_c. The rise in the $C_f \text{Re}_x^{1/2}$ is due to an increment in the nanoparticles colloidal suspension that enhanced the collision of nanoparticle dispersion of ferrofluid. An increase in the nanoparticles volume fraction may physically increase its synergistic effect which, consequently, improves the heat transfer rate. This demonstrates that cooling in hybrid ferrofluid is much faster, whereas cooling in ferrofluid flow may take longer. It can also be seen from Figures 4 and 5 that a non-unique solution (dual solutions) happens to exist for shrinking sheet ($\lambda < -1$), unique (one) solution is observed when $-1 \leq \lambda \leq 1$ and no solution when $\lambda < \lambda_c$, i.e., boundary layer separation is bound to take place. It should be noted that

$\lambda_c = -1.53463, -1.53634$ and -1.53818 are the respective critical values of $\varphi = 0$, 0.01 and 0.02. Accordingly, we can deduce that nanoparticle volume fraction acts in postponing the boundary later separation.

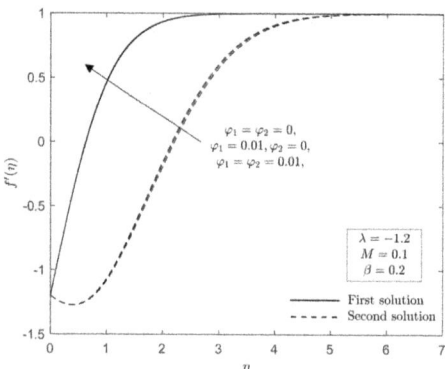

Figure 2. Velocity profile $f'(\eta)$ for various value of φ_1 and φ_2 (Shrinking sheet case) when $M = 0.1$ and $\beta = 0.2$.

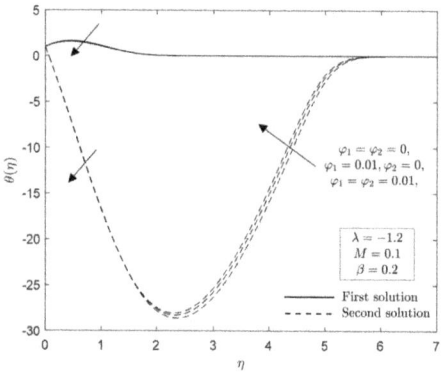

Figure 3. Temperature profile $\theta(\eta)$ for various values of φ_1 and φ_2 (Shrinking sheet case) when $M = 0.1$ and $\beta = 0.2$.

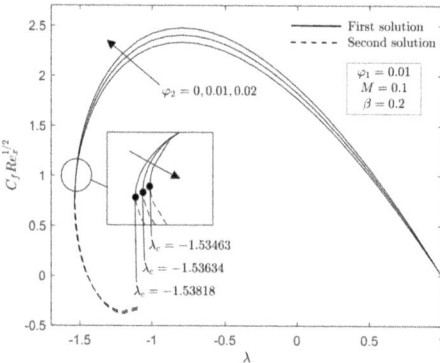

Figure 4. Skin friction coefficient $C_f Re_x^{1/2}$ with λ for some values of $CoFe_2O_4$ nanoparticle volume fraction φ_2 when $M = 0.1$ and $\beta = 0.2$.

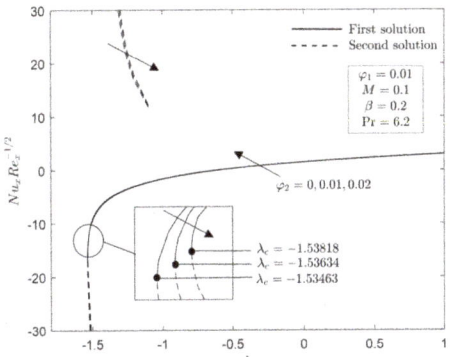

Figure 5. Local Nusselt number $Nu_x Re_x^{-1/2}$ with λ for some values of $CoFe_2O_4$ nanoparticle volume fraction φ_2 when $M = 0.1$ and $\beta = 0.2$.

Figures 6 and 7 depict the graphical representation of the temperature profile $\theta(\eta)$ for selected values of heat source/sink parameter β. The influence of rising values of heat source ($\beta > 0$) is to increase the boundary layer thickness (thermal) for both solutions. As the heat source is increased, the temperature rises, thereby the sheet's temperature also increases. On the contrary, heat sink ($\beta < 0$) leads to decrement of the boundary layer (thermal) in first and second solutions. More heat is removed from the sheet as the heat sink increases, lowering the sheet's temperature. Furthermore, the temperature overshoot is observed for the second solution. This is in line with the fact that the dashed line which indicates the second solution always has a thicker boundary layer than the solid line, i.e., the first solution. The effect of heat source/sink ($\beta = -0.2, 0, 0.2$) on the local Nusselt number $Nu_x Re_x^{-1/2}$ versus stretching/shrinking sheet λ for hybrid ferrofluid is portrayed in Figure 8. One can see that as β is increased, the temperature rises, which consequently lowers $Nu_x Re_x^{-1/2}$. Again, the appearance of the non-unique solution is discovered for the shrinking sheet ($\lambda < -1$) only. In addition, for all heat source/sink parameter values β, the critical value λ_c is the same, i.e., $\lambda_c = -1.53634$.

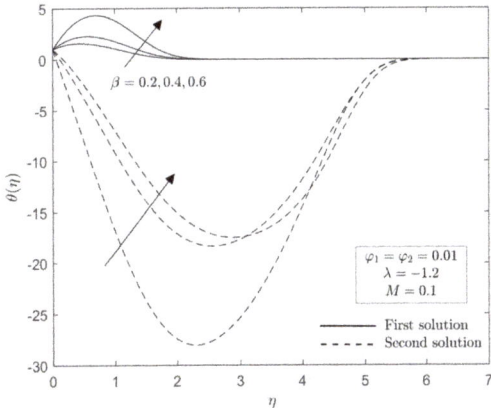

Figure 6. Temperature profile $\theta(\eta)$ for selected values of heat source β (Shrinking sheet case) when $M = 0.1$.

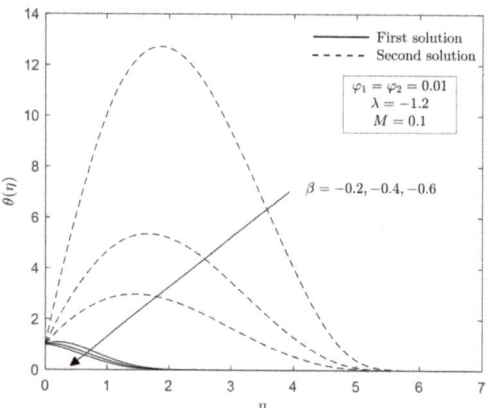

Figure 7. Temperature profile $\theta(\eta)$ for selected values of heat sink β (Shrinking sheet case) when $M = 0.1$.

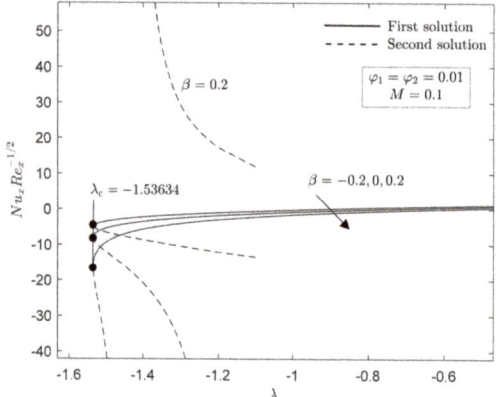

Figure 8. Local Nusselt number $Nu_x Re_x^{-1/2}$ with λ for some values of heat source/sink β when $M = 0.1$.

The influence of magnetic parameter M in the existence of heat source ($\beta = 0.2$) on the velocity $f'(\eta)$ profile and temperature $\theta(\eta)$ profile are depicted in Figures 9 and 10, while skin friction coefficient $C_f Re_x^{1/2}$ and local Nusselt number $Nu_x Re_x^{-1/2}$ are plotted in Figures 11 and 12, respectively. For accumulating amounts of magnetic parameter M, these profiles ($f'(\eta)$ and $\theta(\eta)$) significantly decrease and also cause the boundary layer thickness to reduce in the first solution. Nevertheless, an opposite observation is made for the other solution. The upsurge value of M in the flow causes an increase in the Lorentz force or also known as resistive type force and consequently generates much more resistance to the flow and increases the temperature. Figures 11 and 12 for the skin friction coefficient $C_f Re_x^{1/2}$ and local Nusselt number $Nu_x Re_x^{-1/2}$ demonstrate an increasing behavior for hybrid ferrofluid with an increasing magnetic parameter M. The influence of magnetic parameter M on $Nu_x Re_x^{-1/2}$ is minimal as M is not explicitly occurred in Equation (7). Again, the same observation is observed for the presence of dual solutions (see Figures 4, 5 and 8). It is also clear from these graphs that as the magnetic parameter M intensifies, the domain of the occurrence of dual solutions expands. For instance, the critical values of stretching/shrinking parameter for $M = 0.1$, 0.2 and 0.3 are $\lambda_c = -1.53634, -1.58568$ and -1.63506. This implies that the presence of magnetic parameters can slow down the boundary layer separation to occur.

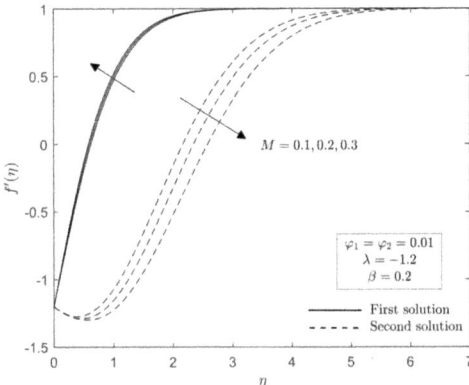

Figure 9. Velocity profile $f'(\eta)$ for selected values of magnetic parameter M (Shrinking sheet case) when $\beta = 0.2$.

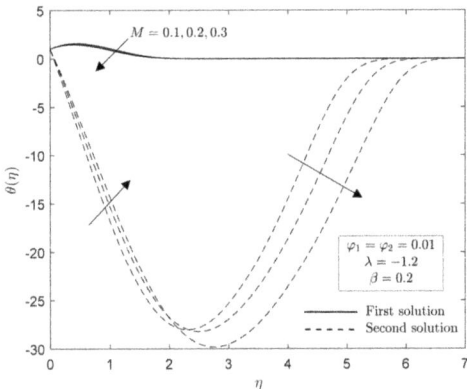

Figure 10. Temperature profile $\theta(\eta)$ for selected values of magnetic parameter M (Shrinking sheet case) when $\beta = 0.2$.

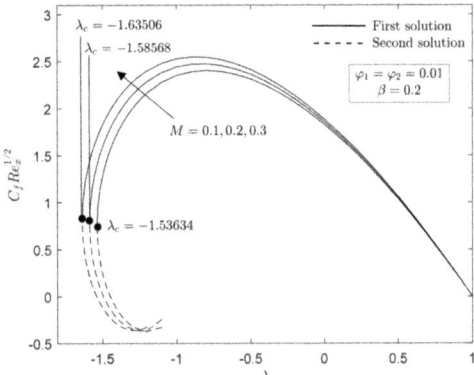

Figure 11. Skin friction coefficient $C_f \mathrm{Re}_x^{1/2}$ with λ for selected values of magnetic parameter M when $\beta = 0.2$.

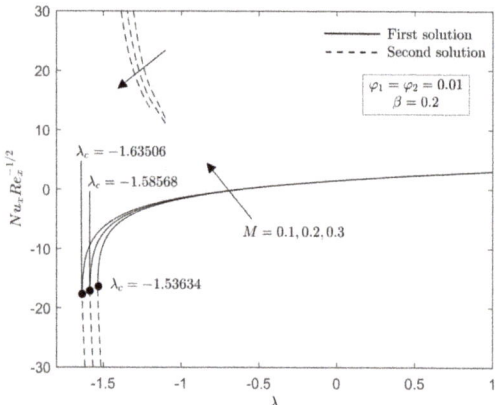

Figure 12. Local Nusselt number $Nu_x \text{Re}_x^{-1/2}$ with λ for selected values of magnetic parameter M when $\beta = 0.2$.

The linearized Equations (19)–(21) are numerically solved using the same numerical approach as before in order to execute the stability of the solutions. To verify the stability of the solutions, a sign of the smallest eigenvalues γ is essential. Hence, Figure 13 is plotted to demonstrate the behavior of the smallest eigenvalues γ when $\beta = 0.2$ and $M = 0.1$ for hybrid ferrofluid ($\varphi_1 = \varphi_2 = 0.01$) concerning λ. Here, the positive eigenvalues indicate the stable solution (i.e., there is only a small disturbance that does not interrupt the flow) while negative eigenvalues convey the unstable solution (which explains the growth of disturbance). Therefore, it can be concluded from Figure 13 that the first solution is a stable solution and the other solution is not. In addition, it can be clearly seen that as stretching/shrinking parameter λ near its critical value λ_c, the value of γ also approximate to zero.

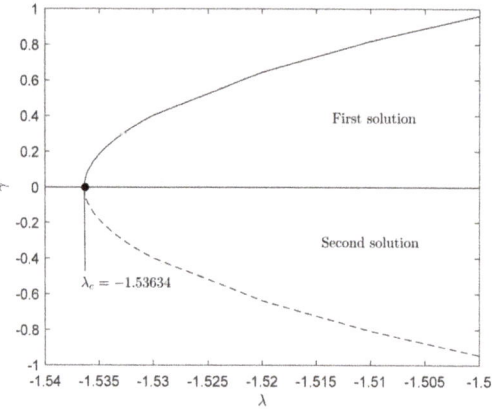

Figure 13. Smallest eigenvalues γ with λ when $\varphi_1 = \varphi_2 = 0.01$, $\beta = 0.2$ and $M = 0.1$.

5. Concluding Remarks

The steady, stagnation point, MHD of hybrid ferrofluid flow caused by an exponentially deformable surface with heat source/sink effect is studied. The similarity transformation is applied to generate self-similar equations, which are then numerically solved with Matlab's built-in solver (bvp4c). The impact of governing parameters such as heat source/sink parameter, nanoparticle volume fraction, magnetic parameter and stretching/shrinking parameter are discussed in detail. We can therefore conclude that:

- Non-unique solution (two solutions) occurs for a specific range of shrinking parameter ($\lambda_c < \lambda < -1$), whereas one solution exists when $\lambda \geq -1$.
- The range of stretching/shrinking parameter λ for which the non-unique solutions are in existence increased as magnetic parameter increase, while it decreased with an increase in $CoFe_2O_4$ nanoparticle volume fraction.
- The heat transfer and skin friction are escalated for increasing of $CoFe_2O_4$ nanoparticle volume fraction and magnetic parameter.
- When the heat source/sink parameter is increased, the surface temperature rises, and the local Nusselt number decreases.
- The first solution is confirmed to be a stable solution from the stability analysis test.

Author Contributions: Conceptualization, N.B. and I.P.; methodology, formal analysis and writing original draft preparation, N.S.A.; validation, N.S.A., N.B. and I.P.; writing—review and editing, supervision, N.B. and I.P.; funding acquisition, N.B. All authors have read and agreed to the published version of the manuscript.

Funding: This research was supported by the Fundamental Research Grant Scheme (FRGS) under Ministry of Higher Education with project number FRGS/1/2018/STG06/UPM/02/4.

Institutional Review Board Statement: Not applicable.

Informed Consent Statement: Not applicable.

Data Availability Statement: Not applicable.

Acknowledgments: The authors would like to express their gratitude to the anonymous reviewers for their valuable comments and suggestions for a betterment of this paper.

Conflicts of Interest: The authors declare no conflict of interest.

References

1. Rosensweig, R.E. *Ferrohydrodynamics*; Cambridge University Press: Cambridge, UK, 1985.
2. Ruuge, E.K.; Rusetski, A.N. Magnetic fluids as drug carriers: Targeted transport of drugs by a magnetic field. *J. Magn. Magn. Mater.* **1993**, *122*, 335–339. [CrossRef]
3. Goodwin, S.; Peterson, C.; Hoh, C.; Bittner, C. Targeting and retention of magnetic targeted carriers (MTCs) enhancing intra-arterial chemotherapy. *J. Magn. Magn. Mater.* **1999**, *194*, 132–139. [CrossRef]
4. Scherer, C.; Figueiredo Neto, A.M. Ferrofluids: Properties and applications. *Braz. J. Phys.* **2005**, *35*, 718–727. [CrossRef]
5. Laroze, D.; Siddheshwar, P.G.; Pleiner, H. Chaotic convection in a ferrofluid. *Commun. Nonlinear Sci. Numer. Simul.* **2013**, *18*, 2436–2447. [CrossRef]
6. Abbas, Z.; Sheikh, M. Numerical study of homogeneous—heterogeneous reactions on stagnation point flow of ferrofluid with non-linear slip condition. *Chin. J. Chem. Eng.* **2017**, *25*, 11–17. [CrossRef]
7. Iqbal, M.S.; Malik, F.; Mustafa, I.; Ghaffari, A.; Riaz, A.; Nisar, K.S. Impact of induced magnetic field on thermal enhancement in gravity driven Fe_3O_4 ferrofluid flow through vertical non-isothermal surface. *Results Phys.* **2020**, *19*, 103472. [CrossRef]
8. Mehrez, Z.; El Cafsi, A. Heat exchange enhancement of ferrofluid flow into rectangular channel in the presence of a magnetic field. *Appl. Math. Comput.* **2021**, *391*, 125634. [CrossRef]
9. Takabi, B.; Salehi, S. Augmentation of the heat transfer performance of a sinusoidal corrugated enclosure by employing hybrid nanofluid. *Adv. Mech. Eng.* **2014**, *6*, 147059. [CrossRef]
10. Devi, S.A.; Devi, S.S.U. Numerical investigation of hydromagnetic hybrid Cu–Al_2O_3/water nanofluid flow over a permeable stretching sheet with suction. *Int. J. Nonlinear Sci. Numer. Simul.* **2016**, *17*, 249–257. [CrossRef]
11. Suresh, S.; Venkitaraj, K.P.; Selvakumar, P.; Chandrasekar, M. Synthesis of Al_2O_3–Cu/water hybrid nanofluids using two step method and its thermo physical properties. *Colloids Surf. A Physicochem. Eng. Asp.* **2011**, *388*, 41–48. [CrossRef]
12. Madhesh, D.; Kalaiselvam, S. Experimental analysis of hybrid nanofluid as a coolant. *Procedia Eng.* **2014**, *97*, 1667–1675. [CrossRef]
13. Esfe, M.H.; Arani, A.A.A.; Rezaie, M.; Yan, W.M.; Karimipour, A. Experimental determination of thermal conductivity and dynamic viscosity of Ag–MgO/water hybrid nanofluid. *Int. Commun. Heat Mass Transf.* **2015**, *66*, 189–195. [CrossRef]
14. Chu, Y.M.; Bilal, S.; Hajizadeh, M.R. Hybrid ferrofluid along with MWCNT for augmentation of thermal behavior of fluid during natural convection in a cavity. *Math. Methods Appl. Sci.* **2020**, *2020*, 1–12. [CrossRef]
15. Kumar, K.A.; Sandeep, N.; Sugunamma, V.; Animasaun, I.L. Effect of irregular heat source/sink on the radiative thin film flow of MHD hybrid ferrofluid. *J. Therm. Anal. Calorim.* **2020**, *139*, 2145–2153. [CrossRef]
16. Nabwey, H.A.; Mahdy, A. Transient flow of micropolar dusty hybrid nanofluid loaded with Fe_3O_4-Ag nanoparticles through a porous stretching sheet. *Results Phys.* **2021**, *21*, 103777. [CrossRef]

17. Rashid, U.; Liang, H.; Ahmad, H.; Abbas, M.; Iqbal, A.; Hamed, Y.S. Study of (Ag and TiO_2)/water nanoparticles shape effect on heat transfer and hybrid nanofluid flow toward stretching shrinking horizontal cylinder. *Results Phys.* **2021**, *21*, 103812. [CrossRef]
18. Anuar, N.S.; Bachok, N.; Arifin, N.M.; Rosali, H. Analysis of Al_2O_3-Cu nanofluid flow behaviour over a permeable moving wedge with convective surface boundary conditions. *J. King Saud Univ.-Sci.* **2021**, *33*, 101370. [CrossRef]
19. Hayat, T.; Fetecau, C.; Sajid, M. Analytic solution for MHD transient rotating flow of a second-grade fluid in a porous space. *Nonlinear Anal. Real World Appl.* **2008**, *9*, 1619–1627. [CrossRef]
20. Kumar, D.; Singh, A.K.; Kumar, D. Influence of heat source/sink on MHD flow between vertical alternate conducting walls with Hall effect. *Phys. A Stat. Mech. Appl.* **2020**, *544*, 123562. [CrossRef]
21. Bhattacharyya, K. Effects of heat source/sink on MHD flow and heat transfer over a shrinking sheet with mass suction. *Chem. Eng. Res. Bull.* **2011**, *15*, 12–17. [CrossRef]
22. Gorla, R.S.R.; Siddiqa, S.; Mansour, M.A.; Rashad, A.M.; Salah, T. Heat source/sink effects on a hybrid nanofluid-filled porous cavity. *J. Thermophys. Heat Transf.* **2017**, *31*, 847–857. [CrossRef]
23. Armaghani, T.; Sadeghi, M.S.; Rashad, A.M.; Mansour, M.A.; Chamkha, A.J.; Dogonchi, A.S.; Nabwey, H.A. MHD mixed convection of localized heat source/sink in an Al_2O_3-Cu/water hybrid nanofluid in L-shaped cavity. *Alex. Eng. J.* **2021**, *60*, 2947–2962. [CrossRef]
24. Jamaludin, A.; Naganthran, K.; Nazar, R.; Pop, I. MHD mixed convection stagnation-point flow of Cu-Al_2O_3/water hybrid nanofluid over a permeable stretching/shrinking surface with heat source/sink. *Eur. J. Mech.-B/Fluids* **2020**, *84*, 71–80. [CrossRef]
25. Reddy, N.N.; Rao, V.S.; Reddy, B.R. Chemical reaction impact on MHD natural convection flow through porous medium past an exponentially stretching sheet in presence of heat source/sink and viscous dissipation. *Case Stud. Therm. Eng.* **2021**, *25*, 100879. [CrossRef]
26. Wang, C.Y. Stagnation flow towards a shrinking sheet. *Int. J. Non-Linear Mech.* **2008**, *43*, 377–382. [CrossRef]
27. Bachok, N.; Ishak, A.; Pop, I. Stagnation-point flow over a stretching/shrinking sheet in a nanofluid. *Nanoscale Res. Lett.* **2011**, *6*, 1–10. [CrossRef]
28. Kamal, F.; Zaimi, K.; Ishak, A.; Pop, I. Stability analysis on the stagnation-point flow and heat transfer over a permeable stretching/shrinking sheet with heat source effect. *Int. J. Numer. Methods Heat Fluid Flow* **2018**, *28*, 2650–2663. [CrossRef]
29. Anuar, N.S.; Bachok, N. Double solutions and stability analysis of micropolar hybrid nanofluid with thermal radiation impact on unsteady stagnation point flow. *Mathematics* **2021**, *9*, 276. [CrossRef]
30. Bhattacharyya, K.; Vajravelu, K. Stagnation-point flow and heat transfer over an exponentially shrinking sheet. *Commun. Nonlinear Sci. Numer. Simul.* **2012**, *17*, 2728–2734. [CrossRef]
31. Bachok, N.; Ishak, A.; Pop, I. Boundary layer stagnation-point flow and heat transfer over an exponentially stretching/shrinking sheet in a nanofluid. *Int. J. Heat Mass Transf.* **2012**, *55*, 8122–8128. [CrossRef]
32. Anuar, N.S.; Bachok, N.; Arifin, N.M.; Rosali, H. Stagnation point flow and heat transfer over an exponentially stretching/shrinking sheet in CNT with homogeneous–heterogeneous reaction: Stability analysis. *Symmetry* **2019**, *11*, 522. [CrossRef]
33. Lund, L.A.; Omar, Z.; Khan, I.; Baleanu, D.; Nisar, K.S. Dual similarity solutions of MHD stagnation point flow of Casson fluid with effect of thermal radiation and viscous dissipation: Stability analysis. *Sci. Rep.* **2020**, *10*, 1–13. [CrossRef] [PubMed]
34. Waini, I.; Ishak, A.; Pop, I. Hybrid nanofluid flow towards a stagnation point on an exponentially stretching/shrinking vertical sheet with buoyancy effects. *Int. J. Numer. Methods Heat Fluid Flow* **2020**, *31*, 216–235. [CrossRef]
35. Merkin, J.H. On dual solutions occurring in mixed convection in a porous medium. *J. Eng. Math.* **1986**, *20*, 171–179. [CrossRef]
36. Weidman, P.D.; Kubitschek, D.G.; Davis, A.M.J. The effect of transpiration on self-similar boundary layer flow over moving surfaces. *Int. J. Eng. Sci.* **2006**, *44*, 730–737. [CrossRef]
37. Harris, S.D.; Ingham, D.B.; Pop, I. Mixed convection boundary-layer flow near the stagnation point on a vertical surface in a porous medium: Brinkman model with slip. *Transp. Porous Media* **2009**, *77*, 267–285. [CrossRef]
38. Anuar, N.S.; Bachok, N.; Arifin, N.M.; Rosali, H. Numerical solution of stagnation point flow and heat transfer over a nonlinear stretching/shrinking sheet in hybrid nanofluid: Stability analysis. *J. Adv. Res. Fluid Mech. Therm. Sci.* **2020**, *76*, 85–98. [CrossRef]
39. Mustafa, I.; Abbas, Z.; Arif, A.; Javed, T.; Ghaffari, A. Stability analysis for multiple solutions of boundary layer flow towards a shrinking sheet: Analytical solution by using least square method. *Phys. A Stat. Mech. Appl.* **2020**, *540*, 123028. [CrossRef]
40. Aladdin, N.A.L.; Bachok, N.; Anuar, N.S. MHD stagnation point flow in nanofluid over shrinking surface using Buongiorno's model: A stability analysis. *J. Adv. Res. Fluid Mech. Therm. Sci.* **2020**, *76*, 12–24. [CrossRef]
41. Aladdin, N.A.L.; Bachok, N.; Pop, I. Boundary layer flow and heat transfer of Cu-Al2O3/water over a moving horizontal slender needle in presence of hydromagnetic and slip effects. *Int. Commun. Heat Mass Transf.* **2021**, *123*, 105213. [CrossRef]
42. Shampine, L.F.; Reichelt, M.W. The matlab ode suite. *SIAM J. Sci. Comput.* **1997**, *18*, 1–22. [CrossRef]
43. Oztop, H.F.; Abu-Nada, E. Numerical study of natural convection in partially heated rectangular enclosures filled with nanofluids. *Int. J. Heat Fluid Flow* **2008**, *29*, 1326–1336. [CrossRef]
44. Sheikholeslami, M.; Gorji-Bandpy, M.; Ganji, D.D. MHD free convection in an eccentric semi-annulus filled with nanofluid. *J. Taiwan Inst. Chem. Eng.* **2014**, *45*, 1204–1216. [CrossRef]
45. Tlili, I.; Mustafa, M.T.; Kumar, K.A.; Sandeep, N. Effect of asymmetrical heat rise/fall on the film flow of magnetohydrodynamic hybrid ferrofluid. *Sci. Rep.* **2020**, *10*, 6477. [CrossRef]

Article

Flow and Heat Transfer Past a Stretching/Shrinking Sheet Using Modified Buongiorno Nanoliquid Model

Natalia C. Roşca [1,*], Alin V. Roşca [2], Emad H. Aly [3] and Ioan Pop [1]

1. Department of Mathematics, Faculty of Mathematics and Computer Science, Babeş-Bolyai University, 400084 Cluj-Napoca, Romania; ipop@math.ubbcluj.ro
2. Department of Statistics-Forecasts Mathematics, Faculty of Economics and Business Administration, Babeş-Bolyai University, 400084 Cluj-Napoca, Romania; alin.rosca@econ.ubbcluj.ro
3. Department of Mathematics, Faculty of Education, Ain Shams University, Roxy, Cairo 11757, Egypt; emad-aly@hotmail.com
* Correspondence: natalia@math.ubbcluj.ro

Abstract: This paper studies the boundary layer flow and heat transfer characteristics past a permeable isothermal stretching/shrinking surface using both nanofluid and hybrid nanofluid flows (called modified Buongiorno nonliquid model). Using appropriate similarity variables, the PDEs are transformed into ODEs to be solved numerically using the function bvp4c from MATLAB. It was found that the solutions of the resulting system have two branches, upper and lower branch solutions, in a certain range of the suction, stretching/shrinking and hybrid nanofluids parameters. Both the analytic and numerical results are obtained for the skin friction coefficient, local Nusselt number, and velocity and temperature distributions, for several values of the governing parameters. It results in the governing parameters considerably affecting the flow and heat transfer characteristics.

Keywords: hybrid nanofluid; stretching/shrinking; buongiorno model; dual solutions

1. Introduction

Owing to the necessary improvement of the thermal conductivity of conventional fluid, the term nanofluid was introduced by Choi [1] in 1995, which aims to provide highly developed heat conductivity. Nanofluids, which are a colloidal mixture of nanoparticles (1–100 nm) and a base liquid (nanoparticle fluid suspensions), are the new class of media of nanotechnology for heat transfer (see for e.g., Buongiorno [2]). In particular, Buongiorno [2] noted that the nanoparticle absolute velocity can be viewed as the sum of the base fluid velocity and a relative velocity. He considered, in turn, seven slip mechanisms: inertia, Brownian diffusion, thermophoresis, diffusion phoresies, Magnus effect, fluid drainage, and gravity settling. He concluded that, in the absence of turbulent effects, it is the Brownian diffusion and the thermophoresis that will be important. Buongiorno proceeded to write down conservation equations based on these two effects. His model is the basis of the present study. Soon after discoveries made by Choi [1], many researchers interested in this new type of working fluid, because of its importance for the emergence and enhancement of thermal properties in practical applications, in various engineering applications such as engine cooling, diesel generator efficiency, cooling of electronics and heat exchanging devices, and solar water heating (see for e.g., Mahian et al. [3]). In a review paper, Manca et al. [4] have shown that cooling is one of the most important technical challenges facing many diverse industries, including microelectronics, transportation, solid-state lighting and manufacturing. Kamel and Lezsovits [5] found that the enrichment of thermophysical properties and heat transfer performance in nanofluid play an essential role in establishing high heat flux with small temperature differences during the boiling process in thermal engineering systems. The addition of nanometre-sized solid metal or metal oxide particles to base fluids elicits a rise in the thermal conductivity of the outgrowth fluids, see for example, Aly and Sayed [6].

To further improve nanofluids that could possess a number of favorable characteristics, researchers developed a new generation heat transfer fluid called hybrid nanofluids (HNF). They are prepared either by dispersing dissimilar nanoparticles as individual constituents or by dispersing nanocomposite particles in the base fluid. HNF may possess better thermal network and rheological properties due to synergistic effect. Researchers, to adjudge the advantages, disadvantages and their suitability for diversified applications, are extensively investigating the behavior and properties of these hybrid nanofluids. Babu et al. [7] have reviewed the contemporary investigations on synthesis, thermophysical properties, heat transfer characteristics, hydrodynamic behavior and fluid flow characteristics reported by researchers on different HNFs. This review also outlines the applications and challenges associated with hybrid nanofluid and makes some suggestions for the future scope of research in this fruitful area. On the other hand, and in an excellent review paper, Huminic and Huminic [8] discussed the HNF, which consists of two solid materials dispersed in a viscous fluid. In this work, it was shown that hybrid nanofluids lead to increased thermal conductivity and finally to a heat transfer enhancement in heat exchangers. Experimental and numerical results show that the hybrid nanofluids are working fluids, which could significantly improve the heat transfer in heat exchangers; however, research concerning to the study of different combinations of hybrid nanoparticles and their stability is still needed.

Numerous researchers have studied the flow and heat transfer of the boundary layer past a stretching/shrinking sheet with applications in manufacturing technology, for instance, glass blowing, extrusion of plastic sheets, drawing plastic films, and hot rolling (see Fisher [9]). As documented by Karwe et al. [10], the outcome quality of the required features is greatly affected by the heat transfer rate along the fluid flow and stretching/shrinking surface. Sakiadis [11] started a boundary layer flow analysis at a steady speed rate through a continuously moving flat surface by employing an integral method. Of all the fundamental fluid flow problems of a linear stretching/shrinking sheet, the current literature testifies that flow behavior due to a non-linear stretching sheet is also a crucial element in most industrial processes. Hybrid nanofluid versus the nanofluid of MHD flow and heat transfer over a stretching/shrinking sheet was introduced by Aly and Pop [12].

Unique and/or multiple (dual) solutions for a stretching/shrinking sheet have recently been presented in the works by Aly et al. [13], Waini et al. [14] and Khashi'ie et al. [15]. These papers show that unique and dual solutions exist for a stretching and shrinking sheet, respectively. In addition, Liao and Pop [16] deduced multiple solutions for both impermeable and permeable shrinking sheets. It should be noted that most of these solutions are based on the boundary layer assumptions and hence do not constitute exact solutions for Navier–Stokes equations (see for e.g., Wang [17]). It is also worth mentioning that Aly [18] has discussed the dual exact solutions of graphene–water nanofluid flow over a stretching/shrinking sheet with a suction/injection and heat source/sink, see also Roşca et al. [19], Aly [20] and Aly and Pop [21].

Finally, we mention here that Pop et al. [22], Zhu et al. [23], Uddin and Rahman [24], Rana et al. [25,26] and Pati et al. [27] have studied the boundary layer flow beneath a uniform free stream permeable continuous moving surface in a nanofluid using both Buongiorno's [2] and Tiwari and Das' [28] nanofluid models. However, we consider in this paper Buongiorno's [2] nanofluid model combined with Devi and Devi's [29] hybrid nanofluid model.

2. Mathematical Model

In this work, we consider the 2D flow and heat transfer of a hybrid nanofluid past a permeable stretching/shrinking surface, as shown in Figure 1, where (x, y) are Cartesian coordinates with associated velocities (u, v). The streamwise flows are directed along the $x-$ direction and y is the plate–normal coordinate. It is assumed that the surface velocity is $u_w(x)$ and the mass flux velocity is v_0 with $v_0 < 0$ for suction and $v_0 > 0$ for the injection or withdraw of the fluid. It is also assumed that the constant temperature and constant nanofluid volume fraction of the surface of the sheet are T_w and C_w while those of the ambient fluid are T_∞ and C_∞.

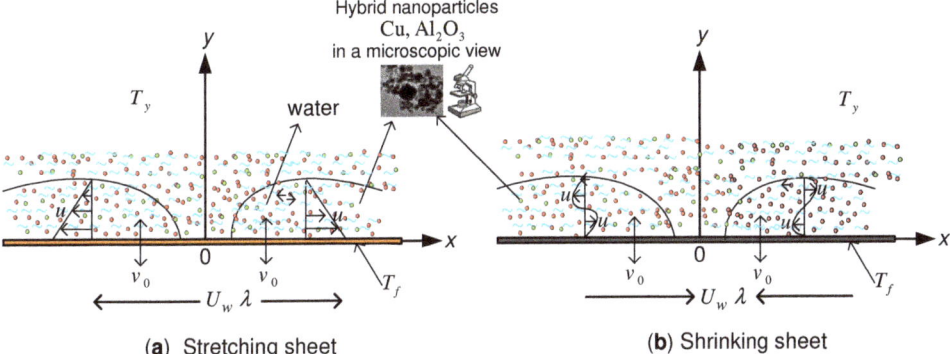

Figure 1. Physical model and coordinate system; (a) stretching sheet and (b) shrinking sheet.

Therefore, the governing equations of the investigating physical model can be written as (Yousefi et al. [30] and Bognár et al. [31])

$$\frac{\partial u}{\partial x} + \frac{\partial v}{\partial y} = 0, \qquad (1)$$

$$u\frac{\partial u}{\partial x} + v\frac{\partial u}{\partial y} = \frac{\mu_{hnf}}{\rho_{hnf}} \frac{\partial^2 u}{\partial y^2} \qquad (2)$$

$$u\frac{\partial T}{\partial x} + v\frac{\partial T}{\partial y} = \frac{k_{hnf}}{(\rho C_p)_{hnf}} \frac{\partial^2 T}{\partial y^2} + \delta\left[D_B \frac{\partial C}{\partial y}\frac{\partial T}{\partial y} + \frac{D_T}{T_\infty}\left(\frac{\partial T}{\partial y}\right)^2\right], \qquad (3)$$

$$u\frac{\partial C}{\partial x} + v\frac{\partial C}{\partial y} = D_B \frac{\partial^2 C}{\partial y^2} + \frac{D_T}{T_\infty}\frac{\partial^2 T}{\partial y^2}, \qquad (4)$$

subject to the following boundary conditions (see for e.g., Kuznetsov and Nield [32])

$$u = u_w(x) = U_w(x)\lambda, \quad v = v_0, \quad T = T_w, \quad D_B \frac{\partial C}{\partial y} + \frac{D_T}{T_\infty}\frac{\partial T}{\partial y} = 0, \quad \text{at} \quad y = 0, \qquad (5a)$$

$$u = u_e(x) \to 0, \quad T = T_\infty, \quad C = C_\infty, \quad \text{as} \quad y \to \infty. \qquad (5b)$$

Here, T is the temperature of the hybrid nanofluid, C is the nanoparticle concentration, D_B is the Brownian diffusion coefficient, D_T is the thermophoretic diffusion coefficient, $\delta = (\rho C_p)_s / (\rho C_p)_f$ is the ratio of nanoparticle heat capacity and the base fluid heat capacity. Further, μ_{hnf} is the dynamic viscosity of the hybrid nanofluids, ρ_{hnf} is the density of the hybrid nanofluids, k_{hnf} is the thermal conductivity of the hybrid nanofluid, $(\rho C_p)_{hnf}$ is the heat capacity of the hybrid nanofluid, λ is the constant stretching/shrinking parameter with $\lambda > 0$ for a stretching sheet, $\lambda < 0$ for a shrinking sheet and $\lambda = 0$ for a static sheet, respectively, and we assume that $U_w(x) = ax$, where a is a positive constant. Equation $D_B \partial C/\partial y + (D_T/T_\infty) \partial T/\partial y = 0$ is a statement that, with thermophoresis taken into account, the normal flux of nanoparticles is zero at the boundary. Furthermore, $(\ )_{hnf}$ denotes the hybrid nanofluid quantities, which are defined as follows (Devi and Devi [29] and Gorla et al. [33])

$$\frac{\rho_{hnf}}{\rho_f} = (1-\varphi_2)\left[1-\varphi_1+\varphi_1\frac{\rho_{s_1}}{\rho_f}\right]+\varphi_2\frac{\rho_{s_2}}{\rho_f}, \tag{6a}$$

$$\frac{\mu_{hnf}}{\mu_f} = \frac{1}{(1-\varphi_1)^{2.5}(1-\varphi_2)^{2.5}}, \tag{6b}$$

$$\frac{k_{hnf}}{k_f} = \frac{k_{s_2}+2k_{bf}+2\varphi_2(k_{s_2}-k_f)}{k_{s_2}+2k_{bf}-\varphi_2(k_{s_2}-k_f)}, \text{ where } \frac{k_{bf}}{k_f} = \frac{k_{s_1}+2k_f+2\varphi_1(k_{s_1}-k_f)}{k_{s_1}+2k_f-\varphi_1(k_{s_1}-k_f)}, \tag{6c}$$

$$\frac{(\rho C_p)_{hnf}}{(\rho C_p)_f} = (1-\varphi_2)\left[1-\varphi_1+\varphi_1\frac{(\rho C_p)_{s_1}}{(\rho C_p)_f}\right]+\varphi_2\frac{(\rho C_p)_{s_2}}{(\rho C_p)_f}, \tag{6d}$$

where φ_1 and φ_2 are the nanoparticle volume fraction for hybrid nanofluid (where $\varphi_1 = \varphi_2 = 0$ correspond to a regular fluid), ρ_f is the density of the base fluid, ρ_{s_1} and ρ_{s_2} are the densities of the hybrid nanoparticles, k_f is the thermal conductivity of the base fluid, k_{s_1} and k_{s_2} are the thermal conductivities of the hybrid nanoparticles, $(\rho C_p)_f$ is the heat capacity of the base fluid. $(\rho C_p)_{s_1}$ and $(\rho C_p)_{s_2}$ are the heat capacitance of the hybrid nanoparticles, and C_p is the heat capacity at the constant pressure of the base fluid. Furthermore, the physical properties of the base fluid (water), alumina (Al_2O_3) and copper (Cu) hybrid nanofluids are given in Table 1. Here, it should be noted that the hybrid nanofluid is assumed to be homogeneous, neglecting internal fluctuations of the particle density or flows.

Table 1. Thermophysical properties of the water and nanoparticles [34].

Physical Properties	Base Fluid	Nanoparticles	
	Water	Al_2O_3	Cu
ρ (kg/m^3)	997.1	3970	8933
C_p (J/kg K)	4179	765	385
k (W/m K)	0.613	40	401
σ (Ω/m)$^{-1}$	0.05	1×10^{-10}	5.96×10^7

Now, we introduce the following similarity variables

$$u = axf'(\eta),\ v = -\sqrt{av_f}f(\eta),\ \theta(\eta) = \frac{T-T_\infty}{T_w-T_\infty},\ \phi(\eta) = \frac{C-C_\infty}{C_\infty},\ \eta = y\sqrt{\frac{a}{v_f}}, \tag{7}$$

so that

$$v_0 = -\sqrt{av_f}S, \tag{8}$$

where S is the constant mass flux parameter with $S > 0$ for suction and $S < 0$ for injection or withdrawal, respectively. Invoking the similarity variables (7), Equations (2)–(4) along with the boundary conditions (5a) are transformed into the following ordinary (similarity) differential equations (see for e.g., Aly [35])

$$\alpha_2 f''' + \alpha_1\left(ff'' - f'^2\right) = 0, \tag{9}$$

$$\frac{\alpha_4}{\alpha_3 Pr}\theta'' + f\theta' + Nb\,\theta'\phi' + Nt\,\theta'^2 = 0, \tag{10}$$

$$\phi'' + Lef\phi' + \frac{Nt}{Nb}\theta'' = 0, \tag{11}$$

which have to be solved subject to the following conditions:

$$f(0) = S, \quad f'(0) = \lambda, \quad \theta(0) = 1, \quad Nb\, \phi'(0) + Nt\, \theta'(0) = 0, \tag{12a}$$
$$f''(\eta) \to 0, \quad \theta(\eta) \to 0, \quad \phi(\eta) \to 0, \quad \text{as} \quad \eta \to \infty, \tag{12b}$$

here, primes denote differentiation with respect to η, $Pr\left(=\frac{\nu}{\alpha}\right)$ is Prandtl number, where $\alpha\left(=\frac{k}{\rho c_p}\right)$ is the thermal diffusivity, $Le\left(=\frac{\nu}{D_B}\right)$ is Lewis number, $Nb\left(=\frac{\delta D_B(\varphi_w - \varphi_\infty)}{\nu}\right)$ is the Brownian motion parameter and $Nt\left(=\frac{\delta D_T(T_w - T_\infty)}{\nu T_\infty}\right)$ is the thermophoresis parameter. Further, α_i, $i = 1$ to 4, are defined as:

$$\alpha_1 = \frac{\rho_{hnf}}{\rho_f}, \quad \alpha_2 = \frac{\mu_{hnf}}{\mu_f}, \quad \alpha_3 = \frac{(\rho C_p)_{hnf}}{(\rho C_p)_f} \quad \text{and} \quad \alpha_4 = \frac{k_{hnf}}{k_f}. \tag{13}$$

The physical quantities of interest are the skin friction coefficient C_f and the local Nusselt number Nu_x, which are defined as:

$$C_f = \frac{\tau_w}{\rho_f U_w^2(x)}, \quad Nu_x = \frac{x q_w}{k_f(T_w - T_\infty)}, \tag{14}$$

where τ_w is the skin friction or shear stress along the plate and q_w is the heat flux from the plate, which are given by:

$$\tau_w = -\mu_{hnf}\left(\frac{\partial u}{\partial y}\right)_{y=0}, \quad q_w = -k_{hnf}\left(\frac{\partial T}{\partial y}\right)_{y=0}. \tag{15}$$

On using (7) and (14), we get:

$$Sr = C_f \sqrt{Re_x} = -\alpha_2 f''(0), \quad Nur = \frac{Nu}{\sqrt{Re_x}} = -\alpha_4 \theta'(0), \tag{16}$$

where $Re_x = \frac{U_w(x) x}{\nu_f}$ is the local Reynolds number.

3. Solutions of the System

On considering conditions of the dimensionless stream function in Equation (12a), $f(\eta)$ can be then deduced as:

$$f(\eta) = S + \frac{\lambda}{\beta}\left(1 - e^{-\beta \eta}\right), \tag{17}$$

where β is a constant to be determined and has to be positive to have a physical meaning. Therefore, by substituting the last relation in Equation (9), β can be obtained as follows:

$$\beta = \frac{1}{2\alpha_2}\left[\alpha_1 S \pm \sqrt{\alpha_1^2 S^2 + 4\alpha_1 \alpha_2 \lambda}\right]. \tag{18}$$

Now, when $\lambda > 0$ (stretching sheet) and for any values of S, one can note that the positive sign of the second root makes β positive. This means that there exists only a unique solution for any combination of the considered parameters (see for e.g., Aly [36]). However, for the shrinking sheet ($\lambda < 0$), suppose that:

$$S_c = \left|2\sqrt{-\frac{\alpha_2}{\alpha_1}\lambda}\right| > 0. \tag{19}$$

Then, we obtain the following three cases;

- There is no any physical solution when $S < S_c$.
- A unique solution is gotten if $S = S_c$.
- Dual solution can be only obtained for $S > S_c$.

Similarly, on supposing that

$$\lambda_c = -\frac{S^2}{4}\frac{\alpha_1}{\alpha_2} < 0, \qquad (20)$$

there is then

- no solution when $[0 > \lambda \geq \lambda_c, S < 0]$ and $[\lambda < \lambda_c, \forall S]$,
- a unique solution if $\lambda = \lambda_c, S > 0$, and
- dual solution at $[0 > \lambda > \lambda_c, S > 0]$,

where the suffix $(\ )_c$ refers the critical value of the specific parameter. Figures 2 and 3 present the regions of no, unique and dual solutions of S as a function of λ and vice versa, respectively, for a stretching/shrinking sheet. Further, 3D of the terminated curve for S as a function of (λ, ϕ_2) for a shrinking sheet is presented in Figure 4.

In addition, from Equation (16), the reduced skin friction coefficient (Sr) is obtained as:

$$Sr = \lambda \, \alpha_2 \, \beta. \qquad (21)$$

With β determined from relation (18), we obtain the analytical solution (17) for $f(\eta)$. Now, in order to calculate θ and ϕ, f from Equation (17) is replaced into Equations (10) and (11) to obtain the following system of differential equations:

$$\frac{\alpha_4}{\alpha_3 Pr} \theta'' + \left[S + \frac{\lambda}{\beta}\left(1 - e^{-\beta \eta}\right) \right] \theta' + Nb\, \theta' \phi' + Nt\, \theta'^2 = 0, \qquad (22)$$

$$\phi'' + Le\left[S + \frac{\lambda}{\beta}\left(1 - e^{-\beta \eta}\right) \right] \phi' + \frac{Nt}{Nb} \theta'' = 0, \qquad (23)$$

along with the following boundary conditions:

$$\theta(0) = 1, \quad Nb\, \phi'(0) + Nt\, \theta'(0) = 0, \qquad (24a)$$
$$\theta(\eta) \to 0, \quad \phi(\eta) \to 0, \quad \text{as} \quad \eta \to \infty. \qquad (24b)$$

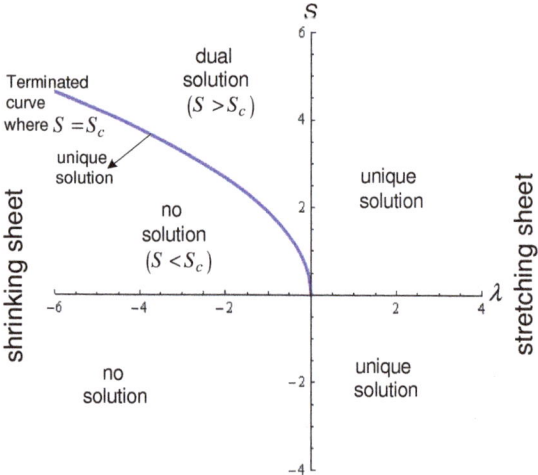

Figure 2. Regions of no, unique and dual solutions of S as a function of λ for stretching/shrinking sheet when $\varphi_1 = 0.1$ and $\varphi_2 = 0.04$.

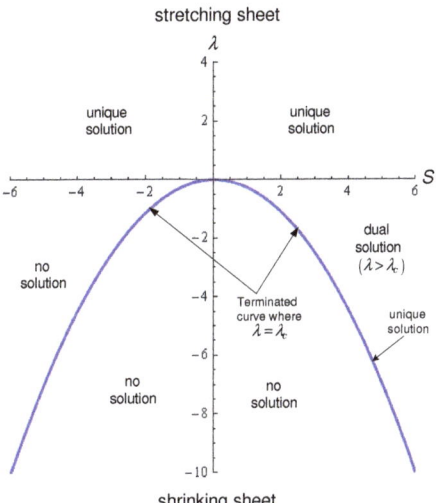

Figure 3. Regions of no, unique and dual solutions of λ as a function of S for stretching/shrinking sheet when $\varphi_1 = 0.1$ and $\varphi_2 = 0.04$.

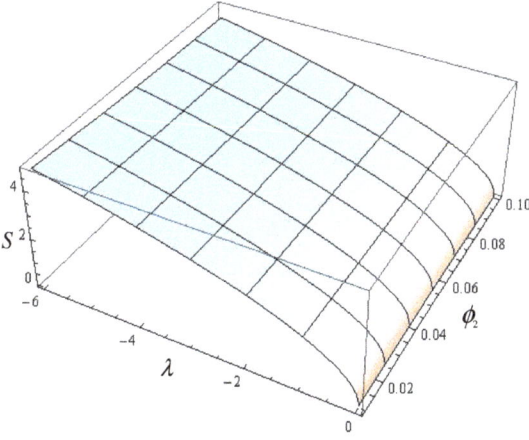

Figure 4. Three-dimensional (3D) of terminated curve for S as a function of (λ, φ_2) for shrinking sheet when $\varphi_1 = 0.1$.

4. Results and Discussion

The boundary value problem (22)–(24) is numerically solved using the function bvp4c from MATLAB (see for e.g., Shampine et al. [37]) for different values of the included parameters λ, S, Pr, Le, Nb, Nt with hybrid nanofluids φ_1 and φ_2. Brief details on the function bvp4c are introduced in the next paragraph.

The function bvp4c is a finite difference code that implements the three-stage Lobatto IIIa formula. This is a collocation formula and the collocation polynomial gives us a C^1–continuous solution, which is fourth-order accurate uniformly in the interval where the function is integrated. Further, in order to apply this routine, the present problem has to be rewritten as systems of first-order ODEs. In particular, we have chosen a suitable finite value of $\eta \to \infty$, namely $\eta = \eta_\infty = 20$, where the relative tolerance is set at 10^{-7}. Mesh selection and error control are based on the residual of the continuous solution. In addition, the starting mesh has 100 points equally distributed on the interval $[0, \eta_\infty = 20]$ and then the mesh is automatically adjusted by the bvp4c routine. It is expected that the present problem may have more than one solution; therefore, a good initial guess is needed to obtain the desired solutions.

It should be noted that the results for $f(\eta)$ are to be analytically obtained from the expression (17), corresponding to the values of β. Therefore, the ODEs, (22) and (23), along with the BCs. (24) have more than one solution when $\lambda < 0$ (shrinking sheet); we use the two analytical solutions described by (17) corresponding to the values of β from (18) to numerically determine the corresponding dual (upper and lower) solutions for θ and ϕ.

The obtained results are displayed in terms of the skin-friction coefficient C_f, local Nusselt number Nu_x, dimensionless velocity $f'(\eta)$ and temperature $\theta(\eta)$ profiles for different values of the parameters S, λ and φ. Both the cases of $\lambda > 0$ (stretching) and $\lambda < 0$ (shrinking) sheets have been studied. Because there are many cases to be considered, we limit presentation to only six figures, namely Figures 5–10. This is also for sewing space.

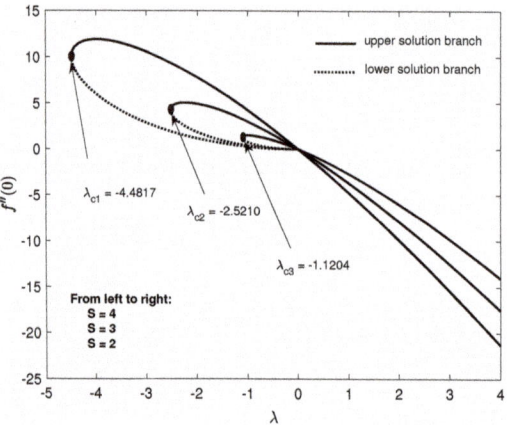

Figure 5. Variation of $f''(0)$ as a function of λ for several values of S for the hybrid nanofluid when $\varphi_1 = 0.025$ and $\varphi_2 = 0.025$.

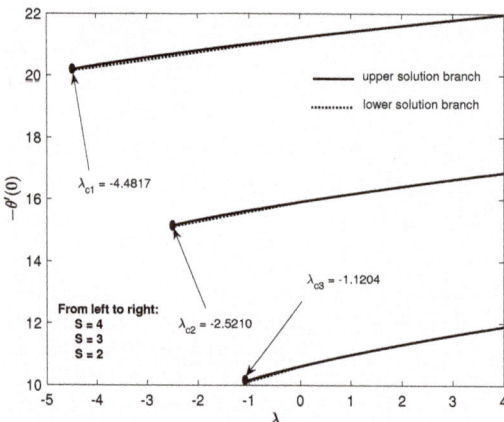

Figure 6. Variation of $-\theta'(0)$ as a function of λ for several values of S for the hybrid nanofluid when $\varphi_1 = 0.025$ and $\varphi_2 = 0.025$.

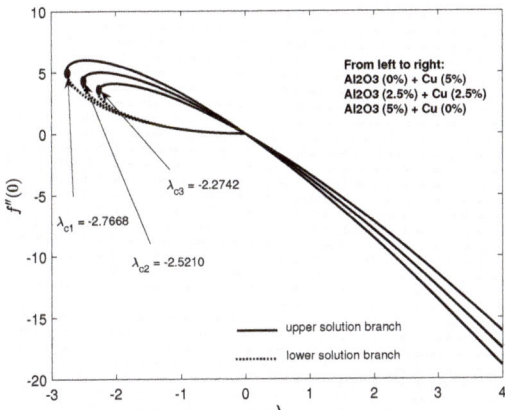

Figure 7. Variation of $f''(0)$ as a function of λ when $S = 3$ and the overall volume fraction of hybrid particles is constant as $\varphi_{hnf} = 0.05$.

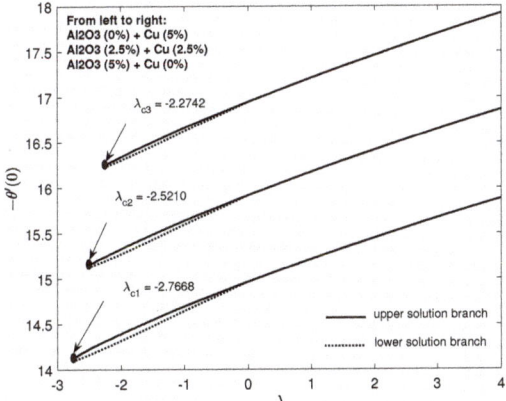

Figure 8. Variation of $-\theta'(0)$ as a function of λ when $S = 3$ and the overall volume fraction of hybrid particles is constant as $\varphi_{hnf} = 0.05$.

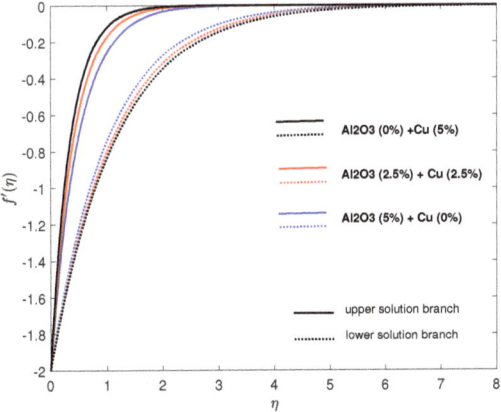

Figure 9. Velocity profiles for the hybrid nanofluid when the overall volume fraction of hybrid nanoparticles is constant as $\varphi_{hnf} = 0.05$ for $\lambda = -2$ and $S = 3$.

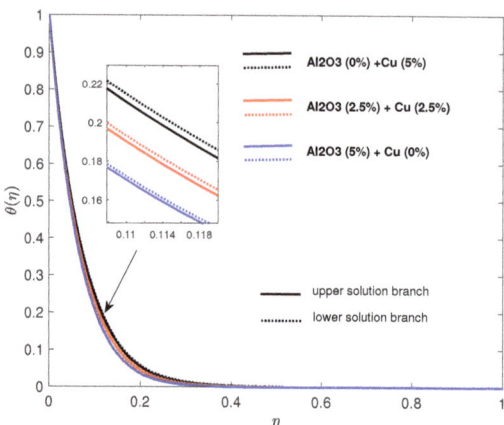

Figure 10. Temperature profiles for the hybrid nanofluid when the overall volume fraction of hybrid nanoparticles is constant as $\varphi_{hnf} = 0.05$ for $\lambda = -2$ and $S = 3$.

Figures 5 and 6 illustrate the variation of the reduced skin friction coefficient $f''(0)$ and reduced heat transfer from the plate $-\theta'(0)$ with the stretching/shrinking parameter λ for several values of the suction parameter S. We can observe that a higher value of suction strength S is necessary to induce the dual steady similarity solutions for the shrinking case. As the shrinking parameter expands from -1.1204 to -4.4817, the required value of the suction parameter contracts from $S = 4$ to $S = 2$. The dual solution regions also expand with the increase of suction parameter S. Figures 7 and 8 show that dual solution regions expand with the increase of the concentration of the Al_2O_3 particles and the decrease of the Cu nanoparticles' concentration when the suction is present. We can see from all Figures 5–8 that the dual solution exists only for the shrinking sheet in the case of suction ($S > 0$). All these figures show that unique solutions exist for Equations (9)–(11) with the boundary conditions (12a,b) when $\lambda > 0$ (stretching sheet), dual solutions (upper and lower branch solutions) exist for $\lambda_c \leq \lambda \leq 0$ (shrinking sheet) and no solutions exist for $\lambda \leq \lambda_c \leq 0$, where $\lambda_c < 0$ is the critical value of $\lambda < 0$ for which the boundary value problems (9)–(12) have no solutions. It should be stated that, for $\lambda < \lambda_c < 0$, the full Navier–Stokes and energy equations have to be solved.

Further, Figures 9 and 10 present the velocity $f'(\eta)$ and temperature $\theta(\eta)$ profiles for shrinking case $\lambda = -2$ when the suction is presented as $S = 3$. In these figures, the solid lines indicate the upper branch solution, while the dot lines refer to the lower branch solution, respectively. It is evident from these figures that the far field boundary conditions (12b) are approached asymptotically. Thus, it supports the numerical results obtained for the boundary value problems (9)–(12). Moreover, it is clearly seen from Figures 9 and 10 that, for both velocity and temperature profiles, the upper branch solution displays a thinner boundary layer thickness compared to the lower branch solution. It is worth pointing out that the solution of the boundary value problem (9)–(12) exists only for large values of suction parameter $S(>0)$. This is in full agreement with the results reported by Fang et al. [38] for the problem of viscous flow over an unsteady shrinking sheet with mass transfer.

5. Conclusions

This paper considered both analytical and numerical solutions of the problem of a permeable stretching/shrinking sheet in both nanofluid and hybrid nanofluids using the mathematical models proposed by Buongiorno [2] and Devi and Devi's [29] hybrid nanofluid model. The important conclusions of the present study are:

- One solution exists for stretching sheet ($\lambda > 0$).
- Dual solutions exist for shrinking case ($\lambda < 0$).

- Skin friction coefficient and the local Nusselt number are increased as the rate of suction $S > 0$ is increased.
- The analysis of the present investigation plays a predominant role in the applications of science and technology. Particularly, the results of the present problem are of great interest for controlled metal welding or the magnetically controlled coating of metals in fusion engineering problems, polymer engineering, metallurgy, and so forth.

Author Contributions: Conceptualization, E.H.A. and I.P.; data curation, E.H.A. and I.P.; formal analysis, E.H.A. and I.P.; funding acquisition, A.V.R.; investigation, E.H.A. and I.P.; methodology, E.H.A.; project administration, A.V.R. and N.C.R.; software, E.H.A.; supervision, E.H.A., N.C.R., A.V.R. and I.P.; validation, E.H.A.; writing—original draft, E.H.A. and I.P.; writing—review and editing, E.H.A., I.P., N.C.R. and A.V.R. All authors have read and agreed to the published version of the manuscript.

Funding: This research received no external funding.

Institutional Review Board Statement: Not applicable.

Informed Consent Statement: Not applicable.

Data Availability Statement: Not applicable.

Conflicts of Interest: The authors declare no conflict of interest.

References

1. Choi, S.U.S. Enhancing thermal conductivity of fluids with nanoparticles. In Proceedings of the 1995 ASME International Mechanical Engineering Congress and Exposition, San Francisco, CA, USA, 12–17 November 1995; ASME FED 231/MD 66; pp. 99–105.
2. Buongiorno, J. Convective transport in nanofluids. *ASME J. Heat Transf.* **2006**, *128*, 240–250. [CrossRef]
3. Mahian, O.; Kianifar, A.; Kalogirou, S.A.; Pop, I.; Wongwises, S. A review of the applications of nanofluids in solar energy. *Int. J. Heat Mass Transf.* **2013**, *57*, 582–594. [CrossRef]
4. Manca, O.; Jaluria, Y.; Poulikakos, D. Heat transfer in nanofluids. *Adv. Mech. Eng.* **2010**, *27*, 380826. [CrossRef]
5. Kamel, M.S.; Lezsovits, F. Boiling heat transfer of nanofluids: A review of recent studies. *Therm. Sci.* **2019**, *23*, 109–124. [CrossRef]
6. Aly, E.H.; Sayed, H.M. Magnetohydrodynamic and thermal radiation effects on the boundary–layer flow due to a moving extensible surface with the velocity slip model: A comparative study of four nanofluids. *J. Magn. Magn. Mater.* **2017**, *422*, 440–451. [CrossRef]
7. Babu, J.A.R.; Kumar, K.K.; Rao, S.S. State-of-art review on hybrid nanofluids. *Renew. Sustain. Energy Rev.* **2017**, *77*, 551–565. [CrossRef]
8. Huminic, G.; Huminic, A. Hybrid nanofluids for heat transfer applications—A state-of-the-art review. *Int. J. Heat Mass. Transfer.* **2018**, *125*, 82–103. [CrossRef]
9. Fisher, E.G. *Extrusion of Plastics*; Wiley: New York, NY, USA, 1976.
10. Karwe, M.V.; Jaluria, Y. Numerical simulation of thermal transport associated with a continuously moving flat sheet in materials. *J. Heat Transf.* **1991**, *113*, 612–619. [CrossRef]
11. Sakiadis, B.C. Boundary-layer behavior on continuous solid surfaces: I. Boundary-layer equations for two-dimensional and axisymmetric flow. *AIChE J.* **1961**, *7*, 26–28. [CrossRef]
12. Aly, E.H.; Pop, I. MHD flow and heat transfer near stagnation point over a stretching/shrinking surface with partial slip and viscous dissipation: Hybrid nanofluid versus nanofluid. *Powder Technol.* **2020**, *367*, 192–205. [CrossRef]
13. Aly, E.H.; Roşca, A.V.; Roşca, N.C.; Pop, I. Convective heat transfer of a hybrid nanofluid over a nonlinearly stretching surface with radiation effect. *Mathematics* **2021**, *9*, 2220. [CrossRef]
14. Waini, I.; Ishak, A.; Pop, I. Hybrid nanofluid flow towards a stagnation point on an exponentially stretching/shrinking vertical sheet with buoyancy effects. *Int. J. Numer. Methods Heat Fluid Flow* **2021**, *31*, 216–235. [CrossRef]
15. Khashi'ie, N.S.; Arifin, N.M.; Pop, I.; Nazar, R. Dual solutions of bioconvection hybrid nanofluid flow due to gyrotactic microorganisms towards a vertical plate. *Chin. J. Phys.* **2021**, *72*, 461–474. [CrossRef]
16. Liao, S.-J.; Pop, I. Explicit analytic solution for similarity boundary layer equations. *Int. J. Heat Mass. Transf.* **2004**, *47*, 75–85. [CrossRef]
17. Wang, C.Y. Similarity stagnation point solutions of the Navier-Stokes equations—Review and extension. *Euro. J. Mech. B/Fluids* **2008**, *27*, 678–683. [CrossRef]
18. Aly, E.H. Dual exact solutions of graphene–water nanofluid flow over stretching/shrinking sheet with suction/injection and heat source/sink: Critical values and regions with stabilit. *Powder Tech.* **2019**, *342*, 528–544. [CrossRef]
19. Roşca, N.C.; Roşca, A.V.; Aly, E.H.; Pop, I. Semi–analytical solution for the flow of a nanofluid over a permeable stretching/shrinking sheet with velocity slip using Buongiorno's mathematical model. *Euro. J. Mech. B/Fluids* **2016**, *58*, 39–49. [CrossRef]

20. Aly, E.H. Catalogue of existence of the multiple physical solutions of hydromagnetic flow over a stretching/shrinking sheet for viscoelastic second–grade and Walter's B fluids. *Phy. Scr.* **2019**, *94*, 105223. [CrossRef]
21. Aly, E.H.; Pop, I. MHD flow and heat transfer over a permeable stretching/shrinking sheet in a hybrid nanofluid with a convective boundary condition. *Int. J. Numer. Meth. Heat Fluid Flow* **2019**, *29*, 3012–3038. [CrossRef]
22. Pop, I.; Seddighi, S.; Bachok, N.; Ismail, F. Boundary layer flow beneath a uniform free stream permeable continuous moving surface in a nanofluid. *J. Heat Mass Transf. Res.* **2014**, *1*, 55–65.
23. Zhu, J.; Yang, D.; Zheng, L.; Zhan, X. Effects of second order velocity slip and nanoparticles migration on flow of Buongiorno nanofluid. *Appl. Math. Lett.* **2016**, *52*, 183–191. [CrossRef]
24. Uddin, M.J.; Rahman, M.M. Numerical computation of natural convective heat transport within nanofluids filled semi-circular shaped enclosure using nonhomogeneous dynamic model. *Therm. Eng. Prog.* **2017**, *1*, 25–38. [CrossRef]
25. Rana, P.; Dhanai, R.; Kumar, L. MHD slip flow and heat transfer of Al_2O_3-water nanofluid over a horizontal shrinking cylinder using Buongiorno's model: Effect of nanolayer and nanoparticle diameter. *Adv. Powder Tech.* **2017**, *28*, 1727–1738. [CrossRef]
26. Rana, P.; Shukla, N.; Bég, O.A.; Bhardwaj, A. Lie group analysis of nanofluid slip flow with Stefan blowing effect via modified Buongiorno's model: Entropy generation analysis. *Diff. Eqs. Dyn. Sys.* **2021**, *29*, 193–210. [CrossRef]
27. Pati, A.K.; Misra, A.; Mishra, S.K. Effect of electrification of nanoparticles on heat and mass transfer in boundary layer flow of a cooper water nanofluid over a stretching cylinder with viscous dissipation. *JP J. Heat Mass. Transf.* **2019**, *17*, 97–117. [CrossRef]
28. Tiwari, R.K.; Das, M.K. Heat transfer augmentation in a two–sided lid–driven differentially heated square cavity utilizing nanofluids. *Int. J. Heat Mass. Transf.* **2007**, *50*, 2002–2018. [CrossRef]
29. Devi, S.S.U.; Devi, S.P.A. Numerical investigation of three-dimensional hybrid Cu–Al_2O_3/water nanofluid flow over a stretching sheet with effecting Lorentz force subject to Newtonian heating. *Can. J. Phys.* **2016**, *94*, 490–496. [CrossRef]
30. Yousefi, R.M.; Dinarvand, S.; Yazdi, M.E.; Pop, I. Stagnation-point flow of an aqueous titania-copper hybrid nanofluid toward a wavy cylinder. *Int. J. Numer. Meth. Heat Fluid Flow* **2018**, *28*, 1716–1735. [CrossRef]
31. Bognár, G.; Klazly, M.; Hriczó, K. Nanofluid Flow Past a Stretching Plate. *Processes* **2020**, *8*, 827. [CrossRef]
32. Kuznetsov, A.V.; Nield, D.A. The Cheng–Minkowycz problem for natural convective boundary layer flow in a porous medium saturated by a nanofluid: A revised model. *Int. J. Heat Mass. Transf.* **2013**, *65*, 682–685. [CrossRef]
33. Gorla, R.S.R.; Siddiqa, S.; Mansour, M.A.; Rashad, A.M.; Salah, T. Heat source/sink effects on a hybrid nanofluid–filled porous cavity. *J. Thermophys. Heat Transf.* **2017**, *31*, 847–857. [CrossRef]
34. Sheikholeslami, S.; Gorji–Bandpy, M.; Ganji, D.D. MHD free convection in an eccentric semi–annulus filled with nanofluid. *J. Taiwan Inst. Chem. Engng.* **2014**, *45*, 1204–1216. [CrossRef]
35. Aly, E.H. Radiation and MHD boundary layer stagnation-point of nanofluid flow towards a stretching sheet embedded in a porous medium: Analysis of suction/injection and heat generation/absorption with effect of the slip model. *Math. Probl. Eng.* **2015**, *2015*, 563547. [CrossRef]
36. Aly, E.H. Existence of the multiple exact solutions for nanofluid flow over a stretching/shrinking sheet embedded in a porous medium at the presence of magnetic field with electrical conductivity and thermal radiation effects. *Powder Tech.* **2016**, *301*, 760–781. [CrossRef]
37. Shampine, L.F.; Gladwell, I.; Thompson, S. *Solving ODEs with MATLAB*; Cambridge University Press: New York, NY, USA, 2003.
38. Fang, T.-G.; Zhang, J.; Yao, S.-S. Viscous flow over an unsteady shrinking sheet with mass transfer. *Chin. Phys. Lett.* **2009**, *26* 014703.

Article
Entropy Analysis and Melting Heat Transfer in the Carreau Thin Hybrid Nanofluid Film Flow

Kohilavani Naganthran [1,2], Roslinda Nazar [3,4], Zailan Siri [1,2] and Ishak Hashim [3,4,*]

1. Institute of Mathematical Sciences, Faculty of Science, Universiti Malaya, Kuala Lumpur 50603, Malaysia; kohi@um.edu.my (K.N.); zailansiri@um.edu.my (Z.S.)
2. Center for Data Analytics Consultancy and Services, Faculty of Science, Universiti Malaya, Kuala Lumpur 50603, Malaysia
3. Department of Mathematical Sciences, Faculty of Science & Technology, Universiti Kebangsaan Malaysia, Bangi 43600 UKM, Malaysia; rmn@ukm.edu.my
4. Centre for Modelling and Data Analysis (DELTA), Faculty of Science & Technology, Universiti Kebangsaan Malaysia, Bangi 43600 UKM, Malaysia
* Correspondence: ishak_h@ukm.edu.my

Abstract: Melting heat transfer has a vital role in forming energy storage devices such as flexible thin film supercapacitors. This idea should be welcomed in the thin film theoretical models to sustain technological advancement, which could later benefit humankind. Hence, the present work endeavors to incorporate the melting heat transfer effect on the Carreau thin hybrid nanofluid film flow over an unsteady accelerating sheet. The mathematical model that obeyed the boundary layer theory has been transformed into a solvable form via an apt similarity transformation. Furthermore, the collocation method, communicated through the MATLAB built-in bvp4c function, solved the model numerically. Non-uniqueness solutions have been identified, and solutions with negative film thickness are unreliable. The melting heat transfer effect lowers the heat transfer rate without affecting the liquid film thickness, while the Carreau hybrid nanofluid contributes more entropy than the Carreau nanofluid in the flow regime.

Keywords: thin film; Carreau fluid; hybrid nanoparticles; melting heat transfer

1. Introduction

The thin film flow research has a great prospect in technological advancement due to its significance in producing electronic devices such as integrated circuits and microscopic fluidic devices [1]. For example, one can see how a solid surface is coated by a thin liquid film in those manufacturing operations. Another potential manufacturing process subset to the thin film flow application is the cast film extrusion that produces polymer sheets and films [2]. Realising the strength of the thin film flow research as an enzyme to attain the next stage of technological development, Wang [3] pioneered the problem of the thin film flow past an accelerating sheet and attested the unavailability of similarity solutions when the flow unsteadiness' rate exceeds 2. Then, Usha and Sridharan [4] revisited the flow problem in [3] asymmetrically and proved that the similarity solutions are absent when the flow unsteadiness' rate exceeds 4. As time went by, the researchers learned that heat transfer analysis is crucial in the thin film flow problem, aligned with the initiative to comprehend the heat exchangers and chemical processing equipment's design. Thus, Andersson et al. [5] solved the thin film flow and heat transfer past an accelerating sheet; they also devised a novel similarity solution for the temperature field. This contribution of [5] is remarkable and highly assists in investigating the heat transfer aspect in the present work. After that, Wang [6] presented the analytic solutions for the thin film flow and heat transfer problem over an unsteady accelerating sheet. The strong contributions of [3–6] are the impetus for the thin film flow and heat transfer research under the following effects: thermocapilarity [7,8], general surface temperature [9,10], thermal radiation [11], magnetohydrodynamics (MHD) [12], viscous dissipation [13], slip effects [14,15].

The strength of the non-Newtonian fluid in illuminating varying fluid viscosity under the applied force has vast industrial applications and managed to attract the researchers' attention to be considered under various settings, such as in [16,17]. On the other hand, the researchers' consideration of the non-Newtonian fluid in the thin film flow problem is raised because the protective coating applied on an extrudate is a non-Newtonian fluid. Therefore, Andersson et al. [18] investigated the power-law thin liquid film flow past an accelerating sheet and found a contradict trend in the fluid velocity when the power-law fluid adapts to the pseudoplastic and dilatant features respectively. Furthermore, Chen [19] enhanced the work of [18] by incorporating the heat transfer characteristic as it is an essential factor to decide the final product's quality. Subsequently, the researchers' consideration of other generalised non-Newtonian fluid models such as the Carreau fluid model increased due to its validity for high and low shear rates. Myers [20] critically analysed the generalised non-Newtonian fluid's potential in the thin film flow and suggested that the Carreau fluid model is a better choice due to its accuracy rate. Accordingly, there is a number of significant works reported within the scope of the Carreau thin film flow; see [21–24].

Besides that, hybrid nanofluid is an incredible invention by humankind to uplift technological advancement to the next level. Choi and Eastman [25] introduced the brilliant idea of suspending the nanosized metal element in the fluid to boost its heat transfer rate. Although nanofluid hits the peak of the researchers' interest due to its applications in the heat transfer equipment, nanofluid is incompatible with some specified real-world applications that require substitution between some nanofluids' properties [26]. Thus, the hybrid nanofluid is proposed to encounter this issue through the experimental works [27,28], and the hybrid nanofluid managed to gain vast interest from the researchers. Shortly, the theoretical works, such as [29] gained momentum in the hybrid nanofluid after the valuable works of Devi and Devi [30,31]. The hybrid nanofluid also succeeded in the thin film flow over an accelerating sheet owing to industrial applications such as microfluidics [32]. For instance, Sadiq et al. [33] explored the Maxwell thin hybrid nanofluid film flow across the Darcy-Forchheimer porous media and inferred that the augmentation of the heat transfer rate in the hybrid Maxwell nanofluid is better than the single-typed Maxwell nanofluid.

Melting heat transfer is a common phase experienced by industrial processes such as casting. Epstein and Cho [34] is one of the earliest works involved in the melting heat transfer effect in the laminar boundary layer flow. Epstein and Cho [34] solved the boundary layer flow problem past the horizontal positioned static flat surface along with the melting heat transfer effect. Ishak et al. [35] extended the work in [29] by considering the flow past the moving sheet and reported that the melting heat transfer effect is the decreasing function of the convective heat transfer rate. Then, Khashi'ie et al. [36] reconsidered the problem solved in [35] by incorporating the presence of hybrid nanoparticles and corroborated the finding as mentioned above in [35]. Even though the melting heat transfer effect has been probed under several settings; see [37,38]; yet, the inspection of the melting heat transfer effect in the thin film flow is scarce. Thus, this motivates the present work to scrutnise the melting heat transfer effect in the thin film flow.

Overall, the present work attempts to solve the problem of the Carreau thin hybrid nanofluid film flow past an accelerating sheet under the influence of the melting heat transfer. The present model is relatively new, and entropy generation analysis is performed. The present work also adapts the similarity transformation suggested by Andersson et al. [5], and the formulated mathematical model has been solved in the built-in collocation method, the bvp4c, to produce the approximate solutions. Furthermore, non-uniqueness solutions have been reported for every case of governing parameters' variations. The findings of the present work may serve as a reference for improving the material processing industry.

2. Mathematical Model

Ruminate the Carreau fluid flow bounded by a thin liquid film and a horizontally placed accelerating sheet from a narrow opening at the Cartesian coordinate system origin. The two-dimensional flow is assumed to be incompressible, unsteady while the thin liquid film has an unvarying thickness, $H(t)$. Figure 1 depicts the flow setup, and y−coordinate is located normal to the x−coordinate. The sheet's accelerated act, which portrays the stretching sheet situation, brings about the fluid motion delimited by the thin film and the accelerating sheet. The sheet is accelerated with speed $U_w(x,t) = \frac{bx}{(1-\sigma t)}$, where b and σ are positive constants with dimension time^{-1}, $\sigma t \neq 1$, while $b > 0$ conveys the stretching rate. The sheet surface is impermeable and melts. The melting surface temperature is denoted by $T_{\tilde{m}}$, whereas T is the fluid temperature. The wall temperature, T_w is defined as $T_w = T_s - T_0\sqrt{\frac{b^2 x^4}{4v_f^2(1-\sigma t)}}$, and $0 \leq T_0 \leq T_s$ [39]. Here, the slit temperature and reference temperature are denoted by T_s and T_0, respectively. Besides, the end effects and gravity are assumed to be very small and thus omitted. The formulated boundary layer model in the present work is only sensible if the liquid film thickness does not overlap with the boundary layer thickness. Otherwise, the present formulated model becomes irrational [40]. Also, the planar thin liquid film is assumed to be smooth and free of any surface waves [5].

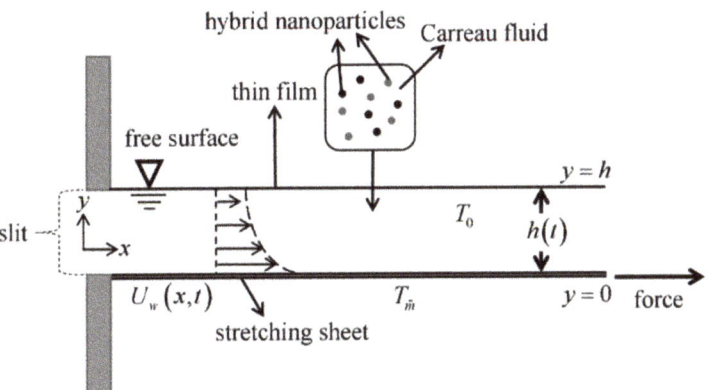

Figure 1. Schematic diagram of the thin film flow past an accelerated sheet.

The Carreau fluid's Cauchy stress tensor is given as [20]

$$\tau = -p\mathbf{I} + \eta \mathbf{A}_1, \qquad (1)$$

where

$$\eta = \eta_\infty + (\eta_0 - \eta_\infty)\left[1 + (\lambda \dot{\gamma})^2\right]^{\frac{n-1}{2}}. \qquad (2)$$

Here, τ is the Cauchy stress tensor, p is the pressure, $\mathbf{I}$ denotes the identity tensor, η_0 signifies the zero-shear-rate viscosity, η_∞ is the infinite-shear-rate viscosity, λ implies the material time constant, and n represents the power-law index. The shear rate, $\dot{\gamma}$ can be elaborated as

$$\dot{\gamma} = \sqrt{\frac{1}{2}(\dot{\gamma}:\dot{\gamma})} = \sqrt{\frac{1}{2}\Pi} = \sqrt{\frac{1}{2}tr\left(\mathbf{A}_1^2\right)} = \sqrt{\frac{1}{2}\sum_i\sum_j \dot{\gamma}_{ij}\dot{\gamma}_{ji}}. \qquad (3)$$

In Equation (3), Π is the second invariant strain rate tensor and $\mathbf{A}_1$ is the Rivlin-Ericksen tensor expressed further as

$$\mathbf{A}_1 = (\text{grad}\mathbf{V}) + (\text{grad}\mathbf{V})^T. \qquad (4)$$

The most practical cases where $\eta_0 \gg \eta_\infty$ is considered. Normally, the value of η_∞ is determined by the extrapolation procedure or chosen to be zero (suggested theoretical value) [41]. Thus, in the present work, the value of η_∞ is set to zero, and affect Equation (1) to become

$$\tau = -p\mathbf{I} + \eta_0 \left[1 + (\lambda\dot{\gamma})^2\right]^{\frac{n-1}{2}} \mathbf{A}_1. \tag{5}$$

The Carreau fluid model shows pseudoplastic, dilatant, and Newtonian features when $0 < n < 1, n > 1$ and $n = 0$, respectively, where n is the power-law index. Under these assumptions, the governing liquid film flow of the Carreau fluid can be written as [42].

$$\frac{\partial u}{\partial x} + \frac{\partial v}{\partial y} = 0, \tag{6}$$

$$\frac{\partial u}{\partial t} + u\frac{\partial u}{\partial x} + v\frac{\partial u}{\partial y} = \frac{\mu_{hnf}}{\rho_{hnf}}\frac{\partial^2 u}{\partial y^2}\left[1 + \lambda^2\left(\frac{\partial u}{\partial y}\right)^2\right]^{\frac{n-1}{2}} + \frac{\mu_{hnf}}{\rho_{hnf}}(n-1)\lambda^2\frac{\partial^2 u}{\partial y^2}\left(\frac{\partial u}{\partial y}\right)^2\left[1 + \lambda^2\left(\frac{\partial u}{\partial y}\right)^2\right]^{\frac{n-3}{2}}, \tag{7}$$

$$\frac{\partial T}{\partial t} + u\frac{\partial T}{\partial x} + v\frac{\partial T}{\partial y} = \frac{k_{hnf}}{(\rho C_p)_{hnf}}\frac{\partial^2 T}{\partial y^2}, \tag{8}$$

where u and v are the velocity components along the x- and y- directions, respectively, λ is a material time constant, n signifies the power-law index. Meanwhile, $(\rho C_p)_{hnf}, \mu_{hnf}, \rho_{hnf}$, and k_{hnf} are the hybrid nanofluid's heat capacity, dynamic viscosity, density and thermal conductivity, respectively. The further definition of $\mu_{hnf}, \rho_{hnf}, k_{hnf}$, and $(\rho C_p)_{hnf}$ are expressed in Table 1.

Table 1. The hybrid nanofluid's correlation properties' definitions (see [43]).

Properties	Au-Cu/(CMC/H$_2$O) Mathematical Relation
Density	$\rho_{hnf} = \left(1 - \phi_{hnf}\right)\rho_f + \phi_1\rho_{s1} + \phi_2\rho_{s2}$
Dynamic viscosity (Brinkman model)	$\mu_{hnf} = \frac{\mu_f}{(1-\phi_{hnf})^{2.5}}$
Thermal capacity	$(\rho C_p)_{hnf} = \left(1 - \phi_{hnf}\right)(\rho C_p)_f + \phi_1(\rho C_p)_{s1} + \phi_2(\rho C_p)_{s2}$
Thermal conductivity (Maxwell model)	$\frac{k_{hnf}}{k_f} = \frac{\left(\frac{\phi_1 k_{s1}+\phi_2 k_{s2}}{\phi_{hnf}}\right)+2k_f+2(\phi_1 k_{s1}+\phi_2 k_{s2})-2\phi_{hnf}k_f}{\left(\frac{\phi_1 k_{s1}+\phi_2 k_{s2}}{\phi_{hnf}}\right)+2k_f-(\phi_1 k_{s1}+\phi_2 k_{s2})+\phi_{hnf}k_f}$

According to Table 1, the nanoparticle volume fraction is ϕ and $\phi = 0$ reduces the model into a regular fluid. Next, ϕ_1 and ϕ_2 signify the Au's and Cu's nanoparticle volume fraction, respectively. The total volume concentration of two types of nanoparticles suspended in the hybrid nanofluid is determined as $\phi_{hnf} = \phi_1 + \phi_2$. Meanwhile, ρ_f and ρ_{hnf} are the densities of the base fluid and the hybrid nanoparticle, respectively, k_f and k_{hnf} are the thermal conductivities of the base fluid and the hybrid nanoparticles, respectively, $(\rho C_p)_f$ and $(\rho C_p)_{hnf}$ are the heat capacitance of the base fluid and the hybrid nanoparticle, respectively. These correlations are based on physical assumptions and agree with the conservation of mass and energy. Thus, the physical properties of the base fluid (water), gold (Au) and copper (Cu) hybrid nanofluids are given in Table 2.

Table 2. The thermophysical properties of selected nanoparticles and base fluid (sodium carboxymethyl cellulose (CMC)/water) (see [44,45]).

Properties	ρ (kg/m^3)	k (W/mK)	$\hat{\beta} \times 10^{-5}$ (mK)	C_p (J/kgK)
Au	19,300	318	1.4	129
Cu	8933	400	1.67	385
CMC/H$_2$O (0–0.3%)	997.1	0.613	21	4179

The Equations (6)–(8) are getting along with the boundary conditions

$$t < 0: \quad u = 0, \ v = 0, \ T = \frac{\partial T}{\partial y} = 0 \text{ for all } x \text{ and } y.$$
$$t \geq 0: \quad u = U_w(x,t), \ \frac{k_{hnf}}{\rho_{hnf}}\left(\frac{\partial T}{\partial y}\right)_{y=0} = [L + (C_p)_s(T_{\tilde{m}} - T_s)]v(x,t), \quad (9)$$
$$T = T_{\tilde{m}} \text{ at } y = 0,$$
$$\frac{\partial u}{\partial y} = 0, \ \frac{\partial T}{\partial y} = 0, \ v = \frac{dh}{dt} \text{ at } y = h,$$

At $y = h$, the kinematic constraint is enforced in the fluid motion through $v = dh/dt$. The wall shear stress and heat flux disappear entirely at the adiabatic free surface and thus $\partial u/\partial y = \partial T/\partial y = 0$ at $y = h$. Next, we introduce the similarity transformations as follows (Andersson et al. [5]):

$$\psi = xf(\zeta)\sqrt{\frac{v_f b}{1-\sigma t}}, \quad u = \frac{\partial \psi}{\partial y} = \frac{bx}{1-\sigma t}f'(\zeta),$$
$$v = -\frac{\partial \psi}{\partial x} = -\sqrt{\frac{v_f b}{1-\sigma t}}f(\zeta), \quad \theta(\zeta) = \frac{T-T_{\tilde{m}}}{T_0 - T_{\tilde{m}}}, \quad (10)$$
$$T = T_s - T_0\left(\frac{bx^2}{2v_f}\right)\frac{1}{\sqrt{(1-\sigma t)^3}}\theta(\zeta),$$

$$\zeta = y\sqrt{\frac{b}{v_f(1-\sigma t)}}, \quad (11)$$

where prime infers the derivative concerning ζ. Employing the similarity conversion as in (10) and (11) into the governing model (6)–(9) satisfies the continuity equation, and the remaining equations are transformed as follows:

$$\left(\frac{\mu_{hnf}/\mu_f}{\rho_{hnf}/\rho_f}\right)\left(1 + nWe^2 f''^2\right)\left(1 + We^2 f''^2\right)^{\frac{n-3}{2}} f''' + \left(ff'' - \frac{\omega \zeta}{2}f'' - f'^2 - \omega f'\right) = 0, \quad (12)$$

$$\frac{k_{hnf}/k_f}{(\rho C_p)_{hnf}/(\rho C_p)_f}\theta'' + \Pr\left(f\theta' - 2f'\theta - \frac{\zeta \omega}{2}\theta' - \frac{3\omega}{2}\theta\right) = 0, \quad (13)$$

with the boundary conditions

$$\Pr f(0) + \frac{k_{hnf}/k_f}{\rho_{hnf}/\rho_f}\chi\theta'(0) = 0, \ f'(0) = 1, \ f(\beta) = \omega\beta/2,$$
$$f''(\beta) = 0, \ \theta(0) = 0, \ \theta'(\beta) = 0, \quad (14)$$

wherein $We = \sqrt{\frac{\lambda^2 b^3 x^2}{v_f(1-\sigma t)^3}}$, is the local Weissenberg number [46], $\omega = \frac{\sigma}{b}$ is the dimensionless measure of unsteadiness, the Prandtl number is defined as $\Pr = \frac{(C_p)_f \mu_f}{k_f}$, while the melting heat transfer parameter is signified by $\chi = \frac{(C_p)_f(T_0-T_{\tilde{m}})}{L+(C_p)_s(T_{\tilde{m}}-T_s)}$. Moreover, β is an unknown constant that conveying the dimensionless film thickness. β also implies the similarity variable (ζ) value at the free surface, and hence the expression in (11) can take the following form:

$$\beta = h\sqrt{\frac{b}{v_f(1-\sigma t)}}, \qquad (15)$$

This unknown constant β must be calculated as an integral part of the boundary-value problem. Thus,

$$\frac{dh}{dt} = -\frac{\beta\sigma}{2}\sqrt{\frac{v_f}{v_f(1-\sigma t)}}, \qquad (16)$$

elucidates the film thickness's rate of change. On the other hand, when $n = 1$ and $We = 0$, the Carreau fluid model in Equations (12) and (13) reveals the Newtonian characteristics. The physical quantities of interest in the present work are the local skin friction coefficient $\left(C_{fx}\right)$ and the local Nusselt number (Nu_x), which can be defined as follows:

$$C_{fx} = \frac{\tau_w}{\rho_f(U_w)^2/2}, \quad Nu_x = \frac{q_w x}{k_f T_0}, \qquad (17)$$

Here, the wall shear stress (τ_w) and the heat flux from the surface of the sheet (q_w) are given by [47].

$$\tau_w = \left\{ \mu_{hnf}\frac{\partial u}{\partial y}\left[1+\lambda^2\left(\frac{\partial u}{\partial y}\right)^2\right]^{\frac{n-1}{2}}\right\}_{y=0}, \quad q_w = -k_{hnf}\left(\frac{\partial T}{\partial y}\right)\bigg|_{y=0}, \qquad (18)$$

By employing (10)–(11) and inducing (19) into (18) provides the following expression.

$$C_{fx}\text{Re}_x^{1/2} = \frac{\mu_{hnf}}{\mu_f}2f''(0)\left\{1+We^2[f''(0)]^2\right\}^{\frac{n-1}{2}}, \quad 2Nu_x\text{Re}_x^{-3/2}(1-\alpha t)^{1/2}\frac{k_f}{k_{hnf}} = \theta'(0). \qquad (19)$$

The local Reynolds number is defined as $\text{Re}_x = \frac{xU_w(x,t)}{v_f}$.

3. Entropy Analysis

The entropy generation analysis is ideal for calculating the dissipated heat energy and measuring any flow systems' performance deterioration. This nonconserved property can be communicated in the following dimensional form [48]:

$$\widehat{S}'''_{gen} = \frac{k_{hnf}}{T_0^2}\left(\frac{\partial T}{\partial y}\right)^2 + \frac{\mu_{hnf}}{T_0}\left[1+\lambda^2\left(\frac{\partial u}{\partial y}\right)^2\right]^{\frac{n-1}{2}}\left(\frac{\partial u}{\partial y}\right)^2, \qquad (20)$$

where terms on heat irreversibility is given followed by the fluid friction irreversibility. By using Equations (10) and (11) into (20), the nondimensional form of the volumetric entropy generation can be formed as follows:

$$\widehat{N}_s = \frac{k_{hnf}}{k_f}\theta'^2(\zeta) + \frac{\mu_{hnf}}{\mu_f}\frac{Br}{\varepsilon}f''^2(\zeta), \qquad (21)$$

Here, the local entropy generation rate $\left(\widehat{N}_s\right)$, the Brinkman number ($Br$), and the temperature difference parameter (ε) are further defined as follows:

$$\widehat{N}_s = \frac{\widehat{S}'''_{gen}T_0^2(1-\sigma t)v_f}{bk_f(T_0-T_{\widetilde{m}})^2}, \quad Br = \frac{\mu_f b^2 x^2}{k_f(1-\sigma t)^2(T_0-T_{\widetilde{m}})}, \quad \varepsilon = \frac{T_0}{T_0-T_{\widetilde{m}}}. \qquad (22)$$

In the entropy generation analysis, it is necessary to compute the Bejan number to identify which entropy generation appears to dominate the flow system, either frictional or thermal entropy generation. Thus, the Bejan number is calculated in the present work, and it takes the following form:

$$Be = \frac{\left(\frac{k_{hnf}}{k_f}\theta'^2(\zeta)\right)}{\left(\frac{k_{hnf}}{k_f}\theta'^2(\zeta) + \frac{\mu_{hnf}}{\mu_f}\frac{Br}{\varepsilon}f''^2(\zeta)\right)} = \frac{1}{1+\Phi}, \quad (23)$$

where $\Phi = \frac{\left(\frac{\mu_{hnf}}{\mu_f}\frac{Br}{\varepsilon}f''^2(\zeta)\right)}{\left(\frac{k_{hnf}}{k_f}\theta'^2(\zeta)\right)}$ is the irreversibility ratio. Expression in (23) signifies the heat transfer irreversibility and total entropy ratio in the flow system. Contact melting, lubrication, and electronic cooling are some heat transfer applications where the Bejan number is vital. Equation (23) also can be utilised to determine the following effects in the flow system (see Table 3):

Table 3. Physical significance of the Bejan number [49].

No.	Condition in Equation (23)	Interpretation
1.	When $\Phi = 0$, $Be = 1$	Heat transfer irreversibility is highly influencing the flow system.
2.	When $\Phi = 1$, $Be = 0.5$	Both heat transfer irreversibility and fluid friction irreversibility are equally influencing the flow system.
3.	When $Be = 0$	Fluid friction irreversibility is highly influencing the flow system.

4. Results and Discussion

The transport phenomena in the thin film flow regime can be learned by plotting the velocity and temperature profiles. In addition, calculating the local skin friction coefficient, the local Nusselt number and the dimensionless film thickness when the pertinent parameters vary is also necessary to inspect the present model's performance. Thus, all numerical outputs were generated by setting the governing parameters' values within the following fixed range: $0 \leq We \leq 0.3, 0 \leq \chi \leq 2.5, 0.8 \leq \omega \leq 1.4$, and $0.6 \leq n \leq 1.6$. The Prandtl number is fixed to 8 throughout the computation process. Also, ϕ_1 and ϕ_2 represents the gold (Au) and copper (Cu) nanoparticle volume fractions, respectively. The numerical outputs are compared between the Carreau hybrid nanofluid case, where $\phi_1 = 0.02, \phi_2 = 0.03$, and the single-typed Carreau nanofluid is considered with $\phi_1 = 0, \phi_2 = 0.03$. These parameter values are chosen based on the availability of the numerical solutions. However, those parameter values lie within the acceptable range established in previously published works. Equations (12)–(14), which convey the simplified form of the present thin film flow problem, are solved using the bvp4c function found in the MATLAB 2019a software. This built-in collocation code eases the solving process even though the present work has dimensionless film thickness as the unknown parameter [50]. Besides that, all computed numerical results are accurate within 1×10^{-10}. In order to test the precision of the present method, the thin film flow problem studied by Wang [6] have been resolved via the bvp4c function, and the comparison of the results is given in Table 4. Table 4 proves that the built-in collocation method agrees well with the numerical results produced via the homotopy analysis method in [6]. Meanwhile, the CPU time for calculating the non-uniqueness solutions is presented in Table 5. In this sample, it is apparent that the CPU time increases from the first to the second solution in every case of n. Before the presentation and discussion of the results go further, it is appropriate to confer about the non-uniqueness numerical solutions. It is undeniable that more than one numerical solutions are obtainable by providing a good set of guess values since that is the built-in bvp4c routine's requirement. The present work found that the second solutions always yield negative film thickness. The negative film thickness implies the thin liquid film's distortion, and hence an ideal thin liquid film cannot be formed [23]. Therefore, the trends showed by the second solution are disregarded.

Table 4. Comparison value of $-\theta'(0)$ in the problem solved by Wang [6].

Pr	$-\theta'(0)$	
	Wang [6]	Present Result
0.01	0.037734	0.0377342
0.1	0.343931	0.3439312
1	1.999590	1.9995914
2	2.975450	2.9759050

Table 5. CPU time for calculating the first and second solutions when $\chi = 1.5, \omega = 0.8, \text{Pr} = 8$, and $We = 0.05$.

n	CPU Time (Seconds)	
	First Solution	Second Solution
0.6	0.491	1.502
0.8	0.499	1.496
1.0	0.502	1.436
1.2	0.508	1.399
1.6	0.512	1.368

Now, Table 6 demonstrates the trend of β for the Carreau hybrid nanofluid and Carreau nanofluid when We increases. The increment of We from 0 to 0.3 affects the dimensionless film thickness to decrease by 0.25% for Carreau hybrid nanofluid and decrement by 0.18% for the Carreau nanofluid. The reason for this occurrence can be collected from Figure 2 and Table 7. Figure 2 shows that the fluid velocity increases insignificantly across the flow regime when We increases. The increment in We elucidates a longer relaxation rate; thus, the Carreau fluid takes more time to react with the external forces. Since the accelerating sheet imposes drag force towards the Carreau fluid (this can be evident by the negative values of $C_{fx}\text{Re}_x^{1/2}$ in Table 7), the fluid velocity increases slightly past the unsteady accelerating sheet, which elevates the wall shear stress and increases the values of $C_{fx}\text{Re}_x^{1/2}$ in a minimal amount.

Table 6. Numerical outputs of β for the hybrid nanofluid ($\phi_1 = 0.02, \phi_2 = 0.03$) and nanofluid when $\omega = 0.8, n = 0.8, \text{Pr} = 8$, and $\chi = 1.5$.

We	β	
	Hybrid Nanofluid	Nanofluid ($\phi_1 = 0, \phi_2 = 0.03$)
0	1.54820137 (−7.56677274)	1.64482153 (−8.69372861)
0.01	1.54819697 (−7.56278525)	1.64481817 (−8.68784901)
0.05	1.54809161 (−7.47673697)	1.64473765 (−8.56397941)
0.1	1.54776380 (−7.28412028)	1.64448683 (−8.30238316)
0.3	1.54439508 (−6.63114764)	1.64188656 (−7.49066700)

^{0} Second solution.

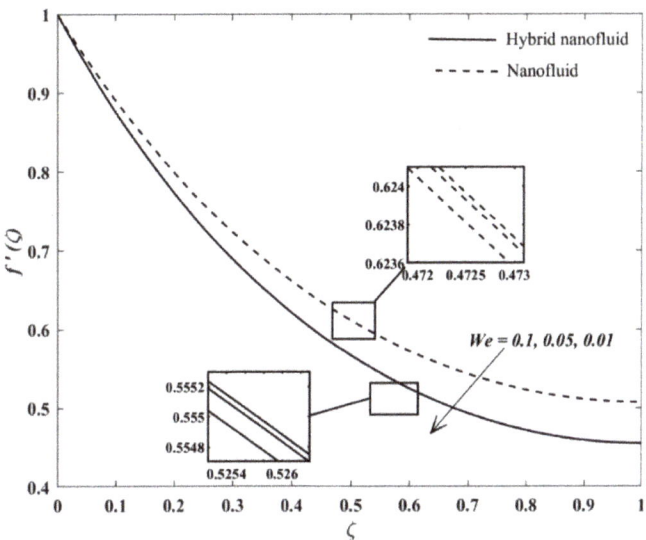

Figure 2. Velocity distribution/profile when $\omega = 0.8, n = 0.8, \Pr = 8$, and $\chi = 1.5$.

Table 7. Numerical outputs of $C_{fx}\mathrm{Re}_x^{1/2}$ for the hybrid nanofluid ($\phi_1 = 0.02, \phi_2 = 0.03$) and nanofluid when $\omega = 0.8, n = 0.8, \Pr = 8$, and $\chi = 1.5$.

We	$C_{fx}\mathrm{Re}_x^{1/2}$	
	Hybrid Nanofluid	Nanofluid ($\phi_1 = 0, \phi_2 = 0.03$)
0	−3.09668738 (−19.16027074)	−2.57368640 (−20.29066744)
0.01	−3.09667513 (−19.13980681)	−2.57367904 (−20.26302661)
0.05	−3.09638151 (−18.69982744)	−2.57350275 (−19.68364588)
0.1	−3.09546813 (−17.72582610)	−2.57295373 (−18.47813713)
0.3	−3.08610125 (−14.52820034)	−2.56727029 (−14.88712835)

^{0} Second solution.

Meanwhile, Figure 3 displays the temperature profiles across the thin film flow vicinity. For the Carreau fluid associated with the hybrid nanoparticles, the temperature increases when We increases. This behavior is evident when $0 \leq \zeta < 0.72727$. It should be noted that the fluid is under the influence of shear thinning effect ($n = 0.8$), and hence the fluid viscosity may decrease with the act of the accelerating sheet and the melting heat transfer's effect. At this moment, when the effect of We is amplified, the fluid temperature augments since the relaxation time is prolonged. A similar result has been reported by Hayat et al. [51]. However, after $\zeta = 0.72727$, the fluid far from the accelerating surface is less affected with the melting heat transfer and thus, the fluid temperature decreases when We increases. On the other hand, in the case of the Carreau nanofluid, fluid temperature increases with declining values of We when $0 \leq \zeta < 0.72727$, and the opposite trend is observed after $\zeta = 0.72727$. Such an interesting difference in the trend might be due to the suspended nanoparticles' thermal conductivity in the base fluid. Besides that, Table 8 tabulates changes in the heat transfer rate at the accelerating impermeable surface. The flow with the copper nanoparticles spectacle a gradual increase in $\theta'(0)$, and this is acceptable because copper has better thermal conductivity and results in an increased rate in heat exchange. However, the hybrid nanofluid does not exhibit a gradual degree of improvement. The heat transfer rate decreases when We's value increases from 0 to 0.3. The increment in the fluid relaxation time affects the Carreau hybrid nanofluid to become warm, which lowers heat flux from the accelerating surface and diminishes $\theta'(0)$.

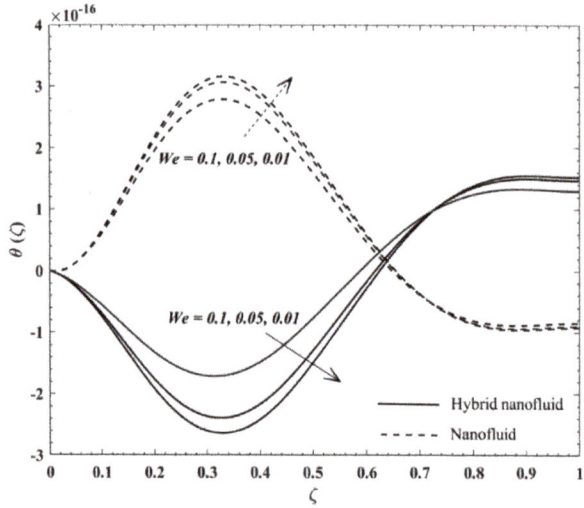

Figure 3. Temperature distribution/profile when $\omega = 0.8, n = 0.8, \Pr = 8$, and $\chi = 1.5$.

Table 8. Numerical outputs of $\theta'(0)$ for the hybrid nanofluid ($\phi_1 = 0.02, \phi_2 = 0.03$) and nanofluid when $\omega = 0.8, n = 0.8, \Pr = 8$, and $\chi = 1.5$.

We	$\theta'(0)$	
	Hybrid Nanofluid	Nanofluid ($\phi_1 = 0, \phi_2 = 0.03$)
0	$-2.323216453 \times 10^{-16}$ $(-1.63498096 \times 10^{-13})$	$-1.98241088 \times 10^{-16}$ $(3.92924247 \times 10^{-16})$
0.01	$-2.34231832 \times 10^{-16}$ $(-1.81621360 \times 10^{-13})$	$-1.97629390 \times 10^{-16}$ $(-4.96367481 \times 10^{-8})$
0.05	$-2.38023218 \times 10^{-16}$ $(-2.65814195 \times 10^{-17})$	$-1.84582892 \times 10^{-16}$ $(-1.16042427 \times 10^{-15})$
0.1	$-2.38200133 \times 10^{-16}$ $(-3.67289115 \times 10^{-15})$	$-1.46101909 \times 10^{-16}$ $(4.52972244 \times 10^{-14})$
0.3	$-9.21786995 \times 10^{-17}$ $(8.12603466 \times 10^{-17})$	$3.65397478 \times 10^{-17}$ $(-3.53683008 \times 10^{-9})$

() Second solution.

The results' discussion is further by examining the behavior of the temperature profiles and $\theta'(0)$ when χ increases. Even though the temperature profiles in Figure 4 reveal an unusual degree of dissonance, Table 9 informs that the convective heat transfer rate at the accelerating sheet increases in the single-typed nanofluid but deteriorates in the Carreau fluid with hybrid suspensions. The increment in χ indicates more cold fluid molecules exist from the melting accelerating sheet towards the warm fluid. Therefore, the nanofluid temperature declines at the moving surface and augments the heat exchange rate. The work of Khan et al. [52] also conveyed such similar result. Conversely, the hybrid nanofluid temperature may have retained a low thermal conductivity, ensuring the low heat flux rate and reducing $\theta'(0)$ at the accelerating surface. Table 10 confirms that when the Carreau fluid with the presence of the nanoparticles changes its character from the shear thinning to the shear thickening feature, the dimensionless film thickness slightly increases, in increments of about 0.035% and 0.025% for the Carreau hybrid nanofluid and Carreau single-typed nanofluid, respectively.

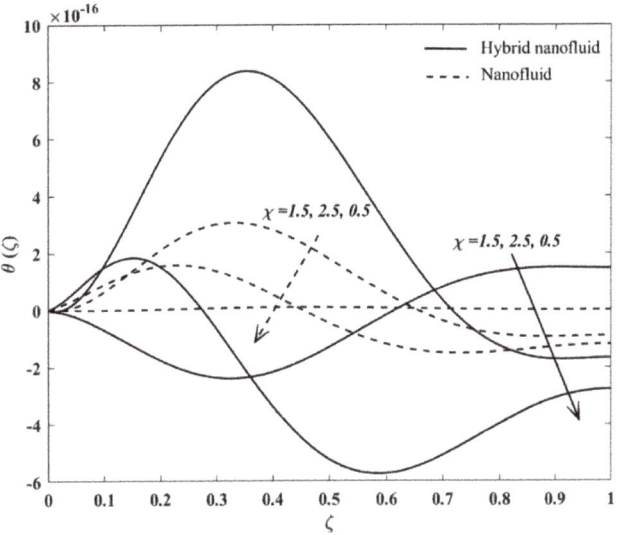

Figure 4. Temperature distribution/profile when $\omega = 0.8, n = 0.8, \Pr = 8$, and $We = 0.05$.

Table 9. Numerical outputs of $\theta'(0)$ for the hybrid nanofluid ($\phi_1 = 0.02, \phi_2 = 0.03$) and nanofluid when $\omega = 0.8, n = 0.8, \Pr = 8$, and $We = 0.05$.

χ	$\theta'(0)$	
	Hybrid Nanofluid	**Nanofluid ($\phi_1 = 0, \phi_2 = 0.03$)**
0.5	$8.06112535 \times 10^{-16}$ $(4.40156253 \times 10^{-9})$	$-2.50887021 \times 10^{-17}$ $(5.80458696 \times 10^{-7})$
1.0	$-1.84797181 \times 10^{-14}$ $(-4.87963701 \times 10^{-8})$	$-3.67551030 \times 10^{-16}$ $(2.33177392 \times 10^{-13})$
1.5	$-2.38023218 \times 10^{-16}$ $(-2.65814195 \times 10^{-17})$	$-1.84582892 \times 10^{-16}$ $(-6.39677735 \times 10^{-15})$
2.0	$-2.90618915 \times 10^{-16}$ $(-4.54529432 \times 10^{-17})$	$3.70535475 \times 10^{-16}$ $(-1.34610120 \times 10^{-14})$
2.5	$-5.43841326 \times 10^{-16}$ $(-2.19788267 \times 10^{-15})$	$6.27111798 \times 10^{-16}$ $(1.09052102 \times 10^{-16})$

^{0} Second solution.

Table 10. Numerical outputs of β for the hybrid nanofluid ($\phi_1 = 0.02, \phi_2 = 0.03$) and nanofluid when $\chi = 1.5, \omega = 0.8, \text{Pr} = 8,$ and $We = 0.05$.

n	β	
	Hybrid Nanofluid	Nanofluid ($\phi_1 = 0, \phi_2 = 0.03$)
0.6	−1.54798177 (−7.39052211)	1.64465370 (−8.44119210)
0.8	1.54809161 (−7.47673697)	1.64473765 (−8.56397941)
1.0	1.54820137 (−7.56677274)	1.64482153 (−8.69372861)
1.2	1.54831102 (−7.66098390)	1.64490536 (−8.83125851)
1.6	1.54853004 (−7.86361369)	1.64507283 (−9.13373232)

^{0} Second solution.

Meanwhile, the temperature profiles in Figure 5 display that when $\zeta \leq 0.444$, the Carreau hybrid nanofluid temperature decreases while n increases from 0.6 to 1.6. This is because the dilatant feature retards the heat energy transmission. However, when the liquid film vicinity travel at $\zeta > 0.444$, the fluid temperature becomes an increasing function of n. The area far from the accelerating sheet is possibly less affected by the shear force from the accelerating sheet, so heat transmission is reduced. Also, from Figure 5, it is observed that the fluid temperature is low at the area far from the accelerating sheet compared to the fluid temperature near the sheet's surface. Table 11 identifies that the heat transfer rate at the accelerating sheet gradually decreases for the Carreau hybrid nanofluid when n increases. This is true because Metzner et al. [53] corroborated that dilatant fluid has a lower heat transfer rate than the shear-thinning fluid. On the other hand, the opposite trend is perceived for the single-typed hybrid nanofluid. In the single-typed nanofluid considered in the present work, the nanoparticle volume fraction is less than the hybrid nanofluid, which may increase the fluid's thermal conductivity as the low-temperature molecules enter the flow stream. Thus, a moderate increase in $\theta'(0)$'s values can be noticed along with the increment of n. Table 12 delivers the decrement of $C_{fx}\text{Re}_x^{1/2}$ along with the increment of n. The strengthening effect of n reduces the wall shear stress at the accelerating sheet. Hence, the values of $C_{fx}\text{Re}_x^{1/2}$ decline.

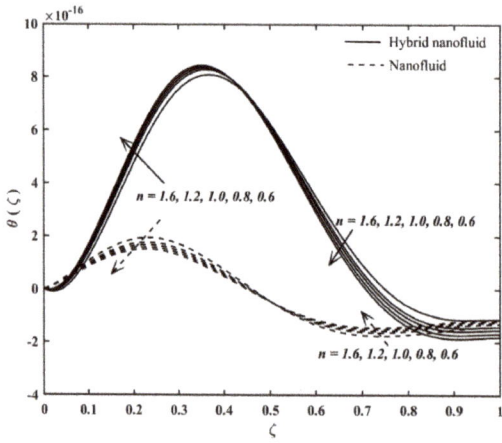

Figure 5. Temperature distribution/profile when $\chi = 1.5, \omega = 0.8, \text{Pr} = 8,$ and $We = 0.05$.

Table 11. Numerical outputs of $\theta'(0)$ for the hybrid nanofluid ($\phi_1 = 0.02, \phi_2 = 0.03$) and nanofluid when $\chi = 1.5, \omega = 0.8, \Pr = 8,$ and $We = 0.05$.

n	$\theta'(0)$	
	Hybrid Nanofluid	Nanofluid ($\phi_1 = 0, \phi_2 = 0.03$)
0.6	$-4.47529129 \times 10^{-16}$ $(-2.02318698 \times 10^{-15})$	$6.06222801 \times 10^{-16}$ $(1.07353816 \times 10^{-14})$
0.8	$-5.43841326 \times 10^{-16}$ $(-2.19788267 \times 10^{-15})$	$6.27111798 \times 10^{-16}$ $(1.09052102 \times 10^{-16})$
1.0	$-6.39204439 \times 10^{-16}$ $(-3.75921582 \times 10^{-14})$	$6.48824224 \times 10^{-16}$ $(1.62156980 \times 10^{-15})$
1.2	$-7.28671413 \times 10^{-16}$ $(2.96819224 \times 10^{-17})$	$6.70578557 \times 10^{-16}$ $(2.17295471 \times 10^{-14})$
1.6	$-9.13862705 \times 10^{-16}$ $(-3.81864083 \times 10^{-9})$	$7.14748340 \times 10^{-16}$ $(2.90372611 \times 10^{-16})$

() Second solution.

Table 12. Numerical outputs of $C_{fx}\mathrm{Re}_x^{1/2}$ for the hybrid nanofluid ($\phi_1 = 0.02, \phi_2 = 0.03$) and nanofluid when $\chi = 1.5, \omega = 0.8, \Pr = 8,$ and $We = 0.05$.

n	$C_{fx}\mathrm{Re}_x^{1/2}$	
	Hybrid Nanofluid	Nanofluid ($\phi_1 = 0, \phi_2 = 0.03$)
0.6	-3.09607536 (-18.26496764)	-2.57331897 (-19.11861939)
0.8	-3.09638151 (-18.69982744)	-2.57350275 (-19.68364589)
1.0	-3.09668738 (-7.56677274)	-2.57368640 (-20.29066744)
1.2	-3.09699297 (-19.64894688)	-2.57386991 (-20.94523474)
1.6	-3.09760332 (-20.72373597)	-2.57423653 (-22.42507737)

() Second solution.

Figures 6–9 show the results of the entropy generation analysis. Figure 6 views the increment in $\widehat{N}_s$ when Br increases. Adding value in Br engenders more heat in the fluid flow vicinity, affecting the system more in chaos and resulting in undesirable flow systems' performance. Moreover, Figure 7 exposes the Bejan number profiles when Br varies, and the values of Be increases along with the increment in Br. It is clear that the heat transfer irreversibility is gradually influencing throughout the flow system when Br rises, except for the case of the Carreau single-typed nanofluid, and $Br = 0.5$. Figure 7 indicates that when Carreau nanofluid at $Br = 0.5$, fluid friction irreversibility dominates the flow system. Figures 8 and 9 present the profiles of $\widehat{N}_s$ and Be profiles when n varies. The variation in n gives insignificant changes on $\widehat{N}_s$ and Be profiles. For example, from Figure 8, the state of the Carreau fluid from portraying the shear-thinning trait and then to the shear-thickening feature yields more heat energy incorporated to the system but minimal. However, the heat transfer irreversibility highly influences the fluid flow system, although Figure 9 shows the minor decrement in Be when the values of n increases.

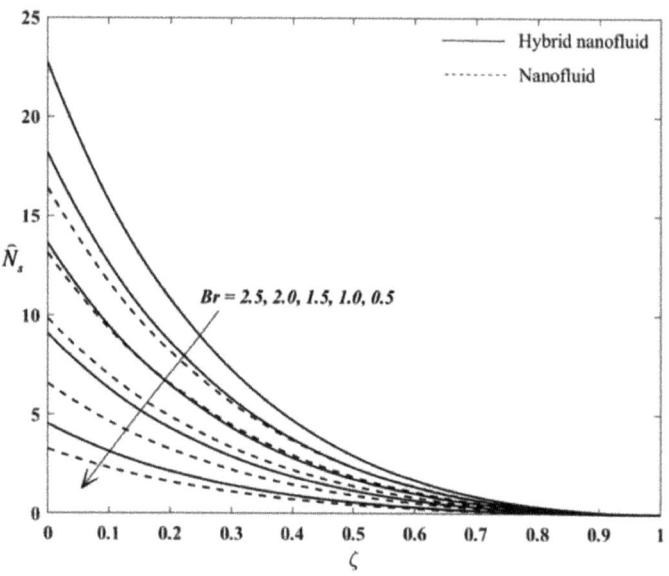

Figure 6. $\widehat{N}_s$ profiles when $\chi = 2.5, \omega = 0.6, \Pr = 8, \varepsilon = 0.2, n = 0.8$ and $We = 0.05$.

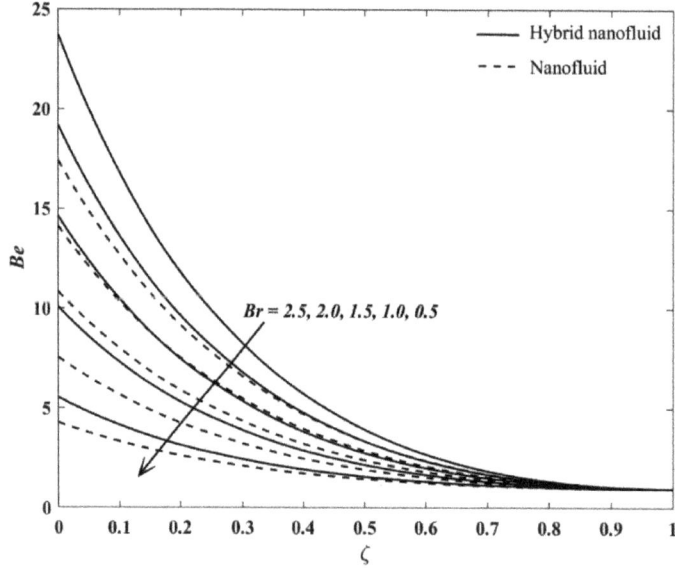

Figure 7. Be profiles when $\chi = 2.5, \omega = 0.6, \Pr = 8, \varepsilon = 0.2$ and $We = 0.05$.

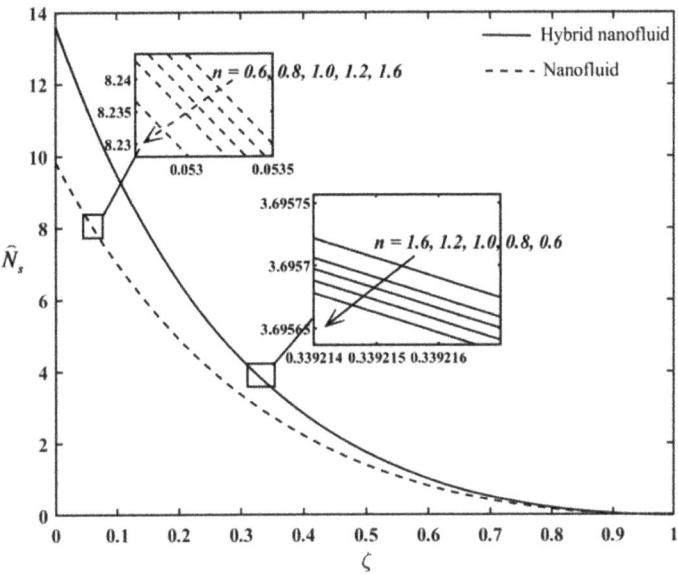

Figure 8. $\widehat{N}_s$ profiles when $\chi = 2.5, \omega = 0.6, \Pr = 8, \varepsilon = 0.2, Br = 1.5$ and $We = 0.05$.

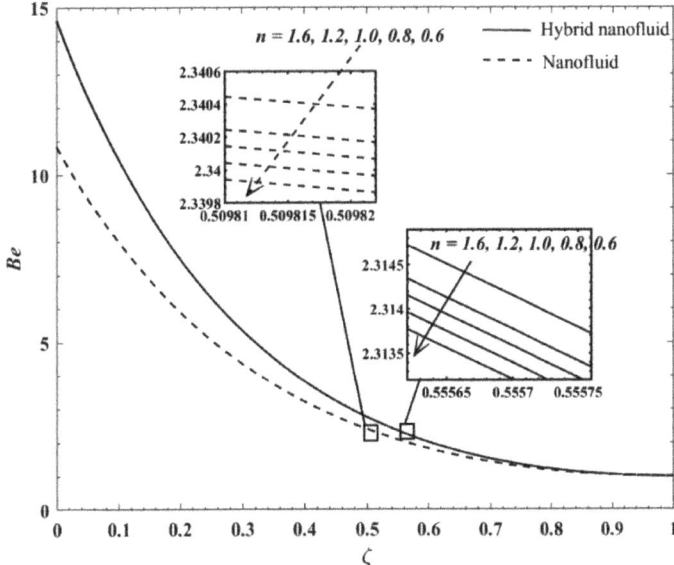

Figure 9. Be profiles when $\chi = 2.5, \omega = 0.6, \Pr = 8, \varepsilon = 0.2, Br = 1.5$ and $We = 0.05$.

5. Conclusions

The present work endeavored to investigate the performance of the Carreau thin hybrid nanofluid film flow and heat transfer while the melting heat transfer effect imposed on the accelerating sheet. Interestingly, this is the original work in the thin film Carreau hybrid nanofluid theoretical model, considering the impact of the melting heat transfer. Two approximate solutions were identified for every variation case. The Carreau hybrid nanofluid's heat transfer rate decreases when the fluid adapts to the dilatant feature.

Besides that, the presence of the hybrid nanoparticles promotes entropy in the flow system compared to the mono-typed nanoparticles. The numerical solutions with negative film thickness indicated defective thin film flow and unreliable. However, the melting heat transfer effect does not affect the liquid film thickness.

Author Contributions: Conceptualisation, K.N. and I.H.; methodology, K.N.; software, K.N.; validation, I.H., R.N. and Z.S.; formal analysis, K.N.; investigation, K.N., R.N., I.H., and Z.S.; writing—original draft preparation, K.N.; writing—review and editing, K.N., I.H., R.N., and Z.S.; funding acquisition, R.N. All authors have read and agreed to the published version of the manuscript.

Funding: This research and APC was funded by Ministry of Higher Education, Malaysia, grant number FRGS/1/2020/STG06/UKM/01/1.

Institutional Review Board Statement: Not applicable.

Informed Consent Statement: Not applicable.

Data Availability Statement: Data sharing not applicable.

Conflicts of Interest: The authors declare no conflict of interest.

Abbreviations

Nomenclature

$\mathbf{A}_1$	first Rivlin-Ericksen tensor (Pa)
Au	gold
b	stretching rate (s^{-1})
Be	Bejan number $(-)$
C_{fx}	local skin friction coefficient $(-)$
C_p	specific heat at constant pressure $\left(Jkg^{-1}K^{-1}\right)$
Cu	copper
$f(\zeta)$	dimensionless stream function $(-)$
$H(t)$	liquid thin film thickness (m)
$\mathbf{I}$	identity tensor $(-)$
k_f	fluid's thermal conductivity $\left(Wm^{-1}K^{-1}\right)$
k_{hnf}	hybrid nanofluid's thermal conductivity $\left(Wm^{-1}K^{-1}\right)$
L	fluid's latent heat (J/kg)
n	power-law index $(-)$
$\widehat{N}_s$	local entropy generation rate
Nu_x	local Nusselt number $(-)$
p	pressure (Pa)
Pr	Prandtl number $(-)$
q_w	wall heat flux $\left(Js^{-1}m^{-2}\right)$
Re_x	local Reynolds number $(-)$
T	temperature (K)
T_s	temperature at slit (K)
T_w	wall temperature (K)
T_0	reference temperature (K)
$T_{\tilde{m}}$	melting surface temperature (K)
t	time (s)
u, v	velocity components at $x-$ and $y-$ axes (ms^{-1})
$U_w(x,t)$	accelerating sheet's velocity (ms^{-1})
$\mathbf{V}$	velocity fields (ms^{-1})
We	local Weissenberg number $(-)$
x, y	Cartesian coordinates (m)
Greek Symbols	
Π	second invariant strain rate tensor (Pa)
β	unknown parameter $(-)$
$\dot{\gamma}$	shear rate (s)

ω	unsteadiness parameter $(-)$
ζ	similarity variable $(-)$
η	apparent viscosity $(\mathrm{kgm^{-1}s^{-1}})$
η_∞	high shear rates viscosity $(\mathrm{kgm^{-1}s^{-1}})$
η_0	zero shear rates viscosity $(\mathrm{kgm^{-1}s^{-1}})$
θ	non-dimensional temperature $(-)$
λ	material time constant (s)
μ_{hnf}	hybrid nanofluid's dynamic viscosity $(\mathrm{kgm^{-1}s^{-1}})$
μ_f	fluid's dynamic viscosity $(\mathrm{kgm^{-1}s^{-1}})$
ν_f	base fluid's kinematic viscosity $(\mathrm{m^2s^{-1}})$
ρ_{hnf}	hybrid nanofluid's density $(\mathrm{kgm^{-3}})$
σ	positive constant $(\mathrm{s^{-1}})$
τ	Cauchy stress tensor (Pa)
τ_w	wall shear stress $(\mathrm{kgm^{-1}s^{-2}})$
ϕ_1	Au's nanoparticle volume fraction $(-)$
ϕ_2	Cu's nanoparticle volume fraction $(-)$
ψ	stream function $(-)$
χ	melting heat transfer parameter $(-)$

Subscripts

w	condition at the stretching sheet's wall
f	base fluid
nf	nanofluid
hnf	hybrid nanofluid
$s1$	Au's solid component
$s2$	Cu's solid component

Superscript

$'$	derivative with respect to ζ

References

1. Diez, J.A.; Kondic, L. Computing three-dimensional thin film flows including contact lines. *J. Comput. Phys.* **2002**, *183*, 274–306. [CrossRef]
2. Cotto, D.; Duffo, P.; Haudin, J.M. Cast film extrusion of polypropylene films. *Int. Polym. Proc.* **1989**, *4*, 103–113. [CrossRef]
3. Wang, C.Y. Liquid film on an unsteady stretching surface. *Q. Appl. Math.* **1990**, *48*, 601–610. [CrossRef]
4. Usha, R.; Sridharan, R. The axisymmetric motion of a liquid film on an unsteady stretching surface. *J. Fluids Eng.* **1995**, *117*, 81–85. [CrossRef]
5. Andersson, H.I.; Aarseth, J.B.; Dandapat, B.S. Heat transfer in a liquid film on an unsteady stretching surface. *Int. J. Heat Mass Transf.* **2000**, *43*, 69–74. [CrossRef]
6. Wang, C. Analytic solutions for a liquid film on an unsteady stretching surface. *Heat Mass Transf.* **2006**, *42*, 759–766. [CrossRef]
7. Dandapat, B.S.; Santra, B.; Vajravelu, K. The effects of variable fluid properties and thermocapillarity on the flow of a thin film on an unsteady stretching sheet. *Int. J. Heat Mass Transf.* **2007**, *50*, 991–996. [CrossRef]
8. Noor, N.F.M.; Hashim, I.H. Thermocapillarity and magnetic field effects in a thin liquid film on an unsteady stretching surface. *Int. J. Heat Mass Transf.* **2010**, *53*, 2044–2051. [CrossRef]
9. Noor, N.F.M.; Abdulaziz, O.; Hashim, I. MHD flow and heat transfer in a thin liquid film on an unsteady stretching sheet by the homotopy analysis method. *Int. J. Numer. Meth. Fluids* **2010**, *63*, 357–373. [CrossRef]
10. Aziz, R.C.; Hashim, I.; Alomari, A.K. Thin film flow and heat transfer on an unsteady stretching sheet with internal heating. *Meccanica* **2011**, *46*, 349–357. [CrossRef]
11. Aziz, R.C.; Hashim, I.; Abbasbandy, S. Effects of thermocapillarity and thermal radiation on flow and heat transfer in a thin liquid film on an unsteady stretching sheet. *Math. Probl. Eng.* **2012**, *2012*, 127320. [CrossRef]
12. Alam, M.K.; Siddiqui, A.M.; Rahim, M.T.; Islam, S. Thin-film flow of magnetohydrodynamic (MHD) Johnson-Segalman fluid on vertical surfaces using the Adomian decomposition method. *Appl. Math. Comput.* **2012**, *219*, 3956–3974. [CrossRef]
13. Rehman, A.; Salleh, Z.; Gul, T.; Zaheer, Z. The impact of viscous dissipation on the thin film unsteady flow of GO-EG/GO-W nanofluids. *Mathematics* **2019**, *7*, 653. [CrossRef]
14. Yusuf, T.A.; Kumar, R.N.; Prasannakumara, B.C.; Adesanya, S.O. Irreversibility analysis in micropolar fluid film along an incline porous substrate with slip effects. *Int. Commun. Heat Mass Transf.* **2021**, *126*, 105357. [CrossRef]
15. Aslani, K.E.; Mahabaleshwar, U.S.; Sakanaka, P.H.; Sarris, I.E. Effect of partial slip and radiation on liquid film fluid flow over an unsteady porous stretching sheet with viscous dissipation and heat source/sink. *J. Porous Media* **2021**, *24*, 1–15. [CrossRef]

16. Aslani, K.E.; Sarris, I.E. Effect of micromagnetorotation on magnetohydrodynamics Poiseuille micropolar flow: Analytical solutions and stability analysis. *J. Fluid Mech.* **2021**, *920*, A25. [CrossRef]
17. Madhukesh, J.K.; Alhadhrami, A.; Kumar, R.N.; Gowda, R.J.P.; Prasannakumara, B.C.; Kumar, R.S.V. Physical insights into the heat and mass transfer in Casson hybrid nanofluid flow induced by a Riga plate with thermophoretic particle deposition. *Proc. Inst. Mech. Eng. E: J. Process Mech. Eng.* **2021**. [CrossRef]
18. Andersson, H.I.; Aarseth, J.B.; Braud, N.; Dandapat, B.S. Flow of a power-law fluid film on an unsteady stretching surface. *J. Non-Newton. Fluid Mech.* **1996**, *62*, 1–8. [CrossRef]
19. Chen, C.H. Heat transfer in a power-law fluid film over a unsteady stretching sheet. *Heat Mass Transf.* **2003**, *39*, 791–796. [CrossRef]
20. Myers, T.G. Application of non-Newtonian models to thin film flow. *Phys. Rev. E* **2005**, *72*, 066302. [CrossRef]
21. Sulochana, C.; Ashwinkumar, G.P. Carreau model for liquid thin film flow of dissipative magnetic-nanofluids over a stretching sheet. *Int. J. Hybrid Inf. Technol.* **2017**, *10*, 239–254. [CrossRef]
22. Sulochana, C.; Ashwinkumar, G.P. Numerical solution of heat transfer characteristics in thin film flow of MHD dissipative Carreau nanofluid past a stretching sheet with $CoFe_2O_4$ nanoparticles. *Int. J. Res. Eng. Technol.* **2016**, *5*, 18–25.
23. Naganthran, K.; Hashim, I.H.; Nazar, R. Non-uniqueness solutions for the thin Carreau film flow and heat transfer over an unsteady stretching sheet. *Int. Commun. Heat Mass Transf.* **2020**, *117*, 104776. [CrossRef]
24. Naganthran, K.; Hashim, I.H.; Nazar, R. Triple solutions of Carreau thin film flow with thermocapillarity and injection on an unsteady stretching sheet. *Energies.* **2020**, *13*, 3177. [CrossRef]
25. Choi, S.U.S.; Eastman, J. Enhancing thermal conductivity of fluids with nanoparticles. *ASME Publ. Fed.* **1995**, *231*, 99–103.
26. Babu, J.A.R.; Kumar, K.K.; Rao, S.S. State-of-art review on hybrid nanofluids. *Renew. Sust. Energ. Rev.* **2017**, *77*, 551–565. [CrossRef]
27. Suresh, S.; Venkitaraj, K.P.; Selvakumar, P.; Chandrasekar, M. Synthesis of Al_2O_3-Cu/water hybrid nanofluids using two step method and its thermo physical properties. *Colloids Surf. A Physicochem. Eng. Asp.* **2011**, *388*, 41–48. [CrossRef]
28. Sundar, L.S.; Singh, M.K.; Sousa, A.C.M. Enhanced heat transfer and friction factor of MWCNT-Fe_3O_4/water hybrid nanofluids. *Int. Commun. Heat Mass Transf.* **2014**, *52*, 73–83. [CrossRef]
29. Hamid, A.; Kumar, R.N.; Gowda, R.J.P.; Kumar, R.S.V.; Khan, S.U.; Khan, M.I.; Prasannakumara, B.C.; Muhammad, T. Impact of Hall current and homogeneous-heterogeneous reactions on MHD flow of GO-MoS_2/water (H_2O)-ethylene glycol ($C_2H_6O_2$) hybrid nanofluid past a vertical stretching surface. *Waves Random Complex Media* **2021**, 1–18. [CrossRef]
30. Devi, S.P.A.; Devi, S.S.U. Numerical investigation of hydromagnetic hybrid Cu-Al_2O_3/water nanofluid flow over a permeable stretching sheet with suction. *Int. J. Nonlinear Sci. Numer. Simul.* **2016**, *17*, 249–257. [CrossRef]
31. Devi, S.U.; Devi, S.P.A. Heat transfer enhancement of Cu-Al_2O_3/water hybrid nanofluid flow over a stretching sheet. *J. Niger. Math. Soc.* **2017**, *36*, 419–433.
32. Kumar, K.A.; Sandeep, N.; Sugunamma, V.; Animasaun, I.L. Effect of irregular heat source/sink on the radiative thin film flow of MHD hybrid ferrofluid. *J. Therm. Anal. Calorim.* **2020**, *139*, 2145–2153. [CrossRef]
33. Sadiq, M.A. The impact of monocity and hybridity of nanostructures on the thermal performance of Maxwellian thin-film flow with memory and Darcy–Forchheimer effects. *J. Therm. Anal. Calorim.* **2021**, *143*, 1261–1272. [CrossRef]
34. Epstein, M.; Cho, D.H. Melting heat transfer in steady laminar flow over a flat plate. *J. Heat Trans.-T ASME* **1976**, *98*, 531–533. [CrossRef]
35. Ishak, A.; Nazar, R.; Bachok, N.; Pop, I. Melting heat transfer in steady laminar flow over a moving surface. *Heat Mass Trans.* **2010**, *46*, 463–468. [CrossRef]
36. Khashi'ie, N.S.; Arifin, N.M.; Pop, I.; Nazar, R. Melting heat transfer in hybrid nanofluid flow along a moving surface. *J. Therm. Anal. Calorim.* **2020**, 1–12. [CrossRef]
37. Hayat, T.; Muhammad, K.; Alsaedi, A. Numerical study of melting heat transfer in stagnation-point flow of hybrid nanomaterial (MWCNTs+Ag+kerosene oil). *Int. J. Numer. Methods Heat Fluid Flow* **2021**, *31*, 2580–2598. [CrossRef]
38. Waqas, H.; Bukhari, F.F.; Farooq, U.; Alqarni, M.S.; Muhammad, T. Numerical computation of melting heat transfer in nonlinear radiative flow of hybrid nanofluids due to permeable stretching curved surface. *Case Stud. Therm. Eng.* **2021**, *27*, 101348. [CrossRef]
39. Tlili, I.; Samrat, S.P.; Sandeep, N.; Nabway, H.A. Effect of nanoparticle shape on unsteady liquid film flow of MHD Oldroyd-B ferrofluid. *Ain Shams Eng. J.* **2021**, *12*, 935–941. [CrossRef]
40. Maity, S.; Ghatani, Y.; Dandapat, B.S. Thermocapillary flow of a thin nanoliquid film over an unsteady stretching sheet. *J. Heat Transf.* **2016**, *138*, 1–8. [CrossRef]
41. Boger, D.V. Demonstration of upper and lower Newtonian fluid behaviour in a pseudoplastic fluid. *Nature.* **1977**, *265*, 126–128. [CrossRef]
42. Khan, M.; Hashim. Boundary layer flow and heat transfer to Carreau fluid over a nonlinear stretching sheet. *AIP Adv.* **2015**, *5*, 107203. [CrossRef]
43. Takabi, B.; Salehi, S. Augmentation of the heat transfer performance of a sinusoidal corrugated enclosure by employing hybrid nanofluid. *Adv. Mech. Eng.* **2014**, *2014*, 1–16. [CrossRef]
44. Oztop, H.F.; Abu-Nada, E. Numerical study of natural convection in partially heated rectangular enclosures filled with nanofluids. *Int. J. Heat Fluid Flow* **2008**, *29*, 1326–1336. [CrossRef]

45. Abo-Elkhair, R.E.; Bhatti, M.M.; Mekheimer, K.S. Magnetic force effects on peristaltic transport of hybrid bio-nanofluid (Au-Cu nanoparticles) with moderate Reynolds number: An expanding horizon. *Int. Commun. Heat Mass Transf.* **2021**, *123*, 105228. [CrossRef]
46. Schlichting, H.; Gersten, K. *Boundary Layer Theory*, 9th ed.; Springer: Berlin, Germany, 2017; pp. 83–85.
47. Khan, M.; Azam, M. Unsteady boundary layer flow of Carreau fluid over a permeable stretching surface. *Results Phys.* **2016**, *6*, 1168–1174. [CrossRef]
48. Das, S.; Chakraborty, S.; Jana, R.N.; Makinde, O.D. Entropy analysis of unsteady magneto-nanofluid flow past accelerating stretching sheet with convective boundary condition. *Appl. Math. Mech.-Engl. Ed.* **2015**, *36*, 1593–1610. [CrossRef]
49. Awad, M.M. The science and the history of the two Bejan numbers. *Int. J. Heat Mass Transf.* **2016**, *94*, 101–103. [CrossRef]
50. Shampine, L.F.; Gladwell, I.; Thompson, S. *Solving ODEs with MATLAB.*; Cambridge University Press: New York, NY, USA, 2003; p. 166.
51. Hayat, T.; Aziz, A.; Muhammad, T.; Alsaedi, A. Numerical simulation for three-dimensional flow of Carreau nanofluid over a nonlinear stretching surface with convective heat and mass conditions. *J. Braz. Soc. Mech. Sci. Eng.* **2019**, *41*, 55. [CrossRef]
52. Khan, M.I.; Waqas, M.; Hayat, T.; Khan, M.I.; Alsaedi, A. Melting heat transfer in stagnation point of Carreau fluid with nonlinear thermal radiation and heat source. *J. Braz. Soc. Mech. Sci. Eng.* **2018**, *40*, 270. [CrossRef]
53. Matzner, A.B.; Vaughn, R.H.; Houghton, G.L. Heat transfer to non-Newtonian fluids. *AIChE J.* **1957**, *3*, 92–100. [CrossRef]

Article

How Does Irrigation Affect Crop Growth? A Mathematical Modeling Approach

Vicente Díaz-González [1,†], Alejandro Rojas-Palma [1,2,*,†] and Marcos Carrasco-Benavides [1,3,†]

1. Doctorado en Modelamiento Matemático Aplicado, Facultad de Ciencias Básicas, Universidad Católica del Maule, Talca 3460000, Chile; jdiazg@ucm.cl (V.D.-G.); mcarrascob@ucm.cl (M.C.-B.)
2. Departamento de Matemática, Física y Estadística, Facultad de Ciencias Básicas, Universidad Católica del Maule, Talca 3460000, Chile
3. Departamento de Ciencias Agrarias, Facultad de Ciencias Agrarias y Forestales, Universidad Católica del Maule, Curicó 3340000, Chile
* Correspondence: amrojas@ucm.cl
† These authors contributed equally to this work.

Abstract: This article presents a qualitative mathematical model to simulate the relationship between supplied water and plant growth. A novel aspect of the construction of this phenomenological model is the consideration of a structure of three phases: (1) The soil water availability, (2) the available water inside the plant for its growth, and (3) the plant size or amount of dry matter. From these phases and their interactions, a model based on a three-dimensional nonlinear dynamic system was proposed. The results obtained showed the existence of a single equilibrium point, global and exponentially stable. Additionally, considering the framework of the perturbation theory, this model was perturbed by incorporating irrigation to the available soil water, obtaining some stability results under different assumptions. Later through the control theory, it was demonstrated that the proposed system was controllable. Finally, a numerical simulation of the proposed model was carried out, to depict the soil water content and plant growth dynamic and its agreement with the results of the mathematical analysis. In addition, a specific calibration for field data from an experiment with wheat was considered, and these parameters were then used to test the proposed model, obtaining an error of about 6% in the soil water content estimation.

Keywords: nonlinear systems; stability; controllability; irrigation strategy; soil–plant-atmosphere continuum

1. Introduction

A clear example of World Climate Change's effects has been the generalized increase in drought in some Mediterranean climatic-type areas of South America [1]. Particularly in Chile, since the end of the 1990s, this phenomenon has produced more frequent and severe droughts that have been referred to as a mega-drought [2,3]. Climate change has serious implications for agricultural production [4]. Agriculture is the activity that consumes the most water worldwide because of irrigation, which has been estimated at around 70% [5]. Irrigation is the artificial application of controlled amounts of water to the soil to replace the water consumed by agricultural crops [6]. Irrigation directly affects the plant's growth, yield, and quality of products, playing a key role in Mediterranean climate-type zones [7]. In Chile, irrigated agriculture represents 52% of the total agricultural surface [8] and 1.7% of the gross domestic product [9], where this economic activity would be impossible without irrigation.

Specific studies have demonstrated the advantages of applying an adequate irrigation strategy [10]. Irrigation scheduling must ideally reflect the crop and climate interactions, considering the water availability, the moment of its application, and the appropriate distribution in the field [6,11,12]. Indeed, several works that analyzed the irrigation strategies used to optimize seasonal water consumption have been developed through engineering crop models, based on biophysical and physiological principles, considering the soil–plant-Atmosphere Continuum (SPAC) system [13,14]. In general, these engineering crop models are computer programs that reliably simulate the growth and development of crops based on specific data. All of them have previously been parameterized and validated, offering reliable results, which have been broadly studied for specific situations [15]. Another alternative to crop modeling is the mathematical approach. Among their advantages are that they enrich the scientific understanding of the phenomena [16] because they manipulate all variables involved, analyzing all the possible responses. To mathematically model how irrigation affects crop growth and the water flow in the SPAC, the phenomenological (or macroscopic) approach is preferred to the mechanistic (or microscopic) one. This is because the phenomenological models are generalist models based on energy and mass transfer principles [17]. Phenomenological models do not require specific soil and plant parameters that may be hard to determine [17,18].

As far as the authors are aware, there are no mathematical models to describe the complete SPAC fluxes. Examples of the effects of the aforementioned mega-drought on agriculture, provided by the development of a generalized mathematical approach, would help to understand water flows in the SPAC. Additionally, these models offer the possibility of analyzing how different irrigation strategies could influence productive parameters such as water productivity, defined as the kilograms of growth per kilogram of water consumed.

We hypothesize that a qualitative mathematical model based on the SPAC interactions will provide reliable trends on the overall relationship among the water in the soil, plant, and growth. Considering that mentioned above, the objective of this work was to develop a phenomenological mathematical model to simulate the relationship between supplied water and plant growth. Taking into account that there are mathematical models that are built to explore, test, and generate hypotheses [19], this tool may provide a useful way of analyzing complex systems and the underlying mechanisms [19,20].

It is important to mention that for simplicity, this model assumes ideal field crop management. Thus, other factors that affect the accumulation of dry matter [21], such as soil nutrients, fertilizers, and so forth were considered ideal, the only limiting factor being the water supply. This model will allow for a description of the effects of different irrigation strategies on crop growth. The main relevance of this study is that it provides a mathematical model in a context in which as far as the authors are aware, there are no similar studies that analyzed the irrigation problem through this approach, coupling between the water supplied to the plant and its dry mass change.

In this work, the development of the model and its analysis is presented as follows. Firstly, we propose a system formulated and studied with an initial available amount of water in the soil. For simplicity, we assumed this concept as being equivalent to the available water capacity (AWC), water holding capacity (SWHC), or total available water (TAW) [6,22]. This initial available amount of water in the soil does not consider external water contributions. This approach is equivalent to assuming, as an initial condition, soil full of water being available for the plant. Additionally, a qualitative analysis of the behavior of the dynamic system was carried out, determining the equilibrium points, the invariant planes, phase diagrams, bounded solutions, and global stability of equilibrium points. Secondly, a system with external water input (i.e., with irrigation) was studied. We started by studying irrigation as a perturbation of the original system, and then it is shown that the said perturbation is a control. Furthermore, simulations were carried out for some parameter values that allowed us to appreciate the dynamics of the system state variables, and then a continuous and periodic irrigation strategy was incorporated to show the effects of irrigation on plant growth. Finally, a calibration and validation example of the resulting parameters of the proposed model will be presented, based on field experiment data obtained from a previous study.

2. Model Formulation

The soil–plant water flow has been traditionally explained by Ohm's law [23], dividing the water flow into three phases that represent the stages of the system: (1) variation of water at the soil root zone; (2) variation of the water inside the plant; and (3) a third phase that corresponds to the effects of this flow on the variation in the plant growth and size [24]. In this case, the studied phenomenon was irrigation, and how the soil water content variations affect the growth of plants. This process is represented by the following abstraction: The process begins by considering that the soil at the root-zone of the plant acts like a pond $v(t)$ that contains the available water for plant water consumption $v(t_0) = v_{max}$. Then the water from the soil fluxes through the plant to the atmosphere, and due to photosynthesis, a proportion of that water is transformed into biomass. The other proportion remains in the plant cells, and a fraction of it allows their growth [25]. The latter has traditionally been assumed as a sigmoidal growing shape. Under these assumptions, a three-phase model is proposed: (1) Soil water availability $v(t)$, (2) water inside the plant available for its growth $w(t)$, and (3) the plant size or amount of dry matter $x(t)$.

2.1. Water Dynamics at the Root Zone

In the development of this model, the soil at the root zone was assumed to act as a pond. This assumption is of an analogy that will be repeatedly used in the text. At the beginning of the growing cycle, it is assumed that this pond starts at full capacity of water $v(t_0) = v_{max}$. Then, during the growing cycle, the variations of the water in the pond $v'(t)$ are composed of two terms: the first is proportional to the amount of water in the soil at the root-zone, and the second term accounts for the interaction of water inside the plant with the water of the pond. Here, it must be considered that for large values $w(t)$, the rate reaches a constant threshold, as follows:

$$v'(t) = -\gamma v(t) - \rho \left(\frac{w(t)}{1 + rw(t)}\right) v(t), \tag{1}$$

where r is a constant that modifies the limiting factor of the water inside the plant, γ is the internal rate of decline in pond water by evaporation, and ρ is the intrinsic rate of water that goes to the plant.

2.2. Water Dynamics Inside the Plant

The water flow from the soil to roots and then to the whole plant is considered as a mass transfer process, where the water that enters the plant is equal to that lost through transpiration, plus that which is stored in the tissues. Then the variation of water $w'(t)$ inside the plant available for its growth, responds to the type,

$$w'(t) = \left\{\begin{array}{c}\text{Water absorption}\\\text{per unit of time}\end{array}\right\} - \left\{\begin{array}{c}\text{Water removed}\\\text{per unit of time}\end{array}\right\}. \tag{2}$$

Water absorption: The plant absorbs the soil-water in proportion to the amount of water $v(t)$ that the pond has in interaction with the water inside the plant $w(t)$; however, the water inside the plant for large values $w(t)$ reaches a constant rate,

$$\left\{\begin{array}{c}\text{Water absorption}\\\text{per unit of time}\end{array}\right\} = \delta \left(\frac{w(t)}{1 + rw(t)}\right) v(t), \tag{3}$$

with δ being the intrinsic rate of increase of the water inside the plant.

Water removed: The water that passes throughout the plant is moved by transpiration, which is considered proportional to the amount of water $w(t)$ that the plant has, and the other is retained in the plant tissues and a fraction of it is utilized for plant growth. This process is considered proportional to the gain of mass $G(x)$ (this term gain will be defined later) in interaction with the amount of water $w(t)$. Then:

$$\left\{ \begin{array}{c} \text{Water removed} \\ \text{per unit of time} \end{array} \right\} = \beta \omega(t) + \mu G(x) \omega(t), \qquad (4)$$

with constant β being the rate of decrease of water inside the plant, and μ is the plant growth rate.

From Equations (2)–(4), we have the following relationship for $\omega'(t)$.

$$\omega'(t) = \delta \left(\frac{\omega(t)}{1 + r\omega(t)} \right) v(t) - \beta \omega(t) - \mu G(x) \omega(t). \qquad (5)$$

2.3. Plant Growth Dynamics

For the growth of the plant, the variation of dry matter is considered, and it is the result of a gain less than a degradation term, where an alternative that includes the Ref. [24] is,

$$x'(t) = \frac{\sigma x(t)}{1 + g x(t)^n} - m x(t), \qquad (6)$$

where $x(t)$ represents the amount of dry mass at time t, the constant σ corresponds to the intrinsic growth rate of the plant, g modifies the limiting factor of plant growth, m corresponds to the rate of degradation of the plant, and factor n allows for modification of the rapidity of growth of the plant.

Let us now discuss the first term of the Equation (6), as in any population, particularly of cells of a plant, the rate of gain of a new mass per unit of time at all times t can be a function of important internal or environmental parameters, also of the same accumulated mass as a limiting element to growth (dense dependence with negative correlation). The form of the function that represents the gain and that corresponds to the first term of (6) is $G(x) = \frac{\vartheta x}{1 + g x^n}$, which can be seen to be very sensitive to the parameter n. The form of G (x) is discussed below for some intervals of n, with constant ϑ.

Next are four cases for different values of n:

(a) If $n < 0$, then $G(x) = \frac{\vartheta x}{1 + g x^{-|n|}}$, which for $x \gg 1$ tends to ϑx, which is not realistic, because the dry mass can not grow forever.
(b) For $n = 0$, it has $G(x) = (\frac{\vartheta}{1+g}) x$, and the dry mass gain increases linearly with the size of the plant, which, like the previous case, does not represent reality.
(c) For $n > 1$, if $x \gg 1$ then $G(x) = \frac{\vartheta}{g} \frac{1}{x^{(n-1)}}$, it tends quickly to zero. This case is unusual, and has been discarded in further analysis.
(d) Finally, the fourth case, with $0 < n \leq 1$, was assumed for the model.

Figure 1 illustrates the effects of parameter n on the function $G(x)$ that represents the mass gain. Five different values of n are taken into account, considering the four previous cases.

In relation to the second term of Equation (6), the literature assumes that the plant in any state of growth has some loss of mass at time t, considered proportional to the size of the plant at time $x(t)$, with a constant degradation rate m.

Figure 2 represents the size of the plant as a function of time, obtained from the relationship (6). It can be seen in Figure 2 that at the beginning of the time scale, the size of the plant tends to grow unlimitedly in a short time interval, for values of $n \leq 0$ (blue, red). This situation does not agree with plants which grow in a common pattern. In nature, plants can present with accelerated growth in their first growth stages, but it then decreases in their maturity until reaching a plateau; after that, there is a decrease in their harvest, or after the end of each growing season [22]. For $n = 2$ (green), the plant's size reaches a constant value very soon (there is no growth), which is not adjusted to the aforementioned pattern of plant growth. By assuming values of $n = 0.8$ (yellow) and $n = 1.0$ (purple), the simulated behavior of the size of the plant over time shows a shape that reflects the natural plant growth pattern.

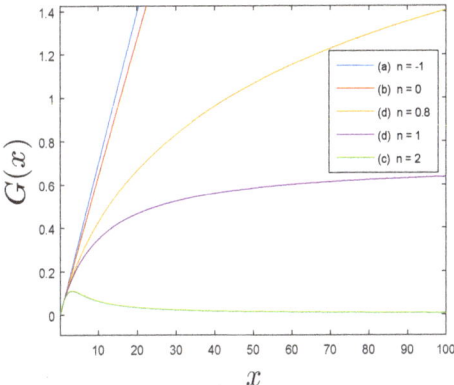

Figure 1. Rate of mass gain as a function of size of the plant, considering the following parameter values: $\vartheta = 0.07$ and $g = 0.1$. This figure shows that for values of $n \leq 0$ (blue, red; cases (a), and (b)), the gain in dry matter grows rapidly (monotonous growth). Similarly, for $n = 2$ (green; case (c)), the dry matter gain falls very quickly to zero. For values of $n = 0.8$ (yellow, case (d)) and $n = 1.0$ (purple; case (d)) the behavior of the gain is more realistic. In this work, a value of $n = 1$ was assumed for the model.

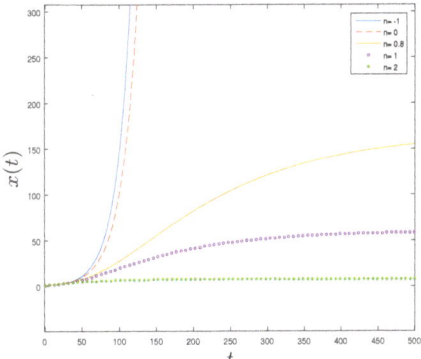

Figure 2. Simulation of dry mass growth as a function of time, where: n is the factor that allows for modification of the plant's rapidity of growth in t time (days), and $x(t)$ is the amount of dry matter (unit of mass). For parameter values $n \in \{-1, 0, 0.8, 1, 2\}$, $\sigma = 0.07$, $g = 0.1$ and $m = 0.01$.

Finally, in the first term of Equation (6), the intrinsic growth rate of the plant σ is considered a function of omega, $\sigma(\omega) = \kappa\omega$, to incorporate an interaction with the water entering the plant, where κ is a proportionality constant that accounts for the influence of water inside the plant on the growth of the crop. In this way, the gain increases when more water enters the plant, then Equation (6) remains:

$$x'(t) = \frac{\kappa\, x(t)\, \omega(t)}{1 + g\, x(t)} - m\, x(t), \tag{7}$$

where one should remember that $0 < n \leq 1$, and for simplicity, we chose $n = 1$.

Assumptions

A1: In relation to the water that flows from the pond to the plant, it is assumed that the water absorption rate of the plant is less than or equal to the rate of loss of water from the pond to the plant, that is, $\delta \leq \rho$.

A2: In relation to the process of photosynthesis and plant growth, it is assumed that the dry matter accumulation rate of the plant is approximately equal to the rate of decrease of the water inside the plant that goes to photosynthesis. This assumption is supported by the equation of photosynthesis [26]. Photosynthesis is the process that occurs in plants (chlorophyll) where the solar energy, through the water hydrolysis, is used for atmospheric carbon dioxide assimilation, resulting in the production of carbohydrate molecules and oxygen. The balanced general equation of this phenomenon, for C3 plants, is as follows: $6H_2O + 6CO_2 \longrightarrow C_6H_2O_6 + 6O_2$, resulting in $\kappa \approx k$.

A3: It is assumed that the rate of water loss through transpiration β is greater than the rate of water loss through evaporation γ, which is $\beta > \gamma$. In addition, it is assumed that the degradation rate of the plant m is greater than the rate of water loss through evaporation γ, which is $m > \gamma$. Finally, it is assumed that $\beta > m$.

2.4. Mathematical Model

From Equations (1)–(7), the following dynamic system is obtained, which represents the coupling between the water supplied to the plant and the change of its dry mass.

$$\begin{cases} x'(t) &= \frac{\kappa x(t) \omega(t)}{1+g x(t)} - m\, x(t), \\ w'(t) &= \delta \frac{\omega(t) v(t)}{1+r \omega(t)} - \beta \omega(t) - \frac{k x(t) \omega(t)}{1+g x(t)}, \\ v'(t) &= -\gamma v(t) - \rho \frac{\omega(t) v(t)}{1+r \omega(t)}. \end{cases} \quad (8)$$

More simply,

$$(x', \omega', v')^T = f(x, \omega, v), \quad (9)$$

where $f(x, \omega, v)$ represents the right side of the system (8).

For obtaining a system of nonlinear differential equations in three dimensions where it has been used, $\mu\, \vartheta = k$ is a constant that represents the intrinsic rate of water decrease by photosynthesis. The parameters are presented in Table 1.

System (8) is defined in the region $\Omega = \{(x, \omega, v) \in \mathbb{R}^3 \mid x, \omega, v \geq 0\}$.

Table 1. Parameters considered in the present study.

Parameters	Meaning	Units
κ	Intrinsic growth rate per unit of water inside the plant	[time × mass]$^{-1}$
g	Limiting factor constant of $x(t)$	[mass]$^{-1}$
m	Plant degradation rate	[time]$^{-1}$
δ	Intrinsic rate of increase of the water inside the plant	[time × mass]$^{-1}$
r	Limiting factor constant of $\omega(t)$	[mass]$^{-1}$
β	Rate of decrease of water inside the plant	[time]$^{-1}$
k	Intrinsic rate of water decrease by photosynthesis	[time × mass]$^{-1}$
γ	Inner rate of decrease of the pond water	[time]$^{-1}$
ρ	Intrinsic rate of water that goes to the plant	[time × mass]$^{-1}$

Remarks

- Plant size variation. In the Equation (8), the first term of x' corresponds to the growth rate of the plant due to the water inside the plant represented by ω, and the expression $(1+g\,x)^{-1}$ is the limiting factor of plant growth. The second term corresponds to the rate of degradation of the plant.
- Variation of water inside the plant. The first term of ω' accounts for the rate of increase of the water inside the plant due to the water coming from the pond v, and the expression $(1+r\,\omega)^{-1}$ corresponds to the limiting factor of the increase in water inside the plant. The second term represents the rate of decrease of the water inside

the plant caused by transpiration. The third term is the rate of water loss inside the plant as a result of photosynthesis, and the expression $kx(1+gx)^{-1}$ represents the rate of decrease per capita, the $x = g^{-1}$ value corresponds to half of the maximum decrease rate kg^{-1}.

- Variation of water in the pond. The first term corresponds to the rate of decrease in pond water due to evaporation losses. The second term is the rate of decrease of the pond water flowing into the plant, the expression $\rho w(1+rw)^{-1}$ represents the rate of decrease per capita of pond water flowing to the plant, and the $w = r^{-1}$ value corresponds to half of the maximum decrease rate ρr^{-1}.

3. Main Results

Lemma 1. *The coordinate planes of the system (8) are invariant.*

Proof. It will be proved that the xw plane is invariant, and the proof is similar for the other planes. On one side, let S_1 be the plane xw with $v = 0$, then the vector $\langle 0, 0, 1 \rangle$ is always normal to S_1. On the other hand, points $(x, w, 0)$ of S_1 comply, $\langle x', w', v' \rangle = \langle \frac{\kappa x w}{1+gx} - mx, -\beta w - \frac{kxw}{1+gx}, 0 \rangle$.

In this way, the following result is obtained:

$$\langle 0, 0, 1 \rangle \cdot \langle x', w', v' \rangle = \langle 0, 0, 1 \rangle \cdot \left\langle \frac{\kappa x w}{1+gx} - mx, -\beta w - \frac{kxw}{1+gx}, 0 \right\rangle = 0,$$

which shows that the plane xw is invariant. □

Proposition 1. *The solutions of system (8) are uniformly bounded.*

Proof. Defining $z(t)$ as:

$$z(t) = \frac{x(t)}{\kappa} + \frac{w(t)}{k} + \frac{\delta}{\rho k} v(t), \quad z(t=0) = z_0 = \frac{x_0}{\kappa} + \frac{w_0}{k} + \frac{\delta}{\rho k} v_0.$$

Then,

$$z'(t) = \frac{x'(t)}{\kappa} + \frac{w'(t)}{k} + \frac{\delta}{\rho k} v'(t) = -\left(\frac{m}{\kappa} x(t) + \frac{\beta}{k} w(t) + \frac{\gamma \delta}{k\rho} v(t) \right),$$

and by assumption A3, the $\min\{m, \beta, \gamma\} = \gamma$. Then, $z'(t)$ satisfies

$$z'(t) \leq -\gamma \left(\frac{x(t)}{\kappa} + \frac{w(t)}{k} + \frac{\delta}{\rho k} v(t) \right) = -\gamma z(t). \tag{10}$$

Using the comparison principle (lemma) [27], then from the differential inequality (10), we obtain

$$0 \leq z(t) \leq z_0 e^{-\gamma t}, \quad \forall t > 0.$$

□

The equilibrium points of the system (8) are:

$$p_0 = (0, 0, 0),$$

$$p_1 = (0, \frac{-\gamma}{\epsilon}, \frac{\beta \rho}{\delta \epsilon}),$$

$$p_2 = (\frac{-\beta}{k+\beta g}, \frac{km}{\kappa(k+\beta g)}, 0),$$

$$p_3 = \left(-\frac{1}{mg}(\frac{\kappa \gamma}{\epsilon} + m), \frac{-\gamma}{\epsilon}, \frac{k\rho}{\kappa g \delta \gamma \epsilon}(\frac{\kappa g \beta \gamma}{k} + \kappa \gamma + m\epsilon) \right),$$

with $\epsilon = \rho + \gamma r$. Considering that the state variables represent non-negative quantities, then only the equilibrium points that are in the first octant are of interest. Thus, the only equilibrium point of interest is $p_0 = (0,0,0)$.

Lemma 2. *The equilibrium point $p_0 = (0,0,0)$ is locally asymptotically stable.*

Proof. The eigenvalues of the Jacobian matrix evaluated at the point $(0,0,0)$ are: $\lambda_1 = -m$, $\lambda_2 = -\beta$, $\lambda_3 = -\gamma$; therefore, $(0, 0, 0)$ is locally stable. □

Proposition 2. *$p_0 = (0,0,0)$ is a globally exponentially stable equilibrium point.*

Proof. Using the direct method of Lyapunov demonstrates the global exponential stability of the system. The following scalar function is considered:

$$V(x, \omega, v) = \left(\frac{k}{\kappa}x + \omega + \frac{\delta}{\rho}v\right)^2. \tag{11}$$

(i) Clearly, $V(0,0,0) = 0$ and $V(x, \omega, v) > 0$ for $(x, \omega, v) \neq (0,0,0)$.

(ii) $V'(x, \omega, v) = -2\left(\frac{k}{\kappa}x + \omega + \frac{\delta}{\rho}v\right)\left(\frac{km}{\kappa}x + \beta\omega + \frac{\gamma\delta}{\rho}v\right)$.
Then, $V'(x, \omega, v) < 0$ in $\Omega - \{(0,0,0)\}$, given that all the parameters: k, κ, δ, ρ, m, β and γ are positive, and the state variables are also positive.

(iii) $V(x,\omega,v) = \left(\frac{k}{\kappa}x + \omega + \frac{\delta}{\rho}v\right)^2 \leq r_1(2(x\omega + xv + \omega v) + (x^2 + \omega^2 + v^2))$. With $r_1 = \max\{(\frac{k}{\kappa})^2, 1, (\frac{\delta}{\rho})^2, \frac{k}{\kappa}, \frac{k\delta}{\kappa\rho}, \frac{\delta}{\rho}\}$, according to the Assumptions $r_1 = 1$, obtaining $V(x,\omega,v) \leq 4\|(x,\omega,v)\|^2$.
On the other hand, $V(x,\omega,v) \geq \left((\frac{k}{\kappa})^2 x^2 + \omega^2 + (\frac{\delta}{\rho})^2 v^2\right) \geq r_2\|(x,\omega,v)\|^2$, with $r_2 = \min\{(\frac{k}{\kappa})^2, 1, (\frac{\delta}{\rho})^2\}$, according to the Assumptions $r_2 = (\frac{\delta}{\rho})^2$, obtaining $V(x,\omega,v) \geq (\frac{\delta}{\rho})^2\|(x,\omega,v)\|^2$.
Obtaining $(\frac{\delta}{\rho})^2\|(x,\omega,v)\|^2 \leq V(x,\omega,v) \leq 4\|(x,\omega,v)\|^2$.

(iv) $V' \leq -2\min\{m, \beta, \gamma\}\left(\frac{k}{\kappa}x + \omega + \frac{\delta}{\rho}v\right)^2$, according to the Assumptions, $\min\{m, \beta, \gamma\} = \gamma$.
Obtaining $V' \leq -2\gamma V$.

(v) Since the Lyapunov function it is strictly increasing, $\lim_{\|(x,\omega,v)\| \to \infty} V(x,\omega,v) = \infty$.
□

4. Modeling with Irrigation

To consider adding external water to the system, in Equation (9), a term $I(t, x, \omega, v)$ is incorporated that accounts for the way in which the water is added.

$$(x', \omega', v')^T = f(x, \omega, v) + I(t, x, \omega, v). \tag{12}$$

The term $I = (0, 0, I_3)^T$ is considered a perturbation of the system. Suppose the perturbation term satisfies the linear growth bound.

$$\|I(t, x, \omega, v)\| < \eta \|(x, \omega, v)\|. \forall\, t \geq 0, \forall\, (x, \omega, v) \in \Omega, \tag{13}$$

where η is a nonnegative constant,

$$\eta < \frac{c_3}{c_4}, \tag{14}$$

where c_3 and c_4 are defined by the Lyapunov function (11) of the nominal system (9) that satisfies the following three conditions,

$$c_1 \|(x, \omega, v)\|^2 \leq V \leq c_2 \|(x, \omega, v)\|^2, \tag{15}$$

$$V' = \frac{\partial V}{\partial t} + \frac{\partial V}{\partial (x,\omega,v)} f(x,\omega,v) \leq -c_3 \|(x,\omega,v)\|^2, \tag{16}$$

$$\left\| \frac{\partial V}{\partial (x,\omega,v)} \right\| \leq c_4 \|(x,\omega,v)\|, \tag{17}$$

where $c_1 = \min\{(\frac{k}{\kappa})^2, 1, (\frac{\delta}{\rho})^2\}$, $c_2 = 4\max\{(\frac{k}{\kappa})^2, 1, (\frac{\delta}{\rho})^2, \frac{k}{\kappa}, \frac{k\delta}{\kappa\rho}, \frac{\delta}{\rho}\}$,
$c_3 = \min\{\frac{mk^2}{\kappa^2}, \beta, \frac{\gamma\delta^2}{\rho^2}\}$, $c_4 = 4\left[\left(\frac{k}{\kappa}\right)^2 + 1 + \left(\frac{\delta}{\rho}\right)^2\right]^{\frac{1}{2}} \max\{\frac{k}{\kappa}, 1, \frac{\delta}{\rho}\}$.

Considering the **Assumptions** of the model, the following is obtained: $c_1 = (\frac{\delta}{\rho})^2$, $c_2 \approx 4$, $c_3 = \gamma(\frac{\delta}{\rho})^2$. For the case c_4, from the **Assumptions** A2, we have that $\frac{k}{\kappa} \approx 1$, where from A1 you get $\frac{\delta}{\rho} \leq 1$, then $\max\{\frac{k}{\kappa}, 1, \frac{\delta}{\rho}\} = 1$, obtaining $c_4 \leq 4\sqrt{3}$; then, we assume that $c_4 \approx 6$.

Lemma 3. *Suppose the perturbation term satisfies $I(t,0,0,0) = 0$, for $t \geq 0$. Then, equilibrium point $p_0 = (0,0,0)$ is globally exponentially stable of the system (12).*

Proof. We use V of the nominal system (9) as a Lyapunov function candidate for (12). Lyapunov function $V(x,\omega,v) = \left(\frac{k}{\kappa}x + \omega + \frac{\delta}{\rho}v\right)^2$.

$$V' = \frac{\partial V}{\partial t} + \frac{\partial V}{\partial (x,\omega,v)}[f(x,\omega,v) + I(t,x,\omega,v)],$$

occupying Equation (16), we obtain

$$V' \leq -c_3\|(x,\omega,v)\|^2 + \left\|\frac{\partial V}{\partial (x,\omega,v)}\right\| \|I(t,x,\omega,v)\|, \tag{18}$$

substituting Equations (17) and (13) into (18)

$$V' \leq (-c_3 + \eta c_4)\|(x,\omega,v)\|^2,$$

using the relation (14) we obtain $V' \leq 0$. □

Now we are going to consider the more general case $I(t,0,0,0) \neq 0$, and we cannot expect the solutions to approach the origin for long times, but we can ensure that the solutions are ultimately confined by a small bound in some sense.

Theorem 1. *Suppose the perturbation $I(t,x,\omega,v)$ satisfies*

$$\|I(t,x,\omega,v)\| < \frac{1}{8\sqrt{2}}\gamma\, r, \tag{19}$$

where equilibrium point $p_0 = (0,0,0)$ is globally asymptotically stable of the system (9). Then, the system solutions (12) satisfy

$$\|(x(t),\omega(t),v(t))\| \leq \tau e^{-\alpha(t-t_0)} \|(x(t_0),\omega(t_0),v(t_0))\|, \quad \forall\, t_0 \leq t < t_0 + T,$$

and

$$\|(x(t),\omega(t),v(t))\| \leq b, \quad \forall\, t \geq t_0 + T,$$

where $\tau = \sqrt{\frac{c_2}{c_1}} = 2(\frac{\rho}{\delta})$, $\alpha = \frac{1}{8}\gamma(1-\theta)(\frac{\delta}{\rho})^2$, $b = \frac{3\sqrt{2}}{4}(\frac{\rho}{\delta})^3 \frac{r}{\theta}$, $0 < \theta < 1$.

Proof. We use V of the nominal system (9) for a perturbed system (12) and using Equation (18), we obtained

$$V' \leq -c_3\|(x,\omega,v)\|^2 + \left\|\frac{\partial V}{\partial (x,\omega,v)}\right\| \|I(t,x,\omega,v)\|.$$

Using Equations (17) and (19), with $\frac{\gamma r}{8\sqrt{2}} \equiv \lambda$ was obtained,

$$V' \leq -(1-\theta)c_3\|(x,\omega,v)\|^2 - \theta c_3\|(x,\omega,v)\|^2 + c_4\lambda\|(x,\omega,v)\|, \ 0 < \theta < 1.$$

For $\|(x,\omega,v)\| \geq \frac{c_4 \lambda}{c_3 \theta} \equiv \mu$ was obtained,

$$V' \leq -(1-\theta)c_3\|(x,\omega,v)\|^2. \tag{20}$$

Now we separate the proof into two cases.
First case: $V \geq c_2 \mu^2$, with (15) is obtained $\|(x,\omega,v)\| \geq \mu$, for all $t_0 \leq t < t_0 + T$.
From Equation (15) and (20), $V' \leq -(1-\theta)\frac{c_3}{c_2} V$ obtaining,

$$V \leq e^{-\frac{c_3}{c_2}(1-\theta)(t-t_0)} V_0, \text{ with } V_0 = V(t_0). \tag{21}$$

Replacing (21) in (15), and using $V_0 \leq c_2 \|(x(t_0), \omega(t_0), v(t_0))\|^2$ is obtained,

$$\|(x,\omega,v)\| \leq \left[\frac{1}{c_1} V\right]^{\frac{1}{2}} \leq \sqrt{\frac{c_2}{c_1}} e^{-\frac{c_3}{2c_2}(1-\theta)(t-t_0)} \|(x(t_0), \omega(t_0), v(t_0))\|. \tag{22}$$

This inequality (22) is valid for the interval $[t_0, t_0 + T)$ during which $V \geq c_2 \mu^2$.
Second case: $V < c_2 \mu^2$, $t \geq t_0 + T$.
From Equation (15), $\|(x,\omega,v)\| \leq \left[\frac{1}{c_1} V\right]^{\frac{1}{2}} \leq \left[\frac{1}{c_1} c_2 \mu^2\right]^{\frac{1}{2}}$, then,

$$\|(x,\omega,v)\| \leq \sqrt{\frac{c_2}{c_1}} \mu \equiv b.$$

□

5. Irrigation as Control

Now the external water added to the system is considered as a control $I(t,x,\omega,v) = h(x,\omega,v) u$, and from (9) the equation of state is obtained, with $h(x,\omega,v) = (0, 0, 1)^T$. Thus, the system (12) assumes the following form:

$$(x', \omega', v')^T = f(x,\omega,v) + h(x,\omega,v) u, \tag{23}$$

with output equation

$$y = l(x,\omega,v) = x. \tag{24}$$

Lemma 4.

(a) The input-affine system model (23) and (24) is linearizable.
(b) Let $(x,\omega,v) \in int(\Omega) = \{(a,b,c) \in \mathbb{R}^3 / a, b, c > 0\}$, the system (23) is feedback linearizable.

Proof. In the first case, using the Lie derivative, we calculate the relative degree of the nonlinear systems (23) and (24).
We define $\Psi_1 = l(x,\omega,v) = x$, then $\frac{\partial \Psi_1}{\partial(x,\omega,v)} = (1\ 0\ 0)$. Thus,

$$\Psi_2 \equiv \frac{\partial \Psi_1}{\partial(x,\omega,v)} f(x,\omega,v) = \frac{\kappa x \omega}{1+gx} - mx,$$

and $\frac{\partial \Psi_2}{\partial(x,\omega,v)} = (\frac{\kappa \omega}{(1+gx)^2} - m \quad \frac{\kappa x}{1+gx} \quad 0)$ is obtained. Finally,

$$\Psi_3 \equiv \frac{\partial \Psi_2}{\partial(x,\omega,v)} f(x,\omega,v),$$
$$= \left(\frac{\kappa\omega}{(1+gx)^2} - m\right)\left(\frac{\kappa x\omega}{1+gx} - mx\right) + \frac{\kappa x}{1+gx}\left(\frac{\delta\omega v}{1+r\omega} - \beta\omega - \frac{k x\omega}{1+gx}\right).$$

Therefore,

$$\frac{\partial \Psi_1}{\partial(x,\omega,v)} h(x,\omega,v) = \frac{\partial \Psi_2}{\partial(x,\omega,v)} h(x,\omega,v) = 0, \quad \text{and}$$

$$\frac{\partial \Psi_3}{\partial(x,\omega,v)} h(x,\omega,v) = \left(\frac{\partial \Psi_3}{\partial x} \ \frac{\partial \Psi_3}{\partial \omega} \ \frac{\partial \Psi_3}{\partial v}\right)\begin{pmatrix}0\\0\\1\end{pmatrix} = \frac{\kappa\delta x\omega}{(1+gx)(1+r\omega)} \neq 0.$$

Therefore, the (23) and (24) system has relative degree 3.

In the second case, we calculate the rank of matrix $\mathcal{G} = \left[h, \ ad_f h, \ ad_f^2 h\right]$ constructed from Lie brackets, and check that the distribution $\mathcal{D} = span\{h, ad_f h\}$ is involutive.

(I) Let's evaluate the second term of $\mathcal{G}$,

$$ad_f h = [f, h] = \frac{\partial h}{\partial(x,\omega,v)} f(x,\omega,v) - \frac{\partial f}{\partial(x,\omega,v)} h(x,\omega,v)$$

$$= \begin{pmatrix} 0 \\ \frac{\delta\omega}{1+r\omega} \\ -\gamma - \frac{\rho\omega}{1+r\omega} \end{pmatrix}. \tag{25}$$

Now let's calculate the third term of $\mathcal{G}$:

$ad_f^2 h = [f, ad_f h]$

$$= \begin{pmatrix} 0 & 0 & 0 \\ 0 & \frac{\delta}{(1+r\omega)^2} & 0 \\ 0 & -\frac{\rho}{(1+r\omega)^2} & 0 \end{pmatrix}\begin{pmatrix}f_1\\f_2\\f_3\end{pmatrix} - \begin{pmatrix}f_{1x} & f_{1\omega} & f_{1v}\\ f_{2x} & f_{2\omega} & f_{2v}\\ f_{3x} & f_{3\omega} & f_{3v}\end{pmatrix}\begin{pmatrix}0\\ \frac{\delta\omega}{1+r\omega}\\ -\gamma - \frac{\rho\omega}{1+r\omega}\end{pmatrix}$$

$$ad_f^2 h = \begin{pmatrix} \frac{\kappa\delta x\omega}{(1+gx)(1+r\omega)} \\ f_2 \frac{\delta}{(1+r\omega)^2} - \frac{\partial f_2}{\partial \omega}\frac{\delta\omega}{1+r\omega} + \frac{\partial f_2}{\partial v}\left(\gamma + \frac{\rho\omega}{1+r\omega}\right) \\ -f_2 \frac{\rho}{(1+r\omega)^2} - \frac{\partial f_3}{\partial \omega}\frac{\delta\omega}{1+r\omega} + \frac{\partial f_3}{\partial v}\left(\gamma + \frac{\rho\omega}{1+r\omega}\right) \end{pmatrix} \equiv \begin{pmatrix}r_1\\r_2\\r_3\end{pmatrix} \tag{26}$$

The matrix remains $\mathcal{G}$

$$\mathcal{G} = \begin{pmatrix} 0 & 0 & r_1 \\ 0 & \frac{\delta\omega}{1+r\omega} & r_2 \\ 1 & \left(-\gamma - \frac{\rho\omega}{1+r\omega}\right) & r_3 \end{pmatrix}.$$

Then $rg(\mathcal{G}) = 3$.

(II) The distribution $\mathcal{D} = span\{h, ad_f h\}$ is involutive, since:

(i) Clearly, $\{h, ad_f h\}$ is linearly independent, with $h = \begin{pmatrix}0\\0\\1\end{pmatrix}$ and

$$ad_f h = \begin{pmatrix}0\\ \frac{\delta\omega}{1+r\omega}\\ -\gamma - \frac{\rho\omega}{1+r\omega}\end{pmatrix}.$$

(ii) Let's evaluate the range of $\left[h, \, ad_f h, \, [h, \, ad_f h]\right]$.

$$rg\left[h, \, ad_f h, \, [h, \, ad_f h]\right] = rg \begin{pmatrix} 0 & 0 & 0 \\ 0 & \frac{\delta\omega}{1+r\omega} & 0 \\ 1 & (-\gamma - \frac{\rho\omega}{1+r\omega}) & 0 \end{pmatrix} = 2.$$

□

Corollary 1. *Under the conditions of the Lemma above the input-affine system, (23) and (24) are controllable.*

Proof. From the input-affine form (23) and (24), the following sets of vector field $\mathcal{L}$ are constructed, formed by the Lie brackets. $\mathcal{L} = \left\{ h, \, ad_f h, \, ad_f^2 h \right\}$. From (25) and (26), we get

$$\mathcal{L} = \left\{ \begin{pmatrix} 0 \\ 0 \\ 1 \end{pmatrix}, \, \begin{pmatrix} 0 \\ \frac{\delta\omega}{1+r\omega} \\ (-\gamma - \frac{\rho\omega}{1+r\omega}) \end{pmatrix}, \, \begin{pmatrix} r_1 \\ r_2 \\ r_3 \end{pmatrix} \right\}.$$

Then, $dim(\mathcal{L}) = 3$. □

6. Numerical Examples and Simulations

6.1. Dynamics of the State Variables of the System

The model (9) was implemented using a script written using Matlab© R2019a (Mathworks Inc., Natick, MA, USA). It is important to highlight that water is the main component of plants—approximately between 80 % and 90 % of the fresh weight in herbaceous plants, and more than 50 % in woody plants [23]. In this simulation, it has been considered for the initial values of the states that 70% corresponds to water inside the plant available for growth, and 30% corresponds to dry mass, then $x(0) = 3.0$, $\omega(0) = 7.0$ and $v(0) = v_{max} = 20.0$ (Figures 3–5). The parameter $g = 0.1$ was taken from Thornley [24]. The parameters β and γ were conditioned by **Assumption** A3, $\beta > m$ and $\gamma < m$, and we took $\beta = 0.1$, $\gamma = 0.000009$ and $m = 0.00001$ and $\kappa = 0.01$. From **Assumption** A2, $k \approx \kappa = 0.01$. Parameters δ, ρ and r were arbitrarily manipulated to fit the curves, and do not necessarily represent values associated with particular cases, with the condition imposed by **Assumption** A1, $\delta \leq \rho$.

Figure 3 presents a simulation of the system without irrigation, which allows us to appreciate the dynamics of the states, for a cultivation period of 300 days. It can be seen that the curve that represents the water available in the soil $v(t)$ (green line) approaches zero for a time t around 35, like the water available inside the plant $\omega(t)$ (black line). Additionally, the amount of dry matter $x(t)$ (red line) has strong growth of t around 30, and then very slowly decays.

The study of the behavior of the long-term solutions and their stability was carried out in order to determine the validity of the model and its construction in qualitative terms, however, for practical application purposes, the behavior of the crops in the short term is of interest for decision-making. This motivated the next numerical scenario.

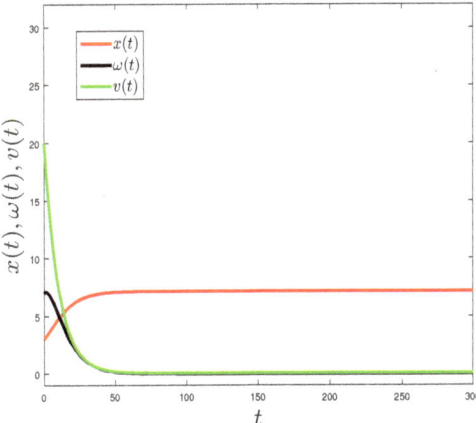

Figure 3. State dynamics for the system without irrigation, time t in days, where $v(t)$ (green line), $\omega(t)$ (black line), and $x(t)$ (red line) are the water available in the soil, the water inside the plant, and the amount of dry matter, respectively. Parameter values: $x(0) = 3.0, \omega(0) = 7.0, v(0) = 20.0$, $\kappa = 0.01, g = 0.1, m = 0.00001, \delta = 1.0, r = 20, \beta = 0.1, k = 0.01, \gamma = 0.000009, \rho = 2.0$.

6.2. Irrigation Strategy

Now we incorporate irrigation in the system (9) to analyze through simulations how irrigation of a farm field influences plant growth. For this, an irrigation function $I(t)$ is incorporated to state variable $v(t)$ of the system (9). We consider a bounded, continuous, differentiable, and periodic irrigation $I(t)$ function, Figure 6. Crop seasons were of 300 days, with irrigation during the first 200 days, an irrigation period of 32 days, with each watering lasting one day, and levels of irrigation of 30 volume units.

When applying the irrigation function $I(t)$ to the system (9), there are fluctuations in the amount of water in the soil available $v(t)$ for the growth of the plant, as shown in Figure 4. The horizontal lines mark the thresholds for the availability of water in the soil; most of the pores of Saturated soils (Sat) were occupied by water, which prevents the uptake of oxygen by the roots; Field Capacity (FC) is the amount of water in the soil after drainage; and Management Allowed Depletion (MAD) is the percentage of depletion without reduction of crop yield [6]. The vertical arrows indicate the times when irrigation is applied. Six irrigation applications were made during the season, where the first irrigation was carried out when the initial amount of water $v(0) = v_{max} = 20.0$ reached the MAD value, approximately at $t = 32$; thus, the irrigation period will be 32. The amount of water supplied in each irrigation slightly exceeds FC.

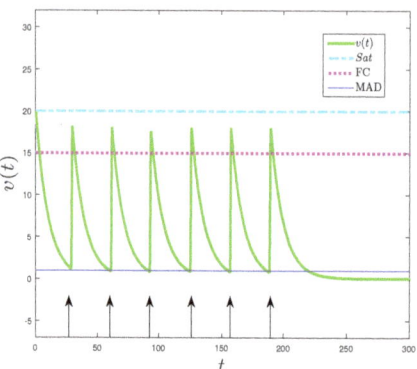

Figure 4. Soil water content $v(t)$ for the plants' growth. The horizontal lines represent the soil water thresholds, Saturated soils (Sat, upper line), Field Capacity (FC), and Management Allowed Depletion (MAD, bottom line). The vertical arrows indicate the times when irrigation is applied. Initial conditions $x(0) = 3.0, \omega(0) = 7.0, v(0) = 20.0$, parameter values $\kappa = 0.01$, $g = 0.1$, $m = 0.00001$, $\delta = 1.0, r = 20, \beta = 0.1, k = 0.01, \gamma = 0.000009, \rho = 2.0$.

Figure 5 shows the dynamics of the states of system (9) when applying the irrigation function of Figure 6. Comparing Figure 5 with Figure 3, it is possible to see how irrigation affects crop growth. The irrigation schedule allows the accumulation of dry matter $x(t)$ to increase during the irrigation period (200 days in the numerical example). When irrigation is suspended, $\omega(t)$ and $v(t)$ tend to zero, and the process of dry matter accumulation stops.

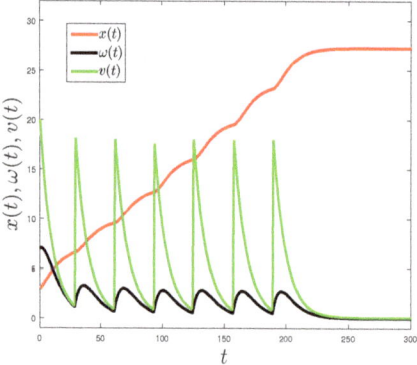

Figure 5. State dynamics for the system with irrigation, time t in days, where $v(t)$ (green line), $\omega(t)$ (black line), and $x(t)$ (red line) are the water available in the soil, the water inside the plant, and the amount of dry matter, respectively. Parameter values: $x(0) = 3.0, \omega(0) = 7.0, v(0) = 20.0, \kappa = 0.01, g = 0.1, m = 0.00001, \delta = 1.0, r = 20, \beta = 0.1, k = 0.01, \gamma = 0.000009, \rho = 2.0$.

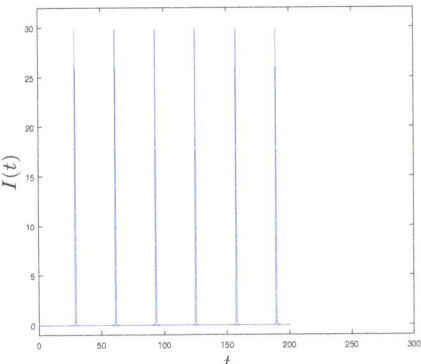

Figure 6. Irrigation function $I(t)$ in days t. This function is considered bounded, continuous, differentiable, and periodic in order to represent a realistic case. Six watering applications were considered during the season.

6.3. Assessment of the Model Performance Using Experimental Data

As our work did not have its own field data, and under the need to evaluate the performance of the proposed model, it was assessed against field data obtained from Andarzian et al. [28]. In this work, the authors presented the results from a field experiment carried out on full and deficit irrigated wheat production in Iran. Mainly, data from this research were obtained from [28] (Figure 1, page 4), which describes the soil moisture dynamics for wheat (1) under full and (2) with water deficit irrigation. The values from this figure were hand-extracted to a Comma Separated Values (CSV) file, using the WebPlotDigitizer webpage (https://automeris.io/WebPlotDigitizer/, accessed on 13 December 2021). Please consult the work of Andarzian et al. [28] for more details.

Data-processing and statistical analysis. The system (9) was solved numerically, adjusting the output $v(t)$ for the soil water content, considering the case under water deficit. This parameterization was carried out using a nonlinear least squares curve-fitting method [29], by occupying a script developed in Matlab© R2019a (Mathworks Inc., Natick, MA, USA). The actual data from the soil moisture obtained from Andarzian et al. [28] were used to fit the parameters to find the best solution. The resulting parameter values of the model that minimized the difference between simulated and measured data are presented in Table 2. The performance of the data fit is presented in Figure 7.

Table 2. Proposed model resulting parameters.

Parameters	Values	Units
κ	0.99373	$[\text{days} \times \text{mm}]^{-1}$
g	0.10390	$[\text{mm}]^{-1}$
m	1.07359	$[\text{days}]^{-1}$
δ	1.02885	$[\text{days} \times \text{mm}]^{-1}$
r	1.22763	$[\text{mm}]^{-1}$
β	1.35470	$[\text{days}]^{-1}$
k	0.01003	$[\text{days} \times \text{mm}]^{-1}$
γ	0.00001	$[\text{days}]^{-1}$
ρ	0.01146	$[\text{days} \times \text{mm}]^{-1}$

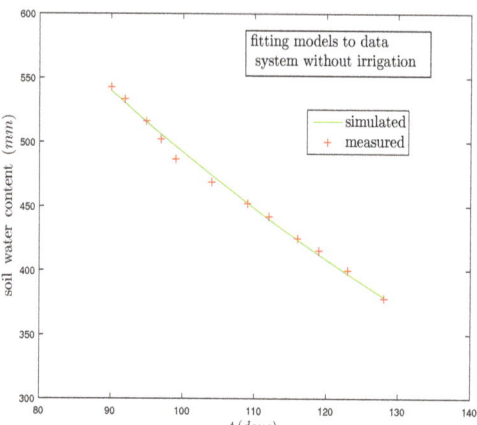

Figure 7. Model fit from the deficit irrigated wheat data (data extracted from Andarzian et al., [28].)

Then the parameters from Table 2 were used to test the proposed model, considering the simulation with irrigation $v(t)$. For this purpose, the data extracted from Andarzian et al. [28] for the experiment with full irrigation were used as ground truth, and they were compared against the proposed model's outputs. The model performance of that simulated against measured data was carried on by the classical curve fit suggested by Mayer and Butler [30]. The statistical parameters used were the Pearson's correlation coefficient (r), the Mean Absolute Error (MAE), and the Root Mean Square Error (RMSE) deviance parameters. Figure 8 shows the graphs of the simulated and measured data.

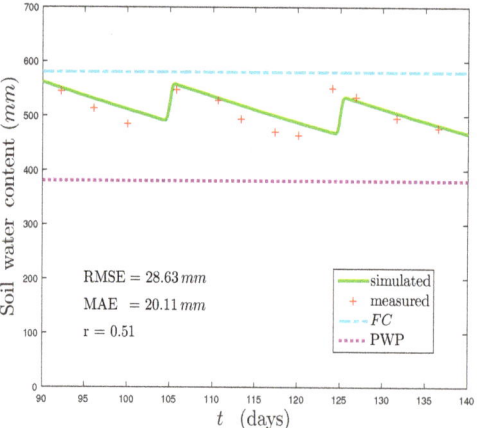

Figure 8. Soil water content trends for modeled and actual data for full irrigated wheat (using the calibrated parameters from Table 2, and measured data from Andarzian et al. [28]). Field Capacity (FC), Permanent Wilting Point (PWP), Root Mean Square Error (RMSE), Mean Absolute Error (MAE), and Pearson's correlation coefficient (r).

The performance of the modeled against measured values, depicted in Figure 8, showed good trends, highlighting the model's capabilities to simulate the soil water content behavior. The green line was very close to the measured values (orange crosses), considering a cycle of two irrigations for the experiment on wheat. Regarding the statistical validation, the r = 0.51, with an RMSE and MAE of 28.63 and 20.11 mm, can be considered acceptable for irrigation purposes [28,31,32].

7. Discussion

As far as the authors are aware, in the literature, there is a large number of works that study the irrigation phenomenon considering the SPAC system from computational simulations [6,15,20,33–36]. The models above have been described as methods to understand and reproduce the water fluxes from the root zone to the atmosphere, evaluating specific climatic scenarios and their influence on plant growth. These approaches can be used to simulate point examples, and are very useful for particular field conditions and management. In our case, the qualitative characteristics of the proposed model could allow for simulations of all situations. In the development of this model, it was assumed that the relation between irrigation and plant growth could be compartmentalized into three parts: The soil water availability, (2) the available water inside the plant for its growth, and (3) the plant size or amount of dry matter. In the construction of the model, it has been considered that the water in the soil only reduces due to the evaporation from the soil and the water consumed by the plant by the transpiration. This last flux allows the plant to photosynthesize. This phenomenon increases the plant's biomass (dry mass amount) due to the water inside the plant available for growth, considering the losses due to degradation. For the relationship between the parameters of the model (8), whose description is given in Table 1, some assumptions have been considered: the rate of flow of water from the pond (soil) to the plant (ρ) being greater or equal to the rate of flow of water entering from the soil to the plant (δ). Furthermore, the rate of accumulation of dry matter (or dry mass) (κ) is approximately equal to the rate of decrease of the water inside the plant that goes towards photosynthesis (k). Finally, the rate of flow of water corresponding to transpiration (β) is greater than the flow rate of evaporated water (γ).

The stability analysis of the proposed model was divided into two parts, with and without an external water supply. The system without an external water supply was first studied (8). Second, it was studied with an external water supply giving rise to the two models (12) and (23) based on the perturbation theory and control theory results.

For the analysis of the model, it was considered that the soil starts with a certain amount of water, the plant starts with a certain size, and at the beginning of the process, there is a certain amount of water inside the plant available for growth. These considerations were both for the system without external water supply (or irrigation) (8) and also for the systems with an external water supply, both the perturbed (12) and control (23).

The proposed mathematical model (8) without an external water supply meets the following properties: The solutions of the system are uniformly bounded, and this indicates that the states' variables do not grow indefinitely. It was also found that the system has a single equilibrium point given by (0,0,0) which is globally exponentially stable, showing that given any initial condition, the water–plant interaction does not persist in the long term.

The simulation shown in Figure 3 indicates that the proposed mathematical model allows to qualitatively account for the expected behavior in the dry matter changes of the plant as a function of the soil water, and the dynamics of the curves are in accordance with what is expected in general for the behavior of plants.

The effect of an external water supply was subsequently studied. In the first place, the external water supply was treated as a perturbation to the original model (8) through an irrigation function, obtaining the system (12). If the perturbation is bounded and null at the origin, that is, at the beginning of the process, there is no external water supply, then the equilibrium point (0,0,0) is globally exponentially stable, maintaining the stability behavior similar to the original system. If the perturbation is not null at the origin, that is, at the beginning of the process there is an external water supply, a bound was found in terms of the system parameters so that said perturbation maintains similar stability to the original system, this bound turned out to be proportional to inner rate of decrease of the soil water content (γ). Second, the irrigation was treated as a control (23) and it was found that the system is controllable by taking the size of the plant as the output state, which implies that it is theoretically possible to achieve a desired plant size level from any initial state through a continuous irrigation strategy dependent on the state variables.

Figures 4 and 5 show that when applying continuous and periodic irrigation, there are fluctuations in the amount of water in the soil available for the plant, that oscillate between the thresholds for the availability of water in the soil FC and MAD, thus achieving sustained growth of the plant. This was most evident when comparing Figures 3 and 5.

After the parameterization, the proposed model obtained an acceptable simulation of the soil water content seasonal trends (Figure 8), considering a specific calibration for field data, from an experiment on wheat. Notwithstanding, this is a specific example. The proposed model's performance should be parameterized and validated whenever tested against field data.

8. Conclusions

In this work, a mathematical model based on the SPAC system was proposed from a phenomenological paradigm to study the effect of irrigation on plant growth from a macroscopic perspective. This mathematical approach has been focused on increasing the understanding of plant–water relation growth dynamics from a qualitative point of view.

A contribution of this work is that it provides a mathematical simplified model to describe the dynamic of the water from the root zone to the plant, their interactions, and how they affect plant growth. This is the first attempt to approximate such a phenomenon in a simple way.

The application of the model to actual data resulted in an acceptable performance for wheat irrigation, considering specific parameters calibration. For future work, it is expected to adjust the model with the results of other field experiments quantitatively. Their potential for use and limitations will depend on its configuration and calibration using ground truth data. Its simplicity, if adequately parameterized, could lead to obtaining representative simulations for more specific purposes, such as irrigation management. As indicated herein, the complex interactions among the soil water availability, water availability, and plant growth open new needs for exploring an adjustment to the proposed model.

Author Contributions: V.D.-G., A.R.-P. and M.C.-B., conceived this research. V.D.-G. and A.R.-P., contributed to the mathematical model development and analyses. All authors worked extensively in the preparation of the whole manuscript, the results interpretation and their discussions. All subsequent revisions were done in the same way. All authors have read and agreed to the published version of the manuscript.

Funding: This study was partially supported by the Doctorate Scholarship of the Universidad Católica del Maule, and the Chilean government through the Agencia Nacional de Investigación y Desarrollo (ANID), throughout the "Programa FONDECYT Iniciación en la Investigación, año 2017" (grant No. 11170323).

Institutional Review Board Statement: Not applicable.

Informed Consent Statement: Not applicable.

Data Availability Statement: Not applicable

Conflicts of Interest: The authors declare no conflict of interest.

References

1. Prudhomme, C.; Giuntoli, I.; Robinson, E.L.; Clark, D.B.; Arnell, N.W.; Dankers, R.; Fekete, B.M.; Franssen, W.; Gerten, D.; Gosling, S.N.; et al. Hydrological droughts in the 21st century, hotspots and uncertainties from a global multimodel ensemble experiment. *Proc. Natl. Acad. Sci. USA* **2014**, *111*, 3262–3267. [CrossRef]
2. Aldunce, P.; Araya, D.; Sapiain, R.; Ramos, I.; Lillo, G.; Urquiza, A.; Garreaud, R. Local perception of drought impacts in a changing climate: The mega-drought in central Chile. *Sustainability* **2017**, *9*, 2053. [CrossRef]
3. Duque-Marín, E.; Rojas-Palma, A.; Carrasco-Benavides, M. Mathematical modeling of fruit trees' growth under scarce watering. *J. Phys. Conf. Ser.* **2021**, *2046*, 012017. [CrossRef]
4. Rosegrant, M.W.; Ringler, C.; Zhu, T. Water for agriculture: Maintaining food security under growing scarcity. *Annu. Rev. Environ. Resour.* **2009**, *34*, 205–222. [CrossRef]

5. FAO. *AQUASTAT Main Database-Food and Agriculture Organization of the United Nations (FAO)*; FAO: Rome, Italy, 2015.
6. Waller, P.; Yitayew, M. *Irrigation and Drainage Engineering*; Springer: Berlin/Heidelberg, Germany, 2015.
7. Romero, M.; Luo, Y.; Su, B.; Fuentes, S. Vineyard Water Status Estimation Using Multispectral Imagery from an UAV Platform and Machine Learning Algorithms for Irrigation Scheduling Management. *Comput. Electron. Agric.* **2018**, *147*, 109–117. [CrossRef]
8. ODEPA. Chilean Agriculture Overview 2017. Available online: https://www.odepa.gob.cl/wp-content/uploads/2017/12/panoramaFinal20102017Web.pdf (accessed on 3 March 2021).
9. ODEPA. Chilean Agriculture Overview 2018. Available online: https://www.odepa.gob.cl/wp-content/uploads/2018/01/ReflexDesaf(_)2030-1.pdf (accessed on 3 March 2021).
10. Kharrou, M.H.; Er-Raki, S.; Chehbouni, A.; Duchemin, B.; Simonneaux, V.; LePage, M.; Ouzine, L.; Jarlan, L. Water use efficiency and yield of winter wheat under different irrigation regimes in a semi-arid region. *Agric. Sci. China* **2011**, *2*, 273–282. [CrossRef]
11. Pereira, L.S. Water, agriculture and food: Challenges and issues. *Water Resour. Manag.* **2017**, *31*, 2985–2999. [CrossRef]
12. Gurovich, L.A.; Riveros, L.F. Agronomic operation and maintenance of field irrigation systems. In *Irrigation-Water Productivity and Operation, Sustainability and Climate Change*; IntechOpen: London, UK, 2019; p. 84997. [CrossRef]
13. Belaqziz, S.; Mangiarotti, S.; Le Page, M.; Khabba, S.; Er-Raki, S.; Agouti, T.; Drapeau, L.; Kharrou, M.; El Adnani, M.; Jarlan, L. Irrigation scheduling of a classical gravity network based on the Covariance Matrix Adaptation—Evolutionary Strategy algorithm. *Comput. Electron. Agric.* **2014**, *102*, 64–72. [CrossRef]
14. Bonan, G.; Williams, M.; Fisher, R.; Oleson, K. Modeling stomatal conductance in the earth system: Linking leaf water-use efficiency and water transport along the soil–plant–atmosphere continuum. *Geosci. Model Dev.* **2014**, *7*, 2193–2222. [CrossRef]
15. Oteng-Darko, P.; Yeboah, S.; Addy, S.; Amponsah, S.; Danquah, E.O. Crop modeling: A tool for agricultural research—A. *J. Agric. Res. Dev.* **2013**, *2*, 001–006.
16. Roose, T.; Schnepf, A. Mathematical models of plant–soil interaction. *Philos. Trans. R. Soc. A* **2008**, *366*, 4597–4611. [CrossRef] [PubMed]
17. Kumar, R.; Jat, M.; Shankar, V. Evaluation of modeling of water ecohydrologic dynamics in soil–root system. *Ecol. Modell.* **2013**, *269*, 51–60. [CrossRef]
18. Shankar, V.; Hari Prasad, K.; Ojha, C.; Govindaraju, R.S. Model for nonlinear root water uptake parameter. *J. Irrig. Drain. Eng.* **2012**, *138*, 905–917. [CrossRef]
19. Enderling, H.; Wolkenhauer, O. Are all models wrong? *Comput. Syst. Oncol.* **2020**, *1*, e1008. [CrossRef] [PubMed]
20. Di Paola, A.; Valentini, R.; Santini, M. An overview of available crop growth and yield models for studies and assessments in agriculture. *J. Sci. Food Agric.* **2016**, *96*, 709–714. [CrossRef] [PubMed]
21. Fourcaud, T.; Zhang, X.; Stokes, A.; Lambers, H.; Körner, C. Plant growth modelling and applications: The increasing importance of plant architecture in growth models. *Ann. Bot.* **2008**, *101*, 1053–1063. [CrossRef]
22. Allen, R.G.; Pereira, L.S.; Raes, D.; Smith, M. *Crop Evapotranspiration-Guidelines for Computing Crop Water Requirements-FAO Irrigation and Drainage Paper 56*; FAO: Rome, Italy, 1998; Volume 300, p. D05109.
23. Azcón-Bieto, J.; Talón, M. *Fundamentos de Fisiología Vegetal España*; 2013. Available online: https://exa.unne.edu.ar/biologia/fisiologia.vegetal/FundamentosdeFisiologiaVegetal2008Azcon..pdf (accessed on 3 March 2021).
24. Thornley, J.; Johnson, I. *Plant and Crop Modelling*; Oxford University Press: Oxford, UK, 1990; pp. 458–462.
25. Nobel, P.S. *Physicochemical & Environmental Plant Physiology*; Academic Press: Cambridge, MA, USA, 1999.
26. Ruben, S.; Randall, M.; Kamen, M.; Hyde, J.L. Heavy oxygen (O18) as a tracer in the study of photosynthesis. *J. Am. Chem. Soc.* **1941**, *63*, 877–879. [CrossRef]
27. Khalil, H.K. *Nonlinear Systems*; Prentice-Hall, Inc.: Hoboken, NJ, USA, 1996; pp. 102–103.
28. Andarzian, B.; Bannayan, M.; Steduto, P.; Mazraeh, H.; Barati, M.; Barati, M.; Rahnama, A. Validation and testing of the AquaCrop model under full and deficit irrigated wheat production in Iran. *Agric. Water Manag.* **2011**, *100*, 1–8. [CrossRef]
29. Harris, D.C. Nonlinear least-squares curve-fitting with Microsoft Excel Solver. *J. Chem. Educ.* **1998**, *75*, 119. [CrossRef]
30. Mayer, D.; Butler, D. Statistical validation. *Ecol. Modell.* **1993**, *68*, 21–32. [CrossRef]
31. Carrasco-Benavides, M.; Ortega-Farías, S.; Gil, P.M.; Knopp, D.; Morales-Salinas, L.; Lagos, L.O.; de la Fuente, D.; López-Olivari, R.; Fuentes, S. Assessment of the vineyard water footprint by using ancillary data and EEFlux satellite images. Examples in the Chilean central zone. *Sci. Total Environ.* **2022**, *811*, 152452. [CrossRef] [PubMed]
32. González-Dugo, M.; González-Piqueras, J.; Campos, I.; Andréu, A.; Balbontín, C.; Calera, A. Evapotranspiration monitoring in a vineyard using satellite-based thermal remote sensing. Remote Sensing for Agriculture, Ecosystems, and Hydrology XIV. *Int. Soc. Opt. Photonics* **2012**, *8531*, 85310N.
33. Vera, J.; Conejero, W.; Mira-García, A.B.; Conesa, M.R.; Ruiz-Sánchez, M.C. Towards irrigation automation based on dielectric soil sensors. *J. Hortic. Sci. Biotechnol.* **2021**, 1–12. [CrossRef]
34. Abioye, E.A.; Abidin, M.S.Z.; Mahmud, M.S.A.; Buyamin, S.; Ishak, M.H.I.; Abd Rahman, M.K.I.; Otuoze, A.O.; Onotu, P.; Ramli, M.S.A. A review on monitoring and advanced control strategies for precision irrigation. *Comput. Electron. Agric.* **2020**, *173*, 105441. [CrossRef]
35. Capraro, F.; Tosetti, S.; Rossomando, F.; Mut, V.; Vita Serman, F. Web-based system for the remote monitoring and management of precision irrigation: A case study in an arid region of Argentina. *Sensors* **2018**, *18*, 3847. [CrossRef] [PubMed]
36. Passot, S.; Couvreur, V.; Meunier, F.; Draye, X.; Javaux, M.; Leitner, D.; Pagès, L.; Schnepf, A.; Vanderborght, J.; Lobet, G. Connecting the dots between computational tools to analyse soil–root water relations. *J. Exp. Bot.* **2019**, *70*, 2345–2357. [CrossRef]

Article

Models of Privacy and Disclosure on Social Networking Sites: A Systematic Literature Review

Lili Nemec Zlatolas *, Luka Hrgarek, Tatjana Welzer and Marko Hölbl

Faculty of Electrical Engineering and Computer Science, University of Maribor, Koroska 46, 2000 Maribor, Slovenia; luka.hrgarek@um.si (L.H.); tatjana.welzer@um.si (T.W.); marko.holbl@um.si (M.H.)
* Correspondence: lili.nemeczlatolas@um.si

Abstract: Social networking sites (SNSs) are used widely, raising new issues in terms of privacy and disclosure. Although users are often concerned about their privacy, they often publish information on social networking sites willingly. Due to the growing number of users of social networking sites, substantial research has been conducted in recent years. In this paper, we conducted a systematic review of papers that included structural equations models (SEM), or other statistical models with privacy and disclosure constructs. A total of 98 such papers were found and included in the analysis. In this paper, we evaluated the presentation of results of the models containing privacy and disclosure constructs. We carried out an analysis of which background theories are used in such studies and have also found that the studies have not been carried out worldwide. Extending the research to other countries could help with better user awareness of the privacy and self-disclosure of users on SNSs.

Keywords: structural equations modeling; social networking sites; privacy; disclosure

Citation: Nemec Zlatolas, L.; Hrgarek, L.; Welzer, T.; Hölbl, M. Models of Privacy and Disclosure on Social Networking Sites: A Systematic Literature Review. *Mathematics* **2022**, *10*, 146. https://doi.org/10.3390/math10010146

Academic Editor: Zhao Kang

Received: 29 November 2021
Accepted: 27 December 2021
Published: 4 January 2022

Publisher's Note: MDPI stays neutral with regard to jurisdictional claims in published maps and institutional affiliations.

Copyright: © 2022 by the authors. Licensee MDPI, Basel, Switzerland. This article is an open access article distributed under the terms and conditions of the Creative Commons Attribution (CC BY) license (https://creativecommons.org/licenses/by/4.0/).

1. Introduction

Nowadays, people use multiple social networking sites (SNSs) and other digital technologies, which have presented an important communication form in recent years, and are also, therefore, of great interest for researchers. SNSs are networked communication platforms where users publish their profiles that include user-supplied content, content provided by other users and data provided by the system; platforms where users can connect with other users; and a platform where users interact with user-generated content on the SNSs [1]. Facebook has been the most popular social network since 2009, with 2.89 billion monthly active users, and it is estimated that, in 2022, SNSs will reach 3.96 billion users [2]. Facebook is just one example of SNSs; however, in most research, it is used as a platform that researchers take as an example while asking users different questions regarding their use of SNSs.

User-generated content raises privacy issues, and questions on what effect privacy issues have on the disclosure of users on SNSs. Privacy is a personal boundary regulation process that regulates private information, and, depending on the context and disclosure of the information is defined as the act of revealing personal information to others [3–5]. The number of social networking users is rising, and although users are often concerned about their privacy, they often publish information on social networking sites willingly, which is also called a privacy paradox [6].

In this paper, we have searched for publications with statistical models containing both privacy and disclosure constructs. Most of the statistical models were structural equations models (SEM). The purpose of SEM is to assess model fit and test the hypotheses of the research [7]. SEM models are used in different areas, including financial operations, vaccination prediction and similar [8,9].

The motivation to start this study was to present a systematic review and analysis of state-of-the-art research in the field of privacy and disclosure on SNSs. In recent years, several studies researching the topic have been published, and the aim of this paper is also to indicate the missing links in the topic, and to show successfully presented research on this topic. This review could help future researchers to establish new models based on the existing models, and also give an overview of where the current studies were carried out and what their main findings were. This paper also presents measurement parameters for the presentation of models, and this could help with a better presentation of the research in this topic.

The systematic review only includes papers or publications containing privacy and disclosure constructs in the statistical models used. We have excluded review type research, discussions and model proposals without confirmation of the models presented. Researchers building new models with privacy and disclosure constructs on SNSs or other technologies could get a better overview of the research that has already been conducted on this topic and the missing research in the field.

The contribution of this study is to present state-of-the-art research where statistical models were formed in regard to SNSs users, their views of privacy and disclosure. Further on, a list of measurement parameters of the papers will be presented, and could be used by researchers as a checklist on what they should report in papers with statistical models.

The rest of the paper is organized as follows. In Section 2, we have reviewed existing literature and presented the background of SNSs, privacy and disclosure. In Section 3, we have defined the methodology for the systematic review, research questions, data sources, evaluation process, study criteria, data collection and literature measurement parameters. In Section 4, we have presented a bibliometric overview of the 98 selected publications, and carried out the analysis of the publications and the parameters of the papers included in the presentation of the models. A discussion of the results and the conclusion is presented in Section 5. In Appendix A, there is a full bibliometric overview of the 98 selected papers, and in Appendix B there is a table with scores for the measurement parameters of the models presented in the papers.

2. Background

This section discusses the fundamentals of privacy and disclosure in SNSs and the fundamentals of structural equations modeling (SEM), to help understand the rest of this paper. There were some systematic literature reviews done on this topic, but none of them include privacy and disclosure constructs in models where SNSs users were used as respondents to a questionnaire. In one study, the privacy paradox was explained by a systematic literature review, and other studies have focused their reviews only on privacy or disclosure constructs separately [10–15].

2.1. Privacy and Disclosure on SNSs

Privacy and disclosure on SNSs have been a topic of interest in many previous studies. Privacy presents an option where a person chooses the information they share and with whom they share it by using privacy controls on the SNSs. This is also similar to offline conversations in communication privacy management theory [16,17]. Many studies use different privacy constructs in their models; in one study there have been significant effects of information collection, profile control and general privacy concerns on privacy concerns and willingness to share users' profiles with Facebook apps [18]. In regard to privacy control, some studies show that users tend to close their profiles on Facebook if their friends also have their profiles closed [19]. The privacy paradox shows that users often have high privacy concerns, but do not put any effort into making their information private [15]. Privacy constructs are often also connected to risk, where a user evaluates the risk of posting their personal information on the SNSs [20,21]. Trust is also a construct often connected to privacy, and has an impact on the user's disclosure [22].

There are different disclosure factors in research connected to SNSs; some of them only involve self-disclosure, others also involve general information disclosure or intention to disclose information on the SNSs. Privacy constructs often have an effect on different disclosure behaviors of users on SNSs. Studies often confirm the effect of privacy concerns on self-disclosure [23,24]. Regarding information disclosure on Facebook, parents' educational influence and frequent use of SNS motivate users to be more concerned about their privacy and to disclose less information [25]. Other constructs that have some impact on the disclosure of information on SNSs are the time being spent on SNSs, the number of friends, perceived risks and benefits, the need for popularity and personality factors [26–28]. The effects of privacy concerns, trusting beliefs and information sensitivity on information disclosure were confirmed in a study on Facebook users [29]. Moreover, other studies found a significant effect of privacy constructs on self-disclosure behaviors [30–32]. Often, data mining techniques are also used for SNSs' network analysis for discovering patterns in users, and these techniques also bring a better understanding of users' behavior on SNSs [33,34].

In research, SEM or regression models are usually based on previous theories, and the theories most often referred to will be presented in the next section.

2.2. Theories on Which the Models for Privacy and Disclosure Are Based

SEM and regression models are usually built based on previously established theories. There are many theories that could be a baseline for creating new SEM or regression models. One of the most used theories is privacy calculus, where it is expected that the users' anticipated benefits and risks have an effect on sharing information on social networking sites, meaning that the users will act accordingly to what they view as costs and benefits of their information disclosure [35–37].

Another highly used theory is communication privacy management (CPM) theory, which defines privacy as the process of opening and closing boundaries to others [17]. First, if a user shares information with others, they extend the co-ownership of that information to other persons with whom they are sharing the information. Next, in the CPM theory, the control of private information is given to an individual, and the individual decides on revealing or concealing that information. Furthermore, boundary turbulence, according to the CPM theory, can occur when information that should be kept private is shared with others without the permission of the owner. This theory aligns well with SNSs, where users can control with whom they share their information.

A technology acceptance model (TAM) is also often used with SNSs. In TAM, external variables have an effect on perceived usefulness and perceived ease of use, and the latter also has an effect on perceived usefulness. Next, perceived usefulness and perceived ease of use have an effect on the attitude toward using technologies, and the attitude has an effect on the behavioral intention to use technology. The latter also has an effect on actual systems use. Although the TAM theory does not predict any privacy constructs, they are often used in the first part as external variables affecting the rest of the constructs in the proposed model. A behavioral intention to use technology is highly connected to information disclosure on SNSs [38,39].

The theory of reasoned action (TRA) proposes the effect of attitude and subjective norm on behavioral intention, and the effect of behavioral intention on actual behavior [40]. This theory separates the belief of what a person believes others would say if they share some information and the motivation of a person to share information. The theory of planned behavior (TPB) is a theory developed a bit later by one of the authors of TRA [41]. TPB uses the same model as in TRA, adding a new construct, perceived behavioral control, which has an effect on behavioral intention and behavior. The new construct presents the opportunities for performing a given behavior, where the individual with more opportunities acts so that their behavioral intention and behavior on the used technology is higher.

The above are the most commonly used theories in newly created models connected to privacy, disclosure and SNSs. There are also other theories, which could be used for creating models, but are not used so often.

2.3. Presentation of Model Results

It is crucial that scientific papers present clear results, so that they can be repeated by other researchers. When building new models and testing the relationships between proposed constructs, it is important that the background of the study is explained very clearly. That is why we looked to see if the papers have information on the constructs used in the model—this is also referred to as content validity. Next, it is important that we do a pre-test of the study on a smaller sample to test the validity of the results. Most often the models involving constructs use quantitative measures, and it is important that the reader of such a paper is informed on what kind of scale they used. Often, they use a 5-point or 7-point Likert scale to get the results for each item in the construct. Normally, people collaborating in the survey see a statement, and they have to evaluate it on a 5- or 7-point scale, for example, 1 meaning "I do not agree" and 5 meaning "I fully agree".

It is also important to know when and where the study to test the model was carried out, so in the presentation of model results, a year and preferably also the month and days of the survey should be presented, as well as the country where the survey was distributed. Next, the authors of papers with models should present their sample frame, which should include information on who was invited to participate in their study. Next, we looked for an explanation if they used random sampling or any other method for sampling. If possible, the response rate should be over 20%, where it is possible to measure this (depending on the sampling method).

In the presentation of the model's results, we were also looking for the number of participants in the survey, to evaluate if the results could be generated to a broader population. Next, it is also important to know from what age range the participants have collaborated in the survey. If, for example, the survey was sent to college students, it can possibly be generalized to a college population, but not to the whole population. Lastly, it is important that the researchers present the gender ratio of participants collaborating in the survey, again to see if this can be generalized to the general public. In the next section, we will present some measures important for presenting the results of structural equations modeling.

2.4. Structural Equations Modeling (SEM)

Quantitative studies can be analyzed in several ways. There are different ways of testing the hypothesis, but the mostly used method for building models for behavior in SNSs is structural equations modeling. There are a few steps that need to be carried out beforehand to prepare the data and analyze it [42]. To understand the steps better, we will present some basic descriptions of measures that should be published in papers presenting their models.

The authors of papers containing SEM should present what items they used to test each construct. Normally, each construct should have more items for testing the whole model. Next, it is important that the convergent validity of items is presented by measuring Cronbach's alpha, composite reliability and average variance extracted measures. Cronbach's alpha is a measure that tests to what extent multiple items for a construct belong together. Cronbach's alpha coefficient ranges from 0 to 1, and the acceptable reliability coefficient is above 0.7; in some research, authors also discuss that a coefficient above 0.6 is sufficient [43,44]. Cronbach's alpha is calculated for each construct in the model. Composite reliability is a measure of the internal consistency required in internally correlated latent variables, and its measure should be greater than 0.7 [45]. The average variance extracted measures the amount of variance captured by a construct in relation to the amount of variance due to measurement error, and it should be greater than 0.5 [46,47].

In the next step, authors of papers should present construct validity with exploratory factor analysis, carried out with factor loadings, where some items could be excluded before continuing to confirmatory factor analysis [48].

Next, confirmatory methods for the proposed model should be presented in papers with model fit to validate the proposed model. Most often presented are the chi-square statistic (C_{min}/df), the normed fit index (NFI), the goodness-of-fit (GFI), the comparative fit index (CFI) and the root mean square error of approximation (RMSEA). The recommended values for these model fits are below 0.3 for chi-square, above 0.9 for NFI, GFI and CFI, and below 0.1 for RMSEA [46,49,50].

In regression or SEM models, the path coefficient analysis and the results of the t-statistic are very important to understand the paths between different constructs. The strength and significance of each path are normally evaluated by the standardized coefficient (β), and by a t value higher than 2.0 or lower than −2.0 [51]. It is important that the authors present these results in the paper, and it is also important how they form the results. If the results are presented as a picture, a reader can see some of the path coefficient results from it right away. If they are presented in a table, the results are readable, but it takes more time to consolidate the results. Some authors also use explanations of path coefficients in text without any supporting materials such as pictures or tables. It is usually quite time consuming to find the results needed from such a form of presentation.

Next to path analysis, the coefficient of determination or variance explained (R^2) for the dependent variable also presents the degree to which the percentage of variance in the dependent variable is accounted for by the independent variables that have an effect on it [42]. The higher this percentage is, the more variance is explained in the specific dependent variable, and the fewer outer independent variables could have an effect on it.

At the end of each paper, it is important that internal validity is discussed—the model results should be compared to existing literature and explained.

3. Methodology

First, we defined the methodology to be used. The objective of our study was to carry out a systematic review of all existing models used on social networking sites with users regarding their views of privacy and disclosure.

3.1. Research Questions

In this study, we intend to answer the following research questions:
- RQ1: To what extent is privacy and disclosure behavior researched in social networking sites?
- RQ2: Which are the most commonly used background theories for the models containing privacy and disclosure constructs?
- RQ3: Do the SEM or regression models on privacy and disclosure include recommended measures for explaining the results of the model?

3.2. Data Sources

The systematic review included the following 6 electronic databases:
- Clarivate Analytics—Web of Science (WoS),
- Elsevier ScienceDirect (SD),
- Springer SpringerLink (Springer),
- Google Scholar,
- IEEE Xplore (IEEE),
- ACM Digital Library (ACM).

The review was conducted by three reviewers, and the search in all databases returned 35,588 results. Due to a lack of advanced search options in Google Scholar and SpringerLink, some results were not related to our search. Therefore, we have only included the 500 most relevant papers from Google Scholar and the 400 most relevant from SpringerLink in our research.

The query strings defined below have been used to search for relevant publications.

The search strings were created by using the research domain and the research questions as a guide.

We used the following search terms:

(("SNS" OR "SNSs" OR "OSN" OR "OSNs" OR "online social networking" OR "online social networks" OR "social networking sites" OR "social networking site" OR "Facebook") AND
 (privacy) AND

("disclosure" OR "self-disclosure" OR "Willingness to provide information" OR "information sharing") AND
("model" OR "path" OR "SEM" OR "coefficient" OR "coefficients" OR "impact" OR "PLS"))

The search in the online digital libraries was conducted in August 2021. The search query was made as broad as possible, to consider as many results as possible related to the research questions posed in this systematic review. The procedure used for searching and the selection of publications are summarized in Figure 1. The summary of the results returned for each database search is presented in Table 1.

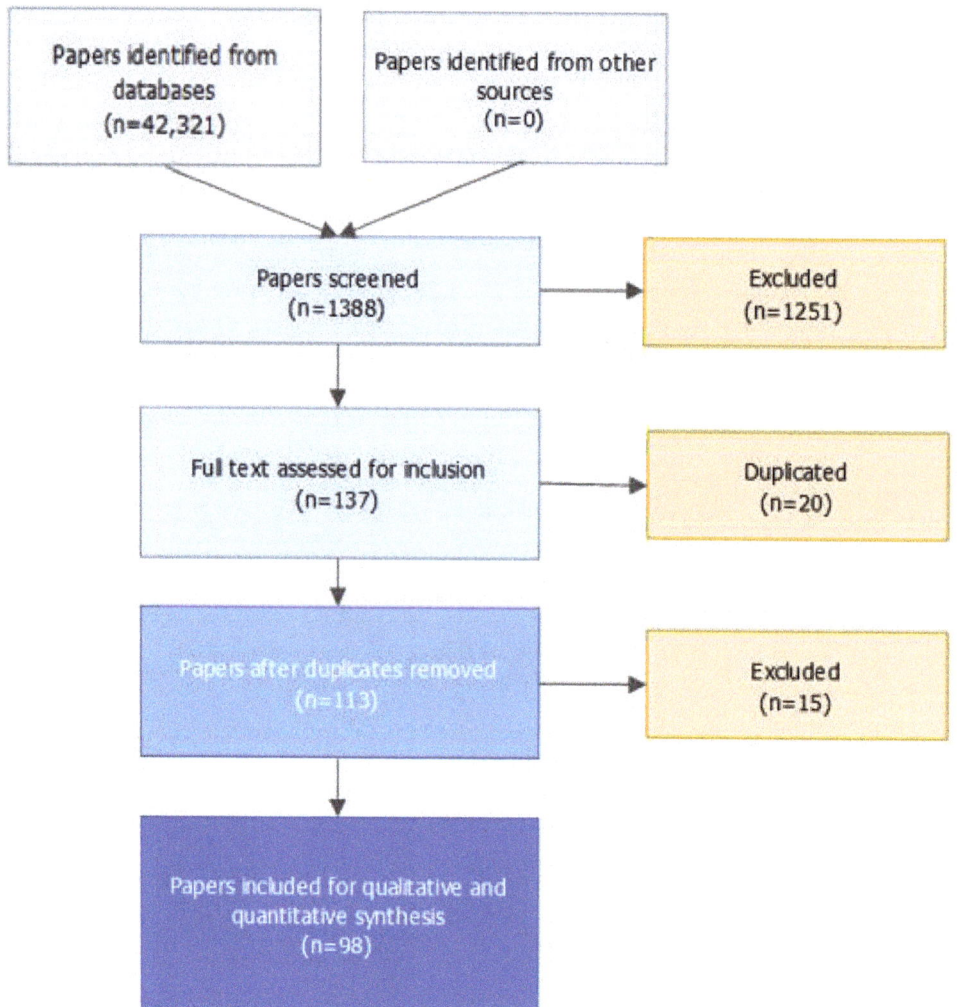

Figure 1. Flow diagram of the search.

Table 1. Summary of search results.

	Springer	IEEE	SD	ACM	WoS	Google Scholar	Total
Search done in	All text	Metadata Only	Title, abstract or keywords	Title, author keywords, abstract	Title/Topic	Relevance	
Search results (Search done on)	6733 (400)	66	47	20	355	35,100 (500)	42,321 (1388)
Number of suitable results for inclusion after screening	20	6	20	2	76	13	137
Percentage of results used for detailed screening	5.00%	9.09%	42.55%	10.00%	21.41%	2.60%	9.87%

3.2.1. Selection of Studies

The selection process started with 1388 publications gathered from online digital libraries. The publications were then included in the systematic review if they fulfilled the selection criteria. The selection process was then divided into four stages:

- Stage 1: The search results were filtered according to the inclusion and exclusion criteria. We limited our systematic review to models, done on social networking sites' users regarding their views of privacy and disclosure. We included studies from 2006 to 2022. The reason for choosing the year 2006 as the beginning of the range is the introduction of modern social networking sites to the general public, such as Facebook in 2006 [52]. The process was reviewed by three researchers.
- Stage 2: We read paper titles and abstracts, and included in the further screening only papers with SEM or regression models done on social networking sites that included privacy and disclosure factors. In cases where relevancy could not be determined from the title and abstract, we studied the entire paper to make sure that all relevant papers were included. We excluded 1251 results.
- Stage 3: We removed the duplicates from 6 different databases. There were 137 publications found, and after removing the duplicates, 113 publications were left for the next phase.
- Stage 4: A thorough reading was used to analyze the remaining results in detail. The analyzed papers had to be related closely to the research topic and questions. The remaining results also had to include social networking sites, SEM models or regression models and privacy and disclosure factors. Some results were excluded, as the models did not include social networking site analysis, or included only one of the factors needed. Altogether, 15 results were excluded.

A total of 98 publications were included in the systematic review. The selection procedure was thorough, in order to ensure that only studies were examined that were relevant and of high quality. The CASP Systematic Review Checklist [53], which addresses the assessment of research in systematic reviews, was used to manage the process of acquiring, selecting, and reviewing data for the review.

3.3. Evaluation Process

In the evaluation process, we had several stages for including the papers into the final selection:

1. Range: We extracted the relevant papers through a comprehensive search in databases and evaluated the studies based on publication date (between 2006 and 2022) and originality (we included only original research).

2. Relevance: The title and abstract were scanned for relevance to the defined objective of including a model with privacy and disclosure constructs and SNSs users.
3. Inclusion: Studies were assessed based on the stage 1 (see Section 3.2.1) rules of selection of studies.
4. Thorough examination: We conducted a full reading of the papers to see if the studies fit the defined objective, and excluded the papers that did not fit the objective.
5. Data: Studies from the selection were analyzed, and we extracted data related to the objective and research questions from each paper.
6. Quality assessment: Studies were assessed thoroughly using the 23 criteria.

3.4. Study Criteria

We set the inclusion and exclusion criteria to form the final selection of the papers. In the inclusion criteria, the following points were checked:

1. Original research study.
2. Publication on the topic of social networking sites, privacy and disclosure.
3. The publication includes a sufficient explanation of the research findings.
4. Publication years range between 2006 and 2022.

We set the inclusion and exclusion criteria to form the final selection of the papers. For the exclusion criteria, the papers with the following characteristics were excluded:

5. Secondary research, review papers and other non-relevant publications.
6. Publications presenting ideas and no results (e.g., research designs).
7. Publications presenting only privacy or only disclosure on models based on users of social networking sites.
8. Publications in any other language but English.

3.5. Data Collection

After the final 98 papers were selected, we extracted data from those papers. First, we extracted the title, authors, year of publication, publication type, publisher and number of citations on Google Scholar. After collecting this information, each paper was analyzed thoroughly, and we extracted data connected to SEM models and regression models from it.

First, we collected the information on which theory the model in the papers was based. Then, we collected data if the factors in the model were discussed. Next, we looked for information if the authors of the papers wrote that they had conducted a pre-test of the questionnaire, and in what form the questionnaire was distributed. We also checked if the authors explained the scale used for validation, and if they have published the year of research. Later, we examined the papers for specification of the sample frame, meaning if the researchers explained who was invited to participate in their survey. We also looked for information on which SNSs platform the questions were referring to, and what kind of sampling the authors used (e.g., convenience, random). Next, we also looked for information whether the response rate was over 20%. Following this, we collected the information on the country of research, the number of participants in the study, the age span of participants and their gender ratio.

Next, we collected data on the model that was presented in the paper. First, we collected the information on the type of model (SEM, PLS-SEM, regression, ...), if the authors used multi-items for testing the model, the number of constructs and number of items in the SEM model. We also collected information if the authors of the selected papers had presented convergent validity by presenting the Cronbach's alpha results, composite reliability and average variance extracted results. Further on, we searched in all papers if construct validity and the results of confirmatory methods were presented. In the latter, we extracted the results of the χ^2, NFI, GFI, CFI and RMSEA tests. Next, we collected the information on what kind of form the results of the model were presented in, and if there was internal validity or a discussion at the end of the paper. We also collected coefficient of determination (R^2) results for privacy and disclosure factors, and all the path coefficients for predictor or consequence factors of privacy or disclosure factor.

3.6. Literature Quality

We assessed the literature quality by observing the measurement parameters based on the criteria defined in Table 2. The parameters for measuring quality were based on the review of the papers involving SEM models, and some papers on how to report the results of SEM and regression models [54,55]. We collected the data from each paper, and assigned the number of points each paper got considering the full paper content. The criteria were designed to measure the quality of each paper by examining if the paper presented all the measures needed for SEM or regression models. All 98 publications were assessed by three reviewers.

Table 2. Measurement parameters.

	Parameters		Possible Points Received
1.	Theory presented		Yes—1.00, No—0.00
2.	Content validity		Yes—1.00, No—0.00
3.	Pre-test		Yes—1.00, No—0.00
4.	Scale explained		Yes—1.00, No—0.00
5.	Year of research		Yes—1.00, No—0.00
6.	Sample frame (who was invited)		Yes—1.00, No—0.00
7.	Random sampling		Yes—1.00, No—0.00
8.	Response rate over 20%		Yes—1.00, No—0.00
9.	Country of research		Yes—1.00, No—0.00
10.	Number of participants who responded to the survey		Number of participants
11.	Age of participants		Yes—1.00, No—0.00
12.	Gender ratio of participants		Yes—1.00, No—0.00
13.	Multi-item variables		Yes—1.00, No—0.00
14.	Average number of items per variable		Number of items per variable
15.		Cronbach's alpha	Yes—1.00, No—0.00
16.	Convergent validity	Composite reliability	Yes—1.00, No—0.00
17.		Average variance extracted	Yes—1.00, No—0.00
18.	Construct validity		Yes—1.00, No—0.00
19.	Confirmatory methods		Yes—1.00, No—0.00
20.	χ^2, NFI, GFI, CFI, RMSEA		0.20 points for each confirmatory method
21.	Form of the presented results		Text—0.30 points, Table—0.50 points, Picture—1.00 points
22.	Internal validity		Yes—1.00, No—0.00
23.	Coefficient of determination (R^2) results		Yes—1.00, No—0.00

Each parameter was presented to the reviewer, who assessed the number of points the paper should get in each line. The reviewers could answer the questions with a number of points. All the parameters were objective and not subject to individual judgment, but the three reviewers were used for double-checking the number of points. A higher score presents a better fulfilment of the criteria.

The reviewers also checked if the year of conducting the survey for the research (5) was written, and the sample frame (6), meaning who was invited to participate in the survey, was explained. The reviewers also checked if the authors of the selected papers stated that they used random sampling (7). The reviewers also looked for the information if the response rate of the invited participants and responding participants was over 20% (8), or the country where the research was conducted (9). For each of the parameters from 1–9 the paper could receive 0 points for not fulfilling the requirement and 1 point for fulfilling it.

Next, the reviewers wrote down the number of participants (10) in the survey from the paper presenting the sample size (the number of participants responded to the survey). If the number of participants was not stated, the paper received 0 points for that parameter. Next, if the demographical data like the age of participants (11) and gender ratio of participants (12) were written in the paper, the paper received 1 point for these two parameters.

The next parameters were oriented towards models' presentation. If the model was built with multi-item variables (13), the paper received 1 point. The average number of items per variable (14) was also collected. Next, the reviewers collected data if convergent validity was presented with three measures—Cronbach's alpha (15), composite reliability (16) and average variance extracted (17). For each of the three measures, the paper received 1 point if the authors presented the results of the measures in the paper. Also, if construct validity (18) was elaborated by exploratory factor analysis with factor loadings, the paper received 1 point. Next, the reviewers searched for information on confirmatory methods (19) in the paper. If some confirmatory methods existed, the paper received 1 point, and if methods χ^2, NFI, GFI, CFI, RMSEA (20) were presented, 0.20 point was given for each of these five methods. Next, if the results of the models (21) were presented in the text, the paper received 0.30 points, if they were presented in a table, the paper received 0.50 points, and if the results were presented in a picture, the paper received 1 point. It is a lot easier for a reader to see a picture with the results presented than to search for the correlation results in a table or text in a long paper. Finally, the paper received 1 point if internal validity (22) was present, meaning that the results were discussed thoroughly, and another point if the coefficient of determination (R^2) results (23) were presented. The analysis of these parameters are presented in Section 4.3.

4. Analysis

4.1. Bibliometric Overview

In this section, a bibliometric overview of the selected publications is presented in Figure 2. The publications from the early years of research on this topic had a higher number of citations than the ones from the last years. The reason for low citation numbers in the last years is that there was not enough time for gathering citations, but we can assume those papers will receive additional citations. Among the 98 final papers, 84 were journal papers, 13 were conference papers, and one was a book section. If we observe the publication type through the years, we can see that, in the first years, there were more conference papers or an equal amount of conference papers to journal papers. This shifted drastically from 2012, where we can see that most of the papers with the topic on social networking sites, privacy and disclosure were published in journals. In 2021, only the first part of the year is included, and that is why the number of papers on the topic is lower, but we can already see some decline in 2020 in the total number of papers, which could also be due to the SARS-CoV-2 pandemic. The research field of social networking sites remains relevant.

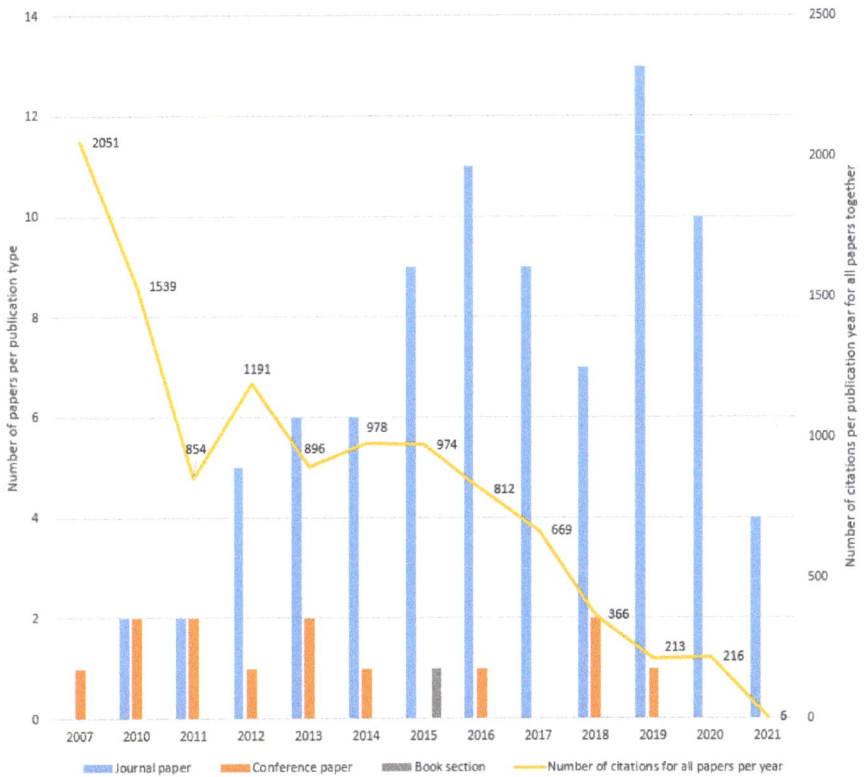

Figure 2. Number of citations for all publications per year for all papers and number of papers per publication type per year.

As presented in Table 3, in the scope of the review we found papers from 65 different publishers. Some journals or conferences published more than one paper with models on privacy and disclosure. The journal Computers in Human Behavior published 11 papers, and the Journal of the Association for Information Science and Technology published five papers on this topic. The conference where most papers with models were published was The Americas Conference on Information Systems.

Table 3. Journals or conferences in which more than one selected paper was published.

Publication Type	Journal/Conference	Number of Papers Published
Journal	Computers in Human Behavior	11
Journal	Journal of the Association for Information Science and Technology	5
Journal	Behaviour & Information Technology	4
Journal	Information Technology & People	4
Conference	AMCIS	3
Journal	International Journal of Information Management	3
Journal	Journal of Computer-Mediated Communication	3
Journal	Decision Support Systems	2
Journal	European Journal of Information Systems	2
Conference	Hawaii International Conference on System Sciences	2
Journal	Information & Management	2
Journal	Information Systems and e-Business Management	2
Journal	New Media & Society	2
Journal	Sustainability	2

4.2. Analysis of Gathered Data

Basic information on the publications is presented in Table A1. The publication ID will be used on graphs and in the tables. Presented also are the authors, the title of the paper, the year of publication and publication type as well as publisher. Out of all the papers, 84 were published in journals, 13 in conferences and one in the book section. The first paper was published in 2007.

We conducted an analysis on which theories the models in the papers were based on. As presented in Table 4, most publications used the privacy calculus theory [37] and communication privacy management (CPM) [17] theory as the basic theory behind their model. Out of 98 papers, in 40 papers, the authors did not present any broader theory as a basis for their model. In 53 papers the authors used one theory, and in five papers the authors used two different theories.

Table 4. Most commonly used background theories for the models.

Theory Used in Papers	Number of Papers the Theory Was Used in
Privacy calculus	20
Communication privacy management (CPM)	18
Technology acceptance model (TAM)	7
Theory of reasoned action (TRA)	5
Theory of planned behavior (TPB)	3
Social capital theory (SCT)	2
Protection motivation theory (PMT)	2
Construal level theory (CLT)	1
Unified Theory of Acceptance and Use of Technology (UTAUT2)	1
Concern about others' privacy (COP)	1
Disclosure of information about others (DIO)	1
Social penetration theory (SPT)	1
Social role theory (SRT)	1

The frequency of theories used in papers by publication year is shown in Figure 3. In recent years, there has been a growth of privacy calculus and CPM theories' use. The theory acceptance model (TAM) theory [38] was used in most cases until 2015.

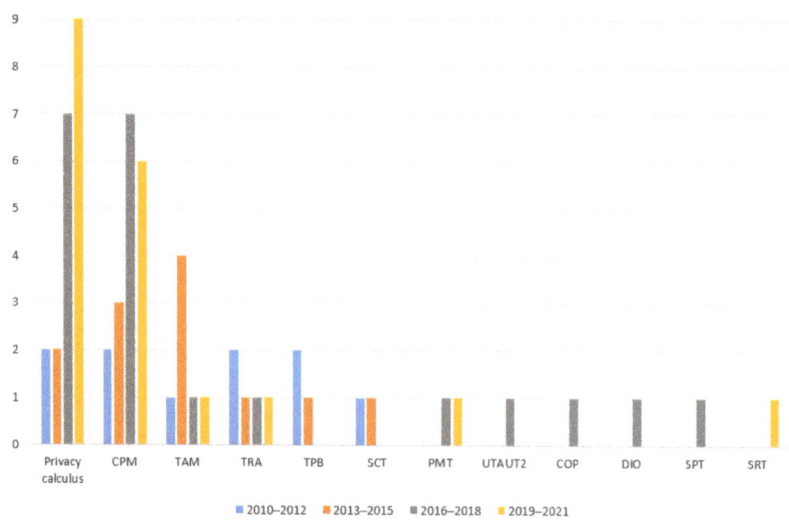

Figure 3. Frequency of theories used in papers by year of publication.

The world map in Figure 4 presents the number of studies carried out in which country. In some studies, more than one country was selected to confirm the models, so all the countries are counted leading to a total of 99 studies in 25 different countries. By continents, there were 38 studies carried out in North America, 36 in Asia, 24 in Europe and one in Africa.

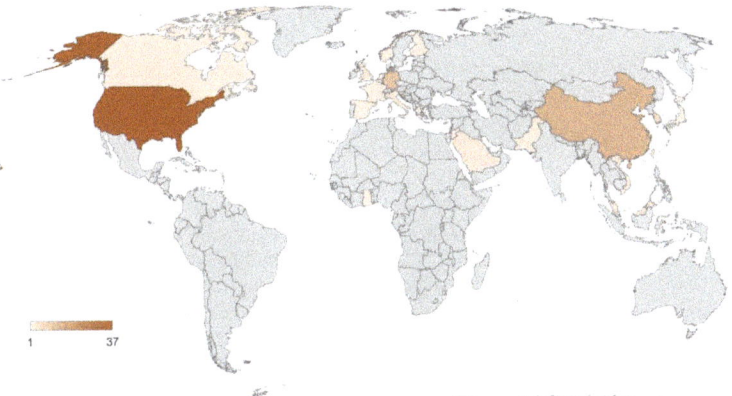

Figure 4. Number of studies done in each country.

After collecting the data from 98 papers, we also collected information on the coefficient of determination (R^2) for privacy factors in each study (if available), and the R^2 for disclosure factor in each study. R^2 presents the percentage of the variation in the dependent variable that is predictable from the independent variables [56]. We collected the R^2 for the privacy factor from 26 studies, and for the disclosure factor from 55 studies. As presented in Figure 5, we created a scatter plot of R^2 and the number of participants in those studies.

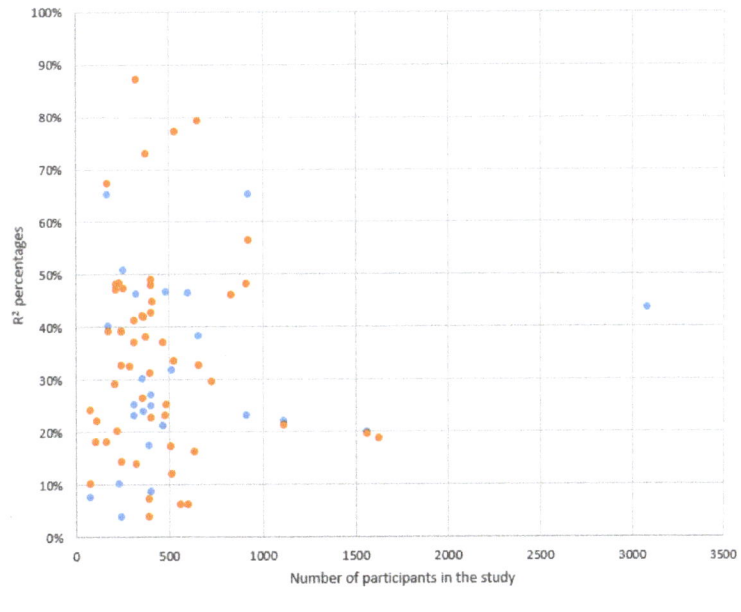

Figure 5. Coefficient of determination (R^2) for privacy and the disclosure factor in studies and the number of participants in the studies.

4.3. Analysis of the Acquired Publications

The last part of the systematic review presents the scores for measuring the number of included parameters in the selected publications in regard to a good presentation of the paper. The used methodology for scores is presented in the Literature Section on quality. In Table 2 the score of the models in the papers is presented, based on the 23 measurement parameters from Table 2.

In Table 5, minimum and maximum values, as well as means and standard deviations are presented for each of the parameters. Since most of the parameters have 0 or 1 values, the mean also presents the percentage in how many papers the measurement parameters of the paper were met. Background theory was presented in 58 papers, while content validity was not presented in just one paper. A pre-test was included in 39 papers, and an explanation of the scale used for the measurements was found in 87 papers. The year of research was presented in 42 papers, and information on who was invited to participate in the survey in all papers. Random sampling was used only in eight papers, and a response rate of over 20% was reported in nine papers. In 85 papers, the country of research was given. The average number of participants in a survey was 522 respondents, and the age of participants was reported in 86 papers. The gender ration was reported in 88 papers.

Table 5. Descriptive statistics of the measurement parameters.

			Min	Max	Mean	S.D.
1.		Theory presented	0.00	1.00	0.59	0.49
2.		Content validity	0.00	1.00	0.99	0.10
3.		Pre-test	0.00	1.00	0.40	0.49
4.		Scale explained	0.00	1.00	0.89	0.32
5.		Year of research	0.00	1.00	0.43	0.50
6.		Sample frame (who was invited)	0.00	1.00	1.00	0.00
7.		Random sampling	0.00	1.00	0.08	0.28
8.		Response rate over 20%	0.00	1.00	0.09	0.29
9.		Country of research	0.00	1.00	0.87	0.34
10.		Number of participants who responded to the survey	66	3085	521.89	527.92
11.		Age of participants	0.00	1.00	0.88	0.33
12.		Gender ratio of participants	0.00	1.00	0.90	0.30
13.		Multi-item variables	0.00	1.00	0.95	0.22
14.		Average number of items per variable	2.00	8.00	4.04	1.02
15.		Cronbach's alpha	0.00	1.00	0.79	0.41
16.	Convergent validity	Composite reliability	0.00	1.00	0.64	0.48
17.		Average variance extracted	0.00	1.00	0.70	0.46
18.		Construct validity	0.00	1.00	0.71	0.45
19.		Confirmatory methods	0.00	1.00	0.45	0.50
20.		χ^2, NFI, GFI, CFI, RMSEA	0.00	1.00	0.33	0.39
21.		Form of the presented results	0.30	1.00	0.90	0.21
22.		Internal validity	0.00	1.00	0.99	0.10
23.		Coefficient of determination (R^2) results	0.00	1.00	0.55	0.50

Multi-item variables were used in 93 papers, and the average amount of items used for models was 4.04. Convergent validity was reported with Cronbach's alpha, and composite reliability and average variance extracted in 77, 63 and 69 papers, respectively. Construct validity was reported in 70 papers, and confirmatory methods were used in 44 papers. Internal validity was discussed in 97 papers and coefficient of determination results were presented in 54 papers.

Next, we performed an ordered probit model with convergent validity (15–17) as a dependent variable, and theory presented (01), construct validity (18) and coefficient of determination (23) as independent variables. Cronbach's alpha, composite reliability and average variance extracted were summed into one dependent variable, convergent validity, having 0, 1, 2 or 3 as a result for this variable for each paper. The results of the omnibus test were significant with the likelihood ratio chi-square 46.15, which means that our proposed model containing the three predictors represents a significant improvement compared to the unconditional model. The relationship between independent variables and the dependent variable were positive, with the p-values lower than 0.05, as presented in Table 6. We can assume that these relationships are statistically significant, and that there is a statistically significant positive linear relationship between theory presented, coefficient of determination, construct validity and convergent validity. Papers that have included theory presented, coefficient of determination and construct validity have a positive effect on convergent validity, meaning that they have also likely presented convergent validity measures if they have also presented the three parameters. All three parameters are statistically significant and were tested with the Wald chi-square test.

Table 6. Results of the probit model.

Dependent Variable: Convergent Validity	B	Std. Dev.	Hypothesis Test	
			Wald Chi-Square	Sig.
Theory presented	0.837	0.256	10.675	0.001
Construct validity	1.072	0.279	14.788	0.000
Coefficient of determination	1.099	0.262	17.605	0.000

We also calculated the sum of scores for each publication by summing all points for the 23 parameters, but we divided the number of participants by 1000 and the average number of items available by 30, so that each of the parameters had similar minimum and maximum values. We also transformed the final scores to percentages for an easier graph reading. This score cannot be interpreted as a measure of quality, but it presents a number of items that were included in papers from the 23 parameters presented in Table 2. Moreover, if the authors exclude one parameter from reporting, it does not mean that it has the same scientific value as the other parameter they are reporting. The parameters are not presented in a balanced scale, but can serve as a checklist of which parameters were included in the reporting. Ideally, all the presented parameters should be included in studies explaining SEM models.

We used the sum of scores per year and per used theory in the papers, and created a graph in Figure 6. The clustered column presents the average score for all the papers that built the model based on a specific theory. In 40 papers, the authors did not use any theory as a background for building a model, and these papers had an average score of 52.95%, which was the lowest average score when comparing it to groups of papers with some background theories. In five papers, the authors used two theories as a background, and those papers were counted in each theory category. The highest sum of scores was received by the paper using the Social penetration theory (SPT). Further on, the average sum of scores per year of publication for each theory used in the papers is presented on the graph.

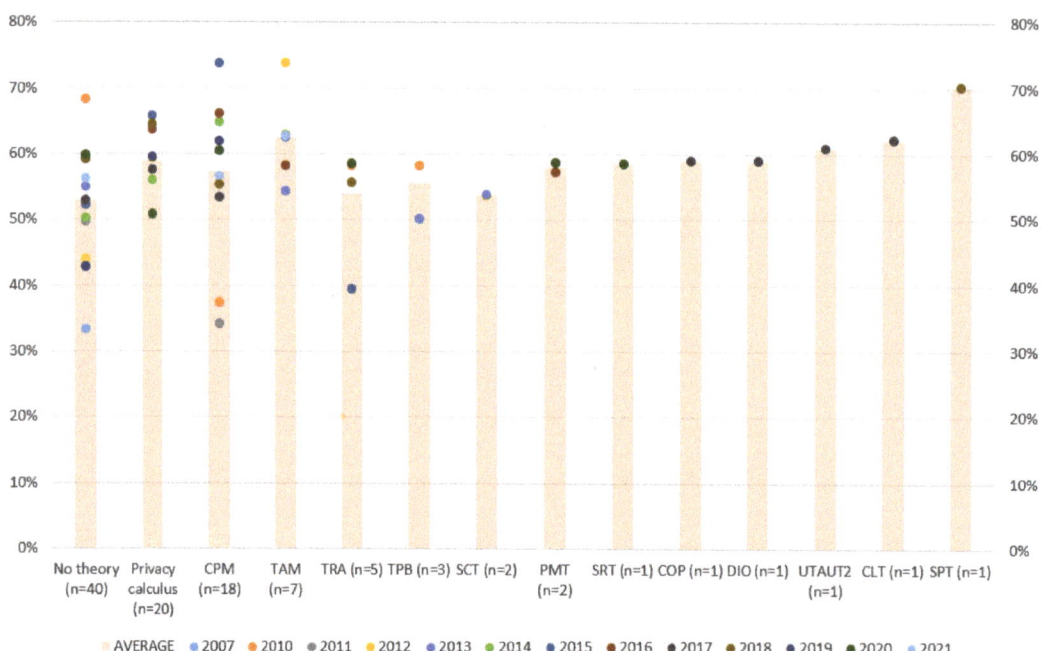

Figure 6. Average sum of scores per year of publication and theory type, and the average sum of scores for papers with theories or no theory behind the model.

As is presented in Figure 7, the graph shows the average scores per publication year and per measurement parameter. All measures have a minimum and maximum value of 0 and 1, except measures 10 and 14. Measure 10 has a minimum of 0.07 and maximum of 3.09, and the highest average of 0.96 in 2018. Measure 14 has a minimum of 0.60 and maximum of 2.40, and the highest average of 1.31. In Figure 7 the orange column presents the average amount of points received in each parameter, and the blue dots present the average amount of points per years of publication. The darker dots present more recent studies, and are more often seen above the average of the specific parameter than the lighter dots. A further detailed analysis of each parameter shows that some measures have been used more often in recent years than they were in the first years. This increase of reporting specific parameters in papers can be seen in: (1) theory presented, (16) composite reliability, (17) average variance extracted, (18) construct validity and (19, 20) confirmatory methods, Moreover, the value for parameter (10), which presents the number of participants who responded to the survey, was increasing until 2018, from 117 to 962 participants on average per year, but after that year, the number of participants decreased to 350, 462 and 356 in the years 2019, 2020 and 2021 respectively. The results show that the authors in the recent publications have improved the quality of reporting SEM or other statistical models on the topic of privacy and disclosure on SNSs.

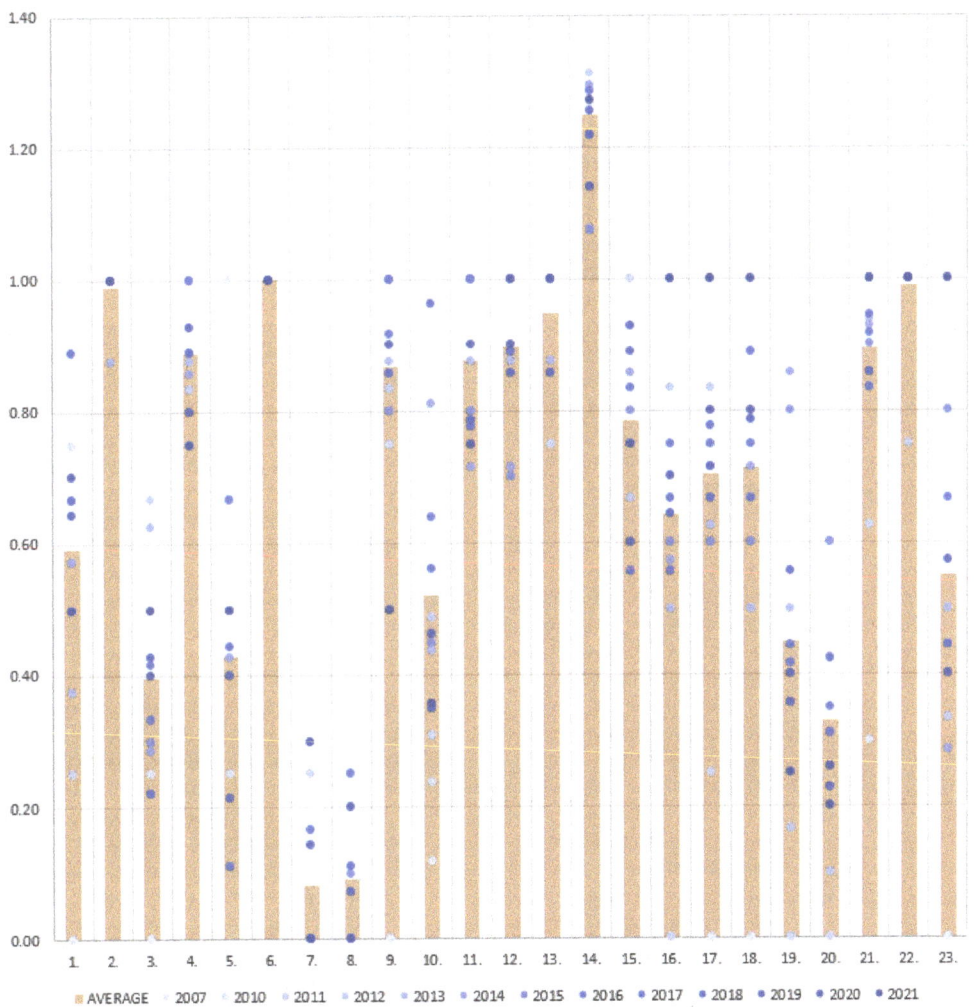

Figure 7. Average scores for each of the 23 measurement parameters by year of publication.

5. Discussion and Conclusion

In this section, we discuss the proposed research questions based on the presented analysis of the papers.

RQ1: To what extent is privacy and disclosure behaviour researched in social networking sites?

The most popular social networking site, Facebook, was founded in 2006, and has been the most popular SNS since 2009. Researchers had already started carrying out research with building models with privacy and disclosure of users in 2007, so the topic has been extensively researched for the past 14 years. In the review process, we included 98 papers containing such papers with models, found in 6 electronic databases. The number of citations these papers received are very high; papers with more than 500 citations up to now have been received by the papers published in 2007, 2010, 2012 and 2014 [57–60]. This shows that the topic is still interesting to other researchers.

The number of citations for all publications per year, summed for all papers in a year and the number of papers per publication type per year are presented in Figure 2. In the first years more conference papers were published, but, later on, journal papers prevailed.

Further on, in Table 3, we found that 65 different publishers have published papers containing models with privacy and disclosure. Among most published papers are the Computers in Human Behavior journal, which published 11 papers, and the Journal of the Association for Information Science and Technology, which published five papers on this topic.

In Figure 4, we also presented a world map, where the number of studies in each country is presented. Some studies did not have that information, and some studies were conducted in more than two countries. Altogether, the studies were carried out in 25 different countries. If we consider the continents, most studies (38) were conducted in North America, followed by 36 in Asia, 24 in Europe and one in Africa.

All our findings show that this is an active field, and none of the studies included all factors that could have an effect on privacy or disclosure factors when considering SNSs because the highest coefficient of determination presented in Figure 5 is 65% for privacy factor and 87% for disclosure factor.

RQ2: Which are the most commonly used background theories for the models containing privacy and disclosure constructs?

In this paper, we also collected information on the background theories used in the models, containing privacy and disclosure constructs, built with SNSs users. Normally, when building a model for SNSs, established theories are used as a background for newly created models. We collected information on which background theories were used in specific papers. In 40 out of 98 papers, the authors did not present any background theory. In 52 papers, the authors used one background theory, and in five papers, the authors used two different theories.

Altogether, the privacy calculus theory has been used in 20 papers, and the communication privacy management theory has been used in 18 papers. There has been a growth of these two theories' usage in the papers in recent years. The technology acceptance model (TAM) has been used in seven studies, the theory of reasoned action (TRA) in five studies, the theory of planned behavior (TPB) in three studies, and social capital theory (SCT) in two studies, but all these four theories were used mostly in the beginning of the research, mainly until 2015. Since 2016, new theories have been used in the papers, such as the protection motivation theory (PMT), the construal level theory (CLT), the unified theory of acceptance and use of technology (UTAUT2), concern about others' privacy (COP), disclosure of information about others (DIO), the social penetration theory (SPT) and the social role theory (SRT).

The analysis of the used background theories are presented in Table 4, where the number of papers the theory was used in is presented, and in Figure 3, where frequency of theories used in papers is presented by year of publication.

RQ3: Do the SEM or regression models on privacy and disclosure include recommended measures for explaining the results of the model?

In the research papers it is very important that the quality of the presented results is high. When presenting SEM or regression models, it is important to include substantial information on how the data were gathered and how the measurement items were established. Further, it is important that the analysis of results is presented in the most detailed way possible for the possibility of replication and better understanding by the reader of the analysis results. Based on the presentation of the results, the papers were given a score for the 23 measurement parameters, which we searched for in each paper. The 23 measurement parameters are presented in Table 2, their analysis in Table 5, and the individual scores given to each of the 98 papers are presented in Table 2.

The parameters with the three lowest average number of points are presented, meaning that these parameters were not presented in the papers often, and further research papers could focus on also including these parameters. First, random sampling was not mentioned in 90 out of 98 papers, which is often hard to achieve. Most commonly the convenience sampling method was used, and this method does not require random sampling. Second, the response rate was not mentioned in 89 papers, which is, again, expected if most papers are using the convenience sampling method where response rate is often difficult to track. Third, in confirmatory methods, information on the results of the $\chi 2$, NFI, GFI, CFI and RMSEA methods were collected, and 54 papers did not present any of the confirmatory methods for their models. The confirmatory methods are used for presenting model fit to validate the proposed model, and it is vital for readers to understand how the proposed model fits within the well-established methods for testing SEM models.

The results also show that papers with some background theory had a better quality of reporting the models, and that, in recent years, the amount of measurement parameters included in reporting has also improved in papers presenting privacy and disclosure in SNSs.

In sum, the research in building models with privacy and disclosure constructs in connection to SNSs is quite broad, but it is still an active field for researchers, because the SNSs are evolving. Also, the theories used as background theories are changing through time, and, most importantly, researchers need to understand that the quality of the results' presentation for statistical models is very important if they want to achieve acknowledgement.

5.1. Conclusions

This research presents a current overview of state-of-the art papers, where models have been built containing privacy and disclosure constructs in regard to SNSs' use. Many users visit Facebook and other SNSs on a daily basis. SNSs users share a great deal of personal information daily, hence the reason for privacy and disclosure being highly researched from the beginning of the use ofSNSs.

In this paper, we collected 98 papers in six online databases published between 2006 and 2022. The papers contain privacy and disclosure constructs, and were tested on SNSs' users. We defined three research questions and analyzed 98 papers according to the research questions. The selected papers are highly cited, and most studies were conducted in North America, Asia and Europe, in 25 different countries.

Our findings also indicate that papers which used background theories for their models also presented their analysis better in the paper, scoring a higher percentage for the sum of scores. In 40 out of 98 papers, the authors did not present any background theory. Next, it is crucial that the researchers present their SEM or regression models with detailed background information and analysis results, for the reader to understand the results better. The parameters that received the lowest score on average for all papers were random sampling, response rate and confirmatory methods. It is difficult to achieve random sampling because most researchers work on a budget, and that is why, usually, response rate is also not calculated, because most papers use convenience sampling methods. However, it is very important that the researchers confirm their built SEM models with confirmatory methods, which did not happen in 54 papers.

The limitation of this paper is that the sum of scores for parameters presents a weighted scale, and because most of the analyzed models were SEM, the scores were established from multiple sources to obtain broader information of the paper presentation and results. The sum of scores for papers was used in two figures and it presents a one-dimensional quality ranking of papers. However, we find that the results in the two figures present a good outline for future papers on this topic.

The limitation of this study is also that papers appearing in database searches up to August 2021 are included in the analysis, while more papers could have been published by the time the paper was published. These papers could be added for further research on this topic to extend the list of 98 extracted papers.

There is greater potential for publishing quality research work regarding privacy and disclosure models. Most of the built models also present a foundation for SNSs developers to understand the users' view of privacy, and, afterwards, users' disclosure of information. The field is still very active and important for researchers to continue their research work on SNSs to get a better understanding of SNSs information development.

Some systematic review studies have already included SEM or regression models for SNSs users, but, to the best of our knowledge, none of the studies included such a sample of models focusing on privacy and disclosure constructs [15]. Some existing literature reviews focus only on privacy constructs or disclosure, or behavior constructs separately [10–14]. No other paper has analyzed SEM and regression models with such methods.

5.2. Future Research Directions

This paper gives future researchers on this topic an overview of state-of-the-art papers containing models with privacy and disclosure constructs tested on SNSs users. In the paper, theories used in such studies as a background are presented, and may be useful for future researchers. Additionally, also presented are journals or conferences that have accepted the most papers, which is useful for authors looking for journals or conferences where they could publish their work.

There is some lack of worldwide research on this topic, because most of the studies were carried out in North America, Asia and Europe, but SNSs are used by most of the population of the world. This is a possibility of constructing the same research in parts of the world where such studies have not yet been conducted and can bring new findings in this topic. It is also important that researchers in the future studies with SEM and other statistical models present their results in detail, so that the paper reaches more readers and acknowledgements. The topic selected for this systematic review is still very active, and new research should be conducted because SNSs are also changing constantly, as well as users' opinions.

For future research, there are many studies that could be carried out to extend the current knowledge on the topic. Our research shows that privacy constructs often have an effect on disclosure constructs in SEM done on SNSs users. The highest coefficients of determination for privacy and disclosure constructs were 65% and 87%, respectively. This shows that there is opportunity for future research on finding new constructs that affect privacy or disclosure.

One systematic literature review on privacy attitude and behavior was carried out in 2017 [15]. The area of systematic literature reviews on privacy, disclosure and SNSs also lacks a thorough review of what factors have an effect on privacy and disclosure constructs, and which privacy and which disclosure constructs are used in existing models. This could give researchers a better idea of what is still not researched in the field of privacy and disclosure on SNSs.

Author Contributions: Conceptualization, L.N.Z.; methodology, L.N.Z., L.H. and M.H.; validation, L.N.Z.; formal analysis, L.N.Z., L.H. and M.H.; data curation, L.N.Z. and M.H.; supervision, T.W.; writing—original draft preparation, L.N.Z.; writing—review and editing, L.N.Z. and M.H.; visualization, L.N.Z.; funding acquisition, T.W. All authors have read and agreed to the published version of the manuscript.

Funding: The authors acknowledge the financial support from the European Union's Horizon 2020 Research and Innovation Program under the CONCORDIA project (GA No. 830927) and the Slovenian Research Agency (Research Core Funding No. P2-0057 and bilateral project BI-US/19-21-017).

Institutional Review Board Statement: Not applicable.

Informed Consent Statement: Not applicable.

Acknowledgments: The authors acknowledge the financial support from the European Union's Horizon 2020 Research and Innovation Program under the CONCORDIA project (GA No. 830927) and the Slovenian Research Agency (Research Core Funding No. P2-0057 and bilateral project BI-US/19-21-017).

Conflicts of Interest: The authors declare no conflict of interest.

Appendix A

Table A1. Bibliometric overview of selected papers.

Publication ID	Reference	Year	Authors	Title	Publication Type	Publisher
1	[57]	2007	Dwyer, C., et al.	Trust and privacy concern within social networking sites: A comparison of Facebook and MySpace	Conference	AMCIS
2	[61]	2010	Lo, J.	Privacy Concern, Locus of Control, and Salience in a Trust-Risk Model of Information Disclosure on Social Networking Sites	Conference	AMCIS
3	[62]	2010	Lo, J. and C. K. Riemenschneider	An Examination of Privacy Concerns and Trust Entities in Determining Willingness to Disclose Personal Information on a Social Networking Site	Conference	AMCIS
4	[58]	2010	Krasnova, H., et al.	Online social networks: Why we disclose	Journal	Journal of Information Technology
5	[63]	2010	Posey, C., et al.	Proposing the online community self-disclosure model: the case of working professionals in France and the U.K. who use online communities	Journal	European Journal of Information Systems
6	[64]	2011	Gibbs, J. L., et al.	First Comes Love, Then Comes Google: An Investigation of Uncertainty Reduction Strategies and Self-Disclosure in Online Dating	Journal	Communication Research
7	[65]	2011	Almadhoun, N. M., et al.	Perceived security, privacy, and trust concerns within Social Networking Sites: The role of Information sharing and relationships development in the Malaysian Higher Education Institutions' marketing	Conference	IEEE International Conference on Control System, Computing and Engineering
8	[29]	2011	McKnight, D. H., et al.	Social Networking Information Disclosure and Continuance Intention: A Disconnect	Conference	Hawaii International Conference on System Sciences
9	[66]	2011	Stutzman, F., et al.	Factors mediating disclosure in social network sites	Journal	Computers in Human Behavior
10	[67]	2012	Becker, L. and K. Pousttchi	Social networks: the role of users' privacy concerns	Conference	International Conference on Information Integration and Web-based Applications & Services

143

Table A1. Cont.

Publication ID	Reference	Year	Authors	Title	Publication Type	Publisher
11	[68]	2012	Chen, R. and S. Sharma	Understanding User Behavior at Social Networking Sites: A Relational Capital Perspective	Journal	Journal of Global Information Technology Management
12	[69]	2012	Krasnova, H., et al.	Self-disclosure and Privacy Calculus on Social Networking Sites: The Role of Culture	Journal	Business & Information Systems Engineering
13	[60]	2012	Lin, S.-W. and Y.-C. Liu	The effects of motivations, trust, and privacy concern in social networking	Journal	Service Business
14	[70]	2012	Vitak, J.	The Impact of Context Collapse and Privacy on Social Network Site Disclosures	Journal	Journal of Broadcasting & Electronic Media
15	[71]	2012	Zhao, L., et al.	Disclosure Intention of Location-Related Information in Location-Based Social Network Services	Journal	International Journal of Electronic Commerce
16	[30]	2013	Chen, R.	Living a private life in public social networks: An exploration of member self-disclosure	Journal	Decision Support Systems
17	[72]	2013	Chen, R. and S. K. Sharma	Self-disclosure at social networking sites: An exploration through relational capitals	Journal	Information Systems Frontiers
18	[73]	2013	Dhami, A., et al.	Impact of trust, security and privacy concerns in social networking: An exploratory study to understand the pattern of information revelation in Facebook	Conference	IEEE International Advance Computing Conference
19	[74]	2013	Kim, J. Y., et al.	Why people use social networking services in Korea: The mediating role of self-disclosure on subjective well-being	Journal	Information Development
20	[75]	2013	Liu, C., et al.	Cognitive, personality, and social factors associated with adolescents' online personal information disclosure	Journal	Journal of Adolescence
21	[76]	2013	Salleh, N., et al.	An Empirical Study of the Factors Influencing Information Disclosure Behaviour in Social Networking Sites	Conference	International Conference on Advanced Computer Science Applications and Technologies

Table A1. Cont.

Publication ID	Reference	Year	Authors	Title	Publication Type	Publisher
22	[23]	2013	Taddei, S. and B. Contena	Privacy, trust and control: Which relationships with online self-disclosure	Journal	Computers in Human Behavior
23	[24]	2013	Xu, F., et al.	Factors affecting privacy disclosure on social network sites: an integrated model	Journal	Electronic Commerce Research
24	[77]	2014	Sriratanaviriyakul, N., et al.	Vietnamese privacy concerns and security in using online social networks	Journal	International Journal of Electronic Security and Digital Forensics
25	[78]	2014	Alarcón-del-Amo, M.-d.-C., et al.	Adoption of social networking sites by Italian	Journal	Information Systems and e-Business Management
26	[26]	2014	Chang, C.-W. and J. Heo	Visiting theories that predict college students' self-disclosure on Facebook	Journal	Computers in Human Behavior
27	[79]	2014	Chang, L. and J. V. Chen	Aligning principal and agent's incentives: A principal–agent perspective of social networking sites	Journal	Expert Systems with Applications
28	[59]	2014	Mamonov, S. and M. Koufaris	The Impact of Perceived Privacy Breach on Sustainability of Social Networking Sites	Conference	Hawaii International Conference on System Sciences
29	[80]	2014	Sharma, S. and R. E. Crossler	Disclosing too much? Situational factors affecting information disclosure in social commerce environment	Journal	Electronic Commerce Research and Applications
30	[81]	2014	Taddicken, M.	The 'Privacy Paradox' in the Social Web: The Impact of Privacy Concerns, Individual Characteristics, and the Perceived Social Relevance on Different Forms of Self-Disclosure*	Journal	Journal of Computer-Mediated Communication
31	[82]	2015	Benson, V., et al.	Information disclosure of social media users: Does control over personal information, user awareness and security notices matter	Journal	Information Technology & People
32	[83]	2015	Azam, A.	Model for individual information privacy disclosure in social commerce environment	Journal	International Journal of Business Environment
33	[84]	2015	Chen, H.-T. and W. Chen	Couldn't or wouldn't? The influence of privacy concerns and self-efficacy in privacy management on privacy protection	Journal	Cyberpsychology, Behavior, and Social Networking

Table A1. Cont.

Publication ID	Reference	Year	Authors	Title	Publication Type	Publisher
34	[85]	2015	Cheung, C., et al.	Self-disclosure in social networking sites: The role of perceived cost, perceived benefits and social influence	Journal	Internet Research
35	[86]	2015	Ernst, C.-P. H.	Risk Hurts Fun: The Influence of Perceived Privacy Risk on Social Network Site Usage	Book section	Springer Fachmedien Wiesbaden
36	[87]	2015	Gerlach, J., et al.	Handle with care: How online social network providers' privacy policies impact users' information sharing behavior	Journal	The Journal of Strategic Information Systems
37	[88]	2015	Gupta, A. and A. Dhami	Measuring the impact of security, trust and privacy in information sharing: A study on social networking sites	Journal	Journal of Direct, Data and Digital Marketing Practice
38	[89]	2015	Min, J. and B. Kim	How are people enticed to disclose personal information despite privacy concerns in social network sites? The calculus between benefit and cost	Journal	Journal of the Association for Information Science and Technology
39	[90]	2015	Nemec Zlatolas, L., et al.	Privacy antecedents for SNS self-disclosure: The case of Facebook	Journal	Computers in Human Behavior
40	[91]	2015	Shibchurn, J. and X. Yan	Information disclosure on social networking sites: An intrinsic–extrinsic motivation perspective	Journal	Computers in Human Behavior
41	[92]	2016	Chen, H., et al.	Protecting Oneself Online:The Effects of Negative Privacy Experiences on Privacy Protective Behaviors	Journal	Journalism & Mass Communication Quarterly
42	[93]	2016	Dienlin, T. and M. J. Metzger	An Extended Privacy Calculus Model for SNSs: Analyzing Self-Disclosure and Self-Withdrawal in a Representative U.S. Sample	Journal	Journal of Computer-Mediated Communication
43	[94]	2016	Hajli, N. and X. Lin	Exploring the Security of Information Sharing on Social Networking Sites: The Role of Perceived Control of Information	Journal	Journal of Business Ethics
44	[28]	2016	Heirman, W., et al.	An open book on Facebook? Examining the interdependence of adolescents' privacy regulation strategies	Journal	Behaviour & Information Technology

Table A1. Cont.

Publication ID	Reference	Year	Authors	Title	Publication Type	Publisher
45	[95]	2016	Hina, S., et al.	A Relational Study of Critical Threats and Risks Affecting the Potential Usage of Collaborative Pattern	Journal	Global Journal of Flexible Systems Management
46	[96]	2016	Kitsiou, A., et al.	Digital privacy and social capital on social network sites. friends or foes?	Conference	ACM
47	[97]	2016	Li, K., et al.	Information privacy disclosure on social network sites: an empirical investigation from social exchange perspective	Journal	Nankai Business Review International
48	[98]	2016	Liou, D.-K., et al.	Investigating information sharing behavior: the mediating roles of the desire to share information in virtual communities	Journal	Information Systems and e-Business Management
49	[99]	2016	Malik, A., et al.	Impact of privacy, trust and user activity on intentions to share Facebook photos	Journal	Journal of Information, Communication and Ethics in Society
50	[100]	2016	Min, J.	Personal information concerns and provision in social network sites: Interplay between secure preservation and true presentation	Journal	Journal of the Association for Information Science and Technology
51	[101]	2016	Ng, M.	Factors influencing the consumer adoption of Facebook: A two-country study of youth markets	Journal	Computers in Human Behavior
52	[21]	2016	Wang, T., et al.	Intention to disclose personal information via mobile applications: A privacy calculus perspective	Journal	International Journal of Information Management
53	[102]	2017	Chen, J. V., et al.	Users' intention to disclose location on location-based social network sites (LBSNS) in mobile environment: privacy calculus and Big Five	Journal	International Journal of Mobile Communications
54	[103]	2017	Hallam, C. and G. Zanella	Online self-disclosure: The privacy paradox explained as a temporally discounted balance between concerns and rewards	Journal	Computers in Human Behavior
55	[104]	2017	Herrero, Á., et al.	Explaining the adoption of social networks sites for sharing user-generated content: A revision of the UTAUT2	Journal	Computers in Human Behavior

Table A1. Cont.

Publication ID	Reference	Year	Authors	Title	Publication Type	Publisher
56	[105]	2017	James, T. L., et al.	Exposing others' information on online social networks (OSNs): Perceived shared risk, its determinants, and its influence on OSN privacy control use	Journal	Information & Management
57	[106]	2017	Koohikamali, M., et al.	Beyond self-disclosure: Disclosure of information about others in social network sites	Journal	Computers in Human Behavior
58	[107]	2017	Liu, Q., et al.	Predicting users' privacy boundary management strategies on Facebook	Journal	Chinese Journal of Communication
59	[108]	2017	Ozdemir, Z. D., et al.	Antecedents and outcomes of information privacy concerns in a peer context: An exploratory study	Journal	European Journal of Information Systems
60	[109]	2017	Trepte, S., et al.	A Cross-Cultural Perspective on the Privacy Calculus	Journal	Social Media + Society
61	[110]	2017	Wang, L., et al.	Let the users tell the truth: Self-disclosure intention and self-disclosure honesty in mobile social networking	Journal	International Journal of Information Management
62	[111]	2018	Chen, H.-T.	Revisiting the Privacy Paradox on Social Media With an Extended Privacy Calculus Model: The Effect of Privacy Concerns, Privacy Self-Efficacy, and Social Capital on Privacy Management	Journal	American Behavioral Scientist
63	[112]	2018	Liu, Z. and X. Wang	How to regulate individuals' privacy boundaries on social network sites: A cross-cultural comparison	Journal	Information & Management
64	[113]	2018	Millham, M. H. and D. Atkin	Managing the virtual boundaries: Online social networks, disclosure, and privacy behaviors	Journal	New Media & Society
65	[114]	2018	Osatuyi, B., et al.	"Fool me once, shame on you . . . then, I learn." An examination of information disclosure in social networking sites	Journal	Computers in Human Behavior
66	[115]	2018	Proudfoot, J. G., et al.	Saving face on Facebook: privacy concerns, social benefits, and impression management	Journal	Behaviour & Information Technology

Table A1. Cont.

Publication ID	Reference	Year	Authors	Title	Publication Type	Publisher
67	[116]	2018	Salehan, M., et al.	A study of the effect of social trust, trust in social networking services, and sharing attitude, on two dimensions of personal information sharing behavior	Journal	The Journal of Supercomputing
68	[117]	2018	Tsay-Vogel, M., et al.	Social media cultivating perceptions of privacy: A 5-year analysis of privacy attitudes and self-disclosure behaviors among Facebook users	Journal	New Media & Society
69	[118]	2018	Z. H, G. O. H., et al.	Regulation of Interpersonal Boundaries and its Effect on Self-Disclosure in Social Networking Sites	Conference	International Conference on Advanced Technologies for Communications
70	[119]	2018	Zhang, N., et al.	Self-disclosure in Social Network Sites: An Integration of Stimulus-Organism-Response Paradigm and Privacy Calculus Model	Conference	WHICEB
71	[120]	2019	Kroll, T. and S. Stieglitz	Digital nudging and privacy: improving decisions about self-disclosure in social networks	Journal	Behaviour & Information Technology
72	[121]	2019	Fianu, E., et al.	The Interplay Between Privacy, Trust and Self-disclosure on Social Networking Sites	Conference	Springer International Publishing
73	[122]	2019	Lankton, N. K., et al.	Understanding the Antecedents and Outcomes of Facebook Privacy Behaviors: An Integrated Model	Journal	IEEE Transactions on Engineering Management
74	[123]	2019	Li, P., et al.	Unpacking the process of privacy management and self-disclosure from the perspectives of regulatory focus and privacy calculus	Journal	Telematics and Informatics
75	[124]	2019	Lin, S. and D. Armstrong	Beyond Information: The Role of Territory in Privacy Management Behavior on Social Networking Sites	Journal	Journal of the Association for Information Systems
76	[125]	2019	Liu, C., Lwin, M. and Ang, R.	Parents' role in teens' personal photo sharing: A moderated mediation model incorporating privacy concern and network size	Journal	Makara Human Behavior Studies In Asia
77	[126]	2019	Liu, Z., et al.	How digital natives make their self-disclosure decisions: a cross-cultural comparison	Journal	Information Technology & People

Table A1. Cont.

Publication ID	Reference	Year	Authors	Title	Publication Type	Publisher
78	[127]	2019	Liu, Z., et al.	The effect of role conflict on self-disclosure in social network sites: An integrated perspective of boundary regulation and dual process model	Journal	Information Systems Journal
79	[128]	2019	Nemec Zlatolas, L., et al.	A Model of Perception of Privacy, Trust, and Self-Disclosure on Online Social Networks	Journal	Entropy
80	[129]	2019	Oghazi, P., et al.	User self-disclosure on social network sites: A cross-cultural study on Facebook's privacy concepts	Journal	Journal of Business Research
81	[130]	2019	Sun, Y., et al.	Investigating privacy and information disclosure behavior in social electronic commerce	Journal	Sustainability
82	[131]	2019	Teubner, T. and C. M. Flath	Privacy in the sharing economy	Journal	Journal of the Association for Information Systems
83	[132]	2019	Wu, P. F.	The privacy paradox in the context of online social networking: A self-identity perspective	Journal	Journal of the Association for Information Science and Technology
84	[133]	2019	Zhang, S., et al.	Does more accessibility lead to more disclosure? Exploring the influence of information accessibility on self-disclosure in online social networks	Journal	Information Technology & People
85	[134]	2020	Li, Y., Rho, E. H. R. and Kobsa, A.	Cultural differences in the effects of contextual factors and privacy concerns on users' privacy decision on social networking sites	Journal	Behaviour & Information Technology
86	[135]	2020	Al-laymoun, O. H. and Aljaafreh, A.	Examining Users' Willingness to Post Sensitive Personal Data on Social Media	Journal	International journal of advanced computer science and applications
87	[136]	2020	Jacobson, J., et al.	Social media marketing: Who is watching the watchers	Journal	Journal of Retailing and Consumer Services
88	[137]	2020	Li, K., et al.	Voluntary sharing and mandatory provision: Private information disclosure on social networking sites	Journal	Information Processing & Management

Table A1. Cont.

Publication ID	Reference	Year	Authors	Title	Publication Type	Publisher
89	[138]	2020	Lin, X. and X. Wang	Examining gender differences in people's information-sharing decisions on social networking sites	Journal	International Journal of Information Management
90	[139]	2020	Mousavi, R., Chen, R., Kim, D. J. and Chen, K.	Effectiveness of privacy assurance mechanisms in users' privacy protection on social networking sites from the perspective of protection motivation theory	Journal	Decision Support Systems
91	[140]	2020	Trepte, S., et al.	The privacy calculus contextualized: The influence of affordances	Journal	Computers in Human Behavior
92	[141]	2020	Youn, S. and W. Shin	Adolescents' responses to social media newsfeed advertising: the interplay of persuasion knowledge, benefit-risk assessment, and ad scepticism in explaining information disclosure	Journal	International Journal of Advertising
93	[142]	2020	Zhang, R., and Fu, J. S.	Privacy Management and Self-Disclosure on Social Network Sites: The Moderating Effects of Stress and Gender	Journal	Journal of Computer-Mediated Communication
94	[143]	2020	Davazdahemami, B., Hammer, B., Kalgotra, P. and Luse, A.	From General to Situational Privacy Concerns: A New Mechanism to Explain Information Disclosure in Social Networks	Journal	Communications of the association for information systems
95	[144]	2021	Chung, K.-C., Chen, C.-H., Tsai, H.-H. and Chuang, Y.-H.	Social media privacy management strategies: A SEM analysis of user privacy behaviors	Journal	Computer Communications
96	[145]	2021	Ibrahim, M., Abdullah, A., Yulong, L., Maryah, A, and Fatmah Hussain, Q.	Gender Differentials on Information Sharing and Privacy Concerns on Social Networking Sites: Perspectives From Users	Journal	Journal of Global Information Management
97	[146]	2021	Sharif, A., Soroya, S. H., Ahmad, S. and Mahmood, K.	Antecedents of Self-Disclosure on Social Networking Sites (SNSs): A Study of Facebook Users	Journal	Sustainability
98	[147]	2021	Thompson, N. and Brindley, J.	Who are you talking about? Contrasting determinants of online disclosure about self or others	Journal	Information technology & people

B.

Table 2. Scores for measurement parameters of the presented models.

Paper ID	1.	2.	3.	4.	5.	6.	7.	8.	9.	10.	11.	12.	13.	14.	15.	16.	17.	18.	19.	20.	21.	22.	23.	Sum of Scores
1	0	1	0	1	1	1	0	0	0	117	1	1	1		1	0	0	0	0	0.0	0.3	1	0	9.42
2	1	1	0	1	0	1	0	0	1	80	1	1	1	4.17	1	1	1	1	0	0.0	1.0	1	1	16.33
3	1	1	0	1	0	1	0	0	1	80	1	1	1	4.75	1	1	1	1	0	0.0	1.0	1	1	16.51
4	0	1	1	1	1	1	0	0	1	259	1	1	1	4.00	1	1	1	1	1	0.8	1.0	1	1	19.26
5	1	1	0	0	0	1	0	0	1	529	1	1	0		0	1	0	0	0	0.0	1.0	1	1	10.53
6	0	1	1	1	1	1	1	1	0	562	1	1	1	4.29	1	0	0	0	0	0.0	0.5	1	1	15.35
7	0	1	1	1	0	1	0	0	1	66	1	1	1	3.75	1	0	0	1	0	0.0	0.5	0	0	11.69
8	0	1	0	1	0	1	0	0	1	481	1	1	1	4.86	1	0	1	1	0	0.0	1.0	1	1	14.94
9	1	1	0	0	1	1	0	0	1	122	1	1	0		1	0	0	0	0	0.0	0.5	1	0	9.62
10	1	1	1	1	1	1	0	0	1	1628	1	1	1	7.25	1	1	1	1	0	0.0	1.0	1	1	20.80
11	1	1	1	1	0	1	0	0	1	222	1	1	1	3.00	1	1	1	0	0	0.0	1.0	1	0	15.12
12	1	1	1	1	1	1	0	0	1	138	1	1	1	4.80	1	1	1	0	0	0.0	0.5	1	0	16.08
13	0	1	1	0	1	1	0	0	0	207	1	1	1		0	1	1	1	0	0.0	0.5	1	0	11.71
14	0	1	0	1	0	1	0	0	1	364	1	1	1	3.60	0	0	0	1	1	0.6	1.0	1	0	13.04
15	1	1	0	1	1	1	0	0	1	368	1	1	1	3.22	1	1	1	1	0	0.0	1.0	1	1	17.33
16	0	1	1	1	0	1	0	0	1	222	1	1	1	3.17	1	1	1	0	0	0.0	1.0	1	1	15.17
17	1	1	1	1	0	1	0	0	1	222	1	1	1	3.25	1	1	1	0	0	0.0	1.0	1	0	15.20
18	1	0	1	1	1	1	0	0	0	246	1	1	1	4.25	1	0	0	0	1	0.8	1.0	1	1	15.32
19	0	1	1	1	1	1	0	0	1	653	1	1	1	3.25	1	1	1	1	1	1.0	1.0	1	1	19.63
20	0	1	1	1	0	1	0	0	1	780	1	1	1	3.00	1	0	0	1	1	0.8	1.0	1	0	15.48
21	0	1	0	1	0	1	0	0	1	486	1	1	1	4.33	0	1	1	1	0	0.0	1.0	1	1	14.79
22	0	1	0	1	1	1	0	0	1	718	1	1	0		0	0	0	0	0	0.0	0.5	1	0	9.22
23	1	1	0	0	1	1	0	0	1	171	0	0	1	3.86	1	0	1	1	1	0.8	1.0	1	0	14.13
24	0	1	0	1	0	1	0	0	1	210	0	0	1	6.00	1	0	1	1	1	0.8	1.0	1	0	13.81
25	1	1	0	1	1	1	0	0	1	675	1	1	1	4.17	1	1	1	0	1	0.8	1.0	1	0	17.73
26	0	1	1	1	1	1	0	0	1	192	0	1	1	3.00	1	0	0	1	1	0.2	0.5	1	0	13.79
27	1	1	1	1	1	1	0	0	1	305	1	1	1	5.43	0	1	1	1	1	0.8	1.0	1	0	18.73
28	0	1	0	1	0	1	0	0	0	638	1	1	1	4.00	1	1	1	1	0	0.0	1.0	1	1	14.84
29	1	1	0	1	0	1	0	0	1	927	1	0	1	3.44	1	1	1	1	1	0.8	1.0	1	1	17.76
30	1	1	0	0	0	1	0	0	1	2739	1	1	1	4.17	1	0	0	0	1	0.8	1.0	1	0	15.79
31	1	1	0	1	0	1	0	0	0	514	0	0	1	3.00	1	0	0	0	1	0.2	0.5	1	1	11.11
32	0	1	1	1	0	1	0	0	1	170	1	0	1	3.29	1	1	1	1	1	0.8	1.0	1	1	16.96
33	0	1	0	1	1	1	0	1	1	515	0	0	1	2.60	0	0	0	0	1	0.4	1.0	1	0	11.70
34	0	1	0	1	0	1	0	0	1	405	1	1	1	3.50	0	1	1	1	0	0.0	1.0	1	1	14.46
35	0	1	0	1	0	1	0	0	1	220	1	1	1	2.67	1	1	1	1	0	0.8	1.0	1	1	16.82
36	0	1	0	1	1	1	0	0	1	1116	1	1	1	3.33	1	0	0	0	0	0.0	0.5	1	1	13.62
37	1	1	0	1	1	1	0	0	0	246	1	1	1	4.25	1	0	0	0	1	0.8	1.0	1	1	15.32

Table 2. *Cont.*

Paper ID	1.	2.	3.	4.	5.	6.	7.	8.	9.	10.	11.	12.	13.	14.	15.	16.	17.	18.	19.	20.	21.	22.	23.	Sum of Scores
39	1	1	1	1	1	1	0	0	1	661	1	1	1	3.71	1	1	1	1	1	1.0	1.0	1	1	20.78
38	1	1	0	1	0	1	0	0	1	362	1	1	1	3.83	1	1	1	1	1	1.0	1.0	1	1	18.51
40	1	1	1	1	1	1	0	0	1	273	1	1	1	5.60	1	1	1	1	1	1.0	1.0	1	0	19.95
41	1	1	0	1	1	1	1	1	1	528	1	1	1		1	0	0	0	1	0.6	1.0	1	0	16.13
42	1	1	0	1	1	1	1	0	1	1156	1	1	1	6.00	1	1	1	0	1	0.6	1.0	1	0	19.56
43	0	1	1	1	0	1	0	1	1	405	1	1	1	3.80	1	1	1	1	0	0.0	1.0	1	1	17.55
44	0	1	0	1	1	1	0	0	1	1564	1	1	1	4.20	1	0	0	1	0	0.0	1.0	1	1	15.82
45	1	1	0	1	0	1	0	0	1	380	1	1	1	3.43	1	1	1	1	0	0.0	1.0	1	1	16.41
46	0	1	1	1	1	1	0	1	1	103	1	1	1	8.00	0	0	0	0	0	0.0	1.0	1	0	14.50
47	1	1	1	1	1	1	0	0	1	291	1	1	1	2.78	1	1	1	1	1	1.0	1.0	1	1	20.12
48	0	1	1	1	1	1	0	0	1	727	1	1	1	4.13	1	1	1	1	1	1.0	1.0	1	1	19.96
49	0	1	0	1	1	1	0	0	1	378	1	1	1	4.50	1	1	1	1	0	0.0	0.5	1	1	16.23
50	1	1	0	1	0	1	0	0	1	396	1	1	1	4.00	1	1	1	1	1	1.0	1.0	1	1	18.60
51	0	1	1	1	1	1	0	0	1	476	1	1	1	3.44	1	1	1	1	0	0.0	0.5	1	0	16.01
52	1	1	0	1	0	1	0	0	0	327	1	1	1	2.86	0	1	1	1	0	0.0	1.0	1	1	14.18
53	1	1	0	0	1	1	0	0	1	298	1	1	1	3.00	0	1	1	1	0	0.0	1.0	1	0	14.20
54	1	1	1	1	0	1	0	0	1	222	1	1	1	5.00	1	0	1	1	1	0.8	1.0	1	0	17.52
55	1	1	0	1	0	1	0	0	1	537	1	1	1	3.38	1	1	1	0	1	0.6	1.0	1	1	17.15
56	1	1	1	1	0	1	0	0	1	1121	1	1	1	4.17	1	1	1	1	0	0.0	1.0	1	0	17.37
57	1	1	0	1	0	1	0	0	1	364	1	1	1	4.18	1	1	1	1	0	0.0	1.0	1	1	16.62
58	1	1	0	1	0	1	0	0	1	432	1	1	1	6.11	0	0	0	1	0	0.0	0.5	1	0	12.77
59	0	1	0	1	0	1	0	0	1	314	1	1	1	5.29	0	1	1	1	0	0.0	1.0	1	1	14.90
60	1	1	0	1	0	1	0	0	1	1550	1	1	1	2.00	1	0	0	1	1	0.6	1.0	1	0	15.75
61	1	1	1	1	0	1	0	0	1	913	1	1	1	3.44	0	1	1	1	1	0.8	1.0	1	1	18.75
62	1	1	0	1	1	1	0	1	1	3085	0	1	1	5.17	0	0	0	0	0	0.0	0.5	1	0	15.14
63	1	1	0	1	0	1	0	0	1	831	1	1	1	4.21	1	1	1	1	0	0.0	0.5	1	1	16.60
64	1	1	0	1	0	1	0	0	1	606	1	0	1	2.57	1	0	0	0	0	0.0	0.5	1	0	10.88
65	1	1	0	1	1	1	0	0	1	326	1	1	1	4.86	1	1	1	1	1	1.0	1.0	1	1	19.78
66	0	1	1	0	0	1	0	0	1	244	1	1	1	4.43	1	1	1	1	1	0.6	1.0	1	1	17.17
67	1	1	0	1	0	1	0	0	1	117	0	1	1	5.17	1	1	1	1	0	0.0	1.0	1	1	15.67
68	0	1	0	1	1	1	0	0	1	2789	1	1	1	4.33	1	0	0	0	1	0.6	1.0	1	0	16.69
69	0	1	0	1	1	1	0	0	1	454	1	1	1	3.75	1	0	1	1	1	0.6	1.0	1	0	16.18
70	1	1	1	1	0	1	0	0	1	210	1	1	1	3.13	1	1	1	1	1	1.0	1.0	1	0	18.15
71	1	1	0	1	1	1	0	0	1	382	1	1	1	3.80	1	0	0	0	0	0.0	0.5	1	0	13.02
72	1	1	0	1	0	1	0	0	1	452	0	0	1	4.71	1	1	1	1	0	0.0	0.5	1	0	13.37
73	1	1	0	1	1	1	1	1	1	305	1	1	1	5.13	1	1	1	1	0	0.0	0.5	1	0	18.34
74	1	1	0	1	1	1	1	0	1	525	1	1	1	3.43	1	0	1	1	1	0.6	1.0	1	0	18.15
75	1	1	1	1	0	1	0	0	1	168	1	1	1	5.78	1	1	1	1	1	0.6	1.0	1	1	19.50
76	0	1	0	1	0	1	0	0	0		0	0	0		1	0	0	0	0	0.0	1.0	1	0	6.00

Table 2. Cont.

Paper ID	1.	2.	3.	4.	5.	6.	7.	8.	9.	10.	11.	12.	13.	14.	15.	16.	17.	18.	19.	20.	21.	22.	23.	Sum of Scores
39	1	1	1	1	1	1	0	0	1	661	1	1	1	3.71	1	1	1	1	1	1.0	1.0	1	1	20.78
77	0	1	0	1	0	1	0	0	1	473	1	1	1	4.22	1	1	1	1	0	0.0	1.0	1	1	15.74
78	0	1	1	1	0	1	0	0	1	110	1	1	1	3.50	1	0	0	1	0	0.0	1.0	1	1	14.16
79	1	1	1	1	0	1	0	0	1	602	1	1	1	3.33	1	1	1	1	1	0.8	1.0	1	1	19.40
80	0	1	1	1	0	1	0	0	1	419	1	1	0		0	0	0	0	0	0.0	0.5	1	0	8.92
81	1	1	0	0	0	1	0	0	1	406	1	1	1	3.50	1	1	1	1	1	1.0	1.0	1	1	17.46
82	1	1	0	1	0	0	0	0	0	237	1	1	1	3.00	1	1	1	1	0	0.0	1.0	1	1	15.14
83	1	1	1	1	0	1	0	0	1	249	1	1	1	3.71	1	1	1	1	1	0.2	1.0	1	1	18.56
84	0	1	1	1	0	1	0	0	1	213	0	1	1	4.60	1	1	1	1	0	0.0	1.0	1	1	15.59
85	0	1	0	1	1	1	0	0	1	1159	1	1	1	4.86	0	0	1	1	1	0.6	1.0	1	0	16.22
86	0	1	1	1	1	0	0	0	1	515	1	1	1	3.57	1	1	1	1	0	0.0	1.0	1	1	17.59
87	0	1	1	1	1	1	1	0	1	751	1	1	1	3.38	0	1	1	1	0	0.0	1.0	1	0	16.77
88	1	1	0	0	0	1	1	1	0	310	1	1	1	2.75	1	1	1	1	0	0.0	1.0	1	0	15.14
89	1	1	1	1	0	1	0	0	1	405	0	1	1	3.57	1	1	1	1	0	0.0	1.0	1	1	16.48
90	1	1	0	1	0	1	0	0	1	315	1	1	1	4.11	1	1	1	1	0	0.0	1.0	1	1	16.55
91	1	1	0	1	0	1	0	0	1	128	1	1	1	3.50	0	0	0	0	1	0.6	1.0	1	0	12.78
92	1	0	1	0	1	0	0	0	1	305	1	0	1	5.20	0	0	0	1	1	0.8	1.0	1	0	13.67
93	1	1	0	1	1	1	1	1	1	556	1	1	1	2.71	1	1	1	0	1	0.6	1.0	1	0	18.97
94	1	1	1	0	0	1	0	0	1	180	1	1	1	4.33	1	1	1	1	0	0.0	1.0	1	1	16.48
95	1	1	1	0	0	1	0	0	0	397	1	1	1	5.17	1	1	1	1	0	0.0	1.0	1	1	15.95
96	0	1	1	1	0	1	0	0	1	412	0	1	1	3.40	1	1	1	1	1	0.8	1.0	1	1	17.23
97	1	1	0	1	1	1	0	0	1	400	1	1	1	4.17	1	1	1	1	0	0.0	1.0	1	1	17.65
98	0	1	0	1	1	1	0	0	0	216	1	1	1	4.20	0	1	1	1	0	0.0	1.0	1	1	14.48

References

1. Ellison, N.B.; Boyd, D.M. Sociality Through Social Network Sites. In *The Oxford Handbook of Internet Studies*; Dutton, W.H., Ed.; OUP Oxford: Oxford, UK, 2013.
2. Most Popular Social Networks Worldwide as of October 2021, Ranked by Number of Active Users. Available online: https://www.statista.com/statistics/272014/global-social-networks-ranked-by-number-of-users (accessed on 19 November 2021).
3. Laufer, R.S.; Wolfe, M. Privacy as a Concept and a Social Issue: A Multidimensional Developmental Theory. *J. Soc. Issues* **1977**, *33*, 22–42. [CrossRef]
4. Altman, I. *The Environment and Social Behavior: Privacy, Personal Space, Territory, and Crowding*; Brooks/Cole Pub. Co.: Monterey, CA, USA, 1975.
5. Archer, J.L. The Self in Social Psychology. In *Self-disclosure*; Wegner, D., Vallacher, R., Eds.; Oxford University: London, UK, 1980; pp. 183–204.
6. Susan, B.B. A privacy paradox: Social networking in the United States. *First Monday* **2006**, *11*, 9. [CrossRef]
7. Byrne, B.M. *Structural Equation Modeling with AMOS: Basic Concepts, Applications, and Programming*, 2nd ed.; Routledge: New York, NY, USA, 2010; p. 396.
8. Valls Martínez, M.D.C.; Martín-Cervantes, P.A.; Sánchez Pérez, A.M.; Martínez Victoria, M.D.C. Learning Mathematics of Financial Operations during the COVID-19 Era: An Assessment with Partial Least Squares Structural Equation Modeling. *Mathematics* **2021**, *9*, 2120. [CrossRef]
9. Nguyen, P.-H.; Tsai, J.-F.; Lin, M.-H.; Hu, Y.-C. A Hybrid Model with Spherical Fuzzy-AHP, PLS-SEM and ANN to Predict Vaccination Intention against COVID-19. *Mathematics* **2021**, *9*, 3075. [CrossRef]
10. Holloway, I.W.; Dunlap, S.; del Pino, H.E.; Hermanstyne, K.; Pulsipher, C.; Landovitz, R.J. Online Social Networking, Sexual Risk and Protective Behaviors: Considerations for Clinicians and Researchers. *Curr. Addict. Rep.* **2014**, *1*, 220–228. [CrossRef]

11. Jain, A.K.; Sahoo, S.R.; Kaubiyal, J. Online social networks security and privacy: Comprehensive review and analysis. *Complex Intell. Syst.* **2021**, *7*, 2157–2177. [CrossRef]
12. Malekhosseini, R.; Hosseinzadeh, M.; Navi, K. An investigation into the requirements of privacy in social networks and factors contributing to users' concerns about violation of their privacy. *Soc. Netw. Anal. Min.* **2018**, *8*, 41. [CrossRef]
13. Masrom, M.B.; Busalim, A.H.; Abuhassna, H.; Mahmood, N.H.N. Understanding students' behavior in online social networks: A systematic literature review. *Int. J. Educ. Technol. High. Educ.* **2021**, *18*, 6. [CrossRef]
14. Rehman, Z.U.; Baharun, R.; Salleh, N.Z.M. Antecedents, consequences, and reducers of perceived risk in social media: A systematic literature review and directions for further research. *Psychol. Mark.* **2020**, *37*, 74–86. [CrossRef]
15. Gerber, N.; Gerber, P.; Volkamer, M. Explaining the privacy paradox: A systematic review of literature investigating privacy attitude and behavior. *Comput. Secur.* **2018**, *77*, 226–261. [CrossRef]
16. James, T.L.; Warkentin, M.; Collignon, S.E. A dual privacy decision model for online social networks. *Inf. Manag.* **2015**, *52*, 893–908. [CrossRef]
17. Petronio, S. *Boundary of Privacy: Dialectics of Disclosure*; State University of New York Press: Albany, NY, USA, 2002.
18. Choi, B.C.F.; Land, L. The effects of general privacy concerns and transactional privacy concerns on Facebook apps usage. *Inf. Manag.* **2016**, *53*, 868–877. [CrossRef]
19. Lewis, K.; Kaufman, J.; Christakis, N. The Taste for Privacy: An Analysis of College Student Privacy Settings in an Online Social Network. *J. Comput-Mediat. Comm.* **2008**, *14*, 79–100. [CrossRef]
20. Sun, Y.; Wang, N.; Shen, X.-L.; Zhang, J.X. Location information disclosure in location-based social network services: Privacy calculus, benefit structure, and gender differences. *Comput. Hum. Behav.* **2015**, *52*, 278–292. [CrossRef]
21. Wang, T.; Duong, T.D.; Chen, C.C. Intention to disclose personal information via mobile applications: A privacy calculus perspective. *Int. J. Inf. Manag.* **2016**, *36*, 531–542. [CrossRef]
22. Lu, Y.; Yang, S.; Chau, P.Y.K.; Cao, Y. Dynamics between the trust transfer process and intention to use mobile payment services: A cross-environment perspective. *Inf. Manag.* **2011**, *48*, 393–403. [CrossRef]
23. Taddei, S.; Contena, B. Privacy, trust and control: Which relationships with online self-disclosure? *Comput. Hum. Behav.* **2013**, *29*, 821–826. [CrossRef]
24. Xu, F.; Michael, K.; Chen, X. Factors affecting privacy disclosure on social network sites: An integrated model. *Electron. Commer. Res.* **2013**, *13*, 151–168. [CrossRef]
25. Feng, Y.; Xie, W. Teens' concern for privacy when using social networking sites: An analysis of socialization agents and relationships with privacy-protecting behaviors. *Comput. Hum. Behav.* **2014**, *33*, 153–162. [CrossRef]
26. Chang, C.-W.; Heo, J. Visiting theories that predict college students' self-disclosure on Facebook. *Comput. Hum. Behav.* **2014**, *30*, 79–86. [CrossRef]
27. Hollenbaugh, E.E.; Ferris, A.L. Facebook self-disclosure: Examining the role of traits, social cohesion, and motives. *Comput. Hum. Behav.* **2014**, *30*, 50–58. [CrossRef]
28. Heirman, W.; Walrave, M.; Vermeulen, A.; Ponnet, K.; Vandebosch, H.; Van Ouytsel, J.; Van Gool, E. An open book on Facebook? Examining the interdependence of adolescents' privacy regulation strategies. *Behav. Inf. Technol.* **2016**, *35*, 706–719. [CrossRef]
29. McKnight, D.H.; Lankton, N.; Tripp, J. Social Networking Information Disclosure and Continuance Intention: A Disconnect. Proceedings of 44th Hawaii International Conference on System Sciences (HICSS), Kauai, HI, USA, 4–7 January 2011; pp. 1–10.
30. Chen, R. Living a private life in public social networks: An exploration of member self-disclosure. *Decis. Support Syst.* **2013**, *55*, 661–668. [CrossRef]
31. Krasnova, H.; Kolesnikova, E.; Guenther, O. "It won't happen to me!": Self-disclosure in online social networks. Proceedings of Americas Conference on Information Systems. San Francisco, CA, USA, 2009., August 6-9.
32. Wu, K.W.; Huang, S.Y.; Yen, D.C.; Popova, I. The effect of online privacy policy on consumer privacy concern and trust. *Comput. Hum. Behav.* **2012**, *28*, 889–897. [CrossRef]
33. Troussas, C.; Virvou, M.; Espinosa, K.J. Using Visualization Algorithms for Discovering Patterns in Groups of Users for Tutoring Multiple Languages through Social Networking. *J. Netw.* **2015**, *10*, 668–674. [CrossRef]
34. Dharsandiya, A.N.; Patel, M.R. A review on Frequent Itemset Mining algorithms in social network data. Proceedings of 2016 International Conference on Wireless Communications, Signal Processing and Networking (WiSPNET), Chennai, India, 23–25 March 2016; pp. 1046–1048.
35. Dinev, T.; Hart, P. An extended privacy calculus model for E-commerce transactions. *Inf. Syst. Res.* **2006**, *17*, 61–80. [CrossRef]
36. Krasnova, H.; Veltri, N.F. Privacy Calculus on Social Networking Sites: Explorative Evidence from Germany and USA. Proceedings of 2010 43rd Hawaii International Conference on System Sciences, Honolulu, HI, USA, 5–8 January 2010; pp. 1–10.
37. Culnan, M.J.; Armstrong, P.K. Information Privacy Concerns, Procedural Fairness, and Impersonal Trust: An Empirical Investigation. *Organ. Sci.* **1999**, *10*, 104–115. [CrossRef]
38. Davis, F.D. *A Technology Acceptance Model for Empirically Testing New End-User Information Systems: Theory and Results*; Massachusetts Institute of Technology: Cambridge, MA, USA, 1985.
39. Polančič, G.; Heričko, M.; Rozman, I. An empirical examination of application frameworks success based on technology acceptance model. *J. Syst. Softw.* **2010**, *83*, 574–584. [CrossRef]
40. Fishbein, M.; Ajzen, I. Belief, attitude, intention, and behavior: An introduction to theory and research. *Philos. Rhetor.* **1977**, *10*, 130–132.

41. Ajzen, I. From Intentions to Actions: A Theory of Planned Behavior. In *Action Control: From Cognition to Behavior*; Kuhl, J., Beckmann, J., Eds.; Springer Berlin Heidelberg: Berlin/Heidelberg, Germany, 1985; pp. 11–39.
42. Lowry, P.B.; Gaskin, J. Partial Least Squares (PLS) Structural Equation Modeling (SEM) for Building and Testing Behavioral Causal Theory: When to Choose It and How to Use It. *IEEE Trans. Prof. Commun.* **2014**, *57*, 123–146. [CrossRef]
43. Nunnaly, J. *Psychometric Theory*; McGraw-Hill: New York, NY, USA, 1978.
44. *Measures of Personality and Social Psychological Attitudes*; Academic Press: Cambridge, UK, 1991; Volume 1.
45. Chin, W.W. The partial least squares approach to structural equation modeling. *Mod. Methods Bus. Res.* **1998**, *295*, 295–336.
46. Hair, J.F. *Multivariate Data Analysis*, 7th ed.; Prentice Hall: Upper Saddle River, NJ, USA, 2010; p. 785.
47. dos Santos, P.M.; Cirillo, M.Â. Construction of the average variance extracted index for construct validation in structural equation models with adaptive regressions. *Commun. Stat. Simul. Comput.* **2021**, 1–13. [CrossRef]
48. DeCoster, J. Overview of Factor Analysis. 1998. Available online: http://www.stat-help.com/notes.html (accessed on 23 December 2021).
49. Segars, A.H.; Grover, V. Re-Examining Perceived Ease of Use and Usefulness: A Confirmatory Factor Analysis. *MIS Q.* **1993**, *17*, 517–525. [CrossRef]
50. Chin, W.W.; Todd, P.A. On the Use, Usefulness, and Ease of Use of Structural Equation Modeling in MIS Research: A Note of Caution. *MIS Q.* **1995**, *19*, 237–246. [CrossRef]
51. Al Omoush, K.S.; Yaseen, S.G.; Atwah Alma'aitah, M. The impact of Arab cultural values on online social networking: The case of Facebook. *Comput. Hum. Behav.* **2012**, *28*, 2387–2399. [CrossRef]
52. Facebook Expands to Include Work Networks. Available online: https://about.fb.com/news/2006/05/facebook-expands-to-include-work-networks-2/ (accessed on 23 August 2021).
53. Programme, C.A.S. CASP Systematic Review Checklist. Available online: https://casp-uk.b-cdn.net/wp-content/uploads/2018/03/CASP-Systematic-Review-Checklist-2018_fillable-form.pdf (accessed on 23 August 2021).
54. Hair, J.F.; Risher, J.J.; Sarstedt, M.; Ringle, C.M. When to use and how to report the results of PLS-SEM. *Eur. Bus. Rev.* **2019**, *31*, 2–24. [CrossRef]
55. Hooper, D.; Coughlan, J.; Mullen, M. Evaluating model fit: A synthesis of the structural equation modelling literature. Proceedings of 7th European Conference on Research Methodology for Business and Management Studies, London, UK, 19–20 June 2008; pp. 195–200.
56. Blunch, N.J. *Introduction to Structural Equation Modeling Using IBM SPSS Statistics and AMOS*, 2nd ed.; SAGE: Los Angeles, CA, USA, 2013; p. 303.
57. Dwyer, C.; Hiltz, S.; Passerini, K. Trust and Privacy Concern within Social Networking Sites: A Comparison of Facebook and Myspace. In *AMCIS 2007 Proceedings*; 2007; p. 339. Available online: https://aisel.aisnet.org/amcis2007/339/ (accessed on 19 November 2021).
58. Krasnova, H.; Spiekermann, S.; Koroleva, K.; Hildebrand, T. Online social networks: Why we disclose. *J. Inf. Technol.* **2010**, *25*, 109–125. [CrossRef]
59. Mamonov, S.; Koufaris, M. The Impact of Perceived Privacy Breach on Sustainability of Social Networking Sites. Proceedings of 2014 47th Hawaii International Conference on System Sciences, Waikoloa, HI, USA, 6–9 January 2014; pp. 1774–1784.
60. Lin, S.-W.; Liu, Y.-C. The effects of motivations, trust, and privacy concern in social networking. *Serv. Bus.* **2012**, *6*, 411–424. [CrossRef]
61. Lo, J. Privacy Concern, Locus of Control, and Salience in a Trust-Risk Model of Information Disclosure on Social Networking Sites. In *AMCIS 2010 Proceedings*; p. 110. Available online: https://citeseerx.ist.psu.edu/viewdoc/download?doi=10.1.1.475.529&rep=rep1&type=pdf (accessed on 19 November 2021).
62. Lo, J.; Riemenschneider, C.K. An Examination of Privacy Concerns and Trust Entities in Determining Willingness to Disclose Personal Information on a Social Networking Site. *AMCIS 2010 Proceedings*. 2010, p. 46. Available online: https://aisel.aisnet.org/amcis2010/46/ (accessed on 19 November 2021).
63. Posey, C.; Lowry, P.B.; Roberts, T.L.; Ellis, T.S. Proposing the online community self-disclosure model: The case of working professionals in France and the U.K. who use online communities. *Eur. J. Inf. Syst.* **2010**, *19*, 181–195. [CrossRef]
64. Gibbs, J.L.; Ellison, N.B.; Lai, C.-H. First Comes Love, Then Comes Google: An Investigation of Uncertainty Reduction Strategies and Self-Disclosure in Online Dating. *Commun. Res.* **2011**, *38*, 70–100. [CrossRef]
65. Almadhoun, N.M.; Dominic, P.D.D.; Lai Fong, W. Perceived security, privacy, and trust concerns within Social Networking Sites: The role of Information sharing and relationships development in the Malaysian Higher Education Institutions' marketing. Proceedings of 2011 IEEE International Conference on Control System, Computing and Engineering, Penang, Malaysia, 25–27 November 2011; pp. 426–431.
66. Stutzman, F.; Capra, R.; Thompson, J. Factors mediating disclosure in social network sites. *Comput. Hum. Behav.* **2011**, *27*, 590–598. [CrossRef]
67. Becker, L.; Pousttchi, K. Social networks: The role of users' privacy concerns. In Proceedings of the 14th International Conference on Information Integration and Web-based Applications & Services, Bali, Indonesia, 3–5 December 2012; pp. 187–195.
68. Chen, R.; Sharma, S. Understanding User Behavior at Social Networking Sites: A Relational Capital Perspective. *J. Glob. Inf. Technol. Manag.* **2012**, *15*, 25–45. [CrossRef]
69. Krasnova, H.; Veltri, N.F.; Günther, O. Self-disclosure and Privacy Calculus on Social Networking Sites: The Role of Culture. *Bus. Inf. Syst. Eng.* **2012**, *4*, 127–135. [CrossRef]

70. Vitak, J. The Impact of Context Collapse and Privacy on Social Network Site Disclosures. *J. Broadcasting Media* **2012**, *56*, 451–470. [CrossRef]
71. Zhao, L.; Lu, Y.; Gupta, S. Disclosure Intention of Location-Related Information in Location-Based Social Network Services. *Int. J. Electron. Comm.* **2012**, *16*, 53–90. [CrossRef]
72. Chen, R.; Sharma, S.K. Self-disclosure at social networking sites: An exploration through relational capitals. *Inf. Syst. Front.* **2013**, *15*, 269–278. [CrossRef]
73. Dhami, A.; Agarwal, N.; Chakraborty, T.K.; Singh, B.P.; Minj, J. Impact of trust, security and privacy concerns in social networking: An exploratory study to understand the pattern of information revelation in Facebook. Proceedings of 2013 3rd IEEE International Advance Computing Conference (IACC), Ghaziabad, India, 22–23 February 2013; pp. 465–469.
74. Kim, J.Y.; Chung, N.; Ahn, K.M. Why people use social networking services in Korea: The mediating role of self-disclosure on subjective well-being. *Inf. Dev.* **2013**, *30*, 276–287. [CrossRef]
75. Liu, C.; Ang, R.P.; Lwin, M.O. Cognitive, personality, and social factors associated with adolescents' online personal information disclosure. *J. Adolesc.* **2013**, *36*, 629–638. [CrossRef]
76. Salleh, N.; Hussein, R.; Mohamed, N.; Aditiawarman, U. An Empirical Study of the Factors Influencing Information Disclosure Behaviour in Social Networking Sites. Proceedings of 2013 International Conference on Advanced Computer Science Applications and Technologies, Kuching, Malaysia, 23–24 December 2013; pp. 181–185.
77. Sriratanaviriyakul, N.; Nkhoma, M.; Felipe, A.L.; Cao, T.K.; Tran, Q.H. Vietnamese privacy concerns and security in using online social networks. *Int. J. Electron. Secur. Digit. Forensics* **2014**, *6*, 306–318. [CrossRef]
78. Alarcón-del-Amo, M.-d.-C.; Lorenzo-Romero, C.; Del Chiappa, G. Adoption of social networking sites by Italian. *Inf. Syst. e-Bus. Manag.* **2014**, *12*, 165–187. [CrossRef]
79. Chang, L.; Chen, J.V. Aligning principal and agent's incentives: A principal–agent perspective of social networking sites. *Expert Syst. Appl.* **2014**, *41*, 3091–3104. [CrossRef]
80. Sharma, S.; Crossler, R.E. Disclosing too much? Situational factors affecting information disclosure in social commerce environment. *Electron. Commer. Res. Appl.* **2014**, *13*, 305–319. [CrossRef]
81. Taddicken, M. The 'Privacy Paradox' in the Social Web: The Impact of Privacy Concerns, Individual Characteristics, and the Perceived Social Relevance on Different Forms of Self-Disclosure*. *J. Comput-Mediat. Comm.* **2014**, *19*, 248–273. [CrossRef]
82. Benson, V.; Saridakis, G.; Tennakoon, H. Information disclosure of social media users: Does control over personal information, user awareness and security notices matter? *Inf. Technol. Amp People* **2015**, *28*, 426–441. [CrossRef]
83. Azam, A. Model for individual information privacy disclosure in social commerce environment. *Int. J. Bus. Environ.* **2015**, *7*, 302–326. [CrossRef]
84. Chen, H.-T.; Chen, W. Couldn't or wouldn't? The influence of privacy concerns and self-efficacy in privacy management on privacy protection. *Cyberpsychology Behav. Soc. Netw.* **2015**, *18*, 13–19. [CrossRef] [PubMed]
85. Cheung, C.; Lee Zach, W.Y.; Chan Tommy, K.H. Self-disclosure in social networking sites: The role of perceived cost, perceived benefits and social influence. *Internet Res.* **2015**, *25*, 279–299. [CrossRef]
86. Ernst, C.-P.H. Risk Hurts Fun: The Influence of Perceived Privacy Risk on Social Network Site Usage. In *Factors Driving Social Network Site Usage*; Springer Fachmedien Wiesbaden: Wiesbaden, Germany, 2015; pp. 45–56.
87. Gerlach, J.; Widjaja, T.; Buxmann, P. Handle with care: How online social network providers' privacy policies impact users' information sharing behavior. *J. Strateg. Inf. Syst.* **2015**, *24*, 33–43. [CrossRef]
88. Gupta, A.; Dhami, A. Measuring the impact of security, trust and privacy in information sharing: A study on social networking sites. *J. Direct Data Digit. Mark. Pract.* **2015**, *17*, 43–53. [CrossRef]
89. Min, J.; Kim, B. How are people enticed to disclose personal information despite privacy concerns in social network sites? The calculus between benefit and cost. *J. Assoc. Inf. Sci. Technol.* **2015**, *66*, 839–857. [CrossRef]
90. Nemec Zlatolas, L.; Welzer, T.; Heričko, M.; Hölbl, M. Privacy antecedents for SNS self-disclosure: The case of Facebook. *Comput. Hum. Behav.* **2015**, *45*, 158–167. [CrossRef]
91. Shibchurn, J.; Yan, X. Information disclosure on social networking sites: An intrinsic–extrinsic motivation perspective. *Comput. Hum. Behav.* **2015**, *44*, 103–117. [CrossRef]
92. Chen, H.; Beaudoin, C.E.; Hong, T. Protecting Oneself Online:The Effects of Negative Privacy Experiences on Privacy Protective Behaviors. *Journal. Mass Commun. Q.* **2016**, *93*, 409–429. [CrossRef]
93. Dienlin, T.; Metzger, M.J. An Extended Privacy Calculus Model for SNSs: Analyzing Self-Disclosure and Self-Withdrawal in a Representative, U.S. Sample. *J. Comput-Mediat. Comm.* **2016**, *21*, 368–383. [CrossRef]
94. Hajli, N.; Lin, X. Exploring the Security of Information Sharing on Social Networking Sites: The Role of Perceived Control of Information. *J. Bus. Ethics* **2016**, *133*, 111–123. [CrossRef]
95. Hina, S.; Dominic, P.D.D.; Ratnam, K.A. A Relational Study of Critical Threats and Risks Affecting the Potential Usage of Collaborative Pattern. *Glob. J. Flex. Syst. Manag.* **2016**, *17*, 373–388. [CrossRef]
96. Kitsiou, A.; Tzortzaki, E.; Sideri, M.; Gritzalis, S. Digital privacy and social capital on social network sites. In friends or foes? In Proceedings of Proceedings of the 6th Workshop on Socio-Technical Aspects in Security and Trust, Los Angeles, CA, USA, 5 December 2016; pp. 3–16.
97. Li, K.; Wang, X.; Li, k.; Che, J. Information privacy disclosure on social network sites: An empirical investigation from social exchange perspective. *Nankai Bus. Rev. Int.* **2016**, *7*, 282–300. [CrossRef]

98. Liou, D.-K.; Chih, W.-H.; Hsu, L.-C.; Huang, C.-Y. Investigating information sharing behavior: The mediating roles of the desire to share information in virtual communities. *Inf. Syst. e-Bus. Manag.* **2016**, *14*, 187–216. [CrossRef]
99. Malik, A.; Hiekkanen, K.; Dhir, A.; Nieminen, M. Impact of privacy, trust and user activity on intentions to share Facebook photos. *J. Inf. Commun. Ethics Soc.* **2016**, *14*, 364–382. [CrossRef]
100. Min, J. Personal information concerns and provision in social network sites: Interplay between secure preservation and true presentation. *J. Assoc. Inf. Sci. Technol.* **2016**, *67*, 26–42. [CrossRef]
101. Ng, M. Factors influencing the consumer adoption of Facebook: A two-country study of youth markets. *Comput. Hum. Behav.* **2016**, *54*, 491–500. [CrossRef]
102. Chen, J.V.; Su, B.C.; Quyet, H.M. Users' intention to disclose location on location-based social network sites (LBSNS) in mobile environment: Privacy calculus and Big Five. *Int. J. Mob. Commun.* **2017**, *15*, 329–353. [CrossRef]
103. Hallam, C.; Zanella, G. Online self-disclosure: The privacy paradox explained as a temporally discounted balance between concerns and rewards. *Comput. Hum. Behav.* **2017**, *68*, 217–227. [CrossRef]
104. Herrero, Á.; San Martín, H.; Garcia-De los Salmones, M.d.M. Explaining the adoption of social networks sites for sharing user-generated content: A revision of the UTAUT2. *Comput. Hum. Behav.* **2017**, *71*, 209–217. [CrossRef]
105. James, T.L.; Wallace, L.; Warkentin, M.; Kim, B.C.; Collignon, S.E. Exposing others' information on online social networks (OSNs): Perceived shared risk, its determinants, and its influence on OSN privacy control use. *Inf. Manag.* **2017**, *54*, 851–865. [CrossRef]
106. Koohikamali, M.; Peak, D.A.; Prybutok, V.R. Beyond self-disclosure: Disclosure of information about others in social network sites. *Comput. Hum. Behav.* **2017**, *69*, 29–42. [CrossRef]
107. Liu, Q.; Yao, M.Z.; Yang, M.; Tu, C. Predicting users' privacy boundary management strategies on Facebook. *Chin. J. Commun.* **2017**, *10*, 295–311. [CrossRef]
108. Ozdemir, Z.D.; Jeff Smith, H.; Benamati, J.H. Antecedents and outcomes of information privacy concerns in a peer context: An exploratory study. *Eur. J. Inf. Syst.* **2017**, *26*, 642–660. [CrossRef]
109. Trepte, S.; Reinecke, L.; Ellison, N.B.; Quiring, O.; Yao, M.Z.; Ziegele, M. A Cross-Cultural Perspective on the Privacy Calculus. *Soc. Media Soc.* **2017**, *3*, 2056305116688035. [CrossRef]
110. Wang, L.; Yan, J.; Lin, J.; Cui, W. Let the users tell the truth: Self-disclosure intention and self-disclosure honesty in mobile social networking. *Int. J. Inf. Manag.* **2017**, *37*, 1428–1440. [CrossRef]
111. Chen, H.-T. Revisiting the Privacy Paradox on Social Media With an Extended Privacy Calculus Model: The Effect of Privacy Concerns, Privacy Self-Efficacy, and Social Capital on Privacy Management. *Am. Behav. Sci.* **2018**, *62*, 1392–1412. [CrossRef]
112. Liu, Z.; Wang, X. How to regulate individuals' privacy boundaries on social network sites: A cross-cultural comparison. *Inf. Manag.* **2018**, *55*, 1005–1023. [CrossRef]
113. Millham, M.H.; Atkin, D. Managing the virtual boundaries: Online social networks, disclosure, and privacy behaviors. *New Media Soc.* **2018**, *20*, 50–67. [CrossRef]
114. Osatuyi, B.; Passerini, K.; Ravarini, A.; Grandhi, S.A. "Fool me once, shame on you … then, I learn." An examination of information disclosure in social networking sites. *Comput. Hum. Behav.* **2018**, *83*, 73–86. [CrossRef]
115. Proudfoot, J.G.; Wilson, D.; Valacich, J.S.; Byrd, M.D. Saving face on Facebook: Privacy concerns, social benefits, and impression management. *Behav. Inf. Technol.* **2018**, *37*, 16–37. [CrossRef]
116. Salehan, M.; Kim, D.J.; Koo, C. A study of the effect of social trust, trust in social networking services, and sharing attitude, on two dimensions of personal information sharing behavior. *J. Supercomput.* **2018**, *74*, 3596–3619. [CrossRef]
117. Tsay-Vogel, M.; Shanahan, J.; Signorielli, N. Social media cultivating perceptions of privacy: A 5-year analysis of privacy attitudes and self-disclosure behaviors among Facebook users. *New Media Soc.* **2018**, *20*, 141–161. [CrossRef]
118. Goh, Z.H.; Cho, H.; Li, P. Regulation of Interpersonal Boundaries and its Effect on Self-Disclosure in Social Networking Sites. In Proceedings of the 2018 International Conference on Advanced Technologies for Communications (ATC), Ho Chi Minh City, Vietnam, 18–20 October 2018; pp. 305–309.
119. Zhang, N.; Pang, J.; Wan, J. Self-Disclosure in Social Network Sites: An Integration of Stimulus-Organism-Response Paradigm and Privacy Calculus Model. In Proceedings of the International Conference on e-Business, Wuhan, China, 30 June 2018.
120. Kroll, T.; Stieglitz, S. Digital nudging and privacy: Improving decisions about self-disclosure in social networks. *Behav. Inf. Technol.* **2021**, *40*, 1–19. [CrossRef]
121. Fianu, E.; Ofori, K.S.; Boateng, R.; Ampong, G.O.A. The Interplay Between Privacy, Trust and Self-disclosure on Social Networking Sites. In *ICT Unbounded, Social Impact of Bright ICT Adoption. TDIT 2019. IFIP Advances in Information and Communication Technology*; Dwivedi, Y., Ayaburi, E., Boateng, R., Effah, J., Eds.; Springer: Cham, Switzerland, 2019; Volume 558. [CrossRef]
122. Lankton, N.K.; McKnight, D.H.; Tripp, J.F. Understanding the Antecedents and Outcomes of Facebook Privacy Behaviors: An Integrated Model. *IEEE Trans. Eng. Manag.* **2020**, *67*, 697–711. [CrossRef]
123. Li, P.; Cho, H.; Goh, Z.H. Unpacking the process of privacy management and self-disclosure from the perspectives of regulatory focus and privacy calculus. *Telemat. Inform.* **2019**, *41*, 114–125. [CrossRef]
124. Lin, S.; Armstrong, D. Beyond Information: The Role of Territory in Privacy Management Behavior on Social Networking Sites. *J. Assoc. Inf. Syst.* **2019**, *20*, 2. [CrossRef]
125. Liu, C.; Lwin, M.; Ang, R. Parents' role in teens' personal photo sharing: A moderated mediation model incorporating privacy concern and network size. *Makara Hum. Behav. Stud. Asia* **2019**, *23*, 145–151. [CrossRef]

126. Liu, Z.; Wang, X.; Liu, J. How digital natives make their self-disclosure decisions: A cross-cultural comparison. *Inf. Technol. Amp People* **2019**, *32*, 538–558. [CrossRef]
127. Liu, Z.; Wang, X.; Min, Q.; Li, W. The effect of role conflict on self-disclosure in social network sites: An integrated perspective of boundary regulation and dual process model. *Inf. Syst. J.* **2019**, *29*, 279–316. [CrossRef]
128. Nemec Zlatolas, L.; Welzer, T.; Hölbl, M.; Heričko, M.; Kamišalić, A. A Model of Perception of Privacy, Trust, and Self-Disclosure on Online Social Networks. *Entropy* **2019**, *21*, 772. [CrossRef] [PubMed]
129. Oghazi, P.; Schultheiss, R.; Chirumalla, K.; Kalmer, N.P.; Rad, F.F. User self-disclosure on social network sites: A cross-cultural study on Facebook's privacy concepts. *J. Bus. Res.* **2019**, *112*, 531–540. [CrossRef]
130. Sun, Y.; Fang, S.; Hwang, Y. Investigating privacy and information disclosure behavior in social electronic commerce. *Sustainability* **2019**, *11*, 3311. [CrossRef]
131. Teubner, T.; Flath, C.M. Privacy in the sharing economy. *J. Assoc. Inf. Syst.* **2019**, *20*, 213–242. [CrossRef]
132. Wu, P.F. The privacy paradox in the context of online social networking: A self-identity perspective. *J. Assoc. Inf. Sci. Technol.* **2019**, *70*, 207–217. [CrossRef]
133. Zhang, S.; Kwok Ron, C.-W.; Lowry Paul, B.; Liu, Z. Does more accessibility lead to more disclosure? Exploring the influence of information accessibility on self-disclosure in online social networks. *Inf. Technol. Amp People* **2019**, *32*, 754–780. [CrossRef]
134. Li, Y.; Rho, E.H.R.; Kobsa, A. Cultural differences in the effects of contextual factors and privacy concerns on users' privacy decision on social networking sites. *Behav. Inf. Technol.* **2020**, 1–23. [CrossRef]
135. Al-laymoun, O.H.; Aljaafreh, A. Examining Users' Willingness to Post Sensitive Personal Data on Social Media. *Int. J. Adv. Comput. Sci. Appl.* **2020**, *11*, 451–458. [CrossRef]
136. Jacobson, J.; Gruzd, A.; Hernández-García, Á. Social media marketing: Who is watching the watchers? *J. Retail. Consum. Serv.* **2020**, *53*, 101774. [CrossRef]
137. Li, K.; Cheng, L.; Teng, C.-I. Voluntary sharing and mandatory provision: Private information disclosure on social networking sites. *Inf. Process. Manag.* **2020**, *57*, 102128. [CrossRef]
138. Lin, X.; Wang, X. Examining gender differences in people's information-sharing decisions on social networking sites. *Int. J. Inf. Manag.* **2020**, *50*, 45–56. [CrossRef]
139. Mousavi, R.; Chen, R.; Kim, D.J.; Chen, K. Effectiveness of privacy assurance mechanisms in users' privacy protection on social networking sites from the perspective of protection motivation theory. *Decis. Support Syst.* **2020**, *135*, 113323. [CrossRef]
140. Trepte, S.; Scharkow, M.; Dienlin, T. The privacy calculus contextualized: The influence of affordances. *Comput. Hum. Behav.* **2020**, *104*, 106115. [CrossRef]
141. Youn, S.; Shin, W. Adolescents' responses to social media newsfeed advertising: The interplay of persuasion knowledge, benefit-risk assessment, and ad scepticism in explaining information disclosure. *Int. J. Advert.* **2020**, *39*, 213–231. [CrossRef]
142. Zhang, R.; Fu, J.S. Privacy Management and Self-Disclosure on Social Network Sites: The Moderating Effects of Stress and Gender. *J. Comput-Mediat. Comm.* **2020**, *25*, 236–251. [CrossRef]
143. Davazdahemami, B.; Hammer, B.; Kalgotra, P.; Luse, A. From General to Situational Privacy Concerns: A New Mechanism to Explain Information Disclosure in Social Networks. *Commun. Assoc. Inf. Syst.* **2020**, *47*, 652–677. [CrossRef]
144. Chung, K.-C.; Chen, C.-H.; Tsai, H.-H.; Chuang, Y.-H. Social media privacy management strategies: A SEM analysis of user privacy behaviors. *Comput. Commun.* **2021**, *174*, 122–130. [CrossRef]
145. Ibrahim, M.; Abdullah, A.; Yulong, L.; Maryah, A.; Fatmah Hussain, Q. Gender Differentials on Information Sharing and Privacy Concerns on Social Networking Sites: Perspectives from Users. *J. Glob. Inf.* **2021**, *29*, 236–255. [CrossRef]
146. Sharif, A.; Soroya, S.H.; Ahmad, S.; Mahmood, K. Antecedents of Self-Disclosure on Social Networking Sites (SNSs): A Study of Facebook Users. *Sustainability* **2021**, *13*, 1220. [CrossRef]
147. Thompson, N.; Brindley, J. Who are you talking about? Contrasting determinants of online disclosure about self or others. *Inf. Technol. People* **2021**, *34*, 999–1017. [CrossRef]

Article

Formulation of Parsimonious Urban Flash Flood Predictive Model with Inferential Statistics

Lloyd Ling [1,*], Sai Hin Lai [2,*], Zulkifli Yusop [3], Ren Jie Chin [1,*] and Joan Lucille Ling [4]

1 Centre of Disaster Risk Reduction (CDRR), Civil Engineering Department, Lee Kong Chian Faculty of Engineering & Science, Universiti Tunku Abdul Rahman, Jalan Sungai Long, Kajang 43000, Malaysia
2 Department of Civil Engineering, Faculty of Engineering, University of Malaya, Kuala Lumpur 50603, Malaysia
3 Centre for Environmental Sustainability and Water Security, Universiti Teknologi Malaysia, Skudai 81310, Malaysia; zulyusop@utm.my
4 American Degree Programme, Department of Liberal Arts and Sciences, Taylor's University, No. 1, Jalan Taylors, Subang Jaya 47500, Malaysia; linglucille@gmail.com
* Correspondence: linglloyd@utar.edu.my (L.L.); laish@um.edu.my (S.H.L.); chinrj@utar.edu.my (R.J.C.)

Citation: Ling, L.; Lai, S.H.; Yusop, Z.; Chin, R.J.; Ling, J.L. Formulation of Parsimonious Urban Flash Flood Predictive Model with Inferential Statistics. *Mathematics* **2022**, *10*, 175. https://doi.org/10.3390/math10020175

Academic Editors: Araceli Queiruga-Dios, Maria Jesus Santos, Fatih Yilmaz, Deolinda M. L. Dias Rasteiro, Jesús Martín Vaquero and Víctor Gayoso Martínez

Received: 31 October 2021
Accepted: 30 December 2021
Published: 6 January 2022

Publisher's Note: MDPI stays neutral with regard to jurisdictional claims in published maps and institutional affiliations.

Copyright: © 2022 by the authors. Licensee MDPI, Basel, Switzerland. This article is an open access article distributed under the terms and conditions of the Creative Commons Attribution (CC BY) license (https://creativecommons.org/licenses/by/4.0/).

Abstract: The curve number (CN) rainfall–runoff model is widely adopted. However, it had been reported to repeatedly fail in consistently predicting runoff results worldwide. Unlike the existing antecedent moisture condition concept, this study preserved its parsimonious model structure for calibration according to different ground saturation conditions under guidance from inferential statistics. The existing CN model was not statistically significant without calibration. The calibrated model did not rely on the return period data and included rainfall depths less than 25.4 mm to formulate statistically significant urban runoff predictive models, and it derived CN directly. Contrarily, the linear regression runoff model and the asymptotic fitting method failed to model hydrological conditions when runoff coefficient was greater than 50%. Although the land-use and land cover remained the same throughout this study, the calculated CN value of this urban watershed increased from 93.35 to 96.50 as the watershed became more saturated. On average, a 3.4% increase in CN value would affect runoff by 44% (178,000 m^3). This proves that the CN value cannot be selected according to the land-use and land cover of the watershed only. Urban flash flood modelling should be formulated with rainfall–runoff data pairs with a runoff coefficient > 50%.

Keywords: curve number; flash flood model; inferential statistics

1. Introduction

Flood and its related disasters are caused by excessive volumes of water (runoff) which are not absorbed by the ground. Residents at low-elevated regions are often at risk of inundation, financial loss, and even the loss of lives. As the pace of urbanisation accelerates around the world, flash flood damage takes place more frequently. Between 1961 and 2020, nearly 10,000 cases were reported with 1.3 million deaths and a minimum of USD 3.3 trillion of financial losses at an equivalent loss rate of almost USD 1800 per second [1]. On average, the total reported deaths worldwide were 23,000/year for the past 6 decades at an equivalent rate of one death every 24 min [1]. Thus, it is important to study the relationship between rainfall and runoff in order to quantify the runoff amount from rainfall with equations or predictive models for water resources management, flood prediction, and risk mitigation to benefit mankind. Although there are many rainfall–runoff models for runoff prediction, this study assessed a popular rainfall–runoff model from the United States Department of Agriculture (USDA), Soil Conservation Services (SCS) for flash flood prediction and benchmarked its runoff prediction accuracy against two parsimonious models which also used two modelling parameters. The main objective is to formulate and identify a parsimonious runoff predictive model which requires the least modelling parameters for urban flash flood prediction.

Near the end of the 1930s and beginning of the 1940s, infiltrometer tests were carried out by the Natural Resources Conservation Service (NRCS) agency, also known as USDA, SCS in order to assess the impact of watershed treatments along with soil conservation measures on the rainfall–runoff process. The US Congress administered a Watershed Protection and Flood Prevention Act (Public Law PL-566) years later in August 1954. Therefore, the SCS had to establish a procedure for national implementation and thus, hydrologic methods that were once an agency procedure to tackle particular scenarios were taken and applied with immediate effect. Having said that, the method did not emerge in the archived literature, nor underwent professional review and critical procedures for a decade and a half [2,3]. The procedure established by the SCS was developed according to available data primarily from watersheds overseen with rain and streamflow gages in the USA. However, the SCS had to overcome most issues in ungagged watersheds. Hydrological models and procedures constructed by early pioneers were therefore adopted and grew into a runoff equation for the SCS curve number (CN) as:

$$Q = \frac{(P - I_a)^2}{P - I_a + S} \quad (1)$$

where

Q = Amount of runoff depth (mm).
P = Depth of rainfall (mm).
I_a = The initial abstraction amount (mm).
S = Maximum potential water retention of a watershed (mm).

Furthermore, the SCS developed a hypothesis whereby $I_a = \lambda S$, λ being the initial abstraction ratio coefficient. The equation was vaguely supported by daily rainfall and runoff data and the sole source of accredited evidence was the NRCS's National Engineering Handbook, Section 4 (NEH-4). In 1954, the SCS also created the CN methodology, although certain preliminary field data and core assumptions emerged undocumented and untraced [2–4].

In addition to that, the SCS proposed that $I_a = \lambda S = 0.20S$ where the initial abstraction ratio coefficient (λ) was 0.20, in which the criterion correlates I_a and S. Field data acquired from different regions in the USA also contributed to the proposed relationship of I_a to S. They determined that $\lambda = 0.20$ due to the simple correlation between I_a and S data points used by the SCS. Notwithstanding the sizeable scatter in the data, $\lambda = 0.20$ was adopted by the SCS with the conclusion that half of the data points fell in range of $0.095 < \lambda < 0.38$ [2,4]. The initial abstraction (I_a) is otherwise the depth of the rainfall event necessary for runoff commencement. Replacing $I_a = 0.20S$ simplifies Equation (1) to become the conventional SCS runoff forecast model that is commonly used in textbooks, certified hydrological design manuals, and is widely used in design software as well as programs following its establishment in 1954 [2–4]. The conventional (simplified) SCS runoff prediction model is:

$$Q = \frac{(P - 0.2S)^2}{P + 0.8S} \quad (2)$$

Equation (2) holds a restriction where $P > 0.20S$, or else Q would be equal to zero. Howbeit, proliferating studies lean against the accuracy of Equation (2)'s predictions as well as the hypothesis where $I_a = 0.20S$. Literature reviews exhibit inconsistency in using Equation (2) to predict runoff results and a number of researchers encouraged the calibration of regional hydrological conditions to be carried out instead of simply following that of the SCS [5,6].

In the past six decades, the CN technique gained wide acceptance and appliance to hydrological problems that were not originally intended to be solved by the SCS. The technique became the most popular method to predict runoff and was widely taught in colleges and universities worldwide. The model was also integrated into many software and USDA SCS systems like the Chemicals, Runoff and Erosion System simulation from the Agricultural Management Systems (CREAMS) model. It is also used in other models, such as the Agricultural

Nonpoint Source model (AGNPS), Hydrologic Engineering Centre–Hydrologic Modelling System (HEC-HMS), USDA Technical Release 20 (TR-20), and USDA Technical Release 55 (TR-55). In fact, it presented a runoff component for successive water quality and erosion models comprising the Areal Nonpoint Source Watershed Environment Response System (ANSWERS), the simulator for Water Resources in Rural Basins (WRRB), the Erosion Productivity Impact Calculator (EPIC), the Pesticide Root Zone model (PRZM), the Water Erosion Prediction Project (WEPP), and the distributed Soil Water Assessment Tool (SWAT) [2–5]. Although not mentioned here, any software and technical handbooks which incorporated Equation (2) are very likely to produce inconsistent runoff prediction results.

Recently, researchers proposed a global gridded CN concept for runoff modelling [7,8]. However, some reported that the usage of the CN in representing a watershed is arbitrary, vague, and often contradictory in describing related areas of land cover [2,9]. Other researchers emphasised the importance to apply a multi-modelling approach and statistical methods with land-use and cover variations in order to achieve better flood modelling results [10,11], while [12] even concluded that even very-fine-resolution topography and high-resolution land cover data may not be able to produce reliable urban flood modelling results using the HEC-RAS software. Some researchers also reported difficulty to determine an optimum λ value [13] in the SCS CN model. Therefore, it is crucial to ameliorate the modelling approach in order to achieve better model applications to manage water resources and river basins.

As Equation (2) was rooted into many fields, the model re-assessment prevents SCS practitioners from committing type II errors (a statistical term used within the context of hypothesis testing that describes the error that occurs when one accepts a null hypothesis that is actually false). The calibration methodology will derive a statistically significant rainfall–runoff model with better runoff prediction accuracy and produce a watershed-specific CN system for an area of interest. Instead of referring to the conventional CN table compiled by SCS which originated from USA, researchers will be able to derive watershed-specific CN anywhere with the presented methodology in this study. The CN derivation methodology will also replace the common unscientific CN adjustments or tweaking practices in order to achieve better runoff prediction results. The approach entails performing "trial and error" CN refining with the observed data to better the results of runoff prediction and assumes that $\lambda = 0.20$ for any watershed. However, such practice lacks statistical justification and often leads to inconsistent runoff prediction results. Study [14] cautioned that a ±10% CN variation could lead to ±50% change in runoff. It would create CN value(s) for a watershed; however, the "calibrated" CN value(s) may not even be able to predict runoff conditions of other watersheds with similar land-use and land cover conditions again. CN values are a better match for traditional agricultural watersheds but less accurate in the estimation of semiarid rangelands and are the worst for forested watersheds [2]. Therefore, CN values should be derived from the local P-Q dataset to reflect realistic situations [6,13,15].

It is not a common practice for practitioners to assess the statistical significance of a predictive model with their dataset. Many engineering students were not taught about the importance of such validation procedures prior to the use of any formulas and equations. The main aim of this study is to emphasise that any formula or predictive model should not be blindly adopted, in order to avoid committing type II error.

2. Methodology and Study Site

When the SCS runoff model was adopted to model rainfall and runoff conditions of a watershed, the assumption of the initial abstraction ratio coefficient ($\lambda = 0.20$) was also accepted. SCS practitioners do not question the validity of the runoff model and therefore, there is a potential of perpetrating a type II error. A hypothesis was used to assess the validity of the existing SCS model according to the rainfall–runoff dataset of this study. The model will be calibrated only when the hypothesis is rejected. In the event that the hypothesis cannot be rejected, the existing SCS model will be adopted for modelling in this study.

Null Hypothesis (H_0): $I_a = \lambda S$ where $\lambda = 0.20$ is valid and applicable for this study. The null hypothesis assesses the validity of Equation (2) as pertaining to the collected dataset. H_0 must be statistically significant at least at alpha (α) significance level of = 0.05 for it to be adopted to model the rainfall–runoff condition at the watershed of study. Otherwise, the model should be calibrated. According to the SCS, λ is a constant value of 0.20 in $I_a = \lambda S$.

In the event of H_0 rejection, a statistically significant initial abstraction ratio coefficient (λ) and total abstraction value (s) will be derived at alpha = 0.01 which will lead to the calculation of the best collective representative CN for the watershed as proposed by the authors' previous study that based model calibration on the non-parametric inferential statistics, the bootstrapping bias corrected, and an accelerated (BCa) procedure [6]. Unlike the existing antecedent moisture condition (AMC) concept which correlates CNI (CN in dry conditions), CNII (CN in normal conditions), and CNIII (CN in wet conditions) to determine the runoff condition of a saturated soil, this study extends the model calibration method proposed previously [6] to model the runoff condition of an urban watershed under different ground saturation conditions without using return period data. Other than that, this study added a new control factor to calibrate the model by limiting the overall model prediction bias near to zero to prevent the newly calibrated model's bias toward a specific dataset under this study. As such, the supervised numerical optimisation algorithm will identify the optimum λ and S value under the model bias control within the bootstrap BCa confidence intervals while keeping the overall runoff predictive model's error and bias near to zero. The BCa technique was chosen as it is the only inferential statistic with a bias correction ability while able to provide a confidence interval (CI) at specific alpha levels for statistical assessments. It is also a data-distribution-free method which is compatible to the nature of any rainfall data distribution and available in the IBM statistical software SPSS used by this study.

The SCS rainfall–runoff model was calibrated previously by US researchers under the recommendation to only consider rainfall depths > 25.4 mm (1 inch) in order to avoid modelling bias towards small rainfall events resulting in higher CNs in rural watersheds [2]. However, the recommended guideline often excludes low-rainfall-depth field data, leading to an insufficient sample size to produce statistically significant results. Some researchers even lowered the limit to 15 mm (arbitrary) with a minimum of 10 events in their study plots [16]. Therefore, this study reviewed the recommended guidelines and demonstrated the possibility to extend the authors' previously proposed calibration methodology and to propose another new model calibration method based on watershed saturation conditions.

A 22.33 km^2 urban watershed (Sungai Kayu Ara) in the capital city of Malaysia, Kuala Lumpur, which consists of a large portion of impervious area, was chosen for this study. Over the years, this urban watershed is plagued by flash flood damages while the return period-based concept to assess the drainage capacity efficiency has neither rectified nor improved the condition. Sungai Kayu Ara watershed covers an area as shown in Figure 1.

The river originates from a forest reserve in the northern upstream and flows toward the relatively flattened developed suburban areas. The outlet of this watershed is marked by a dash circle in Figure 1 under the monitor of a water level station. Ninety-two storm events (1.4 to 90 mm) were collected in this study to produce the rainfall–runoff dataset through the separation of base flow from the hydrograph. A total of 61% (56 rainfall events) of this dataset has a rainfall depth of <25.4 mm (1 inch), but with a measurable runoff amount. Runoff coefficient (Q/P) of this dataset spans from 6% to 97% which is ideal to model runoff change according to the watershed saturation conditions, out of which, thirty-seven (37) rainfall–runoff data pairs have Q/P greater than 50% and twenty-four data pairs are greater than 60%.

This watershed was chosen to show that it is possible to include rainfall depth < 25.4 mm (1 inch) and incorporate watershed saturation conditions into the SCS runoff model calibration for urban runoff prediction. The dataset also contains multiple Q/P (%) data batches in order to reflect the runoff trend and characteristic change due to increasing watershed saturation conditions.

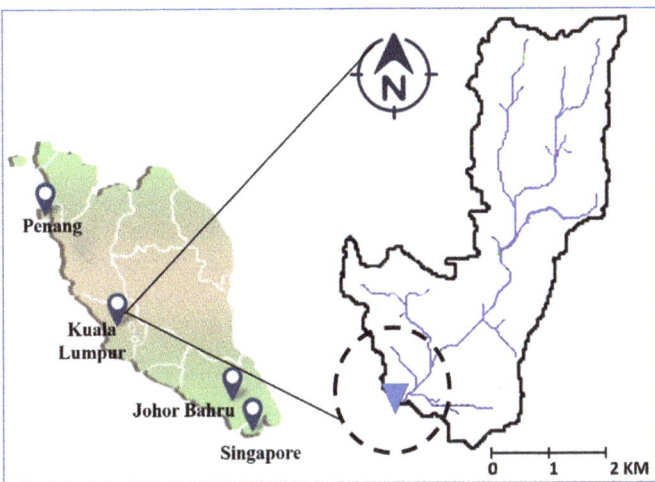

Figure 1. Location of Sungai Kayu Ara Watershed in Kuala Lumpur, Malaysia.

This study highlights the modelling effect on runoff predictions with different saturation-based datasets and advises practitioners against the blind adoption of the authors' previously proposed model calibration methodology [6] for urban flash flood modelling with any rainfall–runoff dataset.

Unlike the Hortonian runoff model, hydrologists have recognised that runoff was the result of rainfall from very wet parts of a watershed since 1960 [17,18]. When the effective soil water-storage capacity is exceeded, runoff will be produced. This runoff generation process is referred to as the saturation-excess runoff. Q/P (%) of a watershed will become larger when effective soil water-storage is reducing [19–22]. Even a medium-sized storm event over a saturated watershed with a high runoff coefficient may cause severe flooding; therefore, it is critical to assess the performance of different runoff models under different runoff coefficient conditions in order to select the best performing parsimonious urban rainfall–runoff model for urban runoff estimation.

This study formulated a feasible runoff predictive model for urban flash flood prediction without using the return period data. Inspired by the saturation-excess runoff concept used by past studies [23–25], the SCS rainfall–runoff model's calibration methodology presented previously [6] was extended to model urban runoff under different ground saturation conditions according to the runoff coefficient which was calculated by dividing runoff amount (Q) to the corresponding rainfall depths (P). The P-Q dataset was then sorted in descending order of the calculated runoff coefficient of each P-Q data pair. A minimum of twenty P-Q events were used to ensure a sufficient sample size for analyses [2,26,27]. The significance of this extended application paved the way for the calibrated SCS runoff model to model urban runoff under different watershed ground saturation conditions (i.e., Q/P > 50%, 60%, and 70% etc.) for urban flash flooding forecasting, the design of hydraulic infrastructures, and drainage capacity assessment.

This study also presented the possibility of developing an urban rainfall–runoff model with a P-Q dataset which includes any rainfall depth that is less than 25.4 mm but with a significant measurable runoff amount. Equation (1) is calibrated with urban hydrological constraints according to the rainfall–runoff dataset to illustrate that the calibrated SCS runoff model could be utilised for modelling urban runoff. In the authors' previous works [6,27], Equation (1) was rearranged into an S general formula, whereby the S and λ values can be derived according to the corresponding P-Q data pairs, the formula is:

$$S_\lambda = \frac{\left[P - \frac{(\lambda-1)Q}{2\lambda}\right] - \sqrt{PQ - P^2 + \left[P - \frac{(\lambda-1)Q}{2\lambda}\right]^2}}{\lambda}$$

. The corresponding S values will be denoted by S_λ

to differentiate from the conventional S value where λ value = 0.20. $S_λ$ must be correlated to the $S_{0.2}$ values prior to the calculation of the CN value [2,6,27]. The non-parametric bootstrapping (BCa) technique was set in SPSS for 2000 random samplings with replacements from the 92 data pairs and produced 99% confidence interval (CI) for parameter optimisation. In another words, the parameter of interest underwent 2000 random validations against its dataset. By utilizing Equation (1), the λ and S optimisation was achieved using the approach of numerical analyses. Model calibration of this study was conducted by removing data pairs of Q/P > 60%, between 40 and 60%, and <40% for model calibration, respectively, with validation against the remaining dataset. Through several iterations of the minimisation of the overall predictive model fitting bias and residual sum of square error (RSS) between the predicted Q against its observed values, the final model was formulated.

Runoff models are compared for their model predictive accuracy in this study. The residual spread of a model is indicated by residual sum of squares (RSS) in which a lower RSS is equivalent to an improved conjecturing model. On the other hand, the model efficiency index (E also known as the Nash–Sutcliffe) lies on a spectrum of minus infinity to 1.0 whereby index value = 1.0 shows an ideal conjectured model. In the instance where E < 0, it is inferior to utilizing an average to predict the dataset. The average residual of a predictive model (BIAS) indicates an altogether model prediction error quantified by the average of its residual to stipulate a pattern in the overall model prediction. A zero value means that it is an ideal error-free overall model prediction, and a negative value demonstrates the under-predictive overall model tendency, and conversely. In addition, a better predictive model will also have smaller residual range and interval, smaller standard deviation in residual, and mean residual near to zero.

2.1. Linear Regression Model

Equation (1) will be calibrated (only if H_0 was rejected) and benchmarked against the linear regression model for runoff prediction accuracy in this study with models of parsimonious interest. For urban rainfall–runoff, the one-dimensional linear regression model was proposed by early pioneers and often utilised, whereby the slope of the regression equation represents a hydrological reduction variable [28] or a proportion in relation to a whole of an impermeable area of a watershed [29]. The intercept on the x-axis estimates a watershed's local depression amount or depression loss [30]. The linear regression model's base form is:

$$Q = mP + c \qquad (3)$$

where

Q = Amount of runoff (mm).
P = Depth of rainfall (mm).
m = Gradient (slope).
c = Constant (intercept on the x-axis).

2.2. Asymptotic Curve Number Modelling

US researcher [31] first pointed out that the most common use of Equation (2) was to calculate runoff from the rainfall depth with the same return period and proposed to perform "frequency matching" by pairing P-Q data pairs with same return periods, while another US researcher [32] reported that CN values decreased against increasing rainfall amounts, and there was a notable pattern in that CN would eventually approach a constant value in most cases. He also proposed a two-parameter asymptotic fitting method (AFM) to sort the rainfall and runoff dataset separately in descending order and pair them up again as "ordered data". The method accepted the SCS proposal where λ = 0.20. Three different patterns were observed and classified as standard behaviour, complacent behaviour, and violent behaviour.

AFM was proposed to determine the representative CN for the watershed of interest through its P-Q dataset (λ value remains as 0.20 under this method) under the theoretical projection when P approaches infinity amount. CN cannot be determined for the complacent behaviour watershed, but standard behaviour watershed follows the following formula for CN determination:

$$CN(P) = CN_\infty + (100 - CN_\infty)e^{(-\frac{P}{k})} \qquad (4)$$

where
$CN(P)$ = Fitted CN value of a specific rainfall depth.]
CN_∞ = CN of a watershed of interest.
P = Rainfall depth (mm).
K = Fitting parameter.

Violent behaviour watershed follows the following formula for CN determination:

$$CN(P) = CN_\infty \left[1 - e^{-k(P-P_{th})}\right] \qquad (5)$$

where
P_{th} = Threshold Rainfall depth (mm).

AFM was chosen to benchmark against the linear regression model and the proposed calibrated model in this study because it is the only CN model that relies on two fitting parameters and has been widely adopted by SCS practitioners.

3. Results

3.1. Linear Regression Model

Using the IBM SPSS, the best fitted model of linear regression for the P-Q dataset of this study based on the basic linear intercept Equation (3) was identified as below while the descriptive and inferential statistics are tabulated in Table 1. Equation (6) has the highest R^2_{adj} of 0.831 and the lowest fitting model standard error (SE) of 4.648.

$$Q = 0.62P - 3.182 \qquad (6)$$

Table 1. Descriptive and Inferential Statistics of Equation (6) at α = 0.05.

Model	Coeff.	p Value	CI Lower	CI Upper	p Value	BCa CI Lower	BCa CI Upper
Constant	−3.182	0.001	−4.956	−1.408	0.004	−5.484	−0.882
Gradient	0.62	0.000	0.561	0.678	0.000	0.531	0.703

From Table 1, both fitting parameters of the linear regression model are statistically significant ($p < 0.01$) and the BCa results reaffirmed the p value significances. Previous researchers [29] used the fitting gradient to estimate the percentage of impervious area while the constant value implies the local depression amount or the watershed's depression loss. However, at alpha = 0.05, the confidence interval (CI) spans 252% and 83% in the respective constant and gradient fitting while the BCa CI results show 622% and 76% variation in those categories. At alpha = 0.05, stringent BCa CI results imply that the local depression, or the depression-loss, of the Sungai Kayu Ara watershed can be any value between 0.89 mm and 5.5 mm (BCa lower-to-upper confidence interval of the fitting constant parameter) while the interpretation of impervious area estimates within the watershed can be any value between 53.1% and 70.3% (BCa lower-to-upper confidence interval of the fitting gradient parameter). Hydrological implications from those two parameters are open to a wide range of interpretations at this point.

3.2. The Existing (Simplified) SCS Runoff Model

Using the entire dataset, the results of BCa established a CI span for derived λ values of the P-Q dataset at the Sungai Kayu Ara watershed (Table 2) can also be used to assess H_0. To implement Equation (2), H_0 must be accepted. The λ confidence interval span and the standard deviation are utilised to assess H_0.

Table 2. BCa results ($\alpha = 0.01$) of derived λ values at Sungai Kayu Ara watershed.

		BCa 99% CI				
	λ	Lower	Upper	S	Lower	Upper
Mean	0.021	0.007	0.051	36.3	28.2	46.7
Median	0.004	0.004	0.006	30.0	22.7	33.7
Skewness	9.020			3.2		
Kurtosis	84.332			16.8		
Std. Deviation	0.097			35.8		

The mean and median CI span (Table 2) did not comprise of a $\lambda = 0.20$. Furthermore, the derived λ dataset's standard deviation is not zero (to indicate that it is a constant), hence H_0 can be rejected at $\alpha = 0.01$, ruling out the validity of Equation (2) to model runoff conditions at this watershed. Therefore, the SCS model must undergo model calibration to avoid the risk of type II errors.

3.3. Calibrated SCS Runoff Model for the Sungai Kayu Ara Watershed

Tabulated in Table 2 are the descriptive statistics regarding the nature of the data distribution of the values of λ and S. The supervised least-square-fitting algorithm has been configured to find the optimum value of λ and S in the confine of the median confidence intervals because of the nature of their skewed data distribution (Table 2). For the Sungai Kayu Ara watershed, the optimum λ value would be 0.004 and the best collective representation of S is 31.47 mm (denoted as $S_{0.004}$), with an overall model bias of zero ($\alpha = 0.01$) to model the entire dataset. As $I_a = \lambda S$, substituting λ and S values produces $I_a = 0.11$ mm.

The calibrated SCS urban rainfall–runoff prediction model, when I_a and S are substituted back to Equation (1), would be:

$$Q_{0.004} = \frac{(P - 0.11)^2}{P + 31.36} \tag{7}$$

where

$Q_{0.004}$ = Runoff amount (mm) of the new model formulated with $\lambda = 0.004$.

The urban runoff model calibrated by the SCS is displayed by Equation (7). It is bound to the condition of $P > 0.11$ mm, otherwise $Q_{0.004} = 0$ mm. Equation (7) has an overall model bias value of zero which implies that it does not have an over- or under-prediction tendency on runoff-amount prediction. The correlation between $S_{0.004}$ and $S_{0.2}$ can be determined with SPSS as: $S_{0.2} = 0.901 \, S_{0.004}{}^{0.87}$ (R^2_{adj} of 0.97, SE of 0.174, and $p < 0.001$). Subsequently, the equivalent $S_{0.2}$ can be calculated as 18.11 mm leading to the derivation of $CN_{0.2} = 93.35$ with the SCS CN formula: $CN_{0.2} = \frac{25,400}{S_{0.2} + 254}$. The 99% BCa CI of $S_{0.004}$ ranges from 22.7 to 33.7 mm (Table 2). Those values can also be used to calculate its equivalent upper and lower $CN_{0.2}$ limits in the same manner; therefore, the best collective $CN_{0.2} = 93.35$ ($\alpha = 0.01$, 99% CI ranges from 92.96 to 94.91) for the urban watershed under this study (The $CN_{0.2}$ value derivation and SCS CN model calibration steps were summarised and listed in a step-wise instruction format in Appendix A (or authors' previous publication [6])).

3.4. Asymptotic Curve Number Modelling

Using the AFM, the derived $CN_{0.2}$ values versus rainfall depths graph (Figure 2) resembles the standard behaviour pattern, hence Equation (4) was adopted to derive CN_∞ as the best representative $CN_{0.2}$ value for the Sungai Kayu Ara watershed and to verify the modelling result in this section. Using the least-square-fitting method, the fitting parameter k was identified to be 19.23 and CN_∞ is 90.27. Rounding to the nearest positive integer, $CN_\infty = CN_{0.2} = 90$. This CN value is in proximity to the equivalent $CN_{0.2}$ value of 93.35 which was derived by the calibrated SCS runoff model in Section 3.3.

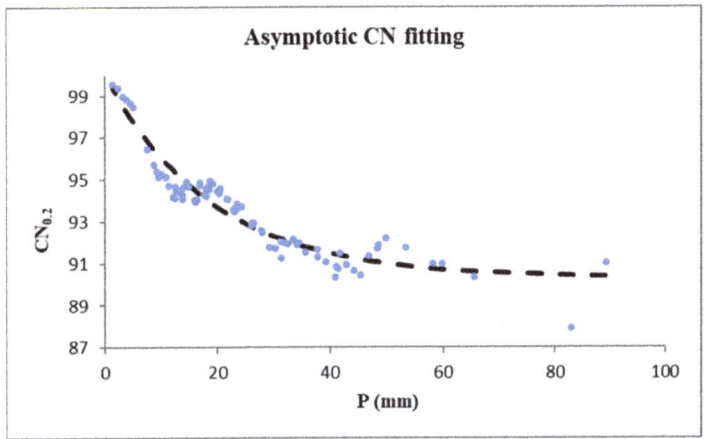

Figure 2. Asymptotic CN fitting of Sungai Kayu Ara watershed: The CN_∞ resembles standard behaviour pattern with $CN_\infty = 90$ near to stable state at the higher rainfall depths.

From the SCS CN formula, the calculated $S_{0.2}$ value is 27.39 mm and $I_a = 0.20 \times 27.39$ mm = 5.48 mm. As such, the AFM runoff predictive model can be formulated from Equation (1) to benchmark the accuracy of the runoff prediction of the original (unsorted) rainfall–runoff dataset against Equations (6) and (7), with the descriptive and inferential statistics of the runoff predictive model's residual listed in Table 3.

Table 3. Runoff Models' BCa 99% residual analyses comparison.

	Equation (6)	Equation (7)	AFM Model
$CN_{0.2}$	N/A	93.35	90.27
E	0.832	0.823	0.784
RSS	1945.06	2052.37	2507.72
Residual Standard Deviation:	4.62	4.75	4.630
Standard Deviation CI:	[3.61, 5.70]	[3.64, 5.84]	[3.55, 5.70]
Skewness	−0.52	0.72	0.554
Mean Residual:	0.008	0.000	−2.460
Residual CI:	[−1.31, 1.23]	[−1.31, 1.29]	[−3.78, −1.19]
Residual: Range	26.84	27.98	28.10

Note: Smaller residual standard deviation and residual range imply a better model. Narrower residual interval shows a model with less error distribution while a residual interval that does not span across zero indicates a model with either an over- or under-prediction tendency.

3.5. Runoff Models Comparison

Inferential statistics results of the runoff models' residual analyses were also generated and tabulated in Table 3. Equation (7), which is the calibrated runoff model (using $\lambda = 0.004$), was benchmarked with the linear intercept model of Equation (6) and AFM. The non-calibrated SCS runoff model of Equation (2) was ruled out as it is not statistically significant, hence it was excluded from the model comparison. The model's prediction efficiency index (E) as well as its residual sum of squared error (RSS) and descriptive statistics were quantified to extract further comparisons.

From Table 3, the model residual of Equations (6) and (7) have skewness values near to zero, implying that each respective residual distribution is almost normally distributed; therefore, the mean residual can be a good indicator of the prediction accuracy of those models. The mean residual's BCa 99% confidence interval range of all three models spanned across zero to indicate the possibility of producing zero residual prediction is significant (α = 0.01), hence all models (except AFM) can achieve an accurate runoff prediction.

The AFM runoff model has a higher RSS, with lower E index when compared to the other two models listed in Table 3. The AFM model shows the runoff amount's underprediction tendency, as its mean residual's confidence interval range fluctuates within a negative range and it also has the widest residual range compared to the other models. According to the SCS, there will be no runoff until a rainfall depth is larger than I_a, but the calculated I_a value of the AFM runoff model is larger than six recorded events (6.5%) of the P-Q dataset, while Equation (7) does not have this issue. Although the AFM runoff model derived a proximate $CN_{0.2}$ as the value from Equation (7), a 3.4% increase in the $CN_{0.2}$ value from 90.27 (AFM model) to 93.35 (Equation (7)) was able to improve the runoff model's E index efficiency by nearly 5% and reduce the RSS by 18% (Table 3).

Up to this point, the linear regression runoff predictive model (Equation (6)) is statistically significant and outperformed against other models to model runoff conditions with the entire dataset. The AFM model is the worst model to predict runoff conditions. To test the robustness of the linear regression runoff predictive model, this study further assessed the runoff prediction ability of Equation (3) against the AFM technique and the newly proposed SCS runoff model calibration method of this study with the same dataset, but regrouped under two different Q/P conditions of >50% and 60%.

4. Further Assessment with Saturation-Excess Runoff Scenarios

Using the same P-Q dataset, the runoff coefficients were calculated to regroup the dataset. The original P-Q dataset has wide distribution range of Q/P from 6% to 97%. Of this, thirty-seven (37) events were found to have Q/P > 50% and twenty-four (24) events were greater than 60%. Thirty-seven (37) and twenty-four (24) P-Q data pairs with runoff coefficients of >50% and >60% were grouped separately to repeat the aforementioned calibration methodology for the rederivation of all rainfall–runoff models for runoff prediction re-assessment. This will further assess the reliability and robustness of all compared runoff predictive models when the watershed becomes increasingly saturated.

4.1. Linear Regression Model

According to the basic linear form of Equation (3), for the given rainfall–runoff dataset, IBM SPSS established the best fitting linear regression model as:

$$\text{For Q/P} > 50\%,\ \mathbf{Q = 0.654P - 0.216} \tag{8}$$

$$\text{For Q/P} > 60\%,\ \mathbf{Q = 0.747P - 0.913} \tag{9}$$

Q and P as defined previously. Equation (8) has R^2_{adj} of 0.936 and SE of 3.549 while Equation (9) has R^2_{adj} of 0.977 and SE of 2.242. The descriptive statistics are tabulated in Table 4.

Table 4. Inferential statistics of Equations (8) and (9) at α = 0.05.

Model Q/P > 50%	Coeff.	p Value	Model Q/P > 60%	Coeff.	p Value
Constant	−0.216	0.834	Constant	−0.913	0.254
Gradient	0.654	0.000	Gradient	0.747	0.000

From Table 4, the constant coefficients are not significant ($p > 0.05$) under both runoff coefficient scenarios for both equations. When the constant becomes insignificant (x-intercept = 0), the fitting constant parameter will be discarded. The linear intercept runoff model relies on the interception on the x-axis (the constant term) to estimate the local depression, initial loss, or the depression loss of a watershed [30]. In the event when the fitting constant becomes statistically insignificant, or local depression, initial loss, or the depression loss becomes zero, the only logically hydrological implication is that 100% rainfall becomes complete runoff (**Q = P**) thereafter.

In order to maintain the proposal of [30], the suitable structure of the alternative linear regression is a regression model through the origin (RTO), with the gradient as the only acceptable model-fitting parameter. The data were assessed with IBM SPSS again under both runoff coefficient conditions and identified the best-fitted RTO given by Equations (10) and (11), and their statistics shown in Tables 5 and 6.

$$\text{For } Q/P > 50\%, \mathbf{Q = 0.649P} \tag{10}$$

$$\text{For } Q/P > 60\%, \mathbf{Q = 0.724P} \tag{11}$$

Table 5. Descriptive statistics of Equations (10) and (11) at $\alpha = 0.05$.

Model	Coeff.	Confidence Interval		p Value
		Lower	Upper	
Q/P > 50% Gradient	0.649	0.616	0.681	0.001
Q/P > 60% Gradient	0.724	0.695	0.753	0.001

Table 6. Inferential statistics of Equations (10) and (11) at $\alpha = 0.05$.

Model	Coeff.	Confidence Interval		BCa p Value
		Lower	Upper	
Q/P > 50% Gradient	0.649	0.605	0.696	0.001
Q/P > 60% Gradient	0.724	0.680	0.756	0.001

According to the assessment statistics in Tables 5 and 6, although both RTO models are significant (p value < 0.01), neither confidence interval span shows a possible inclusion of 1.0 as a fitting gradient for both runoff coefficient scenarios. **Q = P** is not statistically significant and does not fit the modelling dataset under either condition. As such, the 100% complete runoff scenario becomes impossible and posts a conflict with the proposal from [30]. The validity of Equation (3) for runoff prediction is now in question.

On the other hand, complacent behaviour patterns were detected for both runoff coefficient (Q/P > 50% and 60%) scenarios with the AFM. It failed to derive a representative $CN_{0.2}$ value as the value reduced according to the increasing rainfall depths and did not approach any stable value. Both the linear regression (two-parameters) model and the AFM model failed to model the runoff conditions and calculate the $CN_{0.2}$ value for the watershed in this study when Q/P > 50%.

4.2. Calibrated SCS Runoff Model

Although Equation (7) is able to model the Q/P > 50% and Q/P > 60% datasets with zero bias and an E index of 0.854 and 0.851, respectively, the runoff under-prediction tendency is increasing with Q/P (%), which defeats the aim of developing an effective urban flood predictive model. As such, thirty-seven (37) and twenty-four (24) P-Q data pairs of the Sungai Kayu Ara watershed with Q/P > 50% and >60% were grouped separately for λ value rederivation in order to perform SCS model calibration and to formulate statistically significant runoff predictive models again. Optimisation of λ in Equation (1) was conducted within the median confidence interval because of skewed λ datasets of both runoff coefficient scenarios. Tables 7 and 8 illustrate the data distribution of λ values through descriptive statistics analyses conducted with IBM SPSS.

Table 7. Inferential statistics of derived λ at $\alpha = 0.01$ for Q/P > 50% scenario.

Q/P > 50% λ Dataset	Statistics	99% BCa CI of λ Lower	Upper
Mean	0.043	0.011	0.117
Median	0.009	0.005	0.013
Skewness	5.815		
Kurtosis	34.691		
Std. Deviation	0.149		

Table 8. Inferential statistics of derived λ at $\alpha = 0.01$ for Q/P > 60% scenario.

Q/P > 60% λ Dataset	Statistics	99% BCa CI of λ Lower	Upper
Mean	0.061	0.014	0.171
Median	0.013	0.007	0.026
Skewness	4.724		
Kurtosis	22.764		
Std. Deviation	0.184		

The Q/P > 50% dataset (54% dataset with P < 25.4 mm) gave an optimal λ value of 0.005 and an ideal collective S representation of 19.26 mm to yield I_a = 0.104 mm. The optimum λ value and best collective representation of S for Q/P > 60% dataset (63% dataset with P < 25.4 mm) are 0.007 and 12.42 mm, which yield I_a = 0.092 mm. By substituting I_a and S back into Equation (1), the formulation of the calibrated rainfall–runoff prediction models are:

$$\text{For Q/P} > 50\%, \mathbf{Q}_{0.005} = \frac{(\mathbf{P} - 0.104)^2}{\mathbf{P} + 19.159} \quad (12)$$

$$\text{For Q/P} > 60\%, \mathbf{Q}_{0.007} = \frac{(\mathbf{P} - 0.092)^2}{\mathbf{P} + 12.325} \quad (13)$$

$\mathbf{Q}_{0.005}$ = Runoff (mm) where λ = 0.005.
$\mathbf{Q}_{0.007}$ = Runoff (mm) where λ = 0.007.

Equation (12) bounds to a constraint where $\mathbf{P} > 0.104$ mm, else $\mathbf{Q}_{0.005} = 0$, whereas Equation (13) bounds to $\mathbf{P} > 0.092$ mm, else $\mathbf{Q}_{0.007} = 0$. These models were formulated with the extra model bias control factor during the supervised numerical optimisation process under the guiding control of BCa. Both equations have an overall model BIAS value of zero. Conceptualisation of the calibrated SCS runoff prediction Equations (12) and (13) with the optimum λ value hold an identical inherent significant level (α = 0.01). Following the equivalent $CN_{0.2}$ derivation process as stated in Section 3.3, Equation (12) yields the equivalent $CN_{0.2}$ value of 94.89, while Equation (13) derives the value of 96.50 to represent the respective ground saturation conditions of the Sungai Kayu Ara watershed. In Tables 7 and 8, the BCa confidence interval ranges of both scenarios do not consist of the λ value of 0.20, hence Equation (2) is still invalid to model either runoff conditions. As such, it will be excluded from runoff model comparison in this section again.

4.3. Model Comparison under Different Saturation-Excess Runoff Scenarios

The newly calibrated runoff models of Equations (12) and (13) were benchmarked against the RTO linear model $\mathbf{Q} = \mathbf{P}$ only (since the constant-fitting parameter becomes statistically insignificant, refer to Table 4 results) under two different runoff coefficient scenarios. The AFM was excluded as it failed to model the runoff conditions when Q/P > 50% and derive any $CN_{0.2}$ for the watershed. For further comparison, the model's prediction efficiency index (E), RSS, as well as the predictive model BIAS have been formulated, as seen in Table 9.

Table 9. Runoff predictive model's comparison.

Q/P > 50%	Equation (12)	Q = P	Q/P > 60%	Equation (13)	Q = P
E	0.85	0.11	E	0.94	0.59
BIAS	0.000	10.419	BIAS	0.000	7.588
RSS	1051.23	6319.41	RSS	303.25	2056.83

RTO models failed to achieve runoff prediction accuracy with a runoff over-prediction tendency (positive model bias in Table 9). On the contrary, Equations (12) and (13) managed to predict runoff with high E index, and the E index value even improved from 0.85 to 0.94 as the ground saturation condition increased from 50% to 60%. In this study, the proposed calibrated model is the only runoff predictive model that is capable of modelling urban runoff conditions accurately, even when the watershed becomes increasingly saturated.

5. Discussion

5.1. Hydrological Implication of the New Runoff Predictive Models

The new runoff models (Equations (7), (12) and (13)) were derived to represent different hydrological conditions of the Sungai Kayu Ara watershed. Equation (7) modelled the overall runoff condition of the entire dataset. On the other hand, Equations (12) and (13) represent higher ground saturation conditions where runoff coefficients Q/P are >50% and >60%, respectively. The runoff and incremental trend of all the three models are shown in Figure 3. Equation (7) under-predicted runoff amount significantly when compared to Equations (12) and (13), even though it was under the bias control and guided by BCa.

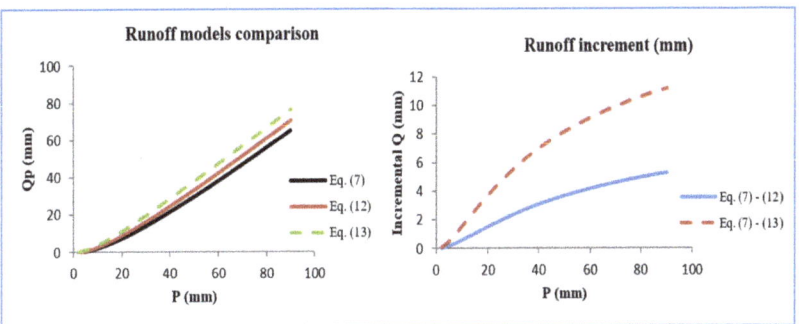

Figure 3. Runoff models using all P-Q data (Equation (7)), Q/P > 50% (Equation (12)), Q/P > 60% (Equation (13)) and runoff depth (mm) increment at Sungai Kayu Ara watershed. By comparing Equations (7) and (13), $CN_{0.2}$ increased 3.4% with an average of 44% (nearly 178,000 m^3) runoff amount increment while $CN_{0.2}$ increased 1.7% from Equations (12) and (13) with an average increment of 15.7% (about 75,000 m^3) in runoff amount. **Note: Runoff depth increment of 1 mm = 22,330 m^3 runoff volume increase at the study site.**

It is noteworthy to highlight that the land-use and land cover of the Sungai Kayu Ara watershed remained the same throughout this study. However, the $CN_{0.2}$ value of this watershed still increased from 93.35 to 94.89 and 96.50 as the watershed became more saturated. This proves that $CN_{0.2}$ value cannot be selected from any handbook according to the land-use and land cover of a watershed only, and it must be derived according to the rainfall–runoff dataset under different ground saturation conditions in order to reflect specific hydrological characteristics of a watershed.

The runoff coefficient distribution for Equation (7) diversifies across a wide range from 6% to 97% (47% on average). Equations (12) and (13) quantify scenarios where the Sungai Kayu Ara watershed becomes more saturated, and the runoff amount from Equation (13) is the highest. The actual incremental runoff from Equations (7)–(13) is also higher than the incremental runoff difference between Equations (7) and (12). Equations (12) and (13) are as postulated by the "saturation-excess runoff" concept—that the runoff coefficient of a watershed becomes larger when effective soil water-storage reduces and induces higher runoff amounts. This proves that runoff predictive models must be formulated with appropriate datasets to reflect ground saturation conditions accurately. The proposed SCS model calibration methodology in this study cannot be adopted blindly for urban flash flood modelling if the Q/P of the dataset is less than 50%.

5.2. Comparison of Rainfall–Runoff Models

The prospects of the Sungai Kayu Ara watershed utilizing a linear regression model for urban runoff analyses is evaluated in this study. Table 3 tabulated comparisons for runoff models. During the saturation-excess assessment, linear intercept regression models had insignificantly fitted constant terms under both runoff coefficient scenarios (Table 4).

According to [30], the constant-fitting parameter is crucial to the x-intercept approach that represents an estimate of initial loss, local depression, or even watershed depression. The absence of an initial- or depression loss at the watershed according to its P-Q dataset is inferred by an insignificant-fitting constant. Further hydrological interpretation shows a completely saturated watershed with 100% of runoff by any volume of rainfall. The only reasonable linear regression runoff model takes the form of **Q = P**, however its RTO equation-fitting results state otherwise (Tables 5 and 6). Best-regressed RTO linear models from IBM SPSS show no possibility to model complete runoff conditions. For the Q/P > 50% dataset, at most Q = 0.696 P where 30.4% of initial loss still exists. For the Q/P > 60% dataset, at most Q = 0.756 P where 24.4% of initial loss still exists. **Q = P** is statistically insignificant ($p > 0.05$) under both runoff coefficient scenarios. The hydrological implications of the linear regression model conflicts and detaches from the statistical justification. As such, hydrological-condition implications based on those two fitting parameters of the linear regression model become inconsistent and unreliable. The linear regression runoff model failed to describe the hydrological conditions of the Sungai Kayu Ara watershed when runoff coefficient is greater than 50%. On the other hand, the AFM did not outperform against compared models in this study (Table 3). It also failed to model the watershed and derive the $CN_{0.2}$ value when the runoff coefficient is greater than 50%.

The original SCS hypothesis where the value of $\lambda = 0.20$ was met with repeated rejections ($\alpha = 0.01$ level) as the BCa 99% confidence interval span did not show the possibility of having the value of 0.20 (Tables 2, 7 and 8), concluding that Equation (2) was not valid and therefore inapplicable for this study. H_0 also faced rejection ($\alpha = 0.01$ level) as its BCa findings indicated a standard deviation of λ that was not equivalent to zero (Table 2), showing the nature of λ's value fluctuations, thus, λ does not meet the requirement of a constant as was suggested in 1954 by the SCS, and is, rather, a variable. As a matter of fact, H_0 in this study was rejected, and thus, it opens the opportunity for SCS model calibration. The notion of approaching this matter based on numerical analysis was also utilised in this study, along with guidance of non-parametric inferential statistics, identifying the ideal collective representation of λ and S values to formulate a calibrated runoff predictive model for the Sungai Kayu Ara watershed.

Many researchers in this field suggested different λ values to recalibrate the SCS runoff predictive model. However, the statistical significance of those new values was not reported [6,27]. This study is also in line with the latest findings in this area which reported the detection of multiple CN and I_a values within a watershed and suggested the practice of using multiple CN and I_a values to represent the heterogeneity of a watershed. Those studies also concluded that the SCS CN model must be calibrated according to local rainfall–runoff data to improve the runoff prediction accuracy [33–35]. As such, Equation (2) can no longer be blindly adopted for runoff prediction modelling according to the SCS with $I_a = 0.2S$. The latest findings of [34,35] increased the SCS CN model calibration difficulty level for SCS practitioners because they can only use one I_a value to calibrate Equation (1) [2,9–13]. The non-parametric inferential statistics model calibration guide proposed by this study offers a solution for SCS practitioners to select statistically significant key parameters of S and λ values from its confidence interval range to calibrate the fundamental SCS CN runoff framework (Equation (1)) according to their rainfall–runoff dataset.

6. Conclusions

1. The hydrological implications of the linear regression model conflicts and detaches from the statistical justification and, therefore, implications based on the two main-fitting parameters of the linear regression model become inconsistent and unreliable. The linear regression runoff model and the AFM technique failed to describe the hydrological conditions of this case study when the runoff coefficient (Q/P) is greater than 50%. On the other hand, $\lambda \neq 0.20$, and the simplified SCS runoff model (Equation (2)) is not statistically significant ($\alpha = 0.01$). These three models are unsuitable in terms of modelling the condition of urban runoff in this study;

2. The decimal $CN_{0.2}$ value can be calculated in order to reflect runoff conditions with higher accuracy. Unlike the antecedent moisture-condition CN concept, $CN_{0.2}$ can be calculated directly and independently to represent the runoff condition of the watershed when it reaches 50% and 60% ground saturation level. The optimum is $\lambda = 0.004$ and $CN_{0.2} = 93.35$ (at $\alpha = 0.01$ level) to model all P-Q data pairs runoff for the Sungai Kayu Ara watershed. Although the land-use and land cover remained the same throughout this study, the $CN_{0.2}$ value of this case study still increased from 94.89 ($\lambda = 0.005$) to 96.50 ($\lambda = 0.007$) as the watershed became more saturated. In line with [14], the $CN_{0.2}$ value was found to be a sensitive parameter. Comparing Equations (7) and (13), the $CN_{0.2}$ value increases by 3.4% with an average of 44% increase in runoff amount, which is almost 178,000 m^3 of the runoff increment. Runoff prediction-difference is more profound toward higher-rainfall-depth storm events. As such, Equation (13) should be used to assess the urban drainage capacity and for flash flood prediction, while $CN_{0.2}$ value cannot be decided according to the land-use and land cover conditions only. It can be derived according to the rainfall–runoff dataset and ground saturation conditions in order to reflect the specific hydrological characteristics of a watershed with the proposed method in this study for urban runoff predictions;

3. This study also demonstrated that it is possible to calibrate Equation (1) and to include rainfall depths less than 1 inch (25.4 mm) in order to formulate a statistically significant urban runoff predictive model. Otherwise, nearly 61% (56 events with measurable runoff) of the P-Q data pairs of this study will be discarded for modelling as the corresponding rainfall values are less than 25.4 mm, out of which, 34% (19 events) with $Q/P > 50$% and 27% (15 events) with $Q/P > 50$% would not be available to formulate Equations (12) and (13) with a sufficient sample size. This study also preserved the parsimonious form of the SCS runoff model for calibration and it emerged as the simplest two-parameter rainfall–runoff predictive model in this study. Flood prediction through rainfall–runoff modelling should be formulated with rainfall–runoff data pairs with runoff coefficients > 50% instead of using datasets with low runoff coefficients;

4. In general, the proposed methodology in this study is applicable to any urban watershed with a measurable runoff amount (even with rainfall depth < 25.4 mm) and enough datasets (at least 20 events) with $Q/P > 50$% or above. It offers a quick and economical runoff assessment in developing areas with rapid land-use and cover change without relying on return period information. Future works may analyse the cost effectiveness of return period-based infrastructure design at urban scale with a longer period rainfall–runoff dataset. The SCS CN model has two parameters (λ and S) only. The proposed model calibration methodology offers a quick quantification of runoff depth from a storm event, whereby SCS practitioners can estimate flood volume at the watershed of interest. Instead of selecting the CN value subjectively by looking at the land-use and land cover, SCS CN model practitioners can derive a range of statistically significant CN values to estimate probable flood volume, assess drainage capacity, and identify probable flood prone area(s). In conjunction, GIS software can be used to assess flood risk, financial losses, and propose needed mitigation strategies;

5. The authors caution that there are several limitations to the proposed methodology. The minimum sample size should be at least 20 to achieve meaningful inferential results. The choice of the statistical software must have the option to conduct bootstrapping BCa procedures and provide confidence intervals for median values. The SCS CN lump model must be used with caution when re-creating the specific features of an actual storm as it does not contain time parameters. It is not a precipitation runoff model to model runoff from snowmelt or rain on frozen ground conditions.

Author Contributions: Conceptualisation, L.L. and Z.Y.; methodology, L.L.; software, L.L. and J.L.L.; validation, L.L., S.H.L., R.J.C. and Z.Y.; formal analysis, L.L.; investigation, L.L., S.H.L., R.J.C. and Z.Y.; resources, L.L. and Z.Y.; data curation, L.L.; writing—original draft preparation, L.L. and J.L.L.; writing—review and editing, L.L., J.L.L., R.J.C. and Z.Y.; visualisation, L.L. and J.L.L.; supervision, Z.Y.; project administration, L.L. and Z.Y.; funding acquisition, L.L. and Z.Y. All authors have read and agreed to the published version of the manuscript.

Funding: The research was supported by Ministry of Higher Education (MoHE) through the Fundamental Research Grant Scheme (FRGS/1/2021/WAB07/UTAR/02/1) and was partly supported by the Brunsfield Engineering Sdn. Bhd., Malaysia (Brunsfield 8013/0002 & 8126/0001).

Institutional Review Board Statement: Not applicable.

Informed Consent Statement: Not applicable.

Data Availability Statement: Please email to request from Ling Lloyd at: linglloyd@utar.edu.my.

Acknowledgments: The authors appreciate the guidance from R. H. Hawkins at The University of Arizona, Tucson, AZ, USA.

Conflicts of Interest: The authors declare no conflict of interest.

Appendix A

The $CN_{0.2}$ value derivation and SCS CN model calibration steps can be summarized as below:

1. Given that: Effective rainfall $(P_e) = P - I_a$ and $I_a = \lambda S$; Equation (1) can be rearranged as: $Q = \frac{P_e^2}{P_e + S}$ where $S = \frac{P_e^2}{Q} - P_e$ and $\lambda = \frac{I_a}{S}$
2. For each P-Q data pair (P_i, Q_i), calculate corresponding λ_i and S_i value;
3. Perform bootstrap, BCa procedure, and normality test in SPSS (version 18.0 or an equivalent statistics software) for (λ_i, S_i);
4. Check the normality test results of S_i to see whether it is normally distributed or not:
   (a) If yes, refer to the mean BCa confidence interval for S_i optimisation.
   (b) Otherwise, refer to the median BCa confidence interval for S_i optimisation;
5. Check the normality test results of λ_i to see whether it is normally distributed or not:
   (a) If yes, refer to the mean BCa confidence interval for λ_i optimisation.
   (b) Otherwise, refer to the median BCa confidence interval for λ_i optimisation;
6. Substitute the $\lambda_{optimum}$ and $S_{optimum}$ value into Equation (1) to formulate the calibrated SCS runoff predictive model;
7. Given (P_i, Q_i) and $\lambda_{optimum}$, compute $S_{\lambda i}$ values with $S_\lambda = \frac{\left[P - \frac{(\lambda-1)Q}{2\lambda}\right] - \sqrt{PQ - P^2 + \left[P - \frac{(\lambda-1)Q}{2\lambda}\right]^2}}{\lambda}$
8. Given (P_i, Q_i) and $\lambda = 0.2$, compute $S_{0.2i}$ values with $S_\lambda = \frac{\left[P - \frac{(\lambda-1)Q}{2\lambda}\right] - \sqrt{PQ - P^2 + \left[P - \frac{(\lambda-1)Q}{2\lambda}\right]^2}}{\lambda}$ again;
9. Correlate $S_{0.2i}$ and $S_{\lambda i}$ to form a S correlation equation in SPSS (or an equivalent statistics software);
10. Substitute the S correlation equation into the SCS curve number formula: $CN_{0.2} = \frac{25,400}{S_{0.2} + 254}$ to derive $CN_{0.2}$ value.

References

1. EM-DAT, CRED/UCLouvain, Brussels, Belgium. International Disasters Database, 1900–2020 Hydrological & Meteorological Categories (Flood, Landslide & Storms). Available online: www.emdat.be (accessed on 16 December 2020).
2. Hawkins, R.H.; Ward, T.J.; Woodward, D.E.; Van Mullem, J.A. *Curve Number Hydrology: State of Practice*; ASCE: Reston, VA, USA, 2009.
3. Hawkins, R.H. Curve number method: Time to think anew? *J. Hydrol. Eng.* **2014**, *19*, 1059. [CrossRef]
4. Natural Resources Conservation Service (NRCS). *National Engineering Handbook, Part 630 Hydrology*; USDA: Washington, DC, USA, 2004.
5. D'Asaro, F.; Grillone, G. Empirical investigation of curve number method parameters in the Mediterranean area. *J. Hydrol. Eng.* **2012**, *17*, 1141–1152. [CrossRef]
6. Ling, L.; Yusop, Z.; Yap, W.S.; Tan, W.L.; Chow, M.F.; Ling, J.L. A Calibrated, Watershed-Specific SCS-CN Method: Application to Wangjiaqiao Watershed in the Three Gorges Area, China. *Water* **2020**, *12*, 60. [CrossRef]
7. Ross, C.W.; Prihodko, L.; Anchang, J.; Kumar, S.; Ji, W.; Hanan, N.P. HYSOGs250m, global gridded hydrologic soil groups for curve-number-based runoff modeling. *Sci. Data* **2018**, *5*, 150091. [CrossRef]
8. Jaafar, H.H.; Ahmad, F.A.; Beyrouthy, N.E. GCN250, new global gridded curve numbers for hydrologic modeling and design. *Sci. Data* **2019**, *6*, 145. [CrossRef] [PubMed]
9. Zelelew, D.G. Spatial mapping and testing the applicability of the curve number method for ungauged catchments in Northern Ethiopia. *Int. Soil Water Conserv. Res.* **2017**, *5*, 293–301. [CrossRef]
10. Hounkpè, J.; Diekkrüger, B.; Afouda, A.A.; Sintondji, L.O.C. Land use change increases flood hazard: A multi-modelling approach to assess change in flood characteristics driven by socio-economic land use change scenarios. *Nat. Hazards* **2019**, *98*, 1021–1050. [CrossRef]
11. Feng, B.; Wang, J.F.; Zhang, Y.; Hall, B.; Zeng, C.Q. Urban flood hazard mapping using a hydraulic–GIS combined model. *Nat. Hazards* **2019**, *100*, 1089–1104. [CrossRef]
12. Yalcin, E. Assessing the impact of topography and land cover data resolutions on two-dimensional HEC-RAS hydrodynamic model simulations for urban flood hazard analysis. *Nat. Hazards* **2020**, *101*, 995–1017. [CrossRef]
13. Durán-Barroso, P.; González, J.; Valdés, J.B. Sources of uncertainty in the NRCS CN Model: Recognition and Solutions. *Hydrol. Process* **2017**, *31*, 3898–3906. [CrossRef]
14. Boughton, W.C. A Review of the USDA SCS Curve Number Method. *Aust. J. Soil Res.* **1989**, *27*, 511–523. [CrossRef]
15. Soulis, K.X.; Valiantzas, J.D. Identification of the SCS-CN parameter spatial distribution using rainfall-runoff data in heterogeneous watersheds. *Water Resour. Manag.* **2013**, *27*, 1737–1749. [CrossRef]
16. Lal, M.; Mishra, S.K.; Pandey, A.; Pandey, R.P.; Meena, P.K.; Chaudhary, A.; Jha, R.K.; Shreevastava, A.J.; Kumar, Y. Evaluation of the Soil Conservation Service curve number methodology using data from agricultural plots. *Hydrogeol. J.* **2016**, *25*, 151–167. [CrossRef]
17. Betson, R.P. What Is Watershed Runoff? *J. Geophys. Res.* **1964**, *68*, 1541–1552. [CrossRef]
18. Hewlett, J.D.; Hibbert, A.R. Factors Affecting the Response of Small Watersheds to Precipitation in Humid Areas. In Proceedings of the International Symposium on Forest Hydrology, State College, PA, USA, 31 August–2 September 1967.
19. Miller, J.D.; Kim, H.; Kjeldsen, T.R.; Packman, J.; Grebby, S.; Dearden, R. Assessing the impact of urbanization on storm runoff in a peri-urban catchment using historical change in impervious cover. *J. Hydrol.* **2014**, *515*, 59–70. [CrossRef]
20. Davidsen, S.; Löwe, R.; Ravn, N.H.; Jensen, L.N.; Arnbjerg-Nielsen, K. Initial conditions of urban permeable surfaces in rainfall-runoff models using Horton's infiltration. *Water Sci. Technol.* **2018**, *77*, 662–669. [CrossRef] [PubMed]
21. Fidal, J.; Kjeldsen, T. Accounting for soil moisture in rainfall-runoff modelling of urban areas. *J. Hydrol.* **2020**, *589*, 125122. [CrossRef]
22. Sumargo, E.; McMillan, H.; Weihs, R.; Ellis, C.J.; Wilson, A.M.; Ralph, F.M. A Soil Moisture Monitoring Network to Assess Controls on Runoff Generation During Atmospheric River Events. *Hydrol. Process* **2020**, *35*, e13998. [CrossRef]
23. Yao, L.; Chen, L.; Wei, W. Assessing the effectiveness of imperviousness on stormwater runoff in micro urban catchments by model simulation. *Hydrol. Processes* **2015**, *30*, 1836–1848. [CrossRef]
24. Ebrahimian, A.; Gulliver, J.S.; Wilson, B.N. Effective impervious area for runoff in urban watersheds. *Hydrol. Processes* **2016**, *30*, 3717–3729. [CrossRef]
25. Hoang, L.; Schneiderman, E.M.; Moore, K.E.B.; Mukundan, R.; Owens, E.M.; Steenhuis, T.S. Predicting saturation-excess runoff distribution with a lumped hillslope model: SWAT-HS. *Hydrol. Processes* **2017**, *31*, 2226–2243. [CrossRef]
26. Schneider, L.; McCuen, R.H. Statistical Guidelines for Curve Number Generation. *J. Irrig. Drain. Eng.* **2005**, *131*, 282–290. [CrossRef]
27. Ling, L.; Yusop, Z.; Ling, J.L. Statistical and Type II Error Assessment of a Runoff Predictive Model in Peninsula Malaysia. *Mathematics* **2021**, *9*, 812. [CrossRef]
28. Harremoës, P.; Arnbjerg-Nielsen, K. Prediction of Hydrological Reduction Factor and Initial Loss in Urban Surface Runoff from Small Ungauged Catchments. *Atmos. Res.* **1996**, *8*, 137–147.
29. Abustan, I.; Ball, J.E. Modelling the Export of Phosphorous From Urban Catchments. In Proceedings of the HydraStorm 98, Adelaide, Australia, 27–30 September 1998.
30. Huber, W.C.; Dickinson, R.E. *Stormwater Management Model, Version 4, Users Manual*; Environmental Research Laboratory, US Environmental Protection Agency: Athens, GA, USA, 1988.

31. Hjelmfelt, A.T. Curve-number procedure as infiltration method. *J. Hydraul. Div.* **1980**, *106*, 1107–1111. [CrossRef]
32. Hawkins, R.H. Asymptotic determination of runoff curve numbers from data. *J. Irrig. Drain. Eng.* **1993**, *119*, 334–345. [CrossRef]
33. ASCE-ASABE (American Society of Agricultural and Biological Engineers)-NRCS (Natural Resources Conservation Service) Task Group on Curve Number Hydrology. *Report of Task Group on Curve Number Hydrology, Chapters 8 (Land Use and Land Treatment Classes), 9 (Hydrologic Soil Cover Complexes), 10 (Estimation of Direct Runoff from Storm Rainfall), 12 (Hydrologic Effects of Land Use and Treatment)*; Hawkins, R.H., Ward, T.J., Woodward, D.E., Eds.; ASCE: Reston, VA, USA, 2017.
34. Santikari, V.P.; Murdoch, L.C. Including effects of watershed heterogeneity in the curve number method using variable initial abstraction. *Hydrol. Earth Syst. Sci.* **2018**, *22*, 4725–4743. [CrossRef]
35. Hawkins, R.H.; Theurer, F.D.; Rezaeianzadeh, M. Understanding the Basis of the Curve Number Method for Watershed Models and TMDLs. *J. Hydrol. Eng.* **2019**, *24*, 06019003. [CrossRef]

Article

A Regularised Total Least Squares Approach for 1D Inverse Scattering

Andreas Tataris [1,*] and Tristan van Leeuwen [1,2]

[1] Mathematical Institite, Utrecht University, 3584 CD Utrecht, The Netherlands; t.van.leeuwen@cwi.nl
[2] Computational Imaging Group, Centrum Wiskunde & Informatica, 1098 XG Amsterdam, The Netherlands
* Correspondence: a.tataris@uu.nl

Abstract: We study the inverse scattering problem for a Schrödinger operator related to a static wave operator with variable velocity, using the GLM (Gelfand–Levitan–Marchenko) integral equation. We assume to have noisy scattering data, and we derive a stability estimate for the error of the solution of the GLM integral equation by showing the invertibility of the GLM operator between suitable function spaces. To regularise the problem, we formulate a variational total least squares problem, and we show that, under certain regularity assumptions, the optimisation problem admits minimisers. Finally, we compute numerically the regularised solution of the GLM equation using the total least squares method in a discrete sense.

Keywords: inverse scattering; Gelfand–Levithan–Marchenko equation; total least squares

1. Introduction

In many scientific, medical and industrial problems, one has to retrieve unknown coefficients of a governing differential equation (PDE) from (partial) measurements of its solution. This way, properties of materials can be studied in a medium that we do not have direct physical access to. In geophysics, for example, a well-known problem is estimating the elastic parameters of the subsurface from surface measurements. The governing PDE is a wave equation, and the measurements consist of a trace of its solution on the boundary of the domain. See, for example, [1] for an overview.

In particular, we focus on the inverse problem for the 1D static wave/Helmholtz equation

$$-\frac{d}{dy}\left\{c^2(y)\frac{d}{dy}v(k,y)\right\} = k^2 v(k,y), \ y \in \mathbb{R},\qquad(1)$$

with $v = v^i + v^s$ and (asymptotic) boundary conditions

$$\lim_{y\to\pm\infty}\left\{\frac{dv^s(k,y)}{dx} \pm ikv^s(k,y)\right\} = 0 \qquad(2)$$

We let $v^i(k,y) = e^{-iky}$, which corresponds to an incoming plane wave from the left. The measurements at $y = 0$ are given by

$$K(t) = \int_{\mathbb{R}} v^s(k,0)e^{2ikt}dk,$$

for $t \in [0, T]$. The goal is now to retrieve c from these measurements.

Various methods for solving the inverse coefficient problem for the wave equation have been developed. A well-known method is full waveform inversion, which poses the inverse problem as a PDE-constrained optimisation problem [2,3]. Other variational formulations for the inverse problem have been proposed as well; see, for example, [4,5]. We refer to such methods as *indirect*, as they are based on an implicit non-linear relation between

data and coefficients that need to be solved iteratively. On the other hand, the inverse problem can be solved using a *direct* method. Here, an explicit formula leads to the exact solution of the inverse problem (for noiseless data). A classical direct method is given by the Gelfand–Levitan–Marchenko (GLM) integral equation [6–8]. This method has its roots in inverse scattering theory, and has recently attracted renewed attention [9–12]. In [13], for example, a GLM-like approach for wavefield redatuming was proposed. Here, boundary measurements are used to estimate the wavefield in the entire domain. Subsequently, such a wavefield can be used to estimate medium parameters by solving the Lippmann–Schwinger integral equation [14].

One advantage of the indirect (variational) methods over the direct ones is that they can handle better situations where there is noise in the data. In direct methods, noise in the data likely gets amplified. To counter such instabilities, one typically adds regularisation. In particular, the GLM approach with noisy data requires a total least squares (TLS) approach, and was studied numerically by [15]. Other regularised approaches for similar integral equations in seismic imaging are discussed in [16].

In this paper, we revisit the classical GLM approach for the 1D inverse medium problem and consider in particular the infinite dimensional case with noisy measurements. To regularise the problem, we formulate a regularised (TLS) approach for it. To solve the resulting variational problem, we use an alternating iterative method [17]. Some numerical examples complete the paper.

Our main contributions are as follows:

- We extend the stability estimates that can be found in [18] to the classical GLM integral equation.
- We show that the variational TLS formulation of the GLM method admits minimisers.

This paper is organised as follows. In Section 2, we state the forward scattering problem and we review some classical results from scattering theory. We also review basic properties of the GLM integral operator. In Section 3, we include our new findings, namely the stability estimate for the GLM inversion assuming having access to noisy scattering data. We then continue studying the variational total least squares problem of reconstructing the solution of the inverse problem from noisy scattering data, and we show the well-posedness of it. We also discuss its analytical limitations. In Section 4 we implement numerically the proposed total least squares regularisation method. In Section 5 we show a number of numerical examples and conclude the paper with a discussion section.

2. Preliminaries

This section summarises mostly known and well-established results in 1D scattering theory. In Section 2.1, we use the travel time coordinate transform to derive the equivalence of the static wave equation with variable velocity to the Schrödinger equation and we formulate the forward scattering problem. In Section 2.2, we repeat the classical procedure of using the Jost solutions to construct the solution of the forward scattering problem. In Section 2.3, we briefly discuss the derivation of the GLM integral equation and we review some basic properties of the GLM integral operator.

2.1. Formulation of the Forward Problem

It has been well-established (see, for example, [7,8]) that the inverse problem for the 1D static wave/Helmholtz equation may equivalently be stated in terms of the 1D Schrödinger equation

$$\left\{-\frac{d^2}{dx^2} + q(x)\right\} u(k,x) = k^2 u(k,x), \quad x \in \mathbb{R}, \tag{3}$$

with boundary conditions

$$\lim_{x \to +\infty} \left\{\frac{du^s(k,x)}{dx} + \imath k u^s(k,x)\right\} = 0, \tag{4}$$

$$\lim_{x \to -\infty} \left\{ \frac{du^s(k,x)}{dx} - \imath k u^s(k,x) \right\} = 0, \tag{5}$$

where

$$u(k, \cdot) = u^i(k, \cdot) + u^s(k, \cdot) \tag{6}$$

with $u^i(k,x) = e^{-\imath k x}$, $x \in \mathbb{R}$. The quantities are related via

$$u(k,x) = \eta(x) v(k, y(x)), \ x \in \mathbb{R}, \tag{7}$$

$$q(x) = \frac{1}{\eta(x)} \frac{d^2 \eta(x)}{dx^2}, x \in \mathbb{R}. \tag{8}$$

where

$$\eta(x) = \{c(y(x))\}^{1/2}, \tag{9}$$

and

$$y(x) = \int_0^x \eta^2(r) dr, \ x \in \mathbb{R}. \tag{10}$$

We assume that the velocity $c > 0$ is bounded and an element of $C^1(\mathbb{R})$. We also assume that c' is bounded and has a compact support and that $c'' \in L^2(\mathbb{R})$ is a bounded function. Therefore, q is bounded and compactly supported since η'' is bounded and compactly supported. We refer to the Appendix A for a discussion on the L^2-validity of the calculations that lead from the static wave equation to the Schrödinger equation. Furthermore, we note that we seek for an element of $H^2_{loc}(\mathbb{R})$ as the solution of the differential equation since the scattering potential is discontinuous in general, and thus, we cannot necessarily obtain a solution of C^2-regularity.

A key result that we will need later on is the absence of bound states.

Theorem 1. *Let the Schrödinger operator*

$$S = -\frac{d^2}{dx^2} + q : H^2(\mathbb{R}) \to L^2(\mathbb{R}), \tag{11}$$

where q is given by relation (8). *Then the discrete spectrum of S is empty.*

We include the proof in the Appendix A. To show Theorem 1, we use the positivity of the static wave operator and its equivalence to the Schrödinger operator. We use this positivity argument thanks to the conversation and the hint given to author [1] (A.T.) from Vassilis Papanicolaou [19]. The result of the absence of bound states for this particular Schrödinger operator can be derived using also physical arguments; see [8].

2.2. Classical Results from Scattering Theory

It is well known that the Schrödinger differential equation can be reduced to the following Schrödinger integral equations at $\pm \infty$.

$$f^+(k,x) = e^{\imath k x} - \int_x^\infty \frac{\sin(k(x-y))}{k} q(y) f^+(k,y) dy, x \in \mathbb{R},$$

and

$$f^-(k,x) = e^{-\imath k x} + \int_{-\infty}^x \frac{\sin(k(x-y))}{k} q(y) f^-(k,y) dy, x \in \mathbb{R}.$$

Such Volterra-type integral equations can be derived using the variation of constants and we refer to [20] for a discussion about the existence and uniqueness of solutions of these integral equations. The functions $f^\pm(\pm k, \cdot)$ are called the Jost solutions, and the solution of the forward scattering problem can be decomposed as a sum of these functions as

$$u(k,x) = T(k) f^-(k,x) = f^+(-k,x) + R(k) f^+(k,x), \ x \in \mathbb{R}, \tag{12}$$

where the functions T, R are called the transmission and reflection coefficients respectively. The transmission and reflection coefficients, as functions of the wavenumber k, satisfy the following relations

$$T(k) = 1 + \frac{1}{2\imath k} \int_{\mathbb{R}} u(k,y)q(y)e^{\imath ky}dy,$$

$$R(k) = \frac{1}{2\imath k} \int_{\mathbb{R}} u(k,y)q(y)e^{-\imath ky}dy, \tag{13}$$

for $k \in \mathbb{R} \setminus \{0\}$ and the conservation of energy

$$|T(k)|^2 + |R(k)|^2 = 1, \; k \in \mathbb{R} \setminus \{0\}. \tag{14}$$

The scattering theory for the Schrödinger equation is a classical mathematical subject that dates back to the 1960s. We refer, for example, to [20–22] and the references therein for introduction and extensive analysis of the quantum scattering problem.

2.3. The Inverse Scattering Problem and the Gelfand–Levitan–Marchenko Inversion Method

The inverse scattering problem is now to retrieve the scattering potential, q, from the reflection coefficient R. The GLM integral equation is the key for solving this inverse scattering problem. In this section, we review the classical inverse scattering problem of the determination of the scattering potential from scattering data, using the GLM integral equation. In Section 2.3.2, we study the integral operator defined by the GLM equation in order to derive properties that will help us to construct an inequality for the error of the solution of the GLM equation as we show in Section 3.1.

2.3.1. Derivation of the GLM Equation

The key ingredient for deriving the GLM integral equation is the scattering identity (12). For fixed x, we get that $\mathbb{C}_{Im>0} \ni k \mapsto f^+(k,x)e^{-\imath kx} - 1$ is an element of the Hardy class $\mathcal{H}_2^+$. Using the Paley–Wiener theorem, we obtain that $f^+(\cdot, x)$ satisfies the following relation

$$e^{-\imath kx}f^+(k,x) = 1 + \int_0^\infty B(x,t)e^{2\imath kt}dt, \; \forall k \in \mathbb{R} \setminus \{0\}, \tag{15}$$

where $B(x, \cdot) \in L^2(0, \infty)$ satisfies

$$-\frac{dB(x,0)}{dx} = q(x). \tag{16}$$

The calculation of the Fourier transform of relation (12) gives the classical GLM integral equation. For more details on the application of the Paley–Wiener theorem to the Jost function $f^+(\cdot, \cdot)$, we refer to [20]. Below, we give the GLM integral equation. For a detailed proof, we refer again to [20], which gives a very detailed exposition of the quantum scattering problem on the line using analytical methods.

Theorem 2. *Let $x \in \mathbb{R}$. Then the function $B(x, \cdot)$ satisfies the GLM integral equation*

$$K(x+t) + \int_0^\infty B(x,z)K(x+t+z)dz + B(x,t) = 0, \; a.e. \text{ for } t \in [0,\infty), \tag{17}$$

where the scattering data $K = K_c + K_d$ are given by

$$K_c(t) = \frac{1}{\pi} \int_{\mathbb{R}} R(k)e^{2\imath kt}dk, \; t \in [0,\infty), \tag{18}$$

$$K_d(t) = 2\sum_{n=1}^N \rho_n e^{-2p_n t}, \; t \in [0,\infty), \tag{19}$$

where $(-\rho_n)_{n=1}^{N}$ are the eigenvalues of the Schrödinger operator $S = -\frac{d^2}{dx^2} + q$ and $(-p_n = -\frac{1}{\|f_n\|_{L^2(\mathbb{R})}})_{n=1}^{N}$, f_n are the eigenfunctions corresponding to the eigenvalues.

Remark 1. *Due to the absence of bound states in our setting, we do not have to consider K_d and will denote the measured scattering data by K, with the understanding that it is directly related to R through a Fourier transform.*

The inverse procedure is as follows. First, the scattering data K are collected by measuring the response at the boundary (i.e., $x = 0$). Then follows the solution of the GLM integral Equation (17). After the GLM kernel is recovered, the scattering potential, q, can be found using relation (16).

2.3.2. Analysing the GLM Operator

In this subsection, we study the GLM integral operator and we review some of its properties. In particular, we use these properties in Section 3.1 for deriving an upper bound for the error of the noisy inverse problem. Since we assume that the scattering potential q is compactly supported, we obtain that for every fixed $x \in \mathbb{R}$, the solution of the GLM equation $B(x, \cdot)$ is compactly supported. In particular, this is justified using the following inequality,

$$|B(x,t)| \leq \int_{x+t}^{\infty} |q(z)|dz \exp\left(\int_{x}^{\infty}(z-x)|q(z)|dz\right), \tag{20}$$

for $x \in \mathbb{R}$ and $t > 0$, see [20]. Consequently, the domain of integration in the GLM integral equation can be reduced to an integration over a finite interval. For a fixed potential q, we assume that the interval of integration is $(0, T_x)$, where T_x depends on the fixed value of $x \in \mathbb{R}$. In addition, since we are interested in reconstructing $B(\cdot, \cdot)$ for the values of x where the scattering potential is supported, it is reasonable to consider the following. Since the set $\{T_x : x \in supp(q)\}$ is bounded from above, we denote with T its supremum. We assume without loss of generality that $(0, T) \supset supp(q)$. We define

$$\mathcal{Y} = \{f \in L^2(\mathbb{R}) : supp(f) \subset (0,T)\}. \tag{21}$$

We also define the set $\mathcal{B}(\mathcal{Y}) = \{L : \mathcal{Y} \to \mathcal{Y} : \text{bounded and linear}\}$. Additionally, for a fixed $x \in (0,T)$ and $f \in \mathcal{Y}$ we define

$$\{A(K)f\}(x,t) := \int_0^T \chi_{(0,T)}(t) K(x+t+z) f(z) dz, \; t \in \mathbb{R}. \tag{22}$$

Since we fix $K \in L^2(\mathbb{R})$, we write for simplicity

$$\{A(K)f\}(x, \cdot) = A_x f. \tag{23}$$

With $\chi_\omega(\cdot)$, we denote the characteristic function which is 1 in ω and 0 in $\mathbb{R} \setminus \omega$. Since the reflection coefficient $R \in L^2(\mathbb{R})$, thus $K \in L^2(\mathbb{R})$, see [20], we find the following.

Lemma 1. *For fixed x, the operator*

$$A_x : \mathcal{Y} \to \mathcal{Y} \tag{24}$$

is compact and self-adjoint.

Lemma 2. *The numbers $\lambda = \pm 1$ are not eigenvalues of A_x.*

Considering the previous lemmas, the following result follows.

Proposition 1. *The operator $I + A_x \in \mathcal{B}(\mathcal{Y})$ is invertible and its inverse is given by the Neumann series expansion in $\mathcal{B}(\mathcal{Y})$.*

3. Main Results

So far, we have summarised mainly known results for the scattering problem of our study. In the following subsection, we provide the reader with a new result regarding the stability of the reconstruction of the GLM kernel from noisy scattering data. In Section 3.2, we show the existence of minimisers for the variational total least squares regularisation of the GLM inversion.

3.1. Stability Estimates

Assuming now that there is an error $\varepsilon \in L^2(\mathbb{R})$ in the measurements of the scattering data K (due to noise, measuring errors, etc.); we are then dealing with the following problem.

$$\text{Given } K^\star = K + \varepsilon \in L^2(\mathbb{R}), \text{ find } B_x^\star \in L^2(0,T): \tag{25}$$

$$B_x^\star(t) + \int_0^T \chi_{(0,T)}(t) K^\star(x+t+z) B_x^\star(z) dz + K^\star(x+t) = 0, \text{ a.e. for } t \text{ in } (0,T), \tag{26}$$

where we let $B_x(\cdot) = B(x, \cdot)$ for ease of notation. We then want to bound $\|B_x^\star - B_x\|_{L^2(\mathbb{R})}$ in terms of $\|\varepsilon\|_{L^2(\mathbb{R})}$. A similar upper bound for the error for a similar GLM equation is given in [18], but not in $L^2(\mathbb{R})$. In addition, we refer to [23] for a discussion on a stability estimate of the Marchenko inversion where the bounds are on the scattering potential. In the application of recovering the scattering potential from scattering data, a pointwise estimate for the error is sufficient in view of relation (16). We denote

$$\Delta B_x = B_x^\star - B_x. \tag{27}$$

and

$$\varepsilon_x(t) = K^\star(x+t) - K(x+t), \text{ a.e for } t \in \mathbb{R}. \tag{28}$$

Assuming further that the error e is real valued, we obtain, as before, that $A_x^\star$ is a compact and self-adjoint operator. We then find the following result.

Lemma 3. *Let the previous assumptions be true. The following inequality holds,*

$$\|A_x^\star - A_x\|_{B(\mathcal{Y})} \leq \sqrt{T} \|\varepsilon_x\|_{L^2(\mathbb{R})}. \tag{29}$$

Proof. Let $f \in \mathcal{Y}$. We obtain

$$\left| [(A_x^\star - A_x) f](t) \right| = \left| \int_0^T \chi_{[0,T]}(z) \left\{ K^\star(x+z+t) - K(x+z+t) \right\} f(z) dz \right| \leq \tag{30}$$

$$\|\varepsilon_{x+t}\|_{L^2(0,T)} \times \|f\|_{L^2(0,T)} \leq \|\varepsilon\|_{L^2(\mathbb{R})} \|f\|_{\mathcal{Y}} \text{ a.e. for } t \in (0,T) \Rightarrow \tag{31}$$

the operator $(A_x^\star - A_x)$ is well defined and

$$\|(A_x^\star - A_x)f\|_{L^2(0,T)} \leq \sqrt{T} \|\varepsilon\|_{L^2(\mathbb{R})} \|f\|_{\mathcal{Y}}, \tag{32}$$

$\forall f \in \mathcal{Y}$. □

With this, we are ready to present the error bound.

Theorem 3. *Under the previous assumptions, we obtain the following:*

$$\|\Delta B_x\|_{\mathcal{Y}} \leq \frac{\|\varepsilon_x\|_{L^2(\mathbb{R})}(1 + \sqrt{T}\|B_x^\star\|_{\mathcal{Y}})}{1 - \|A_x\|_{B(\mathcal{Y})}} \tag{33}$$

Proof. We subtract (17)–(26) to obtain

$$(I + A_x + \{A_x^\star - A_x\}) B_x^\star - (I + A_x) B_x = -\varepsilon_x \iff \tag{34}$$

$$(I + A_x)\Delta B_x = -(A_x^\star - A_x)B_x^\star - \varepsilon_x \Rightarrow \qquad (35)$$

since 1 is not an eigenvalue of A_x

$$\Delta B_x = (I + A_x)^{-1}\{-\varepsilon_x - (A_x^\star - A_x)B_x^\star\} \Rightarrow \qquad (36)$$

$$\|\Delta B_x\|_{\mathcal{Y}} \le \|(I + A_x)^{-1}\|_{\mathcal{B}(\mathcal{Y})}\{\|\varepsilon_x\|_{\mathcal{Y}} + \|A_x^\star - A_x\|_{\mathcal{Y}}\|B_x^\star\|_{\mathcal{Y}}\} \le \qquad (37)$$

$$\frac{\|\varepsilon\|_{L^2(\mathbb{R})}(1 + \sqrt{T}\|B_x^\star\|_{\mathcal{Y}})}{1 - \|A_x\|_{\mathcal{B}(\mathcal{Y})}}. \qquad (38)$$

□

The previous stability estimate gives an upper bound for the error of the solution of the GLM equation, which is proportionate to the L^2-norm of the error in the measurements e. Though, we cannot rule out the case where the operator norm of A_x is almost 1. In general, the operator norm of A_x is determined by K. However, what kind of potential produces scattering data that make the operator norm be closer to 1 is still something to investigate.

3.2. Variational Regularisation

In this section, we define and show well-posedness for the variational total least squares regularisation problem of determining the kernel B from inexact scattering data. Similar work on this subject was done in the finite dimensional setting by [15], where they considered discrete scattering data and they followed a data analytic way for studying the total least squares problem for regularizing the GLM equation. In our approach, we fill the theoretical gap of showing well-posedness of the total least squares regularisation method of the GLM inversion in the infinite dimensional setting.

Now, for a set $\Omega \subset \mathbb{R}^N$, $N = 1, 2$ and a generic function space $\Psi(\Omega) = \{f : \Omega \to \mathbb{C}\}$, we define the extension operator

$$E_0 : \Psi(\Omega) \to \Psi(\mathbb{R}^N), \qquad (39)$$

as the map that extends a function to 0 if the argument is not included in Ω. (This is a bounded operator if, for example, $\Psi(\Omega) = L^2(0, T)$.) Then, we consider the usual Lebesgue space

$$L^2((0,T)^2) = \{f : (0,T) \to L^2(0,T) : \int_0^T \|f(t,\cdot)\|_{L^2(0,T)}^2 dt < \infty\}.$$

The inner product is given by

$$\langle f, g\rangle_{L^2((0,T)^2)} = \int_0^T \langle f(t), g(t)\rangle_{L^2(0,T)} dt = \int_0^T \int_0^T f(x,t)\overline{g(x,t)} dx dt.$$

We also define

$$\Theta : L^2((0,T)^2) \to L^2((0,T), L^2(\mathbb{R})) \qquad (40)$$

with

$$\Theta f = x \mapsto E_0 f(x, \cdot), \text{ for almost all } x \in (0,T). \qquad (41)$$

Lemma 4. Θ *is a bounded linear operator.*

Proof. The linearity is easy to show. Now, for the boundedness, let $f \in L^2((0,T)^2)$

$$\|f\|_{L^2((0,T)^2)}^2 = \int_0^T \int_0^T |f(x,t)|^2 dt dx = \int_0^T \int_{\mathbb{R}} |E_0 f(x,t)|^2 dt dx = \|\Theta f\|_{L^2((0,T),L^2(\mathbb{R}))}^2.$$

□

We define $G : L^2((0,T)^2) \times L^2(\mathbb{R}) \to L^2((0,T), L^2(\mathbb{R}))$ as

$$G(B,K) = \{I + A(K)\}\Theta B =$$

$$x \mapsto \left\{ t \mapsto \Theta B(x,t) + \int_0^T \chi_{(0,T)}(y)\Theta B(x,z)K(x+t+z)dz \right\} \tag{42}$$

Remark 2. *We need Θ in order to have a well-defined convolution type relation in G. In addition, compare this with the setting of the previous section. By using Θ, we avoid the use of the space $\mathcal{Y}$ altogether.*

Proposition 2. $G : L^2((0,T)^2) \times L^2(\mathbb{R}) \to L^2((0,T), L^2(\mathbb{R}))$ *is well defined.*

Proof. Let $(B,K) \in L^2((0,T)^2) \times L^2(\mathbb{R})$. We want to show that $G(B,K) \in L^2((0,T), L^2(\mathbb{R}))$. For almost all $x \in (0,T), t \in \mathbb{R}$, we obtain that

$$|A(K)\Theta B(x,t)| = \left| \int_0^T \chi_{(0,T)}(t)\Theta B(x,z)K(x+t+z)dz \right| \leq$$

$$\|E_0 B(x,\cdot)\|_{L^2(\mathbb{R})} \|K\|_{L^2(\mathbb{R})} = \|B(x,\cdot)\|_{L^2(0,T)} \|K\|_{L^2(\mathbb{R})} \Rightarrow$$

$$\int_0^T \left\{ \int_0^T \chi_{(0,T)}(t)\Theta B(x,z)K(x+t+z)dz \right\}^2 dt \leq T \|B(x,\cdot)\|_{L^2(0,T)}^2 \|K\|_{L^2(\mathbb{R})}^2.$$

Therefore,

$$\left\| x \mapsto \left\{ t \mapsto \int_0^T \chi_{(0,T)}(t)\Theta B(x,z)K(x+t+z)dz \right\} \right\|_{L^2((0,T),L^2(\mathbb{R}))}^2 \leq T \|K\|_{L^2(\mathbb{R})}^2 \|B\|_{L^2((0,T)^2)}^2.$$

Finally,

$$\|G(B,K)\|_{L^2((0,T),L^2(\mathbb{R}))} \leq \sqrt{T} \|K\|_{L^2(\mathbb{R})} \|B\|_{L^2((0,T)^2)} + \|B\|_{L^2((0,T)^2)}.$$

□

Now, for a function $g \in L^2(\mathbb{R})$, we define for almost all $x \in (0,T)$

$$S(g) : x \mapsto g(x + \cdot). \tag{43}$$

Lemma 5. $S : L^2(\mathbb{R}) \to L^2((0,T), L^2(\mathbb{R}))$ *is linear and bounded.*

Proof. Let $g, g_1, g_2 \in L^2(\mathbb{R})$.

$$S(ag)(x,t) = ag(x+t) = aSg(x,t), \text{ a.e. in } (0,T) \times \mathbb{R}.$$

In addition,

$$S(g_1 + g_2)(x,t) = (g_1 + g_2)(x+t) = Sg_1(x,t) + Sg_1(x,t), a.e. \text{ in } (0,T) \times \mathbb{R}.$$

Now, we observe that

$$\|Sg\|_{L^2((0,T),L^2(\mathbb{R}))}^2 = \int_0^T \|g(x+\cdot)\|_{L^2(\mathbb{R})}^2 dx = \tag{44}$$

$$\int_0^T \|g\|_{L^2(\mathbb{R})}^2 dx = T\|g\|_{L^2(\mathbb{R})}^2 \Rightarrow \|Sg\|_{L^2((0,t),L^2(\mathbb{R}))} = \sqrt{T}\|g\|_{L^2(\mathbb{R})}. \tag{45}$$

□

Let $K \in L^2(\mathbb{R})$ given. Let also $\alpha, \beta > 0$. We define the total least squares functional $\phi_K : H^1((0,T)^2) \times H_0^1(0,3T) \to [0,\infty]$ as

$$\phi_K(B,e) :=$$

$$\|G(B, K + E_0 e) + S(K + E_0 e)\|^2_{L^2((0,T), L^2(\mathbb{R}))} + \alpha \|B\|^2_{L^2((0,T)^2)} + \beta \|e\|^2_{L^2(0,3T)}. \quad (46)$$

We assume that we have access to inexact scattering data $K \in L^2(\mathbb{R})$. We will define the solution of the inverse problem of finding the kernel B (in a region where the potential is supported) from K.

Definition 1. *Let $K \in L^2(\mathbb{R})$ inexact scattering data. Let $\alpha, \beta > 0$, and let that there exist functions $\widehat{B} \in H^1((0,T)^2)$ and $\widehat{e} \in H_0^1(0,3T)$ such that*

$$(\widehat{B}, \widehat{e}) \in \operatorname*{argmin}_{B \in \mathcal{U}, e \in \mathcal{V}} \phi_K(B,e), \quad (47)$$

with $\mathcal{U} \subset H^1((0,T)^2)$, $\mathcal{V} \subset H_0^1(0,3T)$, both bounded convex and closed in the respective topologies. Then, we call $\widehat{B}$ a regularised total least squares solution of the GLM integral equation.

Remark 3. *Ideally, we would like to find a perturbation e that will almost cancel out the noise ε which is included in K.*

We state some auxiliary results needed for showing well-posedness for the variational inverse problem (47).

Lemma 6. *Let $K \in L^2(\mathbb{R})$ and let the strongly convergent sequences*

$$B_n \to B \text{ in } L^2((0,T)^2) \quad (48)$$

and

$$e_n \to e \text{ in } L^2(0,3T). \quad (49)$$

Then

$$A(K + E_0 e_n) \Theta B_n \to A(K + E_0 e) \Theta B \text{ in } L^2((0,T), L^2(\mathbb{R})). \quad (50)$$

Proof. For almost all $x \in (0,T), t \in \mathbb{R}$, we take

$$\int_0^T \chi_{(0,T)}(t) \Theta B_n(x,z)(K + E_0 e_n)(x + t + z)dz -$$

$$\int_0^T \chi_{(0,T)}(t) \Theta B(x,z)(K + E_0 e)(x + t + z)dz =$$

$$\int_0^T \chi_{(0,T)}(t) \Theta \{B_n(x,z) - B(x,z)\}(K + E_0 e_n)(x + t + z)dz + \quad (51)$$

$$\int_0^T \chi_{(0,T)}(t) \Theta B(x,z)(K + E_0 e)(x + t + z)dz = \quad (52)$$

Using the triangular inequality and working similarly to Proposition 2, we obtain

$$\|A(K + E_0 e_n) \Theta B_n - A(K + E_0 e) \Theta B\|_{L^2((0,T), L^2(\mathbb{R}))} \leq \quad (53)$$

$$\sqrt{T}\|K + E_0 e_n\|_{L^2(\mathbb{R})}\|B_n - B\|_{L^2((0,T)^2)} + \sqrt{T}\|E_0 e_n - E_0 e\|_{L^2(\mathbb{R})}\|B\|_{L^2((0,T)^2)} \leq$$

$$\sqrt{T}(\|K\|_{L^2(\mathbb{R})} + \|e_n\|_{L^2(0,3T)})\|B_n - B\|_{L^2((0,T)^2)} + \sqrt{T}\|e_n - e\|_{L^2(0,3T)}\|B\|_{L^2((0,T)^2)}. \quad (54)$$

As $n \to \infty$, $\|e_n\|_{L^2(\mathbb{R})}$ is bounded, so we conclude the result. □

Now, using the above auxiliary results, we find the following well-posedness result.

Theorem 4. *The optimisation problem* (47) *admits minimisers.*

Proof. Since
$$0 \leq \phi_K(B,e), \forall (B,e) \in U \times V, \tag{55}$$
we can find a minimizing sequence $(f_n, e_n) \subset U \times V$ with
$$\lim_n \phi_K(B_n, e_n) = \inf_{(e,B) \in \mathcal{U} \times \mathcal{V}} \phi_K(B,e) = \mathcal{M}. \tag{56}$$

Since $\mathcal{U}, \mathcal{V}$, are bounded in their respective spaces these two sequences are bounded. By reflexivity, see ([24] pages 67–68), there exist weak limits f, e such that (passing to subsequences using the same indexing)
$$B_n \rightharpoonup B \text{ in } \sigma(H^1((0,T)^2), H^1((0,T)^2)') \tag{57}$$
and
$$e_n \rightharpoonup e \text{ in } \sigma(H^1(0,3T), H^{-1}(0,3T)). \tag{58}$$

Since U, V are strongly closed and convex subsets of reflexive spaces, they are also weakly closed; see ([24] page 60). Therefore,
$$(B,e) \in \mathcal{U} \times \mathcal{V}. \tag{59}$$

Now, by the following compact embeddings,
$$H_0^1(0,3T) \xhookrightarrow{c} L^2(0,3T)$$
and
$$H^1((0,T)^2) \xhookrightarrow{c} L^2((0,T)^2)$$
we can conclude the strong convergence
$$B_n \to B \text{ in } L^2((0,T)^2) \tag{60}$$
and
$$e_n \to c \text{ in } L^?(0,3T). \tag{61}$$

Using the above lemmas, we obtain that
$$\mathcal{M} = \lim_{n \to \infty} \phi_K(B_n, e_n) = \tag{62}$$

(continuity of the square function and the norm function)

$$\|\lim_n G(B_n, K + E_0 e_n) + S(K) + \lim_n S(E_0 e_n)\|^2_{L^2((0,T),L^2(\mathbb{R}))} +$$

$$\alpha \|\lim_n B_n\|^2_{L^2((0,T)^2)} + \beta \|\lim_n e_n\|^2_{L^2(0,3T)} =$$

$$\|\lim_n B_n + \lim_n A(K + E_0 e_n) B_n + S(K) + \lim_n S(E_0 e_n)\|^2_{L^2((0,T),L^2(\mathbb{R}))} +$$

$$\alpha \|\lim_n B_n\|^2_{L^2((0,T)^2)} + \beta \|\lim_n e_n\|^2_{L^2(0,3T)} =$$

$$\|G(B, K + E_0 e) + S(K) + S(E_0 e)\|^2_{L^2((0,T),L^2(\mathbb{R}))} + \alpha \|B\|^2_{L^2((0,T)^2)} + \beta \|e\|^2_{L^2(0,3T)} \Rightarrow \tag{63}$$

$$\phi_K(B,e) = \mathcal{M}. \quad \square$$

Remark 4. *The set $(0,T)^2 \subset \mathbb{R}^2$ is a bounded Lipschitz domain. By the Rellich–Kondrachov theorem, we conclude the following compact embedding*

$$H^1((0,T)^2) \overset{c}{\hookrightarrow} L^2((0,T)^2),$$

see [25].

Remark 5. *Regarding the choice of $H = H^1((0,T)^2)$ and the choice of $H_0^1(0,3T)$ as the space of the perturbations. We choose in particular these spaces for the space of the GLM kernels (in the total least squares sense) and the perturbations since we have the above compact embedding properties. Otherwise [working, for example, with the $L^2((0,T^2))$ and the $L^2(0,3T)$], we cannot pass to some further strongly convergent subsequences in the proof of existence of minimisers of our variational inverse problem and conclude the existence result. Similar work on this subject was done in [26]. However, the assumptions made in this paper are too strong to require in our application. In particular, the authors considered the existence of minimisers issue for a general class of total least squares problems. Assuming that the inverse problem is described by a bilinear operator with the property that weakly convergent sequences are mapped to strongly convergent sequences, they show existence. However, without working the way we did, the weak to strong continuity property of the forward operator is a very strong assumption to claim, and in general it does not hold. To see that, it is sufficient to pick a weakly convergent sequence of the form $(B_n, 0)_n \subset L^2((0,\tau)^2) \times L^2(\mathbb{R})$ and then observe that $(G(B_n, 0))_n$ is not necessarily norm convergent. Keep also in mind that G is not bilinear. In addition, the convolution type relation between K and B should be carefully studied under the convolution and the weak convergence.*

To sum up our approach, we pick the spaces of interest so that we have a compact embedding property. This way, we do not need to make any assumptions on G.

Remark 6. *Regarding the reasonability of the H^1-regularity assumption for the GLM kernels. Even though a GLM kernel naturally has an L^2-regularity at least in the box of interest, we know that it satisfies a Goursat-type hyperbolic PDE (see [20])*

$$\{\partial_x(\partial_x - \partial_t) - q(x)\}B(x,t) = 0, \ x \in \mathbb{R}, \ t > 0 \quad (64)$$

$$B(x,0) = \int_x^\infty q(z)dz, \ x \in \mathbb{R} \quad (65)$$

$$\lim_{x \to \infty} \|B(x,0)\|_\infty = 0. \quad (66)$$

So either we study the regularity of solutions of the above PDE, or we just view our proposed existence of minimisers result as a relaxed version of the problem of seeking kernels with L^2-regularity (and perturbations).

Remark 7. *Finally, another thing to keep in mind is that it is possible to obtain multiple minimisers of the above optimisation problem since the TLS functional, ϕ_K, is not convex.*

4. Numerical Results

4.1. Numerical Implementation

In this section, we show the discrete form of the GLM equation and its numerical implementation. We also implement numerically the total least squares regularisation method of the GLM equation, using noisy scattering data.

4.1.1. Discretisation of the GLM Equation

We discretise the quantities K and B on a regular grid of samples $t_i = i \cdot \Delta t$. We then denote the discrete scattering data by $\mathbf{k} \in \mathbb{R}^n$. The discrete GLM kernel is denoted by $\mathbf{B} \in \mathbb{R}^{(m+1) \times (m+1)}$. The discrete counterpart to GLM equation is then given by

$$b_{ij} + \Delta t \sum_{l=0}^{m} b_{il} k_{i+j+l} = -k_{i+j}, \tag{67}$$

for $i, j = 0, 1, \ldots m$. We will assume that $n = 3m$ to properly define these relations. The discrete GLM equation can be more compactly expressed using the map $G : \mathbb{R}^{(m+1) \times (m+1)} \times \mathbb{R}^n \to \mathbb{R}^{(m+1)^2}$ and $S : \mathbb{R}^n \to \mathbb{R}^{(m+1)^2}$:

$$G(\mathbf{B}, \mathbf{k}) + S(\mathbf{k}) = \mathbf{0}. \tag{68}$$

For fixed $\mathbf{k}$, this system of equations decouples in m independent systems of equations of the form

$$\left(I_{m+1 \times m+1} + \Delta t \underbrace{\begin{pmatrix} k_i & k_{i+1} & \cdots & k_{i+m} \\ k_{i+1} & k_{i+2} & \cdots & k_{i+m+1} \\ \vdots & & \ddots & \vdots \\ k_{i+m} & k_{i+m+1} & \cdots & k_{i+2m} \end{pmatrix}}_{A_i} \right) \begin{pmatrix} b_{i0} \\ b_{i1} \\ \vdots \\ b_{im} \end{pmatrix} = - \begin{pmatrix} k_i \\ k_{i+1} \\ \vdots \\ k_{i+m} \end{pmatrix},$$

for $i = 0, \ldots, m$. For fixed $\mathbf{B}$, the system of equations takes the following form

$$\begin{pmatrix} T_0 & & 0_{(m+1) \times m} \\ \hline 0_{(m+1) \times 1} & T_1 & 0_{(m+1) \times (m-1)} \\ \hline & & \ddots \\ \hline 0_{(m+1) \times m} & & T_m \end{pmatrix} \begin{pmatrix} k_0 \\ k_1 \\ \vdots \\ k_{3m} \end{pmatrix} = - \begin{pmatrix} b_{00} \\ \vdots \\ b_{0m} \\ b_{10} \\ \vdots \\ b_{1m} \\ \vdots \\ b_{m0} \\ \vdots \\ b_{mm} \end{pmatrix}, \tag{69}$$

with $T_i \in \mathbb{R}^{(m+1) \times (2m+1)}$ defined as

$$T_i = \begin{pmatrix} 1 & 0 & \cdots & & \\ 0 & 1 & 0 & \cdots & \\ & & \ddots & & \\ \cdots & 0 & 1 & 0 & \cdots \end{pmatrix} + \Delta t \begin{pmatrix} b_{i0} & b_{i1} & \cdots & b_{im} & & \\ 0 & b_{i0} & b_{i1} & \cdots & b_{im} & \\ & & \ddots & & & \\ & & & b_{i0} & b_{i1} & \cdots & b_{im} \end{pmatrix}.$$

4.1.2. Numerical Regularisation

Having discretised the GLM equation, we can now define the numerical regularisation strategies. The Tikhonov-regularised problem (LS) reads

$$\min_{\mathbf{B}} \|G(\mathbf{B}, \mathbf{k}) + S(\mathbf{k})\|_2^2 + \alpha \|L\mathbf{B}\|_F^2, \tag{70}$$

where L represents a finite-difference approximation of the second derivative. Due to the special form of the equations for fixed $\mathbf{k}$, this problem separates in m separate least-squares problems for the columns of $\mathbf{B}$. These problems can be readily solved using standard iterative methods, such as LSQR.

The total least-squares (TLS) functional in the discrete setting is given by

$$\phi_k(\mathbf{B}, \mathbf{e}) = \|G(\mathbf{B}, \mathbf{k} + \mathbf{e}) + S(\mathbf{k} + \mathbf{e})\|_2^2 + \alpha \|L\mathbf{B}\|_F^2 + \beta \|\mathbf{e}\|_2^2. \tag{71}$$

To find a minimiser, we apply an alternating minimisation algorithm, as proposed by [17] we repeat for $k = 0, 1, \ldots$

$$\mathbf{B}^{(k+1)} = \underset{\mathbf{B}}{\operatorname{argmin}} \phi_k(\mathbf{B}^{(k)}, \mathbf{e}^{(k)}) \tag{72}$$

$$\mathbf{e}^{(k+1)} = \underset{\mathbf{e}}{\operatorname{argmin}} \phi_k(\mathbf{B}^{(k+1)}, \mathbf{e}^{(k)}). \tag{73}$$

As explained in the previous section, both steps involve a quadratic problem that can easily be solved using an iterative method like LSQR. The convergence of this alternating approach is guaranteed by the bi-convex nature of the functional ϕ_k [17].

Having solved either of the regularised problems for **B** and in view of relation (16), we can compute the scattering potential from the reconstructed kernel by extracting the first column from **B** and using a finite-difference approximation to compute the derivative.

4.1.3. Choice of Regularisation Parameters

Both regularised formulations (LS and TLS) include regularisation parameter(s) that need to be estimated. In particular, for the TLS method, we need to estimate two parameters, α, β. In practice, though we expect that β does not play a significant role, as the problem for **e** is overdetermined, $G(\mathbf{B}, \mathbf{k} + \mathbf{e}) = -S(\mathbf{k} + \mathbf{e})$ defines $(m+1)^2$ equations in $3m + 1$ unknowns. Moreover, the corresponding system matrix consists of an identity matrix plus a small perturbation (cf. (69)), so the system is unlikely to be ill-posed. Thus, we pick a (small) reference value for $\beta = \hat{\beta}$ and focus on estimating the remaining parameter, α.

Ideally, we would pick α to minimise the reconstruction error, i.e.,

$$\hat{\alpha} = \underset{\alpha}{\operatorname{argmin}} \|\widehat{\mathbf{B}}_\alpha - \overline{\mathbf{B}}\|_2, \tag{74}$$

where $\overline{\mathbf{B}}$ is the unregularised solution corresponding to noiseless data, $\overline{\mathbf{k}}$, (i.e., $G(\overline{\mathbf{B}}) = -S(\overline{\mathbf{k}})$), and $\widehat{\mathbf{B}}_\alpha$ denotes the optimal solution of either the LS or the TLS method corresponding to noisy data, $\mathbf{k} = \overline{\mathbf{k}} + \varepsilon$. For the sake of completeness, we mention below a number of commonly used methods for choosing regularisation parameters and how these could potentially be applied in the problem of estimating α.

A posteriori parameter selection methods aim to achieve this by using only knowledge of the data and the noise level. A well-known method in this class is the discrepancy principle. The particular nature of our problem (involving a product of **B** and **k**) makes it difficult to apply such rules, however, as they would require an estimate of the residual at the optimal solution. To see why, note that the residual for (LS) is given by $\|G(\overline{\mathbf{B}}, \varepsilon) + S(\varepsilon)\|_2$. The discrepancy principle then finds an α such that

$$\|G(\widehat{\mathbf{B}}_\alpha, \mathbf{k}) + S(\mathbf{k})\|_2 \approx \|G(\overline{\mathbf{B}}, \varepsilon) + S(\varepsilon)\|_2, \tag{75}$$

but this would require knowledge of the true kernel. For the total least squares approach, we could use the estimated error $\widehat{\mathbf{e}}_\alpha$ and find α such that

$$\|\widehat{\mathbf{e}}_\alpha\|_2 \approx \|\varepsilon\|_2. \tag{76}$$

Heuristic methods such as the L-curve method could be applied. However, it is not clear how well they would perform on problems of this nature, as even for classical ill-posed linear inverse problems, such heuristic methods are not convergent [27]. Despite this theoretical shortcoming, such methods are often applied in practice with success [28].

5. Numerical Examples

In this subsection, we present a couple of numerical examples comparing the regularised approaches (LS and TLS) outlined above. The least-squares (sub-) problems are solved using LSQR. Unless stated otherwise, we use 10 iterations of the alternating method and 10 iterations of LSQR for the sub problems. The scattering potential is obtained by numerically differentiating the reconstructed kernel, as in (16).

We find that the TLS method is not sensitive to the choice of β (as argued in the previous section). We therefore use a fixed value of $\beta = 1 \cdot 10^{-16}$ for all experiments. The remaining regularisation parameter α for each method (LS and TLS) is obtained via (74). Although this requires knowledge of the noiseless data in order to compute $\overline{\mathbf{B}}$, it allows us to make a fair best-case comparison between the methods.

The reconstruction quality of the methods is measured by the relative L^2-error between the reconstructed kernel and the reference solution $\overline{\mathbf{B}}$.

The code used to produce the examples is available on https://github.com/ucsi-consortium/1DInverseScatteringGLM/releases/tag/publication (accessed on 6 December 2021).

5.1. Example 1: The Plasma Wave-Equation with a Smooth Potential

In this first numerical experiment, we consider the case where the scattering data are generated directly by the plasma wave equation. The measured scattering data and the scattering potential are shown in Figure 1.

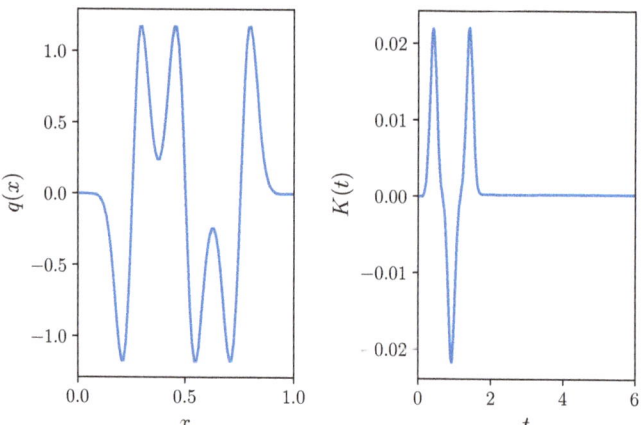

Figure 1. Scattering potential and scattering data. The scattering potential has a relatively smooth profile.

We apply the methods described in the previous subsections, and thus, we solve the GLM integral equation to find the GLM kernel and then the scattering potential. Figure 2 shows the solution of the GLM equation (matrix **B**) and the comparison between the true and the recovered potential. For such a smooth potential, the generated scattering data lead to a good reconstruction.

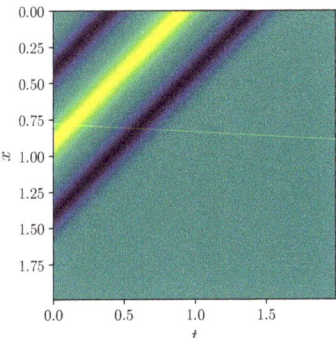 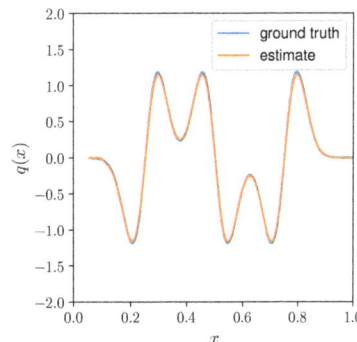

Figure 2. Reconstruction using the unregularised GLM approach from noiseless data. Shown are the kernel (**left**) and corresponding reconstructed scattering potential (**right**). The recovered scattering potential matches well with the ground truth.

As we studied previously, the presence of noise in the scattering data is expected to affect the reconstruction of both the GLM kernel and the potential. To test this, we add i.i.d. normally distributed random noise to the data with mean zero and variance σ^2. Reconstructions using the unregularised, LS and TLS approach for $\sigma = 1 \cdot 10^{-3}$ are shown in Figure 3. The results for various noise levels are summarised in Table 1. In all cases, the TLS approach is superior and requires less regularisation (smaller value of α).

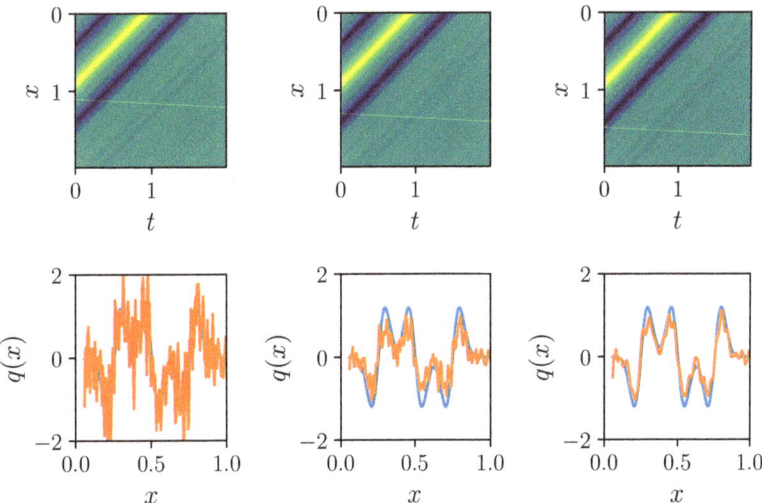

Figure 3. Comparison of the unregularised (**left**), LS (**middle**) and TLS (**right**) approaches on noisy data ($\sigma = 1 \cdot 10^{-3}$). The true potential corresponds to the blue curve.

Table 1. Table for comparing the relative errors of the regularisation methods for various noise levels.

	Unregularised	LS		TLS	
σ	Rel. Error	α	Rel. Error	α	Rel. Error
$1 \cdot 10^{-4}$	$9.30 \cdot 10^{-2}$	$1.99 \cdot 10^{-2}$	$9.30 \cdot 10^{-2}$	$1.68 \cdot 10^{-2}$	$6.48 \cdot 10^{-2}$
$1 \cdot 10^{-3}$	$8.35 \cdot 10^{-1}$	1.34	$4.85 \cdot 10^{-1}$	$2.79 \cdot 10^{-1}$	$2.86 \cdot 10^{-1}$
$1 \cdot 10^{-2}$	7.62	$6.27 \cdot 10^{2}$	$8.89 \cdot 10^{-1}$	$2.94 \cdot 10^{1}$	$7.52 \cdot 10^{-1}$

5.2. Example 2: Data from the Wave Equation

In this second example, we consider scattering data generated from the wave equation with variable density,

$$\rho v_{tt} = \{\rho c^2 v_y\}_y.$$

The coefficients of the wave equation, the corresponding scattering potential and the measured data are shown in Figure 4. This example is more challenging than the previous one, due to significant multiple scattering.

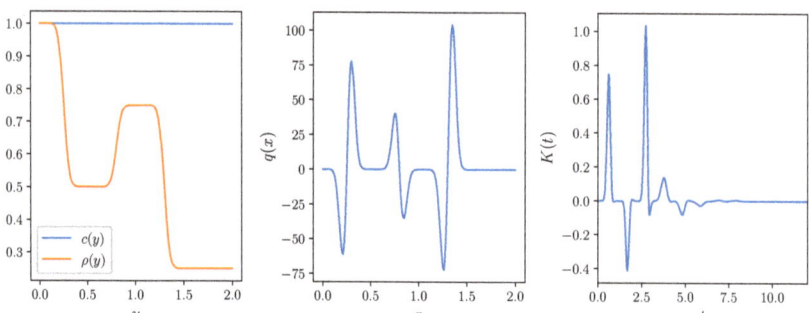

Figure 4. Shown are the the elastic parameters ρ, c (**left**), the corresponding scattering potential (**middle**) and the resulting scattering data (**right**). The chosen elastic parameters result in significant multiple scattering, seen on the right.

The results of the GLM method on noise-free data are shown in Figure 5. The band limitation of our source and the singular behaviour of the potential affects the reconstruction of q.

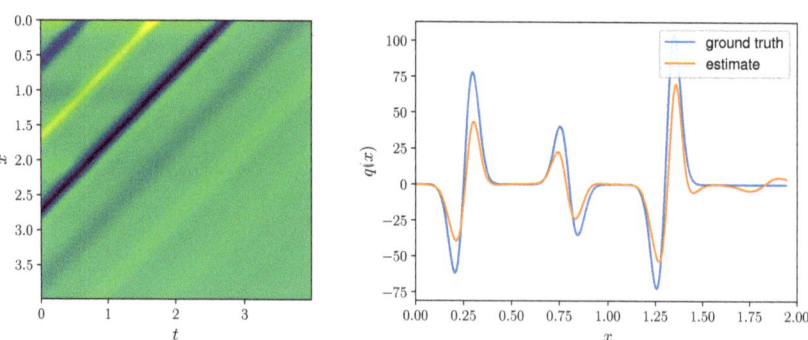

Figure 5. Results for noise-free data. Shown are the reconstructed kernel (**left**) and the reconstructed scattering potential (**right**). The band limitation of our source clearly affects the approximation.

Reconstructions using the unregularised, LS and TLS approach for $\sigma = 1 \cdot 10^{-2}$ are shown in Figure 6. The results for various noise levels are summarised in Table 2. In all cases, the TLS approach is superior.

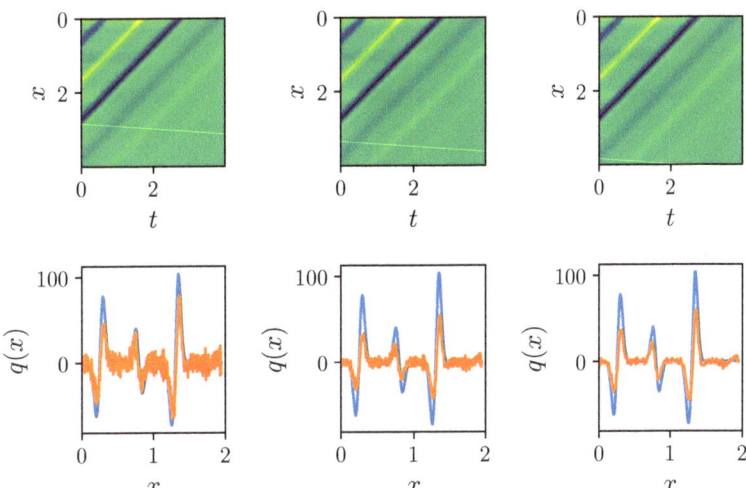

Figure 6. Comparison of the unregularised (**left**), LS (**middle**) and TLS (**right**) approaches on noisy data ($\sigma = 1 \cdot 10^{-2}$). The true potential corresponds to the blue curve.

Table 2. Table for comparing the relative errors of the regularisation methods for various noise levels.

	Unregularised	LS		TLS	
σ	Rel. Error	α	Rel. Error	α	Rel. Error
$1 \cdot 10^{-3}$	$3.81 \cdot 10^{-2}$	$6.56 \cdot 10^{-3}$	$3.91 \cdot 10^{-2}$	$9.52 \cdot 10^{-3}$	$3.26 \cdot 10^{-2}$
$1 \cdot 10^{-2}$	$3.87 \cdot 10^{-1}$	$3.91 \cdot 10^{-1}$	$3.27 \cdot 10^{-1}$	$1.01 \cdot 10^{-1}$	$1.76 \cdot 10^{-1}$
$1 \cdot 10^{-1}$	$3.59 \cdot 10^{0}$	$1.00 \cdot 10^{2}$	$8.05 \cdot 10^{-1}$	$1.68 \cdot 10^{1}$	$7.03 \cdot 10^{-1}$

6. Conclusions and Discussion

We revisited some classical results from inverse scattering to solve the 1D inverse coefficient problem for the wave equation. In particular, we considered the GLM method with noisy data and proposed a regularised total least squares formulation in the infinite dimensional setting. We contributed an error bound for the unregularised GLM approach and have shown existence of minimisers for the variational formulation of the TLS approach. Numerical results illustrate the approach, showing that the TLS approach gives superior results as compared to conventional Tikhonov regularisation.

The results from inverse scattering, in particular a GLM-like approach has recently received renewed attention in the geophysical literature. Noisy data is a significant source of error in these methods, and various discrete regularisation schemes have been proposed to address this issue. While these methods have been shown to work well in practice, careful analysis of the infinite dimensional problem has not been done. We believe that it is important to study this because it will yield new insight in the behaviour of practical approaches as they are pushed to include higher frequency data (and hence finer discretisation). Ultimately, these insights may lead to adaptive methods. Moreover, the 1D problem analysed here serves as a model problem for many practical problems in 2D and 3D, and the insights may inspire new approaches there as well.

Author Contributions: Conceptualisation, A.T. and T.v.L.; methodology, A.T. and T.v.L.; software, A.T. and T.v.L.; validation, A.T. and T.v.L.; formal analysis, A.T.; investigation, A.T.; writing—original draft preparation, A.T.; writing—review and editing, A.T. and T.v.L.; visualisation, A.T. and T.v.L.; supervision, T.v.L.; funding acquisition, T.v.L. All authors have read and agreed to the published version of the manuscript.

Funding: This work was supported by the Utrecht Consortium for Subsurface Imaging (UCSI).

Institutional Review Board Statement: Not applicable.

Informed Consent Statement: Not applicable.

Data Availability Statement: The numerical examples and the code are available here: https://github.com/ucsi-consortium/1DInverseScatteringGLM/releases/tag/publication (accessed on 6 December 2021).

Acknowledgments: Author [1] (Andreas Tataris) would like to thank Vassilis G. Papanicolaou for the discussion and suggestions.

Conflicts of Interest: The authors declare no conflict of interest.

Appendix A. Absence of Bound States Auxiliary Results

In this part of the paper, we include some auxiliary results needed for the proof of Theorem 1. We also provide the proof of Theorem 1 in the end of the Appendix A.

Lemma A1. *Assume that c, c' are bounded, $c \in C^1(\mathbb{R}), c > 0$. Then the travel time coordinate transform*

$$\mathbb{R} \ni y \mapsto x \in \mathbb{R},$$

with

$$c(y)dx(y) = dy, \ y \in \mathbb{R}, \tag{A1}$$

$$x(y) = \int_0^y \frac{1}{c(r)} dr, \ y \in \mathbb{R}, \tag{A2}$$

is a 2-diffeomorphism

Proof. Since the new variable x is defined as a function of the independent variable y and the integrand in (A2) is strictly positive, we get immediately that x is injective. In addition, x', x'' are bounded functions since c, c' are bounded. Since x is a continuous function and since the integrand is in $C^2(\mathbb{R})$, we get that $x \in C^2(\mathbb{R})$. Now, let us study the inverse of x. By the inverse function theorem the inverse of x, x^{-1}, exists and is an element of $C^1(\mathbb{R})$ with the property

$$\frac{dx^{-1}(t)}{dt} = c(x^{-1}(t)), \ t \in \mathbb{R}. \tag{A3}$$

Therefore, $(x^{-1})'$ is bounded since

$$|c(x^{-1}(t))| \leq M, \ t \in \mathbb{R}, \tag{A4}$$

(M is the upper bound of c) and also

$$\frac{d^2 x^{-1}(t)}{dt^2} = c'(x^{-1}(t))(x^{-1})'(t) = c'(x^{-1}(t))c(x^{-1}(t)), \ t \in \mathbb{R}, \tag{A5}$$

which is also bounded since c' is assumed to be bounded. Finally,

$$\frac{dx}{dy} = \frac{1}{c(y)}, y \in \mathbb{R}. \tag{A6}$$

Therefore, since c is bounded from above and from below,

$$\left|\frac{dx(y)}{dy}\right|, \ y \in \mathbb{R}, \tag{A7}$$

is also bounded from above and below. □

Corollary A1. *Let $f \in H^2(\mathbb{R})$. Then $y \mapsto f(x(y)) \in H^2(\mathbb{R})$.*

Now, since
$$(c(y))^{1/2} = \eta(x), \ x \in \mathbb{R}, \tag{A8}$$
we can view $c(y)$ as a function of x as
$$x \stackrel{\text{bijective } x(\cdot)}{\mapsto} y \mapsto c(y). \tag{A9}$$

Since our differential relation is
$$\frac{dy}{dx} = c(y), \tag{A10}$$
we can write
$$\frac{dy}{dx} = \eta^2(x). \tag{A11}$$

Since also
$$y = 0 \text{ if } x = 0, \tag{A12}$$
we can have y as a function of x,
$$y(x) = \int_0^x \eta^2(r) dr, \ x \in \mathbb{R}. \tag{A13}$$

So, similarly to [9], we have established
$$y \stackrel{1-1 \text{ onto}}{\mapsto} x, \tag{A14}$$
$$x \stackrel{1-1 \text{ onto}}{\mapsto} y. \tag{A15}$$

Having that, we can also write
$$\eta(x) = (c(y(x)))^{1/2}, \ x \in \mathbb{R}. \tag{A16}$$

Corollary A2. *The inverse travel time coordinate transform is a 2-diffeomorphism.*

Proof. We have shown that $x(\cdot)$ and its inverse are continuous. We have also shown that their first and second derivatives are continuous and bounded. What is left to show is that the derivative of the inverse is bounded from below. First, we observe that
$$z'(x) = \eta^2(x), \ x \in \mathbb{R}. \tag{A17}$$

However, since $\eta(x)^2 = c(y(x))$ and $c(\cdot)$ is bounded from below, we obtain the result. □

Remark A1. *In view of the differential relations* (A10) *and* (A11), *we can express the one variable as a function of the other.*

The 2-diffeomorphisms given by the travel time coordinate transform and the inverse define bounded linear operators from $H^2(\mathbb{R})$ to $H^2(\mathbb{R})$; see [29]. The static wave operator
$$W = -\frac{d}{dy}\{c^2 \frac{d}{dy}\} : \hat{H} \to L^2(\mathbb{R}), \tag{A18}$$
has domain of definition
$$D(W) = \hat{H} = \{v \in H^1(\mathbb{R}) : c^2 v' \in H^1(\mathbb{R})\}. \tag{A19}$$

We will now show that the relations that lead from the 1D static wave equation to the Schrödinger equation are well defined in the L^2-sense. First, using the 2-diffeomorphism defined by $y(\cdot)$, we can find the following. According to [24] (Proposition 9.6) for $v \in \widehat{H} \subset H^1(\mathbb{R})$, we get the $L^2(\mathbb{R}, dx)$-relation,

$$\frac{dv(y(x))}{dx} = \frac{dv(y(x))}{dy}\frac{dy(x)}{dx} = \frac{dv(y(x))}{dy}c(y(x)), \ x \in \mathbb{R}. \quad (A20)$$

Now, since the function $1/c(y(x)), x \in \mathbb{R}$ defines a multiplication operator $T : L^2(\mathbb{R}, dx) \to L^2(\mathbb{R}, dx)$, we obtain

$$\frac{dv(y(x))}{dx}\frac{1}{c(y(x))} = \frac{dv(y(x))}{dy}, \ x \in \mathbb{R}. \quad (A21)$$

Assuming also that $v \in \widehat{H}$, we obtain the $L^2(\mathbb{R}, dy)$-relation defined by the static wave Equation (1)

$$-\{c^2 v_y\}_y = \lambda v, \quad (A22)$$

with $\lambda \in \mathbb{C}$. Using the inverse travel time coordinate transform, we get that

$$-\Phi\{(c^2 v_y)\}_y = \lambda \Phi v, \quad (A23)$$

with $\Phi g = g \circ y$, with $g \in L^2(\mathbb{R}, dy)$. Now, observe that $c^2 v_y \in H^1(\mathbb{R}, dy)$, therefore we obtain again that

$$\frac{d(c^2 v_y)}{dy}(y(x)) = \frac{d(c^2 v_y)}{dx}\frac{1}{c(y(x))}, x \in \mathbb{R}. \quad (A24)$$

Therefore, combining the above relations, we find that

$$-\Phi\{c^2 v_y\}_y = x \mapsto -\{c^2(y(x))v_y(y(x))\}_y \Rightarrow \quad (A25)$$

$$-\Phi\{c^2 v_y\}_y = x \mapsto -(c(y(x))v_x)_x \frac{1}{c(y(x))} \in L^2(\mathbb{R}, dx). \quad (A26)$$

Therefore, the transformed wave equation has the form

$$-(c(y(x))v_x)_x \frac{1}{c(y(x))} \stackrel{L^2(\mathbb{R}, dx)}{=} \lambda v(y(x)), x \in \mathbb{R}. \quad (A27)$$

Again, using the multiplication operator T, we obtain

$$-(c(y(x))v_x)_x \stackrel{L^2(\mathbb{R}, dx)}{=} \lambda c(y(x))v(y(x)), x \in \mathbb{R}, \quad (A28)$$

which becomes

$$-(\eta^2(x)v_x)_x \stackrel{L^2(\mathbb{R}, dx)}{=} \lambda \eta^2(x)v(y(x)), x \in \mathbb{R}. \quad (A29)$$

Previously, we defined u as

$$u(x) = \eta(x)v(y(x)), \ x \in \mathbb{R}. \quad (A30)$$

Let us view this as a $L^2(\mathbb{R}, dx)$-relation for the moment. It follows that since $v \in \widehat{H}$, then $u \in H^2(\mathbb{R})$ (otherwise we obtain a contradiction by Corollary A3). Now, we can consider the following $L^2(\mathbb{R}, dx)$- relation similarly as above (using again a multiplication operator)

$$v(y(x)) = \eta^{-1}(x)u(x), \ x \in \mathbb{R}, \quad (A31)$$

and since by assumption $c \in C^1(\mathbb{R})$ and $y \in C^1(\mathbb{R})$, then $\eta \in C^1(\mathbb{R})$, and we get pointwise

$$v_x(y(x)) = (\eta^{-1}(x)u(x))_x = \frac{\eta(x)u_x(x) - \eta_x(x)u(x)}{\eta^2(x)}, x \in \mathbb{R}, \quad (A32)$$

since $H^2(\mathbb{R}) \subset C^1(\mathbb{R})$. Since $\eta^{-1}, \eta_x \eta^{-1}$ are bounded, the relation is valid in the $L^2(\mathbb{R}, dx)$-sense. Again, using a multiplication operator, we obtain the $L^2(\mathbb{R}, dx)$ relation

$$\eta^2(x) v_x(y(x)) = \eta(x) u_x(x) - \eta_x(x) u(x), \ x \in \mathbb{R}. \tag{A33}$$

We can weakly differentiate the above relation once more (using density arguments) and we find

$$(\eta^2(x) v_x(y(x)))_x = \eta(x) u_{xx}(x) - \eta_{xx}(x) u(x), \ x \in \mathbb{R}, \tag{A34}$$

which is again valid in $L^2(\mathbb{R}, dx)$. We substitute (A34) in (A29) and using once more a multiplication operator, we find the $L^2(\mathbb{R}, dx)$-relation

$$u_{xx}(x) - \frac{\eta_{xx}(x)}{\eta(x)} u(x) = \lambda u(x), x \in \mathbb{R}, \tag{A35}$$

which is our Schrödinger equation after rearranging. Now, for the sake of completeness we prove the assertions that we used previously.

Lemma A2. *Let $u \in H^2(\mathbb{R})$. The function*

$$y \mapsto v(y) = \eta^{-1}(x(y)) u(x(y))$$

is an element of $\widehat{H}$.

Proof. We need to show that $v, v_y \in L^2(\mathbb{R})$ and $(c^2 v_y)_y \in L^2(\mathbb{R})$. First, we observe that $v \in L^2(\mathbb{R})$. Indeed,

$$\int_{\mathbb{R}} |v(y)|^2 dy = \int_{\mathbb{R}} |\eta^{-1}(x(y)) u(x(y))|^2 dy \leq$$

$$\sup_{y \in \mathbb{R}} \{|\eta^{-2}(x(y))|\} \int_{\mathbb{R}} |u(x(y))|^2 dy < \infty, \tag{A36}$$

since $u \in H^2(\mathbb{R})$, $y \mapsto x(y)$ defines a 2-diffeomorphism and $\eta(x(y)) = \sqrt{c(y)}, y \in \mathbb{R}$ is assumed to be bounded.

Now, we show that $v_y \in L^2(\mathbb{R})$. Let $\phi \in C_c^\infty(\mathbb{R})$. We get

$$(v, \phi')_{L^2} = \int_{\mathbb{R}} c^{-1/2}(y) u(x(y)) \overline{\phi'(y)} dy =$$

$$(u(x(\cdot)), c^{-1/2} \phi')_{L^2}.$$

Since $u(x(\cdot)) \in H^2(\mathbb{R})$, we pick $(f_n)_n \subset C_c^\infty(\mathbb{R})$ with $f_n \xrightarrow{H^2} u(x(\cdot))$. Thus, since $c^{-1/2} \phi$ defines a bounded functional on $L^2(\mathbb{R})$ we obtain

$$(v, \phi')_{L^2} = (u(x(\cdot)), c^{-1/2} \phi')_{L^2} = \lim_n (f_n, c^{-1/2} \phi')_{L^2} =$$

$$\lim_n \int_{\mathbb{R}} f_n(y) c^{-1/2}(y) \overline{\phi'(y)} dy = -\lim_n \int_{\mathbb{R}} (f_n'(y) c^{-1/2}(y) + f_n(y) (c^{-1/2})'(y)) \overline{\phi(y)} dy =$$

$$-\lim_n (f_n', c^{-1/2} \phi) - \lim_n (f_n, (c^{-1/2})' \phi).$$

Since $c^{-1/2} \phi, (c^{-1/2})' \phi$ are in $L^2(\mathbb{R})$, and $f_n \xrightarrow{L^2} u(x(\cdot)), f_n' \xrightarrow{L^2} u(x(\cdot))_y$, we have that

$$(v, \phi')_{L^2} = -\int_{\mathbb{R}} (u(x(y))_y c^{-1/2}(y) + u(x(y)) (c^{-1/2})'(y)) \overline{\phi(y)} dy.$$

Since $c^{-1/2}, (c^{-1/2})'$ are bounded and $u(x(\cdot)) \in H^2(\mathbb{R})$, we obtain that $v \in H^1(\mathbb{R})$. Similarly, $(c^2 v_{\lambda y})_y \in L^2(\mathbb{R})$. We obtain

$$(c^2 v_y, \phi')_{L^2} = \int_{\mathbb{R}} c^2(y)\{c^{-1/2}(y)u(x(y))\}_y \overline{\phi'(y)} dy =$$

$$\int_{\mathbb{R}} c^2(y) c^{-1/2}(y) u(x(y))_y \overline{\phi'(y)} dy + \int_{\mathbb{R}} c^2(y) \left(\frac{1}{c^{1/2}(y)}\right)' u(x(y)) \overline{\phi'(y)} dy \quad \text{(A37)}$$

Let again $(f_n)_n \subset C_c^\infty(\mathbb{R})$, such that $f_n \xrightarrow{H^2} u(x(\cdot))$. We shift our attention to the first term of (A37). Since $c^{-1/2}$ is bounded and is in $C^1(\mathbb{R})$, thus $c^{-1/2} c^2 \phi' = c^{3/2} \phi'$ is in $L^2(\mathbb{R})$, we follow similar steps as before to calculate that

$$\lim_n (f_n', c^{3/2}\phi') = -\lim_n \int_{\mathbb{R}} ((3/2) c^{1/2} c' f_n' + c^{3/2} f_n'') \overline{\phi} dy =$$

$$-\frac{3}{2}\lim_n (f_n', c^{1/2} c' \phi) - \frac{3}{2}\lim_n (f_n'', c^{3/2}\phi),$$

and we continue as before to find

$$\int_{\mathbb{R}} c^2(y) c^{-1/2}(y) u(x(y))_y \overline{\phi'(y)} dy = -\frac{3}{2} \int_{\mathbb{R}} u(x(y)) c^{1/2}(y) c'(y) \overline{\phi(y)} dy -$$

$$\frac{3}{2} \int_{\mathbb{R}} c^{3/2}(y) u_{yy}(x(y)) \overline{\phi(y)} dy. \quad \text{(A38)}$$

Now, we look at the second term of (A37). We first observe that since $c \in C^1(\mathbb{R})$

$$(c^{-1/2}(y))' = -(1/2) c^{-3/2}(y) c'(y), \forall y \in \mathbb{R},$$

thus

$$\int_{\mathbb{R}} c^2(y) c^{1/2'}(y) u(x(y)) \overline{\phi'(y)} dy = -\frac{1}{2} \int_{\mathbb{R}} c^{1/2}(y) c'(y) u(x(y)) \overline{\phi'(y)} dy. \quad \text{(A39)}$$

By assumption we have that $c', u(x(\cdot)) \in H^1(\mathbb{R})$. We already have that $f_n \xrightarrow{H^1} u(x(\cdot))$ and we pick $g_n \subset C_c^\infty(\mathbb{R})$ with $g_n \xrightarrow{H^1} c'$. Similarly to [24], we obtain that

$$f_n g_n \xrightarrow{L^2} u(x(\cdot)) c' \quad \text{(A40)}$$

and

$$(f_n g_n)' = f_n' g_n + f_n g_n' \xrightarrow{L^2} u(x(\cdot))_y c' + u(x(\cdot)) c''. \quad \text{(A41)}$$

Now, we return to (A39). Since $c^{1/2} \phi' \in L^2(\mathbb{R})$, it defines a bounded functional and we obtain that

$$\int_{\mathbb{R}} c^{1/2}(y) c'(y) u(x(y)) \overline{\phi'(y)} dy = \lim_n \int_{\mathbb{R}} (f_n g_n) c^{1/2} \overline{\phi'} dy. \quad \text{(A42)}$$

Since c is an element of $C^1(\mathbb{R})$, we obtain that

$$\lim_n \int_{\mathbb{R}} (f_n g_n) c^{1/2} \overline{\phi'} dy = -\lim_n \int_{\mathbb{R}} \left\{\frac{1}{2} c^{-1/2} c' (f_n g_n) + c^{1/2} (f_n' g_n + f_n g_n')\right\} \overline{\phi} dy =$$

$$-\frac{1}{2}\lim_n (f_n g_n, c^{-1/2} c' \phi) - \lim_n (f_n' g_n + f_n g_n', c^{1/2} \phi) =$$

$$-\int_{\mathbb{R}} \left\{\frac{1}{2}(c'(y))^2 c^{-1/2}(y) u(x(y)) + c'(y) c^{1/2}(y)(u(x(y))_y + c''(y) u(x(y)))\right\} \overline{\phi(y)} dy. \quad \text{(A43)}$$

Combining relations (A38) and (A43) and under our assumptions on c, we conclude that $(c^2 v_y)_y \in L^2(\mathbb{R})$. □

Corollary A3. *Let $v \in \hat{H}$. Then the function*

$$u(x) = \eta(x)v(y(x)), \ x \in \mathbb{R} \tag{A44}$$

is in $H^2(\mathbb{R})$.

Proof. Let $v \in \hat{H}$. Then let $u \in L^2(\mathbb{R}) \setminus H^2(\mathbb{R})$ with u, v related according to (A45). Then, we obtain the L^2-relations

$$u(x) = \eta(x)v(y(x)), \ x \in \mathbb{R} \iff \tag{A45}$$

(we can switch variables through the 2-diffeomorphisms)

$$u(x(y)) = \eta(x(y))v(y), \ y \in \mathbb{R} \iff \tag{A46}$$

(action of a multiplicator operator)

$$v(y) = \eta^{-1}(x(y))u(x(y)), \ y \in \mathbb{R} \tag{A47}$$

Since $u \notin H^2(\mathbb{R})$, then v is not necessarily in $\hat{H}$, according to Lemma A2, which yields a contradiction. □

Since Theorem 1 is not standard, we provide its proof.

Proof of Theorem 1. Let $\lambda = -k^2 < 0$ an eigenvalue of S and $u \in H^2(\mathbb{R})$ the associated eigenfunction such that

$$\left\{-\frac{d^2}{dx^2} + q\right\}u \stackrel{L^2}{=} -k^2 u. \tag{A48}$$

We defined previously the static wave operator as

$$W = -\frac{d}{dy}\{c^2 \frac{d}{dy}\} : \hat{H} \to L^2(\mathbb{R}), \tag{A49}$$

with $\hat{H} = \{v \in H^1(\mathbb{R}) : c^2 v' \in H^1(\mathbb{R})\}$.

We showed above (Lemma A2) that the function v such that $\mathbb{R} \ni x \mapsto v(y(x)) = \eta^{-1}(x)u(x)$ or equivalently

$$y \mapsto v(y) = \eta^{-1}(x(y))u(x(y))$$

belongs to $\hat{H}$. Now, we want to show that if u solves the Schrödinger equation, then v solves the static wave equation. If we assume that v does not solve the wave equation, then since the calculations that lead from the static wave equation to the Schrödinger equation are well defined in the L^2-sense, we obtain that u is not a solution of the Schrödinger equation, which is not true. We will show that W is a positive operator. Indeed $\forall v \in \hat{H}$

$$(Wv, v)_{L^2} = -\int_{\mathbb{R}} \{c^2 v_y\}_y \bar{v} dy = -\lim_{R \to \infty} \int_{-R}^{R} \{c^2 v_y\}_y \bar{v} dy = \tag{A50}$$

$$\lim_{R \to \infty} \left\{\int_{-R}^{R} v_y \overline{c^2 v_y} dy - c^2 v_y \bar{v}\big|_{-R}^{R}\right\} = \int_{\mathbb{R}} c^2 |v_y|^2 > 0. \tag{A51}$$

Considering that $H^1(-R, R)$ is continuously embedded in $H^1(\mathbb{R}), \forall R > 0$, and since the product rule of differentiation is still valid in $H^1(-R, R) \ \forall R > 0$, see [24], we obtain the above result. In addition, note that $c^2 v_y, v \in H^1(\mathbb{R})$ and $H^1(\mathbb{R}) = H_0^1(\mathbb{R})$ is an algebra. Furthermore, the eigenvalues of a positive operator are positive, therefore $\lambda = -k^2$ cannot be an eigenvalue of W. Thus, this contradicts the initial statement of λ being an eigenvalue of S. □

The absence of bound states makes the use of the GLM method applicable in a practical situation of solving an inverse scattering problem from measurements at the surface of an acoustic 1D medium. The only thing required for the inversion is the knowledge of the reflection coefficient, or, equivalently, its Fourier transform.

References

1. Bleistein, N.; Cohen, J.J., Jr. *Mathematics of Multidimensional Seismic Imaging, Migration, and Inversion*; Springer: Berlin/Heidelberg, Germany, 2001; Volume 13.
2. Tarantola, A. Inversion of seismic reflection data in the acoustic approximation. *Geophysics* **1984**, *49*, 1259–1266. [CrossRef]
3. Virieux, J.; Operto, S. An overview of full-waveform inversion in exploration geophysics. *Geophysics* **2009**, *74*, WCC1–WCC26. [CrossRef]
4. Symes, W.W. The seismic reflection inverse problem. *Inverse Probl.* **2009**, *25*, 123008. [CrossRef]
5. Symes, W.W. A differential semblance algorithm for the inverse problem of reflection seismology. *Comput. Math. Appl.* **1991**, *22*, 147–178. [CrossRef]
6. Coen, S.; Cheney, M.; Weglein, A. Velocity and density of a two-dimensional acoustic medium from point source surface data. *J. Math. Phys.* **1984**, *25*, 1857–1861. [CrossRef]
7. Burridge, R. The Gelfand-Levitan, the Marchenko, and the Gopinath-Sondhi integral equations of inverse scattering theory, regarded in the context of inverse impulse-response problems. *Wave Motion* **1980**, *2*, 305–323. [CrossRef]
8. Ware, J.A.; Aki, K. Continuous and Discrete Inverse-Scattering Problems in a Stratified Elastic Medium. I. Plane Waves at Normal Incidence. *J. Acoust. Soc. Am.* **1969**, *45*, 911–921. [CrossRef]
9. Aktosun, T.; Papanicolaou, V. Reconstruction of the wave speed from transmission eigenvalues for the spherically symmetric variable-speed wave equation. *Inverse Probl.* **2013**, *29*, 065007. [CrossRef]
10. Lomas, A.; Curtis, A. An introduction to Marchenko methods for imaging. *Geophysics* **2019**, *84*, F35–F45. [CrossRef]
11. Broggini, F.; Snieder, R. Connection of scattering principles: A visual and mathematical tour. *Eur. J. Phys.* **2012**, *33*, 593–613. [CrossRef]
12. Rose, J.H. 'Single-sided' autofocusing of sound in layered materials. *Inverse Probl.* **2002**, *18*, 1923–1934. [CrossRef]
13. Broggini, F.; Wapenaar, K.; van der Neut, J.; Snieder, R. Data-driven Green's function retrieval and application to imaging with multidimensional deconvolution. *J. Geophys. Res. Solid Earth* **2014**, *119*, 425–441. [CrossRef]
14. Diekmann, L.; Vasconcelos, I.; Cummings, D.; Curtis, A. Towards exact linearized full-waveform inversion via Marchenko redatuming. In *First International Meeting for Applied Geoscience & Energy Expanded Abstracts*; SEG/AAPG/SEPM: Denver, CO, USA, 2021; pp. 3380–3384. [CrossRef]
15. Silvia, M.T.; Tacker, E.C. Regularization of Marchenko's integral equation by total least squares. *J. Acoust. Soc. Am.* **1982**, *72*, 1202–1207. [CrossRef]
16. Vargas, D.; Vasconcelos, I.; Ravasi, M.; Luiken, N. Time-Domain Multidimensional Deconvolution: A Physically Reliable and Stable Preconditioned Implementation. *Remote Sens.* **2021**, *13*, 3683. [CrossRef]
17. Bleyer, I.R.; Ramlau, R. An alternating iterative minimisation algorithm for the double-regularised total least square functional. *Inverse Probl.* **2015**, *31*, 075004. [CrossRef]
18. Carroll, R.; Santosa, F.; Ortega, J. Stability for the one dimensional inverse problem via the gel'fand-levitan equation. *Appl. Anal.* **1982**, *13*, 271–277. [CrossRef]
19. Papanicolaou, V.G. (National Technical University of Athens, Athens, Greece). Personal communication, 2020.
20. Koelink, E. *Scattering Theory*; Radboud University: Nijmegen, The Netherlands, 2008.
21. Drazin, P.G.; Johnson, R.S. *Solitons: An Introduction*, 2nd ed.; Cambridge Texts in Applied Mathematics; Cambridge University Press: Cambridge, UK, 1989.
22. Reed, M.; Simon, B. *III: Scattering Theory*; Methods of Modern Mathematical Physics; Elsevier Science: Amsterdam, The Netherlands, 1979.
23. Aktosun, T. Stability of the Marchenko inversion. *Inverse Probl.* **1987**, *3*, 555–563. [CrossRef]
24. Brezis, H. *Functional Analysis, Sobolev Spaces and Partial Differential Equations*; Springer: Berlin/Heidelberg, Germany, 2010.
25. Baratchart, L.; Bourgeois, L.; Leblond, J. Uniqueness results for inverse Robin problems with bounded coefficient. *J. Funct. Anal.* **2016**, *270*, 2508–2542. [CrossRef]
26. Bleyer, I.R.; Ramlau, R. A double regularization approach for inverse problems with noisy data and inexact operator. *Inverse Probl.* **2013**, *29*, 025004. [CrossRef]
27. Yagola, A.; Leonov, A.; Titarenko, V. Data errors and an error estimation for ill-posed problems. *Inverse Probl. Eng.* **2002**, *10*, 117–129. [CrossRef]
28. Hansen, P.C.; O'Leary, D.P. The Use of the L-Curve in the Regularization of Discrete Ill-Posed Problems. *SIAM J. Sci. Comput.* **1993**, *14*, 1487–1503. [CrossRef]
29. Renardy, M.; Rogers, R.C. *An Introduction to Partial Differential Equations*; Springer: Berlin/Heidelberg, Germany, 2004.

Article

Hybrid Statistical and Numerical Analysis in Structural Optimization of Silicon-Based RF Detector in 5G Network

Tan Yi Liang [1], Nor Farhani Zakaria [1,2,3,*], Shahrir Rizal Kasjoo [1,2], Safizan Shaari [1,2], Muammar Mohamad Isa [1], Mohd Khairuddin Md Arshad [1], Arun Kumar Singh [4] and Sharizal Ahmad Sobri [5,6]

1. Faculty of Electronic Engineering Technology, Universiti Malaysia Perlis (UniMAP), Arau 02600, Perlis, Malaysia; liangtan@studentmail.unimap.edu.my (T.Y.L.); shahrirrizal@unimap.edu.my (S.R.K.); safizan@unimap.edu.my (S.S.); muammar@unimap.edu.my (M.M.I.); mohd.khairuddin@unimap.edu.my (M.K.M.A.)
2. Micro & Nano Electronics (MiNE) Research Group, Faculty of Electronic Engineering Technology, Universiti Malaysia Perlis (UniMAP), Arau 02600, Perlis, Malaysia
3. Advanced Communication Engineering, Centre of Excellence (ACE), Universiti Malaysia Perlis (UniMAP), Kangar 01000, Perlis, Malaysia
4. Department of Electronics and Communication Engineering, Punjab Engineering College (Deemed to be University), Sector-12, Chandigarh 160012, India; arunkumar.singh@outlook.com
5. Advanced Material Research Cluster, Faculty of Bioengineering and Technology, Universiti Malaysia Kelantan, Jeli Campus, Jeli 17600, Kelantan, Malaysia; sharizal.s@umk.edu.my
6. Geopolymer and Green Technology, Centre of Excellence (CEGeoGTech), Universiti Malaysia Perlis (UniMAP), Kangar 01000, Perlis, Malaysia
* Correspondence: norfarhani@unimap.edu.my

Abstract: In this study, a hybrid statistical analysis (Taguchi method supported by analysis of variance (ANOVA) and regression analysis) and numerical analysis (utilizing a Silvaco device simulator) was implemented to optimize the structural parameters of silicon-on-insulator (SOI)-based self-switching diodes (SSDs) to achieve a high responsivity value as a radio frequency (RF) detector. Statistical calculation was applied to study the relationship between the control factors and the output performance of an RF detector in terms of the peak curvature coefficient value and its corresponding bias voltage. Subsequently, a series of numerical simulations were performed based on Taguchi's experimental design. The optimization results indicated an optimized curvature coefficient and voltage peak of 26.4260 V^{-1} and 0.05 V, respectively. The alternating current transient analysis from 3 to 10 GHz showed the highest mean current at 5 GHz and a cut-off frequency of approximately 6.50 GHz, indicating a prominent ability to function as an RF detector at 5G related frequencies.

Keywords: silicon-on-insulator (SOI); self-switching diode (SSD); curvature coefficient; Taguchi method; ANOVA; regression

1. Introduction

The rapid evolution of modern wireless networks and maturing 4G networks has paved the path to the new 5G communication generation, which is no longer exclusively an advancement of legacy 4G mobile networks and behaves as a system with several fresh carrier proficiencies [1]. This emerging 5G technology provides low latency and ultra-high-speed massive connectivity between devices, leading to cross-industry transformations and pervasive processing in an ecosystem where all devices are interconnected. However, it also faces various challenges [2]. To effectively employ these inclusive ideas, a range of applied sciences is required, such as heterogeneous networks, large multiple-input multiple-output, millimeter wave (mmWave) detection, device-to-device communications, software-defined networks, network function visualization, and networking slicing [1]. The motivation of this paper is in the scope of mmWave detection improvement, where a unique, low-cost radio frequency (RF) detector suitable for 5G networks is proposed, both for signal detection and for opportunistically reusing the cellular spectrum and energy efficiency for future RF energy harvesting applications. The critical aspect of this operation is to ensure sufficient efficiency in detecting the received RF signal in the zero-bias condition to convert it into useful energy [3,4]. Zero-bias detectors in 5G networks have been reported using metal oxide semiconductor field effect transistors [5], PN junction diodes [6], and Schottky diodes. Schottky diodes have been most commonly used because of their inherently low turn-on voltages [7]. However, they require a sophisticated nanogate fabrication process that often results in parasitic effects and the coupling of a Schottky device with antennas and waveguides; moreover, the fabrication of large arrays poses additional engineering issues [8]. In addition, self-switching devices (SSDs) have received attention from researchers worldwide as they have been reported to effectively function as zero-bias RF detectors [9–11]. The rectification property of the SSD is dependent on the nonlinear IV characteristic of the device, which can be obtained by controlling the electric-field-independent zone (depletion region) of the SSD asymmetric channel. The L-shaped channel can be simply realized by electron beam lithography and chemical etching and does not involve junctions, doping, or the third gate terminal, being more adequate in terms of fabrication complexity compared to the most-used Schottky diode [12] (more details on the SSD working principle and mechanism can be found in [13]).

Several works on SSDs have focused on the detection and application in the "terahertz (THz) gap" region, the region from 0.1 THz to 10 THz on the electromagnetic spectrum where functionable detectors are scarcely reported [14]. To function in this high-frequency region, the use of high-mobility substrate materials, such as III-V materials (InGaAs, GaAs, InAs, and GaN) [10], is mandatory. Exploration of the usage of SSD in the lower 5G network region, which targets frequencies from approximately 3 to 5 GHz in the sub-6 GHz region in the worldwide communication spectrum [15], has been reported in a small number of studies using silicon as an alternative substrate [16–19], as the mobility of electrons is sufficiently high to accommodate the transition of the sinusoidal RF wave, with the advantage of a considerably lower cost compared to that of III-V materials. Optimization of the structural and material parameters of the SSD is crucial for manipulating nonlinear IV characteristics of the device, which strongly influence the rectification performance of the SSD [20]. Most optimization approaches of the SSD involve varying the channel length, L, channel width, W, and channel trench, W_t, where the depletion region is more affected to control the electron flow. Almost all reported optimization processes were performed using the trial-and-error method, where the parameters were individually varied using a range of values without any structured optimization method [21–24]. In this work, we propose the integration of a statistical analysis using the Taguchi optimization method, supported by the analysis of variance (ANOVA) and regression analysis with a numerical simulation to determine the best structural parameters of a silicon-on-insulator (SOI)-based SSD to achieve the best responsivity in the zero-bias region.

The Taguchi method has been widely used in quantitative research and reported in recent studies on experiment-based procedures to obtain an optimized result and produce high product quality by reducing the production cost using robust design experiments [13,25]. Integration of the Taguchi method with numerical analysis in simulation-based research was also reported using device simulators such as ANSYS [26,27] and ATLAS [20,28]. This shows the capability of the integration between statistical and numerical analysis to reduce the number of simulations and to obtain a prominent result with the aid of the noise ratio analysis in the Taguchi method [14]. Apart from the Taguchi, other designs of experiments (DOE) such as the central composite design and Box–Behnken design, or other quasi-random sequences can be an alternative. These alternatives may offer more precise results in trend prediction involving a higher number of runs and are more complex in design, but are not in the scope of this work. In this study, numerical simulations using the ATLAS device simulator were performed, corresponding to the DOE and analysis of the Taguchi method to obtain the highest curvature coefficient, γ, of a device that is proportional to the responsivity of the detector [28]. In addition, ANOVA and regression analyses were performed to further analyze the sensitivity of the corresponding control factors. By integrating an organized optimization method and numerical simulation, we aimed for an optimized SOI-SSD structure with high responsivity in the 5G network region.

2. Materials and Methods

The SSD was characterized using a Silvaco ATLAS two-dimensional (2D) simulator with a top-view (TV) simulation. Figure 1a shows the geometry of a silicon-based SSD with air as the dielectric in the etched channel of the device (white area), and the cross-section of the device is shown in Figure 1b.

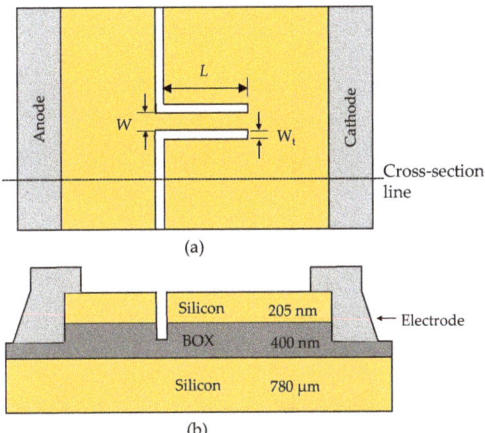

Figure 1. (**a**) Structural parameters of an SOI-based SSD, showing three main control factors: L, W, and W_t, and (**b**) the cross-section of the device.

By considering the three-dimensional (3D) nature of the diode, we assigned an approximate positive background doping of 2.45×10^{16} cm^{-3} and an interface charge density of 3.16×10^{11} cm^{-2} along the channel [16,29]. Physical models such as Klaassen's unified low-field mobility model, the Watt model, Auger recombination, and the energy balance transport model [30] were defined in the simulation to simulate the electron transport and imitate the mechanism of the real device. The materials and physical models used in the simulation were validated by comparing the electrical characteristics with those of a fabricated SOI SSD from [16], and the results were in good agreement, as shown in Figure 2.

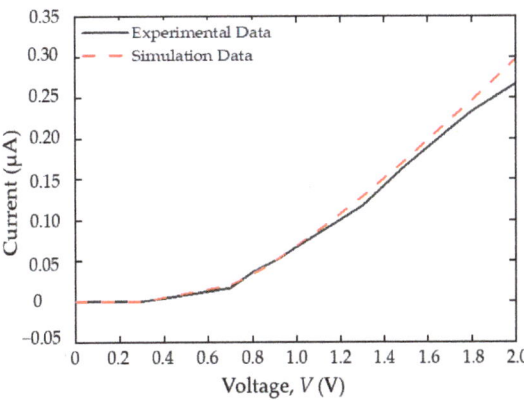

Figure 2. Comparison of IV characteristics between simulation and experimental data of Farhi et al. [16].

2.1. Determination of Control Factors and Levels for the Design of Experiment

Prior to the DOE in the Taguchi method, a series of simulations were conducted by varying the individual geometrical parameters of SSD: channel length, L, channel width, W, and trench width, W_t (refer to Figure 1a). These are the primary parameters affecting the depletion region in the SSD channel, which controls the on–off condition of the device. We have reported the performance of these individually varied parameters and their physical explanation in [19]. The control factors and their levels in this optimization work were selected based on the best electrical performance (high forward current and low leakage current) in each reported variation and are listed in Table 1.

Table 1. Control factors and their level parameters selected from analysis of individual parameters and their electrical performance.

Control Factors	Level (μm)		
	1	2	3
Channel Length, L	1.100	1.200	1.300
Channel Width, W	0.228	0.230	0.232
Trench Width, W_t	0.200	0.150	0.100

2.2. Selection of Suitable Orthogonal Array

To determine a suitable orthogonal array for the DOE, the degrees of freedom must be considered, and they are defined as the number of comparisons between the process parameters of an experiment and the levels [31]. In this study, three control factors and three levels with nine degrees of freedom were used [28]; thus, an L9 orthogonal array of Taguchi's DOE was implemented. The run number and its parameters with their corresponding level values are listed in Table 2.

Table 2. DOE using selected control factors and their level parameters for SSD optimization.

Run No.	Control Factors (Level)			Parameter Values (μm)		
	Channel Length, L	Channel Width, W	Trench Width, W_t	Channel Length, L	Channel Width, W	Trench Width, W_t
1	L_1	W_1	W_{t1}	1.100	0.228	0.200
2	L_1	W_2	W_{t2}	1.100	0.230	0.150
3	L_1	W_3	W_{t3}	1.100	0.232	0.100
4	L_2	W_1	W_{t3}	1.200	0.228	0.100
5	L_2	W_2	W_{t1}	1.200	0.230	0.200
6	L_2	W_3	W_{t2}	1.200	0.232	0.150
7	L_3	W_1	W_{t2}	1.300	0.228	0.150
8	L_3	W_2	W_{t3}	1.300	0.230	0.100
9	L_3	W_3	W_{t1}	1.300	0.232	0.200

2.3. Evaluation of Curvature Coefficient Peak Value and Its Corresponding Voltage

By using the structural parameters from the DOE table, the IV characteristic performance of each run was numerically simulated using the ATLAS device simulator to analyze the rectification performance. The rectification performance in a nonlinear device can be represented by the curvature coefficient, γ, which is proportional to the rectified current [14] and can be calculated as:

$$\gamma = \frac{f^{(2)}}{f^{(1)}}, \tag{1}$$

where $f^{(2)}$ and $f^{(1)}$ are the second and first derivatives, respectively, of the simulated IV characteristics. The peak value of the plotted γ versus voltage (V) and its corresponding bias voltage were recorded for further statistical analysis.

2.4. Evaluation of the Signal-to-Noise Ratio

The signal-to-noise (S/N) ratio in the Taguchi method is used to analyze the quality characteristics of each run [32]. The S/N ratio consists of three quality characteristics: nominal, lower, and higher [33]. To obtain the optimum response for this work, the S/N ratios for γ_{peak} and V_{peak} were calculated using the higher, the better (Equation (2)) and the lower, the better (Equation (3)) quality characteristics, respectively. The higher the γ_{peak}, the better the rectification performance in a nonlinear device, and a lower V_{peak} indicates a lower bias needed in the device to function.

$$\eta_\gamma = -10 \log_{10} \frac{1}{n} \sum \frac{1}{\gamma^2}; \tag{2}$$

$$\eta_v = -10 \log_{10} \frac{1}{n} \sum V^2. \tag{3}$$

3. Results and Discussion

3.1. Analysis of S/N Ratio Using Taguchi Method

The γ_{peak} and V_{peak} calculated from the simulated IV characteristics in each run and their corresponding S/N ratios from the functions of Equations (2) and (3) are listed in Table 3.

Table 3. Curvature coefficient from simulated IV characteristics and corresponding S/N ratio for each run.

Run No.	Peak of Curvature Coefficient, γ_{peak} (V^{-1})	S/N Ratio, η_γ (dB)	Corresponding Peak Voltage, V_{peak} (V)	S/N Ratio, η_v (dB)
1	23.0730	27.2621	0.1100	19.1721
2	23.3971	27.3832	0.0800	21.9382
3	18.9586	25.5561	0.0400	27.9588
4	26.0832	28.3272	0.0600	24.4370
5	24.0095	27.6077	0.1100	19.1721
6	24.2728	27.7024	0.0800	21.9382
7	27.1127	28.6634	0.1000	20.0000
8	26.4260	28.4406	0.0500	26.0206
9	24.8394	27.9028	0.1100	19.1721

The average S/N ratio from individual control factors from each run can be calculated, as shown in Table 4, by adding all similar levels for each factor or parameter according to the results in Table 3. The results are presented in Table 5.

Table 4. S/N ratio equation for each level of the control factors.

Control Factor	Level 1	Level 2	Level 3
Channel Length, L (µm)	$\eta_1 + \eta_2 + \eta_3$	$\eta_4 + \eta_5 + \eta_6$	$\eta_7 + \eta_8 + \eta_9$
Channel Width, W (µm)	$\eta_1 + \eta_4 + \eta_7$	$\eta_2 + \eta_5 + \eta_8$	$\eta_3 + \eta_6 + \eta_9$
Trench Width, W_t (µm)	$\eta_1 + \eta_5 + \eta_9$	$\eta_2 + \eta_6 + \eta_7$	$\eta_3 + \eta_4 + \eta_8$

Table 5. Calculated average S/N ratio for each level of the control factors.

Factors	Average S/N Ratio for γ_{peak} (dB)			Average S/N Ratio for V_{peak} (dB)		
	Level 1	Level 2	Level 3	Level 1	Level 2	Level 3
Channel Length, L	26.7338	27.8791	28.3356	23.0230	21.8491	21.7309
Channel Width, W	28.0842	27.8105	27.0537	21.2030	22.3770	23.0230
Trench Width, W_t	27.5909	27.9164	27.4413	19.1721	21.2921	26.1388

The overall S/N ratios for both γ_{peak} and V_{peak} were calculated using the expression:

$$\eta_{overall} = \frac{(\eta_{\gamma avg} + \eta_{vavg})}{2}. \tag{4}$$

The results are tabulated in Table 6 and plotted in Figure 3 for a better visualization of the S/N values of the levels for each control factor. As observed, the highest S/N ratio level of each control parameter can be determined and used as the optimal parameter of the SSD, as shown in Figure 4, where the L, W, and W_t are 1.30 µm, 0.23 µm, and 0.10 µm, respectively.

Table 6. Overall S/N ratio in each level of the control factors.

Factors	Level			Optimal Parameter
	1	2	3	
Channel Length, L	24.8784	24.8641	25.0333	L_3
Channel Width, W	24.6436	25.0937	25.0384	W_2
Trench Width, W_t	23.3815	24.6042	26.7901	W_{t3}

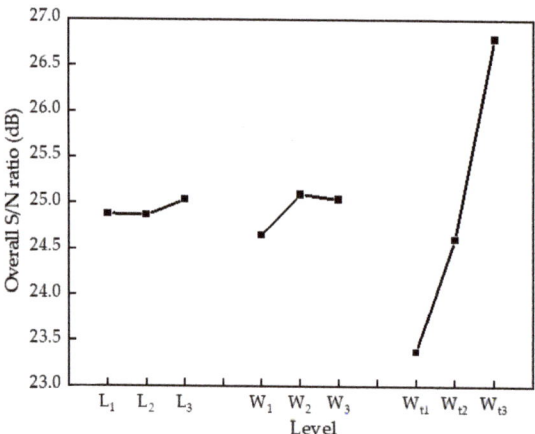

Figure 3. Overall S/N ratio for each control factor level.

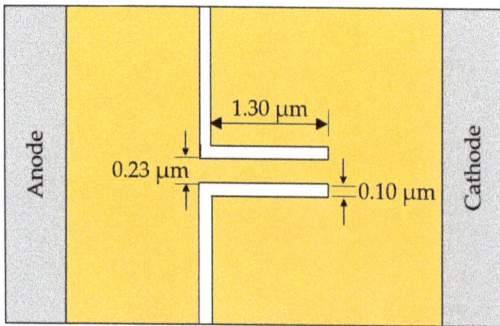

Figure 4. Optimized structure obtained from Taguchi method.

3.2. Taguchi Method with ANOVA and Regression Analysis

3.2.1. Analysis of S/N Ratio

To understand the sensitivity of the involved geometrical parameters to the RF signal response and to validate the optimized structure results obtained from the Taguchi method, ANOVA and regression analysis were conducted using Minitab statistical tool software to assist in solving the statistical and S/N ratio equations.

The S/N ratios for both γ_{peak} and V_{peak} obtained using the Minitab statistical tool were equal to those calculated using the Taguchi method in Table 3, and the average S/N ratio is shown in Table 7. The delta values in the table refer to the difference between the highest average S/N ratio and the lowest S/N ratio for each control factor and were calculated using rank values to determine the most influential control factor for both observed parameters [34,35]. From the delta values, it can be seen that the most influential factors for γ and V are L and W_t, respectively. Figures 5 and 6 show the main effect plots for γ and V, respectively. As observed, the degree of the slope in L for γ and W_t for V is the highest, indicating the presence and proportionality of the main effects [34,35].

Table 7. Response table of S/N ratio for the curvature coefficient γ and corresponding voltage V.

Levels	S/N Ratio for Curvature Coefficient, γ (dB)			S/N Ratio for Corresponding Voltage, V (dB)		
	Channel Length, L	Channel Width, W	Trench Width, W_t	Channel Length, L	Channel Width, W	Trench Width, W_t
1	26.7338	28.0843	27.5909	23.0230	21.2030	19.1721
2	27.8791	27.8105	27.9154	21.8491	22.3770	21.2921
3	28.3356	27.0538	27.4413	21.7309	23.0230	26.1388
Delta	1.60	1.03	0.48	1.29	1.82	6.97
Rank	1	2	3	3	2	1

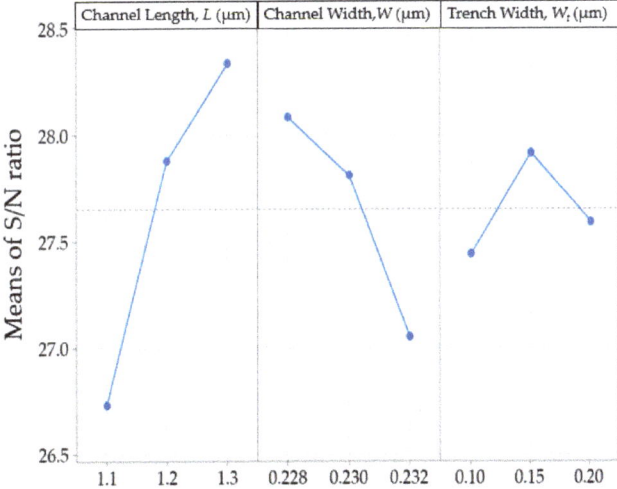

Figure 5. Plot of main effects of S/N ratio for γ.

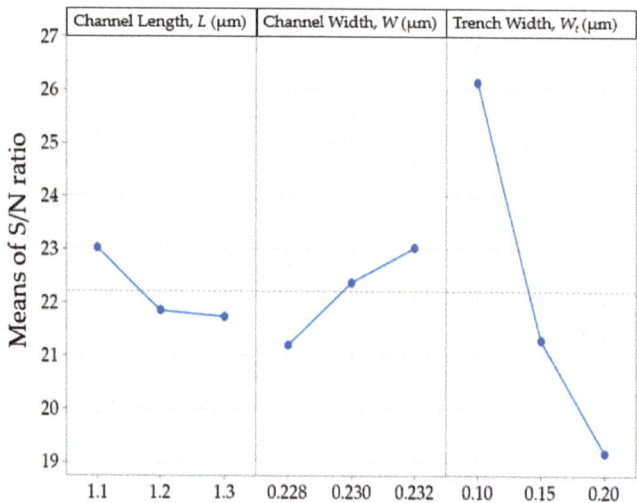

Figure 6. Plot of main effects of S/N ratio for V.

3.2.2. Analysis of Variance for S/N Ratio

To further clarify the sensitivity of geometrical parameters to the RF signal response, an ANOVA was performed for both γ and V using the equations shown in Table 8 with 95% confidence level for the p-test.

Table 8. ANOVA related equations.

	Equation		Notation
Mean Square (MS) Factor	$MS_F = \frac{SS_F}{DF_F}$	SS_F	SS Factor
		DF_F	DF Factor
MS Errors	$MS_E = \frac{SS_E}{DF_E}$	SS_E	SS Error
		DF_E	DF Error
Sum of Square (SS) Factor	$SS_F = \sum n_i (\bar{y}_{i.} - \bar{y}_{..})^2$	$\bar{y}_{i.}$	Mean of the observation at the ith factor level
SS Error	$SS_E = \sum_i \sum_j (y_{ij} - \bar{y}_{i.})^2$	$\bar{y}_{..}$	Mean of all observations
SS Total	$SS_T = \sum_i \sum_j (y_{ij} - \bar{y}_{..})^2$	y_{ij}	Value of the jth observation at the ith factor level
Degree of freedom (DF) Factors	$DF_F = r - 1$	n_T	Total number of observations
DF Error	$DF_E = n_T - r$		
Total DF	$DF_T = n_T - 1$	r	Number of factor levels
F-value	$F = \frac{MS_F}{MS_E}$	MS_F	MS Factor
		MS_E	MS Error
Percentage of contribution	$\% = \frac{SS_F}{SS_T}$	SS_F	SS Factor
		SS_T	SS Total

In ANOVA, the null hypothesis for the p-test is important to determine the relationship between the factors and the signal response, where the null hypothesis is rejected when there is a significant relationship between the factor and the signal response [36]. As observed in the ANOVA results of γ and V (refer to Tables 9 and 10), the null hypothesis was rejected only for W_t and V, which indicates a strong relationship between W_t and the response. However, in terms of % contribution, the % order was similar to the order of the rank from the delta results, and the % contribution for W in the γ showed a high value of 25.19% to the response. Thus, an additional regression analysis was performed to confirm the simultaneous relationship of all control factors with the results.

Table 9. ANOVA results for γ.

Source	DF	Adj SS	Adj MS	F-Value	p-Value	% Contribution
Channel Length, L	2	4.0859	2.0429	6.43	0.1350	60.21
Channel Width, W	2	1.7095	0.8547	2.69	0.2710	25.19
Trench Width, W_t	2	0.3540	0.1770	0.56	0.6420	5.22
Error	2	0.6359	0.3179			
Total	8	6.7852				

Table 10. ANOVA results for V.

Source	DF	Adj SS	Adj MS	F-Value	p-Value	% Contribution
Channel Length, L	2	3.0617	1.5309	5.49	0.1540	3.59
Channel Width, W	2	5.1080	2.5540	9.17	0.0980	5.99
Trench Width, W_t	2	76.5186	38.2593	137.30	0.0070	89.76
Error	2	0.5573	0.2787			
Total	8	85.2456				

3.2.3. Regression Analysis

The p-value hypothesis now involves the regression and control factors. The p-value in the regression analysis explains the changes in the response, where the null hypothesis of the model means that there are no significant changes to the response. As can be observed from Tables 11 and 12, the p-values in both regressions for γ and V reject the null hypothesis, indicating that there are variations in the parameters and responses. For the control factor parameters, L and W for γ_{peak} (refer to Table 11) and W and W_t for V_{peak} (refer to Table 12) reject the null hypothesis. These results are different from the previous analysis from ANOVA, where only W_t in the V_{peak} rejected the null hypothesis. This may occur because in the regression analysis, the coinciding factors from two sets of responses are simultaneously considered in the null hypothesis analysis, whereas in ANOVA, the individual element response is considered [37].

Table 11. Regression ANOVA for the curvature coefficient, γ.

Source	DF	Adj SS	Adj MS	F-Value	p-Value
Regression	3	39.1836	13.0612	8.5700	0.0200
Channel Length, L	1	27.9477	27.9477	18.3300	0.0080
Channel Width, W	1	11.2016	11.2016	7.3500	0.0420
Trench Width, W_t	1	0.0344	0.0344	0.0200	0.8870
Error	5	7.6237	1.5427		
Total	8	46.8073			

Table 12. Regression ANOVA for V.

Source	DF	Adj SS	Adj MS	F-Value	p-Value
Regression	3	0.005817	0.001939	69.800	0.000
Channel Length, L	1	0.000150	0.000150	5.4000	0.068
Channel Width, W	1	0.000267	0.000267	9.6000	0.027
Trench Width, W_t	1	0.005400	0.005400	194.40	0.000
Error	5	0.000139	0.000028		
Total	8	0.005956			

The relationship between the three control factors (L, W, and W_t) and their levels was studied and analyzed using linear regression. The percentages of R-sq, R-sq (adj), and R-sq (pre) values for the linear regression equations of γ and V are listed in Table 13. These values explain the variation in the response, a modification of R-sq by adjusting the number of expressions, and the precision of prediction of the model for a new observation [38]. The results indicated a good prediction percentage of 92.27% in voltage and a lower percentage value of 35.51% in curvature coefficient.

Table 13. Linear regression between control factors and response.

	Regression Equation	R-sq, %	R-sq (adj), %	R-sq (pre), %
Curvature coefficient, γ	$155.2 + 21.58L - 683W + 1.5W_t$	83.71	73.94	35.51
Voltage, V	$0.699 + 0.0500L - 3.33W + 0.6000W_t$	97.67	96.27	92.27

Thus, to determine the validity of the prediction using regression analysis, the simulated and predicted values from the simulation and regression equations were compared, as shown in Figures 7 and 8, respectively. A larger difference between the simulated and predicted results was obtained for γ compared to V, in agreement with the R-sq (pre) values in Table 13. The percentage error between the simulated and predicted results was then calculated using Equation (5):

$$\text{Percentage error} = \left| \frac{simulated\,result - predicted\,result}{predicted\,result} \right| \times 100\%. \tag{5}$$

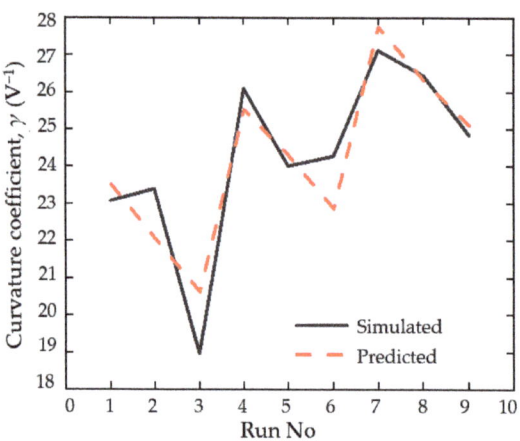

Figure 7. Comparison between predicted and simulated results for curvature coefficient peak, γ_{peak}.

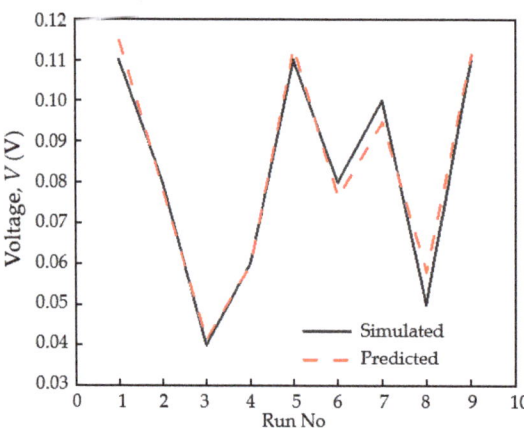

Figure 8. Comparison between predicted and simulated results for corresponding voltage, V_{peak}.

The values of the simulated and predicted results are in good agreement, with average percentage errors (from all runs) of 3.26% and 4.29% for γ and V, respectively, and are considered acceptable for a reliable statistical analysis [39].

Therefore, the response optimizer of the regression analysis was utilized in Minitab (Figure 9). From the optimizer, a high composite desirability of 0.8252 was obtained with a well-balanced rectification performance of γ and V predicted at 26.3239 V^{-1} and 0.0572 V, respectively, using the optimized structure. This balance is beneficial and achieved the objective of having high responsivity in the zero-bias region (lower than 0.3 V). The detection signal of the SOI SSD detector was then evaluated using these optimized structural parameters.

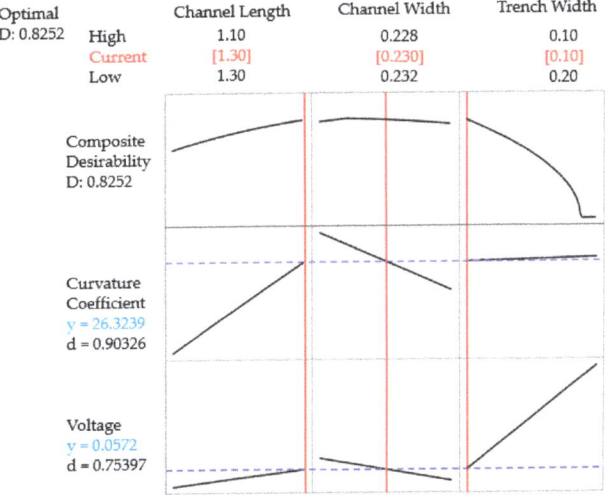

Figure 9. Response optimizer plot for regression analysis using optimized structure of SSD.

3.3. Characterization of the Optimized SSD Structure

The curvature coefficient analysis performed on the optimized structure indicated a prominent rectification performance of γ_{peak} at 26.4260 V^{-1} and V_{peak} of 0.05 V, improved from the highest reported γ value of 25.9172 V^{-1} using the trial-and-error method [19], which shows promising ability to function in zero bias (Figure 10).

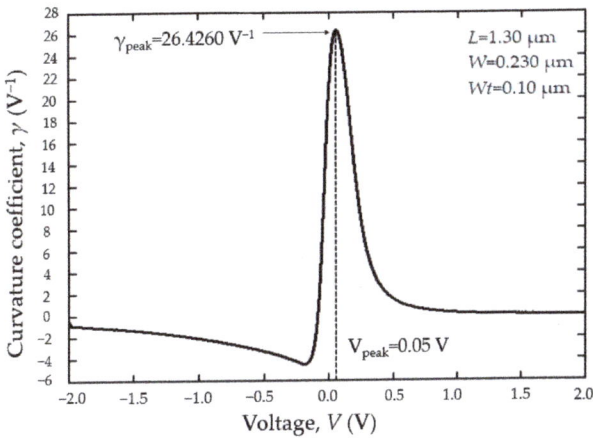

Figure 10. The curvature coefficient, γ, of the optimized SSD structure.

An alternating current (AC) transient analysis was performed on the optimized SSD structure to imitate an RF wave input of 0.30 V with a frequency ranging from 3 to 10 GHz. With 0.30 V input, the device can function in zero bias without an external power supply. In sequence, the current output for each frequency was analyzed using Equation (6) in terms of the mean current, I_{mean}, and plotted (see Figure 11) to obtain the cut-off frequency (the frequency where I_{mean} is equal to 0), which indicates no rectifying current and detection from the RF.

$$I_{mean} = \frac{1}{(t_1 - t_i)} \int_{t_i}^{t_1} f(t_1)dt - \frac{1}{(t_2 - t_1)} \int_{t_1}^{t_2} f(t_2)dt. \qquad (6)$$

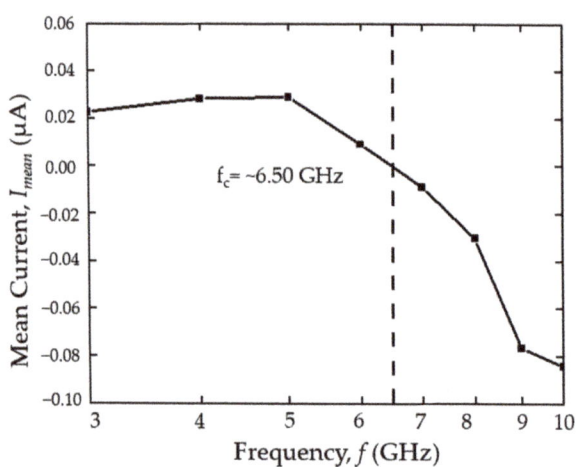

Figure 11. Cutoff frequency and the mean current values in each simulated frequency by using the optimized SSD structure.

As observed, the highest I_{mean} was obtained at 5 GHz, with a cut-off at approximately 6.50 GHz. This cutoff frequency is higher than the previously reported cutoff frequency using the SOI structure [40], which was suggested to be 4 ± 1 GHz. This indicates an improvement in the detection frequency by using an optimized structure, where an increased performance in 5G networks was achieved with the assistance of statistical optimization.

4. Conclusions

In this work, an optimized SSD structure utilized as an RF detector was analyzed by integrating statistical and numerical analyses using the Taguchi method and ATLAS device simulator, respectively. By performing numerical simulations based on Taguchi's DOE using the identified control factors and their corresponding levels, the number of significant simulation frequencies was reduced to nine runs, whereas the trial-and-error method requires a range of varied parameters in each structural parameter. Simulations were performed using the ATLAS device simulator by utilizing the physical models validated with the experimental results. The curvature coefficients, γ, from the resulting IV characteristics from each run were used for the analysis of the S/N ratios of the γ peak, and its corresponding voltage, V, was used for the overall ratio. By performing the overall calculation of the S/N ratios, the give-and-take of both γ and V was considered, where a high γ value in the lower bias voltage region was desired. The optimized structure was 0.23 µm, 1.30 µm, and 0.10 µm in channel width, channel length, and trench width, respectively.

Furthermore, the ANOVA conducted in this study provided an understanding of the sensitivity and the most affected control factors in both observed parameters of the SSD, where the γ peak value and its corresponding voltage were mostly affected by the channel length and trench width, respectively. However, only the *p*-value of the trench width rejected the null hypothesis, despite the high contribution percentage of other control factors. Additional regression analysis was performed to reconfirm the simultaneous relationship of all control factors with the results, which showed the rejection of the null hypotheses in most of the parameters. From the regression analysis, it can be understood that γ was mostly affected by the channel length and width, and its corresponding voltage was dependent on the channel width and trench. The average percentage errors of the predicted and simulated S/N ratios from regression and numerical analyses in all runs were 3.26% and 4.29% for γ and V, respectively, which shows acceptable prediction using regression analysis. Analysis using the response optimizer of the regression analysis showed a favorable composite desirability of 0.8252 with well-balanced performances of γ and V predicted at 26.3239 V^{-1} and 0.0572 V, respectively, using the optimized structure.

Characterization of the optimized SSD from the Taguchi method analysis by means of ATLAS device simulator showed prominent rectification performance with a γ of 26.4260 V^{-1} at 0.05 V bias, which was improved from the highest reported γ value of 25.9172 V^{-1} using the trial-and-error method. The AC analysis of the optimized structure showed a cutoff frequency of ~6.50 GHz, which is higher than the reported cutoff of 4 ± 1 GHz, with a detection peak at 5 GHz. This shows the promising ability of the SOI SSD to function in the 5G network frequency range, which can be a good alternative for a 5G network RF detector with the advantages of fabrication simplicity and low cost.

Author Contributions: Conceptualization, N.F.Z. and S.R.K.; methodology, T.Y.L., N.F.Z. and M.M.I.; software, A.K.S.; writing—original draft preparation, T.Y.L.; writing—review and editing, N.F.Z. and M.K.M.A.; supervision, N.F.Z. and S.R.K.; project administration, S.S. and S.A.S. All authors have read and agreed to the published version of the manuscript.

Funding: This research was funded by the Ministry of Higher Education Malaysia under grant number FRGS/1/2019/STG02/UNIMAP/03/1.

Informed Consent Statement: Not applicable.

Data Availability Statement: Not applicable.

Acknowledgments: The authors would like to acknowledge support from the Fundamental Research Grant Scheme (FRGS) under grant number FRGS/1/2019/STG02/UNIMAP/03/1 from the Ministry of Higher Education Malaysia.

Conflicts of Interest: The authors declare no conflict of interest.

References

1. Pradhan, D.; Sahu, P.K.; Dash, A.; Tun, H.M. Sustainability of 5G Green Network toward D2D Communication with RF- Energy Techniques. In Proceedings of the 2021 International Conference on Intelligent Technologies (CONIT), Hubli, India, 25–27 June 2021. [CrossRef]
2. Vasjanov, A.; Barzdenas, V. A Review of Advanced CMOS RF Power Amplifier Architecture Trends for Low Power 5G Wireless Networks. *Electronics* **2018**, *7*, 271. [CrossRef]
3. Galinina, O.; Tabassum, H.; Mikhaylov, K.; Andreev, S.; Hossain, E.; Koucheryavy, Y. On feasibility of 5G-grade dedicated RF charging technology for wireless-powered wearables. *IEEE Wirel. Commun.* **2016**, *23*, 28–37. [CrossRef]
4. Shafi, M.; Zhang, J.; Tataria, H.; Molisch, A.F.; Sun, S.; Rappaport, T.S.; Tufvesson, F.; Wu, S.; Kitao, K. Microwave vs. Millimeter-Wave Propagation Channels: Key Differences and Impact on 5G Cellular Systems. *IEEE Commun. Mag.* **2018**, *56*, 14–20. [CrossRef]
5. Alaji, I.; Aouimeur, W.; Ghanem, H.; Okada, E.; Lépilliet, S.; Gloria, D.; Ducournau, G.; Gaquière, C. Design of zero bias power detectors towards power consumption optimization in 5G devices. *Microelectron. J.* **2021**, *111*, 105035. [CrossRef]
6. Alaji, I.; Aouimeur, W.; Ghanem, H.; Okada, E.; Lépilliet, S.; Gloria, D.; Ducournau, G.; Gaquière, C. Design of tunable power detector towards 5G applications. *Microw. Opt. Technol. Lett.* **2021**, *63*, 823–828. [CrossRef]
7. Eid, A.; Hester, J.; Tehrani, B.; Tentzeris, M. Flexible W-Band Rectifiers for 5G-powered IoT Autonomous Modules. In Proceedings of the 2019 IEEE International Symposium on Antennas and Propagation and USNC-URSI Radio Science Meeting, Atlanta, GA, USA, 7–12 July 2019.
8. Zakaria, N.F.; Kasjoo, S.R.; Zailan, Z.; Isa, M.M.; Arshad, M.K.M.; Taking, S. InGaAs-based planar barrier diode as microwave rectifier. *Jpn. J. Appl. Phys.* **2018**, *57*, 064101. [CrossRef]

9. Balocco, C.; Kasjoo, S.R.; Lu, X.F.; Zhang, L.Q.; Alimi, Y.; Winnerl, S.; Song, A. Room-temperature operation of a unipolar nanodiode at terahertz frequencies. *Appl. Phys. Lett.* **2011**, *98*, 223501. [CrossRef]
10. Cortes-Mestizo, I.E.; Briones, E.; Briones, J.; Droopad, R.; Perez-Caro, M.; McMurtry, S.; Hehn, M.; Montaigne, F.; Mendez-Garcia, V.H. Study of InAlAs/InGaAs self-switching diodes for energy harvesting applications. *Jpn. J. Appl. Phys.* **2015**, *55*, 014304. [CrossRef]
11. Westlund, A.; Sangaré, P.; Ducournau, G.; de la Torrel, I.; Nilsson, P.A.; Gaquière, C.; Desplanque, L.; Wallart, X.; Millithaler, J.-F.; González, T.; et al. Optimization and small-signal modeling of zero-bias InAs self-switching diode detectors. *Solid State Electron.* **2015**, *104*, 79–85. [CrossRef]
12. Zakaria, N.; Kasjoo, S.; Zailan, Z.; Isa, M.M.; Taking, S.; Arshad, M. Permittivity and temperature effects on rectification performance of self-switching diodes with different geometrical structures using two-dimensional device simulator. *Solid State Electron.* **2017**, *138*, 16–23. [CrossRef]
13. Ku, K.J.; Rao, S.S.; Chen, L. Taguchi-aided search method for design optimization of engineering systems. *Eng. Optim.* **1998**, *30*, 1–23. [CrossRef]
14. Zakaria, N.F.; Kasjoo, S.R.; Isa, M.M.; Zailan, Z.; Arshad, M.K.M.; Taking, S. Self-switching diodes as RF rectifiers: Evaluation methods and current progress. *Bull. Electr. Eng. Inform.* **2019**, *8*, 396–404. [CrossRef]
15. Ancans, G.; Bobrovs, V.; Ancans, A.; Kalibatiene, D. Spectrum Considerations for 5G Mobile Communication Systems. *Procedia Comput. Sci.* **2017**, *104*, 509–516. [CrossRef]
16. Farhi, G.; Saracco, E.; Beerens, J.; Morris, D.; Charlebois, S.; Raskin, J.-P. Electrical characteristics and simulations of self-switching-diodes in SOI technology. *Solid State Electron.* **2007**, *51*, 1245–1249. [CrossRef]
17. Aberg, M.; Saijets, J.; Pursula, E.; Prunnila, M.; Ahopelto, J. Silicon self-switching-device based logic gates operating at room temperature. In Proceedings of the Proceedings Norchip Conference 2004, Oslo, Norway, 8–9 November 2004; pp. 40–43.
18. Zailan, Z.; Kasjoo, S.R.; Zakaria, N.F.; Isa, M.M.; Arshad, M.K.M.; Taking, S. Rectification performance of self-switching diodes in silicon substrate using device simulator. In Proceedings of the 2016 3rd International Conference on Electronic Design (ICED), Phuket, Thailand, 11–12 August 2016; pp. 373–376.
19. Tan, Y.; Zakaria, N.; Kasjoo, S.; Shaari, S.; Isa, M.; Arshad, M.; Rahim, A. Numerical Simulation and Parameters Variation of Silicon Based Self-Switching Diode (SSD) and the Effect to the Physical and Electrical Properties. In Proceedings of the 2020 IEEE International RF and Microwave Conference (RFM), Kuala Lumpur, Malaysia, 14–16 December 2020.
20. Zakaria, N.F.; Kasjoo, S.R.; Zailan, Z.; Isa, M.M.; Arshad, M.K.M.; Taking, S. Rectification performance of self-switching diode in various geometries using ATLAS simulator. In Proceedings of the 2016 3rd International Conference on Electronic Design (ICED), Phuket, Thailand, 11–12 August 2016; pp. 361–364. [CrossRef]
21. IEEE. Nanotechnology Council and Institute of Electrical and Electronics Engineers. In Proceedings of the 2018 IEEE 13th Nanotechnology Materials and Devices Conference (NMDC), Portland, OR, USA, 14–17 October 2018.
22. Zailan, Z.; Zakaria, N.F.; Isa, M.M.; Taking, S.; Arshad, M.K.M.; Kasjoo, S.R. Characterization of self-switching diodes as microwave rectifiers using ATLAS simulator. In Proceedings of the 2016 5th International Symposium on Next-Generation Electronics (ISNE), Hsinchu, Taiwan, 4–6 May 2016.
23. Mateos, J.; Song, A.M.; Vasallo, B.G.; Pardo, D.; Gonzalez, T. THz operation of self-switching nano-diodes and nano-transistors. In *Nanotechnology II*; International Society for Optics and Photonics: Bellingham, WA, USA, 2005; Volume 5838, pp. 145–153.
24. Kimura, Y.; Kiso, T.; Higaki, T.; Sun, Y.; Maemoto, T.; Sasa, S.; Inoue, M.Y. Rectification effects in ZnO-based transparent self-switching nano-diodes. In Proceedings of the 2012 IEEE International Meeting for Future of Electron Devices, Kansai, Suita, Japan, 9 May 2012.
25. Stephanie, F.; Mike, O.; Ben, T.; John, Z. Design of experiments via taguchi methods: Orthogonal arrays—ControlsWiki. In *The Michigan Chemical Process Dynamics and Controls Open Text Book*; 2006; pp. 1–11. Available online: https://controls.engin.umich.edu/wiki/index.php/Design_of_experiments_via_taguchi_methods:_orthogonal_arrays (accessed on 29 November 2021).
26. Liu, S.-J.; Lin, C.-H.; Wu, Y.-C. Minimizing the sinkmarks in injection-molded thermoplastics. *Adv. Polym. Technol.* **2001**, *20*, 202–215. [CrossRef]
27. Fei, N.C.; Mehat, N.M.; Kamaruddin, S. Practical Applications of Taguchi Method for Optimization of Processing Parameters for Plastic Injection Moulding: A Retrospective Review. *ISRN Ind. Eng.* **2013**, *2013*, 462174. [CrossRef]
28. Zakaria, N.F.; Kasjoo, S.R.; Isa, M.M.; Zailan, Z.; Mokhar, M.B.M.; Juhari, N. Application of Taguchi method in optimization of structural parameters in self-switching diode to improve the rectification performance. In Proceedings of the 2nd International Conference on Applied Photonics and Electronics 2019 (Incape 2019), Putrajaya, Malaysia, 22 August 2019; AIP Publishing: Putrajaya, Malaysia, 2020; Volume 2203, p. 020047.
29. Farhi, G.; Morris, D.; Charlebois, S.; Raskin, J.-P. The impact of etched trenches geometry and dielectric material on the electrical behaviour of silicon-on-insulator self-switching diodes. *Nanotechnology* **2011**, *22*, 435203. [CrossRef]
30. ATLAS User's Manual. *Device Simulation Software*; Silvaco Inc.: Santa Clara, CA, USA, 1998; Volume II, pp. 567–1000.
31. Nalbant, M.; Gökkaya, H.; Sur, G. Application of Taguchi method in the optimization of cutting parameters for surface roughness in turning. *Mater. Des.* **2007**, *28*, 1379–1385. [CrossRef]
32. Sorgdrager, A.; Wang, R.-J.; Grobler, A. Taguchi Method in Electrical Machine Design. *SAIEE Afr. Res. J.* **2017**, *108*, 150–164. [CrossRef]

33. Yang, W.; Tarng, Y. Design optimization of cutting parameters for turning operations based on the Taguchi method. *J. Mater. Process. Technol.* **1998**, *84*, 122–129. [CrossRef]
34. Ishrat, S.I.; Khan, Z.A.; Siddiquee, A.N.; Badruddin, I.A.; AlGahtani, A.; Javaid, S.; Gupta, R. Optimising Parameters for Expanded Polystyrene Based Pod Production Using Taguchi Method. *Materials* **2019**, *7*, 847. [CrossRef]
35. Gaaz, T.S.; Sulong, A.B.; Kadhum, A.A.H.; Nassir, M.H.; Al-Amiery, A.A. Optimizing Injection Molding Parameters of Different Halloysites Type-Reinforced Thermoplastic Polyurethane Nanocomposites via Taguchi Complemented with ANOVA. *Materials* **2016**, *9*, 947. [CrossRef]
36. Qidwai, M.O.; Badruddin, I.A.; Khan, N.Z.; Khan, M.A.; Alshahrani, S. Optimization of Microjet Location Using Surrogate Model Coupled with Particle Swarm Optimization Algorithm. *Materials* **2021**, *9*, 2167. [CrossRef]
37. Zerti, O.; Yallese, M.A.; Khettabi, R.; Chaoui, K.; Mabrouki, T. Design optimization for minimum technological parameters when dry turning of AISI D3 steel using Taguchi method. *Int. J. Adv. Manuf. Technol.* **2017**, *89*, 1915–1934. [CrossRef]
38. Mohsin, I.; He, K.; Li, Z.; Zhang, F.; Du, R. Optimization of the Polishing Efficiency and Torque by Using Taguchi Method and ANOVA in Robotic Polishing. *Appl. Sci.* **2020**, *10*, 824. [CrossRef]
39. Ozcelik, B. Optimization of injection parameters for mechanical properties of specimens with weld line of polypropylene using Taguchi method. *Int. Commun. Heat Mass Transf.* **2011**, *38*, 1067–1072. [CrossRef]
40. Aberg, M.; Saijets, J. DC and AC characteristics and modeling of Si SSD-nano devices. In Proceedings of the 2005 European Conference on Circuit Theory and Design, Cork, Ireland, 2 September 2005.

Article

Improving Calculus Curriculum in Engineering Degrees: Implementation of Technological Applications

María Teresa López-Díaz and Marta Peña *

Department of Mathematics, Universitat Politècnica de Catalunya, 08034 Barcelona, Spain; maria.teresa.lopez.diaz@upc.edu
* Correspondence: marta.penya@upc.edu

Abstract: The teaching of mathematics has always concerned all the professionals involved in engineering degrees. Curently students have less interest in these studies, what has caused an increase of this concern. The lack of awareness of students about the significance of mathematics in their careers, provoke the decrease of undergraduate students' motivation, which derives in a low interest in engineering degrees. The aim of this work is that engineering students achieve a greater motivation and involvement in first academic courses, through the implementation of real and technological applications related to their degrees in the learning of mathematical concepts. To this end, the 2019/2020 and 2020/2021 academics years, the seminar "Applications of Multivariable Calculus in Engineering" has been held in Universitat Politècnica de Catalunya-BarcelonaTech (UPC), based on the teaching of Multivariable Calculus by the execution of real problems where calculus concepts are necessary to solve them. With the aim of analyzing students' motivation and assessment of the seminar, anonymous surveys and personal interviews have been conducted. The number of attending students to the sessions in each academic year has been 16 and all of them have been participants in the surveys and interviews. The results show that students' responses were generally positive and they agree that their motivation to the subject Multivariable Calculus has increased with the use of real applications of mathematics. The execution of practical problems with engineering applications improves the acquirement of mathematical concepts, what could imply an increase of students' performance and a decrease of the dropout in the first academic courses of engineering degrees.

Keywords: calculus; engineering education; mathematics education; motivation; STEM

Citation: López-Díaz, M.T.; Peña, M. Improving Calculus Curriculum in Engineering Degrees: Implementation of Technological Applications. *Mathematics* **2022**, *10*, 341. https://doi.org/10.3390/math10030341

Academic Editors: Araceli Queiruga-Dios, Maria Jesus Santos, Fatih Yilma, Deolinda M. L. Dias Rasteiro, Jesús Martín Vaquero and Víctor Gayoso Martínez

Received: 27 November 2021
Accepted: 19 January 2022
Published: 23 January 2022

Publisher's Note: MDPI stays neutral with regard to jurisdictional claims in published maps and institutional affiliations.

Copyright: © 2022 by the authors. Licensee MDPI, Basel, Switzerland. This article is an open access article distributed under the terms and conditions of the Creative Commons Attribution (CC BY) license (https://creativecommons.org/licenses/by/4.0/).

1. Introduction

The economic development of countries is mainly based on technology. Thus, professionals in fields related to science, technology, engineering and mathematics (STEM) are necessary to improve the economy of countries. Technological production implies encouraging and supporting students to become technological professionals. Therefore, STEM disciplines are considered essential for the economic development of technological societies. The potential negative economic impact of undersupply is of concern due to opportunity costs and loss of competitiveness [1]. In addition, STEM education could integrate students' skills and better professional competences. The 21st century, as the age of information technologies, entails new job prospects and upcoming jobs which require new skills from professionals. Nowadays, technology is necessary in many jobs such as science, business, engineering, etc.

Moreover, high occupancy demands for STEM degrees are expected [2,3]. As technological knowledge and expertise is becoming more specialized and economically increasingly important, ever more jobs specialized in STEM disciplines are required and this demand is expected to further increase in the upcoming years, as remarked in [4,5].

However, at the present time in most countries, undergraduate students have less interest in technological degrees [1,6,7], which is mainly due to the lack of awareness of the importance of mathematical subjects in first academic courses of these studies. This lack of awareness derives, in most cases, in the decrease of students' motivation, which has as a result a low performance and a high dropout rate in the first years of these degrees. Thus, the engineering education community work to identify the causes of this situation, as indicates [2].

The worrying dropout in higher education has gained much interest in academic research. One third of undergraduate students leave university without obtaining a degree, mainly during their first academic year [8]. The dropout rate is higher in STEM careers [7].

The importance of students' motivation and engagement has been analyzed in previous studies [9,10], and in particular for technological degrees [11]. In first academic years is essential to promote student engagement [12,13], which involves the improvement of motivation [14,15], relatedness [16], student achievement [17] and academic performance [18], what imply the decrease of the dropout rate.

Practical and real applications used in mathematics subjects of engineering degrees, encourage student engagement and motivation [14], as has been studied in previous works [19–23]. A proper coordination among mathematical subjects and technological subjects of engineering degrees syllabus contribute to the decrease of dropout rates [24]. Active learning has positive results on the rise of students' motivation and on the enhancement of their learning, what entails the improvement of their performance, as it is stated in several studies [25–28]. For instance, the relationship between mathematical creativity and the relevance of problem-solving in the teaching of mathematics has been studied in [29]. Moreover, key employee expected abilities involve problem-solving and analytical thinking skills besides the competences to communicate them. The use of problem-posing in engineering degrees contributes to increase student involvement. This methodology consists of exposing a problem to students, related to technological disciplines, which will lead them to discover what they need to learn to solve this problem. Furthermore, it implies the development of essential abilities and competences for their career, as they are autonomy, continuous learning, critical thinking, planning and communications skills [30,31]. Moreover, the integration of theory and practice entails the improvement of motivation, what implies an increase of academic performance [32–35].

The purpose of this work is to generate an integrated STEM curricula, connecting mathematical applications with STEM education. The aim of the present study is to increase undergraduate engineering students' motivation by contextualization of mathematical subjects with technological applications related to the disciplines taught in the following academic courses of these degrees. The material developed in this work is expected to be introduced for a future adaptation of mathematical subjects' syllabus in engineering degrees.

Engineering students have to solve engineering problems and mathematical methodologies are the tools to solve them. They need to know the usefulness of mathematics and how essential they are for their degrees and their future careers. In this regard, the motivation and involvement of students are considered a key element, clarifying the importance of mathematics for technological subjects and for their future profession.

This study is part of the work "Applications of Mathematics in Engineering", which is formed by two seminars: "Applications of Linear Algebra in Engineering" [36] and "Applications of Multivariable Calculus in Engineering". These two seminars entail the mathematical subjects of first academic courses in technological degrees. This study focuses on the seminar "Applications of Multivariable Calculus in Engineering", whose purpose is to present real and technical applications of Multivariable Calculus related to engineering degrees with the objective of increasing students' motivation towards the learning of mathematics in first academic courses. Knowing the need of mathematical concepts to solve those technical applications, students realized of the importance of mathematics not only for the execution of their degrees but also for the development of their careers as engineers.

This article focuses on these research questions:

- How does the implementation of real and practical applications in mathematical subjects' influence on students' motivation?
- What are the benefits of including real and practical applications in mathematical subjects of first academic courses in technological degrees?

The results of the study show that for students is really motivating to know what they will be capable to do in the next courses of their degree. They also realized of how essential Multivariable Calculus is for their future profession and increased their interest towards the subject.

These results verifies that this experience lets students obtain a greater understanding of mathematical concepts, which increases students' performance in mathematical subjects of engineering degrees.

2. Materials and Methods

The study has been conducted at the Universitat Politècnica de Catalunya-BarcelonaTech (UPC), a public university specialised in STEM degrees. The work "Applications of Mathematics in Engineering" is formed by two seminars: "Applications of Linear Algebra in Engineering" [36] and "Applications of Multivariable Calculus in Engineering", which started in the 2019/2020 academic year and were undertaken in the first and the second semester, respectively. Both seminars were organised in weekly sessions of one hour and a half each session. These sessions have been held also in the 2020/2021 academic year and it is planned to repeat them during the following years.

Thus, since the 2019/2020 academic year, weekly sessions have been given to first-year students of the Industrial Engineering Bachelor's Degree from the Barcelona School of Industrial Engineering (ETSEIB) of the UPC, this degree lasts four years. Currently, the syllabus of mathematical subjects in engineering degrees do not content technological applications. Mathematical subjects focus on mathematical concepts, they are not contextualized in the technological disciplines of engineering degrees. The aim of this work is to contextualize mathematics through the connection of mathematical subjects with technological disciplines, taught in the following academic courses, and with their future technological professions. Thus, students will be able to realize of the importance of mathematics for engineering, as well as they learn engineering applications from the beginning of their degrees.

The two seminars "Applications of Linear Algebra in Engineering" and "Applications of Multivariable Calculus in Engineering" are offered in the same semesters in which the ordinary classes of the compulsory subjects Linear Algebra and Multivariable Calculus are taught, first and second semesters, respectively, so that the students who wish could complement in a parallel way and from a practical point of view the theoretical concepts introduced in the ordinary classes. The seminars have been devised with the aim of increasing students' motivation and involvement in the early stages of engineering studies. In addition to the benefits of these sessions, Universitat Politècnica de Catalunya-BarcelonaTech (UPC) recognizes with 1 European Credit Transfer and Accumulation System (ETCS) the attendance for students.

This article focuses on the seminar "Applications of Multivariable Calculus in Engineering". In each of the sessions of this seminar, applications illustrating the use of mathematical concepts related to multivariable calculus in different engineering areas are explained. The compulsory subject of Multivariable Calculus lasts one semester (14 weeks). Instead, the optional seminar presented in this work consists of 10 weeks. During the first two weeks of the semester, students are informed of the existence of this seminar in order to enable registration; and two other weeks, before the partial and final exams, no seminar sessions are given. So, this seminar consists of 10 sessions, 8 main sessions and 2 review sessions. The 8 main sessions are detailed in Table 1.

Table 1. Applications of Multivariable Calculus in Engineering.

Session	Title
1	"Discontinuous phenomena: hysteresis, caustics"
2	"Thom's catastrophes"
3	"Taylor and Fourier series"
4	"Chain, implicit and inverse theorems"
5	"Inverse kinetics"
6	"Kinematics of mechanisms with links"
7	"Optimization"
8	"Miscellany"

To evaluate the results of this study, anonymous surveys and personal interviews were conducted, with the aim of analyzing students' appreciation of the seminar "Applications of Multivariable Calculus in Engineering".

Surveys were undertaken at the end of each session and evaluate the impact of the experience on the students attending to the sessions, as regards the mathematical and engineering contents, the technological applications and the motivation towards the subject of Multivariable Calculus. These surveys consisted of five questions which must be valued on a 5-point scale (1 = Strongly disagree, 2 = Disagree, 3 = Nor agree nor disagree, 4 = Agree, 5 = Strongly agree). In addition, there is the possibility to include an opinion, where students could explain their impression about the session. The questions set in the surveys were:

Question 1: The assessment of mathematical contents is positive.

Question 2: The assessment of engineering contents is positive.

Question 3: The sessions "Applications of Multivariable Calculus in Engineering" let students know technological applications of different mathematical concepts.

Question 4: The applications of mathematical concepts achieve to increase the motivation to the subject Multivariable Calculus.

Question 5: The execution of practical exercises with technological applications improve the learning of mathematical concepts.

With the aim of extracting more opinions from the students attending the sessions "Applications of Multivariable Calculus in Engineering", personal interviews have been undertaken at the end of all the sessions in 2019/2020 and 2020/2021 academic years, which consisted of several open questions, where students could express in detail their opinion and assessment of the sessions. It should be noted that, in order to avoid bias in the answers, the person who interviewed students was not a professor but a master's student. The main questions set to students were:

1. What aspects do you assess most positively of these sessions?
2. What applications have been more interesting? Why?
3. How have these sessions influenced on your motivation and on your interest toward Multivariable Calculus?
4. Have these sessions helped you understand mathematical concepts of the subject Multivariable Calculus? What applications? What concepts?
5. After these sessions, do you consider that Mathematics are more important and essential to the development of engineering degrees? How? Why?

The influence of the implementation of the seminar "Applications of Multivariable Calculus in Engineering" on the students attending the seminar has been analyzed from the answers to the surveys and to the interviews undertaken after the sessions of this seminar.

3. Results

3.1. Students' Mathematical Contents

The 8 main sessions of the seminar "Applications of Multivariable Calculus in Engineering" consists of real and practical applications of the contents developed in the subject Multivariable Calculus, whose syllabus is:

1. Continuity and derivability of multivariable functions.
2. Integration of multivariable functions.
3. Laplace transform and Fourier series.

The first three sessions of the seminar are focused in discontinuous phenomena. Although they are not still included in mathematical subject programmes, discontinuous phenomena are very common in engineering problems and entail most of the contents of engineering subjects and contribute to illustrate the importance of these mathematical theories to solve real engineering problems. The applications developed in sessions 1, 2 and 3 include the Thom's catastrophes and Taylor and Fourier series.

The sessions 4, 5 and 6 are related to differential calculus and the basic theorems: chain rule, implicit function theorem and inverse function theorem, which are the basis of a great number of classical applications in engineering.

The session 7 is about optimization, which is the most important goal of engineering.

The last session, miscellany, deal with the use of engineering vision to solve applications in order to apply mathematical calculations, concluding that engineers must complement the use of mathematical tools with their engineering knowledge.

Some practical and real applications explained to the students in the sessions "Applications of Multivariable Calculus in Engineering" are explained below. They consist of applications of Multivariable Calculus related to engineering disciplines which can be understood and learnt by undergraduate students in the first academic courses.

3.1.1. Application 1: A Gravitational Machine

The first application is an example of discontinuous phenomena and it was explained in the session 1 (Discontinuous phenomena: hysteresis, caustics), where discontinuous phenomena were introduced highlighting how frequent they are in engineering.

In a gravitational machine appear discontinuous phenomena as it is going to be shown hereunder. A gravitational machine consists of a flat sheet limited by a parabola, leant on a horizontal plane. The most important point of this machine is that the center of gravity (CDG) is variable through the position of a magnet which can be moved on the sheet surface. Supposing the sheet mass negligible, the CDG would be the magnet position (Figure 1).

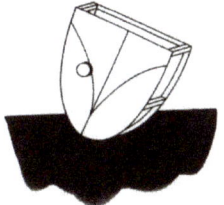

Figure 1. Centre of gravity.

When the CDG is displaced on the sheet, how will the sheet situate in a stable way?

The stability situation will happen when the CDG is placed in a minimum height, therefore the stable equilibrium point P on the parabola outline is the relative minimum of the distance between the CDG and the parabola points, that is, the orthogonal base to the parabola from the CDG, as it is shown in the following figure (Figure 2).

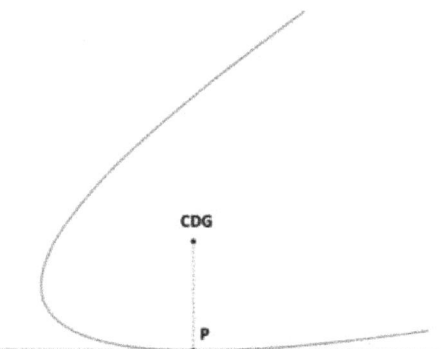

Figure 2. Position of the center of gravity.

If CDG is placed on the parabola vertical axis, the equilibrium point could be stable or instable depending on the CDG height. If the distance between the CDG and the equilibrium point is a relative minimum, there would be stable equilibrium but if this distance is a relative maximum, the equilibrium point is the parabola vertex and it would be instable equilibrium.

If we consider the parabola $\{(z, z^2), |z| \leq 2\}$ and the CDG $= (0, 2)$, the distance between any point on the parabola outline and the CDG placed on the parabola axis would be:

$$E = \left(d\left((z, z^2), (0, 2)\right)\right)^2 = z^2 + \left(z^2 - 2\right)^2 = z^4 - 3z + 4 \tag{1}$$

If we derivate and equal to zero, we obtain:

$$D\left(d\left((z, z^2), (0, 2)\right)\right)^2 = 4z^3 - 6z = 0 \tag{2}$$

where $z = 0$ is a relative maximum and $z = \pm\sqrt{\frac{3}{2}}$ are relative minimums.

Therefore, if CDG is $= (0, 2)$, there is instable equilibrium in the parabola vertex, $V = (0, 0)$. In addition, there is stable equilibrium on the parabola outline points $P_1 = \left(\sqrt{\frac{3}{2}}, \frac{3}{2}\right)$, $P_2 = \left(-\sqrt{\frac{3}{2}}, \frac{3}{2}\right)$. These points are indicated in the following figure (Figure 3):

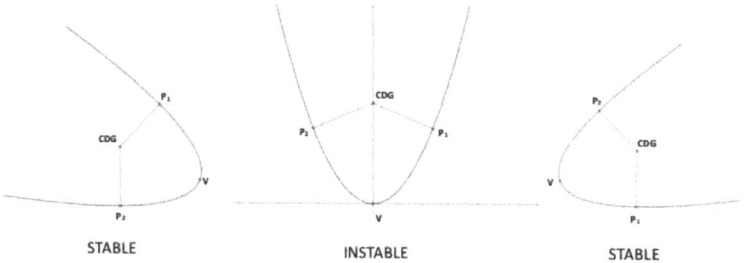

Figure 3. Stability of the center of gravity.

If the CDG height is less than $\frac{1}{2}$. there is only one relative extreme, which is the parabola vertex and, in this case, there would be 1 stable equilibrium point.

Depending on the position of de CDG, there can exist three equilibrium points or only one equilibrium point. This situation happens not only if the CDG is placed on the parabola axis but also on any point inside the parabola.

The question is in what positions of the CDG, there are three equilibrium points (two stable points and one instable point) and in what positions there is only one stable equilibrium point. To answer this question, we must analyze in what positions of the CDG there are three orthogonals, corresponding to two relative minims and one relative maxim and in what positions there is only one equilibrium point, corresponding to a relative minim. To solve it we have to make the orthogonals envelope. We must distinguish the area where there are three orthogonals and the area with only one orthogonal, the separation between these two areas is the orthogonals envelope. To obtain the expression of this envelope, we have to do the following calculations.

The orthogonal in:

$$\left(z, z^2\right) = \left\{(\beta, \alpha) : \frac{\beta - z}{-2z} = \alpha - z^2\right\} \tag{3}$$

The expression of the orthogonal is:

$$0 = \beta - z + 2z\left(\alpha - z^2\right) = \beta + (2\alpha - 1)z - 2z^3 \tag{4}$$

To eliminate z, we calculate the derivative:

$$0 = D^z\left(\beta - z + 2z\left(\alpha - z^2\right)\right) = (2\alpha - 1) - 6z^2 \tag{5}$$

with these 2 expressions, we can obtain that:

$$z^2 = \frac{2\alpha - 1}{6} \Rightarrow 0 = \beta + z\left((2\alpha - 1) - 2\frac{2\alpha - 1}{6}\right) \Rightarrow 0 = \beta + z\frac{2}{3}(2\alpha - 1) \Rightarrow$$
$$\Rightarrow \beta^2 = z^2 \frac{4}{9}(2\alpha - 1)^2 = \frac{2\alpha - 1}{6}\frac{4}{9}(2\alpha - 1)^2 \tag{6}$$

As a result, it can be deduced that the envelope expression is:

$$\beta^2 = \frac{16}{27}\left(\alpha - \frac{1}{2}\right)^3 \tag{7}$$

That is a cusp curve that separates the triple orthogonality area from the simple orthogonality area, as it is shown in this figure (Figure 4):

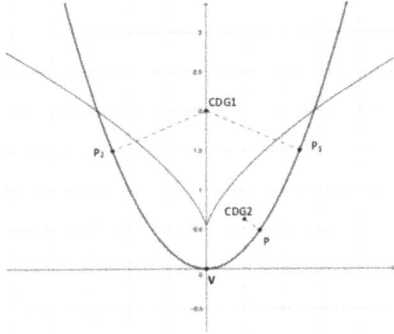

Figure 4. Cusp curve.

If the CDG is placed over the cusp, the gravitational machine will have three equilibrium points. In the figure, CDG1 is placed over the cusp and in this case the two stable equilibrium points are P1 and P2 and the instable equilibrium point is the parabola vertex V.

If the CDG is placed under the cusp, the gravitational machine has one equilibrium point. In the figure, CDG2 is under the cusp and the only one stable point is P.

The following expressions represent these conditions:

$$\text{CDG}(\beta, \alpha) \begin{cases} \beta^2 < \frac{16}{27}\left(\alpha - \frac{1}{2}\right)^3 \Rightarrow \begin{cases} 2\ \text{STABLE} \\ 1\ \text{INSTABLE} \end{cases} \\ \beta^2 > \frac{16}{27}\left(\alpha - \frac{1}{2}\right)^3 \Rightarrow 1\ \text{STABLE} \end{cases} \quad (8)$$

Now we are going to analyze the machine behavior when the CDG moves from a position over the envelope to a position under it. In this case the system will lose one stable equilibrium point. Therefore, it will provoke a discontinuity.

To show it, we are going to study the following figure (Figure 5).

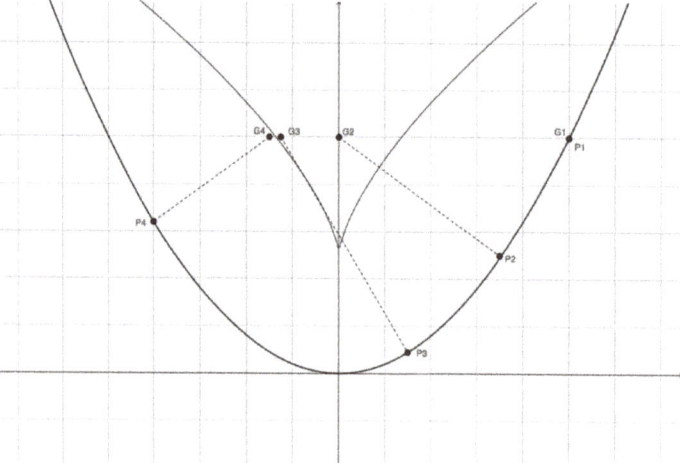

Figure 5. Machine behavior.

If CDG moves slowly among the points G_1, G_2 and G_3, the equilibrium point changes continuously among the points P_1, P_2 and P_3, respectively.

If CDG changes from G_3 to G_4, the parabola falls discontinuously, the equilibrium point jumps from P_3 to P_4. The disruption occurs when $\beta \cong -0.28$.

In the case that $\alpha = 0.4$ and the CDG changes horizontally, there will not be disruption because the CDG is always under the envelope.

3.1.2. Application 2: Euler's Arc

The second example, explained in session 3, is an application of Thom's catastrophes and of Fourier and Taylor's series.

Supposing a compressed arc (with length π) and a load m slightly off-center (ε), as it is represented in the following figure (Figure 6):

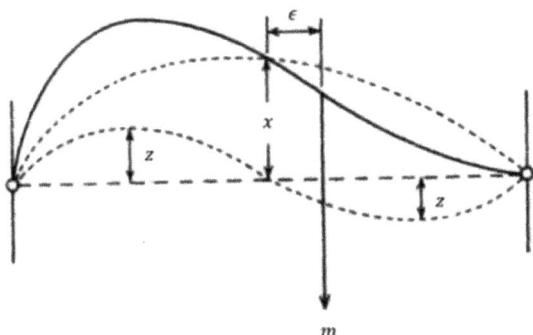

Figure 6. Compressed arc.

The beam resistance depends on two control parameters (m,ε), which must be modelled by the Thom's 2nd catastrophe.

Expressing the arc with the following function:

$$f(s), 0 \leq s \leq \pi \tag{9}$$

Fourier analysis establishes that periodic functions can be modelled by additions of harmonics of different periods. Therefore, the bean function can be expressed as an addition of sinus of different periods:

$$f(s) = \sum c_n \sin ns \tag{10}$$

In this example, supposing one or two harmonics, it is obtained that:

$$m = 0,\ \varepsilon = 0 \Rightarrow f(s) \cong r \sin s \tag{11}$$

If the elastic module is $\mu = \frac{1}{\pi}$, potential energy and elastic energy are:

$$V_P = mf\left(\frac{\pi}{2} + \varepsilon\right) \tag{12}$$

$$V_E = \frac{1}{2\pi} \int_0^\pi (f''(s))^2 \frac{1}{\left(1 + (f'(s))^2\right)^3} ds \tag{13}$$

Applying Taylor ($\varepsilon \ll$):

$$V_P = mx \cos \varepsilon + mz(-\sin 2\varepsilon) \cong mx\left(1 - \frac{\varepsilon^2}{2}\right) + mz(-2\varepsilon) \tag{14}$$

The variable x depends on the variable z because the beam distance does not change when the beam distorts:

$$d = \int_0^\pi \sqrt{1 - (f'(s))^2}\, ds \tag{15}$$

In both cases (considering one or two harmonics) this distance is the same:

$$d = \int_0^\pi \sqrt{1 - (r\cos s)^2}\, ds \cong \int_0^\pi \sqrt{\left(1 + \tfrac{1}{2}r^2 \cos^2 s + \tfrac{-1}{8}r^4 \cos^4 s\right)}\, ds = \\ = \tfrac{\pi}{4}\left(4 - r^3 - \tfrac{3}{16}r^4 - \tfrac{5}{64}r^6\right) \tag{16}$$

$$d = \int_0^\pi \sqrt{1 - (x\cos s + 2z \cos 2s)^2}\, ds \cong \ldots = \\ = \tfrac{\pi}{4}\left(4 - x^2 - 4z^2 - \tfrac{3}{16}x^4 - 3x^2 z^2 - \tfrac{5}{64}x^6\right) \tag{17}$$

Equaling the two expressions below and applying Taylor approximation:

$$x \cong a_0 + a_2 z^2 + a_4 z^4 \Longrightarrow a_0 = r, \; a_2 = -\frac{2}{r} - \frac{3r}{4}, \; a_4 = \frac{-2}{r^3} \tag{18}$$

It is obtained x as an implicit function of z:

$$x \cong r + z^2\left(-\frac{2}{r} - \frac{3r}{4}\right) + z^4 \frac{-2}{r^3} \tag{19}$$

Now we can obtain the elastic energy depending only on z:

$$V_E \cong \ldots = \text{constant} + \left(3 + \frac{13}{8}r^2\right)z^2 \tag{20}$$

The total energy is the addition of the potential and the elastic energy:

$$V = V_P + V_E \cong \text{constant} - 2m\varepsilon z + \left(\left(3 + \frac{13}{8}r^2\right) - m\left(\frac{2}{r} + \frac{3r}{4}\right)\right)z^2 - \frac{2m}{r^3}z^4 \tag{21}$$

which is the expression of the Thom's 2nd catastrophe with vertex (supposing $\varepsilon = 0$):

$$m_0 = \left(3 + \frac{13}{8}r^2\right)\left(\frac{2}{r} + \frac{3r}{4}\right)^{-1} \cong \frac{3}{2}r - \frac{1}{4}r^3 \tag{22}$$

Consequently:

$$V \cong -\frac{3}{r^2}z^4 - \frac{2}{r}(m - m_0)z^2 - 2r\varepsilon z \tag{23}$$

The maxim load decreases quickly when ε increases, as it represents the Thom's cusp represented in the following figure (Figure 7):

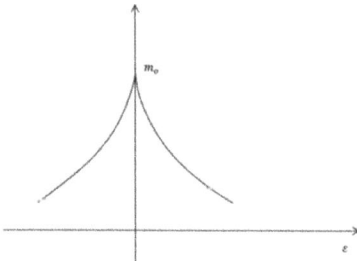

Figure 7. Thom's cusp.

3.1.3. Application 3: Crank and Connecting Rod

This exercise, explained in session 4, is an example of the implicit function theorem, which has many applications in mechanic in order to relation the different parameters operating in a mechanism.

This application is the crank/connecting rod system of explosion motors (see Figure 8), which consists of:

- one crank moving with an angle θ;
- one connecting rod whose movement depends on the crank turn;
- one piston moving horizontally on an axis.

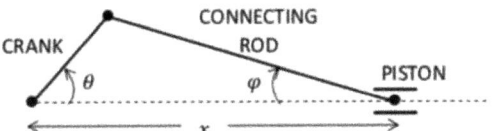

Figure 8. Crank/connecting rod system.

Supposing that the crank length r and the connecting rod length L are known, this system has three position parameters:
- x: piston distance to the crank turn center;
- θ: crank angle;
- φ: connecting rod angle.

These three parameters are related according to the following expressions:

$$\begin{cases} x = r\cos\theta + L\cos\varphi \\ r\sin\theta = L\sin\varphi \end{cases} \quad (24)$$

There are three parameters to determine the position and two equations which relate them. One of the three parameters could be expressed in function of the other two parameters and act as a control parameter determining those two parameters following the equations below.

Fixing the value of one from the three variables, we would obtain a system with two equations and two unknown factors, which would have a unique solution.

Applying the implicit function theorem:

$$(x, \theta, \varphi) \xrightarrow{f} (x - r\cos\theta - L\cos\varphi, r\sin\theta - L\sin\varphi) \quad (25)$$

Calculating the derivative matrix:

$$Df = \begin{pmatrix} 1 & r\sin\theta & L\sin\varphi \\ 0 & r\cos\theta & -L\cos\varphi \end{pmatrix} \quad (26)$$

According to this theorem, one variable acts as implicit (control variable) if the minor formed by the other columns is different to zero.

If we calculate the minor of the variable x:

$$\det\begin{pmatrix} r\sin\theta & L\sin\varphi \\ r\cos\theta & -L\cos\varphi \end{pmatrix} = -rL(\sin\theta\cos\varphi + \cos\theta\sin\varphi) =$$
$$= -rL\sin(\theta + \varphi) \neq 0 \text{ if } (\theta + \varphi) \neq 0, \pi \quad (27)$$

Therefore, x acts as a control parameter except for the neutrals:

$$(\theta + \varphi) = 0, \pi \iff x = \frac{L + r}{L - r} \quad (28)$$

Indeed, the crank turn can be reversed in neutrals.

If we calculate the minor of the variable θ:

$$\det\begin{pmatrix} 1 & L\sin\varphi \\ 0 & -L\cos\varphi \end{pmatrix} = -L\cos\varphi \neq 0 \quad (29)$$

Therefore, the crank angle θ is a control parameter for all the values.

3.1.4. Application 4: Articulated Arm

However, in order to simplify the above computation and the further ones, a key tool is the matrix of the linear map. Let us obtain the matrix of f in ordinary basis.

This example, explained in session 5, is an application of inverse kinetics, which is, calculating input position, speed, etc., from outputs position, speed, etc.

This application explains the work of a robot articulated arm, whose scheme is represented in the following figure (Figure 9), which is composed by:

- a shoulder situated in the coordinates origin;
- an upper arm with length 5 and an angle $\theta > 0$ from the vertical;
- an elbow situated at the end of the upper arm;
- a lower arm with length 4 and angle $\varphi < \pi$ from the upper arm;
- a hand situated at the end of the lower arm, in the coordinates (x, y);
- torsion motors in the articulations (the shoulder and the elbow).

The analysis consists of a direct and an inverse kinetics study of the articulated arm.

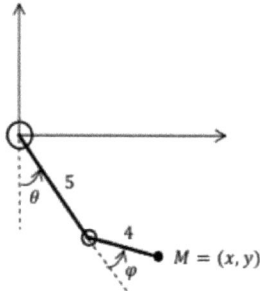

Figure 9. Articulated arm.

The direct kinetics study obtains the hand position from the shoulder and elbow angles, as it is calculated hereunder:

$$]0, \pi[\times]0, \pi[\xrightarrow{f} \Omega. \tag{30}$$

$$(\theta, \varphi) \to (x, y) \tag{31}$$

$$\begin{cases} x = 5\sin\theta + 4\sin(\theta + \varphi) \\ y = 5\cos\theta + 4\cos(\theta + \varphi) \end{cases} \tag{32}$$

The hand speed is calculated applying the chain rule, as it indicated hereunder:

$$\begin{pmatrix} \dot{x} \\ \dot{y} \end{pmatrix} = (Df) \begin{pmatrix} \dot{\theta} \\ \dot{\varphi} \end{pmatrix}, Df = \begin{pmatrix} 5\cos\theta + 4\cos(\theta + \varphi) & 4\cos(\theta + \varphi) \\ -5\sin\theta - 4\sin(\theta + \varphi) & -4\sin(\theta + \varphi) \end{pmatrix} \tag{33}$$

what is really interesting in robots is calculating the shoulder and the elbow rotor speeds from the hand position, that is, the inverse kinetics study. To obtain these speeds, it is necessary to apply the chain rule, the inverse function theorem and the implicit function theorem, as it is carried out in the following example.

If the output is $M = (5, 4)$, it is asked to obtain the shoulder and the elbow speeds $\dot{\theta}$ and $\dot{\varphi}$.

It is clear to see that is a functional dependence between the hand position (x, y) and the shoulder and the elbow positions (θ, φ) since there is only one possible triangle which determine the hand position from the shoulder and the elbow positions. Therefore

$$\Omega \xrightarrow{f^{-1}}]0, \pi[\times]0, \pi[\tag{34}$$

$$(x,y) \to (\theta, \varphi) \tag{35}$$

Applying the inverse function theorem, it is confirmed the f^{-1} derivability:

$$\begin{aligned} \det Df &= -20\cos\theta\,\sin(\theta+\varphi) + 20\sin\theta\,\cos(\theta+\varphi) = \\ &= -20\sin(\theta-(\theta+\varphi)) = -20\sin\varphi \neq 0 \end{aligned} \tag{36}$$

The relation between the shoulder and the elbow speeds, and the hand speed is:

$$\begin{pmatrix} \dot\theta \\ \dot\varphi \end{pmatrix} = (Df)^{-1} \begin{pmatrix} \dot x \\ \dot y \end{pmatrix} \tag{37}$$

The hand position $M = (5,4)$ corresponds to the angles $= \frac{\pi}{2}, \varphi = \frac{\pi}{2}$.
Replacing in the expression below, it is obtained that:

$$\begin{pmatrix} \dot\theta \\ \dot\varphi \end{pmatrix} = \begin{pmatrix} 4 & 4 \\ -5 & 0 \end{pmatrix}^{-1} \begin{pmatrix} \dot x \\ \dot y \end{pmatrix} = \frac{1}{20}\begin{pmatrix} 0 & -4 \\ 5 & 4 \end{pmatrix}\begin{pmatrix} \dot x \\ \dot y \end{pmatrix} \tag{38}$$

$$\dot\theta = -\frac{1}{5}\dot y \tag{39}$$

$$\dot\varphi = \frac{1}{4}\dot x + \frac{1}{5}\dot y \tag{40}$$

3.1.5. Application 5: Electrical Dispatch

This example, explained in session 7, is about the most important goal of engineering, which is the optimization of all the technological process.

The problem of the electrical dispatch deals with assigning the electrical central productions to the required power. All the distributions companies need to calculate the production of each supply central $P_1, \cdots, P_n$ to cover the instant demand P.

In each moment, it must be decided, which centrals act and with what power, considering the cost of productions of those supply centrals. The objective is reaching the minimum production cost.

The production cost of each supply electrical central is defined by the expression:

$$C_j = \alpha_j + \beta_j P_j + \gamma_j P_j^2, \quad 1 \leq j \leq n, \alpha_j, \beta_j, \gamma_j > 0 \tag{41}$$

The problem is, if we have several supply electrical centrals which have quadratic production costs and there is a certain demand P lower than the maximum, knowing the power distribution of the different centrals and the first central that must be stopped.

To illustrate the solving of this problem, we are going to use an example with only three supply electrical centrals, whose costs are hereunder indicated:

$$C_1 = 7 + P_1 + P_1^2. \tag{42}$$

$$C_2 = 4 + 2P_2 + 2P_2^2 \tag{43}$$

$$C_3 = 2 + 4P_3 + 3P_3^2 \tag{44}$$

Total power is the three powers sum:

$$P = P_1 + P_2 + P_3 \tag{45}$$

Total cost production of the three centrals is the cost productions sum:

$$\begin{aligned} C &= (7 + P_1 + P_1^2) + (4 + 2P_2 + 2P_2^2) + + \left(2 + 4(P - P_1 - P_2) + 3(P - P_1 - P_2)^2\right) = \\ &= 13 + 4P - 3P_1 - 2P_2 + P_1^2 + 2P_2^2 + 3(P - P_1 - P_2)^2 \end{aligned} \tag{46}$$

To minimize the cost, the cost partial derivatives are calculated and equaled to zero:

$$D_1 C = -3 + 2P_1 - 6(P - P_1 - P_2) = -3 - 6P + 8P_1 + 6P_2 = 0 \qquad (47)$$

$$D_2 C = -2 + 4P_2 - 6(P - P_1 - P_2) = -2 - 6P + 6P_1 + 10P_2 = 0 \qquad (48)$$

The system obtained is compatible determined, therefore has a unique solution, which is:

$$\begin{array}{l} P_1^* = \tfrac{1}{22}(9 + 12P) \\ P_2^* = \tfrac{1}{22}(-1 + 6P) \end{array} \Rightarrow P_3^* = \frac{1}{22}(-8 + 4P) \qquad (49)$$

This solution is valid only if $P_1^*, P_2^*, P_3^* \geq 0$:

$$P_1^* > 0, \ \forall P \qquad (50)$$

$$P_2^* > 0 \Leftrightarrow P \geq \frac{1}{6} \qquad (51)$$

$$P_3^* > 0 \Leftrightarrow P \geq 2 \qquad (52)$$

Therefore, the solution is valid only if $P \geq 2$.

If P decreases under $P = 2$, the solution below is not valid. From this value, P_3^* turns to be negative, what indicates that the third central must be the first central to stop.

In this case only the other two centrals act and the production cost is:

$$C = 7 + P_1 + P_1^2 + 4 + 2(P - P_1) + 2(P - P_1)^2 \qquad (53)$$

The cost derivative calculation equaled to zero is:

$$P_1^* = \frac{1}{6}(1 + 4P) \qquad (54)$$

$$P_2^* = \frac{1}{6}(-1 + 2P) \Leftrightarrow \frac{1}{2} \leq P \leq 2 \qquad (55)$$

$$P_3^* = 0 \qquad (56)$$

Therefore, if P decreases under $P = \tfrac{1}{2}$, P_2^* turns to be negative, what indicates that the second central must stop.

In this case, the only one central which supplies power is the first central and in this case the distribution is:

$$P_1^* = P, \ P_2^* = P_3^* = 0 \ \text{si} P \leq \frac{1}{2} \qquad (57)$$

3.2. Students' Surveys and Interviews Results

Up to now, two editions of the seminar "Application of Multivariable Calculus in Engineering" have been held, corresponding to the second semester of the 2019/2020 and 2020/2021 academic years. The contents explained in these sessions has been studied considering the answers to the anonymous questionnaires and to the personal interviews conducted to students.

Students' surveys of the sessions undertaken until now have been analyzed. The surveys were held in the 2019/2020 and 2020/2021 academic years, after each of the sessions. The number of attending students to the sessions has been 16 and all of them have been participants in the surveys. The results obtained in these two academic years did not have relevant differences. In the following figures the answers to each question for all the sessions in both years are presented. So, for each figure, 256 represents the total number of cases, which are the answers of 16 students in each of the 8 sessions and during two academic years.

The answers to the first question (Figure 10) show that most of the students, almost 90% of the total 256 answers of students, agree with the mathematical contents developed in the sessions.

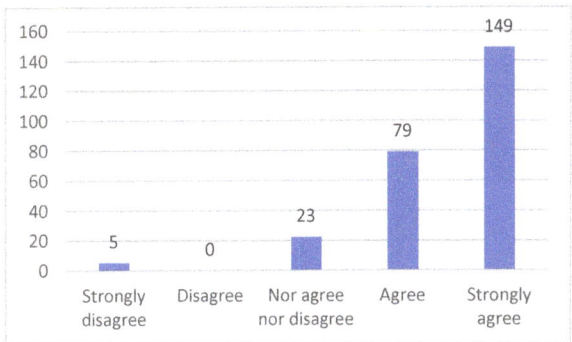

Figure 10. Answers to question 1: The assessment of mathematical contents is positive.

Likewise, in the answers to the second question (Figure 11), it can be observed that almost 90% of the total 256 answers of students agree with the engineering contents explained in the sessions.

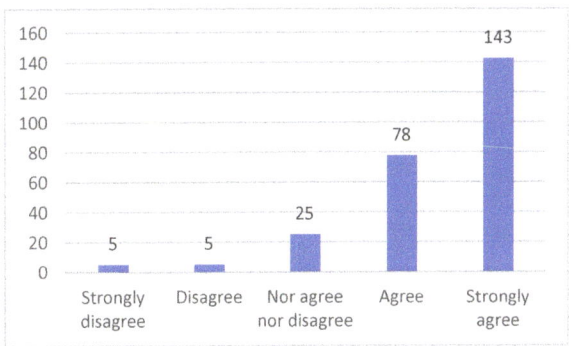

Figure 11. Answers to question 2: The assessment of engineering contents is positive.

According to the answers to question 3, almost 90% of the total 256 answers of students think that the sessions "Applications of Multivariable Calculus in Engineering" let them know technological applications of different mathematical concepts (Figure 12).

Almost 70% of the total 256 answers of students agree that applications of mathematical concepts achieve to increase their motivation to the subject Multivariable Calculus, as the answers to question 4 (Figure 13) show.

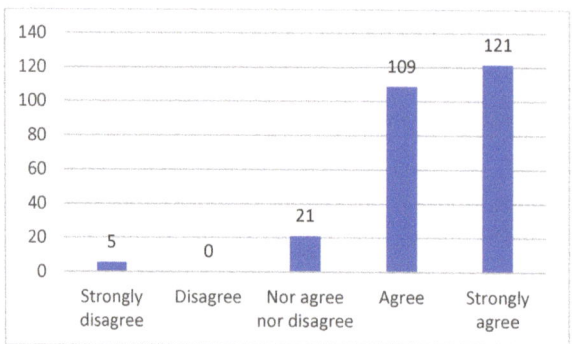

Figure 12. Answers to question 3: The sessions "Applications of Multivariable Calculus in Engineering" let students know technological applications of different mathematical concepts.

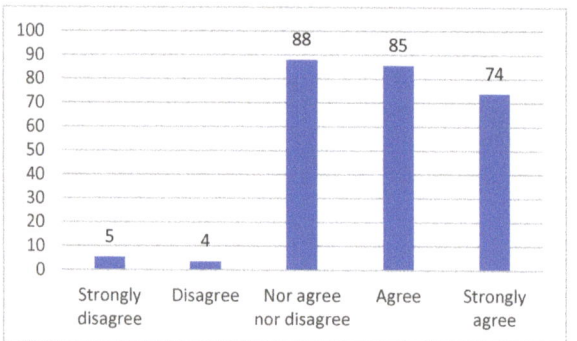

Figure 13. Answers to question 4: The applications of mathematical concepts achieve to increase the motivation to the subject Multivariable Calculus.

More than 70% of the total 256 answers of students state that the execution of practical exercises with technological applications improves the learning of mathematical concepts (Figure 14).

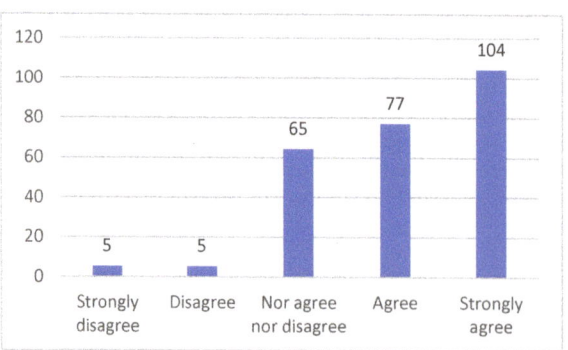

Figure 14. Answers to question 5: The execution of practical exercises with technological applications improve the learning of mathematical concepts.

The response of the attending students to these sessions in 2019/2020 and 2020/2021 academic years has been very positive. As can be observed in the above figures, the number of students who agree or strongly agree with the statements about the seminar is higher than the number of students who nor agree nor disagree, except for the question 4 (Figure 13). The reason is that some students have answered that although they assess positively the contents of the seminar, they were already motivated to the study of Calculus Multivariable before attending to the seminar.

It is also worth mentioning some students' comments expressed in the open questions asked in the anonymous surveys in both years, such as:

- These sessions let know real applications of mathematics in engineering, which gives more sense to the study of mathematics.
- Discovering that discontinuous phenomena produced in engineering processes can be modeled by mathematical theories increases the motivation towards the learning of mathematics.
- The use of mathematical concepts in technological applications, as they are implicit function theorem or Taylor and Fourier series, let students realize about the need of mathematics in engineering.
- Applications of Multivariable Calculus in mechanics and robotics increase the curiosity and the interest of students towards mathematical subjects.

The information extracted from students' answers in personal interviews in both academic years is presented hereunder:

- The real applications shown in the sessions "Applications of Multivariable Calculus in Engineering" let students realize of the usefulness of mathematics for their degree and for their future career.
- Applications studied in this seminar have been very practical and students will use them in their future profession. Learning to solve real engineering problems shows students how essential mathematical subjects are for engineers.
- Seeing how mathematics can be applied in engineering motivates to learn mathematics in order to be able to use them in the future as engineers.
- Seeing technological applications of mathematics increases the interest towards the subject.
- These applications help students understand related mathematical concepts as the implicit function theorem, the Fourier series or the calculations of maximums and minimums in functions defined in compact sets.
- Interesting applications: Zeeman machine solved with Thom's catastrophes theory and Taylor series and the crank/connecting rod system of explosion motors using the implicit function theorem.
- It has been very impressive knowing no technological applications of Thom's catastrophes, such as the analysis of dogs' behavior and sociological applications.
- Students knew that mathematics were necessary for engineering but, attending this seminar, they have discovered that mathematics are also necessary for other different disciplines.
- Mathematics are not subjects to prepare students for beginning the degree, mathematics are applications in the future work of engineers.

4. Discussion

In this work we contribute to develop an integrated STEM curriculum, introducing an implementation of mathematical applications integrated in STEM education. This study provides a connection of mathematical subjects with technological disciplines and with engineering careers, with the objective of enhancing the motivation and engagement of engineering students.

In the present engineering curriculum, the first two academic courses content very few engineering subjects, but consist of mathematics, science, communications and electives subjects. With the implementation developed in this work, mathematical subjects should cover real applications related to the main area of students enrolled degree, offering a wider view in STEM education [37,38], what would involve the improvement of the understanding and learning of mathematical concepts, as [39] states.

The main issue of this work has been the relevance of solving real and technological problems in the teaching of mathematics, since students' analytical thinking skills are enhanced with the use of mathematical problem solving [29,30,40]. In addition, the implementation of real and practical problems in basic sciences subjects promote student engagement and motivation in STEM degrees [14,19–21]. Considering the results shown in Figure 13, it can be seen that almost the 70% of the total 256 answers of students agree that applications of mathematical concepts achieve to increase their motivation to the subject of Multivariable Calculus, what will lead to reduce dropout, since it is connected to motivation [14], student achievement [17] and academic performance [11]. In the results of Figure 14, it has been shown that according to more than the 70% of the total 256 answers of students, the applications explained in the seminar, let them learn mathematical concepts trough practical examples. This fact increases their motivation to mathematics, as it is confirmed in previous studies such as [28]. In addition, as shows Figure 12, almost the 90% of the total 256 answers of students state that with this sessions they have known multiple real application of Multivariable Calculus in engineering and other disciplines, what attain to encourage and motivate them to the learning of the subject, as it was analyzed in several studies [14,19,20].

The answers to the questions taken to the students in the personal interviews after the sessions "Applications of Multivariable Calculus in Engineering", show that most of the practical problems have impressed students because they have discovered that Multivariable Calculus have applications in many different areas. Moreover, it is to highlight that for students is really motivating to know what they will be capable to do in the next academic courses, using the concepts of Multivariable Calculus. They also realized of how essential Multivariable Calculus is for their future career and increased their interest towards the subject.

The results obtained in this study support that this experience contribute to an improvement of students' learning of mathematical concepts, as it was concluded in [33], which involves the increase of students' performance in mathematical subjects of engineering degrees, as it was studied in previous works such as [25].

5. Conclusions

This study was carried out at the Universitat Politècnica de Catalunya-BarcelonaTech (UPC), a university focused on STEM fields. The work is based on the teaching of Multivariable Calculus by the execution of real and technological applications where Calculus concepts are necessary to solve them. The aim of this work is to generate and integrated STEM curriculum, presenting a contribution about the relationship among mathematical applications and STEM education. The work provides evidence that it is possible to increase students' motivation through the implementation of engineering applications in the learning of mathematics, what could imply an improvement of the learning of mathematics and therefore, an increase of students' performance and a decrease of the dropout in the first academic courses of engineering degrees. This entails a rise of interest in STEM degrees, which are essential for the economic growth of technological countries.

In view of the success of the seminar "Applications of Multivariable Calculus in Engineering", more real applications are planned to be developed. These sessions are going to be repeated in the second semester of the next academic year 2021/2022. Likewise, the seminar "Applications of Linear Algebra in Engineering" is going to be repeated in the first semester of the next academic year. These two seminars cover the most mathematical subjects of the first academic course in engineering degrees.

It is also planned to conduct surveys and interviews to the students attending the seminar of the following academic year with the aim of collecting a greater sample of surveys results and more information about students' experience in these sessions.

With the results obtained, it is expected that the contents developed in this work will be included in a future adaptation of mathematical subjects' syllabus in engineering degrees.

Author Contributions: Conceptualization, M.T.L.-D. and M.P.; methodology, M.T.L.-D. and M.P.; formal analysis, M.T.L.-D.; investigation, M.T.L.-D. and M.P.; writing—original draft preparation, M.T.L.-D. and M.P.; writing—review and editing, M.T.L.-D. and M.P.; supervision, M.P. All authors have read and agreed to the published version of the manuscript.

Funding: This research received no external funding.

Institutional Review Board Statement: Not applicable.

Informed Consent Statement: Informed consent was obtained from all subjects involved in the study.

Data Availability Statement: Data and materials available on request from the authors. The data and materials that support the findings of this study are available from the corresponding author upon reasonable request.

Acknowledgments: The authors wish to thank all the students who have been involved in this work. The authors would also like to thank Josep Ferrer for his dedication and contribution to this work.

Conflicts of Interest: The authors declare no conflict of interest.

References

1. Joyce, A. Stimulating interest in STEM careers among students in Europe: Supporting career choice and giving a more realistic view of STEM at work. *European Schoolnet Brussels*. 2014. Available online: https://www.educationandemployers.org/wp-content/uploads/2014/06/joyce_-_stimulating_interest_in_stem_careers_among_students_in_europe.pdf (accessed on 29 October 2021).
2. Marra, R.M.; Rodgers, K.A.; Shen, D.; Bogue, B. Leaving Engineering: A Multi-Year Single Institution Study. *J. Eng. Educ.* **2012**, *101*, 6–27. [CrossRef]
3. Caprile, M. Encouraging STEM studies Labour Market Situation and Comparison of Practices Targeted at Young People in Different Member States. *Policy Dep. A* **2015**, *12*. Available online: https://www.europarl.europa.eu/RegData/etudes/STUD/2015/542199/IPOL_STU (accessed on 29 October 2021).
4. Vennix, J.; Brok, P.D.; Taconis, R. Do outreach activities in secondary STEM education motivate students and improve their attitudes towards STEM? *Int. J. Sci. Educ.* **2018**, *40*, 1263–1283. [CrossRef]
5. Timms, M.; Moyle, K.; Weldon, P.; Mitchell, P. Challenges in STEM Learning in Australian Schools. Policy Insights. May 2018. Available online: https://research.acer.edu.au/policyinsights/7 (accessed on 9 August 2021).
6. Fadzil, H.M.; Saat, R.M.; Awang, K.; Adli, D.S.H. Students' Perception of Learning Stem-Related Subjects through Scientist-Teacher-Student Partnership (STSP). *J. Balt. Sci. Educ.* **2019**, *18*, 537–548. [CrossRef]
7. Ministerio de Universidades. *Datos y Cifras del Sistema Universitario Español*; Ministerio de Universidades: Madrid, Spain, 2021.
8. Bradburn, E.; Washington, D. *Short-Term Enrollment in Postsecondary Education: Student Background and Institutional Differences in Reasons for Early Departure*; U.S. Department of Education, Institute of Education for Education Statistics: Washington, DC, USA, 2002.
9. Zumbrunn, S.; McKim, C.; Buhs, E.S.; Hawley, L.R. Support, belonging, motivation, and engagement in the college classroom: A mixed method study. *Instr. Sci.* **2014**, *42*, 661–684. [CrossRef]
10. Lopez, D. Using Service Learning for Improving Student Attraction and Engagement in STEM Studies. *Eduction Excell. Sustain.* **2017**, *28*, 1053–1060.
11. Wilson, D.; Jones, D.; Bocell, F.; Crawford, J.; Kim, M.J.; Veilleux, N.; Floyd-Smith, T.; Bates, R.; Plett, M. Belonging and Academic Engagement Among Undergraduate STEM Students: A Multi-institutional Study. *Res. High. Educ.* **2015**, *56*, 750–776. [CrossRef]
12. Kuh, G.D.; Cruce, T.M.; Shoup, R.; Kinzie, J.; Gonyea, R.M. Unmasking the Effects of Student Engagement on First-Year College Grades and Persistence. *J. High. Educ.* **2016**, *79*, 540–563. [CrossRef]
13. Tinto, V. Dropout from Higher Education: A Theoretical Synthesis of Recent Research. *Rev. Educ. Res.* **1975**, *45*, 89. [CrossRef]
14. Gasiewski, J.A.; Eagan, K.; Garcia, G.A.; Hurtado, S.; Chang, M.J. From Gatekeeping to Engagement: A Multicontextual, Mixed Method Study of Student Academic Engagement in Introductory STEM Courses. *Res. High. Educ.* **2011**, *53*, 229–261. [CrossRef]
15. Pantziara, M.; Philippou, G.N. Students' Motivation in the Mathematics Classroom. Revealing Causes and Consequences. *Int. J. Sci. Math. Educ.* **2014**, *13*, 385–411. [CrossRef]
16. Ng, B.L.L.; Liu, W.C.; Wang, J. Student Motivation and Learning in Mathematics and Science: A Cluster Analysis. *Int. J. Sci. Math. Educ.* **2015**, *14*, 1359–1376. [CrossRef]
17. Handelsman, M.M.; Briggs, W.L.; Sullivan, N.; Towler, A. A Measure of College Student Course Engagement. *J. Educ. Res.* **2005**, *98*. [CrossRef]

18. Floyd-Smith, T.; Wilson, D.; Campbell, R.; Bates, R.; Jones, D.; Peter, D.; Plett, M.; Scott, E.; Veilleux, N. A Multi Institutional Study of Connection, Community and engagement in Stem Education: Conceptual Model Development. In Proceedings of the ASEE (American Society for Engineering Education) Conference, Arlington, VA, USA, 20 June 2020.
19. Bahamonde, A.D.C.; Aymemí, J.M.F.; Urgellés, J.V.G.I. Mathematical modelling and the learning trajectory: Tools to support the teaching of linear algebra. *Int. J. Math. Educ. Sci. Technol.* **2016**, *48*, 1–15. [CrossRef]
20. Kandamby, T. Enhancement of learning through field study. *JOTSE* **2018**, *8*, 408–419. Available online: https://dialnet.unirioja.es/servlet/articulo?codigo=6623129&info=resumen&idioma=ENG (accessed on 5 August 2021). [CrossRef]
21. Doerr, H.M. What Knowledge Do Teachers Need for Teaching Mathematics through Applications and Modelling? In *Modelling and Applications in Mathematics Education*; Springer: Boston, MA, USA, 2007; pp. 69–78. [CrossRef]
22. Chalmers, C.; Carter, M.; Cooper, T.; Nason, R. Implementing "Big Ideas" to Advance the Teaching and Learning of Science, Technology, Engineering, and Mathematics (STEM). *Int. J. Sci. Math. Educ.* **2017**, *15*, 25–43. [CrossRef]
23. Fan, S.-C.; Yu, K.-C.; Lin, K.-Y. A Framework for Implementing an Engineering-Focused STEM Curriculum. *Int. J. Sci. Math. Educ.* **2020**, *19*, 1523–1541. [CrossRef]
24. Perdigones, A.; Gallego, E.; García, N.; Fernández, P.; Pérez-Martín, E.; del Cerro, J. Physics and Mathematics in the Engineering Curriculum: Correlation with Applied Subjects. *Int. J. Eng. Educ.* **2014**, *30*, 1509–1521.
25. Freeman, S.; Eddy, S.L.; McDonough, M.; Smith, M.K.; Okoroafor, N.; Jordt, H.; Wenderoth, M.P. Active learning increases student performance in science, engineering, and mathematics. *Proc. Natl. Acad. Sci. USA* **2014**, *111*, 8410–8415. [CrossRef]
26. Borda, E.; Schumacher, E.; Hanley, D.; Geary, E.; Warren, S.; Ipsen, C.; Stredicke, L. Initial implementation of active learning strategies in large, lecture STEM courses: Lessons learned from a multi-institutional, interdisciplinary STEM faculty development program. *Int. J. STEM Educ.* **2020**, *7*, 1–18. [CrossRef]
27. Loyens, S.M.M.; Magda, J.; Rikers, R. Self-Directed Learning in Problem-Based Learning and its Relationships with Self-Regulated Learning. *Educ. Psychol. Rev.* **2008**, *20*, 411–427. [CrossRef]
28. Cetin, Y.; Mirasyedioglu, S.; Cakiroglu, E. An Inquiry into the Underlying Reasons for the Impact of Technology Enhanced Problem-Based Learning Activities on Students' Attitudes and Achievement. *Eurasian J. Educ. Res.* **2019**, *19*, 1–18. [CrossRef]
29. Mallart, A.; Font, V.; Diez, J. Case Study on Mathematics Pre-service Teachers' Difficulties in Problem Posing. *Eurasia J. Math. Sci. Technol. Educ.* **2018**, *14*, 1465–1481. [CrossRef]
30. Darhim, D.; Prabawanto, S.; Susilo, B.E. The Effect of Problem-based Learning and Mathematical Problem Posing in Improving Student's Critical Thinking Skills. *Int. J. Instr.* **2020**, *13*, 103–116. [CrossRef]
31. Passow, H.J. Which ABET Competencies Do Engineering Graduates Find Most Important in their Work? *J. Eng. Educ.* **2012**, *101*, 95–118. [CrossRef]
32. López-Díaz, M.; Peña, M. Contextualization of basic sciences in technological degrees. *FIE2020-Front. Educ.* **2020**, 1–5. Available online: https://upcommons.upc.edu/handle/2117/334379 (accessed on 29 October 2021).
33. Lacuesta, R.; Palacios, G.; Fernandez, L. Active learning through problem based learning methodology in engineering education. In Proceedings of the 2009 39th IEEE Frontiers in Education Conference, San Antonio, TX, USA, 18 October 2009; pp. 1–6. [CrossRef]
34. Chen, J.; Kolmos, A.; Du, X. Forms of implementation and challenges of PBL in engineering education: A review of literature. *Eur. J. Eng. Educ.* **2020**, *46*, 90–115. [CrossRef]
35. Chávez, D.A.; Sánchez, V.M.G.; Vargas, A.C. Problem-based learning: Effects on academic performance and perceptions of engineering students in computer sciences. *JOTSE* **2020**, *10*, 306–328. Available online: https://dialnet.unirioja.es/servlet/articulo?codigo=7641626&info=resumen&idioma=ENG (accessed on 5 August 2021).
36. López-Díaz, M.; Peña, M. Mathematics Training in Engineering Degrees: An Intervention from Teaching Staff to Students. *Mathematics* **2021**, *9*, 1475. [CrossRef]
37. Kertil, M.; Gurel, C. Mathematical Modeling: A Bridge to STEM Education. *Int. J. Educ. Math. Sci. Technol.* **2016**, *4*, 44. [CrossRef]
38. Yıldırım, B.; Sidekli, S. Stem applications in mathematics education: The effect of stem applications on different dependent variables. *J. Balt. Sci. Educ.* **2018**, *17*, 200–214. [CrossRef]
39. Kumar, S.; Jalkio, J.A. Teaching Mathematics from an Applications Perspective. *J. Eng. Educ.* **1999**, *88*, 275–279. [CrossRef]
40. Van Der Wal, N.J.; Bakker, A.; Drijvers, P. Which Techno-mathematical Literacies Are Essential for Future Engineers? *Int. J. Sci. Math. Educ.* **2017**, *15*, 87–104. [CrossRef]

Article

Novel Photovoltaic Empirical Mathematical Model Based on Function Representation of Captured Figures from Commercial Panels Datasheet

Ola Hassan [1], Nahla Zakzouk [2] and Ahmed Abdelsalam [2,*]

[1] Basic and Applied Science Department, College of Engineering and Technology, Arab Academy for Science and Technology (AAST), Smart Village Campus, Giza 12577, Egypt; ola.elaraby@aast.edu
[2] Electrical Engineering Department, College of Engineering and Technology, Arab Academy for Science and Technology (AAST), Abo Kir Campus, Alexandria 1029, Egypt; nahlaezzeldin@aast.edu
* Correspondence: ahmed.kadry@aast.edu

Abstract: Photovoltaic (PV) technology is gaining much interest as a clean, sustainable, noise-free source of energy. However, the non-linear behavior of PV modules and their dependency on varying environmental conditions require thorough study and analysis. Many PV modeling techniques have been introduced in the literature, yet they exhibit several complexity levels for parameter extraction and constants estimation for PV power forecast. Comparatively, a simple, accurate, fast, and user friendly PV modeling technique is proposed in this paper featuring the least computational time and effort. Based on function representation of PV curves' available in PV datasheets, an empirical mathematical equation is derived. The proposed formula is considered a generic tool capable of modeling any PV device under various weather conditions without either parameter estimation nor power prediction. The proposed model is validated using experimental data of commercial PV panels' manufacturers under various environmental conditions for different power levels. The obtained results verified the effectiveness of the proposed PV model.

Keywords: PV model; PV datasheet; non-linear PV characteristics; empirical mathematical model; standard testing condition

1. Introduction

With the increasing world-wide demand for renewable energy resources, photovoltaic (PV) systems are gaining much interest. Hence, advances are continuously carried out in the field of their modeling and performance [1]. A PV system includes a PV power source in the form of series and/or parallel combinations of PV modules forming a PV array with the required voltage and amperage [2]. Under uniform environmental conditions, a PV module exerts non-linear electrical characteristic curves, as shown in Figure 1a, where the PV module gives its maximum possible output power at a certain operating point. This maximum power point (MPP) is irradiance and temperature dependent, as presented in Figure 1b [3]. In order to maximize the PV source efficiency under varying environmental conditions, it should be followed by a pulse width modulation (PWM) converter for continuous maximum power point tracking (MPPT) [4].

For robust control of the entire PV system operation, the PV device should be simulated in the virtual environment [5]. Thus, a simple, reliable and precise mathematical model of the PV source is mandatory for accurate analysis of its non-linear characteristics under varying conditions. An efficient PV model is useful in the prediction of PV output power, the analysis of PV converter dynamic behavior and the study of MPP tracking algorithms [6]. PV model accuracy is evaluated by the proximity of the model characteristics to that of the practical device experimental data. Hence, the model should be adjusted using the set of data provided by manufacturers regarding the PV module thermal and electrical characteristics.

However, PV datasheets present a few experimental data that include the nominal open-circuit voltage (V_{OC}), the nominal short-circuit current (I_{SC}), the voltage at the MPP (V_{MPP}), the current at the MPP (I_{MPP}), the maximum experimental peak output power (P_{MPP}), the open-circuit voltage/temperature coefficient (K_V), and the short circuit current/temperature coefficient (K_I) [7]. These data are given under the so-called standard test condition (STC) which is defined by irradiation level of 1000 W/m^2, cell temperature of 25 °C, and air mass value of 1.5 [8]. Some manufacturers may also provide I–V characteristic curves, obtained experimentally under variable operating conditions, to validate and adjust the derived mathematical model. However, obtaining such curves experimentally requires costly and difficult measurements in controlled environmental chambers that should be carried out under certain conditions and according to a number of guidelines [9].

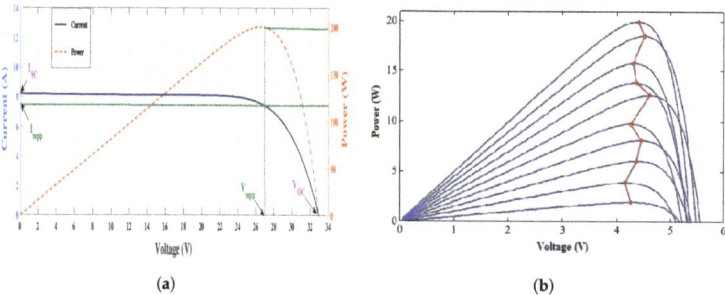

Figure 1. Power versus voltage curves of PV panel under (**a**) uniform conditions, (**b**) varying environmental conditions [3].

Many approaches have been developed for PV modules' modeling and representation as will be illustrated in the following. Equivalent circuit-based PV models, applying the Shockley diode equation for solar cell mathematical representation, have been developed and validated using the experimental data given in manufacturers' datasheets [10]. This equation represents the non-linear characteristics of the PV cell, yet it includes several parameters that are not available in commercial manufacturers' datasheets, hence have to be estimated [7,11]. These parameters include the diode ideality factor (a), diode reverse saturation current (I_o), the light-generated current (I_{PV}), and practical PV device series and shunt resistances. The series resistance (R_s) represents the summation of PV panel structural resistances while the parallel resistance (R_P) mirrors the $p-n$ junction leakage current and depends on the PV cell fabrication method. These unknown parameters differ from one panel to another, thus they should be accurately estimated for correct model adjustment of the considered PV device.

Equivalent circuit-based PV models are either based on single-diode equivalent circuits [12–15], two-diode circuits [16–19], or three-diode circuits [20,21]. When more diodes are included in the model, higher accuracy is obtained, though at the cost of more complexity and computational effort as more parameters have to be estimated (i.e., additional ideality factor and reverse saturation current for each added diode) [22,23]. For simplicity, most developed PV models are based on the single-diode equivalent circuit, as this model offers a satisfactory compromise between simplicity and accuracy [11]. Different mathematical procedures for estimating the unknown PV parameters required are elaborated with different levels of implementation complexity, computational time, and accuracy [24–26]. These procedures can be analytical, numerical, artificial intelligence-based, evolutionary algorithms-based, or hybrid ones.

Normally, analytical mathematical methods give exact solutions by means of algebraic equations. However, due to PV nonlinearity, it is hard to find out the analytical solution of all unknown parameters. Thus, analytical methods apply approximations or simplified assumptions for some PV parameters resulting in fast and simple solution at the cost of relatively less accuracy [27,28]. Generally, the R_P value is high while that of R_s is very low, thus some authors neglect the former [29–32] while others neglect the latter [33,34] or both [35]. In [36–40], an analytical method based on Lambert W function is introduced for parameters extraction, while in [41] transcendental equations for solar cell analysis are presented and solved using Special Tran Function Theory (STFT) to increase estimation accuracy.

Numerical methods develop a set of equations which are solved using numerical or iterative algorithms for precise parameters estimation. In [42], an iterative process is applied where R_s is slowly incremented and corresponding R_P and I_{PV} values are obtained such that the mathematical I–V equation fits specific experimental points on the practical module I–V curve. In [43], an iterative method to find the actual value of the diode ideality factor is presented. Other methods apply optimization numerical algorithms such as Levenberg–Marquardt Algorithm (LMA), Newton Raphson nonlinear, or least-squares algorithm for best curve fitting [27,44]. Although numerical methods outweigh analytical algorithms regarding accuracy, they require long-term time series data, thus consume more time.

Applying artificial intelligence [45–47] and evolutionary techniques [48–53] for PV parameters extraction can be observed as a fast and accurate solution, yet one which lacks simplicity and requires more computational effort, making it less practical. Hybrid techniques are introduced to compromise between simplicity, accuracy, and computational time. In [54] a combination between numerical and analytical methods is presented where PV output current expression is determined by Lambert W function while the PV voltage is computed numerically by the Newton–Raphson method. Lambert W function along with artificial neural network were employed for determination of PV I–V and PV curves [55].

Beside the equivalent circuit-based PV modeling techniques, an alternative PV cell mathematical representation based on trigonometrically function (sine and cosine function based model) is presented in [56,57]. It depends on observing how PV short-circuit current and open-circuit voltage change versus irradiance and temperature, then translating this observation into a trigonometrically property. However, this trigonometric function includes seven constants whose values have to be obtained through PV experimental characteristics which, in turn, adds to the computational efforts and affects its practicality.

Recently, many approaches have been developed to build PV models based on short-term and long-term PV power forecast using ANN and machine learning techniques [58–62]. However, they require complicated implementation, a large number of data samples, and continuous training and fitting results for accurate forecasting. The developed PV modules' modeling approaches and representation can be summarized and listed as shown below:

PV Modeling Approaches:

- Equivalent circuit based model:
  1. Parameters Estimation:
     – Analytical [27–41]
     – Numerical [42–44]
     – Artificial Intelligence [45–47]
     – Evolutionary algorithms [48–53]
     – Hybrid [54,55]
  2. Diodes Number:
     – Single-diode [12–15]
     – Double-diodes [16–19]
     – Triple-diodes [20,21]
- Trigonometric-function based [56,57]
- Short-term or long-term PV power forecast [58–62]
- Proposed empirical PV model

In this paper, a novel generic PV model is presented featuring an empirical mathematical equation based on function representation of captured figures from the datasheet.

This model is able to produce characteristic curves for any PV device at any condition based only on four electrical terms found in any practical PV datasheet at standard testing condition (STC). The proposed approach outweighs other models regarding its simplicity and reduced computational time and effort as none of parameters extraction, constants estimation, or PV power forecast are required. Thus, PV experimental curves at different environmental conditions can be emulated easily with the least cost. The proposed model is tested for different practical PV modules at various power ratings, then compared to a conventional PV model based on a single-diode equivalent circuit. The results validated the proposed approach and verified its competitiveness.

This paper is organized as follows: Section 2 illustrates the methodology adopted for developing the proposed empirical mathematical model of the PV based on captured figures from datasheet. Section 3 includes phase one of the model development of digitizing the captured figures and the data extraction process from the datasheet. Section 4 demonstrates phase two, which presents the formulation of the model through three cases: (i) varying irradiance at fixed STC temperature level, (ii) varying temperature at fixed STC irradiance level, and (iii) specific irradiance and temperature values differ from STC nominal values. Section 5 includes the simulation results of the proposed model compared to the extracted data. Section 6 contains the model validation using various datasheet with different ratings. Section 7 presents a comparison between the proposed mathematical model and a conventional equivalent circuit based PV model. Finally, Section 8 presents the discussion and conclusion.

2. Methodology of the Proposed Empirical Mathematical Model

The process of developing an empirical mathematical model to be used for generating the characteristic I–V curves of the PV panel at different levels of irradiance and temperatures passes through several steps, represented in Figure 2. In this paper, the proposed methodology is performed using the datasheet of KYOCERA PV-model (KK280P-3CD3CG) [63]. The adopted method for developing an empirical mathematical model starts with capturing the curves as images form the datasheet for the irradiance and temperature variations, as shown in Figure 3. We then used software to digitize these curves by transforming the captured images into numerical data points that are used to analyze the curve features in order to represent them in mathematical functions forms, as shown in Figure 4. By investigating the curves' characteristics and linking them with the panel standard test condition (STC) the model is developed to represent the I–V curves for the STC irradiance and temperature values ($G_0 = 1000$ W/m^2 and $T_0 = 25$ °C). Then, the proposed empirical mathematical model is generalized for any irradiance and/or temperature values based on analyzing the effect of the variation in some of I–V curves in the used main datasheet due to the changing in the values of irradiance and temperature. After that, the remaining unused curves of the same datasheet are used to test the proposed model. To validate the developed empirical model, various data from different panels rating datasheets are used [64–67]. The following sections will include a detailed illustration of each stage of the proposed methodology.

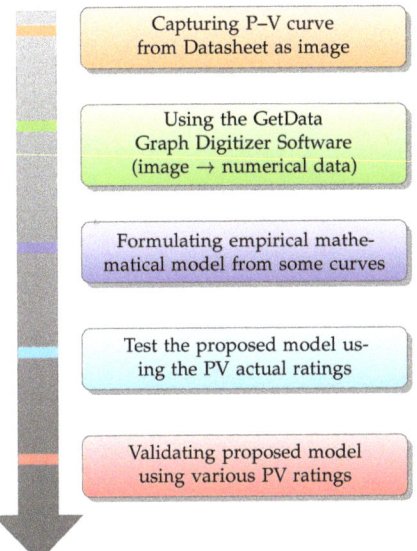

Figure 2. Methodology Work Flow.

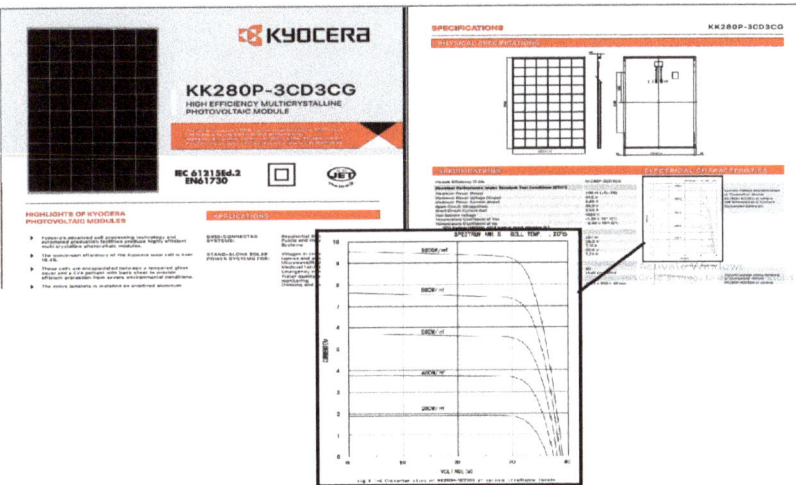

Figure 3. Capturing characteristic curves from datasheet as image.

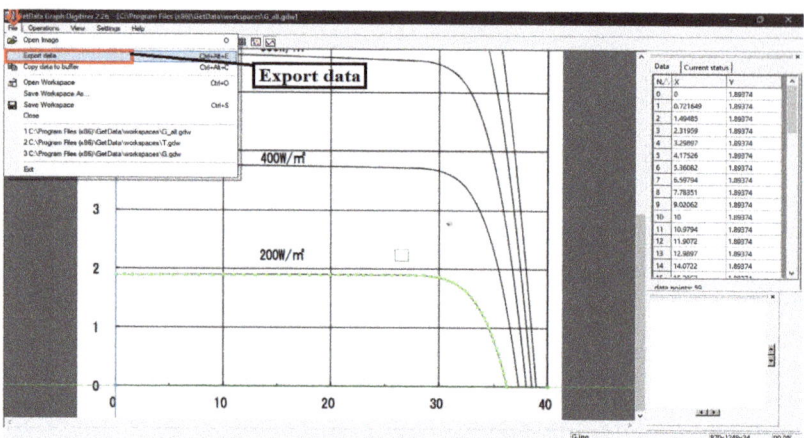

Figure 4. Digitizing the characteristic curves images into numerical data.

3. Stage One: Digitizing the Extracted I–V Curves Images from PV Panel Datasheet

In order to study the I–V curves of the PV-panels presented in datasheet, it is first required to transform them into numerical values. Hence, the software GetData Graph Digitizer® is used. This software is based on manually selecting the points from the curves image. At the beginning, one defines the minimum and maximum values of each axis and sets on image and after that defines its scale values. Then, for each curve in the image, the points are selected by tracing the curve using data pointers. These steps are presented in Figure 5.

A zoom preview exists on the bottom right of this program window to increase the accuracy of selecting the points. The data points are stored in Excel sheet format which can be exported to be used in analyzing and validating the mathematical model. This process of data extraction is used for both curves at various irradiance and temperature values.

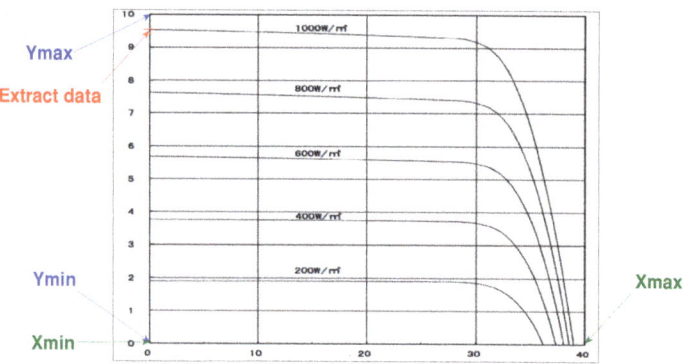

Figure 5. Axis Scale Determination.

The following part of this section includes a step-by-step illustration guide of how to use the program in transforming the datasheet I–V curves images into Excel sheet format aided with screen shoots. The data extraction steps are:

1. Import the datasheet curves to the software as image, then start to set the axes points as shown in Figure 6.
2. Set the minimum and maximum points of the x-axis (default 0, 1) as shown in Figures 7 and 8, respectively.

3. Set the minimum and maximum points of the y-axis (default 0, 1) as shown in Figures 9 and 10, respectively.
4. Adjust the scale of the maximum values of the axes based on datasheet values as shown in Figure 11.
5. Extract the data from each curve for a certain irradiance value by moving the selecting cursor along each curve as shown in Figure 12.
6. For adding more than one curve in the data, select add line to start selecting data for the new curve as shown in Figure 13.
7. Export the data from the software as Excel spreadsheet as two columns for each line, representing x and y values for each pair of points, as shown in Figure 14.

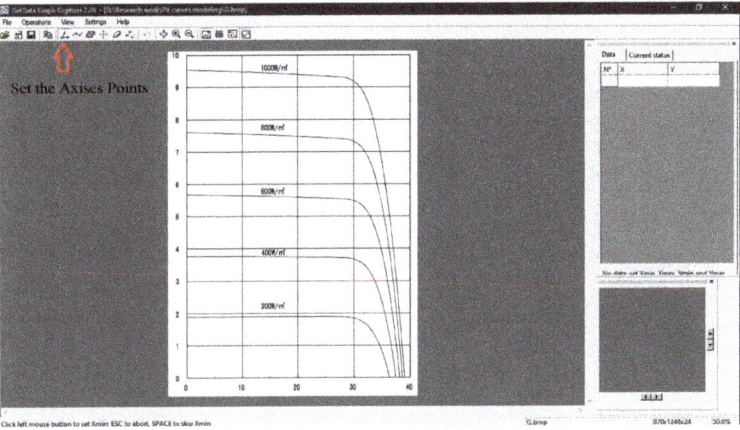

Figure 6. Step (1): Import the datasheet curves image to the software.

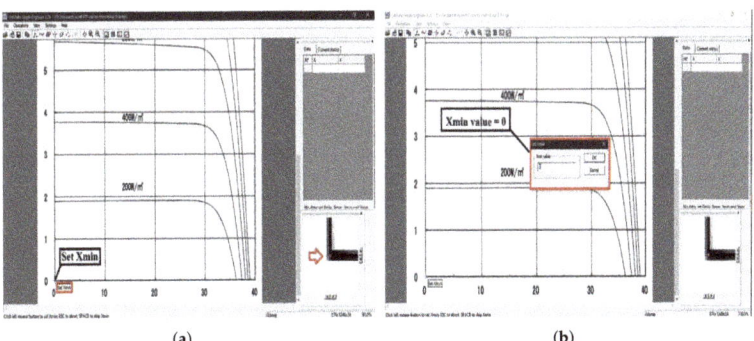

Figure 7. Step (2a): set the minimum value point of x-axis, (**a**) Set the location of the minimum point of x-axis, (**b**) The default value for minimum is 0.

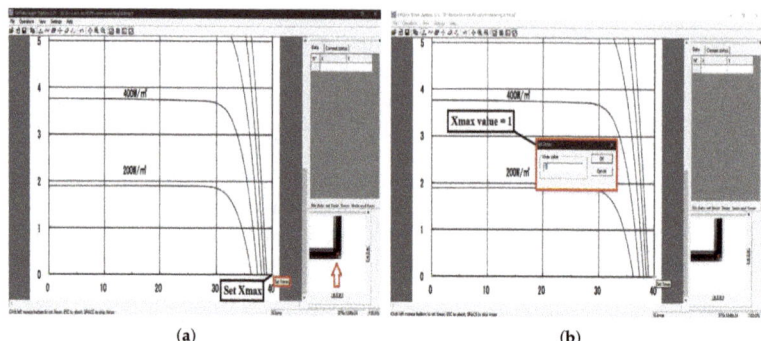

Figure 8. Step (2b): set the maximum value point of x-axis, (**a**) Set the location of the maximum point of x-axis, (**b**) The default value for maximum is 1.

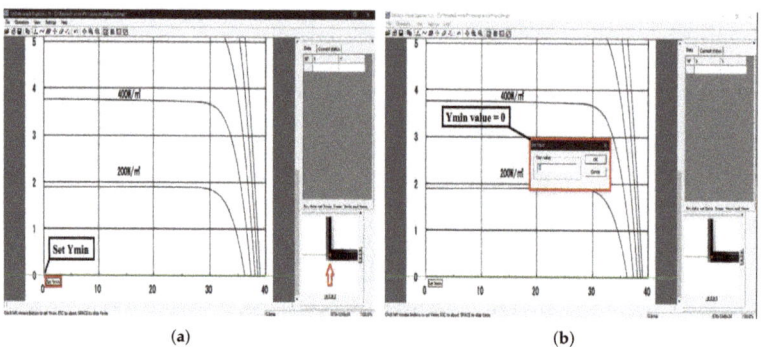

Figure 9. Step (3a): set the minimum value point of y-axis, (**a**) Set the location of the minimum point of y-axis, (**b**) The default value for minimum is 0.

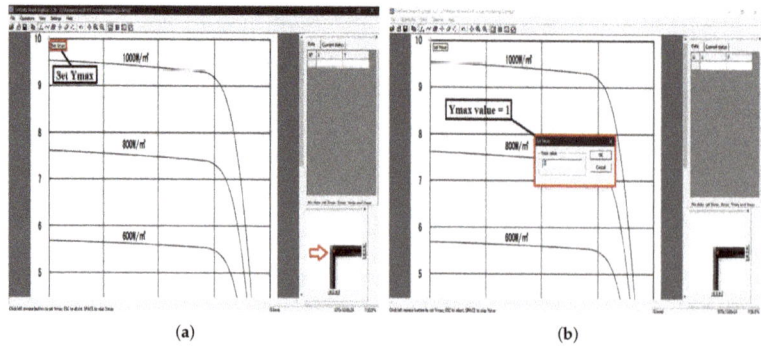

Figure 10. Step (3b): set the maximum value point of y-axis, (**a**) Set the location of the maximum point of y-axis, (**b**) The default value for maximum is 1.

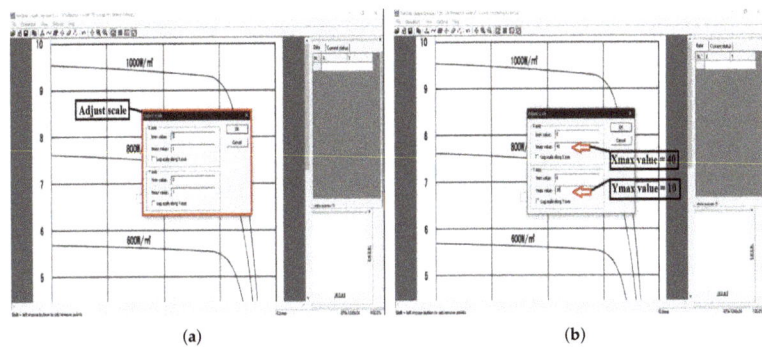

Figure 11. Step (4): Scale the maximum values of x-axis and y-axis, (**a**) Select the dialog box of adjusting the axes limits, (**b**) Set the maximum values according to the captured figures.

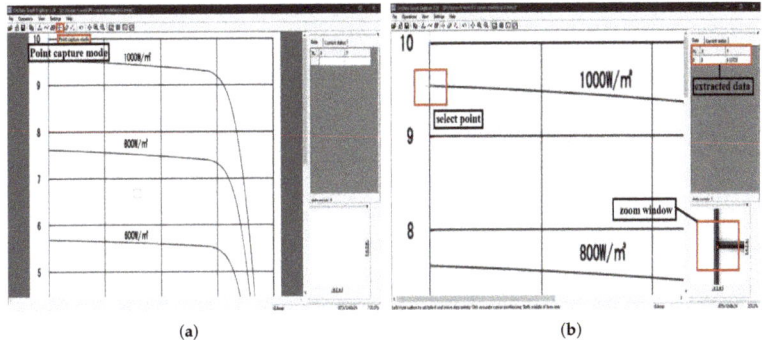

Figure 12. Step (5): Extract the data of each curve, (**a**) Select the point capture mode, (**b**) Start selecting points from the curve.

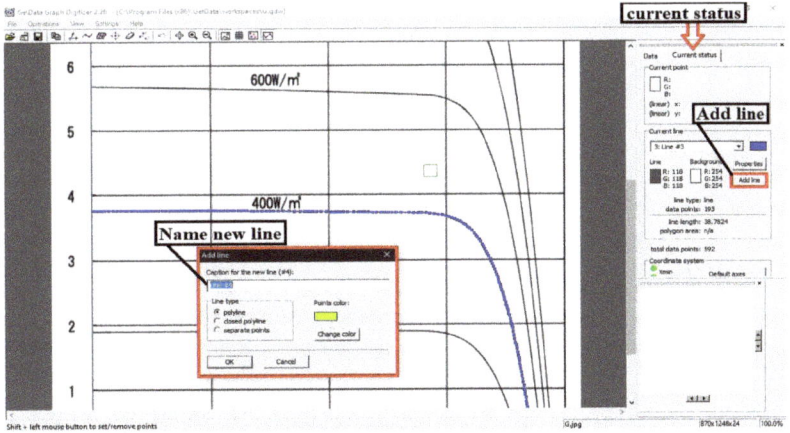

Figure 13. Step (6): Adding curves from the image to be extracted.

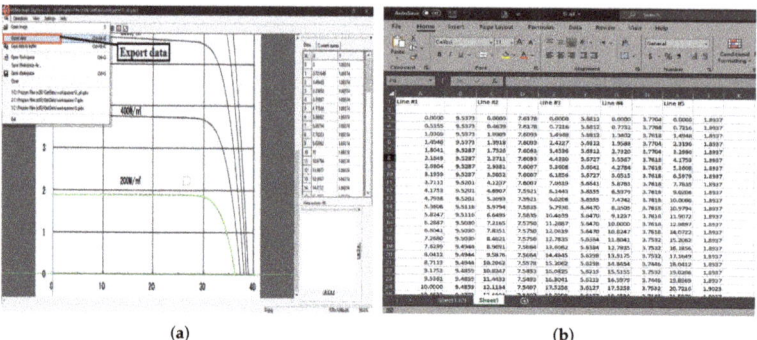

Figure 14. Step (7): Exporting data as excel sheet, (**a**) Select export option rom file menu, (**b**) The exported data in excel sheet format.

4. Stage Two: The Proposed Empirical Mathematical Model of PV Characteristics Curves

The proposed model is developed based on analyzing the I–V curves in several datasheets. By analyzing the curves we observed that the curve can be represented in the form of combination of two mathematical functions. The first function is negative slop straight line and the second one is inverted decaying exponential function. Varying the values of irradiance and temperature have nearly a scaling effect on the I–V curve shape but with preserving the same form. Therefore, the empirical mathematical model proposed in this paper is developed over two stages. The first one is to resemble the curve features in terms of the STC electrical performance terms. The second stage is to represent the impact of varying levels of irradiance and/or temperature on the curves to generalize the model.

In datasheets, it is common to include the curves of the varying irradiance at fixed temperature and/or varying temperature at fixed irradiance. Some datasheets also include a general case at a certain value of irradiance and temperatures which differ from the STC conditions. Therefore, the proposed model is considered over three cases: (i) varying the irradiance levels at STC temperature value, (ii) varying the temperature values at STC irradiance level, and (iii) general form at any value of irradiance and temperature. Each case of them is represented with separate model.

By investigating the first case of different irradiance level at the STC temperature value ($T_0 = 25\ °C$) the effect of this change on the current and voltage is presented for any value of irradiance relative to the STC one as a scale ratio. However, for the second case, the effect of changing the temperature values at the STC irradiance level ($G_0 = 1000\ W/m^2$) is represented in the model with a different ratio of temperature change, producing another form of the model generating the curves at any temperature value at STC irradiance level.

Finally, the general case of producing the curve at any environmental condition different from the STC case is investigated and presented in a general form of the proposed empirical mathematical model after updating the electrical terms used over two passes, one for new irradiance level and STC temperature then for new condition of both new irradiance and temperature required conditions.

The following subsections demonstrate each case of the three models and the used electrical performance terms notations in the models are defined as the following:

G :	Irradiance Level	G_0 :	STC Irradiance Level
T :	Temperature Value	T_0 :	STC Temperature Value
I_{MPP} :	Maximum Power Current	V_{MPP} :	Maximum Power Voltage
I_{SC} :	Short Circuit Current	V_{OC} :	Open Circuit Voltage

4.1. Case One: I–V Characteristics Empirical Mathematical Model for Varying Irradiance Levels

The varying irradiance level leads to varied values of the current produced by the PV panel with the same curve features mentioned early as a combination of two mathematical functions, (i) negative slop straight line and (ii) inverted decaying exponential function. Therefore, with decreasing the irradiance value the current decreases with a ratio of the irradiance level to STC level. In addition, the value of the open circuit voltage reduces with the exponential reduction in the irradiance amount. The maximum power point voltage value is independent of irradiance level, so it is constant for all its values.

The current for any irradiance value at STC temperature value can be calculated using the shown Equation (1):

$$I(G, T_0) = R \times \left[C + M \times V - B \times \left(1 - exp\left(\frac{V}{V_{OC}(G, T_0)}\right)\right) \times (1 - exp(A[V - V_{MPP}(G_0, T_0)]))\right] \quad (1)$$

where,

$$R = \frac{G}{G_0}$$

$$V_{OC}(G, T_0) = V_{OC}(G_0, T_0) - (1 - R) \times \left(\frac{V_{MPP}(G_0, T_0)}{I_{MPP}(G_0, T_0)}\right)^{(1-R)\frac{V_{OC}(G_0, T_0)}{V_{MPP}(G_0, T_0)}}$$

$$C = I_{SC}(G_0, T_0)$$

$$M = \frac{I_{MPP}(G_0, T_0) - I_{SC}(G_0, T_0)}{V_{MPP}(G_0, T_0)}$$

$$B = exp\left(\frac{-V_{MPP}(G_0, T_0)}{V_{OC}(G, T_0)}\right)$$

$$a = \left(1 + \frac{V_{OC}(G, T_0) - V}{V_{MPP}(G_0, T_0)}\right)\left(\frac{1}{V_{OC}(G, T_0) - V_{MPP}(G_0, T_0)}\right)$$

$$A = a \times \ln\left(1 - \frac{(C + M \times V_{OC}(G, T_0))}{B(1-e)}\right)$$

4.2. Case Two: I–V Characteristics Empirical Mathematical Model for Varying Temperature Levels

The same equation previously mentioned in Equation (1) is used to find the I–V curve at fixed level of irradiance (STC level), and any temperature values, but with updated values of some electrical performance terms. The change in temperature at fixed irradiance level has an effect on the values of the short circuit current, open circuit voltage, and maximum power point voltage, although the maximum power point current is constant for various temperature values.

The current for any temperature value at STC irradiance level can be calculated using the shown Equation (2):

$$I(G_0, T) = C + M \times V - B \times \left(1 - e^{\frac{V}{V_{OC}(G_0, T)}}\right) \times \left(1 - e^{A \times (V - V_{MPP}(G_0, T))}\right) \quad (2)$$

where,

$$S = \frac{T - T_0}{T_0}$$

$$I_{SC}(G_0, T) = I_{SC}(G_0, T_0) + 0.1 \times S$$

$$V_{OC}(G_0, T) = V_{OC}(G_0, T_0) - S \times \left(\frac{V_{MPP}(G_0, T_0) - 1}{I_{MPP}(G_0, T_0)}\right)$$

$$V_{MPP}(G_0, T) = V_{MPP}(G_0, T_0) e^{-S * \left(\frac{I_{MPP}(G_0, T_0)}{2V_{MPP}(G_0, T_0)}\right)}$$

$$C = I_{SC}(G_0, T)$$

$$M = \frac{I_{MPP}(G_0, T_0) - I_{SC}(G_0, T)}{V_{mp}(G_0, T)}$$

$$B = e^{\frac{-V_{MPP}(G_0, T)}{V_{OC}(G_0, T)}}$$

$$a = \left(1 + \frac{V_{OC}(G_0, T) - V}{V_{MPP}(G_0, T)}\right) \left(\frac{1}{V_{OC}(G_0, T) - V_{MPP}(G_0, T)}\right)$$

$$A = a \times \ln\left(1 - \frac{(C + M \times V_{OC}(G_0, T))}{B(1 - e)}\right)$$

4.3. Case Three: I–V Characteristics Empirical Mathematical Model for Certain Irradiance and Temperature Values

The current at STC irradiance and temperature values can be produced using either Equation (1) for the case where $[R = 1 \quad at \quad G = G_0]$ or Equation (2) at the case of $[S = 0 \quad at \quad T = T_0]$. However, to generate a curve of PV-panel current output at a certain irradiance and temperature level different from the STC, the same equation is used after updating the model electrical performance terms over two phases, one for updating irradiance to new level, and one updating for the new temperature value, as illustrated below:

Phase one: calculate terms for required irradiance value and at STC temperature (G, T_0), the following equations are used to find the updated values:

$$R = \frac{G}{G_0}$$

$$V_{OC}(G, T_0) = V_{OC}(G_0, T_0) - (1 - R) * \left(\frac{V_{MPP}(G_0, T_0)}{I_{MPP}(G_0, T_0)}\right)^{(1-R)\frac{V_{OC}(G_0, T_0)}{V_{MPP}(G_0, T_0)}}$$

$$I_{SC}(G, T_0) = R * I_{SC}(G_0, T_0)$$

$$I_{MPP}(G, T_0) = R * I_{MPP}(G_0, T_0)$$

$$V_{MPP}(G, T_0) = V_{MPP}(G_0, T_0)$$

Phase two: based on the values generated from phase one to find the terms for the required environmental condition (G, T), the following equations are used, resulting in the updated values:

$$S = \frac{T - T_0}{T_0}$$

$$V_{OC}(G, T) = V_{OC}(G, T_0) - S * \left(\frac{V_{MPP}(G_0, T_0) - 1}{I_{MPP}(G_0, T_0)} \right)$$

$$I_{SC}(G, T) = I_{SC}(G, T_0) + 0.1 * S$$

$$I_{MPP}(G, T) = I_{SC}(G, T_0)$$

$$V_{MPP}(G, T) = V_{MPP}(G, T_0) e^{-S * \left(\frac{I_{MPP}(G_0, T_0)}{2V_{MPP}(G_0, T_0)} \right)}$$

After updating the electrical terms for the required irradiance and temperature values the I–V curve is calculated using the following Equation (3):

$$I(G, T) = C + M \times V - B \times \left(1 - e^{\frac{V}{V_{OC}(G,T)}} \right) \times \left(1 - e^{A*(V - V_{MPP}(G,T))} \right) \qquad (3)$$

where,

$$C = I_{SC}(G, T)$$

$$M = \frac{I_{MPP}(G, T) - I_{SC}(G, T)}{V_{MPP}(G, T)}$$

$$B = e^{\frac{-V_{MPP}(G,T)}{V_{OC}(G,T)}}$$

$$a = \left(1 + \frac{V_{OC}(G, T) - V}{V_{MPP}(G, T)} \right) \left(\frac{1}{V_{OC}(G, T) - V_{MPP}(G, T)} \right)$$

$$A = a \times \ln \left(1 - \frac{(C + M \times V_{OC}(G, T))}{B(1 - e)} \right)$$

5. Proposed Model Simulation

The datasheet of the PV-panel KYOCERA PV-model (KK280P-3CD3CG) [63] is to develop and test the model. Developing the empirical model, at least three curves are needed, including the STC one which the model is based on, scaling it with varying the irradiance or the temperature values. The remaining unused curves are used to test the model. The extracted data versus the curves produced from the proposed mathematical empirical model is presented in the following subsection as follows:

- STC case curve.
- Varying irradiance levels at fixed STC temperature.
- Testing the proposed model with the unused irradiance levels at fixed STC temperature.
- Varying temperature values at fixed STC irradiance.

The standard electrical performance testing condition values used in simulating the curves are listed below in Table 1:

Table 1. Electrical performance values of STCs [63].

Item	Value
G_0	1000 W/m^2
T_0	25 °C
$I_{SC}(G_0, T_0)$	9.53 A
$I_{MPP}(G_0, T_0)$	8.89 A
$V_{MPP}(G_0, T_0)$	31.5 V
$V_{OC}(G_0, T_0)$	38.9 V
$P_{MPP}(G_0, T_0)$	280 W

5.1. Simulation of I–V Characteristics Curves Generated by the Mathematical Model

The STC case ($G = 1000$ W/m^2 and $T_0 = 25$ °C) is simulated using the proposed mathematical model and the produced I–V curve is compared with the data extracted from the datasheet [63], as shown in the following Figure 15.

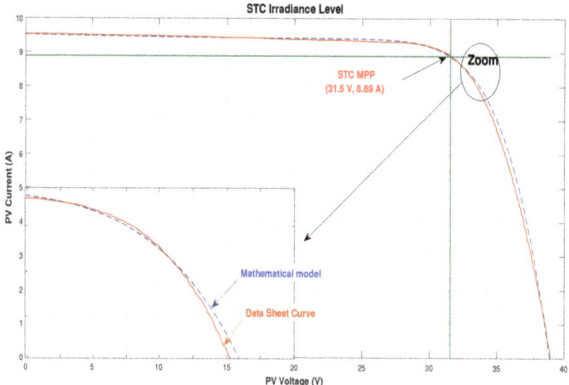

Figure 15. (KK280P-3CD3CG) I–V curves of mathematical model and datasheet for the STC case.

5.2. Simulation of I–V Characteristics Curves for Varying Irradiance Levels at Fixed STC Temperature

Three curves at different levels of irradiance are used to develop the model including the STC one at fixed STC temperature value. The model is simulated for the irradiance levels (G = 400, 800, and 1000 W/m^2) at fixed temperature value of STC case $T_0 = 25$ °C and both the mathematical model and the datasheet current values are presented in Figure 16.

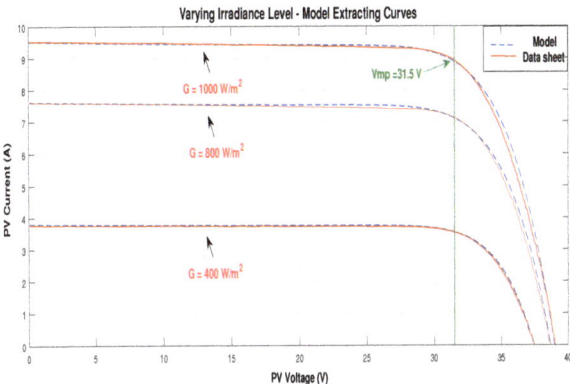

Figure 16. (KK280P-3CD3CG) I–V curves of mathematical model and datasheet for different irradiance levels.

As shown in the results, with the irradiance value decreasing, the current decreases as well. Additionally, the value of the open circuit voltage reduces with a reduction in the irradiance amount on the cell. The maximum power point voltage value is fixed for all irradiance levels.

5.3. Testing the Proposed Model with the Unused Irradiance Levels at Fixed STC Temperature

The model is tested using the rest of the irradiance levels (200, 600 W/m^2) at fixed temperature value of STC case $T_0 = 25$ °C, and both the mathematical model and the datasheet current values are presented in Figure 17.

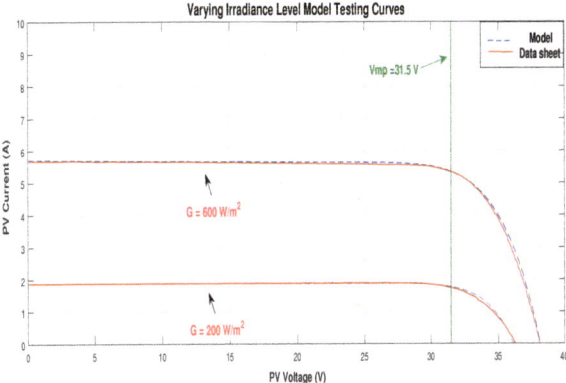

Figure 17. (KK280P-3CD3CG) I–V curves of mathematical model and datasheet for different irradiance levels.

As shown from the simulation, the model is performing reasonably compared to the actual extracted data.

5.4. Simulation of I–V Characteristics Curves for Varying Temperature Values at Fixed STC Irradiance Level

The model is simulated with varying the values of temperature from 25 °C to 75 °C at fixed irradiance level of STC case $G_0 = 1000$ W/m^2 and both the mathematical proposed model and the datasheet current values are shown in Figure 18.

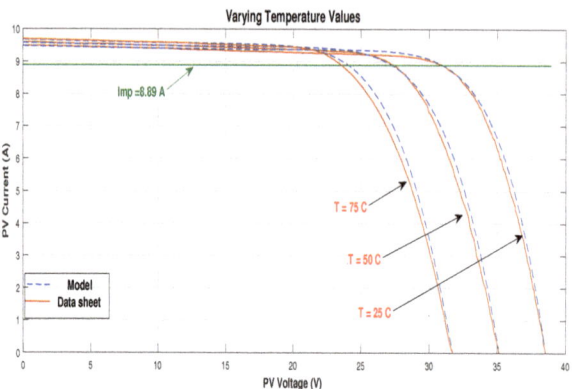

Figure 18. (KK280P-3CD3CG) I–V curves of mathematical model and datasheet for different temperature values.

The results of varying temperatures show that, with increasing temperature, the maximum power point voltage and the value of the open circuit voltage decreases. The maximum power point current value is fixed for different values of temperatures.

6. Model Validation

In this section, various datasheets with different ranges of output power ratings are used to validate the proposed empirical mathematical model. The electrical performance values of STCs of each PV-panel with its rating power are shown in Table 2. Figures 19–22 present the I–V curves of the used datasheet for validating the proposed empirical mathematical model for different irradiance and temperature levels.

Table 2. Electrical performance values of STCs for model validation datasheets.

Datasheet \ Elect. Item	P_{max}	$I_{SC}(G_0, T_0)$	$I_{MPP}(G_0, T_0)$	$V_{MPP}(G_0, T_0)$	$V_{OC}(G_0, T_0)$	Figure
KFSolar (KF245-280P-200) [64]	265 W	9.17 A	8.49 A	31.2 V	37.9 V	Figure 19
Amerisolar (AS-6P30) [65]	275 W	9.2 A	8.79 A	31.3 V	38.5 V	Figure 20
Canadian Solar HiKu (CSL325-350P) [66]	330 W	10.82 A	10.24 A	32.2 V	39.2 V	Figure 21
Trina (TSM-DE18M(II)) [67]	490 W	12.14 A	11.56 A	42.4 V	51.3 V	Figure 22

STC: G_0 = 1000 W/m^2 and T_0 = 25 °C.

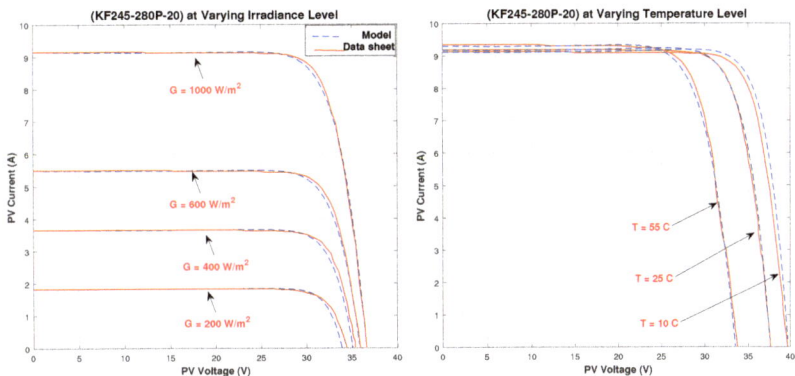

Figure 19. (KF245-280P-20) I–V curves of mathematical model and datasheet one for different irradiance and temperature levels.

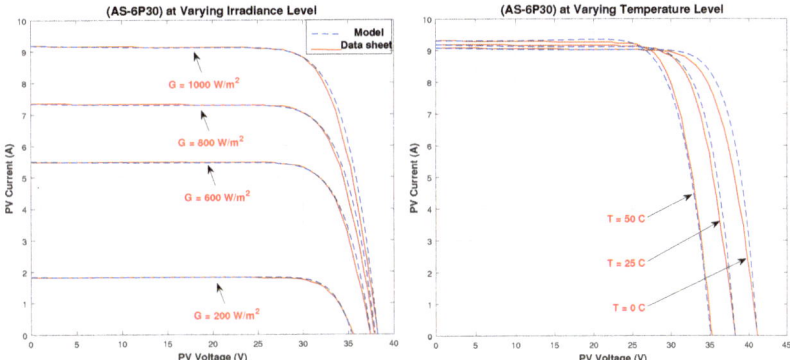

Figure 20. (AS-6P30) I–V curves of mathematical model and datasheet two for different irradiance and temperature levels.

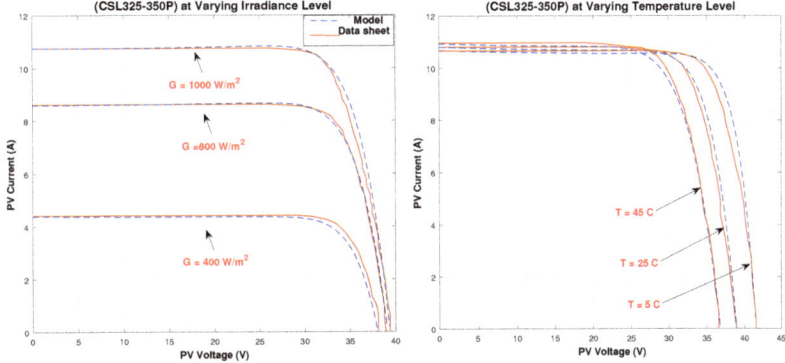

Figure 21. (CSL325-350P) I–V curves of mathematical model and datasheet four for different irradiance and temperature levels.

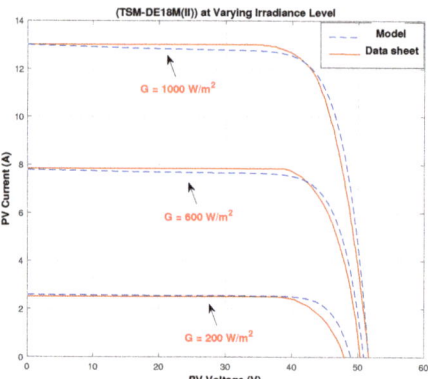

Figure 22. (TSM-DE18M(II)) I–V curves of mathematical model and datasheet three for different irradiance and temperature levels.

To add to the proposed model validation, the root mean square error (RMSE) between the PV I–V curves, modeled by the proposed approach, and their relative experimental datasheet curves are computed and presented in the tables below. The following Tables 3 and 4 present the root mean square error calculated for various irradiance levels and temperature values, respectively. It is noted that, for the tested PV models, the RMSE under different irradiance levels is less than 0.4 in most severe cases (at 1000 W/m^2) which verifies the proposed approach capability during different irradiances. During varying temperatures, the proposed approach shows high performance encountering RMSE less than 0.4 for temperatures ≥ 25 °C. However, at severe temperature cases (temperatures ≤ 10 °C), RMSE reaches high levels which show the proposed model limitations at very low temperatures.

Table 3. Root Mean Square Error Calculated for various irradiance levels.

Irradiance PV Model	200	400	600	800	1000
KYOCERA PV-model (KK280P-3CD3CG) [63]	0.0499	0.1212	0.1896	0.2321	0.3101
KFSolar (KF245-280P-200) [64]	0.0395	0.0789	0.1309		0.1914
Amerisolar (AS-6P30) [65]	0.0434		0.1372	0.2032	0.2105
Canadian Solar HiKu (CSL325-350P) [66]		0.1604		0.310	0.3241
Trina (TSM-DE18M(II)) [67]	0.0715		0.2140		0.3642

$T_0 = 25$ °C.

Table 4. Root Mean Square Error Calculated for various temperature values.

PV Model \ Temperature	0	5	10	25	45	50	55	75
KYOCERA PV-model (KK280P-3CD3CG) [63]				0.313		0.2751		0.0432
KFSolar (KF245-280P-200) [64]			0.727	0.1914			0.0820	
Amerisolar (AS-6P30) [65]	1			0.2105		0.1120		
Canadian Solar HiKu (CSL325-350P) [66]			1	0.3241	0.2266			

$G_0 = 1000 \text{ W/m}^2$.

7. Comparison of the Proposed Model with a Single Diode Equivalent-Circuit Based Model

In this section, a comparison between the proposed empirical mathematical PV model and conventional model is presented in order to verify the proposed model. The conventional model is an equivalent circuit-based iterative approach and it is derived for single diode equivalent circuit with the I–V equation given by Equation (4):

$$I = I_{PV} - I_0 \left[exp\left(\frac{V + R_s I}{V_t a} \right) - 1 \right] - \frac{V + R_s I}{R_P} \quad (4)$$

where, V_t which is equal to $\frac{N_s KT}{q}$, is the PV thermal voltage with N_s PV cells connected in series, q is the electron charge ($1.60217646 \times 10^{-19}$ C), K is the Boltzmann constant ($1.3806503 \times 10^{-23}$ J/°K), T (in °K) is the temperature of the $p - n$ junction.

Unlike the proposed approach, which only requires four electrical terms (V_{OC}, I_{SC}, V_{MPP}, and I_{MPP}) obtained from PV datasheet, the iterative model requires seven electrical terms (V_{OC}, I_{SC}, V_{MPP}, I_{MPP}, K_v, K_I, and N_s) as well as an iterative parameters extraction procedure. The latter puts a random estimation for the ideality factor (a), uses an analytical equation to compute I_o, and finally applies a numerical iterative method to compute R_s then R_p and I_{pv}. The curves fitting steps can be summarized as follows [7]:

- a is selected in the range $1 \leq a \leq 1.5$. In the considered case, a is chosen to be 1.25.
- I_0 is computed using Equation (5)

$$I_0 = \frac{I_{SC} + K_I \Delta T}{exp\left(\frac{V_{OC} + K_V \Delta T}{V_t a} \right) - 1} \quad (5)$$

$\Delta T = T - T_0$ (T and T_0 are the actual and STC temperatures, respectively, (in °K)).

- R_s and R_P are calculated using an iterative method shown in Figure 23.
    - R_s is slowly incremented starting from $R_s = 0$
    - $R_P = R_{P-min} = \frac{V_{MPP}}{I_{SC} - I_{MPP}} - \frac{V_{OC} - V_{MPP}}{I_{MPP}}$

- Several values of R_s and R_p are calculated till the P–V curve peak power P_{MPP} coincides with the experimental peak power P_{MPP-e} given by datasheet (=135 W in the considered case).
- The relation between R_s and R_p, can be found by making $P_{MPP} = P_{MPP-e}$ and solving the resulting equation to find R_P as shown in Equations (6) and (7)

$$P_{MPP} = V_{MPP}\left\{I_{pv} - I_0\left[\exp\left(\frac{q}{KT}\frac{V_{MPP}+R_sI_{MPP}}{N_sa}\right) - 1\right] - \frac{V_{MPP}+R_sI_{MPP}}{R_P}\right\} \quad (6)$$

$$R_P = \frac{V_{MPP}(V_{MPP} + R_sI_{MPP})}{\left\{V_{MPP}I_{pv} - V_{MPP}I_0\exp\left(\frac{q}{KT}\frac{V_{MPP}+R_sI_{MPP}}{N_sa}\right) + V_{MPP}I_0 - P_{MPP-e}\right\}} \quad (7)$$

In the considered case, the resistances are found to be $R_s = 0.18\,\Omega$ and $R_p = 63\,\Omega$ for a peak power tolerance of 0.1 W.

- Calculate the light-generated current at the considered conditions (I_{pv}) from the nominal light-generated current (I_{pv-n}) using Equation (8)

$$I_{pv} = (I_{pv-n} + K_I\Delta T)\frac{G}{G_0} \quad (8)$$

where, $I_{pv-n} = \frac{R_P+R_s}{R_P}I_{SC}$ and (W/m^2) is the irradiation on the device surface, and G_0 is the STC irradiation.

The iterative method flowchart applied for finding R_s and R_p is shown in Figure 23. Both models are validated using the ratings of *KD135SX-UPU* [68] module PV with datasheet parameters shown in Table 5.

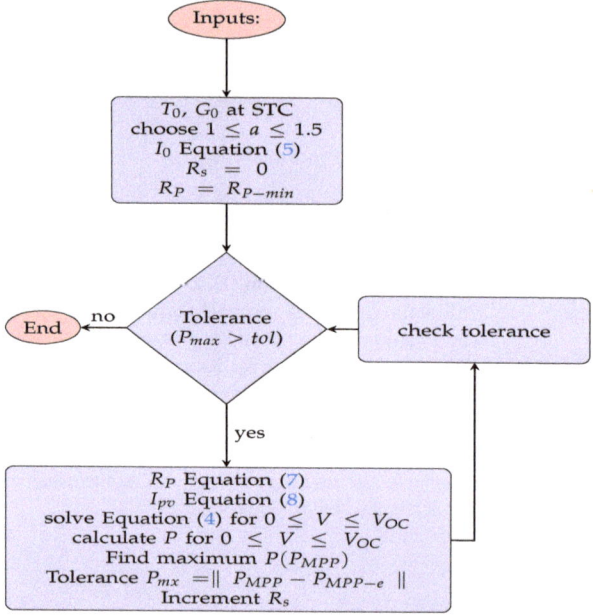

Figure 23. Flowchart of the iterative method applied for finding R_s and R_p [7].

Table 5. $KD135SX$-UPU module specifications at standard test conditions [68].

Item	Notation	Value
STC irradiance	G_0	1000 W/m^2
STC temperature	T_0	25 °C
Nominal Short Circuit Current	I_{SC}	8.37 A
Nominal Open Circuit Voltage	V_{OC}	22.1 V
Maximum Power Current	I_{MPP}	7.63 A
Maximum Power Voltage	V_{MPP}	17.7 V
Maximum Output Power	P_{MPP-e}	135 W
Temperature Coefficient of I_{SC}	K_I	5.02×10^{-3} A/°C
Temperature Coefficient of V_{OC}	K_V	-8×10^{-2} V/°C
Series Cells	N_s	36

The simulation comparison results of the two models are shown in Figure 24 that represents the performance for different irradiance levels and Figure 25 which represents the performance for different temperature values. Each figure include both I–V and P–V curves to illustrate the variance in the performance of the two models. From the simulation results of the conventional model and the proposed mathematical model it was found that the performance of the proposed one deliver better accuracy as its maximum power value is 135.056 W where the conventional model maximum power is 134.15 W for the same datasheet ratings at STC condition. This verifies the proposed model's effectiveness, yet with simpler implementation and less computational time and efforts when compared to the iterative model. The proposed model depends solely on a generic empirical equation that requires only four basic electrical terms found in any PV datasheet without the need for any parameter estimation.

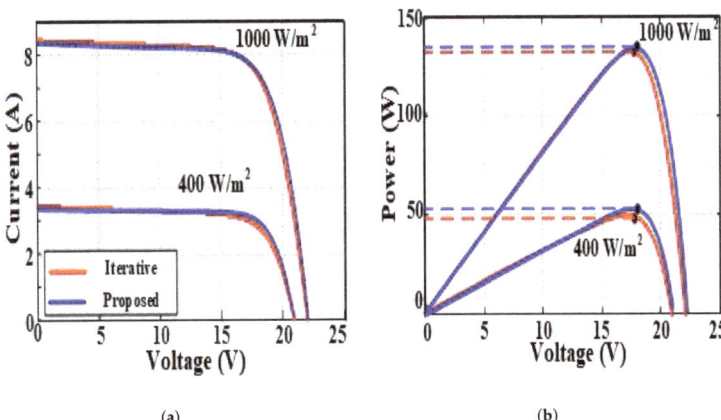

Figure 24. Proposed approach versus iterative method during varying irradiance conditions (a) I–V curves, (b) P–V curves.

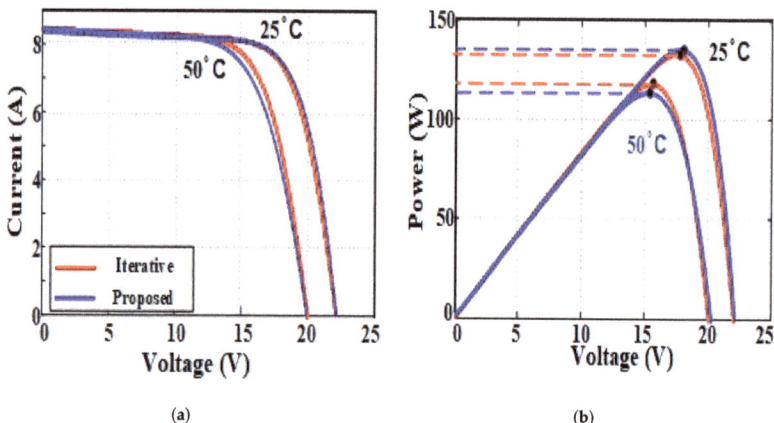

Figure 25. Proposed approach versus iterative method during varying temperature conditions (**a**) I–V curves, (**b**) P–V curves.

The proposed approach-based I–V curves versus the iterative approach-based ones, for $KD135SX$-UPU PV module, are compared to those of the P–V experimental datasheet curves. As shown in Figures 26 and 27, these comparisons are achieved at all the irradiance and temperature levels presented by the experimental datasheet curves which include low irradiance cases. Results show that both approaches gave close I–V curves to those experimental ones presented in datasheet. However, this is achieved with the proposed simpler, faster, less parameter-dependent, and iteration-free empirical method.

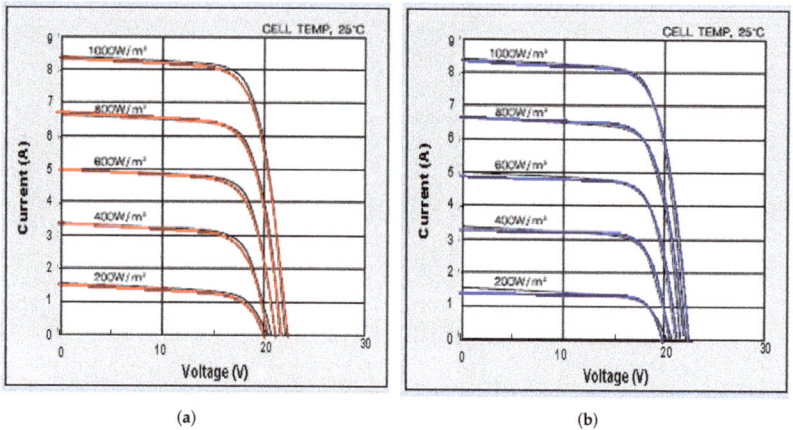

Figure 26. Experimental I–V curves of $KD135SX$-UPU, at T_0 25 °C under varying irradiance, versus those modeled by (**a**) iterative method, (**b**) proposed approach.

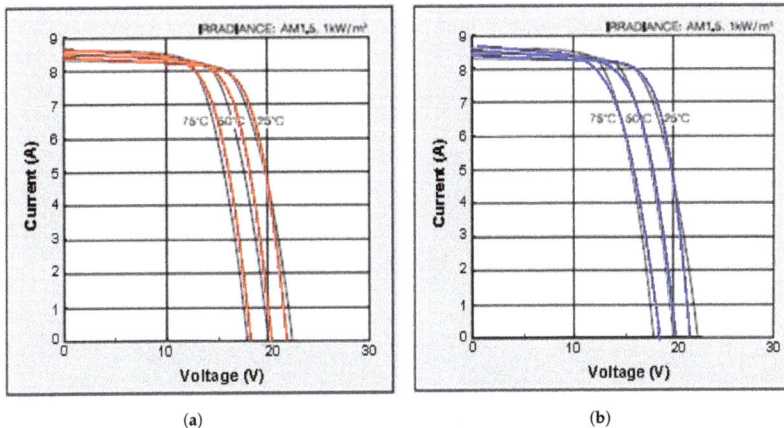

Figure 27. Experimental I–V curves of $KD135SX\text{-}UPU$, at G_0 1000 W/m² under varying temperature, versus those modeled by (**a**) iterative method, (**b**) proposed approach.

For further validation, the latter is retested with a different PV panel with different rating from another manufacturer, the $KC200GT$ PV-module, with specifications presented in Table 6. The experimental I–V curves applied are shown in Figures 28 and 29. Results confirm that both techniques experience relatively close I–V curves which fit onto the experimental curves of this module with the datasheet given below:

Table 6. $KC200GT$ module specifications at standard test conditions [69].

Item	Notation	Value
STC irradiance	G_0	1000 W/m²
STC temperature	T_0	25 °C
Nominal Short Circuit Current	I_{SC}	8.21 A
Nominal Open Circuit Voltage	V_{OC}	32.9 V
Maximum Power Current	I_{MPP}	7.61 A
Maximum Power Voltage	V_{MPP}	26.3 V
Maximum Output Power	P_{MPP-e}	200.143 W
Temperature Coefficient of I_{SC}	K_I	0.0032 A/°C
Temperature Coefficient of V_{OC}	K_V	−0.123 V/°C
Series Cells	N_s	54

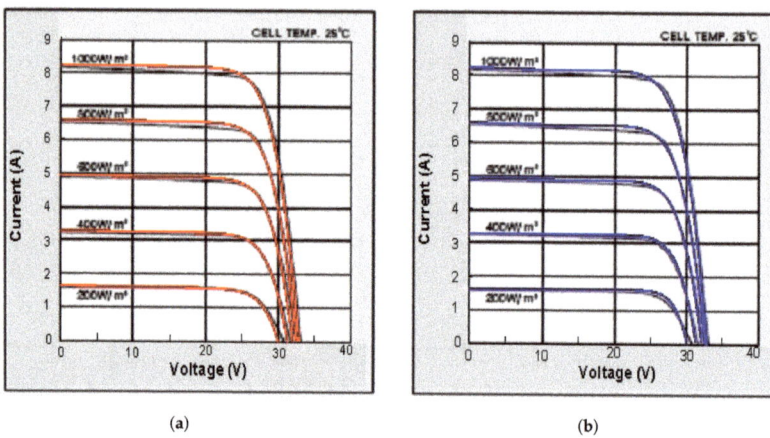

Figure 28. Experimental I–V curves of *KC200GT*, at T_0 25 °C under varying irradiance, versus those modeled by (**a**) iterative method, (**b**) proposed approach.

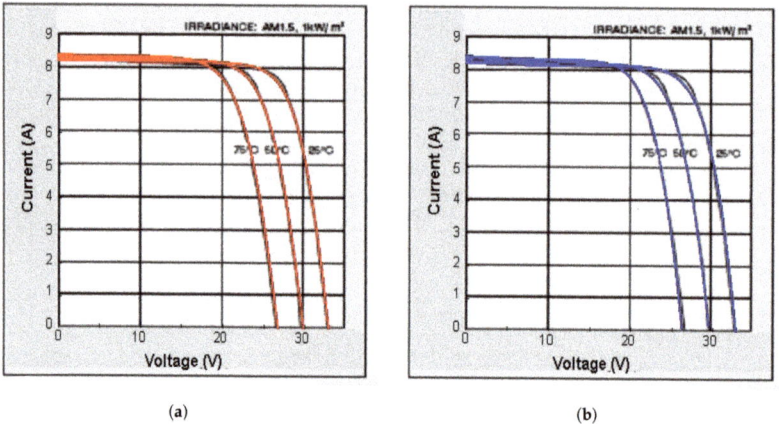

Figure 29. Experimental I–V curves of *KC200GT*, at G_0 1000 W/m^2 under varying temperature, versus those modeled by (**a**) iterative method, (**b**) proposed approach.

8. Privileges and Limitations Discussion

The proposed empirical method is based mainly on the mathematical representation of experimental I–V curves extracted from a PV module datasheet. The model formulates the STC case in mathematical function depending on only four electrical components of the PV-panel (V_{OC}, I_{SC}, V_{MPP}, I_{MPP}). By investigating the STC case I–V curve, it was found that the point of maximum power is a critical point that divides the curve into two parts. The one on the left, starting from the short circuit point and ending at the maximum power point, is a straight line with a negative slope. The equation of this line is formulated based on these two points of the start and end, so it is represented in terms of the electrical terms mentioned earlier. The other curve to the right of the maximum power point is behaving similarly to the inverted decaying exponential function. The two points used to formulate the power of this exponential function are the point of maximum power and the open circuit point. The PV-model proposed in the paper is based on combining these two functions together, that is, the basic equation which is used to generate the STC case curve, as shown in Figure 30. To represent the effect of changing in irradiance or temperature, the authors used other curves and investigated the impact of these changes on the curve relative to the STC case values.

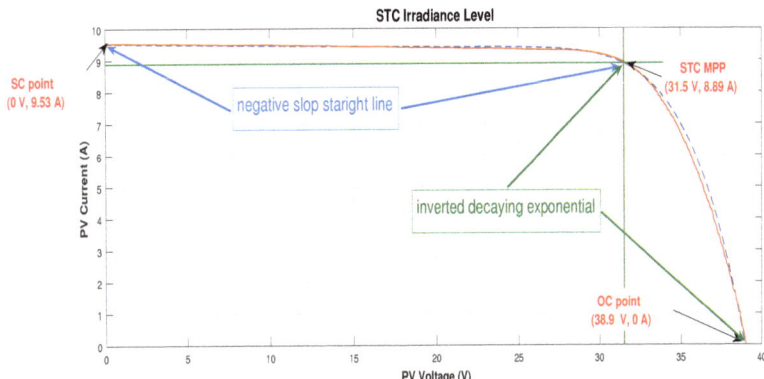

Figure 30. Proposed empirical mathematical model curve mathematical function representation for STC case.

It is worth nothing that this curve extraction is a one-time process, followed by the derivation of empirical equations that mathematically represent this curve for different irradiance and temperature conditions. These equations are valid for any other PV-model and can be applied for all PV ratings from different manufacturers i.e., any PV-module I–V characteristics and curves can be obtained by direct substitution of the new relative (V_{OC}, I_{SC}, V_{MPP}, and I_{MPP}) in the derived empirical equations. Unlike the proposed approach, the physical models depend more on electrical terms, and not all of them are available on datasheets. Thus, they require parameter extraction techniques which depend on iterative and estimation approaches, which in turn adds to system complexity and computational time.

The Table 7 summarizes the main differences between single-diode equivalent circuit-based iterative physical approach presented in Section 7 and the proposed empirical approach regarding approach realization, error cause, implementation complexity, and computational time.

The proposed model relies on data extracted from PV panel manufacturer datasheets available on the market. Commonly, those curves listed in various vendors are experimentally obtained to achieve proper standardized certification as IEC, IEEE, NEC, or UL. In addition, data extraction is only performed once, as stated and performed by the authors. Any further investigation of other PV panels from any other vendors do not require curve extraction, as explained. Only four parameters are needed to substitute in the authors' pre-elaborated proposed formula. Hence, fear form any further unavailability of experimental datasheets is not crucial.

The proposed technique in this paper is developed by using the captured images from the datasheet only once, and then, for generating any graphs at various rating power, the developed proposed model is used directly. There is no need to capture the images from the datasheet every time for reproduction, as this model features the graphs in terms of the electric parameters of the PV-panel (V_{OC}, I_{SC}, V_{MPP}, and I_{MPP}). The developing process of the model used some curves from the main datasheet, then the rest of the curves were used for testing the model. After that, many datasheets at different rating power were used to validate the model. The authors generated the curves using the proposed model and compared them to the datasheet curves so these curves were not used to develop a newer model. The proposed model is formulated for generating I–V curves for three cases: (i) various irradiance level at fixed STC temperature (Equation (1)), (ii) various temperature levels at fixed irradiance level (Equation (2)), and (iii) certain value or irradiance and temperature differ from the STC case (Equation (3)).

Table 7. Comparison between single-diode equivalent circuit-based iterative physical approach and the proposed empirical approach.

Point of Comparison		Iterative Approach	Proposed Model
Parameters required	Parameters	$V_{OC}, I_{SC}, V_{MPP}, I_{MPP},$ $K_v, K_I, N_s, a, I_o, R_s, R_p, I_{pv}$	$V_{OC}, I_{SC}, V_{MPP}, I_{MPP}$
	Number	12	4
	Availability in datasheet	7 are available: $V_{OC}, I_{SC}, V_{MPP}, I_{MPP}, K_v, K_I, N_s$ and 5 are unavailable: a, I_o, R_s, R_p, I_{pv}	All Available
Requires parameter extraction technique?		Yes (to extract a, I_o, R_s, R_p, I_{pv})	NO
Iteration Required		Yes (to calculate R_s, R_p, I_{pv})	NO
Error	Present	YES	YES
	Why?	Random estimation of ideality factor a P_{MPP} tolerance error in the iteration procedure	Captured figure resolution error Manual data selection error
Implementation	Complexity	More complicated	Simpler
	Why?	Every time a new PV is modeled, iterations should be performed to compute the corresponding R_s, R_p, I_{pv}	The proposed empirical model is valid for any PV model, just the new $V_{OC}, I_{SC}, V_{MPP}, I_{MPP}$ are substituted in the proposed equation. So, there is no need to capture any figure from datasheet.
Processing Time	Duration	Longer	Shorter
	Why?	Time required for iterations to compute R_s, R_p, I_{pv}	Direct substitution in the proposed empirical equation

As the developed model is based on digitizing the characteristic curves captured from the datasheet there are some sources of error that affect the data accuracy. The first source of error is the resolution of the captured image from the datasheet. To overcome this source of error, aiming to enhance the accuracy of the extracted data from the datasheet, the authors used image editing software to increase the DPI of the figures.

The second source of error is the manual selection of the graph points in order to extract its numerical value. To mitigate this source of error, the authors used many graph digitizing software packages and compared their output to select the software that delivers the most accurate data extraction. The manual process itself is, unfortunately, unavoidable.

9. Conclusions

In this paper, a novel generic empirical mathematical formula is proposed to model any PV device at varying conditions, based on function representation of captured PV experimental figures. This approach shows simpler implementation and less computational time and efforts when compared to existing PV models that require parameter estimation or power forecast. However, this apporach also offers competitive accuracy. PV curves resulting from the proposed formula show close resemblance to experimental curves of practical PV devices at different environmental conditions. The proposed formula's effectiveness is verified using commercial, market-available PV panels from different manufacturers at various power ratings to highlight the claimed robust performance and accurate PV device modeling features. The proposed PV model can be implemented on a graphical user interface GUI toolbox, presented as a user-friendly block for energy system designers and circuit simulator developers. This facilitates the simulation of PV devices their performance during dynamic shading and address the MPPT problem to assess.

Author Contributions: Conceptualization, A.A.; Data curation, O.H. and N.Z.; Formal analysis, O.H. and A.A.; Investigation, O.H. and A.A.; Methodology, N.Z. and A.A.; Software, O.H.; Supervision, A.A.; Validation, O.H. and N.Z.; Visualization, O.H.; Writing—original draft, O.H. and N.Z.; Writing—review & editing, A.A. All authors have read and agreed to the published version of the manuscript.

Funding: This research received no external funding.

Data Availability Statement: Not applicable.

Conflicts of Interest: The authors declare no conflict of interest.

References

1. *SunShot Vision Study- Photovoltaics: Technologies, Cost, and Performance*; U.S. Department of Energy: Washington, DC, USA, 2012.
2. Hosenuzzaman, M.; Rahim, N.; Selvaraj, J.; Hasanuzzaman, M.; Malek, A.; Nahar, A. Global prospects, progress, policies, and environmental impact of solar photovoltaic power generation. *Renew. Sustain. Energy Rev.* **2015**, *41*, 284–297. [CrossRef]
3. Eltamaly, A.M.; Farh, H.M.H. PV Characteristics, Performance and Modelling. In *Modern Maximum Power Point Tracking Techniques for Photovoltaic Energy Systems*; Eltamaly, A.M., Abdelaziz, A.Y., Eds.; Springer International Publishing: Cham, Switzerland, 2020; pp. 31–63.
4. Onat, N. Recent Developments in Maximum Power Point Tracking Technologies for Photovoltaic Systems. *Int. J. Photoenergy* **2010**, *2010*, 245316. [CrossRef]
5. Jakhrani, A.Q.; Othman, A.K.; Rigit, A.R.H.; Samo, S.R. Model for estimation of global solar radiation in Sarawak, Malaysia. *World Appl. Sci. J.* **2011**, *14*, 83–90.
6. Ramaprabha, R.; Mathur, B.L. Development of an improved model of SPV cell for partially shaded solar photovoltaic arrays. *Eur. J. Sci. Res.* **2010**, *47*, 122–134.
7. Villalva, M.; Gazoli, J.; Filho, E. Comprehensive approach to modeling and Simulation of Photo-voltaic Arrays. *IEEE Trans. Power Electron.* **2009**, *24*, 1198–1208. [CrossRef]
8. Xiao, W.; Dunford, W.; Capel, A. A novel modeling method for photovoltaic cells. In Proceedings of the 2004 IEEE 35th Annual Power Electronics Specialists Conference (IEEE Cat. No.04CH37551), Aachen, Germany, 20–25 June 2004; Volume 3, pp. 1950–1956.
9. *Guidelines for PV Power Measurement in Industry*; European Commission Joint Research Centre (JRC), Institute of Energy: Ispra, Italy, 2010.
10. Soto, W.D.; Klein, S.A.; Beckman, W.A. Improvement and validation of a model for photovoltaic array performance. *Sol. Energy* **2006**, *80*, 78–88. [CrossRef]
11. Carrero, C.; Amador, J.; Arnaltes, S. A single procedure for helping PV designers to select silicon PV modules and evaluate the loss resistances. *Renew. Energy* **2007**, *32*, 2579–2589. [CrossRef]
12. Veerachary, M. PSIM circuit-oriented simulator model for the nonlinear photovoltaic sources. *IEEE Trans. Aerosp. Electron. Syst.* **2006**, *42*, 735–740. [CrossRef]
13. Kim, W.; Choi, W. A novel parameter extraction method for the one diode solar cell model. *Sol. Energy* **2010**, *84*, 1008–1019. [CrossRef]
14. Xiao, W.; Edwin, F.F.; Spagnuolo, G.; Jatskevich, J. Efficient Approaches for Modeling and Simulating Photovoltaic Power Systems. *IEEE J. Photovoltaics* **2013**, *3*, 500–508. [CrossRef]
15. Breitenstein, O. An Alternative One-Diode Model for Illuminated Solar Cells. *IEEE J. Photovoltaics* **2014**, *4*, 899–905. [CrossRef]
16. Sandrolini, L.; Artioli, M.; Reggiani, U. Numerical method for the extraction of photovoltaic module double-diode model parameters through cluster analysis. *Appl. Energy* **2010**, *87*, 442–451. [CrossRef]
17. Ishaque, K.; Salam, Z.; Taheri, H. Simple, fast and accurate two-diode model for photovoltaic modules. *Sol. Energy Mater. Sol. Cells* **2011**, *95*, 586–594. [CrossRef]
18. Romero, B.; Pozo, G.; Arredondo, B. Exact analytical solution of a two diode circuit model for organic solar cells showing S-shape using Lambert Wfunctions. *Sol. Energy* **2012**, *86*, 3026–3029. [CrossRef]
19. Babu, B.C.; Gurjar, S. A Novel Simplified Two-Diode Model of Photovoltaic (PV) Module. *IEEE J. Photovoltaics* **2014**, *4*, 1156–1161. [CrossRef]
20. Nishioka, K.; Sakitani, N.; Uraoka, Y.; Fuyuki, T. Analysis of multicrystalline silicon solar cells by modified 3-diode equivalent circuit model taking leakage current through periphery into consideration. *Sol. Energy Mater. Sol. Cells* **2007**, *91*, 1222–1227. [CrossRef]

21. Soliman, M.A.; Hasanien, H.M.; Alkuhayli, A. Marine Predators Algorithm for Parameters Identification of Triple-Diode Photovoltaic Models. *IEEE Access* **2020**, *8*, 155832–155842. [CrossRef]
22. Manuel Godinho Rodrigues, E.; Godina, R.; Marzband, M.; Pouresmaeil, E. Simulation and Comparison of Mathematical Models of PV Cells with Growing Levels of Complexity. *Energies* **2018**, *11*, 2902. [CrossRef]
23. Bader, S.; Ma, X.; Oelmann, B. A Comparison of One- and Two-Diode Model Parameters at Indoor Illumination Levels. *IEEE Access* **2020**, *8*, 172057–172064. [CrossRef]
24. Cotfas, D.; Cotfas, P.; Kaplanis, S. Methods to determine the dc parameters of solar cells: A critical review. *Renew. Sustain. Energy Rev.* **2013**, *28*, 588–596. [CrossRef]
25. Chin, V.J.; Salam, Z.; Ishaque, K. Cell modelling and model parameters estimation techniques for photovoltaic simulator application: A review. *Appl. Energy* **2015**, *154*, 500–519. [CrossRef]
26. Jordehi, A.R. Parameter estimation of solar photovoltaic (PV) cells: A review. *Renew. Sustain. Energy Rev.* **2016**, *61*, 354–371. [CrossRef]
27. Hasan, M.; Parida, S. An overview of solar photovoltaic panel modeling based on analytical and experimental viewpoint. *Renew. Sustain. Energy Rev.* **2016**, *60*, 75–83. [CrossRef]
28. Ibrahim, H.; Anani, N. Evaluation of Analytical Methods for Parameter Extraction of PV modules. *Energy Procedia* **2017**, *134*, 69–78. [CrossRef]
29. Celik, A.N.; Acikgoz, N. Modelling and experimental verification of the operating current of mono-crystalline photovoltaic modules using four- and five-parameter models. *Appl. Energy* **2007**, *84*, 1–15. [CrossRef]
30. Altas, I.H.; Sharaf, A. A Photovoltaic Array Simulation Model for Matlab-Simulink GUI Environment. In Proceedings of the 2007 International Conference on Clean Electrical Power, Capri, Italy, 21–23 May 2007; pp. 341–345.
31. Ding, K.; Bian, X.; Liu, H.; Peng, T. A MATLAB-Simulink-Based PV Module Model and Its Application Under Conditions of Nonuniform Irradiance. *IEEE Trans. Energy Convers.* **2012**, *27*, 864–872. [CrossRef]
32. Aldwane, B. Modeling, simulation and parameters estimation for Photovoltaic module. In Proceedings of the 2014 First International Conference on Green Energy ICGE 2014, Sfax, Tunisia, 25–27 March 2014; pp. 101–106.
33. Tan, Y.T.; Kirschen, D.; Jenkins, N. A model of PV generation suitable for stability analysis. *IEEE Trans. Energy Convers.* **2004**, *19*, 748–755. [CrossRef]
34. Benavides, N.D.; Chapman, P.L. Modeling the effect of voltage ripple on the power output of photovoltaic modules. *IEEE Trans. Ind. Electron.* **2008**, *55*, 2638–2643. [CrossRef]
35. Saloux, E.; Teyssedou, A.; Sorin, M. Explicit model of photovoltaic panels to determine voltages and currents at the maximum power point. *Sol. Energy* **2011**, *85*, 713–722. [CrossRef]
36. Jain, A.; Kapoor, A. Exact analytical solutions of the parameters of real solar cells using Lambert W-function. *Sol. Energy Mater. Sol. Cells* **2004**, *81*, 269–277. [CrossRef]
37. Jain, A.; Kapoor, A. A new method to determine the diode ideality factor of real solar cell using Lambert W-function. *Sol. Energy Mater. Sol. Cells* **2005**, *85*, 391–396. [CrossRef]
38. Picault, D.; Raison, B.; Bacha, S.; de la Casa, J.; Aguilera, J. Forecasting photovoltaic array power production subject to mismatch losses. *Sol. Energy* **2010**, *84*, 1301–1309. [CrossRef]
39. Chen, Y.; Wang, X.; Li, D.; Hong, R.; Shen, H. Parameters extraction from commercial solar cells I–V characteristics and shunt analysis. *Appl. Energy* **2011**, *88*, 2239–2244. [CrossRef]
40. Batzelis, E.I.; Papathanassiou, S.A. A Method for the Analytical Extraction of the Single-Diode PV Model Parameters. *IEEE Trans. Sustain. Energy* **2016**, *7*, 504–512. [CrossRef]
41. Perovich, S.M.; Djukanovic, M.D.; Dlabac, T.; Nikolic, D.; Calasan, M.P. Concerning a novel mathematical approach to the solar cell junction ideality factor estimation. *Appl. Math. Model.* **2015**, *39*, 3248–3264. [CrossRef]
42. Salilih, E.M.; Birhane, Y.T. Modeling and Analysis of Photo-Voltaic Solar Panel under Constant Electric Load. *J. Renew. Energy* **2019**, *2019*, 9639480. [CrossRef]
43. Matagne, E.; Chenni, R.; El Bachtiri, R. A photovoltaic cell model based on nominal data only. In Proceedings of the 2007 International Conference on Power Engineering, Energy and Electrical Drives, Setubal, Portugal, 12–14 April 2007; pp. 562–565.
44. Can, H.; Ickilli, D. Parameter Estimation in Modeling of Photovoltaic Panels Based on Datasheet Values. *J. Sol. Energy Eng.* **2013**, *136*, 021002. [CrossRef]
45. Elshatter, T.; Elhagry, M.; Abou-Elzahab, E.; Elkousy, A. Fuzzy modeling of photovoltaic panel equivalent circuit. In Proceedings of the Conference Record of the Twenty-Eighth IEEE Photovoltaic Specialists Conference—2000 (Cat. No.00CH37036), Anchorage, AK, USA, 15–22 September 2000; pp. 1656–1659.
46. Balzani, M.; Reatti, A. Neural Network Based Model of a PV Array for the Optimum Performance of PV System. In Proceedings of the Research in Microelectronics and Electronics, 2005 PhD, Lausanne, Switzerland, 28 July 2005; Volume 2, pp. 123–126.
47. Mekki, H.; Mellit, A.; Salhi, H.; Khaled, B. Modeling and simulation of photovoltaic panel based on artificial neural networks and VHDL-language. In Proceedings of the 2007 14th IEEE International Conference on Electronics, Circuits and Systems, Marrakech, Morocco, 11–14 December 2007; pp. 58–61.
48. Zagrouba, M.; Sellami, A.; Bouaïcha, M.; Ksouri, M. Identification of PV solar cells and modules parameters using the genetic algorithms: Application to maximum power extraction. *Sol. Energy* **2010**, *84*, 860–866. [CrossRef]

49. Ishaque, K.; Salam, Z.; Taheri, H.; Shamsudin, M. A critical evaluation of EA computational methods for Photovoltaic cell parameter extraction based on two diode model. *Sol. Energy* **2011**, *85*, 1768–1779. [CrossRef]
50. AlHajri, M.; El-Naggar, K.; AlRashidi, M.; Al-Othman, A. Optimal extraction of solar cell parameters using pattern search. *Renew. Energy* **2012**, *44*, 238–245. [CrossRef]
51. Rajasekar, N.; Krishna Kumar, N.; Venugopalan, R. Bacterial Foraging Algorithm based solar PV parameter estimation. *Sol. Energy* **2013**, *97*, 255–265. [CrossRef]
52. Askarzadeh, A.; Rezazadeh, A. Parameter identification for solar cell models using harmony search-based algorithms. *Sol. Energy* **2012**, *86*, 3241–3249. [CrossRef]
53. Askarzadeh, A.; Rezazadeh, A. Extraction of maximum power point in solar cells using bird mating optimizer-based parameters identification approach. *Sol. Energy* **2013**, *90*, 123–133. [CrossRef]
54. Altas, I.H.; Jakhrani, A.Q.; Samo, S.R.; Kamboh, S.A.; Labadin, J.; Rigit, A.R.H. An Improved Mathematical Model for Computing Power Output of Solar Photovoltaic Modules. *Int. J. Photoenergy* **2014**, *2014*, 346704.
55. Fathabadi, H. Novel neural-analytical method for determining silicon/plastic solar cells and modules characteristics. *Energy Convers. Manag.* **2013**, *76*, 253–259. [CrossRef]
56. Gow, J.; Manning, C. Development of a photovoltaic array model for use in power-electronics simulation studies. *IEEE Proc. Electr. Power Appl.* **1999**, *146*, 193–200. [CrossRef]
57. Babescu, M.; Sorandaru, C.; Musuroi, S.; Svoboda, M.; Olarescu, N.V. An approach on mathematical modeling of photovoltaic solar panels. In Proceedings of the 2013 IEEE 8th International Symposium on Applied Computational Intelligence and Informatics (SACI), Timisoara, Romania, 23–25 May 2013; pp. 239–243.
58. Lee, W.; Kim, K.; Park, J.; Kim, J.; Kim, Y. Forecasting Solar Power Using Long-Short Term Memory and Convolutional Neural Networks. *IEEE Access* **2018**, *6*, 73068–73080. [CrossRef]
59. Wang, Y.; Liao, W.; Chang, Y. Gated Recurrent Unit Network-Based Short-Term Photovoltaic Forecasting. *Energies* **2018**, *11*, 2163. [CrossRef]
60. Kim, Y.; Seo, K.; Harrington, R.J.; Lee, Y.; Kim, H.; Kim, S. High Accuracy Modeling for Solar PV Power Generation Using Noble BD-LSTM-Based Neural Networks with EMA. *Appl. Sci.* **2020**, *10*, 7339. [CrossRef]
61. Hassan, O.E.; Abdelsalam, A.K. New Time Horizon Based Classification of PV Power Generation Forecasting Techniques. In Proceedings of the 2020 30th International Conference on Computer Theory and Applications (ICCTA), Alexandria, Egypt, 12–14 December 2020; pp. 88–95.
62. Tina, G.M.; Ventura, C.; Ferlito, S.; Vito, S.D. A State-of-Art-Review on Machine-Learning Based Methods for PV. *Appl. Sci* **2021**, *11*, 7550. [CrossRef]
63. KYOCERA PV-Model (KK280P-3CD3CG). Available online: https://asia.kyocera.com/products/uploads/Spec_Sheet_KK280P-3CD3CG_3.pdf (accessed on 29 June 2021).
64. KFSolar (KF245-280P-20). Available online: https://www.enfsolar.com/pv/panel-datasheet/crystalline/36949 (accessed on 29 June 2021).
65. Amerisolar (AS-6P30). Available online: https://www.weamerisolar.eu/wp-content/uploads/2017/03/AS-6P30-Module-Specification.pdf (accessed on 29 June 2021).
66. Canadian Solar HiKu (CSL325-350P). Available online: https://www.canadiansolar.com/wp-content/uploads/2019/12/Canadian_Solar-Datasheet-HiKu_CS3L-P_EN.pdf (accessed on 29 June 2021).
67. Trina (TSM-DE18M(II)). Available online: https://www.enfsolar.com/pv/panel-datasheet/crystalline/47504 (accessed on 29 June 2021).
68. KYOCERA PV-Model (KD135SX-UPU). Available online: https://www.manualslib.com/manual/387917/Kyocera-Kd135sx-Upu.html (accessed on 29 June 2021).
69. KYOCERA PV-Model (KC200GT). Available online: https://www.datasheets.com/en/part-details/kc200gt-kyocera-62747508#datasheet (accessed on 29 June 2021).

Article

On Representing Strain Gradient Elastic Solutions of Boundary Value Problems by Encompassing the Classical Elastic Solution

Antonios Charalambopoulos [1], Theodore Gortsas [2] and Demosthenes Polyzos [2,*]

1. School of Applied Mathematics and Physical Sciences, National Technical University of Athens, 15780 Athens, Greece; acharala@math.ntua.gr
2. Department of Mechanical Engineering and Aeronautics, University of Patras, 26504 Patras, Greece; gortsas@upatras.gr
* Correspondence: polyzos@mech.upatras.gr

Abstract: The present work aims to primarily provide a general representation of the solution of the simplified elastostatics version of Mindlin's Form II first-strain gradient elastic theory, which converges to the solution of the corresponding classical elastic boundary value problem as the intrinsic gradient parameters become zero. Through functional theory considerations, a solution representation of the one-intrinsic-parameter strain gradient elastostatic equation that comprises the classical elastic solution of the corresponding boundary value problem is rigorously provided for the first time. Next, that solution representation is employed to give an answer to contradictions arising by two well-known first-strain gradient elastic models proposed in the literature to describe the strain gradient elastostatic bending behavior of Bernoulli–Euler beams.

Keywords: strain gradient elastic theory; general solution representation; Bernoulli–Euler beam; material with microstructure

MSC: 35C05

1. Introduction

It is well known that a structure consisting of a linear, isotropic, classical elastic material, subjected to external time-invariant boundary conditions, behaves according to the Navier–Cauchy equilibrium equation [1–3], which in terms of displacements $\mathbf{u}^{classical}$ and without the presence of body forces reads:

$$\mu \nabla^2 \mathbf{u}^{classical} + (\lambda + \mu) \nabla \nabla \cdot \mathbf{u}^{classical} = 0, \tag{1}$$

where ∇ is the gradient operator, while λ and μ indicate the Lamé constants.

Despite the discrete nature of real materials, the continuum theory of classical elasticity—described by (1) for the elastostatics case—is deduced by considering that the dimensions of the material microstructure are much smaller than a material representative volume element (RVE), which in turn is much smaller than any dimension of the loaded structure. Additionally, the material properties and the generated elastic fields in the RVE are projected, by averaging, around a point $\mathbf{x}$ lying at the center of the RVE. That projection imposes the local nature of the classical theory of elasticity and requires that displacements, stresses, and strains vary constantly or linearly throughout the material RVE [4,5]. Obviously, the situation becomes problematic when the material inhomogeneity is comparable with the size of the structure and the averaging performed in the RVE requires the consideration of strain gradients in the potential energy density and the introduction of internal length scale parameters, which are able to capture size effect phenomena.

At the beginning of 20th century, the Cosserat brothers [6] proposed the idea of an enhanced elastic theory in which, except strains and stresses, the gradient of rotations and the dual in energy, couple stresses should be considered. Their idea reached maturity almost fifty years later with the general works of Toupin [7], Mindlin and Tiersten [8], Green and Rivlin [9] and Koiter [10]. Meanwhile Mindlin [11], while investigating the influence of couple stresses to stress concentrations mentions that "*Also, it would seem to be desirable to explore the consequences of taking into account the remaining components of the strain gradient and, perhaps, second and higher gradients of the strain*". Indeed, one year later, Mindlin [12] published his general dynamic theory for elastic materials with microstructure, where the microstructure is considered as an additional micro-continuum embedded at every point of the macro-continuum, thus justifying, the presence of higher order strain gradients in the expressions of potential energy density. Ignoring inertia terms, the couple stress theory of Toupin [7], Mindlin's elastic theory with microstructure [12] and later the virtual power theory of Germain [13] lead, for a material with microstructural effects, to the same equilibrium equation and boundary conditions. However, the elastostatic Form II version of Mindlin's theory has the very attractive characteristic of retaining the symmetry of the considered total stress tensor as in the classical elasticity case, and concludes in a simple equilibrium equation of the following form:

$$(\lambda + 2\mu)(1 - l_1^2 \nabla^2)\nabla \nabla \cdot \mathbf{u}^{gradient} - \mu(1 - l_2^2 \nabla^2)\nabla \times \nabla \times \mathbf{u}^{gradient} = 0, \quad (2)$$

where l_1^2, l_2^2 are internal length scale parameters that can facilitate microstructural effects for dilatational and shear deformations, respectively.

Considering uniform microstructural effects for all types of deformation, i.e., $l_1^2 = l_2^2 = g$, Equation (2) can be further simplified obtaining the form:

$$\left(1 - g^2 \nabla^2\right)\left[\mu \nabla^2 \mathbf{u}^{gradient} + (\lambda + \mu)\nabla \nabla \cdot \mathbf{u}^{gradient}\right] = 0 \quad (3)$$

Equation (3) and the corresponding boundary conditions of Mindlin's Form II theory consist of an attractive enhanced elastic theory with a microstructure, known as strain gradient elasticity (SGE) or dipolar gradient elasticity (DGE), since it employs only one internal length scale parameter in addition to the two classical Lamé constants, and the most important strains and stresses, appearing in its constitutive equations, are symmetric as in the classical elastic case. During the last thirty years, many authors exploited the simplicity of SGE to solve analytically and/or numerically elastostatic problems with microstructural effects in many fields of linear elastic continuum mechanics, such as fracture and dislocations mechanics [14–20] and structural and material response [21–30], while interesting remarks on SGE can be found in [5,31–34].

Mindlin [11] first proposed a solution representation of Equation (2) based on Papkovich–Neuber type vector and scalar potentials $\mathbf{B}$, B_0 [3,35], which, in the case of Equation (3), is simplified to [30]:

$$\begin{aligned} \mathbf{u}^{gradient} &= \mathbf{B} - \frac{\lambda+\mu}{2(\lambda+2\mu)}\left[\mathbf{r} \cdot \left(1 - g^2 \nabla^2\right)\mathbf{B} + B_0\right] \\ \left(1 - g^2 \nabla^2\right)\nabla^2 \mathbf{B} &= 0 \\ \left(1 - g^2 \nabla^2\right)\nabla^2 B_0 &= 0. \end{aligned} \quad (4)$$

Instead of (4), Charalambopoulos and Polyzos [26] utilized the following representation of the solution of (3):

$$\begin{aligned} \mathbf{u}^{gradient} &= \mathbf{u}^e + \mathbf{u}^g \\ \mu \nabla^2 \mathbf{u}^e + (\lambda + \mu)\nabla \nabla \cdot \mathbf{u}^e &= 0 \\ \left(1 - g^2 \nabla^2\right)\mathbf{u}^g &= 0. \end{aligned} \quad (5)$$

without providing any correlation of (5) with the solution representation (4). The proof of the decomposition (5) is provided in this paper through the proof of theorem 1 in Section 2 and via Papkovich–Neuber type potentials in Appendix A. It should be mentioned at this point that the Papkovich–Neuber type gradient elastic solution (4) agrees with the corresponding one provided by Solyaev et al. [36,37], while the solution decomposition (5) is in agreement with the decomposition proposed by Lazar [38] if one considers that for a classical elastic solution $\mathbf{u}^e$ satisfying Equation (1), the vector function $(1 - g^2 \nabla^2) \mathbf{u}^e$ remains a classical elastic solution. In [34], Gourgiotis et al. solve a sharp notch problem in microstructured solids utilizing a Knein–Williams technique, and mentioned that their asymptotic solution shows significant departure from those of classical elasticity. This statement is basically the motivation for the present work, which, among others, proposes a solution representation of (3) by comprising the solution of the corresponding classical elastic boundary value problem, which is absent in both representations (4) and (5).

The first attempt at incorporating the classical elastic solution in the solution of (3) is that of Ru and Aifantis [39]. More specifically, considering the elastic displacement field $\mathbf{u}^{classical}$ that satisfies (1) and the corresponding classical elastic boundary conditions in a domain Ω confined by a surface $\partial \Omega$, they proposed as strain gradient elastic solution of (3) the vector $\mathbf{u}^{gradient}$ that satisfies the non-homogeneous partial differential equation:

$$(1 - g^2 \nabla^2) \mathbf{u}^{gradient} = \mathbf{u}^{classical}, \tag{6}$$

and the extra boundary condition

$$\frac{\partial^2}{\partial n^2} \mathbf{u}^{gradient} = 0, \tag{7}$$

where $\partial / \partial n$ denotes differentiation with respect to the unit normal vector of $\partial \Omega$.

Comparing (3) with (6), the obvious advantage of this representation is the reduction in the order of the partial differential equation of the problem by two. However, as it is mentioned in Charalambopoulos and Polyzos [26], the representation (6) and (7) is questionable for the following reasons: (i) the solution of the partial differential equation of second order—as Equation (6)—satisfies a boundary condition of second order as the condition (7) is in contradiction with the mathematically accepted condition that the maximal degree of boundary conditions never exceeds the crucial number $n - 1$, where n stands for the degree of the differential equation. (ii) The boundary condition (7) is arbitrary and not the outcome of a variational process. (iii) The classical solution $\mathbf{u}^{classical}$ satisfies the equilibrium Equation (3), but not Equation (6).

Charalambopoulos et al. [30] utilized a representation of the solution that satisfies Equation (3) and the corresponding Form II boundary conditions and comprises the corresponding classical elastic solution, without, however, providing any systematic proof of that representation. This is, among others, the goal of the present work. The possible application of the presented here methodology to Equation (1) and to equations describing the behavior of linear pantographic sheets [40] or obeying to the generalized Hook's law for isotropic second gradient materials [41] will be the subject of future work. The structure of the present work is the following: The next section illustrates the Form II SGE theory of Mindlin with only one internal length scale parameter. Section 3 is entirely devoted to the mathematical establishment of a solution representation of (3), which encompasses the corresponding classical solution and its convergence behavior as the gradient parameter tends to zero. The same solution representation is exploited in Section 4 to show that the bending stiffness of a Form II SGE Bernoulli–Euler beam depends on the material rigidity EI and the internal length scale parameter g and not on EI, g plus the area of the cross-section of the beam.

2. Strain Gradient Elastostatics with One Internal Length Scale Parameter

The present section reports a boundary value problem in terms of the simplest possible strain gradient elastostatic theory with one intrinsic parameter. Mindlin [42] in the second version of his theory considered that the first gradient elastic potential energy density for an elastic body with microstructure is a quadratic form of the strains ε_{ij} and the gradient of strains κ_{ijk}. For isotropic materials, this theory provides a potential energy density containing the two Lamé material constants and five constants that normalize the terms of strain gradients, i.e.,

$$U = \tfrac{1}{2}\lambda \varepsilon_{ii}\varepsilon_{jj} + \mu\varepsilon_{ij}\varepsilon_{ij} + \hat{a}_1 \kappa_{iik}\kappa_{kjj} + \hat{a}_2 \kappa_{ijj}\kappa_{ikk} + \hat{a}_3 \kappa_{iik}\kappa_{jjk}$$
$$+ \hat{a}_4 \kappa_{ijk}\kappa_{ijk} + \hat{a}_5 \kappa_{ijk}\kappa_{kji}$$
$$\varepsilon_{ij} = \tfrac{1}{2}(\partial_i u_j + \partial_j u_i) = \varepsilon_{ji}$$
$$\kappa_{ijk} = \partial_i \varepsilon_{jk} = \tfrac{1}{2}(\partial_i \partial_j u_k + \partial_i \partial_k u_j) = \kappa_{ikj},$$
(8)

where ∂_i denotes spatial differentiation, u_i are the displacement components, λ, μ are the well-known Lamé constants having units N/m^2 and $\hat{a}_1 \div \hat{a}_5$ are five constants having units of force, all explicitly provided in [12].

For the case of $\hat{a}_1 = \hat{a}_3 = \hat{a}_5 = 0$ and $\hat{a}_2 = \lambda g^2$, $\hat{a}_4 = \mu g^2$, the potential energy density U obtains the form

$$U = \tfrac{1}{2}\lambda \varepsilon_{ii}\varepsilon_{jj} + \mu\varepsilon_{ij}\varepsilon_{ij} + \tfrac{1}{2}\lambda g^2 \kappa_{ijj}\kappa_{ikk}$$
$$+ \mu g^2 \kappa_{ijk}\kappa_{ijk},$$
(9)

where g is the only internal length scale parameter that correlates the microstructure with macrostructure, having units of length (m).

Strains and gradient of strains are dual in energy with the Cauchy-like stresses and double stresses, respectively, defined as:

$$\tau_{ij} = \frac{\partial W}{\partial \varepsilon_{ij}} = 2\mu\varepsilon_{ij} + \lambda\varepsilon_{kk}\delta_{ij},$$
(10)

and

$$\mu_{ijk} = \frac{\partial W}{\partial \kappa_{ijk}} = g^2 \partial_i \tau_{jk}$$
(11)

If the Young modulus E and Poisson ratio v are used instead of the Lame constants λ, μ, then the replacements $\lambda = \frac{Ev}{(1+v)(1-2v)}$, $\mu = \frac{E}{2(1+v)}$ should be made.

Considering a material with a microstructure of volume V and external boundary S, the variation of the total potential energy (9) provides, after some algebra [12,43,44], the following relation:

$$\int_V \delta U dV = -\int_V \left[\partial_j \left(\tau_{jk} - \partial_i \mu_{ijk}\right)\right] \delta u_k dV + \int_S R_k D \delta u_k dS$$
$$+ \int_{S_1 \cup S_2} p_k \delta u_k dS + \langle E_k \delta u_k \rangle,$$
(12)

where the vectors p_k, R_k represent the traction and double traction vectors, respectively, defined on the boundary S and written as

$$p_k = n_j\left(\tau_{jk} - \partial_i \mu_{ijk}\right) - D_j\left(n_i \mu_{ijk}\right) + (D_m n_m) n_i n_j \mu_{ijk},$$
(13)

and

$$R_k = n_i n_j \mu_{ijk},$$
(14)

where D_j and D represent the tangential and normal gradient operators on S, respectively, and have the form

$$D_j = (\delta_{jm} - n_j n_m)\partial_m$$
$$D = n_m \partial_m.$$
(15)

The vector E_k in Equation (12) concerns non-smooth boundaries with at least one corner c in two dimensions or at least one closed edge line ℓ in three dimensions, admitting the form:

$$\langle E_k \delta u_k \rangle = \begin{cases} \|n_i m_j \mu_{ijk}\|_{corner\,c} \delta u_k & for\,2D \\ \oint_\ell \|n_i m_j \mu_{ijk}\|_{edge\,\ell} \delta u_k d\ell & for\,3D \end{cases} \tag{16}$$

where $\|\bullet\|$ denotes the difference of $\bullet$ at both sides of the corner c or the edge ℓ, while m_j stands for the tangential vector in both sides of a corner or edge.

Equilibrating (12) with the variation of the work performed by external body force F_k, boundary tractions $\overline{p}_k$, double traction $\overline{R}_k$ and jump traction $\overline{E}_k$, we arrive at the following equilibrium equation:

$$\partial_j (\tau_{jk} - \partial_i \mu_{ijk}) + F_k = 0, \tag{17}$$

accompanied by the classical essential and natural boundary conditions where the displacement vector u_k and/or the traction vector p_k must be defined on the global boundary $S \equiv S_1 \cup S_2$, i.e.,

$$\begin{aligned} u_k(\mathbf{x}) &= \overline{u}_k(\mathbf{x}), & \mathbf{x} \in S_1 \\ p_k(\mathbf{x}) &= \overline{p}_k(\mathbf{x}), & \mathbf{x} \in S_2, \end{aligned} \tag{18}$$

and the non-classical essential and natural boundary conditions where the normal displacement vector $q_k = Du_k$, the double traction vector R_k or jump traction E_k are prescribed on $S \equiv S_3 \cup S_4$, i.e.,

$$\begin{aligned} q_k(\mathbf{x}) &= \overline{q}_k(\mathbf{x}), & \mathbf{x} \in S_3 \\ R_k(\mathbf{x}) &= \overline{R}_k(\mathbf{x}), & \mathbf{x} \in S_4 \\ E_k(\mathbf{x}) &= \overline{E}_k(\mathbf{x}), & \mathbf{x} \in \text{corner or edge}. \end{aligned} \tag{19}$$

In terms of the displacement vector $\mathbf{u}(\mathbf{x})$ and free of body forces, Equation (17) obtains the form

$$\left(1 - g^2 \nabla^2\right) \left[\mu \nabla^2 \mathbf{u}(\mathbf{x}) + (\lambda + \mu) \nabla \nabla \cdot \mathbf{u}(\mathbf{x})\right] = 0. \tag{20}$$

Theorem 1. *The solution of Equation (20) can be written as*

$$\mathbf{u} \equiv \mathbf{u}^{gradient} = \mathbf{u}^{classical} + \mathbf{u}^g, \tag{21}$$

with $\mathbf{u}^{classical} \in \ker(\mu \nabla^2 + (\lambda + \mu) \nabla \nabla \cdot)$ *and* $\mathbf{u}^g \in \ker(1 - g^2 \nabla^2)$.

Proof. We denote as Δ^* the classical elastic elliptic differential operator $\mu \Delta + (\lambda + \mu) \nabla (\nabla \cdot)$. Given that $(1 - g^2 \Delta) \Delta^* \mathbf{u}^{gradient} = \Delta^* (1 - g^2 \Delta) \mathbf{u}^{gradient} = 0$, we infer that

$$\Delta^* \mathbf{u}^{gradient} = \mathbf{w}^g \in \ker\left(1 - g^2 \Delta\right), \tag{22}$$

and

$$\left(1 - g^2 \Delta\right) \mathbf{u}^{gradient} = \mathbf{w}^e \in \ker(\Delta^*). \tag{23}$$

Consequently,

$$\left(1 - g^2 \Delta\right) \mathbf{u}^{gradient} = \mathbf{w}^e \Rightarrow \mu \Delta \mathbf{u}^{gradient} = \frac{\mu}{g^2} \mathbf{u}^{gradient} - \frac{\mu}{g^2} \mathbf{w}^e. \tag{24}$$

Equations (22) and (24) imply that

$$\begin{aligned} &\frac{\mu}{g^2} \mathbf{u}^{gradient} - \frac{\mu}{g^2} \mathbf{w}^e + (\lambda + \mu) \nabla \left(\nabla \cdot \mathbf{u}^{gradient}\right) = \mathbf{w}^g \Rightarrow \\ &\mathbf{u}^{gradient} = -\frac{\lambda + \mu}{\mu} g^2 \nabla \left(\nabla \cdot \mathbf{u}^{gradient}\right) + \mathbf{w}^e + \frac{g^2}{\mu} \mathbf{w}^g. \end{aligned} \tag{25}$$

We consider the Helmholtz decomposition of the field $\mathbf{w}^g$: $\mathbf{w}^g = \nabla H + \nabla \times \mathbf{K}$. Then, Equation (22) leads to

$$\nabla \cdot \left[\mu \Delta \mathbf{u}^{gradient} + (\lambda + \mu)\nabla\left(\nabla \cdot \mathbf{u}^{gradient}\right)\right] = \nabla \cdot (\nabla H + \nabla \times \mathbf{K}) \Rightarrow$$
$$\Delta\left[(\lambda + 2\mu)\nabla \cdot \mathbf{u}^{gradient} - H\right] = 0 \Rightarrow \quad (26)$$
$$(\lambda + 2\mu)\nabla \cdot \mathbf{u}^{gradient} = H + B_0,$$

where B_0, is a harmonic function. Then, Equations (25) and (26) give

$$\mathbf{u}^{gradient} = -\frac{\lambda + \mu}{\mu(\lambda + 2\mu)}g^2 \nabla(H + B_0) + \mathbf{w}^e + \frac{g^2}{\mu}\mathbf{w}^g. \quad (27)$$

Additionally, it holds that $\Delta H = \nabla \cdot \mathbf{w}^g \in \ker(1 - g^2\Delta)$ and therefore $\Delta\left[(1 - g^2\Delta)H\right] = 0 \Rightarrow (1 - g^2\Delta)H = B_1$, where B_1 is another harmonic function. One partial solution of this equation is clearly exactly the function B_1 and so the general solution is $H = u^g + B_1$, with $u^g \in \ker(1 - g^2\Delta)$. Then, (27) is rewritten as

$$\mathbf{u}^{gradient} = -\frac{\lambda + \mu}{\mu(\lambda + 2\mu)}g^2 \nabla(B_0 + B_1) + \mathbf{w}^e$$
$$+ \frac{g^2}{\mu}\mathbf{w}^g - \frac{\lambda + \mu}{\mu(\lambda + 2\mu)}g^2 \nabla u^g. \quad (28)$$

The first two terms of the decomposition (28) form the classical part $\mathbf{u}^e \in \ker\Delta^*$ while the remaining terms form the component $\mathbf{u}^g$ obeying to the homogeneous modified Helmholtz equation. □

3. On Representing Strain Gradient Elastic Solutions via the Solution of the Corresponding Classical Elastic Boundary Value Problem

All the representations of the solution of a strain gradient elastostatic problem appearing in the literature, do not include as a constituent the respective classical elastic solution, while the convergence behavior of these solutions when the gradient parameters fade away is not studied. As in [45,46], in the following, we present a general result considering all the above concerns.

Consider a bounded open region $\Omega \subset R^d$, $d = 2, 3$, with its boundary $\partial\Omega$ being a Lipschitz surface. Assuming that the body forces are absent, we consider the solution of the boundary value problem consisting of the fourth order partial differential Equation (20) and a set of classical and non-classical boundary conditions as those illustrated in Section 2. More precisely, we partition the surface $\partial\Omega$ twice, first in two subdomains $\partial\Omega_D$ and $\partial\Omega_N$ (with $meas(\partial\Omega_D) > 0$), where classical conditions are imposed, and secondly, in the subdomains $\partial\Omega_Q$ and $\partial\Omega_R$, whose common boundary Γ is of dimension $(d-2)$ and represents the corners c or the edges l of the surface $\partial\Omega$. Then, the general set of mixed-type classical conditions can be formulated as

$$\mathbf{u}(\mathbf{x}) = \mathbf{f}(\mathbf{x}), \mathbf{x} \in \partial\Omega_D \ (a)$$
$$\mathbf{P}(\mathbf{x}) = \mathbf{g}(\mathbf{x}), \mathbf{x} \in \partial\Omega_N \ (b), \quad (29)$$

along with the set of non-classical conditions

$$\frac{\partial \mathbf{u}(\mathbf{x})}{\partial n} = \mathbf{h}(\mathbf{x}; g), \ \mathbf{x} \in \partial\Omega_Q \ (a)$$
$$\mathbf{R}(\mathbf{x}) = \mathbf{r}(\mathbf{x}; g), \ \mathbf{x} \in \partial\Omega_R \ (b) \quad (30)$$
$$\mathbf{E}(\mathbf{x}) = \mathbf{s}(\mathbf{x}; g), \ \mathbf{x} \in \Gamma \ (c),$$

where $\mathbf{P} = P_i\hat{\mathbf{x}}_i$, $\mathbf{R} = R_i\hat{\mathbf{x}}_i$ and $\mathbf{E} = E_i\hat{\mathbf{x}}_i$.

The solution $\mathbf{u}(\mathbf{x})$ and the fields $\mathbf{P}(\mathbf{x})$, $\mathbf{R}(\mathbf{x})$, $\mathbf{E}(\mathbf{x})$ depend of course on the parameter g, but this is omitted for simplicity and will be notified only when it is necessary.

It is assumed that the given functions $\mathbf{f}$, $\mathbf{g}$, $\mathbf{h}$, $\mathbf{r}$ and $\mathbf{s}$ share all the required regularity for the well-posedness of the traces of the solution of Equation (20)—and its derivatives—on $\partial\Omega$. To clarify rigorously the last remark, we could additionally invoke the functional theoretic framework of variational problems settled in Sobolev spaces. This approach is described extensively in Wloka [47] for the general case of elliptic boundary value problems of a higher order and is very profitable since it provides results with crucial influence in the solvability of the problem under consideration with existence, uniqueness, and stability. It is out of the scope of the present work to give an extensive investigation via the aforementioned alternative framework, but it would be very helpful to give some brief concepts, facilitating the comprehension of the inner structure of the boundary value problems under investigation. Then, we recall the Sobolev spaces $H^s(\Omega)$ and $H^s(\partial\Omega)$, which are complete Hilbert spaces built by functions (or distributions) with specific integration behavior over Ω and $\partial\Omega$. Among the more recognizable Sobolev spaces, we encounter the space of square integrable measurable functions $H^0(\Omega) = L^2(\Omega)$ and its subspace $H^1(\Omega)$, whose elements possess distributional derivatives with the same square integrable behavior. Every Hilbert space $H^m(\Omega)$, with $m \in \mathbb{N}$, has a usual inner product and an induced norm consisting of the L^2 norms of the derivatives up to degree m. Therefore, the inclusion $H^{m_1}(\Omega) \subset H^{m_2}(\Omega)$ when $m_1 > m_2$ is an obvious relation. For real and positive order s, the norm is defined in a more complicated manner, but generalizes naturally what happens for an integer order. The linear spaces inclusion above still holds. When $s \geq 0$, the elements of the space $H^s(\Omega)$ belong to $L^2(\Omega)$, but this is not the case when $s < 0$ and constitute then pure distributions without functional representative.

Although not necessarily classical functions, the elements of $H^s(\Omega)$ have trace on the boundary $\partial\Omega$, which are generalized functions belonging to $H^{s-\frac{1}{2}}(\partial\Omega)$. The distributional surface normal derivative (of order k) of an element in $H^s(\Omega)$ belongs to $H^{s-k-\frac{1}{2}}(\partial\Omega)$ in the case that the smoothness of the surface allows the induced differentiability. The space $H^s_0(\Omega)$ is a subspace of $H^s(\Omega)$, with elements that, along with all their normal derivatives of order less than s, have zero traces on $\partial\Omega$.

Notice at this point that, for the case of the closed surface $\partial\Omega$, the space $H^{-s}(\partial\Omega)$ is the dual space of $H^s(\partial\Omega)$ and so surface terms of the form $\langle h, f \rangle|_{\partial\Omega}$ naturally arise, where $h \in H^{-s}(\partial\Omega)$ and $f \in H^s(\partial\Omega)$. This term expresses the action of h on f and it is very reminiscent of the virtual work of a force over a displacement. Only when $s = 0$, we have the reduction in the dual pairing $\langle h, f \rangle|_{\partial\Omega}$ to the usual inner product $\int_{\partial\Omega} h(\mathbf{x}) f(\mathbf{x}) dS_\mathbf{x}$.

After this brief discussion, we notice that in the framework of a boundary value problem whose differential equation is of order $2m = 4$, the boundary Equations (29) and (30) involve $m(=2)$ boundary operators (of possibly mixed type) (when $\Gamma = \varnothing$). These operators are characterized by their own orders, which obey to the rule: $0 \leq m_j \leq 2m - 1$. If, for example, we had exactly the boundary conditions (29) and (30) valid on the whole surface $\partial\Omega$ (with $\Gamma = \varnothing$), the involved boundary operators B_j, $j = 1, 2$ would be $B_1 = I$ (with order $m_1 = 0$) and $B_2 = \partial/\partial n$ (with order $m_2 = 1$). This example corresponds to the so called Dirichlet boundary value problem of fourth order. This settlement lies totally in the general framework of the abstract theory of elliptic boundary value problems: The main outcome is the existence and uniqueness of the solution of the problem (20), (29) and (30) with the following regularity general result [47]

$$\|\mathbf{u}\|_{H^s(\Omega)} \leq C_g \Big(\|\mathbf{f}\|_{H^{s-m_1-\frac{1}{2}}(\partial\Omega_D)} + \|\mathbf{g}\|_{H^{s-m_2-\frac{1}{2}}(\partial\Omega_N)} + \|\mathbf{h}\|_{H^{s-m_3-\frac{1}{2}}(\partial\Omega_Q)}$$
$$+ \|\mathbf{r}\|_{H^{s-m_4-\frac{1}{2}}(\partial\Omega_R)} + \|\mathbf{s}\|_{H^{(s-m_4-\frac{1}{2})-\frac{1}{2}}(\Gamma)} \Big),$$

and so, assigning to boundary operators their exact orders, we obtain

$$\|u\|_{H^s(\Omega)} \leq C_g \left(\|f\|_{H^{s-\frac{1}{2}}(\partial\Omega_D)} + \|g\|_{H^{s-\frac{7}{2}}(\partial\Omega_N)} + \|h\|_{H^{s-\frac{3}{2}}(\partial\Omega_Q)} \right.$$
$$\left. + \|r\|_{H^{s-\frac{5}{2}}(\partial\Omega_R)} + \|s\|_{H^{s-3}(\Gamma)} \right). \tag{31}$$

We would like to note the double consecutive dimension reduction $\Omega \to \partial\Omega \to \Gamma$, which takes place in the treatment of the fifth term of the r.h.s of the last equation. The regularity of the solutions depends on the regularity of the data in a specific manner. It is not explicitly apparent, but when the parameter s increases, the validity of Equation (31) passes through further assumptions for additional smoothness of the boundary $\partial\Omega$. The most encountered evocation of the representation (31) is with the selection $s = 2m = 4$ (the order of the differential equation). Therefore, for the solution u to have square integrable (in Ω) derivatives up to fourth order, all the data must belong to "smooth" Sobolev spaces of positive order. Then, the differential equation is satisfied in L^2-sense. However, this is accompanied with the hypothesis of a smooth $C^{1,1}$ boundary. To permit a boundary with corners or edges and to obtain the broader class of admissible solutions, it is preferable to work with $m = 2$. Then,

$$\|u\|_{H^2(\Omega)} \leq C_g \left(\|f\|_{H^{\frac{3}{2}}(\partial\Omega_D)} + \|g\|_{H^{-\frac{3}{2}}(\partial\Omega_N)} \right.$$
$$\left. + \|h\|_{H^{\frac{1}{2}}(\partial\Omega_Q)} + \|r\|_{H^{-\frac{1}{2}}(\partial\Omega_R)} + \|s\|_{H^{-1}(\Gamma)} \right). \tag{32}$$

In this case, the data f, h loose regularity, but still belong to the realm of square integrable functions. However, the data g, r, and s pertaining to stresses and jumps of double stresses over corners (edges) might become not square integrable distributions, ready to act—via the mentioned above dual pairings—on their reciprocal fields. In this point, we would like to say that our analysis has been facilitated from the fact that we are in absence of body forces. The differential equation is not any more valid classically, but in the distributional sense. It is noticeable that due to the special coercivity behavior of the bilinear form corresponding to the gradient elasticity operator, the generic constant C_g appearing in relation (32) cannot present worse behavior than the asymptotic convergence $O(g^{-2})$ for $g \to 0$. In addition, (32) implies a fortiori the boundedness

$$\|u\|_{H^1(\Omega)} \leq C \left(\|f\|_{H^{\frac{3}{2}}(\partial\Omega_D)} + \|g\|_{H^{-\frac{3}{2}}(\partial\Omega_N)} \right.$$
$$\left. + \|h\|_{H^{\frac{1}{2}}(\partial\Omega_Q)} + \|r\|_{H^{-\frac{1}{2}}(\partial\Omega_R)} + \|s\|_{H^{-1}(\Gamma)} \right). \tag{33}$$

It is noticeable here that the constant C is independent of g since suppressing downwards the energy bilinear form and keeping only norms of first derivatives involve exclusively the Lamé constants of classical elasticity.

After the brief introduction of the functional theoretic setting, we are in position to present the two main accomplishments of the current work. First, we are going to present the construction of a very useful decomposition of the unique solution of the problem under consideration. In the sequel, we will state the necessary assumptions on the data so that this representation obtains a stable (with respect to g) behavior, incorporating appropriately the classical solution.

Consider the auxiliary second order classical boundary value problem (titled Problem I), satisfied by the solution $u^{classical}(x)$:

$$\Delta^* u^{classical}(x) = 0, x \in \Omega$$
$$\Delta^* \equiv \mu \nabla^2 + (\lambda + \mu) \nabla \nabla, \tag{34}$$

$$\mathbf{u}^{classical}(\mathbf{x}) = \mathbf{f}(\mathbf{x}), \quad \mathbf{x} \in \partial\Omega_D, \tag{35}$$

$$\mathbf{t}^{classical}(\mathbf{x}) = \mathbf{g}(\mathbf{x}), \quad \mathbf{x} \in \partial\Omega_N, \tag{36}$$

where $\mathbf{t}^{classical} = \tau_{ij}\hat{\mathbf{x}}_i\hat{\mathbf{x}}_j \cdot \hat{\mathbf{n}}$, is the classical surface traction field.

The above defined problem involving Equations (34)–(36) used the classical data from the gradient problem and "ignores" the non-classical ones. We emphasize that in Problem I, the gradient boundary term $\mathbf{P}(\mathbf{x})$ offers its place to its classical counterpart $\mathbf{t}^{classical}(\mathbf{x})$. Applying the classical well-known framework of the preceding analysis concerning this time the traditional second order elliptic boundary value problems, we deduce easily that the unique classical solution satisfies the stability relation

$$\|\mathbf{u}^{classical}\|_{H^1(\Omega)} \leq C \left(\|\mathbf{f}\|_{H^{\frac{1}{2}}(\partial\Omega_D)} + \|\mathbf{g}\|_{H^{-\frac{1}{2}}(\partial\Omega_N)} \right).$$

It is worthwhile to mention here that the last equation defines exactly the needed regularity of the data $\mathbf{f}, \mathbf{g}$ for the stated stability to be guaranteed. However, the gradient problem has already assigned specific regularity assumptions on the data. Compromising the two groups of requirements, we deduce that $\mathbf{f} \in H^{\frac{3}{2}}(\partial\Omega_D) \subset H^{\frac{1}{2}}(\partial\Omega_D)$ as well as $\mathbf{g} \in H^{-\frac{1}{2}}(\partial\Omega_N) \subset H^{-\frac{3}{2}}(\partial\Omega_N)$.

We are in position to state the main representation theorem of this work. We set first, as induced by the discussion above, the broader possible space in which the data are permitted to belong:

$$(\mathbf{f},\mathbf{g},\mathbf{h},\mathbf{r},\mathbf{s}) \in B = H^{\frac{3}{2}}(\partial\Omega_D) \times H^{-\frac{1}{2}}(\partial\Omega_N) \times H^{\frac{1}{2}}(\partial\Omega_Q) \times H^{-\frac{1}{2}}(\partial\Omega_R) \times H^{-1}(\Gamma).$$

The following theorem holds:

Theorem 2. *Let the boundary value problem consist of Equations (20), (29) and (30) where the data $(\mathbf{f},\mathbf{g},\mathbf{h},\mathbf{r},\mathbf{s}) \in B$. This problem is a well-posed fourth order elliptic boundary value problem with a unique solution. This solution can be represented as follows*

$$\begin{aligned}\mathbf{u}(\mathbf{x};g) &= \mathbf{u}^{classical}(\mathbf{x}) + \mathbf{w}(\mathbf{x};g), \quad \mathbf{x} \in \Omega \\ \mathbf{w}(\mathbf{x};g) &= \mathbf{u}^N(\mathbf{x};g) + g^2\mathbf{u}^G(\mathbf{x};g),\end{aligned} \tag{37}$$

where $\mathbf{u}^{classical}$ satisfies Problem I, $\mathbf{u}^N$ satisfies the classical elastostatic equation and $\mathbf{u}^G$ obeys to the modified Helmholtz equation:

$$\mu\nabla^2\mathbf{u}^N(\mathbf{x};g) + (\lambda+\mu)\nabla\nabla\cdot\mathbf{u}^N(\mathbf{x};g) = 0, \quad \mathbf{x} \in \Omega, \tag{38}$$

$$(1 - g^2\nabla^2)\mathbf{u}^g(\mathbf{x};g) = 0, \quad \mathbf{x} \in \Omega. \tag{39}$$

Proof. As explained above, the problem (20), (29) and (30) disposes a unique solution $\mathbf{u}(\mathbf{x},g)$, which is stable with respect to the data as Equations (32) and (33) guarantee. We consider the decomposition

$$\mathbf{u}(\mathbf{x};g) = \mathbf{u}^{classical}(\mathbf{x}) + \mathbf{w}(\mathbf{x};g).$$

The function $\mathbf{w}(\mathbf{x};g)$ satisfies Equation (20) given that both $\mathbf{u}^{classical}(\mathbf{x})$ and the field $\mathbf{u}(\mathbf{x};g)$ obey to this equation too. Based on the Papkovich-type representation [26,30], the field $\mathbf{w}(\mathbf{x};g)$ can be written as

$$\begin{aligned}\mathbf{w}(\mathbf{x};g) = \mathbf{B} - \tfrac{\lambda+\mu}{2(\lambda+2\mu)}\{(1-g^2\nabla^2)\mathbf{B}+ \\ [(1-g^2\nabla^2)\nabla\mathbf{B}]\cdot\mathbf{r} + \nabla B_0\},\end{aligned} \tag{40}$$

where
$$\left(1 - g^2 \nabla^2\right) \nabla^2 \mathbf{B}(\mathbf{x}; g) = 0, \tag{41}$$

$$\left(1 - g^2 \nabla^2\right) \nabla^2 B_0(\mathbf{x}; g) = 0. \tag{42}$$

Working with Equation (41), we have that necessarily $(1 - g^2 \nabla^2) \mathbf{B}(\mathbf{x}; g)$ is a harmonic function $\mathbf{B}^L(\mathbf{x}; g)$. Then,

$$\mathbf{B}(\mathbf{x}; g) = (1 - g^2 \nabla^2) \mathbf{B}(\mathbf{x}; g) + g^2 \nabla^2 \mathbf{B}(\mathbf{x}; g) = \mathbf{B}^L(\mathbf{x}; g) + g^2 \mathbf{B}^G(\mathbf{x}; g),$$

where $\mathbf{B}^G(\mathbf{x}; g)$ satisfies the modified Helmholtz equation $(1 - g^2 \nabla^2) \mathbf{B}^G(\mathbf{x}; g) = 0$.

A similar treatment applies to Equation (42) and the result is that the fields of Equations (41) and (42) have the decomposed form

$$\begin{aligned} \mathbf{B}(\mathbf{x}; g) &= \mathbf{B}^L(\mathbf{x}; g) + g^2 \mathbf{B}^G(\mathbf{x}; g) \\ B_0(\mathbf{x}; g) &= B_0^L(\mathbf{x}; g) + g^2 B_0^G(\mathbf{x}; g), \end{aligned} \tag{43}$$

$$\begin{aligned} \nabla^2 \mathbf{B}^L(\mathbf{x}; g) &= 0, \quad \left(1 - g^2 \nabla^2\right) \mathbf{B}^G(\mathbf{x}; g) = 0 \\ \nabla^2 B_0^L(\mathbf{x}; g) &= 0, \quad \left(1 - g^2 \nabla^2\right) B_0^G(\mathbf{x}; g) = 0. \end{aligned} \tag{44}$$

Inserting these representations in Equation (40) leads to the decomposition

$$\mathbf{w}(\mathbf{x}; g) = \mathbf{u}^N(\mathbf{x}; g) + g^2 \mathbf{u}^G(\mathbf{x}; g), \tag{45}$$

where
$$\mathbf{u}^N = \frac{\lambda + 3\mu}{2(\lambda + 2\mu)} \mathbf{B}^L - \frac{\lambda + \mu}{2(\lambda + 2\mu)} \nabla \mathbf{B}^L \cdot \mathbf{r} - \frac{\lambda + \mu}{2(\lambda + 2\mu)} \nabla B_0^L, \tag{46}$$

and
$$\mathbf{u}^G = \mathbf{B}^G - \frac{\lambda + \mu}{2(\lambda + 2\mu)} \nabla B_0^G. \tag{47}$$

It is evident that $\mathbf{u}^G \in \ker(1 - g^2 \nabla^2)$. In addition, it comes out easily that $\mathbf{u}^N$ belongs to the kernel of the operator ∇^2. Consequently, we deduce that

$$\begin{aligned} 0 &= (1 - g^2 \nabla^2) [\mu \nabla^2 \mathbf{w} + (\lambda + \mu) \nabla \nabla \cdot \mathbf{w}] \\ &= \mu \nabla^2 \mathbf{u}^N + (\lambda + \mu) \nabla \nabla \cdot \mathbf{u}^N + (1 - g^2 \nabla^2) [\mu \nabla^2 \mathbf{u}^G + (\lambda + \mu) \nabla \nabla \cdot \mathbf{u}^G] \\ &= \mu \nabla^2 \mathbf{u}^N + (\lambda + \mu) \nabla \nabla \cdot \mathbf{u}^N, \end{aligned}$$

from where we infer that $\mathbf{u}^N \in \ker[\mu \nabla^2 + (\lambda + \mu) \nabla \nabla \cdot]$. □

As a conclusion, the decomposition (37) with the differential properties (38) and (39) was derived from the point of view of the underlying differential equations and always can be applied to the unique solution of the fourth order boundary value problem under discussion. The implication of boundary conditions is of course the next step. The representation (37) has the advantage that it disposes additional degrees of freedom since the involved "free" functions satisfy the second order differential equations in which the gradient elasticity law decomposes. In addition, the representation (37) involves the classical solution of the problem in the absence of the microstructure $g = 0$ as a cornerstone constituent. It is very interesting to examine whether taking the limit of the expression (37) as $g \to 0$ leads to the classical solution. What matters of course is primary the construction of the solution of the boundary value problem independently of its convergence behavior. Nevertheless, it is essential to construct sufficient conditions on the data assuring this desirable convergence property.

The next theorem verifies that under specific assumptions on the data, convergence is established. The first requirement is in accordance with the underlying constitutive equations concerning double stresses. Indeed, it is natural that the magnitude of the double stresses and the relevant jump fields imposed on the structure obey to specific order analysis with respect to the microstructure parameter. More precisely, the boundary tensors $\mathbf{R}(\mathbf{x})$ and $\mathbf{E}(\mathbf{x})$ are selected as follows:

$$\mathbf{r}(\mathbf{x};s) = g^2 \widetilde{\mathbf{r}}(\mathbf{x}), \ \mathbf{x} \in \partial \Omega_R, \tag{48}$$

$$\mathbf{s}(\mathbf{x};g) = g^2 \widetilde{\mathbf{s}}(\mathbf{x}), \ \mathbf{x} \in \Gamma, \tag{49}$$

and as stated, this choice has a physical origin. The additional requirements are related to the necessary regularity of the rest of the data. It is necessary, in the convergence setting for the boundary data $\mathbf{g}$, to be a genuine square integrable function, in fact an element of $H^{\frac{1}{2}}(\partial \Omega_N)$ and that $\|\mathbf{h}(\cdot,g)\|_{H^{\frac{1}{2}}(\partial \Omega_Q)}$ remains bounded as g varies. In practice, the term $\mathbf{h}(\mathbf{x},g)$ is usually independent of g.

As far as the stated above restriction of $\mathbf{g}$ is concerned, the concept stems from the treatment of the classical solution. As we will see, under this assumption, the function $\frac{\partial}{\partial n} \mathbf{u}^{classical}(\mathbf{x})$ becomes a square integrable function with a crucial role in the convergence analysis.

The following theorem holds.

Theorem 3. *Let the boundary value problem consist of Equations (20), (29) and (30). The data $(\mathbf{f}, \mathbf{g}, \mathbf{h}, \mathbf{r}, \mathbf{s})$ are elements of B with the restriction that $\mathbf{r}$, $\mathbf{s}$ obey to Equations (48) and (49), $\mathbf{g} \in H^{\frac{1}{2}}(\partial \Omega_N) \subset H^{-\frac{1}{2}}(\partial \Omega_N)$ and $\|\mathbf{h}(\cdot,g)\|_{H^{\frac{1}{2}}(\partial \Omega_Q)}$ is a bounded function of g. Two mutually exclusive alternatives arise:*

(A) $\mathbf{h}(\mathbf{x};g) = \mathbf{h}(\mathbf{x}) = \frac{\partial}{\partial n} \mathbf{u}^{classical}(\mathbf{x}), \ \mathbf{x} \in \partial \Omega_Q$ *a.e.*

(B) $\mathbf{h}(\mathbf{x};g) - \frac{\partial}{\partial n} \mathbf{u}^{classical}(\mathbf{x}) \neq 0, \ \mathbf{x} \in \partial \Omega_Q$

In case (B), we impose further regularity on the data by demanding $\mathbf{f} \in H^{\frac{5}{2}}(\partial \Omega_D)$ and $\mathbf{g} \in H^{\frac{3}{2}}(\partial \Omega_N)$.

Let $\mathbf{u}(\mathbf{x};g)$ be the unique solution of the gradient elasticity boundary value problem constructed in Theorem 2. Then, the following asymptotic analysis holds:

$$\mathbf{u}^G = \mathbf{B}^G - \frac{\lambda + \mu}{2(\lambda + 2\mu)} \nabla B_0^G, \tag{50}$$

rendering Problem I, the asymptotic classical limit of the gradient problem, when the impact of the microstructure fades away.

Proof. The classical elastic displacement field satisfies the following stability condition:

$$\|\mathbf{u}^{classical}\|_{H^1(\Omega)} \leq C \left(\|\mathbf{f}\|_{H^{\frac{1}{2}}(\partial \Omega_D)} + \|\mathbf{g}\|_{H^{-\frac{1}{2}}(\partial \Omega_N)} \right), \tag{51}$$

as stated before. However, due to the additional regularity $\mathbf{f} \in H^{\frac{3}{2}}(\partial \Omega_D) \subset H^{\frac{1}{2}}(\partial \Omega_D)$ (valid throughout the work) and the extra requirement $\mathbf{g} \in H^{\frac{1}{2}}(\partial \Omega_N) \subset H^{-\frac{1}{2}}(\partial \Omega_N)$ introduced in the assumptions of the current theorem, we are in position to invoke the well-known regularity theory for second order elliptic boundary value problems guaranteeing that

$$\|\mathbf{u}^{classical}\|_{H^2} \leq C \left(\|\mathbf{f}\|_{H^{\frac{3}{2}}(\partial \Omega_D)} + \|\mathbf{g}\|_{H^{\frac{1}{2}}(\partial \Omega_N)} \right). \tag{52}$$

Consequently, the classical solution has square integrable derivatives of the second order and the theory of traces on the boundary implies that all the terms $\partial_i \partial_j \mathbf{u}^{classical} \big|_{\partial \Omega}$ belong to $H^{-\frac{1}{2}}(\partial \Omega)$ as well as $\partial_i \partial_j \partial_k \mathbf{u}^{classical} \big|_{\partial \Omega} \in H^{-\frac{3}{2}}(\partial \Omega)$.

On the basis of Equation (7) and via tensor symbolism—just for condensing the form of the expressions—the following Betti's form type result, referring to the elastic field $\mathbf{w}$, can be constructed:

$$0 = \int_\Omega (\nabla \cdot (\tilde{\boldsymbol{\tau}}_w - \nabla \cdot \tilde{\boldsymbol{\mu}}_w)) \cdot \mathbf{w}\, dx = \langle \mathbf{R}_w, D\mathbf{w} \rangle|_{\partial\Omega} + \langle \mathbf{P}_w, \mathbf{w} \rangle|_{\partial\Omega}$$
$$+ \langle \mathbf{E}_w, \mathbf{w} \rangle|_\Gamma - \int_\Omega \left(\tilde{\boldsymbol{\tau}}_w : \tilde{\boldsymbol{\varepsilon}}_w + \tilde{\boldsymbol{\mu}}_w \vdots \tilde{\boldsymbol{\varepsilon}}_w \nabla \right) dx. \tag{53}$$

Here, we encounter the dual pairings $\langle \mathbf{R}_w, D\mathbf{w} \rangle|_{\partial\Omega} = \langle \mathbf{R}_w, D\mathbf{w} \rangle|_{H^{-\frac{1}{2}}(\partial\Omega) \times H^{\frac{1}{2}}(\partial\Omega)}$, $\langle \mathbf{P}_w, \mathbf{w} \rangle|_{\partial\Omega} = \langle \mathbf{P}_w, \mathbf{w} \rangle|_{H^{-\frac{3}{2}}(\partial\Omega) \times H^{\frac{3}{2}}(\partial\Omega)}$ and $\langle \mathbf{E}_w, \mathbf{w} \rangle|_\Gamma = \langle \mathbf{E}_w, \mathbf{w} \rangle|_{H^{-1}(\Gamma) \times H^1(\Gamma)}$ between dual spaces that represent surface and curve virtual actions. Only when all the involving fields are regular enough (square integrable functions) these terms give place to the well-known surface L^2 inner products.

On the basis of decomposition (45), the boundary conditions satisfied by the two partners of this decomposition and the splitting imposed by Equation (19), we remark that

$$\mathbf{w}(\mathbf{x}; g) = 0, \ \mathbf{x} \in \partial\Omega_D, \tag{54}$$

$$\mathbf{P}_w(\mathbf{x}; g) = \mathbf{g}(\mathbf{x}) - \mathbf{P}_{\mathbf{u}^{classical}}(\mathbf{x}, g) =$$
$$-((\mathbf{D} \cdot \hat{\mathbf{n}}(\mathbf{x}))\hat{\mathbf{n}}(\mathbf{x})\hat{\mathbf{n}}(\mathbf{x}) - \mathbf{D}\hat{\mathbf{n}}(\mathbf{x})) : \tilde{\boldsymbol{\mu}}_{\mathbf{u}^{classical}}(\mathbf{x}; g)$$
$$+\hat{\mathbf{n}}(\mathbf{x})\hat{\mathbf{n}}(\mathbf{x}) : D\tilde{\boldsymbol{\mu}}_{\mathbf{u}^{classical}}(\mathbf{x}; g) +$$
$$\hat{\mathbf{n}}(\mathbf{x}) \cdot (\mathbf{D} \cdot \tilde{\boldsymbol{\mu}}_{\mathbf{u}^{classical}}(\mathbf{x}; g)) + \hat{\mathbf{n}}(\mathbf{x}) \left(\mathbf{D} \cdot \tilde{\boldsymbol{\mu}}^{213}_{\mathbf{u}^{classical}}(\mathbf{x}; g) \right), \ \mathbf{x} \in \partial\Omega_N \Rightarrow$$
$$\mathbf{P}_w(\mathbf{x}; g) = g^2 (\mathbf{D}\hat{\mathbf{n}}(\mathbf{x}) - (\mathbf{D} \cdot \hat{\mathbf{n}}(\mathbf{x}))\hat{\mathbf{n}}(\mathbf{x})\hat{\mathbf{n}}(\mathbf{x})) : \nabla \tilde{\boldsymbol{\tau}}_{\mathbf{u}^{classical}} \tag{55}$$
$$+ g^2 \hat{\mathbf{n}}(\mathbf{x})\hat{\mathbf{n}}(\mathbf{x}) : D\nabla \tilde{\boldsymbol{\tau}}_{\mathbf{u}^{classical}}$$
$$+ g^2 \hat{\mathbf{n}}(\mathbf{x}) \cdot (\mathbf{D} \cdot \nabla \tilde{\boldsymbol{\tau}}_{\mathbf{u}^{classical}}) + g^2 \hat{\mathbf{n}}(\mathbf{x}) \cdot \left(\mathbf{D} \cdot \nabla \tilde{\boldsymbol{\tau}}^{213}_{\mathbf{u}^{classical}} \right),$$

where $\mathbf{D} = \hat{\mathbf{x}}_i D_i$ (see Equation (13)).

Handling the non-classical boundary conditions of $\mathbf{w}(\mathbf{x}; g)$ leads to

$$D\mathbf{w}(\mathbf{x}; g) = \frac{\partial}{\partial n}\mathbf{u}(\mathbf{x}; g) - \frac{\partial}{\partial n}\mathbf{u}^{classical}(\mathbf{x}) =$$
$$\mathbf{h}(\mathbf{x}; g) - \frac{\partial}{\partial n}\mathbf{u}^{classical}(\mathbf{x}), \ \mathbf{x} \in \partial\Omega_Q,$$

and

$$\mathbf{R}_w(\mathbf{x}; g) = g^2 \tilde{\mathbf{r}}(\mathbf{x}) - \mathbf{R}_{\mathbf{u}^{classical}}(\mathbf{x}; g) =$$
$$g^2 (\tilde{\mathbf{r}}(\mathbf{x}) - \hat{\mathbf{n}}(\mathbf{x})\hat{\mathbf{n}}(\mathbf{x}) : \nabla \tilde{\boldsymbol{\tau}}_{\mathbf{u}^{classical}}), \ \mathbf{x} \in \partial\Omega_R.$$

Then, Equation (53) obtains the form:

$$\int_\Omega \left(\tilde{\boldsymbol{\tau}}_w : \tilde{\boldsymbol{\varepsilon}}_w + \tilde{\boldsymbol{\mu}}_w \vdots \tilde{\boldsymbol{\varepsilon}}_w \nabla \right) dx = g^2 \langle \mathbf{k}(\cdot), \mathbf{w}(\cdot; g) \rangle|_{\partial\Omega_N} +$$
$$+ \left\langle \mathbf{R}_w(\mathbf{x}; g), \mathbf{h}(\mathbf{x}; g) - \frac{\partial}{\partial n}\mathbf{u}^{classical}(\mathbf{x}) \right\rangle\Big|_{\partial\Omega_Q} +$$
$$g^2 \langle (\tilde{\mathbf{r}} - \hat{\mathbf{n}}(\mathbf{x})\hat{\mathbf{n}}(\mathbf{x}) : \nabla \tilde{\boldsymbol{\tau}}_{\mathbf{u}^{classical}}), D\mathbf{w} \rangle|_{\partial\Omega_R} + g^2 \langle \tilde{\mathbf{s}}(\mathbf{x}), \mathbf{w} \rangle|_\Gamma -$$
$$g^2 \langle \mathbf{s}_{\mathbf{u}^{classical}}(\mathbf{x}), \mathbf{w} \rangle|_\Gamma, \tag{56}$$

where

$$\mathbf{k}(\mathbf{x}) = \{ (\mathbf{D}\hat{\mathbf{n}}(\mathbf{x}) - (\mathbf{D} \cdot \hat{\mathbf{n}}(\mathbf{x}))\hat{\mathbf{n}}(\mathbf{x})\hat{\mathbf{n}}(\mathbf{x})) : \nabla \tilde{\boldsymbol{\tau}}_{\mathbf{u}^{classical}}$$
$$+\hat{\mathbf{n}}(\mathbf{x})\hat{\mathbf{n}}(\mathbf{x}) : D\nabla \tilde{\boldsymbol{\tau}}_{\mathbf{u}^{classical}} + \hat{\mathbf{n}}(\mathbf{x}) \cdot (\mathbf{D} \cdot \nabla \tilde{\boldsymbol{\tau}}_{\mathbf{u}^{classical}}) + \hat{\mathbf{n}}(\mathbf{x}) \cdot \left(\mathbf{D} \cdot \nabla \tilde{\boldsymbol{\tau}}^{213}_{\mathbf{u}^{classical}} \right) \}.$$

Thanks to the introductory discussion of this theorem, pertaining to the regularity of surface terms generated by the classical field, it is clear that all the terms participating in $\mathbf{k}(\mathbf{x})$ are well defined and belong to $H^{-\frac{3}{2}}(\partial\Omega_N)$. In addition, given that in our elliptic boundary value problem, every surface norm of traces of the classical field and its derivatives is controlled by the volume norm $\|\mathbf{u}^{classical}\|_{H^2(\Omega)}$, which is bounded by the data as Equation (52) implies, the surface field $g^2 \mathbf{k}(\mathbf{x})$ is uniformly bounded in $H^{-\frac{3}{2}}(\partial \Omega_N)$ with magnitude of order g^2.

The fields $\mathbf{w}$ and $D\mathbf{w}$, on surfaces and (or) curves have appropriate norms, which are bounded by the norm of the solution $\|\mathbf{w}\|_{H^1(\Omega)}$ (due to the continuity of the traces with respect to the solution of the boundary value problem), which is, by its turn, bounded uniformly with respect to the gradient parameter g, via an estimate of the form (33) (applied to $\mathbf{w}$).

If the case (A) holds, the second dual pairing in r.h.s. of Equation (56) disappears and no need to handle the functional $\mathbf{R}_w(\mathbf{x}; g)$ on $\partial\Omega_D$ arises. When we have case (B), we impose further regularity on the displacement and stresses leading to higher regularity on the classical solution. This regularity is optimally selected to guarantee that the crucial field $\frac{\partial}{\partial n}\mathbf{u}^{classical}(\mathbf{x})$ belongs to $H^{\frac{3}{2}}(\partial\Omega)$ (since under this choice, the norm $\|\mathbf{u}^{classical}\|_{H^3(\Omega)}$ is kept bounded).

Finally, the field $\mathbf{R}_w(\mathbf{x}; g)$ on $\partial\Omega_Q$ equals with the field $g^2 \hat{\mathbf{n}}(\mathbf{x})\hat{\mathbf{n}}(\mathbf{x}) : \nabla \tau_w$, which incorporates second order derivatives of $\mathbf{w}$. Then, the adequate surface $H^{-\frac{3}{2}}$—norm of $R_w(\mathbf{x}; g)$ is again uniformly bounded (due to the continuity of the traces with respect to the solution of the boundary value problem) by $g^2 \|\mathbf{w}\|_{H^1(\Omega)}$, which via (33) is bounded by the norms of the data multiplied by $g^2 C$. This coefficient goes to 0 as $g \to 0$, since, as mentioned before, the generic constant does not depend on g.

In any case, taking the limit as $g \to 0$, in expression (56), all the terms of the right-hand side converge uniformly to 0, therefore

$$\int \left(\widetilde{\boldsymbol{\tau}}_{w_{g=0}} : \hat{\boldsymbol{\varepsilon}}_{w_{g=0}} + \widetilde{\boldsymbol{\mu}}_{w_{g=0}} \vdots \hat{\boldsymbol{\varepsilon}}_{w_{g=0}} \nabla \right) dx = 0. \tag{57}$$

The positivity of the bilinear elastic form guarantees that $\widetilde{\boldsymbol{\varepsilon}}_{w_{g=0}} = \widetilde{\mathbf{0}}$, which implies that $\mathbf{w}(\mathbf{x}, 0)$ is a constant. Given that the trace $\mathbf{w}(\mathbf{x}, 0)|_{\partial\Omega_D} = 0$, we infer that

$$\lim_{g \to 0} \mathbf{w}(\mathbf{x}, g) = 0, \; \mathbf{x} \in \Omega, \tag{58}$$

from where we obtain immediately the asymptotic behavior (50). □

Much effort was places in finding the necessary regularity of the data assuring the desired convergence when microstructure behavior disappears. It is interesting that this is necessarily valid when the data are smooth analytic functions of their arguments. Indeed, we have the following corollary, which would be the main outcome of this work if the data were considered analytic, but in our opinion, this could not be proven without the herein adopted generalization to abstract functional spaces.

Corollary 1. *Consider that the boundary value problem consists of Equations (20), (29) and (30). The data $(\mathbf{f}, \mathbf{g}, \mathbf{h}, \mathbf{r}, \mathbf{s})$ are analytic functions of their arguments with the restriction that $\mathbf{r}, \mathbf{s}$ obey to Equations (48) and (49). Let $\mathbf{u}(\mathbf{x}; g)$ be the unique solution of the gradient elasticity boundary value problem, expressed on the basis of the decomposition constructed in Theorem 2. Then, the following asymptotic result is obtained:*

$$\mathbf{u}(\mathbf{x}; g) \to \mathbf{u}^{classical}(\mathbf{x}) \text{ as } g \to 0, \; \mathbf{x} \in \Omega.$$

Proof. The assumed analytic smoothness of the data confirms that the assumptions of the alternative (B) of Theorem 3 are always valid and then the convergence outcome holds in any case. □

Remark 1. As far as the field $\mathbf{R}_w(\mathbf{x};g)$ on $\partial\Omega_Q$ is concerned, we could easily find that the surface $H^{-\frac{1}{2}}$—norm of $\mathbf{R}_w(\mathbf{x};g)$ is again uniformly bounded by $g^2\|\mathbf{w}\|_{H^2(\Omega)}$. On the basis of (24a), this term is bounded by the norms of the data multiplied by $g^2 C_g$. Therefore, if no extra assumption on data was made, the limit $\lim_{g \to 0} g^2 C_g$ would be ambiguous.

Remark 2. We would like to mention once again here that, despite the convergence, which needs some special settlement of the nature of the imposed data, the decomposition (37) is always valid, and when the conditions are arbitrary, what is exactly stated for the participants of the decomposition is that they satisfy the corresponding differential equations, while their superposition satisfies the boundary value problem.

A number of simple one-dimensional problems can reveal the essence of the previous theorems. Let us consider, for example, the elastostatic response of a finite length string. The considered differential equation is given by $u_{xx} - g^2 u_{xxxx} = 0$, $x \in (0,1)$ accompanied by the classical boundary conditions $u(0) = 1$, $u_x(1) - g^2 u_{xxx}(1) = 2$ and the non-classical ones $g^2 u_{xxx}(0) = 3g^2$ and $u_x(1) = 0$.

The solution is

$$u(x) = 2x + 1 - eg^2 + \left[\left(3g^2 + 2ge^{-\frac{1}{g}}\right)e^{-\frac{x}{g}} + g\left(3ge^{-\frac{1}{g}} - 2\right)e^{\frac{x-1}{g}}\right]\left(1 + e^{-\frac{2}{g}}\right)^{-1},$$

while the classical elastic solution that satisfies the conditions $u(0) = 1$ and $u_x(1) = 2$ is $u^{cl}(x) = 2x + 1$.

The same differential equation with the boundary conditions $u(0) = 0$, $u(1) = 1$, $u_x(0) = 2$ and $u_{xxx}(1) = 0$ has the following solution:

$$u(x) = x + g\left[\left(1 - e^{-\frac{2}{g}}\right)(x-1) + e^{-\frac{x}{g}} - e^{\frac{x-2}{g}}\right]\left(g - 1 - (g+1)e^{-\frac{2}{g}}\right)^{-1}$$

with corresponding classical solution, the function $u^{cl\cdot}(x) = x$.

Remark 3. The second example of Remark 2 implies that sometimes it is useful to write Equation (37) in the following form

$$\mathbf{u}(\mathbf{x},g) = (1 + \delta(g))\mathbf{u}^{classical}(\mathbf{x}) + \mathbf{u}^N(\mathbf{x},g) + g^2 \mathbf{u}^G(\mathbf{x},g) \tag{59}$$

with $\delta(g) \to 0$ as $g \to 0$, where $\mathbf{u}^N(\mathbf{x},\xi)$ obeys to the same differential regime. This approach consists of a repartition of the partners of the decomposition, which seems to be more flexible in applications. This reordering is realizable since both fields $\mathbf{u}^{classical}(\mathbf{x})$ and $\mathbf{u}^N(\mathbf{x})$ belong to the kernel of the classical elasticity operator.

Remark 4. The result stated by Theorem 3 could be violated if the boundary conditions are set arbitrarily. As an example, consider the same differential equation as in Remark 2, accompanied with the boundary conditions $u(0) = 0$, $u(1) = 1$, $u_x(0) - g^2 u_{xxx}(0) = 2$ and $u_{xx}(1) = 0$. This problem has the unique solution $u(x) = 2x - 1 + \left[e^{-\frac{x}{g}} - e^{-\frac{1}{g}}e^{\frac{x-1}{g}}\right]\left(1 - e^{-\frac{2}{g}}\right)^{-1}$. However, the classical solution $2x - 1$ satisfies the boundary conditions $u(1) = 1$, $u_x(0) = 2$, but does not satisfy the classical boundary condition $u(0) = 0$. Additionally, the part of the solution containing the displacement $\mathbf{u}^G$ does not converge to zero as $g \to 0$ at the endpoint $x = 0$. The critical factor here, is that two classical boundary conditions are prescribed simultaneously at the same part of the boundary.

Remark 5. In the statement of the theorem, we demanded that $meas(\partial\Omega_D) > 0$. In mathematical terms, this is needed for the uniqueness of the solution. Physically, it reflects the necessity of some anchoring of the structure. However, we would like to say that this condition is not of major *importance for the validity of Theorem 3. The modifications needed could be stated mathematically—they include some compatibility conditions for the data—but the essence is very simple: The results are exactly the same modulo motions of a rigid body. Consequently, imposing a-posteriori a condition not allowing rigid motions is sufficient to construct the unique solution of the problem.*

4. Revisiting Bending Theories of Strain Gradient Elastic Beams

In this section, the solution representation addressed in Section 3 is employed to present an answer to contradictions arising by two well-known first-strain gradient elastic models proposed in the literature to describe the strain gradient elastostatic bending behavior of Bernoulli–Euler beams.

During the last two decades, a plethora of papers dealing with the static and dynamic response of Bernoulli–Euler strain gradient elastic beams have appeared in the literature. Most of them are based on variational approaches and, for the elastostatic case, the equilibrium equation they conclude has either the following form [48–52]

$$EIu'''' - EIg^2 u'''''' + q(x) = 0 \qquad (60)$$

where x coincides with the neutral axis of the beam, E stands for the material Young modulus, I is the moment of inertia of the beam's cross-section A, $u(x)$ is the transverse beam deflection, $q(x)$ is the transverse external load, and g^2 is the intrinsic strain gradient elastic parameter, or the form [53–61]

$$\left(EI + g^2 A\right) u'''' - EIg^2 u'''''' + q(x) = 0. \qquad (61)$$

The essential difference between these two equations is that the first is derived by considering the strain e_{xx} and the gradient of strain e_{xxx} in the expression of the potential energy density of the beam, while the second one considers the strain e_{xx} and the strain gradients e_{xxx}, e_{yxx} with e_{yxx} being the differentiation of e_{xx} with respect to axis y directed along the thickness of the beam. The result is that the bending stiffness in Equation (60) is the same as that of classical elasticity, while the bending stiffness in (61) depends on the internal length scale parameter g^2 and the cross-section of beam A. The interesting point here is that the same categorization is valid for other works dealing with the bending of strain gradient elastic Timoshenko beams and plates, as well as for experimental and numerical validations on the bending response of strain gradient elastic beams. Here, one can mention the works of Papargyri-Beskou and Beskos [62], Papargyri-Beskou et al. [63], Triantafyllou and Giannakopoulos [64], and Gortsas et al. [29] for the strain gradient model of Equation (60), and the works of Lazopoulos and Lazopoulos [65], Khakalo and Niiranen [57,58,60,66], and Korshunova et al. [67] for the model of Equation (61).

Since there is a principal difference between the two above-mentioned bending models, the question here is which of them is the correct one. Lurie et al. [68] and Lurie and Solyaev [69,70] proposed elegant answers to that question by proving that Equation (60) is the only correct one for the bending response of a strain gradient elastic Bernoulli–Euler beam. Among others, they mentioned that " … *a formal variational procedure for obtaining the governing equilibrium equations in the beam theories, ignoring boundary conditions on the top and bottom surfaces of the beam leads to an erroneous result of abnormal increasing of the beam normalized bending stiffness with decreasing its thickness.* … ". Polizzotto [31] upholds this argument because the normal derivative of displacements identically vanishes at the beam lateral surface, and thus cannot play any role as a boundary layer. In the present section, we reach the same conclusion under the light of the theorems proved in the previous section.

The starting point of our analysis is the pure bending of a classical elastic, isotropic two-dimensional orthogonal rectangle subjected to pure bending under plane strain conditions, as depicted in Figure 1. The boundary conditions of the problem are $p_k(x_1, \pm a) = 0$ and

$p_2(0, x_2) = p_2(L, x_2) = 0$, $p_1(0, x_2) = p_1(L, x_2) = P_1 x_2/a$ and the corresponding solution is provided by Selvadurai [3] in the following form:

$$u_1^{classical} = \frac{P_1(1-\nu^2)}{Ea} x_1 x_2$$
$$u_2^{classical} = -\frac{P_1}{2Ea}\left[\nu(1+\nu)x_2^2 + (1-\nu^2)x_1^2\right].$$
(62)

Figure 1. Pure bending of an elastic beam.

Consider a rectangular 3D plate of length L and cross-section $2a \times b$. The torque at both boundaries of the plate is defined as

$$M = \int_{-a}^{a} x_2 \left(P_1 \frac{x_2}{a}\right) dS = \int_{-a}^{a} x_2 \left(P_1 \frac{x_2}{a}\right) b \, dx_2 = \frac{P_1 I}{a}$$
(63)

with $I = 2ba^3/3$ being the moment of inertia of the cross-section $2a \times b$. Equation (62), valid for the midplane of the plate, obtain the form

$$u_1^{classical} = \frac{M(1-\nu^2)}{EI} x_1 x_2$$
$$u_2^{classical} = -\frac{M}{2EI}\left[\nu(1+\nu)x_2^2 + (1-\nu^2)x_1^2\right]$$
(64)

while the deflection of the neutral axis is given by $u_2^{classical}$ for $x_2 = 0$, i.e.,

$$u_2^{classical} = -\frac{M}{2EI}(1-\nu^2)x_1^2$$
(65)

which, for $\nu = 0$, is identical to the deflection of a classical elastic Bernoulli–Euler beam subjected to pure bending [3,69], i.e.,

$$u_{Bernoulli-Euler}^{classical} = -\frac{M}{2EI} x_1^2.$$
(66)

Next, we consider the same pure bending problem presented in Figure 1, however, for a strain gradient elastic material. The classical boundary conditions remain the same as in the classical elastic problem, i.e.,

$$p_k(x_1, \pm a) = 0$$
$$p_2(0, x_2) = p_2(L, x_2) = 0$$
$$p_1(0, x_2) = p_1(L, x_2) = \frac{M}{I} x_2$$
(67)

while in non-classical boundary conditions, we consider the zeroing of double tractions at all the external boundaries, for example:

$$R_k(x_1, \pm a) = 0$$
$$R_k(0, x_2) = R_k(0, x_2) = 0. \tag{68}$$

According to the theorem presented in Section 3, the strain gradient elastic solution of this problem is written as

$$u_1(x_1, x_2; g) = u_1^{classical}(x_1, x_2) + u_1^N(x_1, x_2; g) + g^2 u_1^G(x_1, x_2; g)$$
$$u_2(x_1, x_2; g) = u_2^{classical}(x_1, x_2) + u_2^N(x_1, x_2; g) + g^2 u_2^G(x_1, x_2; g). \tag{69}$$

Evidently, the solution (69) imposes the following forms for tractions and double tractions, respectively

$$p_1(\hat{n}, x_1, x_2; g) = p_1^{classical}(\hat{n}, x_1, x_2; g) + p_1^N(\hat{n}, x_1, x_2; g)$$
$$+ g^2 p_1^G(\hat{n}, x_1, x_2; g)$$
$$p_2(\hat{n}, x_1, x_2; g) = p_2^{classical}(\hat{n}, x_1, x_2; g) + p_2^N(\hat{n}, x_1, x_2; g)$$
$$+ g^2 p_2^G(\hat{n}, x_1, x_2; g) \tag{70}$$

$$R_1(\hat{n}, x_1, x_2; g) = R_1^{classical}(\hat{n}, x_1, x_2; g) + R_1^N(\hat{n}, x_1, x_2; g)$$
$$+ g^2 R_1^G(\hat{n}, x_1, x_2; g)$$
$$R_2(\hat{n}, x_1, x_2; g) = R_2^{classical}(\hat{n}, x_1, x_2; g) + R_2^N(\hat{n}, x_1, x_2; g)$$
$$+ g^2 R_2^G(\hat{n}, x_1, x_2; g) \tag{71}$$

with $\hat{n}$ being the unit normal vector of the surface, to which both tractions and double tractions are referred.

Concentrating our attention on the classical part of the solution (69), it is easy to observe that [30]

$$\begin{aligned}\tau_{11}^{classical} &= (\lambda + 2\mu)\partial_1 u_1^{classical} + \lambda \partial_2 u_2^{classical} &= \tfrac{M}{I} x_2 \\ \tau_{22}^{classical} &= \lambda \partial_1 u_1^{classical} + (\lambda + 2\mu)\partial_2 u_2^{classical} &= 0 \\ \tau_{12}^{classical} &= \tau_{21}^{classical} = \mu(\partial_2 u_1^{classical} + \partial_1 u_2^{classical}) &= 0\end{aligned} \tag{72}$$

and

$$\begin{aligned}\mu_{111}^{classical} &= (\lambda + 2\mu)g^2 \partial_1^2 u_1^{classical} + \lambda g^2 \partial_1 \partial_2 u_2^{classical} &= 0 \\ \mu_{222}^{classical} &= \lambda g^2 \partial_1 \partial_2 u_1^{classical} + (\lambda + 2\mu)g^2 \partial_2^2 u_2^{classical} &= 0 \\ \mu_{112}^{classical} &= \mu_{121}^{classical} = \mu g^2 (\partial_1 \partial_2 u_1^{classical} + \partial_1^2 u_2^{classical}) &= 0 \\ \mu_{122}^{classical} &= \lambda g^2 \partial_1^2 u_1^{classical} + (\lambda + 2\mu)g^2 \partial_1 \partial_2 u_2^{classical} &= 0 \\ \mu_{211}^{classical} &= (\lambda + 2\mu)g^2 \partial_1 \partial_2 u_1^{classical} + \lambda g^2 \partial_2^2 u_2^{classical} &= g^2 \tfrac{M}{I} \\ \mu_{212}^{classical} &= \mu_{221}^{classical} = \mu g^2 (\partial_2^2 u_1^{classical} + \partial_1 \partial_2 u_2^{classical}) &= 0.\end{aligned} \tag{73}$$

As it is explained by Charalambopoulos et al. [30], the two components of the gradient elastic traction and double traction vectors, defined on a surface with unit normal vector $\hat{n}(n_1, n_2)$, have the form, respectively,

$$\begin{aligned}p_1 &= n_1 \tau_{11} + n_2 \tau_{21} + n_1(n_1^2 - 2)\partial_1 \mu_{111} + n_2(n_2^2 - 2)\partial_2 \mu_{221} \\ &+ n_2(n_1^2 - 1)(\partial_1 \mu_{121} + \partial_1 \mu_{211}) + n_1(n_2^2 - 1)(\partial_2 \mu_{121} + \partial_2 \mu_{211}) \\ &+ n_2 n_1^2 \partial_2 \mu_{111} + n_1 n_2^2 \partial_1 \mu_{221} \\ p_2 &= n_2 \tau_{22} + n_1 \tau_{12} + n_1(n_1^2 - 2)\partial_1 \mu_{112} + n_2(n_2^2 - 2)\partial_2 \mu_{222} \\ &+ n_2(n_1^2 - 1)(\partial_1 \mu_{212} + \partial_1 \mu_{122}) + n_1(n_2^2 - 1)(\partial_2 \mu_{122} + \partial_2 \mu_{212}) \\ &+ n_2 n_1^2 \partial_2 \mu_{112} + n_1 n_2^2 \partial_1 \mu_{222}\end{aligned} \tag{74}$$

and
$$R_1 = n_1^2 \mu_{111} + n_1 n_2 \mu_{121} + n_1 n_2 \mu_{211} + n_2^2 \mu_{221}$$
$$R_2 = n_2^2 \mu_{222} + n_1^2 \mu_{112} + n_1 n_2 \mu_{122} + n_1 n_2 \mu_{212} \tag{75}$$

In view of (72)–(75), the classical part of the gradient elastic traction and double traction vectors defined on a surface with unit normal vector $\hat{n}(n_1, n_2)$ exhibit the following forms, respectively

$$R_1 = n_1^2 \mu_{111} + n_1 n_2 \mu_{121} + n_1 n_2 \mu_{211} + n_2^2 \mu_{221}$$
$$R_2 = n_2^2 \mu_{222} + n_1^2 \mu_{112} + n_1 n_2 \mu_{122} + n_1 n_2 \mu_{212} \tag{76}$$

and
$$R_1^{classical}(\hat{n}, x_1, x_2; g) = n_1 n_2 \mu_{211}^{classical} = n_1 n_2 \frac{M}{T}$$
$$R_2^{classical}(\hat{n}, x_1, x_2; g) = 0. \tag{77}$$

Inserting Equations (76) and (77) into (70) and (71), respectively, and satisfying the boundary conditions (67) and (68) one obtains:

$$p_k^N(n_2, x_1, \pm a; g) + g^2 p_k^G(n_2, x_1, \pm a; g) = 0, \; k = 1, 2$$
$$p_k^N(n_1, 0, x_2; g) + g^2 p_k^G(n_1, 0, x_2; g) = 0, \; k = 1, 2 \tag{78}$$
$$p_k^N(n_1, L, x_2; g) + g^2 p_k^G(n_1, L, x_2; g) = 0, \; k = 1, 2$$

and
$$R_k^N(n_2, x_1, \pm a; g) + g^2 R_k^G(n_2, x_1, \pm a; g) = 0, \; k = 1, 2$$
$$R_k^N(n_1, 0, x_2; g) + g^2 R_k^G(n_1, 0, x_2; g) = 0, \; k = 1, 2 \tag{79}$$
$$R_k^N(n_1, L, x_2; g) + g^2 R_k^G(n_1, L, x_2; g) = 0, \; k = 1, 2.$$

Equations (78) and (79) indicate that the parts $u_k^N(x_1, x_2; g)$, $u_k^G(x_1, x_2; g)$ satisfy a homogeneous system of algebraic equations for arbitrary material properties. Apparently, this leads to the conclusion that

$$u_k^N(x_1, x_2; g) = u_k^G(x_1, x_2; g) = 0 \tag{80}$$

which means that the pure bending of the strain gradient elastic plate presented in Figure 1 has absolutely the same response as that of the classical elastic one.

Extending this result to the behavior of the neutral axis of the plate for $\nu = 0$, we obtain

$$u_{Bernoulli-Euler}^{classical} \equiv u_{Bernoulli-Euler}^{gradient} = -\frac{M}{2EI} x_1^2. \tag{81}$$

This result is possible only when Equation (60) is valid. Equation (61) is misleading since the double stress μ_{yxx} does not contribute to the solution of the problem.

5. Conclusions

A material with microstructural effects obeys the simplified elastostatic version of Mindlin's Form II first-strain gradient elastic theory, and its displacement field $\mathbf{u}(\mathbf{x})$ satisfies the fourth-order partial differential Equation (3) and the relevant classical and non-classical boundary conditions. In the present work, it has been rigorously proved that the solution of Equation (3) admits the following representation:

$$\mathbf{u}(\mathbf{x}, g) = (1 + \delta(g))\mathbf{u}^{classical}(\mathbf{x}) + \mathbf{u}^N(\mathbf{x}, g) + g^2 \mathbf{u}^G(\mathbf{x}, g), \tag{82}$$

which has the following convenient advantages:

1. Incorporates the solution $\mathbf{u}^{classical}(\mathbf{x})$ of the respective classical elastic boundary value problem, that satisfies the same classical boundary conditions with the strain gradient elastic problem.
2. Converges to the classical elastic solution as $g \to 0$.

3. Comprises two displacements fields $\mathbf{u}^N(\mathbf{x}, g)$, $\mathbf{u}^G(\mathbf{x}, g)$, which satisfy the simpler equations $\mu \nabla^2 \mathbf{u}^N + (\lambda + \mu) \nabla \nabla \cdot \mathbf{u}^N = 0$ and $(1 - g^2 \nabla^2) \mathbf{u}^G = 0$, respectively.

The representation of the solution presented above was employed to prove that a strain gradient elastic Bernoulli–Euler beam subjected to pure bending does not present microstructural effects and its behavior is identical to that of a classical elastic Bernoulli–Euler beam. This result is in full agreement with the corresponding conclusions provided by Lurie and Solyaev [69] on the same subject.

Author Contributions: Conceptualization, D.P.; Data curation, A.C.; Formal analysis, A.C. and D.P.; Funding acquisition, D.P.; Investigation, A.C. and T.G.; Writing—original draft, A.C., T.G. and D.P. All authors have read and agreed to the published version of the manuscript.

Funding: This research was funded by the Hellenic Foundation for Research and Innovation (HFRI) under the "First Call for HFRI. Research Projects to support Faculty members and Researchers and the procurement of high-cost research equipment grant" (Project Number: 2060).

Institutional Review Board Statement: Not applicable.

Informed Consent Statement: Not applicable.

Data Availability Statement: Not applicable.

Conflicts of Interest: The authors declare no conflict of interest.

Appendix A

In this Appendix, the proof of decomposition (5) through the solution representation (4) is provided.

It is well known that the solution of Equation (1), via Papkovich–Neuber potentials, has the form [3,64]

$$\mathbf{u}^{classical} = \mathbf{B}^{classical} - \frac{1}{4(1-v)} \nabla \left(\mathbf{r} \cdot \mathbf{B}^{classical} + B_0^{classical} \right), \tag{A1}$$

with

$$\begin{aligned} \nabla^2 \mathbf{B}^{classical} &= 0 \\ \nabla^2 B_0^{classical} &= 0. \end{aligned} \tag{A2}$$

On the other hand, the solution representation (4) reads

$$\mathbf{u}^{gradient} = \mathbf{B}^{gradient} - \frac{1}{4(1-v)} \left[\mathbf{r} \cdot \left(1 - g^2 \nabla^2 \right) \mathbf{B}^{gradient} + B_0^{gradient} \right], \tag{A3}$$

with

$$\begin{aligned} (1 - g^2 \nabla^2) \nabla^2 \mathbf{B}^{gradient} &= 0 \\ (1 - g^2 \nabla^2) \nabla^2 B_0^{gradient} &= 0. \end{aligned} \tag{A4}$$

Comparing (A2) with (A4), it is apparent that $(1 - g^2 \nabla^2) \mathbf{B}^{gradient} \equiv \mathbf{B}^{classical}$, and subsequently (A3) can be written as

$$\mathbf{u}^{gradient} = \mathbf{B}^{gradient} - \frac{1}{4(1-v)} \left[\mathbf{r} \cdot \mathbf{B}^{classical} + B_0^{gradient} \right]. \tag{A5}$$

By adding and subtracting $\mathbf{B}^{classical}$ and $B_0^{classical}$ in (A5), we obtain

$$\mathbf{u}^{gradient} = \mathbf{B}^{gradient} + \mathbf{B}^{classical} - \mathbf{B}^{classical}$$
$$- \tfrac{1}{4(1-v)} \left[\mathbf{r} \cdot \mathbf{B}^{classical} + B_0^{gradient} + B_0^{classical} - B_0^{classical} \right] \Rightarrow$$
$$\mathbf{u}^{gradient} = \mathbf{B}^{classical} - \tfrac{1}{4(1-v)} \nabla \left[\mathbf{r} \cdot \mathbf{B}^{classical} + B_0^{classical} \right]$$
$$+ \mathbf{B}^{gradient} - \mathbf{B}^{classical} - \tfrac{1}{4(1-v)} \nabla \left[B_0^{gradient} - B_0^{classical} \right],$$

and because of (A1), it is apparent that

$$\mathbf{u}^{gradient} = \mathbf{u}^{classical} + \mathbf{B}^{gradient} - \mathbf{B}^{classical} - \frac{1}{4(1-v)}\nabla\left[B_0^{gradient} - B_0^{classical}\right]. \quad (A6)$$

However,

$$\left.\begin{array}{l}(1-g^2\nabla^2)\left(\mathbf{B}^{gradient} - \mathbf{B}^{classical}\right) \\ (1-g^2\nabla^2)\left(B_0^{gradient} - B_0^{classical}\right)\end{array}\right\} \stackrel{(A.4)}{=} \left.\begin{array}{l}\mathbf{B}^{classical} - \mathbf{B}^{classical} \\ B_0^{classical} - B_0^{classical}\end{array}\right\} = 0. \quad (A7)$$

Equations (A6) and (A7) easily imply that

$$\begin{aligned}\mathbf{u}^{gradient} &= \mathbf{u}^{classical} + \mathbf{u}^g \\ \mathbf{u}^{classical} &\in \ker\left(\mu\nabla^2(\lambda+\mu)\nabla\nabla\cdot\right) \\ \mathbf{u}^g &\in \ker\left(1-g^2\nabla^2\right)\end{aligned} \quad (A8)$$

which confirms (5).

References

1. Timoshenko, S.P.; Goodier, J.N. *Theory of Elasticity*, 3rd ed.; McGraw-Hill: New York, NY, USA, 1970.
2. Gurtin, M.E. *An Introduction to Continuum Mechanics*, 1st ed.; Academic Press: Cambridge, UK, 1981.
3. Selvadurai, A.P.S. *Partial Differential Equations in Mechanics 2*, 1st ed.; Springer: Heidelberg, Germany, 2000.
4. Exadaktylos, G.E.; Vardoulakis, I. Microstructure in linear elasticity and scale effects: A reconsideration of basic rock mechanics and rock fracture mechanics. *Tectonophysics* 2001, *335*, 81–109. [CrossRef]
5. Polyzos, D.; Fotiadis, D.I. Derivation of Mindlin's gradient elastic theory via simple lattice and continuum models. *Int. J. Solids Struct.* 2012, *49*, 470–480. [CrossRef]
6. Cosserat, E.; Cosserat, F. *Theorie des Corps Deformables*; A. Hermann et Fils: Paris, France, 1909; Volume 81.
7. Toupin, R.A. Elastic materials with couple stresses. *Arch. Ration. Mech. Anal.* 1962, *11*, 385–414. [CrossRef]
8. Mindlin, R.D.; Tiersten, H.F. Effects of couple-stresses in linear elasticity. *Arch. Ration. Mech. Anal.* 1962, *11*, 415–448. [CrossRef]
9. Green, A.E.; Rivlin, R.S. Multipolar continuum mechanics. *Arch. Ration Mech. Anal.* 1964, *17*, 113–147. [CrossRef]
10. Koiter, W.T. Couple-stresses in the theory of elasticity, I&II. *Philos. Trans. R. Soc. Lond. B* 1964, *67*, 17–44.
11. Mindlin, R.D. Influence of couple stresses on stress concentrations. *Exp. Mech.* 1963, *3*, 1–7. [CrossRef]
12. Mindlin, R.D. Micro-structure in linear elasticity. *Arch. Rat. Mech. Anal.* 1964, *16*, 51–78. [CrossRef]
13. Germain, P. The method of virtual power in the mechanics of continuous media, I: Second-gradient theory. *Math. Mech. Complex Syst.* 2020, *8*, 153–190. [CrossRef]
14. Vardoulakis, I.; Exadaktylos, G.; Aifantis, E. Gradient elasticity with surface energy: Mode-III crack problem. *Int. J. Solids Struct.* 1996, *33*, 4531–4559. [CrossRef]
15. Exadaktylos, G. Gradient elasticity with surface energy: Mode-I crack problem. *Int. J. Solids Struct.* 1998, *35*, 421–456. [CrossRef]
16. Aravas, N.; Giannakopoulos, A.E. Plane asymptotic crack-tip solutions in gradient elasticity. *Int. J. Solids Struct.* 2009, *46*, 4478–4503. [CrossRef]
17. Gourgiotis, P.A.; Georgiadis, H.G. Plane-strain crack problems in microstructured solids governed by dipolar gradient elasticity. *J. Mech. Phys.* 2009, *57*, 1898–1920. [CrossRef]
18. Karlis, G.; Tsinopoulos, S.V.; Polyzos, D.; Beskos, D.E. Boundary Element Analysis of Mode I and Mixed Mode (I and II) Crack Problem of 2-D Gradient Elasticity. *Comput. Methods Appl. Mech. Eng.* 2007, *196*, 5092–5103. [CrossRef]
19. Karlis, G.; Tsinopoulos, S.V.; Polyzos, D.; Beskos, D.E. 2D and 3D Boundary Element Analysis of Mode-I Cracks in Gradient Elasticity. *CMES* 2008, *26*, 189–208.
20. Lazar, M.; Maugin, G.A.; Aifantis, E.C. Dislocations in second strain gradient elasticity. *Int. J. Solids Struct.* 2006, *43*, 1787–1817. [CrossRef]
21. Gao, X.L.; Park, S. Variational formulation of a simplified strain gradient elasticity theory and its application to a pressurized thick-walled cylinder problem. *Int. J. Solids Struct.* 2007, *44*, 7486–7499. [CrossRef]
22. Georgiadis, H.G.; Anagnostou, D.S. Problems of Flamant–Boussinesq and Kelvin type in dipolar gradient elasticity. *J. Elast.* 2008, *90*, 71–98. [CrossRef]
23. Gao, X.L.; Ma, H.M. Solution of Eshelby's inclusion problem with a bounded domain and Eshelby's tensor for a spherical inclusion in a finite spherical matrix based on a simplified strain gradient elasticity theory. *J. Mech. Phys. Solids* 2010, *58*, 779–797. [CrossRef]

24. Karlis, G.F.; Charalambopoulos, A.; Polyzos, D. An advanced boundary element method for solving 2D and 3D static problems in Mindlin's strain-gradient theory of elasticity. *Int. J. Numer. Methods Eng.* **2010**, *83*, 1407–1427. [CrossRef]
25. Papargyri-Beskou, S.; Tsinopoulos, S.V. Lame's strain potential method for plain gradient elasticity problems. *Arch. Appl. Mech.* **2015**, *9–10*, 1399–1419. [CrossRef]
26. Charalambopoulos, A.; Polyzos, D. Analytical solutions for a plane strain gradient elastic rectangle in tension. *Arch. Appl. Mech.* **2015**, *85*, 1421–1438. [CrossRef]
27. Anagnostou, D.S.; Gourgiotis, P.A.; Georgiadis, H.G. The Cerruti problem in dipolar gradient elasticity. *Math. Mech. Solids* **2015**, *20*, 1088–1106. [CrossRef]
28. Khakalo, S.; Niiranen, J. Gradient-elastic stress analysis near cylindrical holes in a plane under bi-axial tension fields. *Int. J. Solids Struct.* **2017**, *110–111*, 351–366. [CrossRef]
29. Gortsas, T.; Tsinopoulos, S.V.; Rodopoulos, D.; Polyzos, D. Strain gradient elasticity and size effects in the bending of fiber composite plates. *Int. J. Solids Struct.* **2018**, *143*, 103–112. [CrossRef]
30. Charalambopoulos, A.; Tsinopoulos, S.V.; Polyzos, D. Plane strain gradient elastic rectangle in bending. *Arch. Appl. Mech.* **2020**, *90*, 967–986. [CrossRef]
31. Polizzotto, C. A hierarchy of simplified constitutive models within isotropic strain gradient elasticity. *Eur. J. Mech. A Solids* **2017**, *61*, 92–109. [CrossRef]
32. Zhou, S.; Li, A.; Wang, B. A reformulation of constitutive relations in the strain gradient elasticity theory for isotropic materials. *Int. J. Solids Struct.* **2016**, *80*, 28–37. [CrossRef]
33. Lazar, M.; Po, G. On Mindlin's isotropic strain gradient elasticity: Green tensors, regularization, and operator-split. *J. Micromechanics Mol. Phys.* **2018**, *3*, 1840008. [CrossRef]
34. Gourgiotis, P.A.; Sifnaiou, M.D.; Georgiadis, H.G. The problem of sharp notch in microstructured solids governed by dipolar gradient elasticity. *Int. J. Fract.* **2010**, *166*, 179–201. [CrossRef]
35. Andreou, E.; Dassios, G.; Polyzos, D. Korn's constant for a spherical shell. *Q. Appl. Math.* **1988**, *XLVI*, 583–591. [CrossRef]
36. Solyaev, Y.; Lurie, S.; Korolenko, V. Three-phase model of particulate composites in second gradient elasticity. *Eur. J. Mech. A Solids* **2019**, *78*, 103853. [CrossRef]
37. Solyaev, Y.; Lurie, S.; Altenbach, H.; dell'Isola, F. On the elastic wedge problem within simplified and incomplete strain gradient elasticity theories. *Int. J. Solids Struct.* **2022**, *239–240*, 111433. [CrossRef]
38. Lazar, M. On gradient field theories: Gradient magnetostatics and gradient elasticity. *Philos. Mag.* **2014**, *94*, 2840–2874. [CrossRef]
39. Ru, C.Q.; Aifantis, E.C. A simple approach to solve boundary value problems in gradient elasticity. *Acta Mech.* **1993**, *101*, 59–68. [CrossRef]
40. Eremeyev, V.A.; Dell'Isola, F.; Boutin, C.; Steigmann, D. Linear pantographic sheets: Existence and uniqueness of weak solutions. *J. Elast.* **2018**, *132*, 175–196. [CrossRef]
41. Dell'Isola, F.; Sciarra, G.; Vidoli, S. Generalized Hook's law for isotropic second gradient materials. *Proc. R. Soc. A Math. Phys. Eng. Sci.* **2009**, *465*, 2177–2196.
42. Mindlin, R.D. Second gradient of strain and surface-tension in linear elasticity. *Int. J. Solids Struct.* **1965**, *1*, 417–438. [CrossRef]
43. Polyzos, D.; Tsepoura, K.G.; Tsinopoulos, S.V.; Beskos, D.E. A Boundary Element Method for Solving 2D and 3D Static Gradient Elastic Problems, Part 1: Integral formulation. *Comput. Methods Appl. Mech. Eng.* **2003**, *192*, 2845–2873. [CrossRef]
44. Polyzos, D. A Boundary Element Formulation for Solving Dipolar Gradient Elastic Problems. *Comput. Mech.* **2005**, *35*, 292–304. [CrossRef]
45. Marin, M.; Othman, M.I.A.; Seadawy, A.R.; Carstea, C. A domain of influence in the Moore-Gibson-Thompson theory of dipolar bodies. *J. Taibah Univ. Sci.* **2020**, *14*, 653–660. [CrossRef]
46. Ghita, C.; Pop, N.; Cioban, H. Quasi-static behavior as a limit process of a dynamical one for an anisotropic hardening material. *Comput. Mater. Sci.* **2012**, *52*, 217–225. [CrossRef]
47. Wloka, J. *Partial Differential Equations*; Cambridge University Press: Cambridge, UK, 1987.
48. Papargyri-Beskou, S.; Tsepoura, K.G.; Polyzos, D.; Beskos, D.E. Bending and stability analysis of gradient elastic beams. *Int. J. Solids Struct.* **2003**, *40*, 385–400, Erratum in *Int. J. Solids Struct.* **2005**, *42*, 4911–4912. [CrossRef]
49. Challamel, N.; Wang, C.M. The small length scale effect for a non-local cantilever beam: A paradox solved. *Nanotechnology* **2008**, *19*, 345703. [CrossRef] [PubMed]
50. Giannakopoulos, A.E.; Stamoulis, K. Structural analysis of gradient elastic components. *Int. J. Solids Struct.* **2007**, *44*, 3440–3451. [CrossRef]
51. Challamel, N. Variational formulation of gradient or/and nonlocal higher-order shear elasticity beams. *Compos. Struct.* **2013**, *105*, 351–368. [CrossRef]
52. Polizzotto, C. Stress gradient versus strain gradient constitutive models within elasticity. *Int. J. Solids Struct.* **2014**, *51*, 1809–1818. [CrossRef]
53. Lazopoulos, K.A.; Lazopoulos, A.K. Bending and buckling of thin strain gradient elastic beams. *Eur. J. Mech. A Solids* **2010**, *29*, 837–843. [CrossRef]
54. Shokrieh, M.M.; Zibaei, I. Determination of the Appropriate Gradient Elasticity Theory for Bending Analysis of Nano-beams by Considering Boundary Conditions Effect. *Lat. Am. J. Solids Struct.* **2015**, *12*, 2208–2230. [CrossRef]

55. Akgoz, B.; Civalek, O. Strain gradient elasticity and modified couple stress models for buckling analysis of axially loaded micro-scaled beams. *Int. J. Eng. Sci.* **2011**, *49*, 1268–1280. [CrossRef]
56. Akgoz, B.; Civalek, O. A size-dependent shear deformation beam model based on the strain gradient elasticity theory. *Int. J. Eng. Sci.* **2013**, *70*, 1–14. [CrossRef]
57. Khakalo, S.; Niiranen, J. Form II of Mindlin's second strain gradient theory of elasticity with a simplification: For materials and structures from nano- to macro-scales. *Eur. J. Mech. A Solids* **2018**, *71*, 292–319. [CrossRef]
58. Khakalo, S.; Balobanov, V.; Niiranen, J. Modelling size-dependent bending, buckling and vibrations of 2D triangular lattices by strain gradient elasticity models: Applications to sandwich beams and auxetics. *Int. J. Eng. Sci.* **2018**, *127*, 33–52. [CrossRef]
59. Zhao, B.; Liu, T.; Chen, J.; Peng, X.; Song, Z. A new Bernoulli–Euler beam model based on modified gradient elasticity. *Arch. Appl. Mech.* **2019**, *89*, 277–289. [CrossRef]
60. Niiranen, J.; Balobanov, V.; Kiendl, J.; Hosseini, S.B. Variational formulations, model comparisons and numerical methods for Euler–Bernoulli micro- and nano-beam models. *Math. Mech. Solids* **2019**, *24*, 312–335. [CrossRef]
61. Fu, G.; Zhou, S.; Qi, L. On the strain gradient elasticity theory for isotropic materials. *Int. J. Eng. Sci.* **2020**, *154*, 103348. [CrossRef]
62. Papargyri-Beskou, S.; Beskos, D.E. Static Analysis of Gradient Elastic Bars, Beams, Plates and Shells. *Open Mech. J.* **2010**, *4*, 65–73.
63. Papargyri-Beskou, S.; Giannakopoulos, A.E.; Beskos, D.E. Variational analysis of gradient elastic flexural plates under static loading. *Int. J. Solids Struct.* **2010**, *47*, 2755–2766. [CrossRef]
64. Triantafyllou, A.; Giannakopoulos, A.E. Structural analysis using a dipolar elastic Timoshenko beam. *Eur. J. Mech. A Solids* **2013**, *39*, 218–228. [CrossRef]
65. Lazopoulos, K.A.; Lazopoulos, A.K. On a strain gradient elastic Timoshenko beam model. *ZAMM Z. Angew. Math. Mech.* **2011**, *91*, 875–882. [CrossRef]
66. Khakalo, S.; Niiranen, J. Lattice structures as thermoelastic strain gradient metamaterials: Evidence from full-field simulations and applications to functionally step-wise-graded beams. *Compos. Part B* **2019**, *177*, 107224. [CrossRef]
67. Korshunova, N.; Alaimo, G.; Hosseini, S.B.; Carraturo, M.; Reali, A.; Niiranen, J.; Auricchio, F.; Rank, E.; Kollmannsberger, S. Bending behavior of octet-truss lattice structures: Modelling options, numerical characterization and experimental validation. *Mater. Des.* **2021**, *205*, 109693. [CrossRef]
68. Lurie, S.A.; Volkov-Bogorodsky, D.B.; Belov, P.; Lykosova, E. Do nanosized rods have abnormal mechanical properties? on some fallacious ideas and direct errors related to the use of the gradient theories for simulation of scale-dependent rods. *Nanosci. Technol. Int. J.* **2016**, *7*, 261–295. [CrossRef]
69. Lurie, S.; Solyaev, Y. Revisiting bending theories of elastic gradient beams. *Int. J. Eng. Sci.* **2018**, *126*, 1–21. [CrossRef]
70. Lurie, S.; Solyaev, Y. On the formulation of elastic and electroelastic gradient beam theories. *Contin. Mech. Thermodyn.* **2019**, *31*, 1601–1613. [CrossRef]

Article

Analysis of Industrial Engineering Students' Perception after a Multiple Integrals-Based Activity with a Fourth-Year Student

Anuar R. Giménez [1], Jesús Martín-Vaquero [1,*] and Manuel Rodríguez-Martín [2]

1. ETSII Béjar, University of Salamanca, 37700 Béjar, Spain; anuargimenez@usal.es
2. Department of Mechanical Engineering, University of Salamanca, 49029 Zamora, Spain; ingmanuel@usal.es
* Correspondence: jesmarva@usal.es

Abstract: In industrial engineering degrees in Spain, mathematics subjects are usually taught during the first two academic years. Consequently, it is often the case that students sometimes do not feel motivated to learn subjects such as Mathematics II (calculus). Nevertheless, this subject is fundamental for understanding other subjects in the degree study plan, as well as for the graduate's future professional career as an engineer. To address this, a problem-based teaching methodology was carried out with the help of a fourth-year student who explained an activity to first-year students in a manner which was both friendly and approachable. In this experiment, the student went through a series of practical problems taken from different engineering subjects, which required multivariable integrals to be calculated and which he had learned in mathematics as a first-year student. In addition, a method based on pre-test and post-test assessments was applied. From this work, various benefits were observed in terms of learning, as well as an increase in the level of motivation of first-year students. There was a greater appreciation of the usefulness of calculus and computer programs to solve real-life problems, and the students generally responded positively to this type of activity.

Keywords: multivariable integrals; interdisciplinary activities; engineering and science students; problem-based teaching

MSC: 97I10; 97I50

Citation: Giménez, A.R.; Martín-Vaquero, J.; Rodríguez-Martín, M. Analysis of Industrial Engineering Students' Perception after a Multiple Integrals-Based Activity with a Fourth-Year Student. *Mathematics* **2022**, *10*, 1764. https://doi.org/10.3390/math10101764

Academic Editor: Antonio Rodríguez Fuentes

Received: 6 April 2022
Accepted: 16 May 2022
Published: 21 May 2022

Publisher's Note: MDPI stays neutral with regard to jurisdictional claims in published maps and institutional affiliations.

Copyright: © 2022 by the authors. Licensee MDPI, Basel, Switzerland. This article is an open access article distributed under the terms and conditions of the Creative Commons Attribution (CC BY) license (https://creativecommons.org/licenses/by/4.0/).

1. Introduction

Engineering degrees involve studies that are extremely oriented toward problem solving. As such, problem-based learning (PBL) strategies were introduced after the Second World War as a means to reform universities, involving new educational models established between 1965 and 1975 [1]. This specific approach uses constructivist principles that encourage the application of prior knowledge, collaborative learning, and active engagement [2], and it feeds into another important methodology directly applicable in engineering degrees, namely, project-based learning. These two methodologies serve as inspiration for each other [3]. Therefore, the activities to be developed in the context of PBL should be associated with recurrent topics related to work the students may encounter in their future careers or a real situation with, for example, missing information or unclear answers [4–6].

In teaching engineering, it is important to integrate activities that reflect real-life situation rather than purely theoretical aspects [7]. In this regard, the use of PBL to teach mathematic subjects has also been called realistic mathematics education [8–12], which has been shown to have a positive effect on student motivation and participation in the classroom [13–16].

Mathematics is usually seen as being one of the most abstract and difficult subjects [17] and can cause students to experience negative feelings such as self-doubt and anxiety [18]. Thus, the manner in which an individual perceives their own competence in relation to the subject can influence final outcomes [19–21].

Intrinsic motivation can be defined as the satisfaction inherent to the performance of an activity, as opposed to that which is caused by the consequences or profits gained by the activity. When intrinsically motivated, a person is driven to act for reasons of satisfaction or challenge, rather than external rewards, pressures, or products [22]. By contrast, extrinsic motivation is that provoked by external factors. Intrinsic motivation is beneficial for the student because it favors student involvement in learning through satisfaction and enjoyment [23,24].

In this work, a learning methodology based on problem solving is proposed, using software to improve mathematical competence and an approach similar to that proposed by other authors [13,14]. The study was carried out on students enrolled in the subject entitled Mathematics II (calculus in one and several variables), which is a compulsory subject in the first academic year for the following degrees: mechanical engineering, electrical engineering, and electronic and automatic engineering. It has been observed that students do not always understand the reason why they must study such complicated mathematics, as they tend to prefer to solve more applied problems related to engineering. In addition, the students often do not realize they are being provided with tools for building a solid foundation for future studies.

The flow work employed for this activity is unique in that a fourth-year student, supervised by the teacher, was asked to teach an activity to the students. In doing so, they shared their experiences and perspective about the usefulness of math throughout a particular degree course. In this way, the learning experience became more relevant and real and could help to change our students' opinion and level of motivation regarding the importance of mathematics in engineering. This is the main focus of this research.

In Section 2, the methodology used to carry out this work is explained, including a description of the context and participants. In Section 3, the main details of the activity undertaken are provided, and the perception that our students had about calculus is examined, in addition to whether the strategy helped them. The questionnaire and its results are analyzed in Section 4, and our conclusions are presented in Section 5.

2. Methodology

2.1. Context and Participants

During the academic year 2020–2021, 63 students were enrolled in the subject Mathematics II (calculus) distributed among the following three degrees: 21 students were studying for a bachelor's degree in electrical engineering, 13 were studying for a bachelor's degree in electronical and automatic engineering, and 29 were studying for a bachelor's degree in mechanical engineering. University of Salamanca students can also study for double degrees such as electrical and mechanical engineering or electrical and electronic engineering. It should be noted that all these degrees fall within what in Spain is called "degrees of the field of industrial engineering" due to previous professional regulations maintained in the new context of the European Higher Education Area. All these degrees in Spain are distributed over 4 years, and Mathematics I (algebra) and Mathematics II (calculus) are always taught in the first year.

Even though the students were enrolled in different degree programs, they were grouped together in the same classroom, since Mathematics II is a compulsory subject for all students. This educational context (with students taking different degrees but all related to industrial engineering) is ideal for educational research. For this reason, other studies have been successfully conducted on a multidisciplinary group of students such as the one used here [25].

To this end, we asked the students to participate in the activity and to take the pre- and post-test described in Section 4. Additionally, we explained to the students that all of their answers would be treated anonymously according to the ethical code for carrying out questionnaires used by our university. Furthermore, participation in the study was totally optional; thus, only 17 of the 63 students decided to answer the survey. They were

13 men and four women within the age range of 18 to 22 years old. None of the students were excluded from the study.

Consequently, the study sample comprised 17 students out of the 63 students (27%) enrolled in Mathematics II (Table 1). Double degree corresponds to students in electrical and mechanical engineering.

Table 1. Distribution of the sample.

Degree Program	ECTS *	Academic Year	Students Number	Percentage of the Total Study Group
Bachelor in Mechanical Engineering	240	4	9	52.9%
Bachelor in Electrical Engineering	240	4	1	5.9%
Bachelor in Electronic and Automatic Engineering	240	4	4	23.5%
Double degree	276	4	3	17.6%

* ECTS is the number of credits according to the European Credit Transfer System. It serves to measure the work that students must complete in order to acquire the knowledge, skills, and abilities necessary to pass their curriculum. One credit according to ECTS corresponds to 25–30 h of student work. Thus, 240 credits according to ECTS corresponds to 4 years, and most of our students in the double degree require at least 5 years to complete their studies.

Prior to conducting the experiment and to gather more information about the sample, a questionnaire was filled out by the students, yielding the following results:

- On a Likert scale [26] of 1–5, students answered the following question: "I think my level of digital competence is high". The average response value was 3, and the standard deviation was 0.75.
- Students were asked if they had previous experience using the package Wolfram Mathematica [27], of which 94.1% answered no.
- Finally, students were asked if they were currently enrolled in any second, third, or fourth subjects, of which 88.2% answered no.

The competencies to be acquired specific to this subject are based on Spanish regulations that are drawn from the regulations of the European Higher Education Area (EHEA). The three university degrees programs belong to the field of industrial engineering; hence, the first two academic years are common to all degrees. By contrast, the subjects taken during the first 2 years are specific to each specialization and, therefore, are different.

In addition, double degrees are also offered at our school. In this case, students enrolled in the double degree program in electrical and mechanical engineering are included in the sample as a different group.

According to Spanish regulations for engineers, some engineering projects and tasks can be performed by any of the engineers in the industrial field. However, other more specialized projects and tasks can only be carried out by specialists in the field; for example, low-voltage electrical projects can be carried out by any industrial field engineer, but high-voltage electric projects can only be carried out by electrical engineers. Please note that a degree in chemical engineering belongs to degrees within the branch of industrial engineering but is not offered by the School of Industrial Engineering of the University of Salamanca and, as such, was not included in this research.

2.2. Analysis of the Methodology

2.2.1. Interdisciplinary Problems to Teach Calculus

The students studying our degree programs will be future engineers. In [28], it is stated that the work of an engineer "is predominantly intellectual and varied and not of a routine mental or physical character. It requires the exercise of original thought and judgement and the ability to supervise the technical and administrative work of others". For this reason, we consider teaching competences through interdisciplinary problems to be beneficial. Additionally, we are of the opinion that the first academic year of an engineering degree should provide general tools that allow engineers to solve a large array of daily problems: "their education and training will have been such that they will have acquired a broad and general appreciation of the engineering sciences, as well as thorough insight into the special features of their own branch" [28].

Students are constantly asking questions such as the following: "Why is this concept or topic interesting?" "Why do I need to study this part of the subject?" "Am I going to use this in the future and, if so, how?"

Additionally, some of our subjects are taught in the first 2 years of the degree program, which is the case of the subject calculus taught in the industrial engineering degree program in Béjar, Spain. This subject is included in the first year, and most of our students are not yet aware of the real situations that require engineers to know calculus in several variables, for example. The usefulness of some of the operations learnt in calculus does not become obvious until later on during the final stages of the degree.

Since multivariable (calculus) integrals are used by engineers in many situations to solve real problems, we decided it would be useful for third- and fourth-year students, as well as professors teaching other specialty subjects, to share their experiences with the use of calculus (in this case multivariable (calculus) integrals in several variables) to younger students. Obviously, this subject is only a tool for the students and not a main topic of study; therefore, it needs to be remembered that the students' appreciation of integrals in several variables may differ greatly from that of a mathematician's.

For this reason, multivariable (calculus) integrals were initially taught to the students in the normal fashion: theory, properties of integrals, and the most common ways to calculate some types of integrals. Additionally, some exercises in one dimension were shown, followed on by integrals in several variables, as well as solving some common exercises of integrals in several variables. Forming part of the experiment, an interdisciplinary activity was included, together with another teacher and a fourth-year student. The workflow for this activity is shown in Figure 1.

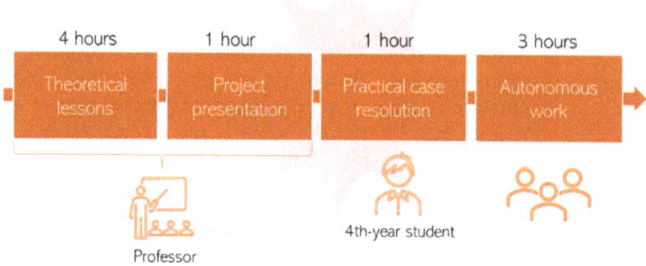

Figure 1. Workflow of the activity.

The aim of this work was to analyze the results of this activity, where it was proposed to evaluate not only how real problem solving can improve (or decrease) but also the motivation of engineering students in relation to the learning of mathematical subjects. In addition, we also wanted to measure the effect of the use of mathematical software in calculus classes. Computers are useful for assisting in two-step problem solving: first, consider the steps needed to solve the problem; then, use the acquired technical skills to control the computer to help solve the problem [29]. In this way, using computer tools, we can solve more complex problems; additionally, we are teaching our students the use of mathematical and computation software that they will have to use in other subjects and possibly also in their future profession as engineers, allowing the development of mathematical thinking. Doing so moves away from more theoretical exercises, permitting the student to have a change from classes that they consider to be more tedious. In addition, the group of researchers who carried out this activity included a professor from the Department of Applied Mathematics, a professor from the Department of Mechanical Engineering and a fourth-year student who had an interest in educational research. Consequently, a broader view was achieved, from the perspective of mathematical education, the specific technological application of integrals to mechanical engineering, and the student's experience, perception, and interaction with the other students. The instructor teaching mechanical engineering and the student shared their experiences with using integrals in other engineering subjects from both points of view. Moreover, we asked the students to anonymously answer a pre-test and post-test survey as a means to measure whether this new method was helpful in increasing their motivation and becoming more active in the teaching–learning process.

2.2.2. Computer Tools

Many of the problems related to mathematics in the world of engineering are advanced. Thus, engineers need to use several competencies/skills to resolve these kinds of problems, such as the need to formulate the problem mathematically and knowledge about useful tools. However, currently, in many cases, this is not enough, and, depending on the difficulty of the problem at hand, in most cases, specific mathematical software is required to calculate some difficult operations.

In [13], the authors used operations and properties of matrices (which are complex and abstract concepts for our students) with the help of an application in digital imaging and data processing. Obviously, the resulting matrices have very large dimensions, and it would make no sense to do these calculations by hand. Today, computers are very much a part of the life of our students, and more and more computer tools are being used not only in teaching engineering but also by professionals.

At the University of Salamanca, during the activity, we had a license for Wolfram Mathematica [29], as well as MATLAB®. Additionally, Wolfram Alpha is available for use in the classroom for carrying out some small and fast calculations. Since our students solve many more simple exercises, we also teach them how to check their results using this software. Hence, the students are able to use these computer mathematical tools together with codes such as those described in Appendix A.

These codes and corresponding manuals are uploaded to the Moodle Learning Platform [30] and are available to students. Thus, students and teachers can access the work and activities at any time, and students have all resources available, allowing them to organize their work.

In this way, codes are provided to enhance the learning of students, but the goal is for them to develop the code that allows them to solve the problem. Codes can be uploaded to the Campus Virtual Studium (our Moodle platform) for the students to see, and the teacher can directly explain real problems and discuss how they should be solved. Therefore, the students come into contact with much more complicated calculations.

Wolfram Mathematica allows the student to work with code which is executed line by line. Modifications can be made in previous lines without the need to repeat introducing all the commands or generate scripts. In addition, the definition of functions is simpler and does not need to be raised separately. Therefore, this program was considered more suitable for carrying out this activity rather than other alternatives like MATLAB or similar free applications such as Octave or SciLab. These programs are very useful and can be used in other activities and subjects, especially those in which the use of matrices is necessary. However, Wolfram Mathematica was chosen in this case owing to its intuitiveness and the ability to introduce functions. In the past, other authors used Mathematica for very similar activities to teach algebra or calculus [13,14].

3. Development of Our Activities and Results

An increasingly technological and competitive environment requires the industrial engineer to pose very diverse problems. In its modeling and resolution, one of the most frequently used mathematical tools is multivariable (calculus) integrals. Therefore, engineering students must understand its importance and practical applications, as well as the computer tools available to facilitate their work.

However, many students, mainly in the first year, do not understand the importance of multivariable (calculus) integrals in engineering and limit themselves to learning mostly repetitive problems. Subsequently, this situation ends up causing the students to become less focused and motivated throughout the course.

Thus, we decided to introduce different real-life engineering problems where multivariable integral calculus is used and to show its different applications. Obviously, solving some of these problems can be quite complex and iterative; hence, the use of mathematical software was required.

The problem-based activity was carried out after having taught all the theoretical lessons on the basic principles of calculus in several variables, Thereby helping the students to link the knowledge acquired through real-life engineering cases.

This session lasted 2 h, with a 10 min break in the middle. In the first half (Section 3.1), the fourth-year student explained to the class several real-life exercises that he faced during the engineering degree, in which multivariable integration was needed to find the solution. For each problem, he first introduced the basic principles required to fully understand the path to the solution and, then, the answer was explained step by step. Finally, the fourth-year student talked about the different degree subjects each problem belonged to and what the students would learn from each one. In the second half of the class (Section 3.2), a complex topography problem was addressed, in which not only interpolation in several variables and integration was needed, but also computational mathematical tools (this exercise is described in Section 3.2 and solved in Appendix A with the help of Mathematica).

3.1. Real-Life Engineering Problems

Industrial engineering studies encompass very diverse areas of knowledge structured in different subjects, some of which were used in this activity.

Fluid mechanics is a second-year subject in which students learn the scientific fundamentals of the design and calculation of fluid systems and installations. To delve into these problems, it is first necessary to be able to characterize the properties of a given fluid. For this reason, the exercise proposed consisted of designing a coaxial cylinder viscosimeter to determine the properties of a lubricant. This apparatus works by rotating an internal cylinder immersed in some given fluid and measuring the power needed to turn it at a certain speed. By knowing the rotation speed of the cylinder and the properties of the lubricant, students are easily able to calculate the power required by the device using the shear stress of the fluid. To do so, double integrals are needed: one for the lateral surface of the cylinder and another one for the bottom surface.

Theory of machines and mechanisms is also a second-year course in which students learn about the modeling, calculation, and design of mechanisms and machines from a static, kinematic, and dynamic point of view. The suggested problem in this area consists of balancing the crankshaft of an engine with the help of CAD/CAE Software such as Autodesk Inventor. An initial model of a simplified and unbalanced engine crankshaft is given, which means that its center of gravity is not aligned with its axis of rotation. Using the design software mentioned and multivariable integrals, students come up with a fixed design by changing the geometry of the initial mechanism to move the centroid. As the center of gravity is above the axis, a semi-cylindrical volume is added in the lower bar, forcing it downward. Therefore, they calculate the diameter of the added volume so that the centroid matches the rotation shaft. For that, triple integrals are needed to obtain the center of mass of the half cylinder.

Other real engineering examples mentioned during the first half of the activity were about the following:

- Industrial robots and manipulators. One of the most important features of these automatons is their work range, i.e., the surface or volume represented by all the robot's positions in space. To calculate this, a manipulator position study is carried out obtaining a cloud of points with its limit positions. These data are interpolated, and, with multivariable integration, the range surface or volume can be obtained.
- Self-driving cars and LIDAR sensors. These active sensors scan their surroundings with an infrared laser, mapping thousands of points. The point cloud obtained is treated in a similar way to the previous problem.
- Metrology. Laser interferometers can be used to measure roughness. These perform a micrometric scan of the part to be analyzed creating a point cloud that approximates its surface. To calculate the volume of material that needs to be removed in a grinding operation to improve its finish, it is necessary to apply multivariable integration.
- Calculation of structures. It is increasingly common to see constructions with a quadric surface shape, since they have very interesting properties. For instance, the cooling towers of nuclear power plants are shaped like hyperboloids, to boost natural convection and expel hot gases outside.

All of these cases were described in different subjects using mechanical and electrical engineering examples. Anuar R. Giménez (the first author of this paper) made a collection and briefly described them in the first hour of the practical case activity (third section in the whole activity; see Figure 1). During the second hour of the activity, Anuar described and explained in detail how he solved the problem that appears in Section 3.2. This was a problem the students had already solved in the subject topography which is compulsory in the mechanical engineering degree. However, in this subject, they solved it with computer tools, and the mathematical aspects were not explained in detail.

3.2. Estimating the Volume of a Building Excavation, from a Point Cloud Collected by Topography Measurements

Among the attributes and competencies of an industrial engineer is the ability to design, build, and operate structures and buildings for industrial use. The construction process consists of several phases. One of the most important stages is the taking of measurements directly on the ground and precisely transferring them to paper. This basic operation is known as topographic surveying. That is why topography is part of the curricula in these studies.

The activity that we developed consists of estimating the volume of excavated material needed to raise an industrial building, from a series of measurements made with a theodolite on a plot of a nearby town. The provided data are the Cartesian coordinates (X, Y, Z) of a series of points (identified with signals on the ground) referred to an origin, which will determine the depth of emptying.

Indeed, the position of each point is obtained in polar coordinates (r, φ, θ). The device used gives, for each point, an azimuthal and a zenithal angle measurement, as well as the distance between the instrument and the point of sight, using the stadia method. Applying basic trigonometry, the projections of each point are obtained on cardinal directions axes. Therefore, cartesian coordinates are calculated.

To ease understanding and simplify the calculations, only 13 terrain signals were set, as can be seen in Figure 2.

The procedure used to solve the suggested problem can be structured in three steps:

(i) Finding an interpolating polynomial that fits the point cloud set up by the previous coordinates. For this, the least squares adjustment method is used. We calculate the coefficients of the polynomial (introduced in Appendix A) so that they minimize the quadratic error between the interpolating function and the data points. The approximation obtained is shown in Figure 2. This is a fourth-order polynomial in x and y, with 12 terms (12 unknown coefficients determined).

(ii) Determining the equations of the different lines between the perimeter points, in order to establish the limits of integration with which the volume will be calculated later.
(iii) Subdividing the prismoid formed by the coordinates of each plot point and the origin plane in different integrable prisms. Its edges are defined by the equations of the line obtained previously. The total volume of the excavation is calculated as the sum of the volumetric integrals of these bodies.

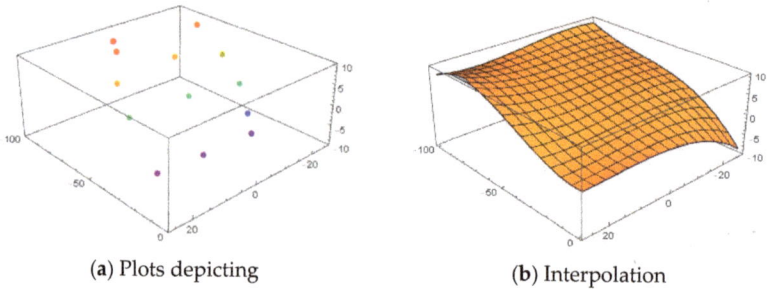

(a) Plots depicting (b) Interpolation

Figure 2. (a) Representation of the plot's relief, with a 13-point cloud in cartesian coordinates. (b) Its numerical approximation with an interpolating polynomial obtained with the least squares method.

When it comes to developing the scripts for doing the calculations, interesting setbacks arose that were successfully solved. The values of the obtained coordinates were measured on the field using a reference origin with a position of (500 m, 500 m, 500 m). This resulted in very high values during the calculation which the program truncated. Therefore, we obtained an inconsistent final result. To solve this, the points were transferred to an equivalent reference system centered at (0, 0, 0), obtaining more congruent values. If the coordinate origin was not changed, some numbers in matrix A were O (10^{10}). These types of difficulties and related mishaps appear in the daily work of an engineer, and the results provided by software may be erroneous if they are not correctly interpreted.

There are commercial programs available to the engineer such as TopoCal 2016 [31], capable of resolving the issue raised. However, students are not aware of the mathematics behind this type of software. After carrying out the activity, it is interesting that students acquire a general idea of the different calculation tools used by these programs, such as multivariable integration or interpolation, as seen with the mentioned example.

It is also important to familiarize the students with mathematical software from the subjects in the first year, as they are very powerful tools that are used to solve some real problems in engineering, also in addition to complementing their training. That is why, in Appendix A, some small scripts examples are included, so that they can complete calculations in mathematics.

3.3. Questionnaire

Since the purpose of this paper was to analyze the methodology explained above, we conducted a pre-test and post-test questionnaire on students in different bachelor's degrees of industrial engineering. This included 15 questions about different items that were to be measured. The questionnaire was carried out in Salamanca before and after the use of the activities proposed in this study.

Students were able to answer each one of these questions using a scale from 1 to 5, where 1 meant the student totally disagreed and 5 meant they totally agreed. Question Q1 measures the student's opinion about mathematics. Q2 and Q3 measure extrinsic motivation, while Q4 measures intrinsic motivation. Q5 measures the usefulness of the practical class using software with respect to the theoretical one. Q6 measures the student's opinion about using a computer. Q7 and Q8 measure the student's perception about how useful the activity is to solve real problems. Q9 addresses the scalability of the activity. Q10 assesses the student's perception about their computer skills. Finally, Q11 and Q12 address student's the opinion on the part of the activity taught by the fourth-year student. This questionnaire was completed by the students before (pre-test) and after the activity (post-test) in order to identify possible differences in the students' responses.

The questions included in the survey are shown in Table 2, and the descriptive statistics for the responses to the pre-test and post-test questionnaire are shown in Table 3.

Table 2. All questions included in the questionnaire with a Likert scale.

Code	Question	Category
Q1	I think mathematics is a field closely related to engineering.	Motivation
Q2	I think that integral calculus is related to other subjects in my degree course.	Motivation
Q3	I think that integral calculus will be important in my professional career.	Motivation
Q4	The math classes are fun and catch my interest.	Motivation
Q5	I think a math class with practical applications, like this one, is more useful than a conventional class.	Usability
Q6	I think computers are needed when teaching math.	Usability
Q7	The activities of this subject serve to organize my learning and to be able to approach solving problems of different types in a structured way (and not just learn mathematical content).	Critical thinking
Q8	Knowing the formulas of the surface and the length of the line in different types of coordinates (cartesian, parametric, and polar) can help me solve real-life problems.	Critical thinking
Q9	Activities that mix engineering and mathematics should also be included when learning other subjects.	Usability
Q10	I think my computer skills are high.	Usability
Q11	I think it is a good idea for a senior classmate to teach a math class.	Usability
Q12	When I am a fourth-year student grade and see the usefulness of mathematics in other subjects, I would like the opportunity to give a class to first-year students.	Usability

Table 3. Questions included in the questionnaire. All of them were evaluated using a Likert scale.

Question		Mean	Standard Deviation	Standard Error
Q1	Pre-test	4.29	0.77	0.19
	Post-test	4.47	0.62	0.15
Q2	Pre-test	3.77	1.09	0.26
	Post-test	4.35	0.49	0.12
Q3	Pre-test	3.06	1.25	0.30
	Post-test	4.12	0.78	0.19
Q4	Pre-test	2.24	1.15	0.28
	Post-test	3.18	1.13	0.27
Q5	Pre-test	3.76	1.03	0.25
	Post-test	4.06	0.75	0.18
Q6	Pre-test	3.41	0.87	0.21
	Post-test	3.65	0.93	0.22
Q7	Pre-test	3.35	0.79	0.19
	Post-test	3.59	0.87	0.21
Q8	Pre-test	2.71	0.99	0.24
	Post-test	3.82	1.01	0.25
Q9	Pre-test	3.77	0.97	0.24
	Post-test	4.18	0.81	0.20
Q10	Pre-test	3.00	1.00	0.24
	Post-test	2.88	1.11	0.27
Q11	Pre-test	4.00	0.71	0.17
	Post-test	4.24	0.75	0.18
Q12	Pre-test	2.65	1.37	0.33
	Post-test	2.71	1.31	0.32

Through these questions, the authors attempted to measure several important issues related to the teaching–learning process such as motivation, usability, and critical thinking.

4. Discussion on the Results

4.1. Questionnaire Given to First-Year Students

In the case of the pre-test, a standardized Cronbach's alpha coefficient of 0.71955 was obtained. In the post-test, a standardized alpha equal to 0.83614 was obtained. These results can be considered good and are in line with other results reported for questionnaires of a similar type [13].

In general terms, the students, after carrying out the activity, considered that mathematics is close to engineering ($\bar{x} = 4.294$, $SE = 0.151$), and that integrals are related to other subjects of their degree course ($\bar{x} = 4.353$, $SE = 0.120$).

The students also believe that multivariable (calculus) integrals will be useful for their future professional career ($\bar{x} = 4.118$, $SE = 0.190$), and that lessons based on practical applications are more useful than theoretical classes ($\bar{x} = 4.06$, $SE = 0.181$). They also are of the opinion that activities that mix both mathematics and engineering should be included when teaching or learning other subjects ($\bar{x} = 4.060$, $SE = 0.181$). The students also considered the proposed methodology (shown by a fourth-year student) to be a good idea ($\bar{x} = 4.000$, $SE = 0.171$). However, they were not interested in participating as a fourth-year student in the future ($\bar{x} = 2.7059$, $SE = 0.318$). In this last question, the dispersion results were noticeably higher than in other questions; hence, a high polarization in terms of the answer was expected (hypothetically motivated by the fact that some students have teacher vocation and others do not). Lastly, there is no clear position regarding the consideration of mathematics as fun and attractive ($\bar{x} = 3.177$, $SE = 0.274$), although the score was higher after the activity was carried out.

It can be observed that the mean results of the post-test were more favorable than those of the pre-test for all questions raised, except for question Q10. According to the students' responses, the activity caused students to consider their computer skills to be inferior. This may hypothetically be due to the complexity of the software and the need to use programming code to solve the activity.

Once the descriptive analysis of both pre-test and post-test responses were analyzed (Table 3), a hypothesis contrast based on Levene's test for equality of variances (to check the homoscedasticity) and on the *t*-test for equality of means was applied.

Statistically significant differences were detected between the pre- and post-test results for questions Q3, Q4, and Q8. The results showed that the activity changed the students' perception about the importance of mathematics for their professional career (Q3) (T(28.86) = 2.964, *p*-value = 0.006) and about the perception that math could be fun and appealing (Q4) (T(32) = 2.409, *p*-value = 0.022). Please note that question Q4 was related to the intrinsic motivation of the student, while questions Q2 and Q3 were related to the extrinsic motivation. Lastly, differences were detected regarding specific issues about the activity (Q8) (T(32) = 3.258, *p*-value = 0.003).

Since the parametric statistical treatment of Likert type data can be a controversial issue when an ordinal scale is used, two approaches were applied: parametric and nonparametric tests [32]. An interval scale is handled using parametric statistics [33], but some authors have argued that nonparametric statistics should be used [34]. In this way, different nonparametric tests (median test, Mann–Whitney U test, Kolmogorov–Smirnov test, and Kruskal–Wallis test) were also applied. The results of these tests are shown in Table 4.

Table 4. The *p*-values of all questions included in the survey were rated using a Likert scale. Results in bold are those where the *p*-value was below the significance level (0.05).

Test	Q1	Q2	Q3	Q4	Q5	Q6	Q7	Q8	Q9	Q10	Q11	Q12
Kolmogorov–Smirnov	1.00	0.454	**0.046**	0.240	0.954	0.954	0.954	**0.046**	0.954	1.00	0.954	1.00
Median test	1.00	0.707	0.396	0.120	1.00	0.493	0.493	**0.016**	0.463	0.463	1.000	1.000
Mann–Whitney U	0.586	0.131	**0.012**	**0.024**	0.540	0.433	0.413	**0.003**	0.259	0.786	0.375	0.838
Kruskal–Wallis	0.542	0.087	**0.008**	0.200	0.495	0.403	0.366	**0.002**	0.223	0.774	0.332	0.830

First, the Kolmogorov–Smirnov test was applied, which showed that questions Q4 and Q8 did not conform to a normal distribution. The Mann–Whitney test (like the t-test for the parametric approach) also showed the existence of statistically significant differences between pre-test and post-test for questions Q3 (p-value = 0.012), Q4 (p-value = 0.024), and Q8 (p-value = 0.003), while the median test only detected the existence of significant differences in the median for question Q8 (p-value = 0.016). The Kruskal–Wallis test showed statistically significant differences for Q3 (p-value = 0.008) and Q8 (p-value = 0.002). According to the results, the existence of statistically significant differences in the questions Q3, Q4, and Q8 was demonstrated for a nonparametric approach based on different statistics. These results are compatible with those obtained by the parametric tests.

4.2. Participant Observation

Through the results obtained from the questionnaires, a quantitative analysis of the proposed methodology was carried out. The fourth-year student taking part in the activity and the professor teaching the subject assessed the feedback received from a qualitative point of view. Once the activity was completed, the student wrote a report on the observations made.

The fourth-year student found the activity rewarding, as it allowed him to empathize with his fellow students by sharing his experience and making it easier for them to face difficult mathematical concepts in a more enjoyable and practical way. He stated the following:

"I consider that these teaching methodologies are very enriching for both students and teachers. The mathematics subjects taught in the first years of engineering are usually very theoretical and overwhelm many students. In my opinion, exploring real-world problems and challenges from early grades drives students to obtain a deeper knowledge of the subjects they are studying and encourages them to develop confidence and motivation. Personally, I would have loved to participate in this type of activity when I first entered college.

At the beginning of the activity, I noticed how the students seemed curious and were excited to do something new, outside the usual routine. As the session progressed, although some of them were rather clueless, most students remained attentive and really seemed to be interested in what we were doing. Overall, the atmosphere was quite welcoming. I would highly recommend other senior students to continue carrying out these experiences."

It is worth stressing that the exercise that seemed to motivate the students the most was about balancing the crankshaft of an engine, perhaps because many of them were enrolled in mechanical engineering. When the class finished, the fourth-year student had a good overall feeling. Even a few days later, a couple of students asked him questions about different subjects they would be taking the following year.

The fourth-year student also mentioned how his perspective on calculus in several variables had changed during each subject over the course of this university degree. When he was first introduced to this area, he had problems understanding its theoretical basis and found the subject complex; therefore, he became discouraged. Moreover, he did not find it useful in other engineering subjects. It was not until third year, while studying surveying, that he realized its importance, as he needed multivariable integration to estimate the volume of an industrial building excavation.

In sum, he considered these activities to be helpful for most students, not only in terms of realizing the relationship between mathematical tools taught in first year subjects and other engineering areas, but also in appreciating the relevance of this subject in terms of their future career. As a student in his last year of a mechanical and electrical engineering double degree, he realized that calculus is a key tool for solving many real problems in all branches of industrial engineering. Therefore, associating real engineering applications with mathematical concepts that might seem complex could help first-year students to better understand them. Since some of the activities carried out included complex and iterative operations, mathematical software was required. This could also help the students understand the mathematical operations behind certain functions of some commercial programs that they might use in their studies and professional career, drawing their attention to programing.

This teaching experience allowed the fourth-year student to gain mathematical knowledge as he had to return to studying calculus in several variables, in a more in-depth way and from a different point of view. The experience also permitted him to improve his public communication skills and sparked an interest in teaching. For this reason, he suggested that it might be very enriching for future fourth-year students to take part in similar activities.

At the end of the activity, the professor asked several students their opinion about the experience. The students who responded affirmed their preference for this type of activity rather than solving more theoretical exercises, and they liked hearing from a more experienced peer about the usefulness of calculus in other types of subjects normally associated with their engineering degrees. His comments confirmed the results later observed in the questionnaire described above.

5. Conclusions

Students should be able to solve daily mathematical-related problems throughout their professional careers. Therefore, as instructors, we are obliged to provide them with the tools for solving real problems and teach students how to apply them for the benefit of society. Additionally, new university programs and requirements, as well as societal demands, require the subjects to be as practical as possible. This in turn has encouraged teachers to redesign and rethink how subjects are taught, where subjects are made more attractive to students. This is particularly true for a topic like mathematics, since students generally have problems understanding the concepts and do not like the theoretical part of math-related subjects. For this reason, in this work, an activity was carried out aimed at improving motivation for learning mathematics in a group of students studying in different degrees associated with the field of industrial engineering. The activity involved the participation of a fourth-year student, who is a coauthor of this paper, who explained how to resolve problems to first-year students. During his explanation of the activity, the fourth-year student also tried to explain to the students his perception regarding the importance of mathematics in terms of the subjects he had taken over the course of his degree. At the same time, the teacher responsible for the subject observed the behavior of the students and the progress of the activity.

The activity was based on solving different real-life engineering problems in which multivariable integrals were needed to find the solution, enriching the knowledge acquired in a competency-based mathematics subject using a problem-based teaching method. The exercises carried out covered quite different areas, such as fluid mechanics or construction and topography, some of them involving several calculations; therefore, mathematical software was required.

First, the students completed a pre-test questionnaire, and, once the activity had been completed, the students then completed a post-test questionnaire with the same questions as those presented in the pre-test questionnaire. The results of the questionnaire indicated that the students on a general level do not perceive mathematics as a fun subject. This response is in line with other published reports on the topic [14]. Additionally, the results of the questionnaire were consistent with what both the fourth-year student and the professor observed in the classroom during the activity, showing that, overall, the activity was satisfactory and motivating in general terms. The students indicated that they would like to carry out more activities of this type, which they considered to be helpful for problem solving, although the results also indicated that the students did not wish to participate in the future as a fourth-year student.

The results of pre-test and post-test questionnaire were compared using parametric and nonparametric inferential techniques. Both tests provided similar results, the most remarkable being that statistically significant differences were found for questions measuring intrinsic motivation, extrinsic motivation, and the usefulness of the activity to solve real problems similar to those reported in other studies [13,14,34].

Lastly, protocols should be developed if we want that students in the latest years of our degrees show specific tasks/problems to the first-year students related to the practical application of mathematics in engineering.

Author Contributions: All authors contributed equally to this work. All authors have read and agreed to the published version of the manuscript.

Funding: This research received no external funding.

Institutional Review Board Statement: Not applicable.

Informed Consent Statement: Not applicable.

Conflicts of Interest: The authors declare no conflict of interest.

Appendix A

Estimating the volume of a building excavation

The comments in the code used in the classroom are in Spanish for academic purposes. In this work, they have been translated into English to allow readers to understand them.

(* From the Excel file, we import data that the students previously calculated in another third-year subject. *)

data = Import["C:\\data_palomares.xlsx"][[1]]

{{−0.937085, −5.90457, 0.492498}, {13.5512, −7.28953, 0.326174}, {25.4282, −9.473, 0.168468}, {18.6554, −40.5825, 3.69048}, {−6.18117, −16.894, 1.41553}, {−13.2269, −33.8948, 3.37329}, {−7.95319, −66.4691, 6.04395}, {12.8675, −61.5239, 5.9983}, {2.85255, −84.6279, 7.25412}, {−0.12187, −93.8704, 7.74539}, {−26.3122, −86.2181, 7.02484}, {−19.8547, −56.455, 5.19855}, {1.05622, −39.5746, 3.50618}}

data = {{−0.93708456`, −5.90457219`, 0.49249848`}, {13.551175`, −7.28952502`, 0.32617372`}, {25.4281851`, −9.47299653`, 0.16846814`}, {18.6554001`, −40.5824811`, 3.69047693`}, {−6.18117493`, −16.8939747`, 1.41553061`}, {−13.2268731`, −33.8947756`, 3.37329311`}, {−7.95318955`, −66.4691303`, 6.04395385`}, {12.8674808`, −61.5238784`, 5.99830393`}, {2.85254857`, −84.6279358`, 7.25411933`}, {−0.12186975`, −93.8704137`, 7.74539119`}, {−26.312194`, −86.2180903`, 7.02483645`}, {−19.8547003`, −56.4550142`, 5.1985514`}, {1.056217`, −39.574576`, 3.506184`}};

(* We must choose how we want the polynomials to be. We want the polynomials to be like the one below (for example). *)

pol[x_, y_] = a1 + a2*x + a3*y + a4*x^2 + a5*x*y + a6*y^2 + a7*x^3 + a8*x^2*y + a9*x*y^2 + a10*y^3 + a11*x*y^3 + a12*x^2*y^2;

(* Thus, the system of vectors, the generators of our vector space, is formed by means of the below phi functions. *)

phi[i_, x_, y_] =
Which[i == 1, 1, i == 2, x, i == 3, y, i == 4, x^2, i == 5, x*y,
i == 6, y^2, i == 7, x^3, i == 8, x^2*y, i == 9, x*y^2, i == 10,
y^3, i == 11, x*y^3, i == 12, x^2*y^2];

(* Now, we can calculate the coefficients of the polynomial that reaches (or is closest to all the points from our Excel file, depending on the dimensions of our problem). We evaluate our basis in all the points and solve the least squares problem. *)

A = Table[phi[j, data[[i, 1]], data[[i, 2]]], {i, 1, Length[data]}, {j, 1, 12}];

b = Table[data[[i, 3]], {i, 1, Length[data]}];

LeastSquares[A, b]

{0.0565949, 0.0797015, −0.070381, −0.00583912, 0.00981652, 0.000672554, 0.000107678, −0.000217221, 0.00022677, 5.86501*10^−6, 1.46394*10^−6, −1.51735*10^−6}

(* This problem can also be solved as an optimization problem, and Plot3D can be used to draw our polynomial and compare it with the real points as shown in Figure A1. *)

NMinimize[dist, {a1, a2, a3, a4, a5, a6, a7, a8, a9, a10, a11, a12}]

{0.00415069, {a1 -> 0.0565949, a2 -> 0.0797015, a3 -> −0.070381, a4 -> −0.00583912, a5 -> 0.00981652, a6 -> 0.000672554, a7 -> 0.000107678, a8 -> −0.000217221, a9 -> 0.00022677, a10 -> 5.86501*10^−6, a11 -> 1.46394*10^−6, a12 -> −1.51735*10^−6}}

In[11]:= Z[x_, y_] = pol[x, y] /. {a1 → 0.05659488760297747`, a2 → 0.07970150315538359`, a3 → -0.07038101175614282`, a4 → -0.005839117879023703`, a5 → 0.009816523263871687`, a6 → 0.0006725538797118747`, a7 → 0.0001076776122910887`, a8 → -0.00021722071036437375`, a9 → 0.00022677038687355584`, a10 → 5.865014189925957`*^-6, a11 → 1.463936133060352`*^-6, a12 → -1.5173512154792845`*^-6}

Out[11]= 0.0565949 + 0.0797015 x - 0.00583912 x² + 0.000107678 x³ - 0.070381 y + 0.00981652 x y - 0.000217221 x² y + 0.000672554 y² + 0.00022677 x y² - 1.51735×10⁻⁶ x² y² + 5.86501×10⁻⁶ y³ + 1.46394×10⁻⁶ x y³

In[71]:= Plot3D[Z[x, y], {x, -27, 27}, {y, -100, 0}, PlotRange → {-10, 10}, ColorFunction → "Rainbow"]

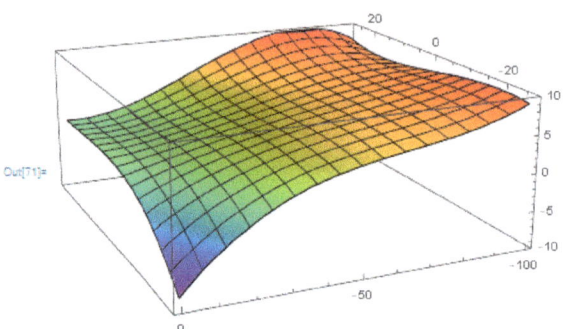

Figure A1. Approximation of the plot´s relief with an interpolating polynomial obtained previously with the least squares method.

(* Finally, we are ready to approximate the volume. *)

ord1 = Ordering[data]; (* Order of the coordinates *)
data2 = {{−26.312194`, −86.2180903`, 7.02483645`},{−19.8547003`, −56.4550142`, 5.1985514`}, {−13.2268731`, −33.8947756`, 3.37329311`},{−0.93708456`, −5.90457219`, 0.49249848`}, {13.551175`, −7.28952502`, 0.32617372`},{25.4281851`, −9.47299653`, 0.16846814`},{18.6554001`, −40.5824811`, 3.69047693`}, {−6.18117493`, −16.8939747`, 1.41553061`},{12.8674808`, −61.5238784`, 5.99830393`}, {2.85254857`, −84.6279358`, 7.25411933`},{−0.12186975`, −93.8704137`, 7.74539119`},{−26.312194`, −86.2180903`, 7.02483645`}};

(* We calculate the lines that will be used in the integration. *)
For[i = 1,i < Length[data2],i++,
m[i] = (data2[[i + 1,2]]-data2[[i,2]])/(data2[[i + 1,1]]-data2[[i,1]]);
b[i] = data2[[i,2]]-m[i]*data2[[i,1]]
];
Integrate[Z[x, y],{x,data2[[1,1]],data2[[2,1]]},{y,(m [11]*x + b [11]),(m [1]*x + b [1])}] +
Integrate[Z[x, y],{x,data2[[2,1]],data2[[3,1]]},{y,(m [11]*x + b [11]),(m [2]*x + b [2])}] +
Integrate[Z[x, y],{x,data2[[3,1]],data2[[4,1]]},{y,(m [11]*x + b [11]),(m [3]*x + b [3])}] +
Integrate[Z[x, y],{x,data2[[4,1]],data2[[5,1]]},{y,(m [11]*x + b [11]),(m [4]*x + b [4])}] +
Integrate[Z[x, y],{x,data2[[5,1]],data2[[11,1]]},{y,(m [11]*x + b [11]),(m [5]*x + b [5])}] +

Integrate[Z[x, y],{x,data2[[11,1]],data2[[10,1]]},{y,(m [10]*x + b [10]),(m [5]*x + b [5])}] +
Integrate[Z[x, y],{x,data2[[10,1]],data2[[9,1]]},{y,(m [9]*x + b [9]),(m [5]*x + b [5])}] +
Integrate[Z[x, y],{x,data2[[9,1]],data2[[6,1]]},{y,(m [8]*x + b [8]),(m [5]*x + b [5])}] +
Integrate[Z[x, y],{x,data2[[6,1]],data2[[8,1]]},{y,(m [8]*x + b [8]),(m [6]*x + b [6])}] +
Integrate[Z[x, y],{x,data2[[8,1]],data2[[7,1]]},{y,(m [7]*x + b [7]),(m [6]*x + b [6])}]

10070.1

(* The result is similar to others obtained using engineering software. *)

References

1. Kolmos, A.; De Graaff, E. Problem-Based and Project-Based Learning in Engineering Education: Merging Models. In *Cambridge Handbook of Engineering Education Research*; Johri, A.A., Olds, B., Eds.; Cambridge University Press: Cambridge, UK, 2014.
2. Seibert, S.A. Problem-based learning: A strategy to foster generation Z's critical thinking and perseverance. *Teach. Learn. Nurs.* **2021**, *16*, 85–88. [CrossRef] [PubMed]
3. Kolmos, A. Reflections on Project Work and Problem-based Learning. *European J. Eng. Educ.* **1996**, *21*, 141–148. [CrossRef]
4. Miner-Romanoff, K.; Rae, A.; Zakrzewski, C.E. A holistic and multifaceted model for ill-structured experiential problem-based learning: Enhancing student critical thinking and communication skills. *J. Probl. Based Learn. High. Educ.* **2019**, *7*, 70–96. [CrossRef]
5. Ballester, E.; Castro-Palacio, J.C.; Velázquez-Abad, L.; Giménez, M.H.; Monsoriu, J.A.; Sánchez-Ruiz, L.M. Smart physics with smartphone sensors. In Proceedings of the IEEE Frontiers in Education Conference (FIE), Madrid, Spain, 22–25 October 2014; pp. 1–4. [CrossRef]
6. Chans, G.M.; Bravo-Gutiérrez, M.E.; Orona-Navar, A.; Sánchez-Rodríguez, E.P. Compilation of Chemistry Experiments for an Online Laboratory Course: Student's Perception and Learning Outcomes in the Context of COVID-19. *Sustainability* **2022**, *14*, 2539. [CrossRef]
7. Mandavgane, S. Fun with fluid: An innovative assignment in fluid mechanics. *Educ. Chem. Eng.* **2020**, *30*, 40–48. [CrossRef]
8. Freudenthal, H. Geometry between the devil and the deep sea. In *The Teaching of Geometry at the Pre-College Level*; Springer: Dordrecht, The Netherlands, 1971; pp. 137–159.
9. Freudenthal, H. *Weeding and Sowing: Preface to a Science of Mathematical Education*; Springer: Dordrecht, The Netherlands, 1977.
10. Freudenthal, H. *Revisiting Mathematics Education: China Lectures*; Kluwer: Dordrecht, The Netherlands, 1991.
11. Van den Heuvel-Panhuizen, M.; Drijvers, P. Realistic mathematics education. In *Encyclopedia of Mathematics Education*; Springer: Dordrecht, The Netherlands, 2014; pp. 521–525.
12. Queiruga-Dios, A.; Encinas, A.H.; Rodríguez, G.; del Rey, A.M.; Martín-Vaquero, J.; Encinas, L.H. Case study: Malware propagation models for undergraduate engineering students. In Proceedings of the 4th International Conference on Technological Ecosystems for Enhancing Multiculturality (TEEM '16), Salamanca, Spain, 2–4 November 2016; Association for Computing Machinery: New York, NY, USA, 2016; pp. 931–935. [CrossRef]
13. Caridade, C.M.; Encinas, A.H.; Martín-Vaquero, J.; Queiruga-Dios, A. CAS and real life problems to learn basic concepts in Linear Algebra course. *Comput. Appl. Eng. Educ.* **2015**, *23*, 567–577. [CrossRef]
14. Caridade, C.; Encinas, A.H.; Martín-Vaquero, J.; Queiruga-Dios, A.; Rasteiro, D. Project-based teaching in Calculus courses: Estimation of the surface and perimeter of the Iberian Peninsula. *Comput. Appl. Eng. Educ.* **2018**, *26*, 1350–1361. [CrossRef]
15. English, L.D. Interdisciplinary Problem Solving: A Focus on Engineering Experiences. In Proceedings of the 31st Annual Conference of the Mathematics Education Research Group of Australasia, Brisbane, Australia, 28 June–1 July 2008.
16. Niss, M. Mathematical competencies and the learning of mathematics: The Danish KOM project. In Proceedings of the 3rd Mediterranean Conference on Mathematical Education, Athens, Greece, 3–5 January 2003; pp. 115–124.
17. Wang, C.K.J.; Liu, C.W.; Nie, Y.; Chye, Y.L.S.; Lim, B.S.C.; Liem, G.A.; Tay, E.-G.; Hong, Y.; Chiu, C. Latent profile analysis of students' motivation and outcomes in mathematics: An organismic integration theory perspective. *Heliyon* **2017**, *3*, e00308. [CrossRef]
18. Rodríguez, S.; Estévez, I.; Piñeiro, I.; Valle, A.; Vieites, T.; Regueiro, B. Perceived Competence and Intrinsic Motivation in Mathematics: Exploring Latent Profiles. *Sustainability* **2021**, *13*, 8707. [CrossRef]
19. Recber, S.; Isiksal, M.; Koç, Y. Investigating self-efficacy, anxiety, attitudes and mathematics achievement regarding gender and school type. *Ann. Psychol.* **2018**, *34*, 41–51. [CrossRef]
20. Rosário, P.; Lourenço, A.; Paiva, O.; Rodrigues, A.; Valle, A.; Tuero Herrero, E. Prediction of mathematics achievement: Effect of personal, socio educational and contextual variables. *Psicothema* **2012**, *24*, 289–295. [PubMed]
21. Talsma, K.; Schüz, B.; Schwarzer, R.; Norris, K. I believe, therefore I achieve (and vice versa): A meta-analytic cross-lagged panel analysis of self-efficacy and academic performance. *Learn. Individ. Differ.* **2018**, *61*, 136–150. [CrossRef]
22. Ryan, R.M.; Deci, E.L. Motivaciones intrínsecas y extrínsecas: Definiciones clásicas y nuevas direcciones. *Contemp. Educ. Psychol.* **2000**, *25*, 54–67. [CrossRef] [PubMed]
23. Ryan, R.M.; Deci, E.L. Intrinsic and extrinsic motivations: Classic definitions and new directions. *Contemp. Educ. Psychol.* **2000**, *25*, 54–67. [CrossRef] [PubMed]

24. Ryan, R.M.; Deci, E.L. Intrinsic and extrinsic motivation from a self-determination theory perspective: Definitions, theory, practices, and future directions. *Contemp. Educ. Psychol.* **2020**, *61*, 101860. [CrossRef]
25. Rodríguez-Martín, M.; Rodríguez-Gonzálvez, P.; Sánchez-Patrocinio, A.; Sánchez, J.R. Short CFD Simulation Activities in the Context of Fluid-Mechanical Learning in a Multidisciplinary Student Body. *Appl. Sci.* **2019**, *9*, 4809. [CrossRef]
26. Lubke, H.L.; Muthén, B. Applying multigroup confirmatory factor models for continuous outcomes to Likert scale data complicates meaningful group comparisons. *Struct. Equ. Modeling* **2004**, *11*, 514–515. [CrossRef]
27. *Mathematica, Version 12.11.2*; Wolfram Research, Inc.: Champaign, IL, USA, 2020.
28. Christensen, S.H.; Didier, C.; Jamison, A.; Meganck, M.; Mitcham, C.; Newberry, B. *Engineering Identities, Epistemologies and Values: Engineering Education and Practice in Context*; Springer: Berlin/Heidelberg, Germany, 2015; Volume 2, p. 170.
29. Hsu, T.C.; Chang, S.C.; Hung, Y.T. How to learn and how to teach computational thinking: Suggestions based on a review of the literature. *Comput. Educ.* **2018**, *126*, 296–310. [CrossRef]
30. Moodle. Moodle Help Guides for Staff. 2020. Available online: https://workspace.nottingham.ac.uk/display/Moodlehelp/Moodle+Help+Guides+for+staff (accessed on 3 May 2022).
31. *TopoCal, Version 5.0.404, Badajoz, EXT*; Cando Design, Inc.: South Shields, UK, 2016. Available online: http://www.topocal.com/ (accessed on 3 May 2022).
32. Rodríguez-Martín, M.; Vergara, D.; Rodríguez-Gonzálvez, P. Simulation of a Real Call for Research Projects as Activity to Acquire Research Skills: Perception Analysis of Teacher Candidates. *Sustainability* **2020**, *12*, 7431. [CrossRef]
33. Jamieson, S. Likert scales: How to (ab)use them. *Med. Educ.* **2004**, *38*, 1217–1218. [CrossRef]
34. Lee, Y.; Capraro, R.M.; Bicer, A. Affective mathematics engagement: A comparison of STEM PBL versus non-STEM PBL instruction. *Can. J. Sci. Math. Technol. Educ.* **2019**, *19*, 270–289. [CrossRef]

Article

Team Control Problem in Virtual Ellipsoid and Its Numerical Simulations

Zhiqing Dang, Zhaopeng Dai *, Yang Yu *, Long Zhang, Ang Su, Zhihang You and Hongwei Gao

School of Mathematics and Statistics, Qingdao University, Qingdao 266071, China; 2020020279@qdu.edu.cn (Z.D.); zhanglong_note@qdu.edu.cn (L.Z.); 2020020275@qdu.edu.cn (A.S.); 2020020276@qdu.edu.cn (Z.Y.); gaohongwei@qdu.edu.cn (H.G.)
* Correspondence: dzpeng@amss.ac.cn (Z.D.); yuyang1988@qdu.edu.cn (Y.Y.)

Abstract: There is tremendous interest in designing feedback strategy control for clusters in modern control theory. We propose a novel numerical solution to target team control problems by using the Hamilton formalism methods. In order to ensure the smooth wireless information exchange, all members of the team are located in a virtual ellipsoidal container during the whole movement process. An ellipsoidal container tube is constructed as the external state constraint of the team. The corresponding value function is then formulated based on collision avoidance conditions and energy constraints in the process of the team motion. Time-dependent partial differential equations are formulated based on Hamilton formalism, which have been solved numerically by using the traditional finite difference method (FDM). The objective of the presented method is to obtain optimal control and motion trajectory of the cluster at each moment. Lastly, we conduct a simulation study of unmanned aerial vehicles (UAVs) to demonstrate the performance of the proposed method.

Keywords: ellipsoidal trajectory; team control; value function; finite difference method

MSC: 93-10; 93A16; 49L12

1. Introduction

The control problem has always been an important research object in the field of mathematics. Many new theoretical results have been made such as Virtual Reference Feedback Tuning (VRFT) [1] and indirect adaptive iterative learning control (iAILC) scheme [2]. In particular, the feedback strategy design of the control system is one of the most important parts in modern mathematical control theory. It is widely used in synthesizing controls, for example, team motion in biological systems such as flocks of geese or schools of fish [3]. In this study, we focus on the method of guiding the team with members (named as "cluster") to move towards the given target set [4] by avoiding the collision among the cluster member, which is the key to realize the optimal control of the bionics cluster. This paper proposes a decentralized cluster control scheme with strong scalability, which can be widely used in aerospace engineering problems, such as the formation of unmanned aerial vehicles (UAVs), multiple spacecrafts cooperation in a specific orbit, multiple small satellites cooperation in the cavity of a large satellite, and so on.

The intelligent objects investigated in the team control problem include but are not limited to UAVs, ships, satellites, robots [5–7], and their applications in the fields of military, aerospace, and industry [8–10]. This kind of problem studies the control of a multi-agent system according to the requirements of distributed tasks during the process of moving to a specific target or direction given the constraints of maintaining a predetermined geometric form and other environmental limitations at the same time. The research scope of formation control mainly includes the following five aspects: formation generation, formation keeping, formation switching, formation obstacle avoidance, and formation adaptive problems. In the present literature, formation control methods mainly include leader–follower strategy [11–17], behavior-based method [18,19], virtual structure method [20–23], and artificial potential field method [24–26].

On the basis of Hamilton formalism, Kurzhanski et al. [27] described this kind of cluster motion by the terms of the corresponding Hamilton–Jacobi–Bellman (HJB) equation. Based on the duality theory of convex analysis [28], the solvable conditions for the trajectory of virtual ellipsoid were given in [29], where the optimal control model and the corresponding numerical simulation procedures were also provided. Although the mathematical model and solvable conditions of the cluster motion were available in [4,30], obtaining accurate and efficient numerical solutions is still a challenging problem that should develop new numerical techniques, which is pointed out by Kurzhanski in [30,31].

This work applies the Hamilton formalism methods to the numerical solutions of target team control problems described above. In this problem, the formation of clusters is decentralized and all members of the cluster should be located within the preset virtual ellipsoid container [4] during the entire movement process to ensure the smooth wireless information exchange among the members. Given the collision avoidance conditions and energy constraints, we present a mathematical model to formulate how the cluster members achieve the given target set. By solving the corresponding value function, we obtain the optimal controls of the members. Besides this, a numerical simulation based on the classical finite difference method (FDM) is provided. We then simulate algorithm by applying it to the formation of UAVs. This algorithm can be used to realize the formation of UAVs and control the entire UAV group to move to a preset target position simultaneously while maintaining the formation. The algorithm guarantees the optimal control of UAVs under the current constraints, which further proves the successful application of this algorithm to aerospace engineering problems.

Our study provides an alternative approach to solve decentralized cluster control problem and demonstrate the scalability and practical feasibility of the model. This model can be widely used in aerospace engineering problems. The method ensures the flexible and dynamic adjustment of the members' relative position, given the whole formation shape of the cluster remains stable. Finally, several extended applications of the model are provided to demonstrate the variability of the model.

Our method has significant advantages in dealing with such problems. It overcomes the inflexibility in the traditional rigid structure motion model in which the relative positions of the cluster members are fixed, thus, limiting the movement of the cluster when the obstacle avoidance or the formation strategy change is required, despite that the formation can be maintained to a certain extent. Compared with the traditional artificial potential field method [24–26], we solve the problem that the target is unreachable when the obstacle is too close to the target set while maintaining good formation. Besides this, the cluster control method proposed in this paper is a decentralized method, which has the advantages of high anti-interference and fault tolerance compared with the leader–follower strategy [11–17]. In addition, the traditional virtual structure method [20–23] cannot solve the obstacle avoidance problem well, but the cluster formation algorithm proposed in this paper can be solved by adding constraints in the value function.

The paper is organized as follows: The basic model is described in Section 2. The detailed problem statement is provided in Section 3, and the control problem of cluster members in the ellipsoid is solved in Section 4. We verify accuracy of the proposed method through comprehensive numerical examples in Section 5. In Section 6, we conduct a simulation study to demonstrate effectiveness of the proposed method. Lastly, concluding remarks are offered in the Section 7.

2. Basic Model

Define a non-degenerate ellipsoid [32] in $\mathbb{R}^n$:

$$\varepsilon(q, Q) = \{p \in \mathbb{R}^n : \langle p - q, Q^{-1}(p - q)\rangle \leq 1\}, q \in \mathbb{R}^n, Q \in \mathbb{R}^{n \times n}, Q = Q' > 0, \quad (1)$$

with center q and configuration matrix Q [33]. On a given finite time interval $[t_0, \theta]$, suppose functions $q(t)$, $Q(t)$ are piece-wise continuous differentiable and satisfy the following dynamic system of equations [29]:

$$\dot{q}(t) = A(t)q(t) + C(t)v(t), \quad q(t_0) = q^0, \tag{2}$$

$$\dot{Q}(t) = T(t)Q(t) + Q(t)T'(t) + B(t)V(t)B'(t), \tag{3}$$

$$T(t) = T'(t), V(t) = V'(t), Q(t_0) = Q^0, \tag{4}$$

where the coefficient matrices $A(t)$, $B(t)$, $C(t)$ and $T(t)$ are assumed to be continuously differentiable, $E_c[t] = \varepsilon(q(t), Q(t))$ represents the motion of the virtual ellipsoid whose continuity is given in Appendix A, and $v(t) \in \mathbb{R}^n$, $V(t) \in \mathbb{R}^{n \times n}$ control the trajectory of the center $q(t)$ of the ellipsoid and the configuration matrix $Q(t)$ of the ellipsoid, respectively. Systems (2)–(4) are considered under the constraints [29]:

$$\langle v(t), v(t) \rangle \leq \mu^2(t), \quad [V(t), V(t)] \leq v^2(t), \tag{5}$$

$$[Q(t), Q(t)] \leq \lambda_+^2, \quad \lambda_+ > 0, \tag{6}$$

$$[Q(t), Q(t)] \geq \lambda_-^2, \quad \lambda_+ > \lambda_- > 0, \tag{7}$$

where and elsewhere, angle brackets represent the inner product of vectors, and square brackets stand for the inner product of matrices. The inner product of matrices A and B is defined as $[A, B] = tr(A'B)$, where $tr(A'B)$ denotes the trace of matrix $A'B$ [34], suppose that functions $\mu^2(t)$ and $v^2(t)$ are piece-wise continuous functions with only finite first kind discontinuities. In summary, the inequality condition (5) is a constraint on energy consumption; conditions (6) and (7) are constraints of ellipsoid volume, where λ_+ and λ_- are given constants.

Consider the following equations of joint motions for a family of control systems:

$$\dot{x}(t) = u(t), \quad x \in \mathbb{R}^{n \times m}, u \in \mathbb{R}^{n \times m}, \tag{8}$$

$$x(t_0) = x^0, \tag{9}$$

$$x = \{x_1, x_2, \cdots, x_m\}, u = \{u_1, u_2, \cdots, u_m\}, \tag{10}$$

$$x_i = \begin{pmatrix} x_{i1} \\ x_{i2} \\ \vdots \\ x_{in} \end{pmatrix}, u_i = \begin{pmatrix} u_{i1} \\ u_{i2} \\ \vdots \\ u_{in} \end{pmatrix}, i = 1, \cdots, m, \tag{11}$$

and Equations (8)–(11) describe a joint motion of m systems with phase vectors $x_i, \dot{x}_i \in \mathbb{R}^n$, and controls $u_i \in \mathbb{R}^n (i = 1, \cdots, m)$ subject to hard geometrical constraints

$$u_i \in \mathcal{P}_i, i = 1, \cdots, m, \tag{12}$$

in which $\mathcal{P}_i \subset \mathbb{R}^n$ stands for a symmetric convex compact set.

Definition 1 ([4]). *A solution $x(t)$ of systems (8)–(11) described by m trajectories $x_i(t)$ is called a team motion on the interval $t \in [t_0, \theta]$ if the following constraints are fulfilled:*

$$\gamma^2 \leq d^2(x_j(t), x_k(t)), \quad 1 \leq j < k \leq m, \tag{13}$$

$$x_i(t) \in E_c[t] = \varepsilon(q(t), Q(t)) \subset R^n, \quad i = 1, \cdots, m, \tag{14}$$

where $d(x_j(t), x_k(t))$ is the Euclidean distance between points $x_j(t)$ and $x_k(t)$, and γ is a given constant. The team members satisfying the constraints (13) and (14) are named as a 'cluster'. Constraint (13) provides collision avoidance condition for each of the members located inside the cluster, while condition (14) ensures that every member is close to each other to maintain the overall formation shape. These two conditions must be consistent. The ellipsoid $E_c[t] = \varepsilon(q(t), Q(t))$, as shown in Equation (14), can represent a virtual structure which contains all cluster members and also satisfies the above-mentioned collision avoidance condition of the cluster members.

3. Problem Statement

Given a finite time interval $[t_0, \theta]$, a positive number $\sigma > 0$, an initial ellipsoid $E_c[t_0] = \varepsilon(q(t_0), Q(t_0))$, and the initial state $x(t_0)$ of cluster members, our goal is to find optimal controls $u_i(t)(i = 1, \cdots, m)$ over the above systems $x_i(t)(i = 1, \cdots, m)$ so that the cluster motion reaches a given target set under constraints (13) and (14), which is

$$\mathcal{M}_\sigma = \{q, Q : \langle q - m_f, q - m_f \rangle + [Q - M, Q - M] \leq \sigma^2, M = M' > 0\}. \tag{15}$$

Here the target set $\mathcal{M}_\sigma$ is given in the form of the neighborhood of an ellipsoid $E_M = \varepsilon(m_f, M)$.

This problem mentioned above can be divided into two sub-problems. The first is to find the control of the ellipsoid so as to obtain the motion of the virtual ellipsoid in the time interval $[t_0, \theta]$ and satisfy $E_c(\theta) \in \mathcal{M}_\sigma$, that is, the system (2)–(4) with the constraints (5)–(7) reaches the preset set of targets. Solving this problem is equivalent to minimizing the following function:

$$\begin{aligned}\Psi(t, q, Q | \alpha_1, \alpha_2, \beta_1, \beta_2, v(\cdot), V(\cdot)) = \int_t^\theta \Big(\alpha_1 \langle v(\tau), v(\tau) \rangle \\ + \alpha_2 [V(\tau), V(\tau)] + \beta_1(\lambda_+^2 - [Q(\tau), Q(\tau)]) + \beta_2([Q(\tau), Q(\tau)] - \lambda_-^2) \Big) d\tau \\ + (\langle q(\theta) - m_f, D(q(\theta) - m_f) \rangle + [Q(\theta) - M, \mathcal{D}(Q(\theta) - M)]),\end{aligned} \tag{16}$$

where the constant coefficients $\alpha_1, \alpha_2, \beta_1, \beta_2 \geq 0$, the configuration parameters $D = D' > 0$, and $\mathcal{D} = \mathcal{D}' > 0$. The solution to this problem has been given in [29]. The second is to obtain the numerical solutions of target team control problems under the constraints (13) and (14), which is another important part of the present paper.

4. Control of Cluster Members in the Ellipsoid

The solution of the first problem generates function $E_c(t)$, which is the virtual ellipsoid tube containing the cluster $x(t)$ and finally moving to the target set $\mathcal{M}_\sigma$. The main idea of the method to solve the second problem is using the pre-constructed motion $E_c(t)$ as the reference motion. Therefore, the problem can be divided into two situations: One is when the initial state of the cluster satisfies $x(t_0) \notin E_c(t_0)$, the cluster members gather towards the virtual ellipsoid. The other is when the initial state of the cluster satisfies $x(t_0) \in E_c(t_0)$, the cluster members follow the virtual ellipsoid tube to reach the given target set.

Consider the dynamic equations of the systems (8)–(11) with the constraints (13) and (14). Different to the methods available in existing literatures, which are to maximize the distance between m members, this paper considers minimizing the following function:

$$\begin{aligned}\varphi(t, x, u) = \int_t^\theta \Big(\omega \sum_{i=1}^m \langle u_i(\tau), u_i(\tau) \rangle + \sum_{i=1}^m \beta_i \langle x_i(\tau) - q(\tau), Q^{-1}(\tau)(x_i(\tau) - q(\tau)) \rangle \\ - \frac{1}{2} \Big(\sum_{1 \leq i < j \leq m} \kappa_{ij} \langle x_i(\tau) - x_j(\tau), x_i(\tau) - x_j(\tau) \rangle \\ + \sum_{1 \leq i < j \leq m} \kappa_{ji} \langle x_j(\tau) - x_i(\tau), x_j(\tau) - x_i(\tau) \rangle \Big) \Big) d\tau \\ + \sum_{i=1}^m \langle x_i(\theta) - m_i, x_i(\theta) - m_i \rangle,\end{aligned} \tag{17}$$

where $\omega, \beta_i, \kappa_{ij}, \kappa_{ji} \geq 0 (i, j = 1, \cdots, m)$ are constant coefficients, $m_i \in \mathcal{M}_\sigma (i, j = 1, \cdots, m)$ are the terminal targets of each cluster member, $\langle u_i(\tau), u_i(\tau) \rangle$ depicts the energy consumed during the movement of the cluster members, $\langle x_i(\tau) - q(\tau), Q^{-1}(\tau)(x_i(\tau) - q(\tau))\rangle$ describes the distance between the cluster members and the virtual ellipsoid, $\langle x_i(\tau) - x_j(\tau), x_i(\tau) - x_j(\tau)\rangle$ represents the distance between cluster members, and the last one $\langle x_i(\theta) - m_i, x_i(\theta) - m_i \rangle$ figures the gap between the terminal state of the cluster members and the terminal target.

According to the above analysis, the corresponding value function (objective function) can be established as follows:

$$\begin{aligned}
V_E(t,x) = \min_{u_i(\cdot)} \Big\{ &\int_t^\theta \Big(\omega \sum_{i=1}^m \langle u_i(\tau), u_i(\tau)\rangle + \sum_{i=1}^m \beta_i \langle x_i(\tau) - q(\tau), Q^{-1}(\tau)(x_i(\tau) - q(\tau))\rangle \\
&- \frac{1}{2}\Big(\sum_{1 \le i < j \le m} \kappa_{ij} \langle x_i(\tau) - x_j(\tau), x_i(\tau) - x_j(\tau)\rangle \\
&+ \sum_{1 \le i < j \le m} \kappa_{ji} \langle x_j(\tau) - x_i(\tau), x_j(\tau) - x_i(\tau)\rangle \Big) \Big) d\tau \\
&+ \sum_{i=1}^m \langle x_i(\theta) - m_i, x_i(\theta) - m_i\rangle \Big\},
\end{aligned}$$
(18)

with the terminal condition $V_E(\theta, x) = \sum_{i=1}^m \langle x_i(\theta) - m_i, x_i(\theta) - m_i \rangle$. It is interesting to note that the value function (18) is the solution of the following HJB equation:

$$\begin{aligned}
\frac{\partial V_E}{\partial t} + \min_{u_i(\cdot)} \Big\{ &\sum_{i=1}^m \langle \frac{\partial V_E}{\partial x_i}, \dot{x}_i \rangle + \omega \sum_{i=1}^m \langle u_i(t), u_i(t) \rangle + \sum_{i=1}^m \beta_i \langle x_i - q, Q^{-1}(x_i - q)\rangle \\
&- \frac{1}{2}\Big(\sum_{1 \le i < j \le m} \kappa_{ij}\langle x_i - x_j, x_i - x_j\rangle + \sum_{1 \le i < j \le m} \kappa_{ji} \langle x_j - x_i, x_j - x_i\rangle \Big) \\
&\Big| x_i = x_i(t), q = q(t), Q = Q(t) \Big\} = 0.
\end{aligned}$$
(19)

For briefly, assume

$$\begin{aligned}
F = &\sum_{i=1}^m \langle \frac{\partial V_E}{\partial x_i}, \dot{x}_i\rangle + \omega \sum_{i=1}^m \langle u_i(t), u_i(t)\rangle + \sum_{i=1}^m \beta_i \langle x_i - q, Q^{-1}(x_i - q)\rangle \\
&- \frac{1}{2}\Big(\sum_{1 \le i < j \le m} \kappa_{ij} \langle x_i - x_j, x_i - x_j\rangle + \sum_{1 \le i < j \le m} \kappa_{ji} \langle x_j - x_i, x_j - x_i\rangle \Big),
\end{aligned}$$
(20)

and from

$$\frac{\partial F}{\partial u_i(t)} = 0, \quad i = 1, \cdots, m,$$
(21)

we can obtain

$$u_i(t) = -\frac{1}{2\omega} \frac{\partial V_E}{\partial x_i}, \quad i = 1, \cdots, m.$$
(22)

According to the quadratic form of x_i in Equation (18), we construct the value function $V_E(t,x)$ as

$$\begin{aligned}
V_E(t,x) = &\sum_{i=1}^m \langle x_i, s_{ii}(t)x_i\rangle + \sum_{i=1}^m \langle x_i, k_i(t)\rangle + \frac{1}{2}\Big(\sum_{1 \le i < j \le m} \langle x_i, s_{ij}(t)x_j\rangle \\
&+ \sum_{1 \le i < j \le m} \langle x_j, s_{ji}(t)x_i\rangle \Big) + r(t),
\end{aligned}$$
(23)

where the parameters $s_{ii}(t) = s'_{ii}(t) > 0$, $k_i(t)$, $r(t)$ and $s_{ij}(t) = s'_{ij}(t) > 0$ are continuously differentiable and satisfy $s_{ij}(t) = s_{ji}(t)$, $\kappa_{ij} = \kappa_{ji}$. Taking the partial derivative of the above equation for t and $x_i (i = 1, \cdots, m)$ respectively, we obtain:

$$\frac{\partial V_E}{\partial t} = \sum_{i=1}^{m} \langle x_i, \dot{s}_{ii}(t) x_i \rangle + \sum_{i=1}^{m} \langle x_i, \dot{k}_i(t) \rangle + \frac{1}{2} \Big(\sum_{1 \leq i < j \leq m} \langle x_i, \dot{s}_{ij}(t) x_j \rangle + \sum_{1 \leq i < j \leq m} \langle x_j, \dot{s}_{ji}(t) x_i \rangle \Big) + \dot{r}(t), \tag{24}$$

$$\frac{\partial V_E}{\partial x_i} = 2 s_{ii}(t) x_i + k_i(t) + \frac{1}{2} \Big(\sum_{j \in B_i} s_{ij}(t) x_j + \sum_{j \in B_i} s_{ji}(t) x_j \Big), \quad i = 1, \cdots, m, \tag{25}$$

where set B_i as $B_i = \{ j \in \{1, \cdots, m\} | j \neq i \}$. Substituting Equations (22) into (26) provides

$$\frac{\partial V_E}{\partial t} + \Big\{ \sum_{i=1}^{m} \langle \frac{\partial V_E}{\partial x_i}, -\frac{1}{2\omega} \frac{\partial V_E}{\partial x_i} \rangle + \omega \sum_{i=1}^{m} \langle -\frac{1}{2\omega} \frac{\partial V_E}{\partial x_i}, -\frac{1}{2\omega} \frac{\partial V_E}{\partial x_i} \rangle + \sum_{i=1}^{m} \beta_i \langle x_i - q, Q^{-1}(x_i - q) \rangle$$

$$- \frac{1}{2} \Big(\sum_{1 \leq i < j \leq m} \kappa_{ij} \langle x_i - x_j, x_i - x_j \rangle + \sum_{1 \leq i < j \leq m} \kappa_{ji} \langle x_j - x_i, x_j - x_i \rangle \Big) \tag{26}$$

$$\Big| x_i = x_i(t), q = q(t), Q = Q(t) \Big\} = 0.$$

Then, substituting Equations (24) and (25) into (26), yields

$$\sum_{i=1}^{m} \langle x_i, \dot{s}_{ii}(t) x_i \rangle + \sum_{i=1}^{m} \langle x_i, \dot{k}_i(t) \rangle + \frac{1}{2} \Big(\sum_{1 \leq i < j \leq m} \langle x_i, \dot{s}_{ij}(t) x_j \rangle + \sum_{1 \leq i < j \leq m} \langle x_j, \dot{s}_{ji}(t) x_i \rangle \Big) + \dot{r}(t)$$

$$- \frac{1}{4\omega} \sum_{i=1}^{m} \langle (2 s_{ii}(t) x_i + k_i(t) + \frac{1}{2} (\sum_{j \in B_i} s_{ij}(t) x_j + \sum_{j \in B_i} s_{ji}(t) x_j)), 2 s_{ii}(t) x_i + k_i(t)$$

$$+ \frac{1}{2} (\sum_{j \in B_i} s_{ij}(t) x_j + \sum_{j \in B_i} s_{ji}(t) x_j) \rangle + \sum_{i=1}^{m} \beta_i \langle x_i - q, Q^{-1}(x_i - q) \rangle \tag{27}$$

$$- \frac{1}{2} \Big(\sum_{1 \leq i < j \leq m} \kappa_{ij} \langle x_i - x_j, x_i - x_j \rangle + \sum_{1 \leq i < j \leq m} \kappa_{ji} \langle x_j - x_i, x_j - x_i \rangle \Big) = 0.$$

For the above equation, matching the coefficients of like powers of $x_i(t) (i = 1, \cdots, m)$, the following differential equations can be obtained:

$$\dot{s}_{ii}(t) - \frac{1}{4\omega} \Big(4 s'_{ii}(t) s_{ii}(t) + \sum_{j \in B_i} s_{ij}(t) s_{ji}(t) \Big) + \beta_i Q^{-1} - \frac{1}{2} \sum_{j \in B_i} (\kappa_{ij} + \kappa_{ji}) I = 0, \quad s_{ii}(\theta) = I, \tag{28}$$

$$\dot{k}_i(t) - \frac{1}{4\omega} \Big(4 s'_{ii}(t) k_i(t) + \sum_{j \in B_i} (s_{ij}(t) + s_{ji}(t)) k_j(t) \Big) - 2 \beta_i Q^{-1} q = 0, \quad k_i(\theta) = -2 \beta_i m_i, \tag{29}$$

$$\dot{s}_{ij}(t) - \frac{1}{4\omega} \Big(4 s'_{ii}(t) (s_{ij}(t) + s_{ji}(t)) + 2 \sum_{l \neq i, j} s_{il}(t) s_{jl}(t) \Big) + (\kappa_{ij} + \kappa_{ji}) I = 0, \quad s_{ij}(\theta) = 0, \tag{30}$$

$$\dot{r}(t) - \frac{1}{4\omega} \Big(\sum_{i=1}^{m} k'_i(t) k_i(t) \Big) + \sum_{i=1}^{m} \beta_i q' Q^{-1} q = 0, \quad r(\theta) = \sum_{i=1}^{m} m'_i m_i, \tag{31}$$

where $1 \leq i < j \leq m$. The differential Equations (28)–(31) can be solved here numerically using the traditional finite difference method (FDM) by Explicit Euler's method:

$$\begin{aligned}
\dot{s}_{ii}(t_{k+1}) &= (s_{ii}(t_k) - s_{ii}(t_{k+1}))/(\Delta t), \\
\dot{k}_i(t_{k+1}) &= (k_i(t_k) - k_i(t_{k+1}))/(\Delta t), \\
\dot{s}_{ij}(t_{k+1}) &= (s_{ij}(t_k) - s_{ij}(t_{k+1}))/(\Delta t), \\
\dot{r}(t_{k+1}) &= (r(t_k) - r(t_{k+1})/(\Delta t),
\end{aligned} \qquad (32)$$

the specific solution process is provided in Appendix B.

Theorem 1. *The value function (23) in which the parameters are determined by system (28)–(31) specifies a solution of the optimization problem (18). In this case, the optimal controls $u_i(t)(i = 1, \cdots, m)$ are given by (22), namely,*

$$u_i(t) = -\frac{1}{2\omega}(2s_{ii}(t)x_i + k_i(t) + \frac{1}{2}(\sum_{j \in B_i} s_{ij}(t)x_j + \sum_{j \in B_i} s_{ji}(t)x_j)), \quad i = 1, \cdots, m, \qquad (33)$$

where the parameters $s_{ii}(t), k_i(t), r(t), s_{ij}(t)$ and $s_{ji}(t)$ are solved by differential Equations (28)–(31).

Thus, for given $\omega, \beta_i, \kappa_{ij}, \kappa_{ji} \geq 0 (i, j = 1, \cdots, m)$, we can obtain the trajectory of system members. In this way, for a given m, the numerical solution of team control can be obtained. The optimality proof for controls $u_i(t)(i = 1, \cdots, m)$ is given in Appendix C.

5. Numerical Results and Discussions

Numerical results for the problem are given below using the Matlab R2014b software. We consider a two-dimensional (2D) problem defined on the time interval $t \in [0,1]$ with $m = 3$. We first calculate the trajectory of the virtual ellipsoid according to the calculation method given in [29], and then use the computed result as the reference motion of the cluster in this paper. The initial states of the cluster members are taken to be $x_1(0) = [0, 0.5]$, $x_2(0) = [0.5, 0]$, $x_3(0) = [0, 0]$. For terminal targets, we here set $m_1 = [0.75, 0.75]$, $m_2 = [1.25, 1.25]$, $m_3 = [1, 1]$. The parameters here are chosen as $\omega = 0.1$, $\beta_1 = 5.87$, $\beta_2 = 5.88$, $\beta_3 = 5.85$, $\kappa_{12} = 1.13$, $\kappa_{13} = 1.15$, $\kappa_{23} = 1.10$. Taking the state information of the virtual ellipsoid and the above numerical values as known conditions, and substituting them into the algorithm given in this paper for derivation, the problem can be transformed into a differential equation system of the form (28)–(31). Solving them by Explicit Euler's method, the numerical results for the team motion of all cluster members can be seen in Figure 1. If the initial state of the cluster members changes to $x_1(0) = [0, 1.5]$, $x_2(0) = [2, 0]$, $x_3(0) = [0, 0]$, the team motion shown in Figure 2 can be obtained. If the parameters κ_{12}, κ_{13}, κ_{23} are taken to be $\kappa_{12} = 1.03$, $\kappa_{13} = 1.05$, $\kappa_{23} = 1.00$, the resulting team motion can be found in Figure 3, where we can observe from Figure 4 that there is still no collision between each of the cluster members.

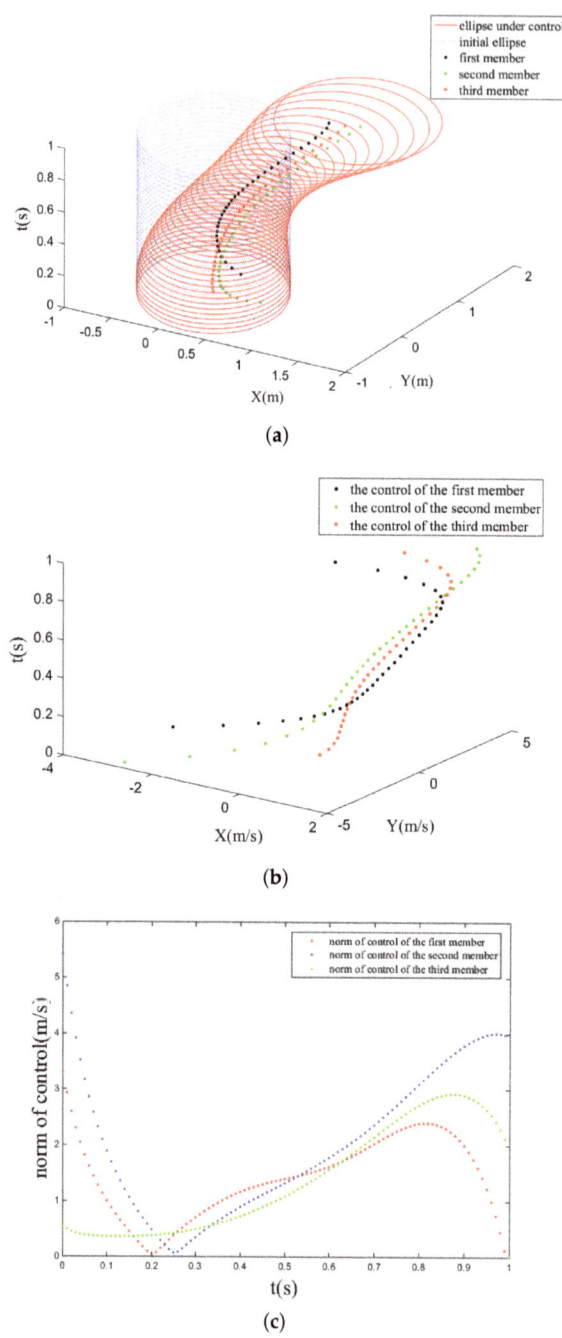

Figure 1. Team motion with initial states $x_1(0) = [0, 0.5]$, $x_2(0) = [0.5, 0]$, $x_3(0) = [0, 0]$ and parameters $\omega = 0.1$, $\beta_1 = 5.87$, $\beta_2 = 5.88$, $\beta_3 = 5.85$, $\kappa_{12} = 1.13$, $\kappa_{13} = 1.15$, $\kappa_{23} = 1.10$. (**a**) The state-time relationship diagram of the cluster. (**b**) The control-time relationship diagram of the cluster. (**c**) The norm of the control-time relationship diagram of the cluster.

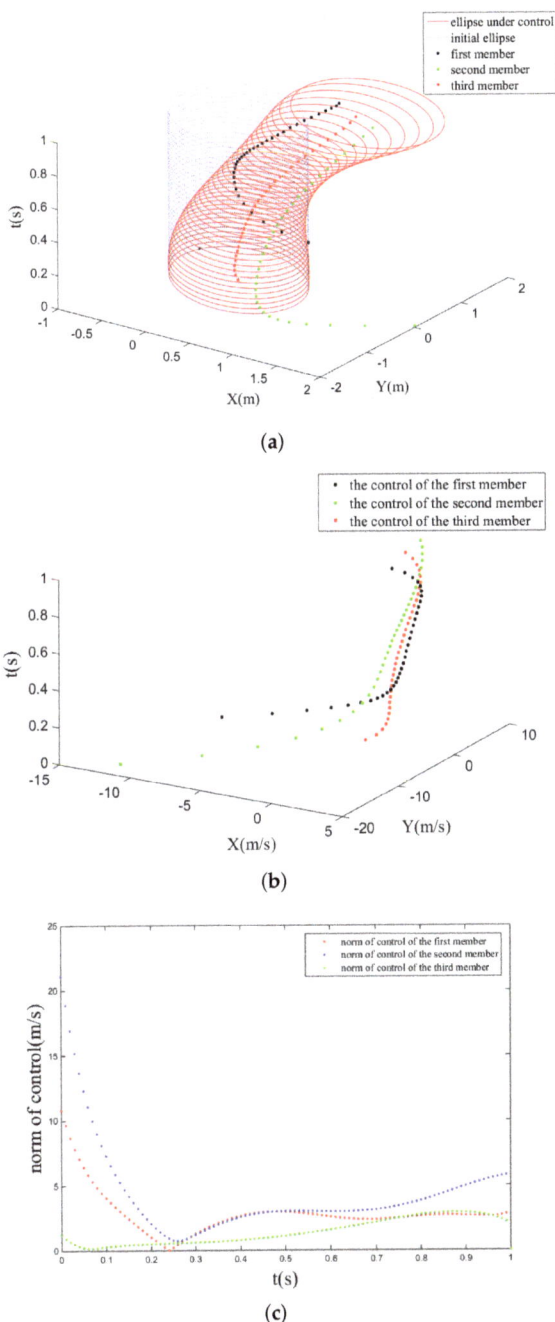

Figure 2. Team motion with initial states $x_1(0) = [0, 1.5]$, $x_2(0) = [2, 0]$, $x_3(0) = [0, 0]$ and parameters $\omega = 0.1$, $\beta_1 = 5.87$, $\beta_2 = 5.88$, $\beta_3 = 5.85$, $\kappa_{12} = 1.13$, $\kappa_{13} = 1.15$, $\kappa_{23} = 1.10$. (**a**) The state-time relationship diagram of the cluster. (**b**) The control-time relationship diagram of the cluster. (**c**) The norm of the control-time relationship diagram of the cluster.

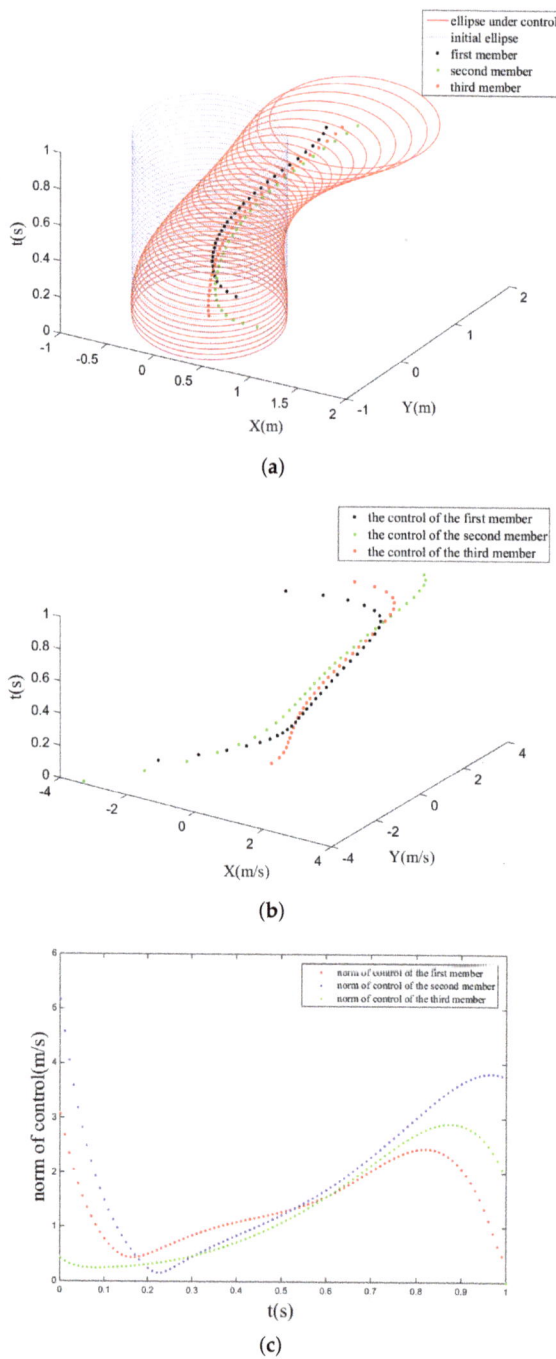

Figure 3. Team motion with initial states $x_1(0) = [0, 0.5]$, $x_2(0) = [0.5, 0]$, $x_3(0) = [0, 0]$ and parameters $\omega = 0.1$, $\beta_1 = 5.87$, $\beta_2 = 5.88$, $\beta_3 = 5.85$, $\kappa_{12} = 1.03$, $\kappa_{13} = 1.05$, $\kappa_{23} = 1.00$. (**a**) The state-time relationship diagram of the cluster. (**b**) The control-time relationship diagram of the cluster. (**c**) The norm of the control-time relationship diagram of the cluster.

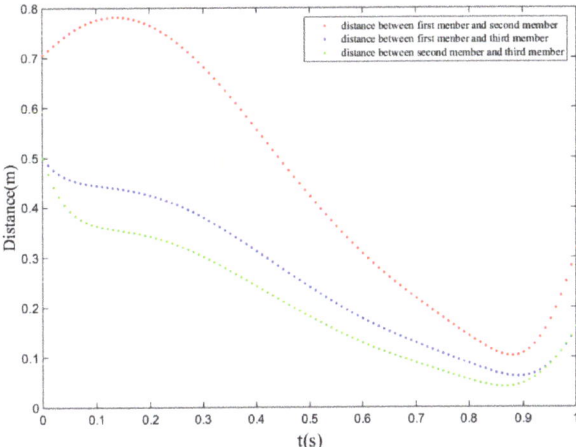

Figure 4. Distance between cluster members with parameters $\omega = 0.1$, $\beta_1 = 5.87$, $\beta_2 = 5.88$, $\beta_3 = 5.85$, $\kappa_{12} = 1.03$, $\kappa_{13} = 1.05$, $\kappa_{23} = 1.00$.

In Figures 1–3, the vertical axis stands for the time direction. The X axis represents the first component of the state vector of the cluster members, while the Y axis represents the second in three Figures 1a, 2a and 3a, and they represent the two components of the control vector of the cluster members, respectively, in Figures 1b, 2b and 3b. The vertical elliptical tube depicts the initial ellipse, and the curved elliptical tube depicts the elliptical orbit under optimal control, which can be obtained according to [29]. The three curves represent the trajectories of the three members in the cluster respectively. In Figure 4, the horizontal axis denotes the time direction, and the vertical axis is the distance between each of the member during the movement. In summary, based on the value function constructed in this article, the optimal control obtained by the convex analysis technique and the Hamilton method can achieve the preconceived goals.

In summary, based on the value function constructed in this paper, the optimal control obtained by the convex analysis technique and the Hamilton method can achieve the preconceived goals: The first is to control the system members whose initial state are inside the initial ellipsoid to follow the movement of the virtual ellipsoid to reach a predetermined target set. The second is that, for cluster members whose initial state are not in the initial ellipsoid, they can enter the ellipsoid trajectory and follow the movement of the virtual ellipsoid to reach a predetermined target set through the applied control. In the above-mentioned movement process, the cluster members satisfy all the constraints.

6. Aerospace Applications

The swarm formation algorithm provided in this article can be widely used in aerospace engineering problems, such as the formation of UAVs, the problem of multiple spacecrafts working together in a specific orbit, and the formation of multiple small satellites wrapped in the cavity of a large satellite. Taking the UAV formation problem as an example, the cluster described in this paper represents the UAV swarm, and the virtual ellipsoid where the cluster is located can represent the safe area where the UAV can move. We verify the application of the algorithm in this article to the formation of UAV swarms through the AirSim&Unreal Engine simulation platform. Taking three UAVs as an example, we choose to simulate numerical examples shown in Figures 1 and 2. The unit of distance is ten meters and the entire simulation process takes ten seconds. We use the geodetic coordinate system and assume that the drone remains at an altitude of fifty meters throughout the simulation. Here, the state vs. time of the three UAVs are shown in Figures 1a and 2a, the control vs. time of the three UAVs are shown in Figures 1b and 2b. Lastly, the norm of control vs. time of the three UAVs are shown in Figures 1c and 2c. The results are shown in Figures 5 and 6, which demonstrate the feasibility of this algorithm in a real environment.

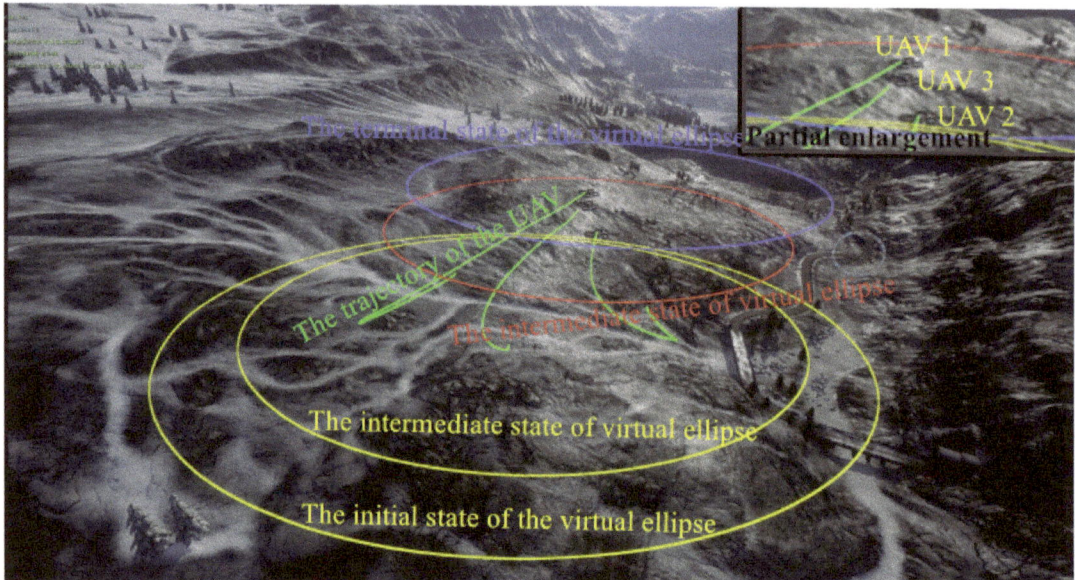

Figure 5. The movement of the UAV swarm corresponding to Figure 1.

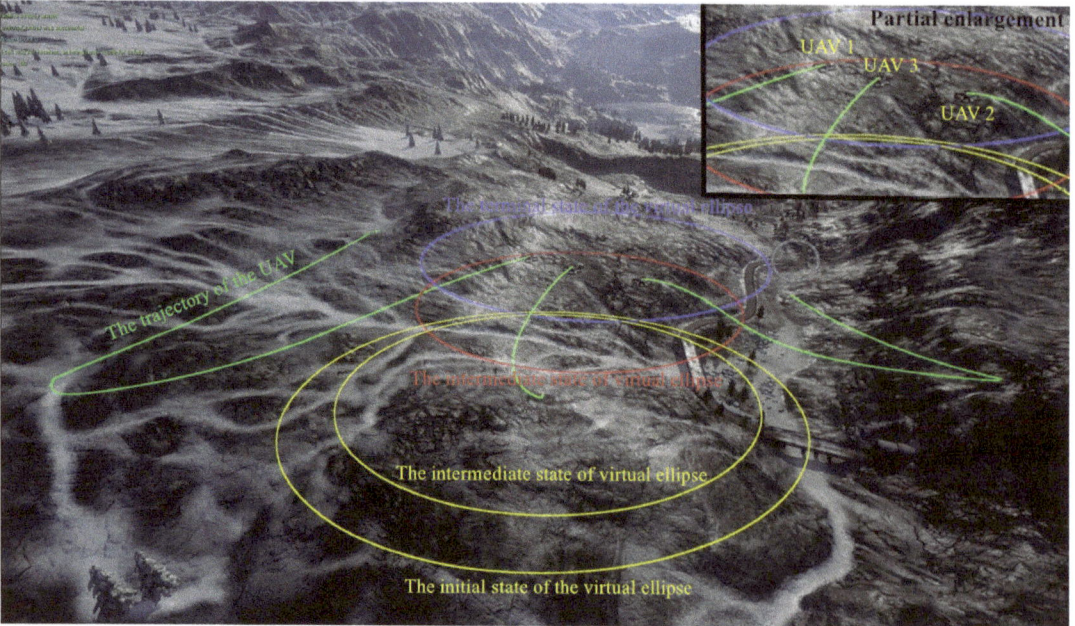

Figure 6. The movement of the UAV swarm corresponding to Figure 2.

Figure 5 shows the trajectory when the initial state of the UAV swarm is in the initial ellipse, and Figure 6 shows the trajectory when the initial state of the UAV swarm is not in the initial ellipse. The upper left corner of both figures is a partial enlarged view of the figure. In these figures, the four ellipses correspond to the security area of the UAV cluster at four instants ($t = 0.00, t = 0.40, t = 0.85$ and $t = 1.00$). We can observe that for the UAV swarm whose initial state is in the initial ellipse, the given set of targets can be reached by the control we exert on it and the entire movement process remains within the virtual ellipse. On the contrary, for the UAV swarm whose initial state is not in the initial ellipse, the control we exert on it will make it gradually enter the virtual ellipse first, and then move to the given target set. It is worth mentioning here that the control strategy of the UAV swarm given in this article is decentralized and the control strategy of each UAV is optimized in real-time.

In addition to the problems described in this article, considering the complex real environment, we list the following situations for different practical needs. For each situation, corresponding problem-solving ideas are given.

Case 1: Considering that the movement of the UAV swarm will be affected by the wind field, we can rewrite the system dynamic Equation (8) as:

$$\dot{x}(t) = u(t) + w(x,t), \ x \in \mathbb{R}^{n \times m}, \ u \in \mathbb{R}^{n \times m}, \ w \in \mathbb{R}^{n \times m}, \tag{34}$$

where $w(x,t)$ is the expression for the wind field which the cluster is subjected. It depends not only on time, but also on the state of the cluster. Assuming the remaining conditions keep unchanged, according to the optimization algorithm given in this paper, the optimal trajectory of the UAV swarm under the influence of the wind field can be obtained.

Case 2: If the UAV swarm needs to avoid obstacles (such as enemy fighters or radar areas) during the movement, we can add an obstacle term to the integral term of Equation (16) to achieve the effect of avoiding obstacles for the entire UAV swarm. Take the example of avoiding an obstacle χ, we could add the term $-\varsigma D(E_c[t], O)$ to the integrand in Equation (16). Here, ς is a constant coefficient, O denotes the minimal convex compact set containing the external obstacle χ, and $D(E_c[t], O)$ is defined as:

$$D(E_c[t], O) = inf\{\|z^* - z^{**}\|, z^* \in E_c[t], z^{**} \in O\}. \tag{35}$$

Following the calculation process given in this work, the ellipsoidal trajectory that satisfies the collision avoidance of the external obstacle can be calculated in advance forms a reference motion, and then the cluster motion on the premise of avoiding the collision between cluster and the external obstacle can be obtained.

Case 3: Considering the fact that the dimension of the control input is different from the dimension of the UAV state, we can replace Equation (8) with

$$\dot{x}(t) = A(t)x(t) + B(t)u(t), \ x \in \mathbb{R}^{n \times m}, \ u \in \mathbb{R}^{p \times m}, \tag{36}$$

where the coefficient matrices $A(t) \in \mathbb{R}^{n \times n}$ and $B(t) \in \mathbb{R}^{n \times p}$ are assumed to be continuously differentiable.

Case 4: The term $\beta_1(\lambda_+^2 - [Q(\tau), Q(\tau)]) + \beta_2([Q(\tau), Q(\tau)] - \lambda_-^2)$ in Equation (16) in this paper is the constraint on the volume of the virtual ellipsoid, and we can also constrain the sum of squares of semiaxes of the ellipsoid by replacing it with $\beta_1(\lambda_+^2 - trQ(\tau)) + \beta_2(trQ(\tau) - \lambda_-^2)$.

In short, we can achieve different practical needs by transforming the system dynamic equation or value function, and the algorithm framework provided in this work is still applicable. On the other hand, it also shows that our proposed model has strong variability and is more suitable for environments with high scalability requirements.

7. Conclusions

This work proposes a solving model of the decentralized cluster control problem and demonstrates the scalability and practical feasibility of the model. It is mainly to construct a new matrix valued function based on the comprehensive consideration of cluster member collision avoidance and energy constraints. Applying the Hamilton formalism methods, the model and the optimization algorithm of the cluster objective control problem are given, and the numerical method of the optimal control of the cluster members satisfying the constraints is established. Furthermore, the algorithm provided in this article can meet the different needs of practical problems. In addition to the aforementioned, we can also flexibly adjust the distance between cluster members by adjusting parameters in value function. As a consequence, the proposed method provides a new framework for general team control problems and also provides an efficient alternative for cluster problems in bionics. Simultaneously, this paper offers research ideas for the study of military combat formations or ecological groups.

Several problems remain to be addressed in future work. Firstly, we may improve computational efficiency by applying the proposed method in parallel computing system. Secondly, our algorithm focuses on single-cluster coordinated movement under static reorganization. It is of interest to study potentials of the presented method in multi-cluster and dynamic reorganization setting. Lastly, we want to combine this control problem with game theory to study the obstacle avoidance problem in the movement of virtual ellipsoid, including fixed obstacles and moving obstacles.

Author Contributions: Conceptualization, Z.D. (Zhiqing Dang); Methodology, Z.D. (Zhiqing Dang), Z.D. (Zhaopeng Dai), and Y.Y.; Software, A.S. and Z.Y.; Formal analysis, L.Z.; Validation, Z.D. (Zhiqing Dang) and H.G.; Writing—original draft preparation, Z.D. (Zhiqing Dang); Writing—review and editing, Z.D. (Zhiqing Dang), Z.D. (Zhaopeng Dai), and Y.Y.; Supervision, H.G. All authors have read and agreed to the published version of the manuscript.

Funding: This research was supported by National Natural Science Foundation of China (Nos. 72171126, 11872220).

Institutional Review Board Statement: Not applicable.

Informed Consent Statement: Not applicable.

Data Availability Statement: Not applicable.

Conflicts of Interest: The authors declare no conflict of interest.

Appendix A

In this appendix, the proof of the continuity of the virtual ellipsoid is given.

It is known that the center and the configuration matrix of the ellipsoid satisfy the dynamic equations:

$$\dot{q}(t) = A(t)q(t) + C(t)v(t), \; q(t_0) = q^0, \tag{A1}$$

$$\dot{Q}(t) = T(t)Q(t) + Q(t)T'(t) + B(t)V(t)B'(t), \tag{A2}$$

$$T(t) = T'(t), V(t) = V'(t), Q(t_0) = Q^0, \tag{A3}$$

where the given coefficient matrices $A(t)$, $B(t)$, $C(t)$, $T(t)$, $\mu(t)$, and $v(t)$ are bounded. For the convenience of description, we assume that the time interval $t \in [t_0, \theta]$ was divided into n sections, the step length is recorded as Δt.

Let $\|A(t)\| \leq \mathcal{A}, \|B(t)\| \leq \mathcal{B}, \|C(t)\| \leq \mathcal{C}, \|T(t)\| \leq \mathcal{T}, \sqrt{\langle v(t), v(t) \rangle} \leq |\mu(t)| \leq \mu_0$. For the center of the virtual ellipsoid $q(t), t \in [t_0, \theta]$, $\Delta t = \frac{\theta - t_0}{n_t}$ where n_t denotes the number of time steps, the following inequality holds:

$$\begin{aligned}
\|q(t_0 + \Delta t)\| &\leq \|q(t_0)\| + \Delta t \|\dot{q}(t_0)\| \\
&\leq \|q(t_0)\| + \Delta t (\|A(t_0)q(t_0)\| + \|C(t_0)v(t_0)\|) \\
&\leq \|q(t_0)\| + \Delta t (\mathcal{A}\|q(t_0)\| + \mathcal{C}\mu_0) \\
&\leq (1 + \mathcal{A}\Delta t)\|q(t_0)\| + \mathcal{C}\mu_0 \Delta t,
\end{aligned} \quad (A4)$$

$$\begin{aligned}
\|q(t_0 + \Delta t + \Delta t)\| &\leq (1 + \mathcal{A}\Delta t)\|q(t_0 + \Delta t)\| + \mathcal{C}\mu_0 \Delta t \\
&\leq (1 + \mathcal{A}\Delta t)[(1 + \mathcal{A}\Delta t)\|q(t_0)\| + \mathcal{C}\mu_0 \Delta t] + \mathcal{C}\mu_0 \Delta t \\
&\leq (1 + \mathcal{A}\Delta t)[(1 + \mathcal{A}\Delta t)\|q(t_0)\| + \mathcal{C}\mu_0 \Delta t] + \mathcal{C}\mu_0 \Delta t \\
&\leq (1 + \mathcal{A}\Delta t)^2 \|q(t_0)\| + (1 + \mathcal{A}\Delta t)\mathcal{C}\mu_0 \Delta t + \mathcal{C}\mu_0 \Delta t,
\end{aligned} \quad (A5)$$

...

$$\begin{aligned}
\|q(t_0 + n_t \Delta t)\| &\leq (1 + \mathcal{A}\Delta t)^{n_t} \|q(t_0)\| + (1 + \mathcal{A}\Delta t)^{n_t - 1} \mathcal{C}\mu_0 \Delta t \\
&\quad + (1 + \mathcal{A}\Delta t)^{n_t - 2} \mathcal{C}\mu_0 \Delta t + \ldots + \mathcal{C}\mu_0 \Delta t \\
&= (1 + \mathcal{A}\Delta t)^{n_t} \|q(t_0)\| + \mathcal{C}\mu_0 \Delta t \frac{1 - (1 + \mathcal{A}\Delta t)^{n_t}}{1 - (1 + \mathcal{A}\Delta t)} \\
&= (\|q(t_0)\| + \frac{\mathcal{C}\mu_0}{\mathcal{A}})(1 + \mathcal{A}\Delta t)^{n_t} - \frac{\mathcal{C}\mu_0}{\mathcal{A}},
\end{aligned} \quad (A6)$$

It is obvious that $(1 + \mathcal{A}\Delta t)^{n_t} = (1 + \mathcal{A}\frac{\theta - t_0}{n_t})^{n_t}$ is monotone increasing with n_t, and

$$\lim_{n_t \to \infty} (1 + \mathcal{A}\Delta t)^{n_t} = \lim_{n_t \to \infty} (1 + \mathcal{A}\frac{\theta - t_0}{n_t})^{n_t} = e^{\mathcal{A}(\theta - t_0)}. \quad (A7)$$

Thus,

$$\|q(t_0 + n_t \Delta t)\| \leq (\|q(t_0)\| + \frac{\mathcal{C}\mu_0}{\mathcal{A}})e^{\mathcal{A}(\theta - t_0)} - \frac{\mathcal{C}\mu_0}{\mathcal{A}} \quad (A8)$$

is bounded. The same boundedness holds for any $q(t_0 + i\Delta t), i = 0, 1, \ldots n_t$. Let $n_t \to \infty$ this gives proof that $q(t)$ is bounded over $[t_0, \theta]$.

Therefore,

$$\begin{aligned}
\|q(t + \Delta t) - q(t)\| &\leq \Delta t \|\dot{q}(t)\| \leq \Delta t (\|A(t)\|\|q(t)\| + \|C(t)\|\|v(t)\|) \\
&\leq \Delta t (\mathcal{A}\|q(t)\| + \mathcal{C}\mu_0)
\end{aligned} \quad (A9)$$

gives proof that the function $q(t)$ satisfies the Lipschitz continuity condition, and the function $q(t)$ is continuously proved.

The continuity of $Q(t)$ can be proved in a similar way. Thus, the continuity of the virtual ellipsoid $E_c(t) = \varepsilon(q(t), Q(t))$ is proved.

Appendix B

Algorithm A1 Algorithmic Steps for Numerical Computing

Require: The total time interval $[t_0, \theta]$, the number of time step n_t, the center $\mathbf{q}(t)$ and configuration matrix $Q(t)$ for the ellipsoid $\varepsilon(\mathbf{q}, Q)$, the number of cluster members m, the destination $\mathbf{m}_i$ for every member, and the coefficients $\omega, \beta_i, \kappa_{ij}$ for $i = 1, 2, ..., m, j = 1, 2, ..., m$.

Ensure: The optimal control $u_i^*(t)$ for the cluster member with index $i = 1, 2, ..., m$ at the following time node: $t_0, t_0 + \Delta t, t_0 + 2\Delta t, ..., t_0 + n\Delta t = \theta$.

1: $\Delta t = \frac{\theta - t_0}{n_t}$;
2: s=0;
3: for $(i = 1; i <= m; i++)$
4:     $s+ = \mathbf{m}_i' \mathbf{m}_i$;
5: $r(\theta) = s$;
6: $\mathbf{k}_i(\theta) = -2\beta_i \mathbf{m}_i$;
7: for $(t = \theta; t > t_0; t- = \Delta t)$\{
8:     for $(i = 1; i <= m; i++)$\{
9:         $s_{ii}(\theta) = I_m$;
10:        $M_1 = M_2 = zeros(m,m), z_1 = z_2 = z_3 = 0, \mathbf{v}_1 = \mathbf{v}_2 = zeros(m,1)$;
11:        //zeros(m,n) stands for $0_{m \times n}$
12:        for $(j = 1; j <= m; j++)$\{
13:            $s_{ij}(\theta) = 0$;
14:            $z_1 = \mathbf{k}_i'(t)\mathbf{k}_i(t)$;
15:            $z_2 = \beta_i \mathbf{q}'(t) Q^{-1}(t) \mathbf{q}(t)$;\}
16:            for $l = 1; l <= m; l++$;
17:                $z_3+ = s_{il}(t) s_{jl}(t)$;
18:            if(i!=j)\{
19:                $M_1+ = s_{ij}(t) s_{ji}(t)$;
20:                $M_2+ = (\kappa_{ij} + \kappa_{ji}) I_m$;
21:                $\mathbf{v}_1+ = [s_{ij}(t) + s_{ji}(t)]\mathbf{k}_j(t)$;
22:        $s_{ii}(t - \Delta t) = s_{ii}(t) + \{\frac{1}{4\omega}[4s_{ii}'(t) s_{ii}(t)] - M_1 - \beta_i Q^{-1}(t) + \frac{1}{2} M_2\} * \Delta t$;
23:        $r(t)(t - \Delta t) = r(t) + (\frac{1}{4\omega} z_1 - z_2) * \Delta t$;
24:        $\mathbf{k}_i(t - \Delta t) = \mathbf{k}_i(t) + \{\frac{1}{4\omega}[4s_{ii}'(t)\mathbf{k}_i(t) - \mathbf{v}_1] + 2\beta_i Q^{-1}(t)\mathbf{q}(t)]\} * \Delta t$;
25:        $s_{ij}(t - \Delta t) = s_{ij}(t) + \{\frac{1}{4\omega} 4 s_{ii}'(t)[s_{ij}(t) + s_{ji}(t)] + 2z_3 + (\kappa_{ij} + \kappa_{ji}) I_m\} * \Delta t$;
26:        for $(j = 1; j <= m; j++)$
27:            if $(j! - i)$
28:                $\mathbf{v}_2+ = (s_{ij}(t - \Delta t) + s_{ji}(t - \Delta t))\mathbf{x}_j$;
29:        $\mathbf{u}_i(t)(t - \Delta t) = -\frac{1}{2\omega}[2s_{ii}(t - \Delta t)\mathbf{x}_i + \mathbf{k}_i(t - \Delta t) + \frac{1}{2}\mathbf{v}_2]$;\}\}

Appendix C

In this Appendix, we give the conditions and proofs for the optimality of the control. For simplicity in the proof process, we define the following notation:

$$F(x(t), u(t), t) = \omega \sum_{i=1}^{m} \langle \mathbf{u}_i(t), \mathbf{u}_i(t) \rangle + \sum_{i=1}^{m} \beta_i \langle \mathbf{x}_i(t) - \mathbf{q}(t), Q^{-1}(t)(\mathbf{x}_i(t) - \mathbf{q}(t)) \rangle \\ - \frac{1}{2} \Big(\sum_{1 \leq i < j \leq m} \kappa_{ij} \langle \mathbf{x}_i(t) - \mathbf{x}_j(t), \mathbf{x}_i(t) - \mathbf{x}_j(t) \rangle \\ + \sum_{1 \leq i < j \leq m} \kappa_{ji} \langle \mathbf{x}_j(t) - \mathbf{x}_i(t), \mathbf{x}_j(t) - \mathbf{x}_i(t) \rangle \Big) \quad (A10)$$

and

$$f(x(t), u(t), t) = \dot{x} = u(t). \quad (A11)$$

Set

$$H[x(t), u(t), t] = \sum_{i=1}^{m} \langle \frac{\partial V_E}{\partial x_i}, \dot{x}_i \rangle + \omega \sum_{i=1}^{m} \langle u_i(t), u_i(t) \rangle + \sum_{i=1}^{m} \beta_i \langle x_i - q, Q^{-1}(x_i - q) \rangle \\ - \frac{1}{2} \Big(\sum_{1 \leq i < j \leq m} \kappa_{ij} \langle x_i - x_j, x_i - x_j \rangle + \sum_{1 \leq i < j \leq m} \kappa_{ji} \langle x_j - x_i, x_j - x_i \rangle \Big), \quad (A12)$$

we can obtain the relation

$$H[x(t), u(t), t] = F(x(t), u(t), t) + \lambda(t) f(x(t), u(t), t), \quad (A13)$$

where $\lambda(t) = \frac{\partial V_E}{\partial x}|_{x=x^*}$ with $x^*(t)$ being the optimal trajectory. Assuming u^* is the control obtained in the text, then we have

$$H[x(t), u^*(t), t] = -\frac{1}{4\omega} \sum_{i=1}^{m} \langle (2s_{ii}(t)x_i + k_i(t) + \frac{1}{2}(\sum_{j \in B_i} s_{ij}(t)x_j + \sum_{j \in B_i} s_{ji}(t)x_j)), \\ 2s_{ii}(t)x_i + k_i(t) + \frac{1}{2}(\sum_{j \in B_i} s_{ij}(t)x_j + \sum_{j \in B_i} s_{ji}(t)x_j) \rangle + \sum_{i=1}^{m} \beta_i \langle x_i - q, Q^{-1}(x_i - q) \rangle \quad (A14) \\ - \frac{1}{2} \Big(\sum_{1 \leq i < j \leq m} \kappa_{ij} \langle x_i - x_j, x_i - x_j \rangle + \sum_{1 \leq i < j \leq m} \kappa_{ji} \langle x_j - x_i, x_j - x_i \rangle \Big).$$

At the same time, we mark

$$S(x, \theta) = \sum_{i=1}^{m} \langle x_i(\theta) - m_i, x_i(\theta) - m_i \rangle, \quad (A15)$$

then, the following theorem holds.

Theorem A1. *u^* is an optimal control if $H[x(t), u^*(t), t]$ is convex in x for each t and $S(x, \theta)$ is convex in x.*

Proof. From the above definition we know

$$H[x(t), u(t), t] \geq H[x(t), u^*(t), t]. \quad (A16)$$

Since $H[x(t), u^*(t), t]$ is differential and convex in x and we assume that $x^*(t)$ is the optimal trajectory, we can use the definition of convex function to obtain

$$H[x(t), u(t), t] \geq H[x^*(t), u(t), t] + H_x[x^*(t), u(t), t][x(t) - x^*(t)], \quad (A17)$$

hence we have

$$H[x(t), u(t), t] \geq H[x^*(t), u^*(t), t] + H_x[x^*(t), u^*(t), t][x(t) - x^*(t)]. \quad (A18)$$

By definition of H in (A13), yields

$$F(x(t), u(t), t) + \lambda(t) f(x(t), u(t), t) \geq F(x^*(t), u^*(t), t) + \lambda(t) f(x^*(t), u^*(t), t) \\ - \dot{\lambda}(t)[x(t) - x^*(t)]. \quad (A19)$$

Using Equation (A11), transposing, and regrouping,

$$F(x^*(t), u^*(t), t) - F(x(t), u(t), t) \leq \dot{\lambda}(t)[x(t) - x^*(t)] + \lambda(t)[\dot{x}(t) - \dot{x}^*(t)]. \quad (A20)$$

Furthermore, since $S(x, \theta)$ is a differential and convex function, we have

$$S(x(\theta), \theta) \geq S(x^*(\theta), \theta) + S_x(x^*(\theta), \theta)[x(\theta) - x^*(\theta)] \quad \text{(A21)}$$

or,

$$S(x^*(\theta), \theta) - S(x(\theta), \theta) \leq -S_x(x^*(\theta), \theta)[x(\theta) - x^*(\theta)]. \quad \text{(A22)}$$

Integrating both sides of (A20) from t_0 to θ and adding (A21), we have

$$\int_{t_0}^{\theta}[F(x^*(t), u^*(t), t)dt + S(x^*(\theta), \theta)] - \int_{t_0}^{\theta}[F(x(t), u(t), t)dt + S(x(\theta), \theta)]$$
$$\leq [\lambda(\theta) - S_x(x^*(\theta), \theta)][[x(\theta) - x^*(\theta)]] - \lambda(t_0)[x(t_0 - x*(t_0)] \quad \text{(A23)}$$

or,

$$V_E(u^*) - V_E(u) \leq [\lambda(\theta) - S_x(x^*(\theta), \theta)][[x(\theta) - x^*(\theta)]] - \lambda(t_0)[x(t_0 - x*(t_0)], \quad \text{(A24)}$$

where $V_E(u)$ is the value of the value function (objective function) associated with a control u. Since $x(t_0) = x^*(t_0) = x_0$, the initial condition, and since $\lambda(\theta) = S_x(x^*(\theta), \theta)$, we have

$$V_E(u^*) \leq V_E(u). \quad \text{(A25)}$$

Thus, u^* is an optimal control. This completes the proof. □

In the numerical example of this paper, we know

$$H[x(t), u^*(t), t] = -\frac{1}{4\omega}\sum_{i=1}^{3}\langle(2s_{ii}(t)x_i + k_i(t) + \frac{1}{2}(\sum_{j \in B_i}s_{ij}(t)x_j + \sum_{j \in B_i}s_{ji}(t)x_j)),$$

$$2s_{ii}(t)x_i + k_i(t) + \frac{1}{2}(\sum_{j \in B_i}s_{ij}(t)x_j + \sum_{j \in B_i}s_{ji}(t)x_j)\rangle + \sum_{i=1}^{3}\beta_i\langle x_i - q, Q^{-1}(x_i - q)\rangle \quad \text{(A26)}$$

$$-\frac{1}{2}(\sum_{1 \leq i < j \leq 3}\kappa_{ij}\langle x_i - x_j, x_i - x_j\rangle + \sum_{1 \leq i < j \leq 3}\kappa_{ji}\langle x_j - x_i, x_j - x_i\rangle),$$

and

$$S(x, \theta) = \sum_{i=1}^{3}\langle x_i(\theta) - m_i, x_i(\theta) - m_i\rangle. \quad \text{(A27)}$$

After numerical verification, the algorithm in this paper satisfies the above theorem conditions. The optimality of control u provided in this paper is proved.

References

1. Roman, R.-C.; Precup, R.-E.; Petriu, E.M. Hybrid Data-Driven Fuzzy Active Disturbance Rejection Control for Tower Crane Systems. *Eur. J. Control* **2021**, *58*, 373–387. [CrossRef]
2. Chi, R.; Li, H.; Shen, D.; Hou, Z.; Huang, B. Enhanced P-type Control: Indirect Adaptive Learning from Set-point Updates. *IEEE Trans. Automat. Control* **2022**. doi:10.1109/TAC.2022.3154347 [CrossRef]
3. Olfati-Saber, R. Flocking for multi-agent dynamic systems: Algorithms and theory. *IEEE Trans. Automat. Control* **2006**, *51*, 401–420. [CrossRef]
4. Kurzhanski, A.B. On a team control problem under obstacles. *Proc. Steklov Inst. Math.* **2015**, *51*, 128–142. [CrossRef]
5. Adhikari, M.P.; de Ruiter, A.H. Online feasible trajectory generation for collision avoidance in fixed-wing unmanned aerial vehicles. *J. Guid. Control Dyn.* **2020**, *43*, 1201–1209. [CrossRef]
6. Ahn, C.; Kim, Y. Point targeting of multisatellites via a virtual structure formation flight scheme. *J. Guid. Control Dyn.* **2009**, *32*, 1330–1344. [CrossRef]
7. Zhang, F.; Huang, P.; Meng, Z.; Zhang, Y.; Liu, Z. Dynamics analysis and controller design for maneuverable tethered space net robot. *J. Guid. Control Dyn.* **2017**, *40*, 2828–2843. [CrossRef]
8. Kluever, C.; Horneman, K. Terminal trajectory planning and optimization for an unpowered reusable launch vehicle. In Proceedings of the AIAA Guidance, Navigation, and Control Conference and Exhibit, San Francisco, CA, USA, 15–18 August 2005; p. 6058.

9. Vian, J.L.; Moore, J.R. Trajectory optimization with risk minimization for military aircraft. *J. Guid. Control Dyn.* **1989**, *12*, 311–317. [CrossRef]
10. Levy, M.; Shima, T.; Gutman, S. Linear quadratic integrated versus separated autopilot-guidance design. *J. Guid. Control Dyn.* **2013**, *36*, 1722–1730. [CrossRef]
11. Gustavi, T.; Hu, X. Observer-based leader-follower formation control using onboard sensor information. *IEEE Trans. Robot.* **2008**, *24*, 1457–1462. [CrossRef]
12. Mariottini, G. L.; Morbidi, F.; Prattichizzo, D.; Valk, N. V.; Michael, N.; Pappas, G.; Daniilidis, K. Vision-based localization for leader-follower formation control. *IEEE Trans. Robot.* **2009**, *25*, 1431–1438. [CrossRef]
13. Chen, X.; Yan, P.; Serrani, A. On input-to-state stability-based design for leader/follower formation control with measurement delays. *Int. J. Robust Nonlinear Control* **2013**, *23*, 1433–1455. [CrossRef]
14. Lee, D.; Sanyal, A. K.; Butcher, E. A. Asymptotic tracking control for spacecraft formation flying with decentralized collision avoidance. *J. Guid. Control Dyn.* **2015**, *38*, 587–600. [CrossRef]
15. Panagou, D.; Kumar, V. Cooperative visibility maintenance for leader-follower formations in obstacle environments. *IEEE Trans. Robot.* **2014**, *30*, 831–844. [CrossRef]
16. Wang, X.; Zhang, J.; Zhang, D.; Shen, L. UAV formation: From numerical simulation to actual flight. In Proceedings of 2015 IEEE International Conference on Information and Automation, Lijiang, China, 8–10 August 2015; pp. 475–480.
17. Du, H.; Chen, M.Z.; Wen, G. Leader–following attitude consensus for spacecraft formation with rigid and flexible spacecraft. *J. Guid. Control Dyn.* **2016**, *39*, 944–951. [CrossRef]
18. Giulietti, F.; Innocenti, M.; Pollini, L. Formation flight control-a behavioral approach. In Proceedings of the AIAA Guidance, Navigation, and Control Conference and Exhibit, Montreal, QC, Canada, 6–9 August 2001; p. 4239.
19. Lawton, J.R.; Beard, R.W.; Young, B.J. A decentralized approach to formation maneuvers. *IEEE Trans. Robot. Autom.* **2003**, *19*, 933–941. [CrossRef]
20. Ren, W.; Beard, R.W. Decentralized scheme for spacecraft formation flying via the virtual structure approach. *J. Guid. Control Dyn.* **2004**, *27*, 73–82. [CrossRef]
21. Sadowska, A.; den Broek, T.V.; Huijberts, H.; van de Wouw, N.; Kostić, D.; Nijmeijer, H. A virtual structure approach to formation control of unicycle mobile robots using mutual coupling. *Int. J. Control* **2011**, *84*, 1886–1902. [CrossRef]
22. Watanabe, Y.; Amiez, A.; Chavent, P. Fully-autonomous coordinated flight of multiple UAVs using decentralized virtual leader approach. In Proceedings of 2013 IEEE/RSJ International Conference on Intelligent Robots and Systems, Tokyo, Japan, 3–7 November 2013; pp. 5736–5741.
23. Ren, W.; Beard, R. Virtual structure based spacecraft formation control with formation feedback. In Proceedings of the AIAA Guidance, Navigation, and Control Conference and Exhibit, Monterey, CA, USA, 5–8 August 2002; p. 4963.
24. Olfati-Saber, R.; Murray, R. M. Distributed cooperative control of multiple vehicle formations using structural potential functions. *Ifac Proc. Vol.* **2002**, *35*, 495–500. [CrossRef]
25. Gazi, V. Swarm aggregations using artificial potentials and sliding-mode control. *IEEE Trans. Robot.* **2005**, *21*, 1208–1214. [CrossRef]
26. Mabrouk, M.; McInnes, C. Solving the potential field local minimum problem using internal agent states. *Robot. Auton. Syst.* **2008**, *56*, 1050–1060. [CrossRef]
27. Kurzhanski, A.B.; Mesyats, A.I. Ellipsoidal motions for applied control: From theory to computation. In Proceedings of the 52nd IEEE Conference on Decision and Control, Firenze, Italy, 10–13 December 2013; pp. 5816–5821.
28. Rockafellar, R.T.; Wets, R.J.-B. *Variational Analysis*; Springer Science & Business Media: Berlin/Heidelberg, Germany, 2009.
29. Kurzhanski, A.B.; Mesyats, A.I. Optimal control of ellipsoidal motions. *Diff. Equat.* **2012**, *48*, 1502–1509. [CrossRef]
30. Kurzhanski, A.B.; Mesyats, A.I. The hamiltonian formalism for problems of group control under obstacles. *IFAC-PapersOnLine* **2016**, *49*, 570–575. [CrossRef]
31. Kurzhanski, A.B. On the problem of optimization in group control. In *Control Techniques in Complex Engineering Systems: Theory and Applications*; Springer: Berlin/Heidelberg, Germany, 2019; pp. 51–61.
32. Poznyak, A.; Ordaz, P. 'KL'-gain adaptation for attractive ellipsoid method. *IMA J. Math. Control I.* **2015**, *32*, 447–469.
33. Kurzhanski, A.B.; Vályi, I. *Ellipsoidal Calculus for Estimation and Control*; Springer: Berlin/Heidelberg, Germany, 1997.
34. Bellman, R. *Introduction to Matrix Analysis*; SIAM: Philadelphia, PA, USA, 1997.

Article

A Refined Closed-Form Solution for the Large Deflections of Alekseev-Type Annular Membranes Subjected to Uniformly Distributed Transverse Loads: Simultaneous Improvement of Out-of-Plane Equilibrium Equation and Geometric Equation

Bo Li [1], Qi Zhang [1], Xue Li [1], Xiao-Ting He [1,2] and Jun-Yi Sun [1,2,*]

[1] School of Civil Engineering, Chongqing University, Chongqing 400045, China; 202116131339@cqu.edu.cn (B.L.); 202016021045@cqu.edu.cn (Q.Z.); 20161602025t@cqu.edu.cn (X.L.); hexiaoting@cqu.edu.cn (X.-T.H.)

[2] Key Laboratory of New Technology for Construction of Cities in Mountain Area (Chongqing University), Ministry of Education, Chongqing 400045, China

* Correspondence: sunjunyi@cqu.edu.cn; Tel.: +86-(0)23-65120720

Citation: Li, B.; Zhang, Q.; Li, X.; He, X.-T.; Sun, J.-Y. A Refined Closed-Form Solution for the Large Deflections of Alekseev-Type Annular Membranes Subjected to Uniformly Distributed Transverse Loads: Simultaneous Improvement of Out-of-Plane Equilibrium Equation and Geometric Equation. *Mathematics* 2022, 10, 2121. https://doi.org/10.3390/math10122121

Academic Editors: Araceli Queiruga-Dios, Maria Jesus Santos, Fatih Yilmaz, Deolinda M. L. Dias Rasteiro, Jesús Martín Vaquero and Víctor Gayoso Martínez

Received: 7 May 2022
Accepted: 14 June 2022
Published: 17 June 2022

Publisher's Note: MDPI stays neutral with regard to jurisdictional claims in published maps and institutional affiliations.

Copyright: © 2022 by the authors. Licensee MDPI, Basel, Switzerland. This article is an open access article distributed under the terms and conditions of the Creative Commons Attribution (CC BY) license (https://creativecommons.org/licenses/by/4.0/).

Abstract: The Alekseev-type annular membranes here refer to annular membranes fixed at outer edges and connected with a movable, weightless, stiff, con-centric, circular thin plate at inner edges, which were proposed originally by Alekseev for bearing centrally concentrated loads. They are used to bear the pressure acting on both membranes and plates, which was proposed originally in our previous work for developing pressure sensors. The pressure is applied onto an Alekseev-type annular membrane, resulting in the parallel movement of the circular thin plate. Such a movement can be used to develop a capacitive pressure sensor using the circular thin plate as a movable electrode plate of a parallel plate capacitor. The pressure applied can be determined by measuring the change in capacitance of the parallel plate capacitor, based on the closed-form solution for the elastic behavior of Alekseev-type annular membranes. However, the previous closed-form solution is unsuitable for annular membranes with too large deflection, which limits the range of pressure operation of the developed sensors. A new and more refined closed-form solution is presented here by improving simultaneously the out-of-plane equilibrium equation and geometric equation, making it possible to develop capacitive pressure sensors with a wide range of pressure operations. The new closed-form solution is numerically discussed in its convergence and effectiveness and compared with the previous one. Additionally, its beneficial effect on developing the proposed capacitive pressure sensors is illustrated.

Keywords: annular membrane; uniform transverse loading; large deflection; power series method; closed-form solution

MSC: 74G10; 74K15

1. Introduction

Membrane structures can be used in civil engineering, aerospace engineering, technical applications and other fields, among which, axisymmetric membrane structures are often preferred for some technical applications, such as the bulge tests [1–3], blister tests [4–6] or constrained blister tests [7–10], and non-contact or contact capacitive pressure sensors [11–14]. The problem of axisymmetric deformation of membranes in these technical applications often has strong nonlinearity due to the concomitant of large deflection. So, analytical solutions to these membrane problems are available only in a few cases, and there are far fewer analytical solutions in the literature for annular membrane problems than for circular membrane problems. However, analytical solutions are often found to be necessary to implement these technical applications. This paper is devoted to the analytical study to the problem of axisymmetric deformation with large deflection of the Alekseev-type annular membrane structures under uniformly distributed transverse loads. The analytical solution of this problem can be used to develop a kind of capacitive pressure sensor [15], but the available analytical solution in the existing literature is not suitable for the case where the annular membranes exhibit too large deflection or rotation angle [15], which limits the range of pressure operation of the developed sensors. The purpose or significance of this work is to provide a new and more refined closed-form solution for developing capacitive pressure sensors with a wide range of pressure operation.

There are two methods for analytically solving the problem of axisymmetric deformation of circular or annular membranes in the existing literature—one is the power series solution, and the other is the algebraic solution. Hencky is the first person who used the power series method to solve circular membrane problems. He presented a power series solution of a circular membrane fixed at its outer edge and loaded transversely and uniformly in 1915 [16], where a computational error was corrected, respectively, by Chien in 1948 [17] and Alekseev in 1953 [18]. This is the first solution of circular membrane problems. This solution is often referred to as the well-known Hencky's solution and is cited in related studies [19–22]. Sun et al. improved the well-known Hencky's solution many times to make it suitable for heavily loaded membranes [23]. The peripherally fixed and uniformly normally loaded circular membranes are another type of circular membrane problems [24,25], where the direction of normally loading is always perpendicular to the membrane with deflection (while the direction of transversely loading is always perpendicular to the membrane without deflection). Gas pressure is typical normal loading while structural dead weight is typical transverse loading.

According to the Mathematics Subject Classification (MSC), membranes and thin films belong to different categories in the mechanics of deformable solids of the MSC database. A membrane is not necessarily as thin as a thin film, and can be a thin film, a thin plate or even a thick plate, but must have rigid edges that do not produce displacement under transverse loads. Annular membrane problems are often more complicated than circular membrane problems because circular membranes have only outer edges while annular membranes have both outer edges and inner edges. The outer edges of annular membranes are all fixed and, thus, rigid, just like that of circular membranes, while their inner edges are all movable rigid edges, which can be divided into two types. The first type is the inner edges attached to a weightless, stiff, concentric, circular thin plate, which is proposed originally by Alekseev [26]; while the second type is those attached to a weightless stiff ring, which is proposed originally by Sun et al. [27]. For convenience, the annular membranes with the first type of inner edges are referred to simply as Alekseev-type annular membranes (or annular membrane structures) [15,26], and those with the second type of inner edges are referred to simply as Sun-type annular membranes (or annular membrane structures) [27]. In this study, only the Alekseev-type annular membranes are involved.

Alekseev is the first person to deal with annular membrane problems [26], who algebraically solved the axisymmetric deformation problem of a peripherally fixed annular membrane, connected with a movable, weightless, stiff, concentric, circular thin plate at its inner edge, and transversely loaded at the center point of the circular thin plate. However, the closed-form solution presented in [26] is valid only for membranes with Poisson's ratios less than 1/3. Sun et al. [28] algebraically solved the problem dealt with originally by Alekseev [26] again and presented a global or complete closed-form solution that is valid for membranes with Poisson's ratio less than, equal to, or greater than 1/3. Yang et al. [29] extended the closed-form solution presented by Sun et al. [28] to the more general case of annular membranes with or without initial in-plane stress. In fact, many widely used thin films, such as polymers, often have Poisson's ratios greater than 1/3, and all the structures constituted more or less have some initial in-plane stresses. It is worth mentioning that the solutions presented by Alekseev [26], Sun et al. [28] and Yang et al. [29] are the only three algebraic solutions for membrane problems in the literature so far, which are derived from directly solving nonlinear differential equations by the algebraic method. As mentioned above, all these three solutions apply only to the problem of axisymmetric deformation of Alekseev-type annular membrane structures under concentrated forces, the case where the external loads (the concentrated forces) are applied at the center point of the weightless, stiff, concentric, circular thin plates and do not directly contact the annular membranes.

Lian et al. [15] proposed to use Alekseev-type annular membrane structures to design a membrane elastic deflection and parallel plate capacitor-based capacitive pressure sensor, where the uniformly distributed transverse loads are synchronously applied onto both the weightless, stiff, concentric, circular thin plate and the annular membrane, resulting in the parallel movement of the circular thin plate. It is obvious that the distance of parallel movement of the circular thin plate, wich is caused by the application of uniformly distributed transverse loads, is exactly equal to the maximum deflection of the annular membrane. Therefore, the circular thin plate, if made of conductive materials, can be used as a movable electrode plate of a parallel plate capacitor. The change in the capacitance of the parallel plate capacitor corresponds to the distance of parallel movement of the circular thin plate, also the maximum deflection of the annular membrane, and the uniformly distributed transverse loads applied. In this way, the pressure applied, i.e., the applied uniformly distributed transverse loads, may be determined by measuring the capacitance of the parallel plate capacitor, as long as the closed-form solution of the axisymmetric elastic deformation of the Alekseev-type annular membrane under uniformly distributed transverse loads can be obtained. Such a closed-form solution has been given by Lian et al. [15], which is in the form of power series. This closed-form solution is also the first power series solution for annular membrane problems. The derivation of this power series solution was a salutary reminder of the convergence of annular membrane problems: the power series method for annular membrane problems is more difficult to converge than that for circular membrane problems, due to the fact that the stress, strain or deflection in annular membrane problems can not be expanded into a power series at the center of the membranes while that in circular membrane problems can. This limitation means that the annular membrane problems solved by using the power series method must be first examined in convergence before the convergence of their power series solutions can be tested.

However, the closed-form solution presented by Lian et al. [15] is not applicable to the case where the annular membranes exhibit a too large rotation angle or deflection, because it was derived from the assumption of a small rotation angle of membrane which is usually adopted in membrane problems. This assumption will affect the accuracy of the closed-form solution and introduce large computational errors, especially when heavily loaded membranes exhibit a large rotation angle or deflection. In the derivation of the closed-form solution presented by Lian et al. [15], the out-of-plane and in-plane equations and geometric equations are established by using the assumption of a small rotation angle, except that the physical equations are established by using the assumption of a small deformation (the stress–strain relationships are assumed to satisfy Hooke's law). In this paper, the physical equations are still assumed to satisfy Hooke's law, but the assumption of a small rotation angle of membrane is given up during the establishments of the out-of-plane equilibrium equation and geometric equations, resulting in a new and more refined closed-form solution. Furthermore, our attempt to simultaneously give up the assumption of a small rotation angle in the establishments of the geometric equation, in-plane equation and out-of-plane equilibrium equation failed to achieve a closed-form solution. This suggests, to some extent, that the power series method for annular membrane problems is much more complicated than the power series method for circular membrane problems.

The paper is organized as follows: The problem of axisymmetric deformation with large deflection of an Alekseev-type annular membrane under uniformly distributed transverse loads is reformulated and solved in the following section, where the out-of-plane equilibrium equation and geometric equations are re-established with the assumption of a small rotation angle of membrane given up, and finally, a new and more refined closed-form solution of the problem under consideration is given. In Section 3, the convergence and effectiveness of the closed-form solution given in Section 2 are discussed. A numerical comparison between the present and previous closed-form solutions was conducted. The beneficial effect of the improved closed-form solution in Section 2 on developing the capacitive pressure sensors proposed by Lian et al. [15] is investigated by comparing the pressure values, which are, under the same deflection, calculated by using the closed-form solution presented in this paper and using the one presented by Lian et al. [15]. Concluding remarks are given in Section 4.

The innovation of this paper is mainly reflected in the following two aspects: one is the contribution to thin film mechanics, and the other is the practical applications that can be derived from this study. The new closed-form solution derived in Section 2 can be used for heavily loaded annular membranes with larger rotation angles, while the previous closed-form solution is only suitable for lightly loaded annular membranes with smaller rotation angles, thus, developing and enriching the theory of annular membranes. On the other hand, by simultaneously improving the out-of-plane equilibrium equation and geometric equation, the computational accuracy of the new closed-form solution is greatly improved. Therefore, if the new closed-form solution is used to design the capacitive pressure sensors proposed by Lian et al. [15], the pressure measurement error of the sensors designed may be reduced by up to 40% in comparison with the use of the previous closed-form solution, which is also the application significance and value of the work presented here.

2. Membrane Equation and Its Solution

A linearly elastic, initially flat annular membrane with inner radius b, outer radius a, thickness h, Young's modulus of elasticity E and Poisson's ratio v is fixed at its outer edge and connected at its inner edge with a movable, concentric, weightless, stiff, circular thin plate, forming an Alekseev-type annular membrane structure. A loads q is uniformly, transversely and quasi-statically applied onto the circular thin plate and the annular membrane, resulting in an out-of-plane displacement (deflection) of the annular membrane and a parallel movement of the circular thin plate, as shown in Figure 1, where the origin o of the introduced cylindrical coordinate system (r, φ, w) sits at the centroid of the initially flat annular membrane, the geometric middle plane of the initially flat annular membrane is located in the polar coordinate plane (r, φ), the radial coordinate is denoted by r, the angle coordinate is denoted by φ but not shown in Figure 1, and the axial coordinate is denoted by w that also denotes the deflection of the deflected annular membrane. Suppose a free body of a deflected annular membrane of radius r ($b \leq r \leq a$) is taken from the central portion of the deflected annular membrane, to study the static equilibrium of this free body under the joint action of the external active force $\pi r^2 q$ and internal reactive force $2\pi r \sigma_r h$, which are produced by the uniformly distributed transverse loads q and the membrane force $\sigma_r h$ at the boundary r, as shown in Figure 2, where θ is the rotation angle of the deflected annular membrane and σ_r is the radial stress.

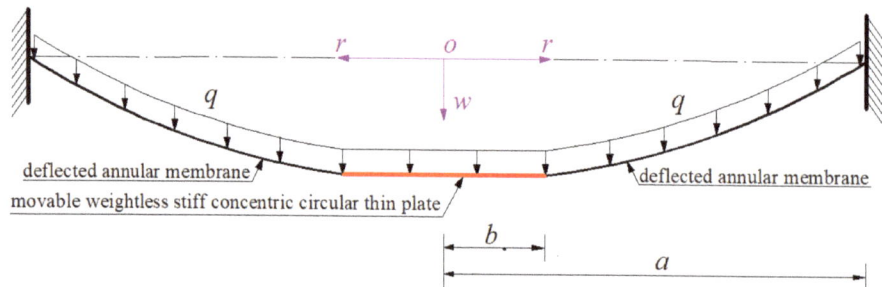

Figure 1. Deflection profile along a diameter of an Alekseev-type annular membrane under loads q.

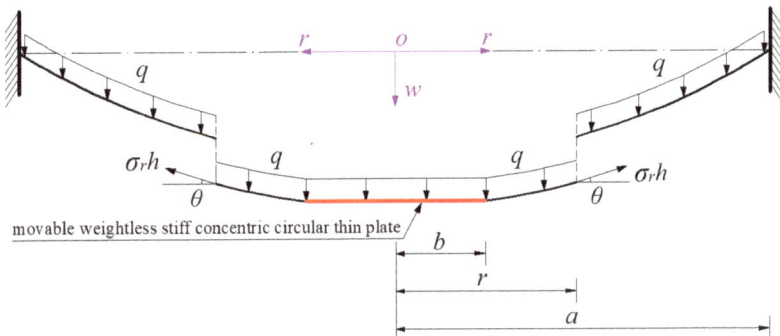

Figure 2. Equilibrium diagram of the free body with radius r ($b \leq r \leq a$).

In the transverse (vertical) direction, there are only two opposing forces, i.e., $\pi r^2 q$ and $2\pi r \sigma_r h \sin\theta$. Therefore, the equilibrium condition in this direction is that the resultant force of these two opposing forces is equal to zero, i.e.,

$$\pi r^2 q - 2\pi r \sigma_r h \sin\theta = 0. \quad (1)$$

If $w(r)$ is used to denote the deflection of the annular membrane at r, then

$$\tan\theta = -\frac{dw(r)}{dr}. \quad (2)$$

It is well known from trigonometric functions that $\sin\theta = 1/\sqrt{1 + 1/\tan^2\theta}$. Therefore, from Equations (1) and (2), the so-called out-of-plane equilibrium equation can be written as

$$2\sigma_r h = rq\sqrt{1 + 1/(-dw/dr)^2}. \quad (3)$$

By comparing Equation (3) in this paper and Equation (4) in [15], it can be found that the out-of-plane equilibrium equation in [15], i.e., Equation (4) in [15], uses the assumption of $\sin\theta = \tan\theta$. Obviously, this assumption is valid only when the rotation angle of membrane, θ, is small. For instance, the error caused by the assumption of $\sin\theta = \tan\theta$ can be written as $(\tan\theta - \sin\theta)/\sin\theta$ and is about 1.54% when $\theta = 10°$, 6.42% when $\theta = 20°$, 15.47% when $\theta = 30°$, and 30.54% when $\theta = 40°$. However, Equation (3) is not affected by this assumption, since this assumption is given up during the establishment of Equation (3).

If the circumferential stress is denoted by σ_t, then the in-plane equilibrium equation may be written as [15]

$$\frac{d}{dr}(r\sigma_r h) - \sigma_t h = 0. \quad (4)$$

If the radial displacement and strain and circumferential strain are denoted by $u(r)$, e_r and e_t, respectively, then the geometric equations may be written as [23]

$$e_r = [(1 + \frac{du}{dr})^2 + (\frac{dw}{dr})^2]^{1/2} - 1 \quad (5)$$

and

$$e_t = \frac{u}{r} \quad (6)$$

By comparing Equation (5) in this paper and Equation (6a) in [15], it can be found that the radial relationship between strain and displacement has been changed. The classical radial relationship between strain and displacement, i.e., Equation (6a) in [15], is heavily dependent on the assumption of small rotation angle of membrane, see [23] for details.

Moreover, the physical equations are still assumed to be linearly elastic [15]

$$\sigma_r = \frac{E}{1-v^2}(e_r + v e_t) \tag{7}$$

and

$$\sigma_t = \frac{E}{1-v^2}(e_t + v e_r). \tag{8}$$

In the above physical equations, geometric equations, in-plane equilibrium equation and out-of-plane equilibrium equation, there are six equations and six variables, i.e., $\sigma_r, \sigma_t, e_r, e_t, u(r)$ and $w(r)$. Therefore, this boundary value problem can be solved. Substituting Equations (5) and (6) into Equations (7) and (8) yields

$$\sigma_r = \frac{E}{1-v^2}\left\{\left[(1+\frac{du}{dr})^2 + (\frac{dw}{dr})^2\right]^{1/2} - 1 + v\frac{u}{r}\right\} \tag{9}$$

and

$$\sigma_t = \frac{E}{1-v^2}\left\{\frac{u}{r} + v\left[(1+\frac{du}{dr})^2 + (\frac{dw}{dr})^2\right]^{1/2} - v\right\}. \tag{10}$$

Eliminating u/r from Equations (9) and (10) and using Equation (4) yields

$$\frac{u}{r} = \frac{1}{Eh}(\sigma_t h - v\sigma_r h) = \frac{1}{Eh}\left[\frac{d}{dr}(r\sigma_r h) - v\sigma_r h\right]. \tag{11}$$

After the u in Equation (11) is substituted into Equation (9), then the so-called consistency equation can be written as

$$\frac{v-1}{E}\sigma_r + \frac{vr}{E}\frac{d\sigma_r}{dr} + \left\{[1 + \frac{(1-v)}{E}\sigma_r + \frac{(3-v)r}{E}\frac{d\sigma_r}{dr} + \frac{r^2}{E}\frac{d^2\sigma_r}{dr^2}]^2 + (\frac{dw}{dr})^2\right\}^{1/2} - 1 = 0. \tag{12}$$

σ_r, σ_t and w can be obtained by solving Equations (3), (4) and (12). The boundary conditions of solving Equations (3), (4) and (12) are

$$e_t = 0\left(\frac{u}{r} = 0\right) \text{ at } r = b, \tag{13}$$

$$e_t = 0\left(\frac{u}{r} = 0\right) \text{ at } r = a \tag{14}$$

and

$$w = 0 \text{ at } r = b. \tag{15}$$

The following dimensionless variables are introduced

$$Q = \frac{aq}{Eh}, W = \frac{w}{a}, S_r = \frac{\sigma_r}{E}, S_t = \frac{\sigma_t}{E}, \alpha = \frac{b}{a}, x = \frac{r}{a}, \tag{16}$$

and transform Equations (3), (4), (11)–(15) into

$$2S_r = xQ\sqrt{1 + 1/(-dW/dx)^2}, \tag{17}$$

$$\frac{d(xS_r)}{dx} - S_t = 0, \tag{18}$$

$$\frac{u}{r} = (1-v)S_r + x\frac{dS_r}{dx}, \tag{19}$$

$$(v-1)S_r + vx\frac{dS_r}{dx} + \left\{[1 + (1-v)S_r + (3-v)x\frac{dS_r}{dx} + x^2\frac{d^2S_r}{dx^2}]^2 + (\frac{dW}{dx})^2\right\}^{1/2} - 1 = 0, \tag{20}$$

$$(1-v)S_r + x\frac{dS_r}{dx} = 0 \text{ at } x = \alpha, \tag{21}$$

$$(1-v)S_r + x\frac{dS_r}{dx} = 0 \text{ at } x = 1 \tag{22}$$

and
$$W = 0 \text{ at } x = 1. \tag{23}$$

For practical physical problems, the displacement, strain and stress are all finite within $\alpha \leq x \leq 1$. Therefore, S_r and W can be expanded into the power series of the $x - \beta$

$$S_r = \sum_{i=0}^{\infty} c_i (x - \beta)^i \tag{24}$$

and

$$W = \sum_{i=0}^{\infty} d_i (x - \beta)^i, \tag{25}$$

where $\beta = (1 + \alpha)/2$. After introducing $X = x - \beta$, then Equations (17), (20), (24) and (25) can be transformed into

$$[4S_r^2 - (X + \beta)^2 Q^2](-\frac{dW}{dX})^2 - (X + \beta)^2 Q^2 = 0, \tag{26}$$

$$[1 + (1-\nu)S_r + (3-\nu)(X+\beta)\frac{dS_r}{dX} + (X+\beta)^2 \frac{d^2 S_r}{dX^2}]^2 + (\frac{dW}{dX})^2 \\ -[1-(\nu-1)S_r - \nu(X+\beta)\frac{dS_r}{dX}]^2 = 0 \tag{27}$$

$$S_r = \sum_{i=0}^{\infty} c_i X^i \tag{28}$$

and

$$W = \sum_{i=0}^{\infty} d_i X^i. \tag{29}$$

After substituting Equations (28) and (29) into Equations (26) and (27), the sums of the coefficients of the same powers of the X can be obtained by merging similar terms. A system of equations for determining the recursion formulas of the coefficients c_i and d_i may be obtained by letting all the sums of the coefficients be equal to zero. The resulting recursion formulas for the coefficients c_i and d_i are listed in Appendix A. It can be seen from Appendix A that the coefficients c_i ($i = 2, 3, 4, \ldots$) and d_i ($i = 1, 2, 3, \ldots$) can be expressed in terms of the first two coefficients c_0 and c_1.

The remaining coefficients c_0, c_1 and d_0 are three undetermined constants. Their values depend on the problem being dealt with, and are determined by Equations (21)–(23), the boundary conditions. After expressing the coefficients d_i ($i = 1, 2, 3, \ldots$) and c_i ($i = 2, 3, 4, \ldots$) in terms of c_0 and c_1, substituting Equation (24) into Equations (21) and (22) yields

$$(1-\nu)\sum_{i=0}^{\infty} c_i (\alpha - \beta)^i + \alpha \sum_{i=1}^{\infty} i c_i (\alpha - \beta)^{i-1} = 0 \tag{30}$$

and

$$(1-\nu)\sum_{i=0}^{\infty} c_i (1-\beta)^i + \sum_{i=1}^{\infty} i c_i (1-\beta)^{i-1} = 0, \tag{31}$$

and further, substituting Equation (25) into Equation (23) yields

$$d_0 = -\sum_{i=1}^{\infty} d_i (1-\beta)^i. \tag{32}$$

Because Equations (30) and (31) contain only c_0 and c_1, therefore, the values of c_0 and c_1 can be determined by simultaneously solving Equations (30) and (31). Further, with the known c_0 and c_1, all the values of c_i ($i = 2, 3, 4, \ldots$) and d_i ($i = 1, 2, 3, \ldots$) can be determined, and the value of d_0 can, thus, be determined by Equation (32).

Finally, with the known c_i and d_i, the particular solution of stress $\sigma_r(r)$ and deflection $w(r)$ can be determined. As for the expression of $\sigma_t(r)$, it can easily be determined with the known expression of $\sigma_r(r)$ and Equation (4). It is not necessary to address this easy problem here. Obviously, the maximum deflection, w_m, should be at $x = \alpha$, and from Equations (16) and (25), is given by

$$w_m = a \sum_{i=0}^{\infty} d_i \left(\frac{b-a}{2a}\right)^i. \tag{33}$$

From Equations (16) and (24), the maximum stress, σ_m, is given by

$$\sigma_m = \sigma_r(b) = E \sum_{i=0}^{\infty} c_i \left(\frac{b-a}{2a}\right)^i. \tag{34}$$

3. Results and Discussions

This section will first analyze the convergence of the closed-form solution given in Section 2, then investigate its effectiveness (asymptotic behavior) and, finally, make a comparison between the present and previous closed-form solutions.

3.1. Convergence Analysis

As mentioned in the introduction, the annular membrane problems solved by using the power series method are usually difficult to converge. Therefore, they must be first examined in convergence before their power series solutions are tested in convergence. To this end, an annular membrane problem is considered of an Alekseev-type annular membrane with Poisson's ratio $v = 0.47$, Young's modulus of elasticity $E = 7.84$ MPa, outer radius $a = 70$ mm, inner radius $b = 40$ mm, and thickness $h = 0.2$ mm subjected to the loads $q = 0.0001$ MPa. After the values of E, v, a, b, h and q are substituted into Equation (16), it is found that $\alpha = 4/7$, $\beta = (1+\alpha)/2 = 11/14$ and $Q = 0.00446429$.

First, let us truncate the infinite power series in Equations (30)–(32) to the nth terms, i.e.,

$$(1-v)\sum_{i=0}^{n} c_i (\alpha - \beta)^i + \alpha \sum_{i=1}^{n} i c_i (\alpha - \beta)^{i-1} = 0, \tag{35}$$

$$(1-v)\sum_{i=0}^{n} c_i (1-\beta)^i + \sum_{i=1}^{n} i c_i (1-\beta)^{i-1} = 0 \tag{36}$$

and

$$d_0 = -\sum_{i=1}^{n} d_i (1-\beta)^i. \tag{37}$$

The parameter n in Equations (35)–(37) can first take 2 to start the numerical calculations of the undetermined constants c_0, c_1 and d_0, then take 3, 4, ... until 11. The results of the numerical calculations of c_0, c_1 and d_0 are listed in Table 1. The variations of c_0, c_1 and d_0 with n are shown in Figures 3–5, where the dash-dotted lines show the convergence trends of the data points of even terms ($n = 2, 4, 6 \ldots$) and the dashed lines show that of odd terms ($n = 3, 5, 7 \ldots$). From Figures 3–5, it can be seen that the data sequences for c_0, c_1 and d_0 have a very good convergence trend and show a very good saturation when the parameter n takes 8 or 9, which indicates that the undetermined constants c_0, c_1 and d_0 when $q = 0.0001$ MPa can take the numerical values calculated by $n = 8$ or 9.

Table 1. The results of numerical calculation of c_0, c_1 and d_0 for $q = 0.0001$ MPa.

n	c_0	c_1	d_0
2	0.01197985	−0.00943991	0.03886790
3	0.01492981	−0.00851534	0.03058498
4	0.01287976	−0.00753818	0.03579442
5	0.01323855	−0.00739810	0.03468850
6	0.01301745	−0.00730386	0.03531982

Table 1. Cont.

n	c_0	c_1	d_0
7	0.01306394	−0.00728509	0.03517532
8	0.01303710	−0.00727377	0.03525289
9	0.01304256	−0.00727152	0.03523588
10	0.01303968	−0.00727034	0.03524527
11	0.01304025	−0.00726945	0.03524248

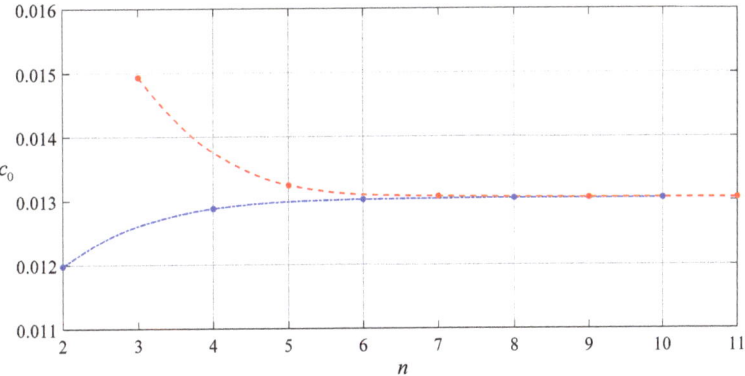

Figure 3. Variation of c_0 with n for $q = 0.0001$ MPa, where the dash-dotted line shows the convergence trend of the data points of even terms ($n = 2, 4, 6 \ldots$) and the dashed line shows that of odd terms ($n = 3, 5, 7 \ldots$).

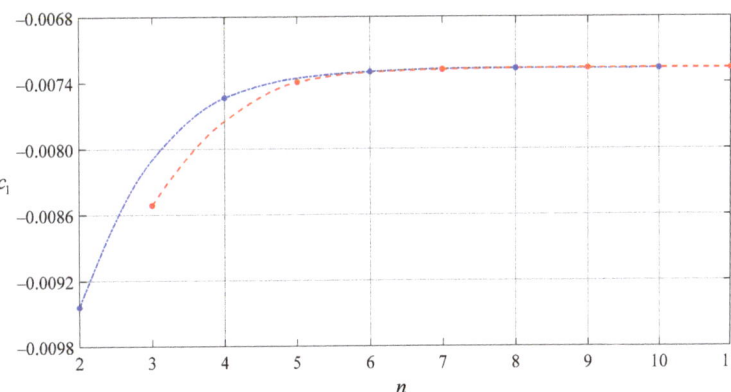

Figure 4. Variation of c_1 with n for $q = 0.0001$ MPa, where the dash-dotted line shows the convergence trend of the data points of even terms ($n = 2, 4, 6 \ldots$) and the dashed line shows that of odd terms ($n = 3, 5, 7 \ldots$).

It is well known that higher order equations can generate multiple roots, meaning, multiple roots of c_0 and c_1 could be generated when solving Equations (35) and (36) simultaneously. In boundary value problems, however, there are usually no judgment conditions that can be used to determine which of these roots is a valid root. However, it can be believed that since the power of the power series in Equations (35)–(37) is continuously increasing at equal intervals (i.e., the parameter n in Equations (35)–(37) consecutively takes values from 2 to 11), the corresponding results of numerical calculations of c_0, c_1 and d_0 should also be consecutively changing. Therefore, the variations of the numerically calculated values of c_0, c_1 and d_0 with n should obey some continuous and smooth functions, and, if expressed graphically, should follow some continuous and smooth curves. So, continuity and smoothness can be used to judge and determine valid roots, and the results of numerical calculations of c_0, c_1 and d_0 listed in Table 1 are obtained in such a way (invalid roots are not listed in Table 1). Of course, we can also make no distinction between odd and even terms when drawing Figures 3–5. This will give oscillation convergence trends, as shown in Figures 6–8. However, doing so is not conducive to the full demonstration of smoothness in some cases, as shown in Figure 7 (please compare to Figure 4).

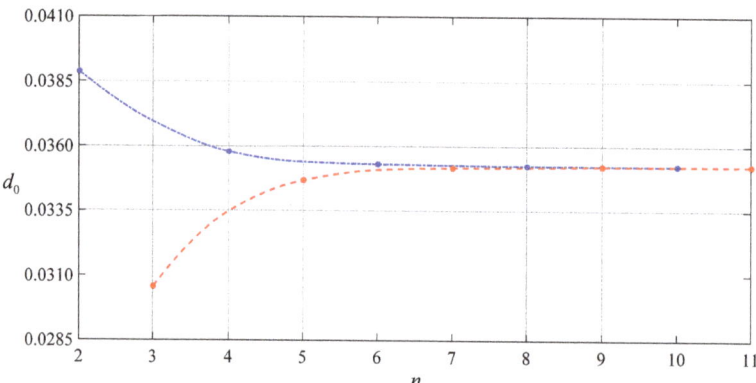

Figure 5. Variation of d_0 with n for q = 0.0001 MPa, where the dash-dotted line shows the convergence trend of the data points of even terms (n = 2, 4, 6 ...) and the dashed line shows that of odd terms (n = 3, 5, 7 ...).

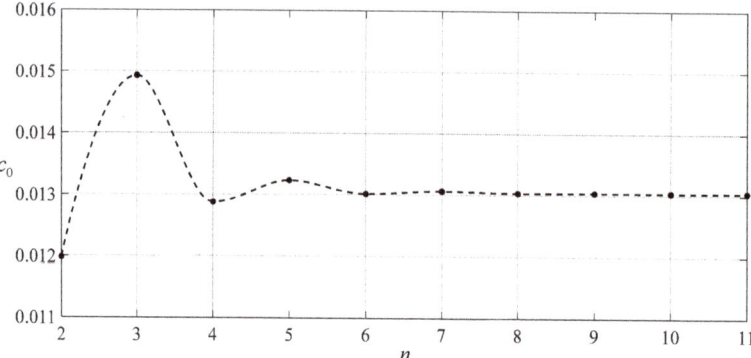

Figure 6. Variation of c_0 with n for q = 0.0001 MPa.

It should be pointed that for the boundary value problems solved by the power series method, the convergence of the particular solutions can be checked only after the convergence values of the undetermined constants $c0$, $c1$ and $d0$ are determined. From Figures 3–5 or Figures 6–8, it can be seen that the data sequences of $c0$, $c1$ and $d0$ have been converging well at about n = 8 or 9, therefore, the undetermined constants $c0$, $c1$ and $d0$ when q = 0.0001 MPa can take the numerical values calculated by $n \geq 8$ or 9. Here, we take the numerical values at n = 11 in Table 1 as the convergence values of the undetermined constants $c0$, $c1$ and $d0$ when q = 0.0001 MPa, that is, $c0$ = 0.01304025, $c1 = -0.00726945$ and $d0 = 0.03524248$. Obviously, the power series particular solutions of stress and deflection converge throughout the closed interval [4/7, 1] as long as they converge at the two ends of the closed interval. Tables 2 and 3 show the numerical values of stress and deflection at the two ends of the closed interval [4/7, 1], which are calculated by using Equations (24) and (25). Figures 9–12 show the variations of $ci(1 - \beta)^i$,

$c_i(\alpha - \beta)^i$, $d_i(1 - \beta)^i$ and $d_i(\alpha - \beta)^i$ with i, indicating that the power series particular solutions of stress and deflection converge very quickly.

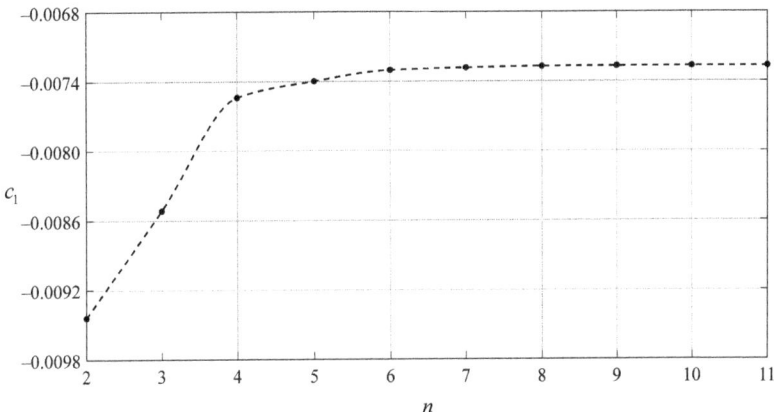

Figure 7. Variation of c_1 with n for $q = 0.0001$ MPa.

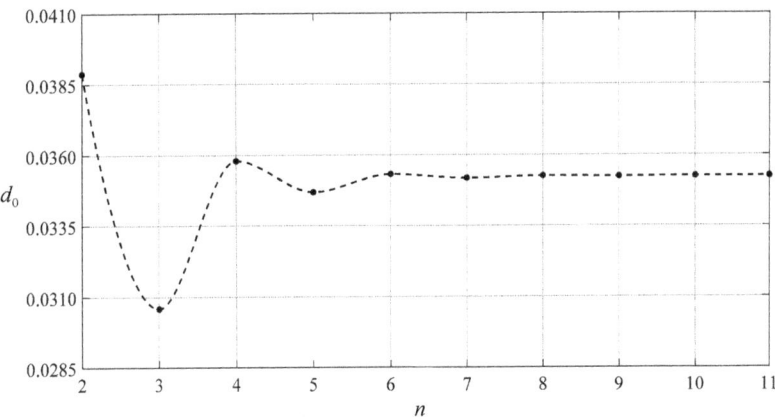

Figure 8. Variation of d_0 with n for $q = 0.0001$ MPa.

Table 2. The numerically calculated values of $c_i(1 - \beta)^i$ and $c_i(\alpha - \beta)^i$ when $q = 0.0001$ MPa, $\alpha = 4/7$ and $\beta = 11/14$.

i	$c_i(1 - \beta)^i$	$c_i(\alpha - \beta)^i$
0	0.01304025	0.01304025
1	-0.00155774	0.00155774
2	0.00029641	0.00029641
3	-0.00016810	0.00016810
4	$5.29538927 \times 10^{-5}$	$5.29538927 \times 10^{-5}$
5	$-1.80161742 \times 10^{-5}$	$1.80161742 \times 10^{-5}$
6	$5.60599264 \times 10^{-6}$	$5.60599264 \times 10^{-6}$
7	$-1.75933493 \times 10^{-6}$	$1.75933493 \times 10^{-6}$
8	$5.35507803 \times 10^{-7}$	$5.35507803 \times 10^{-7}$
9	$-1.62632278 \times 10^{-7}$	$1.62632278 \times 10^{-7}$
10	$4.86626780 \times 10^{-8}$	$4.86626780 \times 10^{-8}$
11	$-1.44986110 \times 10^{-8}$	$1.44986110 \times 10^{-8}$

Table 3. The numerically calculated values of $d_i(1-\beta)^i$ and $d_i(\alpha-\beta)^i$ when $q = 0.0001$ MPa, $\alpha = 4/7$ and $\beta = 11/14$.

i	$d_i(1-\beta)^i$	$d_i(\alpha-\beta)^i$
0	0.03524248	0.03524248
1	−0.02908424	0.02908424
2	−0.00580824	−0.00580824
3	−0.00028009	0.00028009
4	$-5.91427706 \times 10^{-5}$	$-5.91427706 \times 10^{-5}$
5	$-9.23001859 \times 10^{-6}$	$9.23001859 \times 10^{-6}$
6	$-8.68232313 \times 10^{-7}$	$-8.68232313 \times 10^{-7}$
7	$-4.31388327 \times 10^{-7}$	$4.31388327 \times 10^{-7}$
8	$-3.77046968 \times 10^{-9}$	$-3.77046968 \times 10^{-9}$
9	$-1.85145370 \times 10^{-8}$	$1.85145370 \times 10^{-8}$
10	$-1.25152469 \times 10^{-10}$	$-1.25152469 \times 10^{-10}$
11	$-5.73606617 \times 10^{-10}$	$5.73606617 \times 10^{-10}$

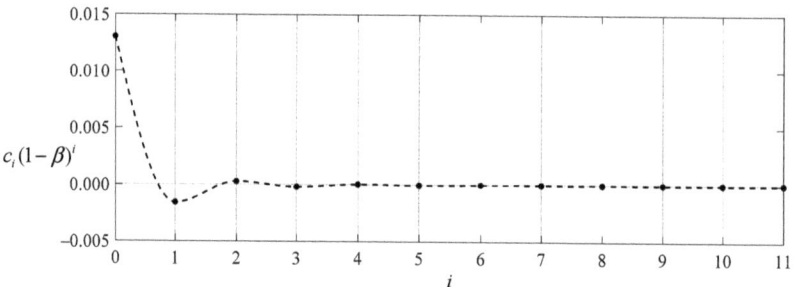

Figure 9. Variation of $c_i(1-\beta)^i$ with i for $q = 0.0001$ MPa and $\beta = 11/14$.

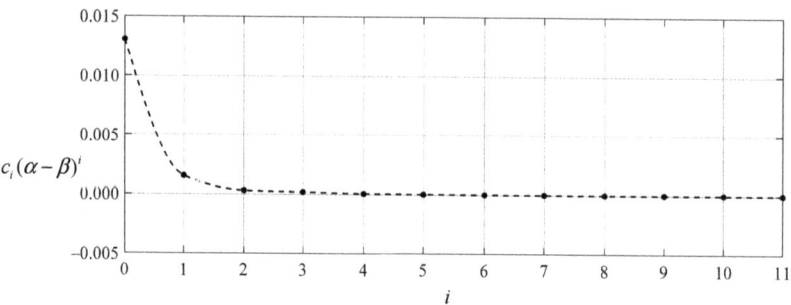

Figure 10. Variation of $c_i(\alpha-\beta)^i$ with i for $q = 0.0001$ MPa, $\alpha = 4/7$ and $\beta = 11/14$.

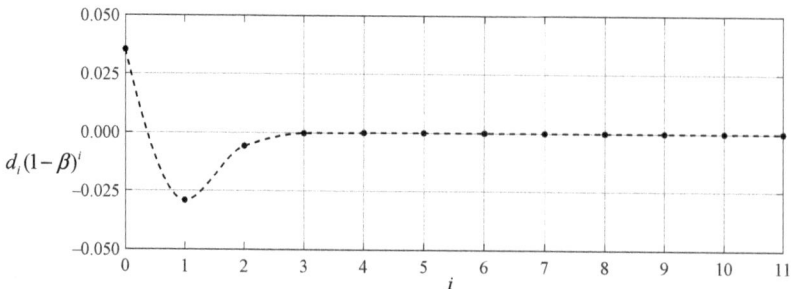

Figure 11. Variation of $d_i(1-\beta)^i$ with i for $q = 0.0001$ MPa and $\beta = 11/14$.

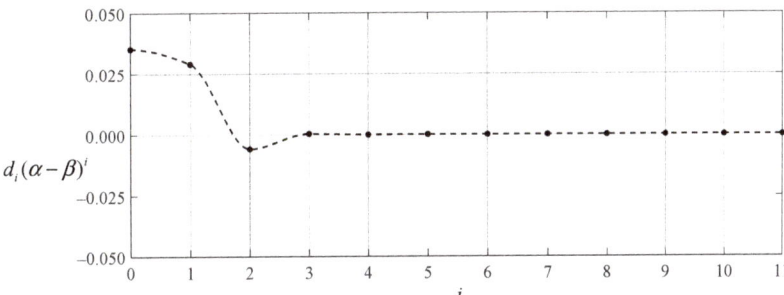

Figure 12. Variation of $d_i(\alpha - \beta)^i$ with i for $q = 0.0001$ MPa, $\alpha = 4/7$ and $\beta = 11/14$.

In fact, the magnitude of the applied loads q (corresponding to the different geometry of a deflected annular membrane) has a certain effect on the convergence values of the undetermined constants c_0, c_1 and d_0, which can be seen from the calculations below. Let us continue with the example above but increase the loads q from 0.0001 MPa to 0.008 MPa. Table 4 shows the results of the numerical calculation of the undetermined constants c_0, c_1 and d_0 for the problem of an Alekseev-type annular membrane with Poisson's ratio $v = 0.47$, Young's modulus of elasticity $E = 7.84$ MPa, outer radius $a = 70$ mm, inner radius $b = 40$ mm and thickness $h = 0.2$ mm, where $q = 0.008$ MPa, $\alpha = 4/7$, $\beta = (1 + \alpha)/2 = 11/14$ and $Q = aq/Eh = 0.35714286$. The variations of c_0, c_1 and d_0 with n are shown in Figures 13–15, where the dash-dotted lines show the convergence trend of the data points of even terms ($n = 2, 4, 6 \ldots$) and the dashed line show that of odd terms ($n = 3, 5, 7 \ldots$). From Figures 13–15, it can be seen that the data sequences of c_0, c_1 and d_0 have a very good convergence trend and show a very good saturation when the parameter n takes 9 or 10, which indicates that the undetermined constants c_0, c_1 and d_0 when $q = 0.008$ MPa can take the numerical values calculated by $n = 9$ or 10.

Table 4. The results of the numerical calculation of c_0, c_1 and d_0 when $q = 0.008$ MPa.

n	c_0	c_1	d_0
2	0.24525643	−0.19325783	0.19851576
3	0.29529305	−0.16306971	0.14895366
4	0.26747513	−0.14877045	0.17425372
5	0.27846455	−0.14657377	0.16504231
6	0.27237181	−0.14333397	0.17021351
7	0.27426590	−0.14246365	0.16824011
8	0.27364233	−0.14211856	0.16936731
9	0.27435725	−0.14198977	0.16918853
10	0.27420479	−0.14206417	0.16928792
11	0.27422132	−0.14202197	0.16921323
12	0.27421202	−0.14205290	0.16926132
13	0.27421591	−0.14203814	0.16923154

From the comparison between Figures 13–15 and Figures 3–5, it can be seen that due to the increase from $q = 0.0001$ MPa to $q = 0.008$ MPa, the convergence points have been moved slightly back, i.e., from $n = 8$ or 9 at $q = 0.0001$ MPa (see Figures 3–5) to $n = 9$ or 10 at $q = 0.008$ MPa (see Figures 13–15). This means that the magnitude of the applied loads q has a certain effect on the convergence values of the undetermined constants c_0, c_1 and d_0.

From Figures 13–15, it can be seen that the data sequences of c_0, c_1 and d_0 have been converging well at about $n = 9$ or 10, indicating that the undetermined constants c_0, c_1 and d_0 when $q = 0.008$MPa can take the numerical values calculated by $n \geq 9$ or 10. Therefore, the numerical values at $n = 13$ in Table 4, i.e., $c_0 = 0.27421591$, $c_1 = -0.14203814$ and $d_0 = 0.16923154$, can be taken as the convergence values of the undetermined constants c_0, c_1 and d_0 when $q = 0.008$ MPa to determine the power series particular solutions of stress and deflection. The results of numerical calculation of stress and deflection at the two ends of the closed interval [4/7, 1], which are calculated by using Equations (24) and (25), are listed in Tables 5 and 6. Figures 16–19 show the variations of $c_i(1-\beta)^i$, $c_i(\alpha-\beta)^i$, $d_i(1-\beta)^i$ and $d_i(\alpha-\beta)^i$ with i, indicating that the power series particular solutions of stress and deflection when $q = 0.008$ MPa still converge very quickly in comparison with Figures 9–12 ($q = 0.0001$ MPa).

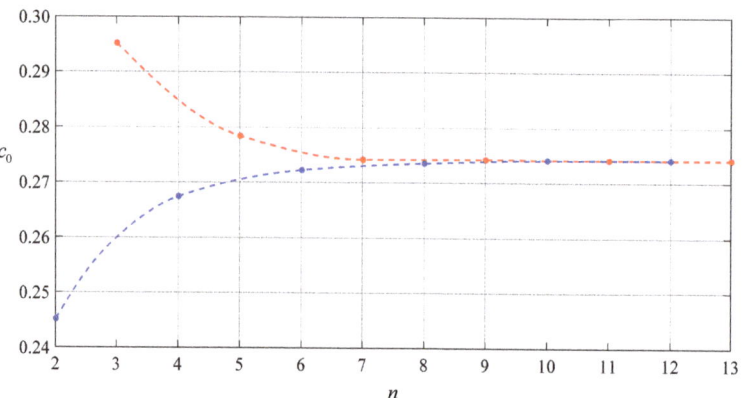

Figure 13. Variation of c_0 with n for $q = 0.008$ MPa, where the dash-dotted line shows the convergence trend of the data points of even terms ($n = 2, 4, 6 \dots$) and the dashed line shows that of odd terms ($n = 3, 5, 7 \dots$).

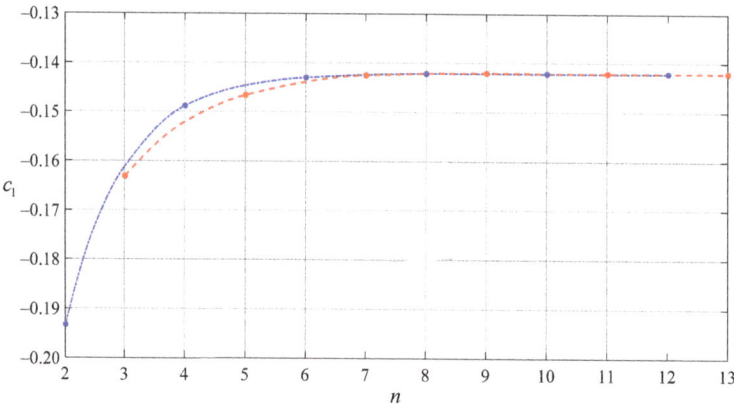

Figure 14. Variation of c_1 with n for $q = 0.008$ MPa, where the dash-dotted line shows the convergence trend of the data points of even terms ($n = 2, 4, 6 \dots$) and the dashed line shows that of odd terms ($n = 3, 5, 7 \dots$).

Combining the above, it can be concluded that the increase in the loads q from 0.0001 MPa to 0.008 MPa mainly affects the determination of the convergence values of the undetermined constants c_0, c_1 and d_0, but has little influence on the convergence of the power series particular solutions of stress and deflection. Therefore, regardless of the magnitude of the applied loads q (corresponding to the different geometry of a deflected annular membrane), the convergence values of the undetermined constants c_0, c_1 and d_0 should be determined in terms of the convergence on the scatter diagrams (such as Figures 3–5 or Figures 13–15). From this point of view, drawing a scatter diagram is a very important work for the power series solution of ordinary differential equations, but in practice, its importance is often ignored.

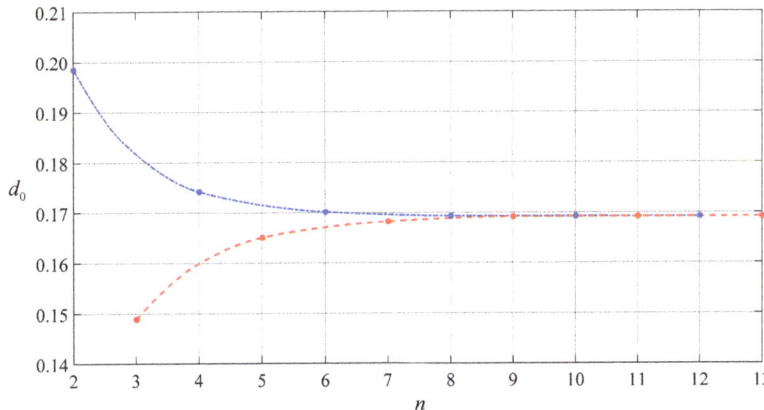

Figure 15. Variation of d_0 with n for $q = 0.008$ MPa, where the dash-dotted line shows the convergence trend of the data points of even terms ($n = 2, 4, 6 \ldots$) and the dashed line shows that of odd terms ($n = 3, 5, 7 \ldots$).

Table 5. The numerically calculated values of $c_i(1 - \beta)^i$ and $c_i(\alpha - \beta)^i$ when $q = 0.008$ MPa, $\alpha = 4/7$ and $\beta = 11/14$.

i	$c_i(1 - \beta)^i$	$c_i(\alpha - \beta)^i$
0	0.27421591	0.27421591
1	−0.03043674	0.03043674
2	0.00655555	0.00655555
3	−0.00409301	0.00409301
4	$9.57948254 \times 10^{-4}$	$9.57948254 \times 10^{-4}$
5	$-4.72257108 \times 10^{-4}$	$4.72257108 \times 10^{-4}$
6	$8.39765267 \times 10^{-5}$	$8.39765267 \times 10^{-5}$
7	$-5.62440026 \times 10^{-5}$	$5.62440026 \times 10^{-5}$
8	$2.39571485 \times 10^{-6}$	$2.39571485 \times 10^{-6}$
9	$-8.48354140 \times 10^{-6}$	$8.48354140 \times 10^{-6}$
10	$1.71560584 \times 10^{-6}$	$1.71560584 \times 10^{-6}$
11	$-1.92778425 \times 10^{-6}$	$1.92778425 \times 10^{-6}$
12	$8.75934218 \times 10^{-7}$	$8.75934218 \times 10^{-7}$
13	$-6.26245384 \times 10^{-7}$	$6.26245384 \times 10^{-7}$

Table 6. The numerically calculated values of $d_i(1 - \beta)^i$ and $d_i(\alpha - \beta)^i$ when $q = 0.008$ MPa, $\alpha = 4/7$ and $\beta = 11/14$.

i	$d_i(1 - \beta)^i$	$d_i(\alpha - \beta)^i$
0	0.16923154	0.16923154
1	−0.12761152	0.12761152
2	−0.03316675	−0.03316675
3	−0.00559019	0.00559019
4	−0.00186868	−0.00186868
5	$-6.72098886 \times 10^{-4}$	$6.72098886 \times 10^{-4}$
6	$-2.62267256 \times 10^{-4}$	$-2.62267256 \times 10^{-4}$
7	$-1.11698057 \times 10^{-4}$	$1.11698057 \times 10^{-4}$
8	$-4.86768405 \times 10^{-5}$	$-4.86768405 \times 10^{-5}$
9	$-2.22870953 \times 10^{-5}$	$2.22870953 \times 10^{-5}$
10	$-1.04435147 \times 10^{-5}$	$-1.04435147 \times 10^{-5}$
11	$-5.03839569 \times 10^{-6}$	$5.03839569 \times 10^{-6}$
12	$-2.48735974 \times 10^{-6}$	$-2.48735974 \times 10^{-6}$
13	$-1.25620215 \times 10^{-6}$	$1.25620215 \times 10^{-6}$

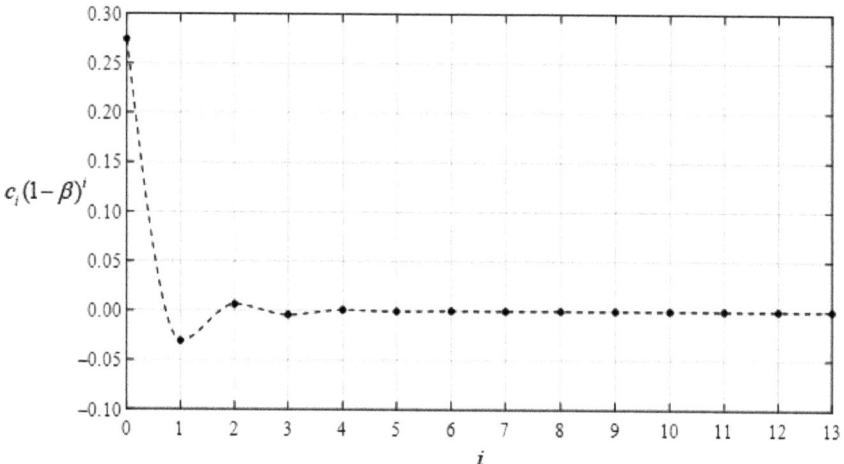

Figure 16. Variation of $c_i(1-\beta)^i$ with i when $q = 0.008$ MPa and $\beta = 11/14$.

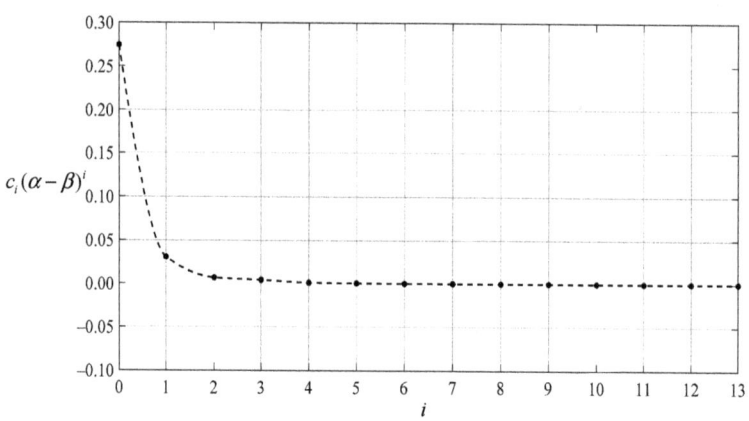

Figure 17. Variation of $c_i(\alpha-\beta)^i$ with i when $q = 0.008$ MPa, $\alpha = 4/7$ and $\beta = 11/14$.

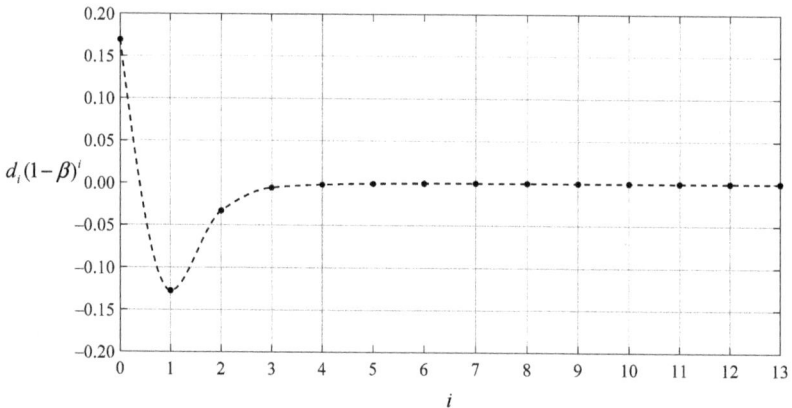

Figure 18. Variation of $d_i(1-\beta)^i$ with i when $q = 0.008$ MPa and $\beta = 11/14$.

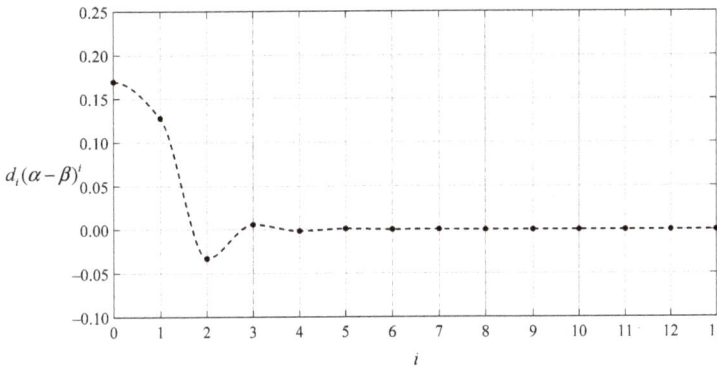

Figure 19. Variation of $d_i(\alpha - \beta)^i$ with i when $q = 0.008$ MPa, $\alpha = 4/7$ and $\beta = 11/14$.

3.2. Asymptotic Behavior of the Closed-Form Solution

The effectiveness of the closed-form solution obtained in Section 2 may be proved by its asymptotic behavior from an annular membrane to a circular membrane, that is, the closed-form solution of an Alekseev-type annular membrane with outer radius a and inner radius b, which is given in Section 2, should be equivalent to the closed-form solution of a circular membrane with outer radius a, when the inner radius of the annular membrane approaches zero ($b\rightarrow 0$). To this end, the closed-form solution of circular membranes presented by Lian et al. in 2020 [23] is specially used here, which is obtained by using the same out-of-plane, in-plane, geometric and physical equations used in this paper. The circular membrane and Alekseev-type annular membrane are subjected to the same action of loads $q = 0.0002$ MPa and have the same thickness $h = 0.2$ mm, outer radius $a = 70$ mm, Poisson's ratio $v = 0.47$, and Young's modulus of elasticity $E = 7.84$ MPa, and the inner radius of the Alekseev-type annular membrane takes $b = 60$ mm, 40 mm, 20 mm and 10 mm, respectively. Their deflection profiles along a diameter are shown in Figure 20, where the solid lines ("Present study") refer to the deflection curves of the Alekseev-type annular membranes, which are calculated by the closed-form solution given in Section 2, and the dash-dotted solid line ("Lian et al., 2020") refers to the deflection curve of the circular membrane, which is calculated by the closed-form solution given by Lian et al. in 2020 [23]. From Figure 20, it can be seen that as the inner radius of the Alekseev-type annular membranes gradually approach zero ($b\rightarrow 0$), their deflection curves are gradually closed to the deflection curve of the circular membrane. This indicates that the derivation of the closed-form solution given in Section 2 is, to some extent, correct and reliable.

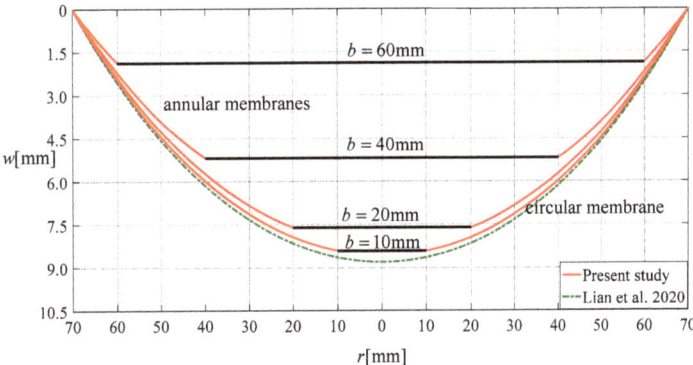

Figure 20. Deflection profiles along a diameter of four Alekseev-type annular membranes and a circular membrane when $q = 0.0002$ MPa.

3.3. Comparison between Closed-Form Solutions before and after Improvement

To quantitatively analyze the difference between the closed-form solutions before and after improvement (i.e., the closed-form solutions presented by Lian et al. [15] and in this paper), an example is considered of an Alekseev-type annular membrane with thickness $h = 0.2$ mm, inner radius $b = 40$ mm, outer radius $a = 70$ mm, Poisson's ratio $v = 0.47$ and Young's modulus of elasticity $E = 7.84$ MPa, which is subjected to the loads $q = 0.0002$ MPa, 0.008 MPa and 0.035 MPa, respectively. Figures 21 and 22 show the variations of deflection and stress differences with loads q, where the dashed lines ("Lian et al., 2017") are calculated by using the closed-form solution which was presented by Lian et al. in 2017 [15] and the solid lines ("Present study") by using the closed-form solution given in Section 2. It can be seen from Figure 21 that as the uniformly distributed transverse loads q increase from 0.0002 MPa to 0.035 MPa, the differences in deflection also increase, and the differences in maximum deflection are about 5.195 mm − 5.162 mm = 0.033 mm when $q = 0.0002$ MPa, 18.761 mm − 17.654 mm = 1.107 mm when $q = 0.008$ MPa, and 32.346 mm − 28.873 mm = 3.473 mm when $q = 0.035$ MPa. Additionally, it can be seen from Figure 22 that as the uniformly distributed transverse loads q increase from 0.0002 MPa to 0.035 MPa, the differences in stress also increase. The differences in maximum stress are about 0.189518 MPa − 0.187173 MPa = 0.002345 MPa when $q = 0.0002$ MPa, 2.484320 MPa − 2.189192 MPa = 0.295128 MPa when $q = 0.008$ MPa, and 8.142192 MPa − 5.856020 MPa = 2.286172 MPa when $q = 0.035$ MPa, while the differences in minimum stress are about 0.145827 MPa − 0.143930 MPa = 0.001897 MPa when $q = 0.0002$ MPa, 1.934280 MPa − 1.684316 MPa = 0.250864 MPa when $q = 0.008$ MPa, and 6.483791 MPa − 4.503084 MPa = 1.980707 MPa when $q = 0.035$ MPa. Figures 21 and 22 suggest that the closed-form solutions, which are presented by Lian et al. [15] and in this paper, are very close to each other for lightly loaded membranes and diverge gradually as the loads q applied intensifies. Therefore, the closed-form solution presented in this paper should be used preferentially for heavily loaded Alekseev-type annular membranes with larger rotation angles.

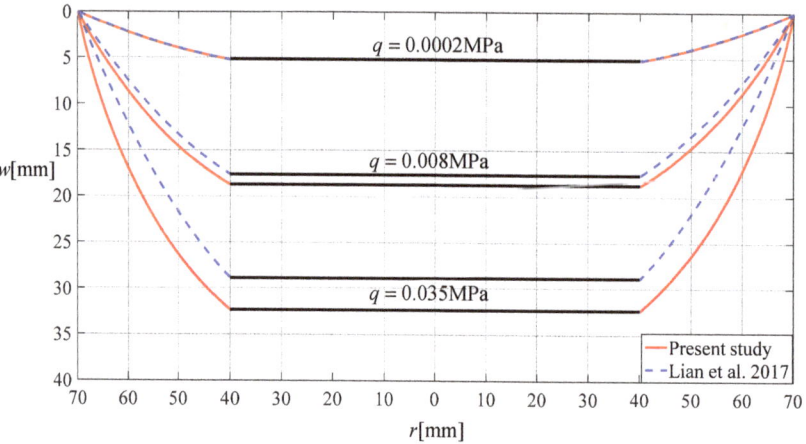

Figure 21. Variations of differences in deflection with loads q.

Now, let us analyze qualitatively the difference between the closed-form solutions before and after improvement from the point of view of the asymptotic behavior of annular membrane solutions gradually approaching circular membrane solutions. We continue with the example in Section 3.2 but increase the loads q from 0.0002 MPa to 0.01 MPa. The deflection profiles along a diameter are shown in Figure 23, where the solid lines ("Present study") refer to the deflection curves of four Alekseev-type annular membranes with outer radius $a = 70$ mm and inner radius $b = 60$ mm, 40 mm, 20 mm and 10 mm under $q = 0.01$ MPa, which are calculated by using the closed-form solution given in Section 2, the dashed lines ("Lian et al., 2017") refer to the deflection curves of four Alekseev-type annular membranes with outer radius $a = 70$ mm and inner radius $b = 60$ mm, 40 mm, 20 mm and 10 mm under $q = 0.01$ MPa, which are calculated by using the closed-form solution presented by Lian et al. in 2017 [15], and the dash-dotted solid line ("Lian et al., 2020") refers to the deflection curve of the circular membrane with outer radius $a = 70$ mm under $q = 0.01$ MPa, which is calculated by using the closed-form solution given by Lian et al. in 2020 [23]. It can be seen from Figure 23 that the asymptotic behavior of the "Present study" gradually approaching the "Lian et al., 2020" can still remain constant when $q = 0.01$ MPa.

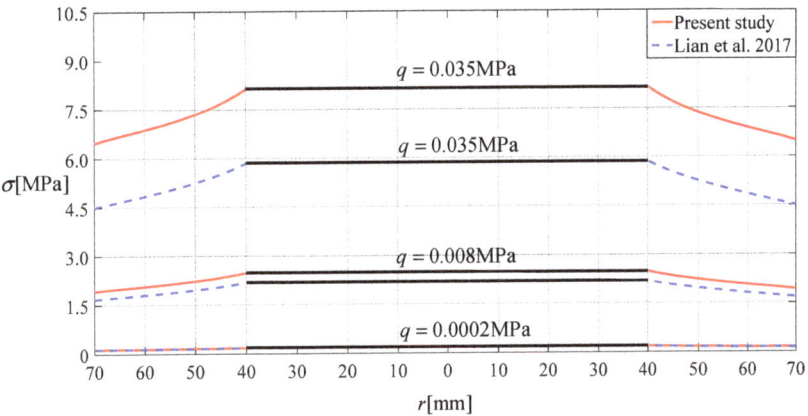

Figure 22. Variations of differences in stress with loads q.

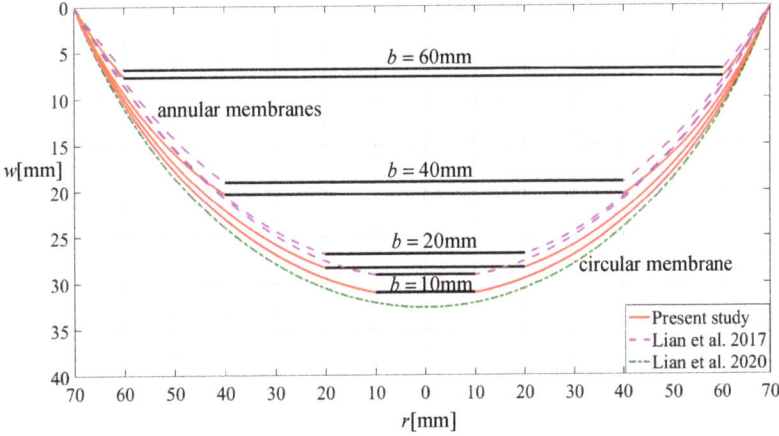

Figure 23. Deflection profiles along a diameter of eight Alekseev-type annular membranes and a circular membrane when $q = 0.01$ MPa.

However, from Figure 23 it can also be seen that the asymptotic behavior of the "Lian et al., 2017" gradually approaching the "Lian et al., 2020" is, in terms of the effect, inferior to the asymptotic behavior of the "Present study" gradually approaching the "Lian et al., 2020". The gap between the two gradually increases as the inner radius b of the Alekseev-type annular membranes gradually decreases, see Figure 23. So, in theory, when $b \to 0$, if the "Present study" can be close to the "Lian et al., 2020", then the "Lian et al., 2017" will never be close to the "Lian et al., 2020". Therefore, from this point of view, if the "Lian et al., 2020" is used as the benchmark (the closed-form solution of circular membranes presented by Lian et al. in 2020 [23] has certain credibility because it is an improvement on a classic well-established solution, the well-known Hencky solution, see [23] for details), then it can be qualitatively concluded as follows: under the same conditions the closed-form solution presented in this paper has higher computational accuracy than the closed-form solution presented by Lian et al. in 2017 [15].

3.4. Beneficial Effect of Improved Closed-Form Solution on Pressure Measurement

In the pressure measurement systems (using the capacitive pressure sensors proposed by Lian et al. [15]), the maximum deflection w_m of the Alekseev-type annular membranes under pressure q can be determined by capacitance measurement, then the pressure q applied can be determined with the determined maximum deflection w_m and the closed-form solution of the elastic behavior of the Alekseev-type annular membranes under pressure q. Therefore, the beneficial effect of the improved closed-form solution presented in this paper on developing the pressure measurement systems (using the capacitive pressure sensors proposed by Lian et al. [15]) can be directly reflected by the difference of the pressure calculation values, where the closed-form solutions presented in this paper and presented by Lian et al. [15] are used for the pressure calculations under the same maximum deflection w_m.

To this end, the Alekseev-type annular membrane used in Section 3.3 is used again, i.e., thickness h = 0.2 mm, inner radius b = 40 mm, outer radius a = 70 mm, Poisson's ratio v = 0.47 and Young's modulus of elasticity E = 7.84 MPa. Let this Alekseev-type annular membrane first subjected to the loads q = 0.0002 MPa, 0.008 MPa and 0.035 MPa, respectively, where the maximum deflections produced are w_m = 5.195 mm for q = 0.0002 MPa, w_m = 18.761 mm for q = 0.008 MPa, and w_m = 32.346 mm for q = 0.035 MPa, which are calculated by using the closed-form solution presented in this paper. Then, use the closed-form solution presented by Lian et al. [15] to calculate the pressure q required when this Alekseev-type annular membrane produces the same maximum deflections w_m, i.e., w_m = 5.195 mm, 18.761 mm and 32.346 mm, respectively. These calculations result in that w_m = 5.195 mm requires about q = 0.000204 MPa, w_m = 18.761 mm requires about q = 0.0096 MPa, and w_m = 32.346 mm requires about q = 0.0492 MPa, respectively. For the sake of intuition and clarity, the calculation results are listed in Table 7 and shown in Figure 24, where the "Present study" refers to the results calculated by using the closed-form solution given in Section 2 and the "Lian et al., 2017" refers to the results calculated by using the closed-form solution which was given by Lian et al. in 2017 [15]. It can be seen from Table 7 that as the maximum deflection w_m increases from 5.195 mm to 32.346 mm (the ratio of maximum deflection to diameter of the annular membrane is about 0.037 to 0.231), the relative errors of "Lian et al., 2017" with respect to "Present study" increases from 2% to 40.57%. This is because the increase in the maximum deflection w_m makes the rotation angle of the annular membrane bigger and bigger, so that the small rotation angle assumption used for establishing the out-of-plane equilibrium equation and geometric equation in [15], i.e., Equations (4) and (6) in [15], is less and less valid due to the bigger and bigger rotation angle. So, if the closed-form solution which was presented by Lian et al. in 2017 [15] is used to predict the pressure q required for a certain maximum deflection w_m determined by capacitance measurement, then the resulting error will increase with the increase in the maximum deflection w_m. Therefore, the closed-form solution presented in this paper should be used preferentially for the pressure measurement systems using the capacitive pressure sensors proposed in [15].

Table 7. Required pressures q and their relative errors under the same maximum deflections w_m.

Maximum Deflections w_m [mm]	Required Pressures q [MPa]		Relative Errors
	Lian et al., 2017	Present Study	
5.195	0.000204	0.0002	2%
18.761	0.0096	0.008	20%
32.346	0.0492	0.035	40.57%

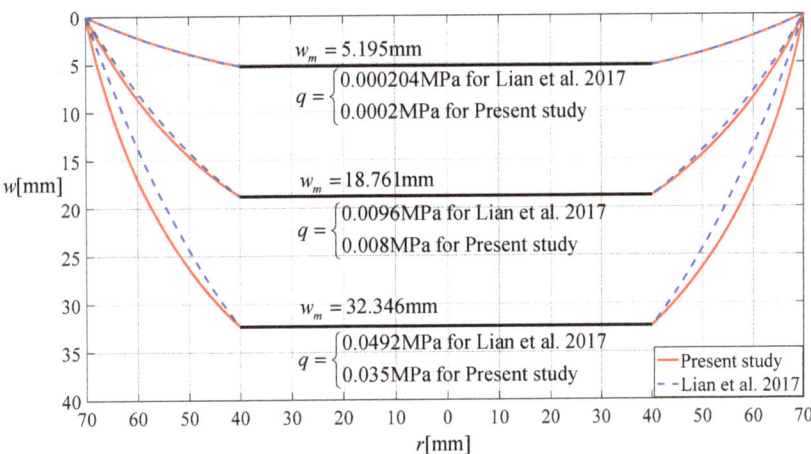

Figure 24. Variations of differences in pressure q with maximum deflection w_m.

4. Concluding Remarks

In this paper, the axisymmetric deformation problem of an Alekseev-type annular membrane structure under uniformly distributed transverse loads, which was originally proposed in our previous work [15], is investigated again. The main improvement on our previous work is that the assumption of small rotation angle of membrane, which was used in the establishment of the previous out-of-plane equilibrium equation and geometric equations, is given up, resulting in a new and more refined closed-form solution. The following main conclusions can be drawn from this study.

Since the size of the rotation angle of the annular membrane corresponds to the size of the maximum deflection of the annular membrane, the assumption of small rotation angle of membrane will become less and less valid with the increase in the maximum deflection of the annular membrane, making the previous closed-form solution obtained by using the assumption of small rotation angle of membrane become less and less accurate. Therefore, the closed-form solution, which is presented in this paper, should be preferred for the design of the capacitive pressure sensors proposed in [15], in order to reduce pressure measurement error. When the ratio of maximum deflection to diameter of the annular membrane is in the range of 0.037 to 0.231, the pressure measurement error is reduced by about 2% to 40%, indicating that the improvement on our previous work has produced a significant beneficial effect.

The work presented here can be further combined with the design of the capacitive pressure sensors proposed in [15].

Author Contributions: Conceptualization, J.-Y.S.; methodology, B.L., Q.Z. and J.-Y.S.; validation, X.L. and X.-T.H.; writing—original draft preparation, B.L. and Q.Z.; writing—review and editing, X.L. and X.-T.H.; visualization, B.L. and Q.Z.; funding acquisition, J.-Y.S. All authors have read and agreed to the published version of the manuscript.

Funding: This research was funded by the National Natural Science Foundation of China (Grant No. 11772072).

Institutional Review Board Statement: Not applicable.

Informed Consent Statement: Not applicable.

Data Availability Statement: Not applicable.

Conflicts of Interest: The authors declare no conflict of interest.

Nomenclature

a	Outer radius of the annular membrane
b	Inner radius of the annular membrane
h	Thickness of the annular membrane
v	Poisson's ratio
E	Young's modulus of elasticity
q	Uniformly distributed transverse loads
r	Radial coordinate
φ	Angle coordinate
w	Transverse coordinate and deflection
o	Coordinate origin
π	Pi (ratio of circumference to diameter)
σ_r	Radial stress
σ_t	Circumferential stress
θ	Rotation angle of the deflected membrane
e_r	Radial strain
e_t	Circumferential strain
u	Radial displacement
Q	Dimensionless q (aq/hE)
W	Dimensionless w (w/a)
S_r	Dimensionless σ_r (σ_r/E)
S_t	Dimensionless σ_t (σ_t/E)
α	Ratio v of b to a (b/a)
x	Dimensionless r (r/a)
β	Introduced parameter $\beta=(1+\alpha)/2$
c_i	Coefficients of the power series for S_r
d_i	Coefficients of the power series for W

Appendix A

$$d_1 = -\frac{\beta Q}{\sqrt{-Q^2\beta^2 + 4c_0^2}},$$

$$c_2 = \frac{1}{2\beta^2}(\sqrt{\beta^2 v^2 c_1^2 + 2\beta v^2 c_0 c_1 - 2\beta v c_0 c_1 + v^2 c_0^2 - 2\beta v c_1 - 2v c_0^2 - 2v c_0 + c_0^2 - d_1^2 + 2c_0 + 1}$$
$$+ \beta v c_1 - 3\beta c_1 + v c_0 - c_0 - 1),$$

$$d_2 = -\frac{Q^2\beta d_1^2 - 4c_0c_1d_1^2 + Q^2\beta}{2d_1(Q^2\beta^2 - 4c_0^2)},$$

$$c_3 = \frac{1}{6\beta^2(2\beta^2 c_2 - \beta v c_1 + 3\beta c_1 - v c_0 + c_0 + 1)}(4\beta^3 v c_2^2 - 20\beta^3 c_2^2 + 20\beta^2 v c_1 c_2 - 38\beta^2 c_1 c_2$$
$$+ 10\beta v c_0 c_2 + 9\beta v c_1^2 - 10\beta c_0 c_2 - 12\beta c_1^2 + 3v c_0 c_1 - 10\beta c_2 - 3c_0 c_1 - 2d_1 d_2 - 3c_1),$$

$$d_3 = -\frac{1}{6d_1(Q^2\beta^2 - 4c_0^2)}(4Q^2\beta^2 d_2^2 + 8Q^2\beta d_1 d_2 + Q^2 d_1^2 - 16c_0^2 d_2^2$$
$$- 32c_0c_1d_1d_2 - 8c_0c_2d_1^2 - 4c_1^2 d_1^2 + Q^2),$$

$$c_4 = -\frac{1}{24\beta^2(2\beta^2 c_2 - \beta v c_1 + 3\beta c_1 - v c_0 + c_0 + 1)}(36\beta^4 c_3^2 - 36\beta^3 v c_2 c_3 + 204\beta^3 c_2 c_3$$
$$- 84\beta^2 v c_1 c_3 - 52\beta^2 v c_2^2 + 174\beta^2 c_1 c_3 + 136\beta^2 c_2^2 - 42\beta v c_0 c_3 - 86\beta v c_1 c_2 + 42\beta c_0 c_3$$
$$+ 134\beta c_1 c_2 - 16 v c_0 c_2 - 12 v c_1^2 + 42\beta c_3 + 16 c_0 c_2 + 15 c_1^2 + 6 d_1 d_3 + 4 d_2^2 + 16 c_2),$$

$$d_4 = -\frac{1}{2d_1(Q^2\beta^2 - 4c_0^2)}(3Q^2\beta^2 d_2 d_3 + 3Q^2\beta d_1 d_3 + 2Q^2\beta d_2^2 + Q^2 d_1 d_2 - 12c_0^2 d_2 d_3$$
$$- 12c_0 c_1 d_1 d_3 - 8c_0 c_1 d_2^2 - 8c_0 c_2 d_1 d_2 - 2c_0 c_3 d_1^2 - 4c_1^2 d_1 d_2 - 2c_1 c_2 d_1^2),$$

$$c_5 = -\frac{1}{20\beta^2(2\beta^2c_2-\beta vc_1+3\beta c_1-vc_0+c_0+1)}(72\beta^4c_3c_4 - 32\beta^3vc_2c_4 - 18\beta^3vc_3^2$$
$$+192\beta^3c_2c_4 + 126\beta^3c_3^2 - 72\beta^2vc_1c_4 - 98\beta^2vc_2c_3 + 156\beta^2c_1c_4 + 296\beta^2c_2c_3$$
$$-36\beta vc_0c_4 - 78\beta vc_1c_3 - 46\beta vc_2^2 + 36\beta c_0c_4 + 132\beta c_1c_3 + 90\beta c_2^2 - 15vc_0c_3$$
$$-25vc_1c_2 + 36\beta c_4 + 15c_0c_3 + 35c_1c_2 + 4d_1d_4 + 6d_2d_3 + 15c_3),$$

$$d_5 = -\frac{1}{10d_1(Q^2\beta^2-4c_0^2)}(16Q^2\beta^2d_2d_4 + 9Q^2\beta^2d_3^2 + 16Q^2\beta d_1d_4 + 24Q^2\beta d_2d_3 + 6Q^2d_1d_3$$
$$+4Q^2d_2^2 - 64c_0^2d_2d_4 - 36c_0^2d_3^2 - 64c_0c_1d_1d_4 - 96c_0c_1d_2d_3 - 48c_0c_2d_1d_3 - 32c_0c_2d_2^2$$
$$-32c_0c_3d_1d_2 - 8c_0c_4d_1^2 - 24c_1^2d_1d_3 - 16c_1^2d_2^2 - 32c_1c_2d_1d_2 - 8c_1c_3d_1^2 - 4c_2^2d_1^2),$$

$$c_6 = -\frac{1}{60\beta^2(2\beta^2c_2-\beta vc_1+3\beta c_1-vc_0+c_0+1)}(240\beta^4c_3c_5 + 144\beta^4c_4^2 - 100\beta^3vc_2c_5$$
$$-120\beta^3vc_3c_4 + 620\beta^3c_2c_5 + 936\beta^3c_3c_4 - 220\beta^2vc_1c_5 - 316\beta^2vc_2c_4 - 174\beta^2vc_3^2$$
$$+490\beta^2c_1c_5 + 1036\beta^2c_2c_4 + 633\beta^2c_3^2 - 110\beta vc_0c_5 - 246\beta vc_1c_4 - 314\beta vc_2c_3 + 110\beta c_0c_5$$
$$+438\beta c_1c_4 + 698\beta c_2c_3 - 48vc_0c_4 - 84vc_1c_3 - 48vc_2^2 + 110\beta c_5 + 48c_0c_4 + 126c_1c_3 + 80c_2^2$$
$$+10d_1d_5 + 16d_2d_4 + 9d_3^2 + 48c_4),$$

$$d_6 = -\frac{1}{6d_1(Q^2\beta^2-4c_0^2)}(10Q^2\beta^2d_2d_5 + 12Q^2\beta^2d_3d_4 + 10Q^2\beta d_1d_5 + 16Q^2\beta d_2d_4 + 9Q^2\beta d_3^2$$
$$+4Q^2d_1d_4 + 6Q^2d_2d_3 - 40c_0^2d_2d_5 - 48c_0^2d_3d_4 - 40c_0c_1d_1d_5 - 64c_0c_1d_2d_4 - 36c_0c_1d_3^2$$
$$-32c_0c_2d_1d_4 - 48c_0c_2d_2d_3 - 24c_0c_3d_1d_3 - 16c_0c_3d_2^2 - 16c_0c_4d_1d_2 - 4c_0c_5d_1^2 - 16c_1^2d_1d_4$$
$$-24c_1^2d_2d_3 - 24c_1c_2d_1d_3 - 16c_1c_2d_2^2 - 16c_1c_3d_1d_2 - 4c_1c_4d_1^2 - 8c_2^2d_1d_2 - 4c_2c_3d_1^2),$$

$$c_7 = -\frac{1}{42\beta^2(2\beta^2c_2-\beta vc_1+3\beta c_1-vc_0+c_0+1)}(180\beta^4c_3c_6 + 240\beta^4c_4c_5 - 72\beta^3vc_2c_6$$
$$-90\beta^3vc_3c_5 - 48\beta^3vc_4^2 + 456\beta^3c_2c_6 + 750\beta^3c_3c_5 + 432\beta^3c_4^2 - 156\beta^2vc_1c_6 - 232\beta^2vc_2c_5$$
$$-270\beta^2vc_3c_4 + 354\beta^2c_1c_6 + 802\beta^2c_2c_5 + 1098\beta^2c_3c_4 - 78\beta vc_0c_6 - 178\beta vc_1c_5$$
$$-238\beta vc_2c_4 - 129\beta vc_3^2 + 78\beta c_0c_6 + 328\beta c_1c_5 + 574\beta c_2c_4 + 336\beta c_3^2 - 35vc_0c_5$$
$$-63vc_1c_4 - 77vc_2c_3 + 78\beta c_6 + 35c_0c_5 + 99c_1c_4 + 143c_2c_3 + 6d_1d_6 + 10d_2d_5 + 12d_3d_4 + 35c_5),$$

$$d_7 = -\frac{1}{14d_1(Q^2\beta^2-4c_0^2)}(24Q^2\beta^2d_2d_6 + 30Q^2\beta^2d_3d_5 + 16Q^2\beta^2d_4^2 + 24Q^2\beta d_1d_6$$
$$+40Q^2\beta d_2d_5 + 48Q^2\beta d_3d_4 + 10Q^2d_1d_5 + 16Q^2d_2d_4 + 9Q^2d_3^2 - 96c_0^2d_2d_6$$
$$-120c_0^2d_3d_5 - 64c_0^2d_4^2 - 96c_0c_1d_1d_6 - 160c_0c_1d_2d_5 - 192c_0c_1d_3d_4 - 80c_0c_2d_1d_5$$
$$-128c_0c_2d_2d_4 - 72c_0c_2d_3^2 - 64c_0c_3d_1d_4 - 96c_0c_3d_2d_3 - 48c_0c_4d_1d_3 - 32c_0c_4d_2^2$$
$$-32c_0c_5d_1d_2 - 8c_0c_6d_1^2 - 40c_1^2d_1d_5 - 64c_1^2d_2d_4 - 36c_1^2d_3^2 - 64c_1c_2d_1d_4 - 96c_1c_2d_2d_3$$
$$-48c_1c_3d_1d_3 - 32c_1c_3d_2^2 - 32c_1c_4d_1d_2 - 8c_1c_5d_1^2 - 24c_2^2d_1d_3 - 16c_2^2d_2^2 - 32c_2c_3d_1d_2$$
$$-8c_2c_4d_1^2 - 4c_3^2d_1^2),$$

$$c_8 = -\frac{1}{112\beta^2(2\beta^2c_2-\beta vc_1+3\beta c_1-vc_0+c_0+1)}(504\beta^4c_3c_7 + 720\beta^4c_4c_6 + 400\beta^4c_5^2$$
$$-196\beta^3vc_2c_7 - 252\beta^3vc_3c_6 - 280\beta^3vc_4c_5 + 1260\beta^3c_2c_7 + 2196\beta^3c_3c_6 + 2760\beta^3c_4c_5$$
$$-420\beta^2vc_1c_7 - 640\beta^2vc_2c_6 - 772\beta^2vc_3c_5 - 408\beta^2vc_4^2 + 966\beta^2c_1c_7 + 2296\beta^2c_2c_6$$
$$+3382\beta^2c_3c_5 + 1896\beta^2c_4^2 - 210\beta vc_0c_7 - 486\beta vc_1c_6 - 670\beta vc_2c_5 - 762\beta vc_3c_4$$
$$+210\beta c_0c_7 + 918\beta c_1c_6 + 1710\beta c_2c_5 + 2202\beta c_3c_4 - 96vc_0c_6 - 176vc_1c_5 - 224vc_2c_4$$
$$-120vc_3^2 + 210\beta c_7 + 96c_0c_6 + 286c_1c_5 + 448c_2c_4 + 255c_3^2 + 14d_1d_7 + 24d_2d_6 + 30d_3d_5$$
$$+16d_4^2 + 96c_6),$$

$$d_8 = -\frac{1}{4d_1(Q^2\beta^2-4c_0^2)}(7Q^2\beta^2 d_2 d_7 + 9Q^2\beta^2 d_3 d_6 + 10Q^2\beta^2 d_4 d_5 + 7Q^2\beta d_1 d_7$$
$$+12Q^2\beta d_2 d_6 + 15Q^2\beta d_3 d_5 + 8Q^2\beta d_4{}^2 + 3Q^2 d_1 d_6 + 5Q^2 d_2 d_5 + 6Q^2 d_3 d_4 - 28c_0{}^2 d_2 d_7$$
$$-36c_0{}^2 d_3 d_6 - 40c_0{}^2 d_4 d_5 - 28c_0 c_1 d_1 d_7 - 48c_0 c_1 d_2 d_6 - 60c_0 c_1 d_3 d_5 - 32c_0 c_1 d_4{}^2$$
$$-24c_0 c_2 d_1 d_6 - 40c_0 c_2 d_2 d_5 - 48c_0 c_2 d_3 d_4 - 20c_0 c_3 d_1 d_5 - 32c_0 c_3 d_2 d_4 - 18c_0 c_3 d_3{}^2$$
$$-16c_0 c_4 d_1 d_4 - 24c_0 c_4 d_2 d_3 - 12c_0 c_5 d_1 d_3 - 8c_0 c_5 d_2{}^2 - 8c_0 c_6 d_1 d_2 - 2c_0 c_7 d_1{}^2 - 12c_1{}^2 d_1 d_6$$
$$-20c_1{}^2 d_2 d_5 - 24c_1{}^2 d_3 d_4 - 20c_1 c_2 d_1 d_5 - 32c_1 c_2 d_2 d_4 - 18c_1 c_2 d_3{}^2 - 16c_1 c_3 d_1 d_4$$
$$-24c_1 c_3 d_2 d_3 - 12c_1 c_4 d_1 d_3 - 8c_1 c_4 d_2{}^2 - 8c_1 c_5 d_1 d_2 - 2c_1 c_6 d_1{}^2 - 8c_2{}^2 d_1 d_4 - 12c_2{}^2 d_2 d_3$$
$$-12c_2 c_3 d_1 d_3 - 8c_2 c_3 d_2{}^2 - 8c_2 c_4 d_1 d_2 - 2c_2 c_5 d_1{}^2 - 4c_3{}^2 d_1 d_2 - 2c_3 c_4 d_1{}^2),$$

$$c_9 = -\frac{1}{72\beta^2(2\beta^2 c_2 - \beta v c_1 + 3\beta c_1 - v c_0 + c_0 + 1)}(336\beta^4 c_3 c_8 + 504\beta^4 c_4 c_7 + 600\beta^4 c_5 c_6$$
$$-128\beta^3 v c_2 c_8 - 168\beta^3 v c_3 c_7 - 192\beta^3 v c_4 c_6 - 100\beta^3 v c_5{}^2 + 832\beta^3 c_2 c_8 + 1512\beta^3 c_3 c_7$$
$$+2016\beta^3 c_4 c_6 + 1100\beta^3 c_5{}^2 - 272\beta^2 v c_1 c_8 - 422\beta^2 v c_2 c_7 - 522\beta^2 v c_3 c_6 - 572\beta^2 v c_4 c_5$$
$$+632\beta^2 c_1 c_8 + 1556\beta^2 c_2 c_7 + 2412\beta^2 c_3 c_6 + 2912\beta^2 c_4 c_5 - 136\beta v c_0 c_8 - 318\beta v c_1 c_7$$
$$-448\beta v c_2 c_6 - 526\beta v c_3 c_5 - 276\beta v c_4{}^2 + 136\beta c_0 c_8 + 612\beta c_1 c_7 + 1192\beta c_2 c_6$$
$$+1636\beta c_3 c_5 + 900\beta c_4{}^2 - 63 v c_0 c_7 - 117 v c_1 c_6 - 153 v c_2 c_5 - 171 v c_3 c_4 + 136\beta c_8$$
$$+63 c_0 c_7 + 195 c_1 c_6 + 323 c_2 c_5 + 399 c_3 c_4 + 8 d_1 d_8 + 14 d_2 d_7 + 18 d_3 d_6 + 20 d_4 d_5 + 63 c_7),$$

$$d_9 = -\frac{1}{18 d_1(Q^2\beta^2-4c_0^2)}(32Q^2\beta^2 d_2 d_8 + 42Q^2\beta^2 d_3 d_7 + 48Q^2\beta^2 d_4 d_6 + 25Q^2\beta^2 d_5{}^2$$
$$+32Q^2\beta d_1 d_8 + 56Q^2\beta d_2 d_7 + 72Q^2\beta d_3 d_6 + 80Q^2\beta d_4 d_5 + 14Q^2 d_1 d_7 + 24Q^2 d_2 d_6$$
$$+30Q^2 d_3 d_5 + 16Q^2 d_4{}^2 - 128 c_0{}^2 d_2 d_8 - 168 c_0{}^2 d_3 d_7 - 192 c_0{}^2 d_4 d_6 - 100 c_0{}^2 d_5{}^2$$
$$-128 c_0 c_1 d_1 d_8 - 224 c_0 c_1 d_2 d_7 - 288 c_0 c_1 d_3 d_6 - 320 c_0 c_1 d_4 d_5 - 112 c_0 c_2 d_1 d_7 - 192 c_0 c_2 d_2 d_6$$
$$-240 c_0 c_2 d_3 d_5 - 128 c_0 c_2 d_4{}^2 - 96 c_0 c_3 d_1 d_6 - 160 c_0 c_3 d_2 d_5 - 192 c_0 c_3 d_3 d_4 - 80 c_0 c_4 d_1 d_5$$
$$-128 c_0 c_4 d_2 d_4 - 72 c_0 c_4 d_3{}^2 - 64 c_0 c_5 d_1 d_4 - 96 c_0 c_5 d_2 d_3 - 48 c_0 c_6 d_1 d_3 - 32 c_0 c_6 d_2{}^2$$
$$-32 c_0 c_7 d_1 d_2 - 8 c_0 c_8 d_1{}^2 - 56 c_1{}^2 d_1 d_7 - 96 c_1{}^2 d_2 d_6 - 120 c_1{}^2 d_3 d_5 - 64 c_1{}^2 d_4{}^2 - 96 c_1 c_2 d_1 d_6$$
$$-160 c_1 c_2 d_2 d_5 - 192 c_1 c_2 d_3 d_4 - 80 c_1 c_3 d_1 d_5 - 128 c_1 c_3 d_2 d_4 - 72 c_1 c_3 d_3{}^2 - 64 c_1 c_4 d_1 d_4$$
$$-96 c_1 c_4 d_2 d_3 - 48 c_1 c_5 d_1 d_3 - 32 c_1 c_5 d_2{}^2 - 32 c_1 c_6 d_1 d_2 - 8 c_1 c_7 d_1{}^2 - 40 c_2{}^2 d_1 d_5 - 64 c_2{}^2 d_2 d_4$$
$$-36 c_2{}^2 d_3{}^2 - 64 c_2 c_3 d_1 d_4 - 96 c_2 c_3 d_2 d_3 - 48 c_2 c_4 d_1 d_3 - 32 c_2 c_4 d_2{}^2 - 32 c_2 c_5 d_1 d_2 - 8 c_2 c_6 d_1{}^2$$
$$-24 c_3{}^2 d_1 d_3 - 16 c_3{}^2 d_2{}^2 - 32 c_3 c_4 d_1 d_2 - 8 c_3 c_5 d_1{}^2 - 4 c_4{}^2 d_1{}^2),$$

$$c_{10} = -\frac{1}{180\beta^2(2\beta^2 c_2 - \beta v c_1 + 3\beta c_1 - v c_0 + c_0 + 1)}(864\beta^4 c_3 c_9 + 1344\beta^4 c_4 c_8$$
$$+1680\beta^4 c_5 c_7 + 900\beta^4 c_6{}^2 - 324\beta^3 v c_2 c_9 - 432\beta^3 v c_3 c_8 + 2124\beta^3 c_2 c_9$$
$$+3984\beta^3 c_3 c_8 + 5544\beta^3 c_4 c_7 + 6420\beta^3 c_5 c_6 - 684\beta^2 v c_1 c_9 - 1076\beta^2 v c_2 c_8$$
$$-1356\beta^2 v c_3 c_7 - 1524\beta^2 v c_4 c_6 - 790\beta^2 v c_5{}^2 + 4465\beta^2 c_5{}^2 + 3170\beta c_2 c_7 + 4554\beta c_3 c_6$$
$$-160 v c_0 c_8 - 300 v c_1 c_7 - 400 v c_2 c_6 - 460 v c_3 c_5 + 18 d_1 d_9 + 32 d_2 d_8 + 42 d_3 d_7 + 48 d_4 d_6,$$
$$+1602\beta^2 c_1 c_9 + 4052\beta^2 c_2 c_8 + 6522\beta^2 c_3 c_7 + 8292\beta^2 c_4 c_6 - 342\beta v c_0 c_9 - 806\beta v c_1 c_8$$
$$-1154\beta v c_2 c_7 - 1386\beta v c_3 c_6 - 1502\beta v c_4 c_5 + 342\beta c_0 c_9 + 1574\beta c_1 c_8 + 5342\beta c_4 c_5$$
$$+342\beta c_9 + 1150 c_3 c_5 + 160 c_8 - 504\beta^3 v c_4 c_7 - 540\beta^3 v c_5 c_6 - 240 v c_4{}^2 + 160 c_0 c_8$$
$$+510 c_1 c_7 + 880 c_2 c_6 + 624 c_4{}^2 + 25 d_5{}^2)$$

$$d_{10} = -\frac{1}{10d_1(Q^2\beta^2-4c_0^2)}(18Q^2\beta^2 d_2 d_9 + 24Q^2\beta^2 d_3 d_8 + 28Q^2\beta^2 d_4 d_7 + 30Q^2\beta^2 d_5 d_6$$
$$+18Q^2\beta d_1 d_9 + 32Q^2\beta d_2 d_8 + 42Q^2\beta d_3 d_7 + 48Q^2\beta d_4 d_6 + 25Q^2\beta d_5^2 + 8Q^2 d_1 d_8$$
$$+14Q^2 d_2 d_7 + 18Q^2 d_3 d_6 + 20Q^2 d_4 d_5 - 72c_0^2 d_2 d_9 - 96c_0^2 d_3 d_8 - 112c_0^2 d_4 d_7$$
$$-120c_0^2 d_5 d_6 - 72c_0 c_1 d_1 d_9 - 128c_0 c_1 d_2 d_8 - 168c_0 c_1 d_3 d_7 - 192c_0 c_1 d_4 d_6 - 100c_0 c_1 d_5^2$$
$$-64c_0 c_2 d_1 d_8 - 112c_0 c_2 d_2 d_7 - 144c_0 c_2 d_3 d_6 - 160c_0 c_2 d_4 d_5 - 56c_0 c_3 d_1 d_7 - 96c_0 c_3 d_2 d_6$$
$$-120c_0 c_3 d_3 d_5 - 64c_0 c_3 d_4^2 - 48c_0 c_4 d_1 d_6 - 80c_0 c_4 d_2 d_5 - 96c_0 c_4 d_3 d_4 - 40c_0 c_5 d_1 d_5$$
$$-64c_0 c_5 d_2 d_4 - 36c_0 c_5 d_3^2 - 32c_0 c_6 d_1 d_4 - 48c_0 c_6 d_2 d_3 - 24c_0 c_7 d_1 d_3 - 16c_0 c_7 d_2^2$$
$$-16c_0 c_8 d_1 d_2 - 4c_0 c_9 d_1^2 - 32c_1^2 d_1 d_8 - 56c_1^2 d_2 d_7 - 72c_1^2 d_3 d_6 - 80c_1^2 d_4 d_5 - 56c_1 c_2 d_1 d_7$$
$$-96c_1 c_2 d_2 d_6 - 120c_1 c_2 d_3 d_5 - 64c_1 c_2 d_4^2 - 48c_1 c_3 d_1 d_6 - 80c_1 c_3 d_2 d_5 - 96c_1 c_3 d_3 d_4$$
$$-40c_1 c_4 d_1 d_5 - 64c_1 c_4 d_2 d_4 - 36c_1 c_4 d_3^2 - 32c_1 c_5 d_1 d_4 - 48c_1 c_5 d_2 d_3 - 24c_1 c_6 d_1 d_3$$
$$-16c_1 c_6 d_2^2 - 16c_1 c_7 d_1 d_2 - 4c_1 c_8 d_1^2 - 24c_2^2 d_1 d_6 - 40c_2^2 d_2 d_5 - 48c_2^2 d_3 d_4 - 40c_2 c_3 d_1 d_5$$
$$-64c_2 c_3 d_2 d_4 - 36c_2 c_3 d_3^2 - 32c_2 c_4 d_1 d_4 - 48c_2 c_4 d_2 d_3 - 24c_2 c_5 d_1 d_3 - 16c_2 c_5 d_2^2$$
$$-16c_2 c_6 d_1 d_2 - 4c_2 c_7 d_1^2 - 16c_3^2 d_1 d_4 - 24c_3^2 d_2 d_3 - 24c_3 c_4 d_1 d_3 - 16c_3 c_4 d_2^2 - 16c_3 c_5 d_1 d_2$$
$$-4c_3 c_6 d_1^2 - 8c_4^2 d_1 d_2 - 4c_4 c_5 d_1^2)$$

$$c_{11} = -\frac{1}{110\beta^2(2\beta^2 c_2 - \beta v c_1 + 3\beta c_1 - v c_0 + c_0 + 1)}(-200\beta^3 v c_2 c_{10} - 270\beta^3 v c_3 c_9$$
$$-320\beta^3 v c_4 c_8 - 350\beta^3 v c_5 c_7 - 420\beta^2 v c_1 c_{10} - 854\beta^2 v c_3 c_8 - 978\beta^2 v c_4 c_7$$
$$-1040\beta^2 v c_5 c_6 + 5598\beta^2 c_4 c_7 - 210\beta v c_0 c_{10} - 498\beta v c_1 c_9 - 722\beta v c_2 c_8$$
$$-882\beta v c_3 c_7 - 978\beta v c_4 c_6 - 505\beta v c_5^2 + 2034\beta c_2 c_8 + 3024\beta c_3 c_7 + 3714\beta c_4 c_6$$
$$+99c_9 + 540\beta^4 c_3 c_{10} + 864\beta^4 c_4 c_9 + 1260\beta^4 c_6 c_7 - 668\beta^2 v c_2 c_9 + 6350\beta^2 c_5 c_6$$
$$+210\beta c_0 c_{10} - 99v c_0 c_9 - 187v c_1 c_8 - 253v c_2 c_7 - 297v c_3 c_6 - 319v c_4 c_5 - 180\beta^3 v c_6^2$$
$$+1120\beta^4 c_5 c_8 + 4238\beta^2 c_3 c_8 + 2558\beta^2 c_2 c_9 + 10d_1 d_{10} + 18d_2 d_9 + 24d_3 d_8 + 28d_4 d_7$$
$$+30d_5 d_6 + 2340\beta^3 c_6^2 + 990\beta^2 c_1 c_{10} + 1980\beta c_5^2 + 99c_0 c_9 + 323c_1 c_8 + 575c_2 c_7$$
$$+783c_3 c_6 + 899c_4 c_5 + 210\beta c_{10} + 1320\beta^2 c_2 c_{10} + 2538\beta^2 c_3 c_9 + 3648\beta^3 c_4 c_8$$
$$+984\beta c_1 c_9 + 4410\beta^3 c_5 c_7)$$

$$d_{11} = -\frac{1}{22d_1(Q^2\beta^2-4c_0^2)}(40Q^2\beta^2 d_2 d_{10} + 54Q^2\beta^2 d_3 d_9 + 64Q^2\beta^2 d_4 d_8 + 70Q^2\beta^2 d_5 d_7$$
$$+36Q^2\beta^2 d_6^2 + 40Q^2\beta d_1 d_{10} + 72Q^2\beta d_2 d_9 + 96Q^2\beta d_3 d_8 + 112Q^2\beta d_4 d_7 + 120Q^2\beta d_5 d_6$$
$$+18Q^2 d_1 d_9 + 32Q^2 d_2 d_8 + 42Q^2 d_3 d_7 + 48Q^2 d_4 d_6 + 25Q^2 d_5^2 - 160c_0^2 d_2 d_{10} - 216c_0^2 d_3 d_9$$
$$-256c_0^2 d_4 d_8 - 280c_0^2 d_5 d_7 - 144c_0^2 d_6^2 - 160c_0 c_1 d_1 d_{10} - 288c_0 c_1 d_2 d_9 - 384c_0 c_1 d_3 d_8$$
$$-448c_0 c_1 d_4 d_7 - 480c_0 c_1 d_5 d_6 - 144c_0 c_2 d_1 d_9 - 256c_0 c_2 d_2 d_8 - 336c_0 c_2 d_3 d_7 - 384c_0 c_2 d_4 d_6$$
$$-200c_0 c_2 d_5^2 - 128c_0 c_3 d_1 d_8 - 224c_0 c_3 d_2 d_7 - 288c_0 c_3 d_3 d_6 - 320c_0 c_3 d_4 d_5 - 112c_0 c_4 d_1 d_7$$
$$-192c_0 c_4 d_2 d_6 - 240c_0 c_4 d_3 d_5 - 128c_0 c_4 d_4^2 - 96c_0 c_5 d_1 d_6 - 160c_0 c_5 d_2 d_5 - 192c_0 c_5 d_3 d_4$$
$$-80c_0 c_6 d_1 d_5 - 128c_0 c_6 d_2 d_4 - 72c_0 c_6 d_3^2 - 64c_0 c_7 d_1 d_4 - 96c_0 c_7 d_2 d_3 - 48c_0 c_8 d_1 d_3$$
$$-32c_0 c_8 d_2^2 - 32c_0 c_9 d_1 d_2 - 8c_0 c_{10} d_1^2 - 72c_1^2 d_1 d_9 - 128c_1^2 d_2 d_8 - 168c_1^2 d_3 d_7 - 192c_1^2 d_4 d_6$$
$$-100c_1^2 d_5^2 - 128c_1 c_2 d_1 d_8 - 224c_1 c_2 d_2 d_7 - 288c_1 c_2 d_3 d_6 - 320c_1 c_2 d_4 d_5 - 112c_1 c_3 d_1 d_7$$
$$-192c_1 c_3 d_2 d_6 - 240c_1 c_3 d_3 d_5 - 128c_1 c_3 d_4^2 - 96c_1 c_4 d_1 d_6 - 160c_1 c_4 d_2 d_5 - 192c_1 c_4 d_3 d_4$$
$$-80c_1 c_5 d_1 d_5 - 128c_1 c_5 d_2 d_4 - 72c_1 c_5 d_3^2 - 64c_1 c_6 d_1 d_4 - 96c_1 c_6 d_2 d_3 - 48c_1 c_7 d_1 d_3$$
$$-32c_1 c_7 d_2^2 - 32c_1 c_8 d_1 d_2 - 8c_1 c_9 d_1^2 - 56c_2^2 d_1 d_7 - 96c_2^2 d_2 d_6 - 120c_2^2 d_3 d_5 - 64c_2^2 d_4^2$$

$$-96c_2c_3d_1d_6 - 160c_2c_3d_2d_5 - 192c_2c_3d_3d_4 - 80c_2c_4d_1d_5 - 128c_2c_4d_2d_4 - 72c_2c_4d_3^2$$
$$-64c_2c_5d_1d_4 - 96c_2c_5d_2d_3 - 48c_2c_6d_1d_3 - 32c_2c_6d_2^2 - 32c_2c_7d_1d_2 - 8c_2c_8d_1^2 - 40c_3^2d_1d_5$$
$$-64c_3^2d_2d_4 - 36c_3^2d_3^2 - 64c_3c_4d_1d_4 - 96c_3c_4d_2d_3 - 48c_3c_5d_1d_3 - 32c_3c_5d_2^2 - 32c_3c_6d_1d_2$$
$$-8c_3c_7d_1^2 - 24c_4^2d_1d_3 - 16c_4^2d_2^2 - 32c_4c_5d_1d_2 - 8c_4c_6d_1^2 - 4c_5^2d_1^2),$$

$$c_{12} = -\frac{1}{264\beta^2(2\beta^2c_2 - \beta\nu c_1 + 3\beta c_1 - \nu c_0 + c_0 + 1)}(1320\beta^4 c_3 c_{11} + 2160\beta^4 c_4 c_{10}$$
$$+2880\beta^4 c_5 c_9 + 3360\beta^4 c_6 c_8 - 660\beta^3 \nu c_3 c_{10} - 924\beta^3 \nu c_6 c_7 + 3212\beta^3 c_2 c_{11} + 6300\beta^3 c_3 c_{10}$$
$$+11600\beta^3 c_5 c_8 + 12852\beta^3 c_6 c_7 - 1356\beta^2 \nu c_6^2 + 2398\beta^2 c_1 c_{11} + 6304\beta^2 c_2 c_{10}$$
$$+10686\beta^2 c_3 c_9 + 14536\beta^2 c_4 c_8 + 17134\beta^2 c_5 c_7 - 506\beta\nu c_0 c_{11} - 1206\beta\nu c_1 c_{10} + 506\beta c_0 c_{11}$$
$$+2406\beta c_1 c_{10} + 5078\beta c_2 c_9 + 9858\beta c_4 c_7 - 240\nu c_0 c_{10} + 240c_{10} - 484\beta^3 \nu c_2 c_{11}$$
$$-880\beta^3 \nu c_5 c_8 + 9288\beta^3 c_4 c_9 - 1012\beta^2 \nu c_1 c_{11} - 1624\beta^2 \nu c_2 c_{10} - 2100\beta^2 \nu c_3 c_9$$
$$-2440\beta^2 \nu c_4 c_8 - 2644\beta^2 \nu c_5 c_7 - 1766\beta\nu c_2 c_9 - 2186\beta\nu c_3 c_8 - 2466\beta\nu c_4 c_7$$
$$-2606\beta\nu c_5 c_6 + 7754\beta c_3 c_8 + 11006\beta c_5 c_6 - 456\nu c_1 c_9 - 624\nu c_2 c_8 - 744\nu c_3 c_7 - 816\nu c_4 c_6$$
$$+36d_6^2 - 792\beta^3 \nu c_4 c_9 + 1295c_5^2 + 1764\beta^4 c_7^2 + 506\beta c_{11} + 9024\beta^2 c_6^2 - 420\nu c_5^2$$
$$+240c_0 c_{10} + 798c_1 c_9 + 1456c_2 c_8 + 2046c_3 c_7 + 2448c_4 c_6 + 22d_1 d_{11} + 40d_2 d_{10} + 54d_3 d_9$$
$$+64d_4 d_8 + 70d_5 d_7),$$

$$d_{12} = -\frac{1}{6d_1(Q^2\beta^2 - 4c_0^2)}(11Q^2\beta^2 d_2 d_{11} + 15Q^2\beta^2 d_3 d_{10} + 18Q^2\beta^2 d_4 d_9 + 20Q^2\beta^2 d_5 d_8$$
$$+21Q^2\beta^2 d_6 d_7 + 11Q^2\beta d_1 d_{11} + 20Q^2\beta d_2 d_{10} + 27Q^2\beta d_3 d_9 + 32Q^2\beta d_4 d_8 + 35Q^2\beta d_5 d_7$$
$$+18Q^2\beta d_6^2 + 5Q^2 d_1 d_{10} + 9Q^2 d_2 d_9 + 12Q^2 d_3 d_8 + 14Q^2 d_4 d_7 + 15Q^2 d_5 d_6 - 44c_0^2 d_2 d_{11}$$
$$-60c_0^2 d_3 d_{10} - 72c_0^2 d_4 d_9 - 80c_0^2 d_5 d_8 - 84c_0^2 d_6 d_7 - 44c_0 c_1 d_1 d_{11} - 80c_0 c_1 d_2 d_{10}$$
$$-108c_0 c_1 d_3 d_9 - 128c_0 c_1 d_4 d_8 - 140c_0 c_1 d_5 d_7 - 72c_0 c_1 d_6^2 - 40c_0 c_2 d_1 d_{10} - 72c_0 c_2 d_2 d_9$$
$$-96c_0 c_2 d_3 d_8 - 112c_0 c_2 d_4 d_7 - 120c_0 c_2 d_5 d_6 - 36c_0 c_3 d_1 d_9 - 64c_0 c_3 d_2 d_8 - 84c_0 c_3 d_3 d_7$$
$$-96c_0 c_3 d_4 d_6 - 50c_0 c_3 d_5^2 - 32c_0 c_4 d_1 d_8 - 56c_0 c_4 d_2 d_7 - 72c_0 c_4 d_3 d_6 - 80c_0 c_4 d_4 d_5$$
$$-28c_0 c_5 d_1 d_7 - 48c_0 c_5 d_2 d_6 - 60c_0 c_5 d_3 d_5 - 32c_0 c_5 d_4^2 - 24c_0 c_6 d_1 d_6 - 40c_0 c_6 d_2 d_5$$
$$-48c_0 c_6 d_3 d_4 - 20c_0 c_7 d_1 d_5 - 32c_0 c_7 d_2 d_4 - 18c_0 c_7 d_3^2 - 16c_0 c_8 d_1 d_4 - 24c_0 c_8 d_2 d_3$$
$$-12c_0 c_9 d_1 d_3 - 8c_0 c_9 d_2^2 - 8c_0 c_{10} d_1 d_2 - 2c_0 c_{11} d_1^2 - 20c_1^2 d_1 d_{10} - 36c_1^2 d_2 d_9 - 48c_1^2 d_3 d_8$$
$$-56c_1^2 d_4 d_7 - 60c_1^2 d_5 d_6 - 36c_1 c_2 d_1 d_9 - 64c_1 c_2 d_2 d_8 - 84c_1 c_2 d_3 d_7 - 96c_1 c_2 d_4 d_6$$
$$-50c_1 c_2 d_5^2 - 32c_1 c_3 d_1 d_8 - 56c_1 c_3 d_2 d_7 - 72c_1 c_3 d_3 d_6 - 80c_1 c_3 d_4 d_5 - 28c_1 c_4 d_1 d_7$$
$$-48c_1 c_4 d_2 d_6 - 60c_1 c_4 d_3 d_5 - 32c_1 c_4 d_4^2 - 24c_1 c_5 d_1 d_6 - 40c_1 c_5 d_2 d_5 - 48c_1 c_5 d_3 d_4$$
$$-20c_1 c_6 d_1 d_5 - 32c_1 c_6 d_2 d_4 - 18c_1 c_6 d_3^2 - 16c_1 c_7 d_1 d_4 - 24c_1 c_7 d_2 d_3 - 12c_1 c_8 d_1 d_3$$
$$-8c_1 c_8 d_2^2 - 8c_1 c_9 d_1 d_2 - 2c_1 c_{10} d_1^2 - 16c_2^2 d_1 d_8 - 28c_2^2 d_2 d_7 - 36c_2^2 d_3 d_6 - 40c_2^2 d_4 d_5$$
$$-28c_2 c_3 d_1 d_7 - 48c_2 c_3 d_2 d_6 - 60c_2 c_3 d_3 d_5 - 32c_2 c_3 d_4^2 - 24c_2 c_4 d_1 d_6 - 40c_2 c_4 d_2 d_5$$
$$-48c_2 c_4 d_3 d_4 - 20c_2 c_5 d_1 d_5 - 32c_2 c_5 d_2 d_4 - 18c_2 c_5 d_3^2 - 16c_2 c_6 d_1 d_4 - 24c_2 c_6 d_2 d_3$$
$$-12c_2 c_7 d_1 d_3 - 8c_2 c_7 d_2^2 - 8c_2 c_8 d_1 d_2 - 2c_2 c_9 d_1^2 - 12c_3^2 d_1 d_6 - 20c_3^2 d_2 d_5 - 24c_3^2 d_3 d_4$$
$$-20c_3 c_4 d_1 d_5 - 32c_3 c_4 d_2 d_4 - 18c_3 c_4 d_3^2 - 16c_3 c_5 d_1 d_4 - 24c_3 c_5 d_2 d_3 - 12c_3 c_6 d_1 d_3$$
$$-8c_3 c_6 d_2^2 - 8c_3 c_7 d_1 d_2 - 2c_3 c_8 d_1^2 - 8c_4^2 d_1 d_4 - 12c_4^2 d_2 d_3 - 12c_4 c_5 d_1 d_3 - 8c_4 c_5 d_2^2$$
$$-8c_4 c_6 d_1 d_2 - 2c_4 c_7 d_1^2 - 4c_5^2 d_1 d_2 - 2c_5 c_6 d_1^2).$$

$$c_{13} = -\frac{1}{156\beta^2(2\beta^2 c_2 - \beta v c_1 + 3\beta c_1 - v c_0 + c_0 + 1)}(792\beta^4 c_3 c_{12} + 1320\beta^4 c_4 c_{11}$$
$$+1800\beta^4 c_5 c_{10} + 2160\beta^4 c_6 c_9 + 2352\beta^4 c_7 c_8 + 1920\beta^3 c_2 c_{12} + 3828\beta^3 c_3 c_{11} - 970\beta^2 v c_2 c_{11}$$
$$+1428\beta^2 c_1 c_{12} + 3808\beta^2 c_2 c_{11} + 6576\beta^2 c_3 c_{10} + 9156\beta^2 c_4 c_9 + 11116\beta^2 c_5 c_8 + 12168\beta^2 c_6 c_7$$
$$-1060\beta v c_2 c_{10} - 834\beta v c_6{}^2 + 300\beta c_0 c_{12} + 1444\beta c_1 c_{11} + 3100\beta c_2 c_{10} + 4836\beta c_3 c_9$$
$$+143 c_{11} - 288\beta^3 v c_2 c_{12} - 396\beta^3 v c_3 c_{11} - 576\beta^3 v c_6 c_8 - 294\beta^3 v c_7{}^2 + 5760\beta^3 c_4 c_{10}$$
$$+7380\beta^3 c_5 c_9 + 8448\beta^3 c_6 c_8 - 600\beta^2 v c_1 c_{12} - 1488\beta^2 v c_4 c_9 - 300\beta v c_0 c_{12} - 1630\beta v c_5 c_7 \quad ,$$
$$+6316\beta c_4 c_8 + 7300\beta c_5 c_7 - 143 v c_0 c_{11} - 273 v c_1 c_{10} - 377 v c_2 c_9 - 455 v c_3 c_8 - 533 v c_5 c_6$$
$$-480\beta^3 v c_4 c_{10} - 540\beta^3 v c_5 c_9 + 4410\beta^3 c_7{}^2 - 1266\beta^2 v c_3 c_{10} - 1636\beta^2 v c_5 c_8 - 1710\beta^2 v c_6 c_7$$
$$-718\beta v c_1 c_{11} - 1326\beta v c_3 c_9 - 1516\beta v c_4 c_8 + 3822\beta c_6{}^2 - 507 v c_4 c_7 + 300\beta c_{12} + 143 c_0 c_{11}$$
$$+483 c_1 c_{10} + 899 c_2 c_9 + 1295 c_3 c_8 + 1599 c_4 c_7 + 1763 c_5 c_6 + 12 d_1 d_{12} + 22 d_2 d_{11} + 30 d_3 d_{10}$$
$$+36 d_4 d_9 + 40 d_5 d_8 + 42 d_6 d_7)$$

$$d_{13} = -\frac{1}{26 d_1 (Q^2 \beta^2 - 4 c_0{}^2)}(48 Q^2 \beta^2 d_2 d_{12} + 66 Q^2 \beta^2 d_3 d_{11} + 80 Q^2 \beta^2 d_4 d_{10}$$
$$+90 Q^2 \beta^2 d_5 d_9 + 96 Q^2 \beta^2 d_6 d_8 + 49 Q^2 \beta^2 d_7{}^2 + 48 Q^2 \beta d_1 d_{12} + 88 Q^2 \beta d_2 d_{11} + 120 Q^2 \beta d_3 d_{10}$$
$$+144 Q^2 \beta d_4 d_9 + 160 Q^2 \beta d_5 d_8 + 168 Q^2 \beta d_6 d_7 + 22 Q^2 d_1 d_{11} + 40 Q^2 d_2 d_{10} + 54 Q^2 d_3 d_9$$
$$+64 Q^2 d_4 d_8 + 70 Q^2 d_5 d_7 + 36 Q^2 d_6{}^2 - 192 c_0{}^2 d_2 d_{12} - 264 c_0{}^2 d_3 d_{11} - 320 c_0{}^2 d_4 d_{10}$$
$$-360 c_0{}^2 d_5 d_9 - 384 c_0{}^2 d_6 d_8 - 196 c_0{}^2 d_7{}^2 - 192 c_0 c_1 d_1 d_{12} - 352 c_0 c_1 d_2 d_{11} - 480 c_0 c_1 d_3 d_{10}$$
$$-576 c_0 c_1 d_4 d_9 - 640 c_0 c_1 d_5 d_8 - 672 c_0 c_1 d_6 d_7 - 176 c_0 c_2 d_1 d_{11} - 320 c_0 c_2 d_2 d_{10} - 432 c_0 c_2 d_3 d_9$$
$$-512 c_0 c_2 d_4 d_8 - 560 c_0 c_2 d_5 d_7 - 288 c_0 c_2 d_6{}^2 - 160 c_0 c_3 d_1 d_{10} - 288 c_0 c_3 d_2 d_9 - 384 c_0 c_3 d_3 d_8$$
$$-448 c_0 c_3 d_4 d_7 - 480 c_0 c_3 d_5 d_6 - 144 c_0 c_4 d_1 d_9 - 256 c_0 c_4 d_2 d_8 - 336 c_0 c_4 d_3 d_7 - 384 c_0 c_4 d_4 d_6$$
$$-200 c_0 c_4 d_5{}^2 - 128 c_0 c_5 d_1 d_8 - 224 c_0 c_5 d_2 d_7 - 288 c_0 c_5 d_3 d_6 - 320 c_0 c_5 d_4 d_5 - 112 c_0 c_6 d_1 d_7$$
$$-192 c_0 c_6 d_2 d_6 - 240 c_0 c_6 d_3 d_5 - 128 c_0 c_6 d_4{}^2 - 96 c_0 c_7 d_1 d_6 - 160 c_0 c_7 d_2 d_5 - 192 c_0 c_7 d_3 d_4$$
$$-80 c_0 c_8 d_1 d_5 - 128 c_0 c_8 d_2 d_4 - 72 c_0 c_8 d_3{}^2 - 64 c_0 c_9 d_1 d_4 - 96 c_0 c_9 d_2 d_3 - 48 c_0 c_{10} d_1 d_3$$
$$-32 c_0 c_{10} d_2{}^2 - 32 c_0 c_{11} d_1 d_2 - 8 c_0 c_{12} d_1{}^2 - 88 c_1{}^2 d_1 d_{11} - 160 c_1{}^2 d_2 d_{10} - 216 c_1{}^2 d_3 d_9 - 256 c_1{}^2 d_4 d_8$$
$$-280 c_1{}^2 d_5 d_7 - 144 c_1{}^2 d_6{}^2 - 160 c_1 c_2 d_1 d_{10} - 288 c_1 c_2 d_2 d_9 - 384 c_1 c_2 d_3 d_8 - 448 c_1 c_2 d_4 d_7$$
$$-480 c_1 c_2 d_5 d_6 - 144 c_1 c_3 d_1 d_9 - 256 c_1 c_3 d_2 d_8 - 336 c_1 c_3 d_3 d_7 - 384 c_1 c_3 d_4 d_6 - 200 c_1 c_3 d_5{}^2$$
$$-128 c_1 c_4 d_1 d_8 - 224 c_1 c_4 d_2 d_7 - 288 c_1 c_4 d_3 d_6 - 320 c_1 c_4 d_4 d_5 - 112 c_1 c_5 d_1 d_7 - 192 c_1 c_5 d_2 d_6$$
$$-240 c_1 c_5 d_3 d_5 - 128 c_1 c_5 d_4{}^2 - 96 c_1 c_6 d_1 d_6 - 160 c_1 c_6 d_2 d_5 - 192 c_1 c_6 d_3 d_4 - 80 c_1 c_7 d_1 d_5$$
$$-128 c_1 c_7 d_2 d_4 - 72 c_1 c_7 d_3{}^2 - 64 c_1 c_8 d_1 d_4 - 96 c_1 c_8 d_2 d_3 - 48 c_1 c_9 d_1 d_3 - 32 c_1 c_9 d_2{}^2$$
$$-32 c_1 c_{10} d_1 d_2 - 8 c_1 c_{11} d_1{}^2 - 72 c_2{}^2 d_1 d_9 - 128 c_2{}^2 d_2 d_8 - 168 c_2{}^2 d_3 d_7 - 192 c_2{}^2 d_4 d_6$$
$$-100 c_2{}^2 d_5{}^2 - 128 c_2 c_3 d_1 d_8 - 224 c_2 c_3 d_2 d_7 - 288 c_2 c_3 d_3 d_6 - 320 c_2 c_3 d_4 d_5 - 112 c_2 c_4 d_1 d_7$$
$$-192 c_2 c_4 d_2 d_6 - 240 c_2 c_4 d_3 d_5 - 128 c_2 c_4 d_4{}^2 - 96 c_2 c_5 d_1 d_6 - 160 c_2 c_5 d_2 d_5 - 192 c_2 c_5 d_3 d_4$$
$$-80 c_2 c_6 d_1 d_5 - 128 c_2 c_6 d_2 d_4 - 72 c_2 c_6 d_3{}^2 - 64 c_2 c_7 d_1 d_4 - 96 c_2 c_7 d_2 d_3 - 48 c_2 c_8 d_1 d_3$$
$$-32 c_2 c_8 d_2{}^2 - 32 c_2 c_9 d_1 d_2 - 8 c_2 c_{10} d_1{}^2 - 56 c_3{}^2 d_1 d_7 - 96 c_3{}^2 d_2 d_6 - 120 c_3{}^2 d_3 d_5 - 64 c_3{}^2 d_4{}^2$$
$$-96 c_3 c_4 d_1 d_6 - 160 c_3 c_4 d_2 d_5 - 192 c_3 c_4 d_3 d_4 - 80 c_3 c_5 d_1 d_5 - 128 c_3 c_5 d_2 d_4 - 72 c_3 c_5 d_3{}^2$$
$$-64 c_3 c_6 d_1 d_4 - 96 c_3 c_6 d_2 d_3 - 48 c_3 c_7 d_1 d_3 - 32 c_3 c_7 d_2{}^2 - 32 c_3 c_8 d_1 d_2 - 8 c_3 c_9 d_1{}^2 - 40 c_4{}^2 d_1 d_5$$
$$-64 c_4{}^2 d_2 d_4 - 36 c_4{}^2 d_3{}^2 - 64 c_4 c_5 d_1 d_4 - 96 c_4 c_5 d_2 d_3 - 48 c_4 c_6 d_1 d_3 - 32 c_4 c_6 d_2{}^2 - 32 c_4 c_7 d_1 d_2$$
$$-8 c_4 c_8 d_1{}^2 - 24 c_5{}^2 d_1 d_3 - 16 c_5{}^2 d_2{}^2 - 32 c_5 c_6 d_1 d_2 - 8 c_5 c_7 d_1{}^2 - 4 c_6{}^2 d_1{}^2)$$

$$\begin{aligned}
c_{14} = &-\frac{1}{364\beta^2(2\beta^2 c_2 - \beta v c_1 + 3\beta c_1 - v c_0 + c_0 + 1)}(-676\beta^3 v c_2 c_{13} - 936\beta^3 v c_3 c_{12}\\
&-1144\beta^3 v c_4 c_{11} - 1300\beta^3 v c_5 c_{10} - 1404\beta^3 v c_6 c_9 - 1456\beta^3 v c_7 c_8 - 1404\beta^2 v c_1 c_{13}\\
&-2284\beta^2 v c_2 c_{12} - 3004\beta^2 v c_3 c_{11} - 3564\beta^2 v c_4 c_{10} - 3964\beta^2 v c_5 c_9 - 4204\beta^2 v c_6 c_8\\
&-2506\beta v c_2 c_{11} - 3162\beta v c_3 c_{10} - 3654\beta v c_4 c_9 - 3982\beta v c_5 c_8 - 4146\beta v c_6 c_7\\
&-1872\beta^4 c_3 c_{13} + 3168\beta^4 c_4 c_{12} + 4400\beta^4 c_5 c_{11} + 5400\beta^4 c_6 c_{10} + 6048\beta^4 c_7 c_9\\
&+16401\beta^2 c_7^2 - 702\beta v c_0 c_{13} - 1686\beta v c_1 c_{12} + 3414\beta c_1 c_{12} + 7434\beta c_2 c_{11} + 11802\beta c_3 c_{10}\\
&+15750\beta c_4 c_9 + 18702\beta c_5 c_8 - 336 v c_0 c_{12} - 644 v c_1 c_{11} - 896 v c_2 c_{10} - 1092 v c_3 c_9\\
&-1232 v c_4 c_8 - 1316 v c_5 c_7 + 336 c_0 c_{12} + 1150 c_1 c_{11} + 2176 c_2 c_{10} + 3198 c_3 c_9 + 4048 c_4 c_8\\
&+4606 c_5 c_7 + 23184\beta^3 c_7 c_8 + 3354\beta^2 c_1 c_{13} + 9052\beta^2 c_2 c_{12} + 15874\beta^2 c_3 c_{11} + 22524\beta^2 c_4 c_{10}\\
&+27994\beta^2 c_5 c_9 + 31564\beta^2 c_6 c_8 + 702\beta c_0 c_{13} + 20274\beta c_6 c_7 - 672 v c_6^2 + 702\beta c_{13} + 26 d_1 d_{13}\\
&+48 d_2 d_{12} + 66 d_3 d_{11} + 80 d_4 d_{10} + 3136\beta^4 c_8^2 + 4524\beta^3 c_2 c_{13} + 9144\beta^3 c_3 c_{12} + 13992\beta^3 c_4 c_{11}\\
&+18300\beta^3 c_5 c_{10} + 21492\beta^3 c_6 c_9 - 2142\beta^2 v c_7^2 + 2400 c_6^2 + 90 d_5 d_9 + 96 d_6 d_8 + 49 d_7^2\\
&+336 c_{12})
\end{aligned}$$

$$\begin{aligned}
d_{14} = &-\frac{1}{14 d_1(Q^2\beta^2 - 4 c_0^2)}(26 Q^2\beta^2 d_2 d_{13} + 36 Q^2\beta^2 d_3 d_{12} + 44 Q^2\beta^2 d_4 d_{11}\\
&+50 Q^2\beta^2 d_5 d_{10} + 54 Q^2\beta^2 d_6 d_9 + 56 Q^2\beta^2 d_7 d_8 + 26 Q^2\beta d_1 d_{13} + 48 Q^2\beta d_2 d_{12} + 66 Q^2\beta d_3 d_{11}\\
&+80 Q^2\beta d_4 d_{10} + 90 Q^2\beta d_5 d_9 + 96 Q^2\beta d_6 d_8 + 49 Q^2\beta d_7^2 + 12 Q^2 d_1 d_{12} + 22 Q^2 d_2 d_{11}\\
&+30 Q^2 d_3 d_{10} + 36 Q^2 d_4 d_9 + 40 Q^2 d_5 d_8 + 42 Q^2 d_6 d_7 - 104 c_0^2 d_2 d_{13} - 144 c_0^2 d_3 d_{12}\\
&-176 c_0^2 d_4 d_{11} - 200 c_0^2 d_5 d_{10} - 216 c_0^2 d_6 d_9 - 224 c_0^2 d_7 d_8 - 104 c_0 c_1 d_1 d_{13} - 192 c_0 c_1 d_2 d_{12}\\
&-264 c_0 c_1 d_3 d_{11} - 320 c_0 c_1 d_4 d_{10} - 360 c_0 c_1 d_5 d_9 - 384 c_0 c_1 d_6 d_8 - 196 c_0 c_1 d_7^2 - 96 c_0 c_2 d_1 d_{12}\\
&-176 c_0 c_2 d_2 d_{11} - 240 c_0 c_2 d_3 d_{10} - 288 c_0 c_2 d_4 d_9 - 320 c_0 c_2 d_5 d_8 - 336 c_0 c_2 d_6 d_7 - 88 c_0 c_3 d_1 d_{11}\\
&-160 c_0 c_3 d_2 d_{10} - 216 c_0 c_3 d_3 d_9 - 256 c_0 c_3 d_4 d_8 - 280 c_0 c_3 d_5 d_7 - 144 c_0 c_3 d_6^2 - 80 c_0 c_4 d_1 d_{10}\\
&-144 c_0 c_4 d_2 d_9 - 192 c_0 c_4 d_3 d_8 - 224 c_0 c_4 d_4 d_7 - 240 c_0 c_4 d_5 d_6 - 72 c_0 c_5 d_1 d_9 - 128 c_0 c_5 d_2 d_8\\
&-168 c_0 c_5 d_3 d_7 - 192 c_0 c_5 d_4 d_6 - 100 c_0 c_5 d_5^2 - 64 c_0 c_6 d_1 d_8 - 112 c_0 c_6 d_2 d_7 - 144 c_0 c_6 d_3 d_6\\
&-160 c_0 c_6 d_4 d_5 - 56 c_0 c_7 d_1 d_7 - 96 c_0 c_7 d_2 d_6 - 120 c_0 c_7 d_3 d_5 - 64 c_0 c_7 d_4^2 - 48 c_0 c_8 d_1 d_6\\
&-80 c_0 c_8 d_2 d_5 - 96 c_0 c_8 d_3 d_4 - 40 c_0 c_9 d_1 d_5 - 64 c_0 c_9 d_2 d_4 - 36 c_0 c_9 d_3^2 - 32 c_0 c_{10} d_1 d_4\\
&-48 c_0 c_{10} d_2 d_3 - 24 c_0 c_{11} d_1 d_3 - 16 c_0 c_{11} d_2^2 - 16 c_0 c_{12} d_1 d_2 - 4 c_0 c_{13} d_1^2 - 48 c_1^2 d_1 d_{12}\\
&-88 c_1^2 d_2 d_{11} - 120 c_1^2 d_3 d_{10} - 144 c_1^2 d_4 d_9 - 160 c_1^2 d_5 d_8 - 168 c_1^2 d_6 d_7 - 88 c_1 c_2 d_1 d_{11}\\
&-160 c_1 c_2 d_2 d_{10} - 216 c_1 c_2 d_3 d_9 - 256 c_1 c_2 d_4 d_8 - 280 c_1 c_2 d_5 d_7 - 144 c_1 c_2 d_6^2 - 80 c_1 c_3 d_1 d_{10}\\
&-144 c_1 c_3 d_2 d_9 - 192 c_1 c_3 d_3 d_8 - 224 c_1 c_3 d_4 d_7 - 240 c_1 c_3 d_5 d_6 - 72 c_1 c_4 d_1 d_9 - 128 c_1 c_4 d_2 d_8\\
&-168 c_1 c_4 d_3 d_7 - 192 c_1 c_4 d_4 d_6 - 100 c_1 c_4 d_5^2 - 64 c_1 c_5 d_1 d_8 - 112 c_1 c_5 d_2 d_7 - 144 c_1 c_5 d_3 d_6\\
&-160 c_1 c_5 d_4 d_5 - 56 c_1 c_6 d_1 d_7 - 96 c_1 c_6 d_2 d_6 - 120 c_1 c_6 d_3 d_5 - 64 c_1 c_6 d_4^2 - 48 c_1 c_7 d_1 d_6\\
&-80 c_1 c_7 d_2 d_5 - 96 c_1 c_7 d_3 d_4 - 40 c_1 c_8 d_1 d_5 - 64 c_1 c_8 d_2 d_4 - 36 c_1 c_8 d_3^2 - 32 c_1 c_9 d_1 d_4\\
&-48 c_1 c_9 d_2 d_3 - 24 c_1 c_{10} d_1 d_3 - 16 c_1 c_{10} d_2^2 - 16 c_1 c_{11} d_1 d_2 - 4 c_1 c_{12} d_1^2 - 40 c_2^2 d_1 d_{10}\\
&-72 c_2^2 d_2 d_9 - 96 c_2^2 d_3 d_8 - 112 c_2^2 d_4 d_7 - 120 c_2^2 d_5 d_6 - 72 c_2 c_3 d_1 d_9 - 128 c_2 c_3 d_2 d_8\\
&-168 c_2 c_3 d_3 d_7 - 192 c_2 c_3 d_4 d_6 - 100 c_2 c_3 d_5^2 - 64 c_2 c_4 d_1 d_8 - 112 c_2 c_4 d_2 d_7 - 144 c_2 c_4 d_3 d_6\\
&-160 c_2 c_4 d_4 d_5 - 56 c_2 c_5 d_1 d_7 - 96 c_2 c_5 d_2 d_6 - 120 c_2 c_5 d_3 d_5 - 64 c_2 c_5 d_4^2 - 48 c_2 c_6 d_1 d_6\\
&-80 c_2 c_6 d_2 d_5 - 96 c_2 c_6 d_3 d_4 - 40 c_2 c_7 d_1 d_5 - 64 c_2 c_7 d_2 d_4 - 36 c_2 c_7 d_3^2 - 32 c_2 c_8 d_1 d_4\\
&-48 c_2 c_8 d_2 d_3 - 24 c_2 c_9 d_1 d_3 - 16 c_2 c_9 d_2^2 - 16 c_2 c_{10} d_1 d_2 - 4 c_2 c_{11} d_1^2 - 32 c_3^2 d_1 d_8 - 56 c_3^2 d_2 d_7
\end{aligned}$$

$$-72c_3{}^2d_3d_6 - 80c_3{}^2d_4d_5 - 56c_3c_4d_1d_7 - 96c_3c_4d_2d_6 - 120c_3c_4d_3d_5 - 64c_3c_4d_4{}^2 - 48c_3c_5d_1d_6$$
$$-80c_3c_5d_2d_5 - 96c_3c_5d_3d_4 - 40c_3c_6d_1d_5 - 64c_3c_6d_2d_4 - 36c_3c_6d_3{}^2 - 32c_3c_7d_1d_4$$
$$-48c_3c_7d_2d_3 - 24c_3c_8d_1d_3 - 16c_3c_8d_2{}^2 - 16c_3c_9d_1d_2 - 4c_3c_{10}d_1{}^2 - 24c_4{}^2d_1d_6 - 40c_4{}^2d_2d_5$$
$$-48c_4{}^2d_3d_4 - 40c_4c_5d_1d_5 - 64c_4c_5d_2d_4 - 36c_4c_5d_3{}^2 - 32c_4c_6d_1d_4 - 48c_4c_6d_2d_3 - 24c_4c_7d_1d_3$$
$$-16c_4c_7d_2{}^2 - 16c_4c_8d_1d_2 - 4c_4c_9d_1{}^2 - 16c_5{}^2d_1d_4 - 24c_5{}^2d_2d_3 - 24c_5c_6d_1d_3 - 16c_5c_6d_2{}^2$$
$$-16c_5c_7d_1d_2 - 4c_5c_8d_1{}^2 - 8c_6{}^2d_1d_2 - 4c_6c_7d_1{}^2)$$

$$c_{15} = -\frac{1}{210\beta^2(2\beta^2c_2 - \beta vc_1 + 3\beta c_1 - vc_0 + c_0 + 1)}(2632\beta^3c_2c_{14} + 8352\beta^3c_4c_{12}$$
$$+11110\beta^3c_5c_{11} + 13320\beta^3c_6c_{10} + 14742\beta^3c_7c_9 - 1758\beta^2vc_3c_{12} - 2102\beta^2vc_4c_{11}$$
$$-2360\beta^2vc_5c_{10} - 2532\beta^2vc_6c_9 - 2618\beta^2vc_7c_8 - 406\beta vc_0c_{14} - 978\beta vc_1c_{13} + 6720\beta c_7{}^2$$
$$+406\beta c_{14} + 195c_0c_{13} + 675c_1c_{12} + 1295c_2c_{11} + 1935c_3c_{10} + 2499c_4c_9 + 2915c_5c_8 + 3135c_6c_7$$
$$+26d_2d_{13} + 36d_3d_{12} + 44d_4d_{11} + 195c_{13} + 1872\beta^4c_4c_{13} - 448\beta^3vc_8{}^2 + 5382\beta^3c_3c_{13}$$
$$+13586\beta^2c_4c_{11} + 406\beta c_0c_{14} + 1992\beta c_1c_{13} + 4390\beta c_2c_{12} + 7072\beta c_3c_{11} + 9606\beta c_4c_{10}$$
$$+11656\beta c_5c_9 + 12982\beta c_6c_8 - 195vc_0c_{13} - 375vc_1c_{12} - 525vc_2c_{11} - 645vc_3c_{10} - 735vc_4c_9$$
$$-795vc_5c_8 - 825vc_6c_7 - 1281\beta vc_7{}^2 + 9426\beta^2c_3c_{12} + 1946\beta^2c_1c_{14} + 19866\beta^2c_6c_9$$
$$+17210\beta^2c_5c_{10} + 5306\beta^2c_2c_{13} + 21266\beta^2c_7c_8 + 4032\beta^4c_8c_9 + 2640\beta^4c_5c_{12} + 3780\beta^4c_7c_{10}$$
$$+3300\beta^4c_6c_{11} + 1092\beta^4c_3c_{14} - 1328\beta^2vc_2c_{13} - 812\beta^2vc_1c_{14} + 14d_1d_{14} + 7616\beta^3c_8{}^2 + 50d_5d_{10}$$
$$+54d_6d_9 + 56d_7d_8 - 392\beta^3vc_2c_{14} - 546\beta^3vc_3c_{13} - 672\beta^3vc_4c_{12} - 770\beta^3vc_5c_{11} - 840\beta^3vc_6c_{10}$$
$$-882\beta^3vc_7c_9 - 1462\beta vc_2c_{12} - 1858\beta vc_3c_{11} - 2166\beta vc_4c_{10} - 2386\beta vc_5c_9 - 2518\beta vc_6c_8)$$

$$d_{15} = -\frac{1}{30d_1(Q^2\beta^2 - 4c_0{}^2)}(120Q^2\beta^2d_6d_{10} + 104Q^2\beta d_2d_{13} - 336c_0c_6d_3d_7 - 128c_0c_7d_1d_8$$
$$-192c_0c_9d_3d_4 - 128c_0c_{10}d_2d_4 - 64c_0c_{11}d_1d_4 - 96c_0c_{11}d_2d_3 - 176c_1c_3d_1d_{11} - 384c_1c_4d_3d_8$$
$$-128c_1c_7d_4{}^2 - 192c_1c_8d_3d_4 - 72c_1c_9d_3{}^2 - 160c_2{}^2d_2d_{10} - 216c_2{}^2d_3d_9 - 256c_2{}^2d_4d_8$$
$$-64c_4c_7d_1d_4 - 8c_4c_{10}d_1{}^2 - 40c_5{}^2d_1d_5 - 64c_5{}^2d_2d_4 - 8c_5c_9d_1{}^2 - 4c_7{}^2d_1{}^2 + 96Q^2\beta^2d_4d_{12}$$
$$-312c_0{}^2d_3d_{13} - 440c_0{}^2d_5d_{11} - 504c_0{}^2d_7d_9 - 224c_0c_1d_1d_{14} - 352c_0c_3d_2d_{11} - 448c_0c_5d_4d_7$$
$$-256c_0c_6d_2d_8 - 352c_1c_2d_2d_{11} - 512c_1c_3d_4d_8 - 32c_1c_{11}d_2{}^2 - 8c_1c_{13}d_1{}^2 - 88c_2{}^2d_1d_{11}$$
$$-280c_2{}^2d_5d_7 - 200c_2c_4d_5{}^2 - 128c_2c_6d_4{}^2 - 224c_3c_4d_2d_7 - 160c_3c_6d_2d_5 - 32c_3c_{10}d_1d_2$$
$$-32c_4c_9d_1d_2 - 48c_5c_7d_1d_3 + 200Q^2\beta d_5d_{10} - 160c_0c_5d_1d_{10} - 480c_0c_5d_5d_6 - 128c_0c_8d_4{}^2$$
$$-72c_0c_{10}d_3{}^2 - 384c_1{}^2d_6d_8 - 288c_1c_4d_2d_9 - 480c_1c_4d_5d_6 - 144c_1c_5d_1d_9 - 160c_1c_8d_2d_5$$
$$-80c_1c_9d_1d_5 - 128c_1c_9d_2d_4 - 64c_2c_9d_1d_4 - 8c_2c_{12}d_1{}^2 - 128c_3{}^2d_2d_8 - 128c_3c_4d_1d_8$$
$$-240c_3c_5d_3d_5 - 64c_4{}^2d_4{}^2 - 192c_4c_5d_3d_4 - 36c_5{}^2d_3{}^2 - 16c_6{}^2d_2{}^2 + 176Q^2\beta d_4d_{11}$$
$$-224c_0{}^2d_2d_{14} - 480c_0{}^2d_6d_{10} - 192c_0c_3d_1d_{12} - 512c_0c_4d_4d_8 - 288c_0c_5d_2d_9 - 384c_0c_6d_4d_6$$
$$-320c_0c_7d_4d_5 - 192c_1{}^2d_2d_{12} - 264c_1{}^2d_3d_{11} - 320c_1c_3d_2d_{10} - 448c_1c_4d_4d_7 - 32c_2c_{11}d_1d_2$$
$$-96c_3c_6d_1d_6 - 32c_3c_9d_2{}^2 - 56c_4{}^2d_1d_7 - 96c_4{}^2d_2d_6 - 96c_4c_5d_1d_6 - 48c_4c_8d_1d_3 - 32c_4c_8d_2{}^2$$
$$-96c_5c_6d_2d_3 + 56Q^2\beta d_1d_{14} + 144Q^2\beta d_3d_{12} + 224Q^2\beta d_7d_8 - 320c_0c_4d_2d_{10} - 288c_0c_4d_6{}^2$$
$$-384c_0c_5d_3d_8 - 200c_0c_6d_5{}^2 - 112c_0c_8d_1d_7 - 240c_0c_8d_3d_5 - 96c_0c_9d_1d_6 - 360c_1{}^2d_5d_9$$
$$-192c_1c_2d_1d_{12} - 640c_1c_2d_5d_8 - 64c_1c_{10}d_1d_4 - 144c_2{}^2d_6{}^2 - 112c_3c_5d_1d_7 - 192c_3c_5d_2d_6$$
$$-80c_3c_7d_1d_5 - 160c_4c_5d_2d_5 - 80c_4c_6d_1d_5 + 110Q^2\beta^2d_5d_{11} + 126Q^2\beta^2d_7d_9 + 49Q^2d_7{}^2$$
$$-416c_0c_1d_2d_{13} - 576c_0c_1d_3d_{12} - 480c_0c_3d_3d_{10} - 576c_0c_3d_4d_9 - 432c_0c_4d_3d_9 - 144c_0c_6d_1d_9$$
$$-288c_0c_7d_3d_6 - 320c_1{}^2d_4d_{10} - 196c_1{}^2d_7{}^2 - 672c_1c_2d_6d_7 - 288c_1c_3d_6{}^2 - 200c_1c_5d_5{}^2$$

$$\begin{aligned}
&-64c_3c_8d_1d_4 - 96c_3c_8d_2d_3 - 128c_4c_6d_2d_4 - 32c_5c_8d_1d_2 - 8c_6c_8d_1{}^2 + 64Q^2\beta^2d_8{}^2 + 26Q^2d_1d_{13} \\
&+48Q^2d_2d_{12} + 66Q^2d_3d_{11} + 80Q^2d_4d_{10} + 90Q^2d_5d_9 + 96Q^2d_6d_8 - 384c_0{}^2d_4d_{12} - 392c_0c_2d_7{}^2 \\
&-640c_0c_3d_5d_8 - 224c_0c_7d_2d_7 - 192c_0c_8d_2d_6 - 48c_0c_{12}d_1d_3 - 32c_0c_{13}d_1d_2 - 432c_1c_3d_3d_9 \\
&-160c_1c_4d_1d_{10} - 288c_3c_4d_3d_6 - 48c_3c_9d_1d_3 - 96c_4c_7d_2d_3 - 32c_6c_7d_1d_2 + 78Q^2\beta^2d_3d_{13} \\
&-256c_0{}^2d_8{}^2 - 672c_0c_3d_6d_7 - 160c_0c_9d_2d_5 - 32c_0c_{12}d_2{}^2 - 8c_0c_{14}d_1{}^2 - 104c_1{}^2d_1d_{13} \\
&-480c_1c_2d_3d_{10} - 576c_1c_2d_4d_9 - 560c_1c_3d_5d_7 - 96c_1c_8d_1d_6 - 192c_2c_7d_3d_4 - 80c_2c_8d_1d_5 \\
&-128c_2c_8d_2d_4 - 72c_2c_8d_3{}^2 - 48c_2c_{10}d_1d_3 - 32c_2c_{10}d_2{}^2 - 100c_3{}^2d_5{}^2 - 192c_3c_6d_3d_4 - 120c_4{}^2d_3d_5 \\
&-72c_4c_6d_3{}^2 - 704c_0c_1d_4d_{11} - 800c_0c_1d_5d_{10} - 864c_0c_1d_6d_9 - 896c_0c_1d_7d_8 - 208c_0c_2d_1d_{13} \\
&-384c_0c_2d_2d_{12} - 528c_0c_2d_3d_{11} - 640c_0c_2d_4d_{10} - 720c_0c_2d_5d_9 - 768c_0c_2d_6d_8 - 224c_2c_5d_2d_7 \\
&-288c_2c_5d_3d_6 - 320c_2c_5d_4d_5 - 112c_2c_6d_1d_7 - 192c_2c_6d_2d_6 - 240c_2c_6d_3d_5 - 96c_2c_7d_1d_6 \\
&-160c_2c_7d_2d_5 - 288c_1c_6d_3d_6 - 320c_1c_6d_4d_5 - 112c_1c_7d_1d_7 - 192c_1c_7d_2d_6 - 240c_1c_7d_3d_5 \\
&-96c_1c_{10}d_2d_3 - 48c_1c_{11}d_1d_3 - 32c_1c_{12}d_1d_2 - 160c_2c_3d_1d_{10} - 288c_2c_3d_2d_9 - 384c_2c_3d_3d_8 \\
&-448c_2c_3d_4d_7 - 480c_2c_3d_5d_6 - 144c_2c_4d_1d_9 - 256c_2c_4d_2d_8 - 336c_2c_4d_3d_7 - 384c_2c_4d_4d_6 \\
&-128c_2c_5d_1d_8 + 56Q^2\beta^2d_2d_{14} + 216Q^2\beta d_6d_9 - 176c_0c_4d_1d_{11} - 560c_0c_4d_5d_7 - 80c_0c_{10}d_1d_5 \\
&-256c_1c_5d_2d_8 - 336c_1c_5d_3d_7 - 384c_1c_5d_4d_6 - 128c_1c_6d_1d_8 - 224c_1c_6d_2d_7 - 96c_2c_9d_2d_3 \\
&-72c_3{}^2d_1d_9 - 168c_3{}^2d_3d_7 - 192c_3{}^2d_4d_6 - 320c_3c_4d_4d_5 - 128c_3c_5d_4{}^2 - 128c_3c_7d_2d_4 \\
&-72c_3c_7d_3{}^2 - 8c_3c_{11}d_1{}^2 - 64c_5c_6d_1d_4 - 32c_5c_7d_2{}^2 - 24c_6{}^2d_1d_3)
\end{aligned}$$

References

1. Delfani, M.R. Nonlinear elasticity of monolayer hexagonal crystals: Theory and application to circular bulge test. *Eur. J. Mech. A Solid.* **2018**, *68*, 117–132. [CrossRef]
2. Dai, Z.; Lu, N. Poking and bulging of suspended thin sheets: Slippage, instabilities, and metrology. *J. Mech. Phys. Solids* **2021**, *149*, 104320. [CrossRef]
3. Gutscher, G.; Wu, H.C.; Ngaile, G.; Altan, T. Determination of flow stress for sheet metal forming using the viscous pressure bulge (VPB) test. *J. Mater. Process. Technol.* **2004**, *146*, 1–7. [CrossRef]
4. Sun, J.Y.; Qian, S.H.; Li, Y.M.; He, X.T.; Zheng, Z.L. Theoretical study of adhesion energy measurement for film/substrate interface using pressurized blister test: Energy release rate. *Measurement* **2013**, *46*, 2278–2287. [CrossRef]
5. Ma, Y.; Wang, G.R.; Chen, Y.L.; Long, D.; Guan, Y.C.; Liu, L.Q.; Zhang, Z. Extended Hencky solution for the blister test of nanomembrane. *Extrem. Mech. Lett.* **2018**, *22*, 69–78. [CrossRef]
6. Cao, Z.; Tao, L.; Akinwande, D.; Huang, R.; Liechti, K.M. Mixed-mode traction-separation relations between graphene and copper by blister tests. *Int. J. Solids Struct.* **2016**, *84*, 147–159. [CrossRef]
7. Napolitanno, M.J.; Chudnovsky, A.; Moet, A. The constrained blister test for the energy of interfacial adhesion. *J. Adhes. Sci. Technol.* **1988**, *2*, 311–323. [CrossRef]
8. Pervier, M.L.A.; Hammond, D.W. Measurement of the fracture energy in mode I of atmospheric ice accreted on different materials using a blister test. *Eng. Fract. Mech.* **2019**, *214*, 223–232. [CrossRef]
9. Zhu, T.T.; Li, G.X.; Müftü, S.; Wan, K.T. Revisiting the constrained blister test to measure thin film adhesion. *J. Appl. Mech. T ASME* **2017**, *84*, 071005. [CrossRef]
10. Zhu, T.T.; Müftü, S.; Wan, K.T. One-dimensional constrained blister test to measure thin film adhesion. *J. Appl. Mech. T ASME* **2018**, *85*, 054501. [CrossRef]
11. Molla-Alipour, M.; Ganji, B.A. Analytical analysis of mems capacitive pressure sensor with circular diaphragm under dynamic load using differential transformation method (DTM). *Acta Mech. Solida Sin.* **2015**, *28*, 400–408. [CrossRef]
12. Lee, H.Y.; Choi, B. Theoretical and experimental investigation of the trapped air effect on air-sealed capacitive pressure sensor. *Sens. Actuators A* **2015**, *221*, 104–114. [CrossRef]
13. Mishra, R.B.; Khan, S.M.; Shaikh, S.F.; Hussain, A.M.; Hussain, M. Low-cost foil/paper based touch mode pressure sensing element as artificial skin module for prosthetic hand. In Proceedings of the 2020 3rd IEEE International Conference on Soft Robotics (RoboSoft), New Haven, CT, USA, 15 May–15 July 2020; pp. 194–200.
14. Meng, G.Q.; Ko, W.H. Modeling of circular diaphragm and spreadsheet solution programming for touch mode capacitive sensors. *Sens. Actuators A* **1999**, *75*, 45–52. [CrossRef]

15. Lian, Y.S.; Sun, J.Y.; Ge, X.M.; Yang, Z.X.; He, X.T.; Zheng, Z.L. A theoretical study of an improved capacitive pressure sensor: Closed-form solution of uniformly loaded annular membranes. *Measurement* **2017**, *111*, 84–92. [CrossRef]
16. Hencky, H. On the stress state in circular plates with vanishing bending stiffness. *Z. Angew. Math. Phys.* **1915**, *63*, 311–317.
17. Chien, W.Z. Asymptotic behavior of a thin clamped circular plate under uniform normal pressure at very large deflection. *Sci. Rep. Natl. Tsinghua Univ.* **1948**, *5*, 193–208.
18. Alekseev, S.A. Elastic circular membranes under the uniformly distributed loads. *Eng. Corpus* **1953**, *14*, 196–198.
19. Huang, P.F.; Song, Y.P.; Li, Q.; Liu, X.Q.; Feng, Y.Q. A theoretical study of circular orthotropic membrane under concentrated load: The relation of load and deflection. *IEEE Access* **2020**, *8*, 126127–126137. [CrossRef]
20. Rao, Y.; Qiao, S.; Dai, Z.; Lu, N. Elastic wetting: Substrate-supported droplets confined by soft elastic membranes. *J. Mech. Phys. Solids* **2021**, *151*, 104399. [CrossRef]
21. Chen, S.L.; Zheng, Z.L. Large deformation of circular membrane under the concentrated force. *Appl. Math. Mech.* **2003**, *24*, 25–28.
22. Chien, W.Z.; Wang, Z.Z.; Xu, Y.G.; Chen, S.L. The symmetrical deformation of circular membrane under the action of uniformly distributed loads in its central portion. *Appl. Math. Mech.* **1981**, *2*, 599–612.
23. Lian, Y.S.; Sun, J.Y.; Zhao, Z.H.; He, X.T.; Zheng, Z.L. A revisit of the boundary value problem for Föppl–Hencky membranes: Improvement of geometric equations. *Mathematics* **2020**, *8*, 631. [CrossRef]
24. Campbell, J.D. On the theory of initially tensioned circular membranes subjected to uniform pressure. *Q. J. Mech. Appl. Math.* **1956**, *9*, 84–93. [CrossRef]
25. Fichter, W.B. *Some Solutions for the Large Deflections of Uniformly Loaded Circular Membranes*; NASA: Washington, DC, USA, 1997; TP-3658.
26. Alekseev, S.A. Elastic annular membranes with a stiff centre under the concentrated force. *Eng. Corpus* **1951**, *10*, 71–80.
27. Sun, J.Y.; Zhang, Q.; Li, X.; He, X.T. Axisymmetric large deflection elastic analysis of hollow annular membranes under transverse uniform loading. *Symmetry* **2021**, *13*, 1770. [CrossRef]
28. Sun, J.Y.; Hu, J.L.; He, X.T.; Zheng, Z.L. A theoretical study of a clamped punch-loaded blister configuration: The quantitative relation of load and deflection. *Int. J. Mech. Sci.* **2010**, *52*, 928–936. [CrossRef]
29. Yang, Z.X.; Sun, J.Y.; Zhao, Z.H.; Li, S.Z.; He, X.T. A closed-form solution of prestressed annular membrane internally-connected with rigid circular plate and transversely-loaded by central shaft. *Mathematics* **2020**, *8*, 521. [CrossRef]

Article

Prediction of Splitting Tensile Strength of Self-Compacting Recycled Aggregate Concrete Using Novel Deep Learning Methods

Jesús de-Prado-Gil [1,*], Osama Zaid [2], Covadonga Palencia [1] and Rebeca Martínez-García [3]

[1] Department of Applied Physics, Campus of Vegazana s/n, University of León, 24071 León, Spain; c.palencia@unileon.es
[2] Department of Structure Engineering, Military College of Engineering, Risalpur, National University of Sciences and Technology, Islamabad 44000, Pakistan; Osama.zaid@scetwah.edu.pk
[3] Department of Mining Technology, Topography and Structures, Campus de Vegazana s/n, University of León, 24071 León, Spain; rmartg@unileon.es
* Correspondence: jdeprg00@estudiantes.unileon.es

Citation: de-Prado-Gil, J.; Zaid, O.; Palencia, C.; Martínez-García, R. Prediction of Splitting Tensile Strength of Self-Compacting Recycled Aggregate Concrete Using Novel Deep Learning Methods. *Mathematics* **2022**, *10*, 2245. https://doi.org/10.3390/math10132245

Academic Editors: Araceli Queiruga-Dios, Maria Jesus Santos, Fatih Yilmaz, Deolinda M. L. Dias Rasteiro, Jesús Martín Vaquero and Víctor Gayoso Martínez

Received: 14 June 2022
Accepted: 24 June 2022
Published: 27 June 2022

Publisher's Note: MDPI stays neutral with regard to jurisdictional claims in published maps and institutional affiliations.

Copyright: © 2022 by the authors. Licensee MDPI, Basel, Switzerland. This article is an open access article distributed under the terms and conditions of the Creative Commons Attribution (CC BY) license (https:// creativecommons.org/licenses/by/ 4.0/).

Abstract: The composition of self-compacting concrete (SCC) contains 60–70% coarse and fine aggregates, which are replaced by construction waste, such as recycled aggregates (RA). However, the complexity of its structure requires a time-consuming mixed design. Currently, many researchers are studying the prediction of concrete properties using soft computing techniques, which will eventually reduce environmental degradation and other material waste. There have been very limited and contradicting studies regarding prediction using different ANN algorithms. This paper aimed to predict the 28-day splitting tensile strength of SCC with RA using the artificial neural network technique by comparing the following algorithms: Levenberg–Marquardt (LM), Bayesian regularization (BR), and Scaled Conjugate Gradient Backpropagation (SCGB). There have been very limited and contradicting studies regarding prediction by using and comparing different ANN algorithms, so a total of 381 samples were collected from various published journals. The input variables were cement, admixture, water, fine and coarse aggregates, and superplasticizer; the data were randomly divided into three sets—training (60%), validation (10%), and testing (30%)—with 10 neurons in the hidden layer. The models were evaluated by the mean squared error (MSE) and correlation coefficient (R). The results indicated that all three models have optimal accuracy; still, BR gave the best performance (R = 0.91 and MSE = 0.2087) compared with LM and SCG. BR was the best model for predicting TS at 28 days for SCC with RA. The sensitivity analysis indicated that cement (30.07%) was the variable that contributed the most to the prediction of TS at 28 days for SCC with RA, and water (2.39%) contributed the least.

Keywords: artificial neural network; self-compacting concrete; recycled aggregates; tensile strength; Levenberg–Marquardt; Bayesian regularization; scaled conjugate gradient backpropagation

MSC: 68T07

1. Introduction

Concrete is the most widely used construction material in the world. One of the main arduous tasks is to produce durable concrete without excessive voids and with a long service life [1]. Due to extensive research, concrete design technology has improved in past years by adding certain admixtures [2,3]. Self-compacting concrete, created in Japan in the 1980s to achieve high-performance, long-lasting concrete buildings, is one of the outcomes of improved concrete design technology [4–6]. The main distinction between self-compacting concrete and conventional concrete is the mixing proportions of the materials [7–9]. SCC is known as the innovative concrete of the era and has the property of self-settlement in construction areas without vibratory force. SCC settles under its weight by making its path like fluid [10–12]. SCC is considered innovative because it can easily be used in congested areas where concreting is not easy. In SCC, noise pollution reduces and improves the filling capability and enhances the construction speed [13–15]. The population is growing at an alarming rate worldwide, along with the adoption and implementation of new concrete design technologies, resulting in increased resource consumption and environmental degradation. In consequence, there has been an increase in the amount of building and construction waste [16,17]. In terms of the composition of concrete, coarse aggregate (natural crushed stone) and fine aggregate (sand) make up most of the self-compacting concrete, approximately 60–70% [18–20]. Simultaneously, natural resources are being depleted at a high speed due to modern urbanization [21–23]. The primary source of well-quality aggregates, i.e., mountains, are being depleted at an alarming rate [24–26]. Because of this, natural catastrophes have struck many countries worldwide [27–29]. On the other hand, many buildings are demolished yearly due to earthquakes or after completing their service life [19,27,30]. Therefore, a considerable amount of construction waste is generated annually. To counter such things, the most sustainable revolution is to use recycled aggregates in self-compacting concrete. Recycled aggregates (RA) are abundant waste products developed by demolishing the building and then crushing, sieving, and adequately cleaning [31]. The second procedure is to bypass all these experimental works, thus reducing environmental degradation and other wastage of natural materials.

Currently, many researchers are working on using soft computing techniques. One such method is using an artificial neural network (ANN) to validate and predict specific parameters of concrete. The artificial neural network technique is generally motivated by the human brain, which is composed of billions of neurons. The ANN works similarly, learning from experiences and then utilizing the data to predict different parameters [32,33].

2. Background Literature

2.1. Artificial Neural Network

Artificial neural networks (ANNs) are a fundamental technique in deep learning. Deep learning (DL) is a subset of machine learning (ML) that allows for the computation of multi-layer neural networks. Machine learning is a subset of artificial intelligence (AI) that uses statistical methods to enable computers to develop over time, unlike the primary subject of AI, which allows machines to mimic human behavior. The primary difference between ML and DL is that in deep learning, the machine performs feature extraction and classification. Still, in machine learning, we must perform the feature extraction ourselves, and the machine performs the classification and prediction [34].

An artificial neural network (ANN) is a mathematical or computer model inspired by the human brain's enormous biological neural network [35]. It can improve its performance by learning from its mistakes, which is how an artificial neural network receives information, i.e., by learning. It comprises several functions and weights that operate as artificial neurons and are connected in a network. They are primarily used in artificial intelligence projects that solve complicated and complex issues [32]. ANN can be operated using specific algorithms that are unique in their way. From this paper's point of view, LM, BR, and SCGB are discussed below.

2.1.1. Levenberg–Marquardt Algorithm

The Levenberg–Marquardt (LM) algorithm is a procedure composed of several iterations. These iterations are used to find the minimum value of a multivariate function written as the sum of squares of non-linear real-valued functions [36,37]. Researchers recently adopted this approach to solve nonlinear least square complex problems across a wide range of fields [38]. In the LM algorithm, two methods are combined to speed up the iterations and minimize errors, i.e., the steepest descent and the Gauss–Newton method. When the present outcome is correct, the algorithm becomes the Gauss–Newton method faster than another. When the outcome is incorrect, it behaves like the steepest descent, which is relatively slow but always converges [39]. This algorithm generally uses more memory but less time.

2.1.2. Bayesian Regularization

Standard backpropagation nets are less reliable than Bayesian regularized artificial neural networks (BRANNs), which can decrease or eliminate the requirement for prolonged cross-validation [40]. In the same way that ridge regression makes a nonlinear regression into a "well-posed" statistical issue, Bayesian regularization does the same for nonlinear regression. It takes more time, but the model has numerous benefits over complex data [41]. The advantage of using BRANNs is that the models are reliable, and a validation procedure is not required [40,42]. These networks address various issues that emerge in Quantitative Structure–Activity Relationship (QSAR) modeling, including model selection, robustness, validation set selection, and network architectural optimization [43]. Bayesian criteria are stopped during training by empirical processes, making the network impossible to over train.

2.1.3. Scaled Conjugate Gradient Backpropagation

The weights are attuned in the steepest descent direction, i.e., the most negative of the gradients, via the fundamental backpropagation method. This is the fastest reducing path for the performance function. It is noted that while the function reduces the quickest along with the negative of the gradient, this does not lead to the fastest convergence [44].

The conjugate gradient algorithms search in a path that generally yields quicker convergence than the sharpest descent direction while sustaining the error reduction made in the previous phases [45]. The conjugate direction is the name given to this direction. The step size is modified in most conjugate gradient algorithms through each iteration. A search is conducted along the conjugate gradient direction to calculate the step size that will lessen the performance function along the line [46]. It is also reasonable to approximate the step size using a method other than the line search methodology. The goal is to merge the Levenberg algorithm's model trust region method with the conjugate gradient technique. SCG is the name given to this method, which was first described in the literature by Møller (1993) [47]. At every iteration user, design parameters are updated independently, which is critical for the algorithm's success. This is an essential benefit of line search-based algorithms [47].

3. Research Significance

This research aimed to validate and predict the splitting tensile strength of self-compacting concrete incorporated with recycled aggregates by artificial neural networks. From the author's best information related to the present literature, no significant studies have been conducted on applying different deep learning methods to predict the split tensile strength of SCC with RA. For this purpose, different algorithms were implemented, namely Levenberg–Marquardt (LM), Bayesian regularization (BR), and Scaled Conjugate Gradient Backpropagation (SCGB) algorithms. The best model was selected after comparing them using statistical indicators: correlation coefficient (R-value) and mean squared error (MSE). In the end, sensitivity analysis was performed to see how each input variable affected the output variable.

4. Methodology

4.1. Data Collection

The data were collected from various research articles. Table 1 shows the database containing a total of 381 samples comprised of the tensile strength of self-compacting concrete with recycled aggregates with several variables, such as water, cement, admixtures, coarse aggregates, water, fine aggregates, and superplasticizers. The database includes the Sr No., indicating the total number of research papers, authors' references, amount of data (# data) contributing from each article, and percentage (% data) of the overall data.

Table 1. Experimental database.

No.	Reference	# Data	% Data	No.	Reference	# Data	% Data
1	Ali et al., 2012 [48]	18	4.72	22	Nieto et al., 2019 [49]	22	5.77
2	Aslani et al., 2018 [50]	15	3.94	23	Nili et al., [51]	10	2.62
3	Babalola et al., 2020 [52]	14	3.67	24	Pan et al., 2019 [53]	6	1.57
4	Bahrami et al., 2020 [54]	10	2.62	25	Revathi et al., 2013 [55]	5	1.31
5	Behera et al., 2019 [56]	6	1.57	26	Revilla Cuesta et al., 2020 [57]	5	1.31
6	Chakkamalayath et al., 2020 [58]	6	1.57	27	Sadeghi-Nik et al., 2019 [59]	12	3.15
7	Duan et al., 2020 [60]	10	2.62	28	Señas et al., 2016 [61]	6	1.57
8	Fiol et al., 2018 [62]	12	3.15	29	Sharific et al., 2013 [63]	6	1.57
9	Gesoglu et al., 2015 [64]	24	6.30	30	Khafaga, S.A., 2014 [65]	15	3.94
10	Grdic et al., 2010 [66]	3	0.79	31	Silva et al., 2016 [67]	5	1.31
11	Guneyisi et al., 2014 [68]	5	1.31	32	Singh et al., 2019 [69]	12	3.15
12	Guo et al., 2020 [70]	11	2.89	33	Sun et al., 2020 [71]	10	2.62
13	Katar et al., 2021 [72]	4	1.05	34	Surendar et al., 2021 [73]	7	1.84
14	Khodair et al., 2017 [74]	20	5.25	35	Tang et al., 2016 [75]	5	1.31
15	Kou et al., 2009 [76]	13	3.41	36	Thomas et al., 2016 [77]	4	1.05
16	Krishna et al., 2018 [78]	5	1.31	37	Tuyan et al., 2014 [79]	12	3.15
17	Kumar et al., 2017 [80]	4	1.05	38	Uygunoglu et al., 2014 [81]	8	2.10
18	Long et al., 2016 [82]	4	1.05	39	Wang et al., 2020 [83]	5	1.31
19	Mahakavi and Chitra, 2019 [84]	25	6.56	40	Yu et al., 2014 [85]	3	0.79
20	Manzi et al., 2017 [86]	4	1.05	41	Zhou et al., 2013 [87]	6	1.57
21	Martínez-García et al., 2020 [88]	4	1.05		Total	381	100

Table 2 presents the statistical characteristics, such as the minimum, maximum, mean, median, mode, and standard deviation, of certain variables as inputs (water, cement, admixtures, coarse aggregates, water, fine aggregates, and superplasticizers) and one possible output from these published research articles, i.e., the tensile strength of self-compacting recycled aggregate concrete. Their graphical representation is shown in Figures 1 and 2.

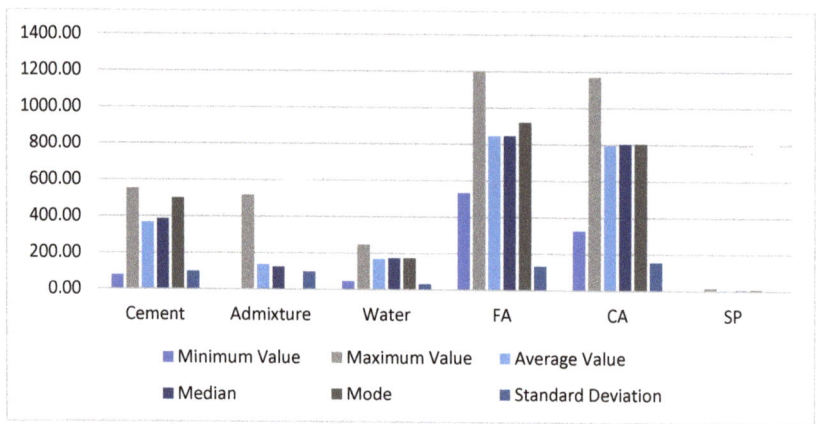

Figure 1. Statistical characteristics of input variables.

4.2. Data Visualization

The correlation between the input variables—i.e., water, cement, admixtures, coarse aggregates, water, fine aggregates, and superplasticizers—and output—i.e., splitting tensile strength (TS)—was investigated to see whether there was a link between them; this statistical analysis assisted in the creation of the predictive model by increasing the accuracy of the outcome's prediction [89]. For this purpose, the Pearson correlation matrix (heat map) was generated, as shown in Figure 3, which analyzed the correlation between the independent input variables. A correlation (|r| > 0.8) between input variables might indicate that there is currently multicollinearity between variables, which could alter modeling findings and bias the model. As seen in the heat map, although there was a substantial connection between some of the characteristics, such as between admixtures and cement (r = −0.608) and between coarse aggregates and fine aggregates (r = −0.685), none of the characteristics had a correlation greater than 0.80, showing that multicollinearity did not occur [90,91].

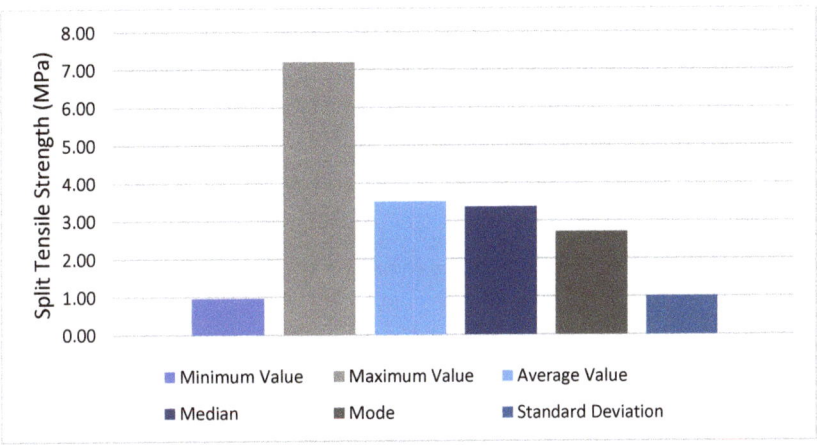

Figure 2. Statistical characteristics of the output variable.

Table 2. Statistical characteristics of input and output variables.

	Variables	Abbreviation	Minimum	Mean	Maximum	Median	Mode	Standard Deviation
	Cement	C	78.00	368.73	550.00	385.00	500.00	98.38
	Admixture	A	0.00	138.27	515.00	123.00	0.00	94.95
Input	Water	W	45.50	167.29	246.00	172.00	172.00	31.02
(kg/m^3)	Fine Aggregates	FA	532.20	844.71	1200.00	846.00	919.00	130.52
	Coarse Aggregates	CA	328.00	196.05	1170.00	803.00	803.00	154.06
	Super Plasticizer	SP	0.00	5.07	16.00	4.55	7.50	3.12
Output (MPa)	Tensile Strength	TS	0.96	3.52	7.20	3.37	2.70	1.00

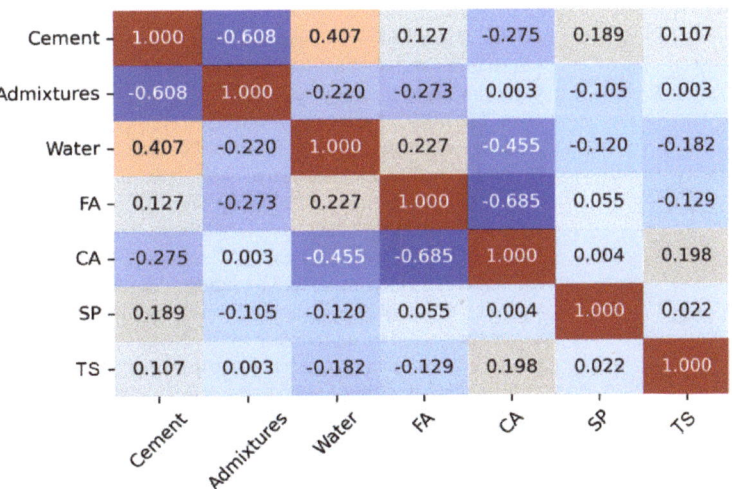

Figure 3. Correlation coefficient heat map between the input and output variables.

4.3. Artificial Neural Network for the Training, Validation, and Prediction of the Tensile Strength

An artificial neural network (ANN) is a mathematical or computational model influenced by biological neural networks' structural and/or functional characteristics. It can improve its performance by learning from its mistakes. Artificial neural networks, like human brains, acquire knowledge through learning. They are made up of a network of artificial neurons that communicate with one another and analyze data using a connectionist approach to computation. They are primarily employed to simulate complicated input–output interactions or data patterns in data [14]. Training, validation, and testing are the three phases of ANNs. The model is repeated until it reaches the desired outcome in the training phase. The validation step's mistakes are detected during the training phase [92].

An ANN model generally comprises several layers, the first of which is input and output, which contains input and output data. Depending on the model, one or more hidden layers exist between these layers. It is made up of neurons that are linked by weights. The output of each neuron is determined by its activation function. Activation functions come in several different forms. Nonlinear activation functions, such as sigmoid and step, are commonly employed [1]. The general structure of an ANN is shown in Figure 4.

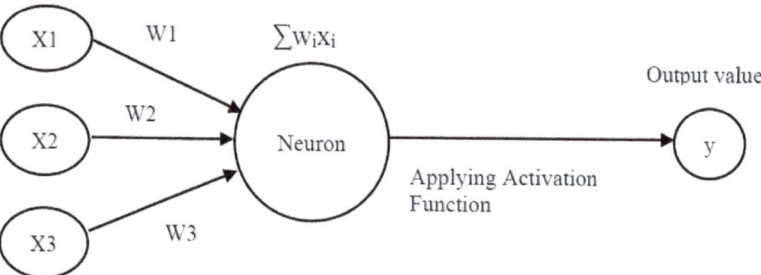

Figure 4. General structure of ANN.

A variety of factors must be considered while creating an ANN model. The first step is selecting the most appropriate structure for the ANN model. Then, the data are inserted into the selected ANN model in terms of input and output. Then, in the activation function, the number of layers and the number of hidden layers, as well as some neurons in each hidden layer, must be selected by experience [93,94].

In this research, concerning Tables 1 and 2, the network was made utilizing six input parameters and one output parameter with one hidden layer. The input layer consists of variables such as cement, admixtures, water, fine and coarse aggregates, and superplasticizer. The output parameter was selected by splitting the tensile strength of self-compacting recycled aggregate concrete. The feedforward backpropagation neural network was used in this study. The architecture of the current research on ANN is shown in Figure 5.

It should be noted that three algorithms were used and compared in this study, namely Levenberg–Marquardt (LM), Bayesian regularization (BR), and Scaled Conjugate Gradient backpropagation (SCG). Designing and performing the network were performed on MATLAB software. The Levenberg–Marquardt algorithm usually necessitates more memory, but it takes less time. Training terminates when generalization stops improving, as demonstrated by an increase in the mean square error of the validation samples. But in the case of Bayesian regularization, although this technique takes longer, it can provide strong generalization for complex, tiny, or noisy datasets. Adaptive weight reduction causes training to come to an end (regularization). On the other hand, the Scaled Conjugate Gradient Backpropagation algorithm uses less memory than the previous one. Training automatically terminates when generalization stops improving, as shown by a rise in the mean square error of the validation sample [45,46,94,95].

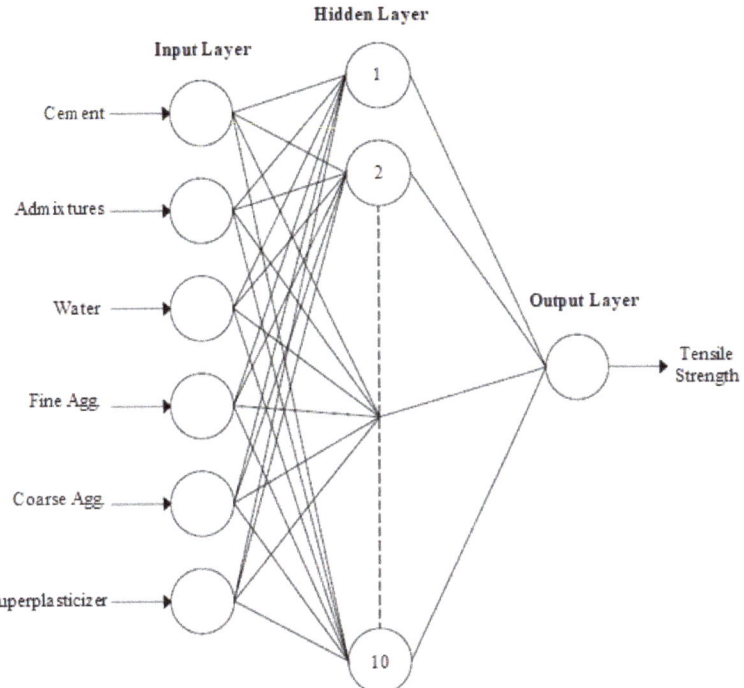

Figure 5. Artificial neural network architecture.

The models were developed and performed in MATLAB. The network was divided into three phases, i.e., training, validation, and testing. Sixty percent of data was selected for training, and the remaining 10% and 30% of data were selected for the validation and testing stage, respectively. In the training stage, 10 neurons were selected for the hidden layer. The network randomly chose data for training, validation, and testing according to its selected percentage, with 229 samples for training, 38 samples for validation, and 114 samples for the testing stage. In the case of Bayesian regularization (BR), validation is not required, so the numbers of samples taken for training and testing were 267 and 114, respectively. This is because validation is often employed as a type of regularization, while BR algorithms have their built-in form of validation. The splitting of data is summarized in Table 3.

4.4. ANN Network Model Evaluation

Using the ANN tool to develop the neural network; the models' performance was assessed using two measures; coefficient of correlation (R-value) and mean squared error (MSE) [96,97], as given in Equation (1).

$$\text{MSE} = \frac{1}{n}\sum(y_i - \hat{y}_i)^2 \quad (1)$$

where n = number of data points, y_i = observed values, and $\hat{y}_i$ = predicted values.

Regression is considered the best evaluation measurement to check the accuracy of the overall network. The correlation between outputs and predicted targets was measured using R-values. A strong relationship has an R-value of 1, whereas a random relationship has an R-value of 0 [48,96].

The average squared discrepancy between outputs and objectives is known as the mean squared error. The lower the value, the better. There is no error if the value is zero.

Table 3. Data split for model testing.

Step	Percentage %	No. of Specimens
Levenberg–Marquardt Algorithm		
Train	60	229
Validation	10	38
Test	30	114
Total	100	381
Bayesian Regularization		
Train	70	267
Validation	-	0
Test	30	114
Total	100	381
Scaled Conjugate Gradient Backpropagation		
Train	60	229
Validation	10	38
Test	30	114
Total	100	381

5. Results and Discussion

The model was run on the basis of three algorithms, namely LM, BR, and SCG, separately, and their results are compared and discussed below.

5.1. Levenberg–Marquardt Algorithm

The network was trained again and again to find the best-fit model. The performance of the model is shown in Figure 6 with 10 neurons. The plot contains different colored lines indicating training, validation, and testing. The model started training with a high MSE, which was eventually reduced by the validation parameters preventing overfitting data. It shows that after 44 epochs, the training error was still decreasing, but the validation and testing errors were increasing. Therefore, after six more epochs, the model training was stopped, and an optimized model was produced with minimum MSE.

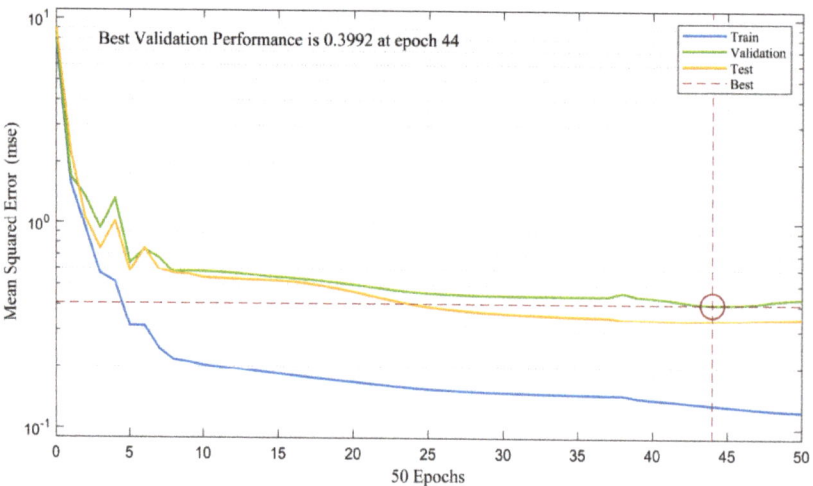

Figure 6. LM algorithm model performance.

The model error histogram is shown in Figure 7 between training, validation, and testing. The graph shows that the error bars converge to the zero-error line. The performance criteria results show that the model is suitable for predicting the outcomes of splitting tensile strength of SCC with RA.

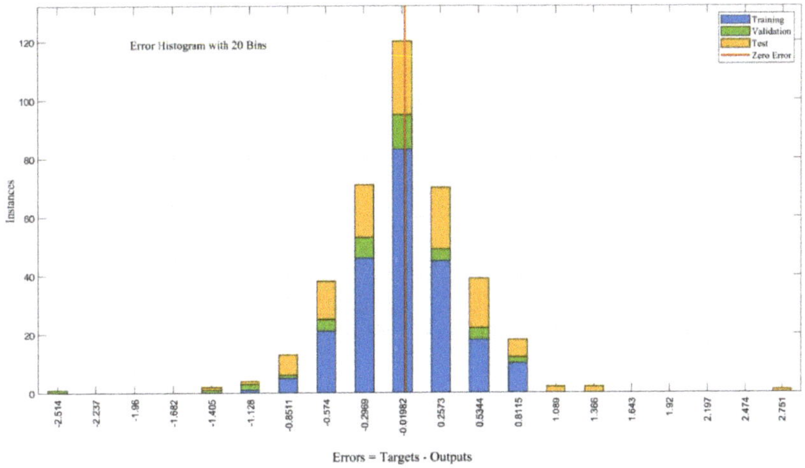

Figure 7. LM algorithm model error histogram.

After that, a regression analysis was performed. Figure 8a–c shows the correlation of training, validation, and testing between the input and output values of the model. The model's overall accuracy, i.e., correlation, is shown in Figure 8d. In each scenario, a black-colored linear fit is displayed. It should be noted that the overall R-value was found to be 0.86, which shows that the correlation was very close to a linear fit, confirming a good model for predicting values of the splitting tensile strength of SCC using RA. Finally, all the performance parameters results, i.e., the R-value and MSE of the overall model with training, validation, and testing, are summarized in Table 4. Overall, these results indicate that the Levenberg–Marquardt algorithm is a good algorithm for predicting the splitting tensile strength of self-compacting recycled aggregate concrete.

Table 4. Summary of different model evaluation parameters of LM Algorithm.

Step	Function	MSE	R
Training	trainlm	0.1508	0.9267
Validation	trainlm	0.3992	0.7899
Testing	trainlm	0.3282	0.8294
Overall	trainlm	0.2927	0.8573

5.2. Bayesian Regularization

In the same manner, the model was trained using the Bayesian regularization approach. The model's performance is shown in Figure 9 with the same number of neurons. The plot consists of two colored lines indicating training and testing only, as BR does not need a validation step because it has a built-in form of validation in the training step. The model started training with high MSE, which was eventually reduced by the training parameters preventing overfitting data. As BR takes more time, the graph shows that the model took several epochs, and after 100 epochs, training and testing error lines were reduced considerably and approximately became a straight line. The model is trained further to validate thoroughly, and training is stopped at 190 epochs. An optimized model has a 0.14403 performance indicator at 189 epochs.

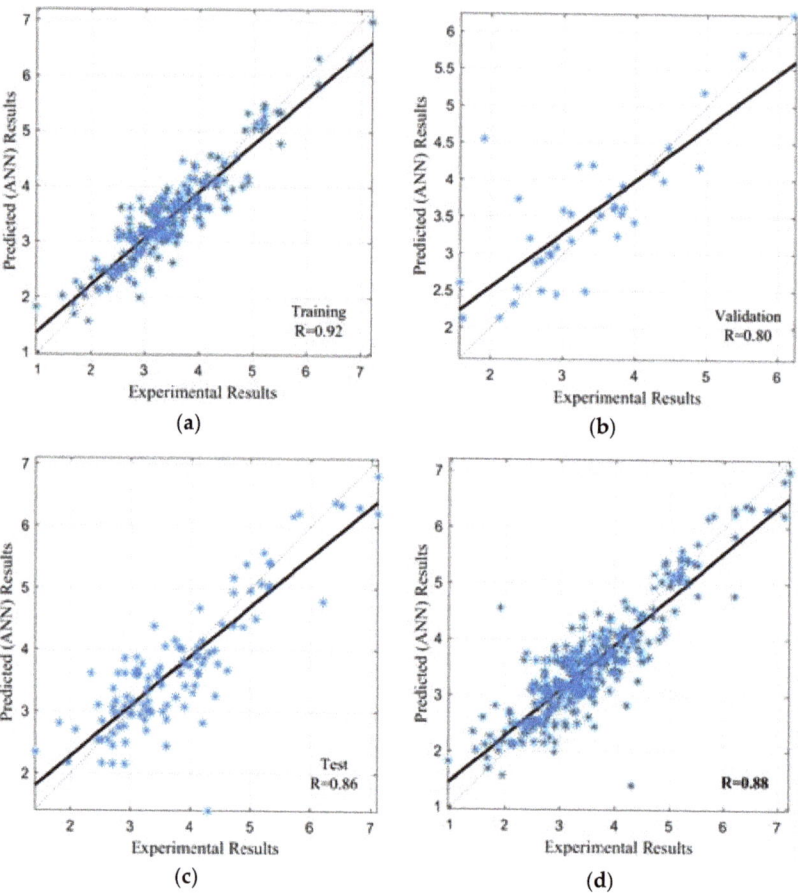

Figure 8. LM algorithm regression graphs between the experimental and predicted tensile strength: (**a**) training; (**b**) validation; (**c**) testing, and (**d**) overall dataset.

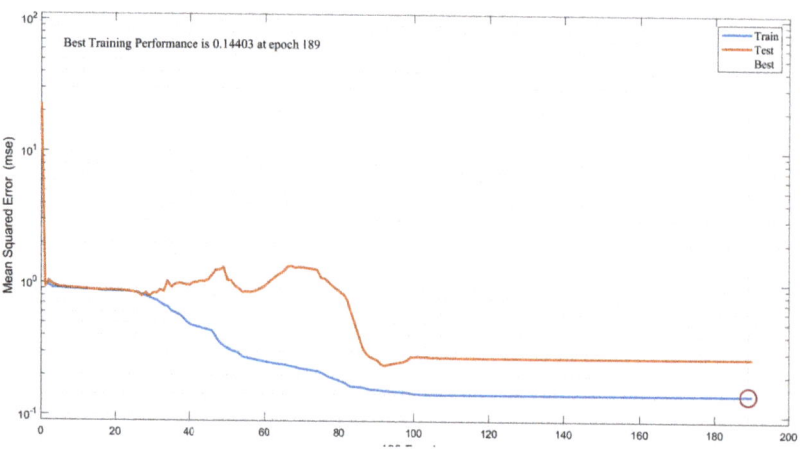

Figure 9. BR model performance.

The model error histogram is shown in Figure 10 between training and testing. The graph shows that the bins convergence to the zero-error line is excellent, and the error is also small compared to the LM algorithm. The results of this performance criteria are shown that the model is perfect for predicting the outcomes of splitting tensile strength of SCC with RA. After that, a regression analysis is performed in the same manner. Figure 11a,b show the correlation of training and testing between the input and output values of the model. Overall correlation is shown in Figure 11c. In each scenario, a black-colored linear fit is displayed. It is noted that the overall R-value is found to be 0.91. The model trained by Bayesian regularization has excellent accuracy for predicting output, i.e., splitting tensile strength of SCC with RA. Finally, all the performance parameters results, i.e., R-value and MSE of the overall model with training and test, are summarized in Table 5. Overall, these results indicate that Bayesian regularization can be adopted for predicting the splitting tensile strength of self-compacting recycled aggregate concrete.

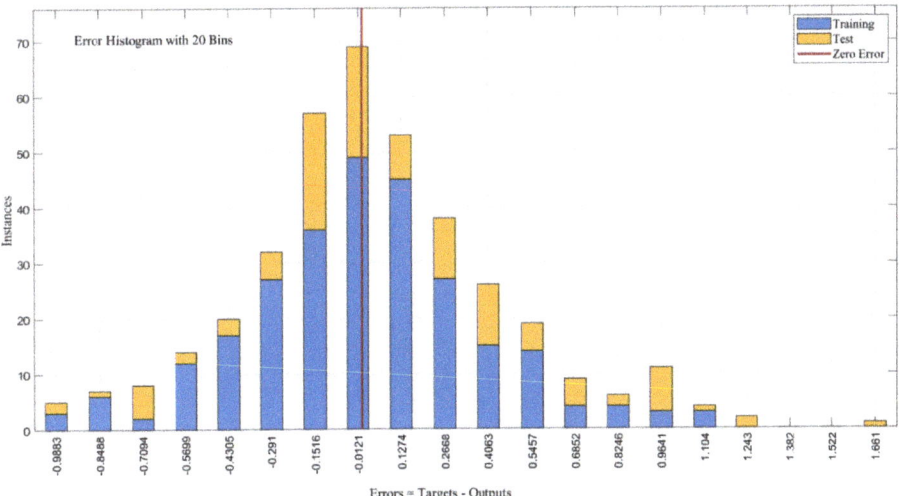

Figure 10. BR model error histogram.

Table 5. Summary of different model evaluation parameters of BR.

Step	Function	MSE	R
Training	trainbr	0.1440	0.9254
Testing	trainbr	0.2734	0.8638
Overall	trainbr	0.2087	0.9049

5.3. Scaled Conjugate Gradient Backpropagation

The model is trained by using the Scaled Conjugate Gradient Backpropagation approach. The performance of the model is shown in Figure 12 with 10 neurons. The plot contains different color lines indicating training, validation, and testing. The model starts training with high MSE, which is eventually reduced by the validation parameters preventing overfitting data. The graph shows that MSE did not reduce much compared with the other two algorithms. It shows that after 66 epochs, the training errors were decreasing, but the validation and testing errors were increasing a little bit. Therefore, after eight more epochs, the model training was stopped, and an optimized model was produced, with a minimum MSE achieved.

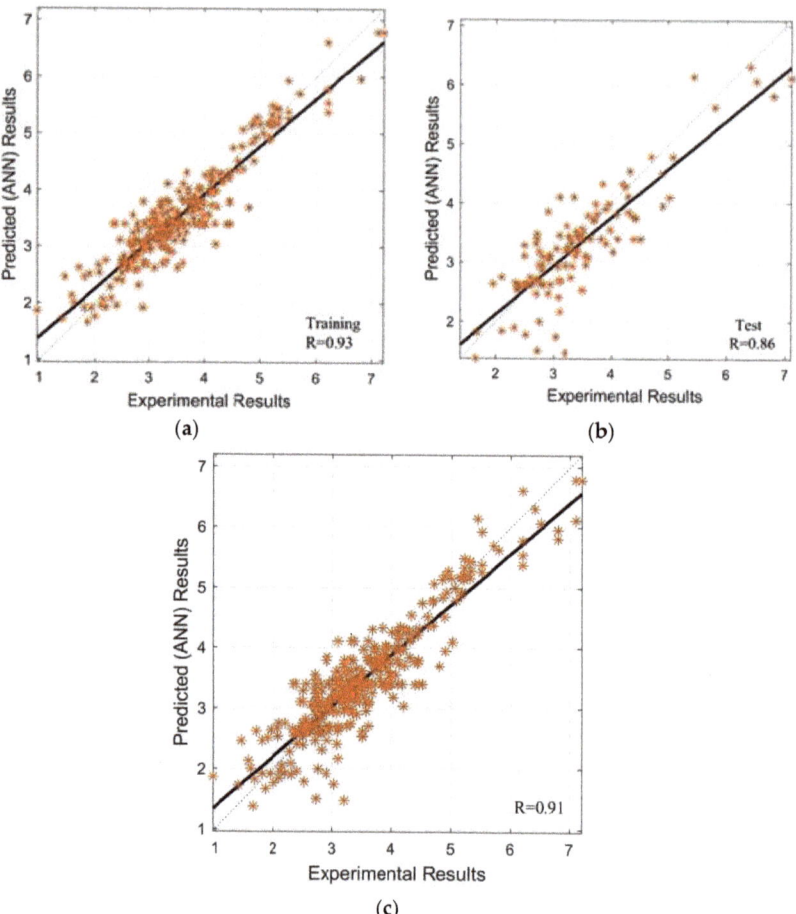

Figure 11. Bayesian regularization regression graphs between the experimental and predicted tensile strength: (**a**) training, (**b**) testing, and (**c**) overall dataset.

The model error histogram is shown in Figure 13 between training, validation, and testing. The graph shows that the error bar bins converge to the zero-error line with low accuracy. The results of this performance criteria indicate that the model has high error values compared with other algorithms and is below par for predicting the outcomes of splitting tensile strength of SCC with RA. After that, a regression analysis was performed. Figure 14a–c show the correlation of training, validation, and testing between the input and output values of the model. The model's overall accuracy, i.e., correlation, is shown in Figure 14d. In each scenario, a maroon-colored linear fit is displayed. It should be noted that the overall R-value was found to be 0.64, which shows that the correlation was far from a linear fit, confirming a below-par or average model for predicting values of splitting tensile strength of SCC using RA.

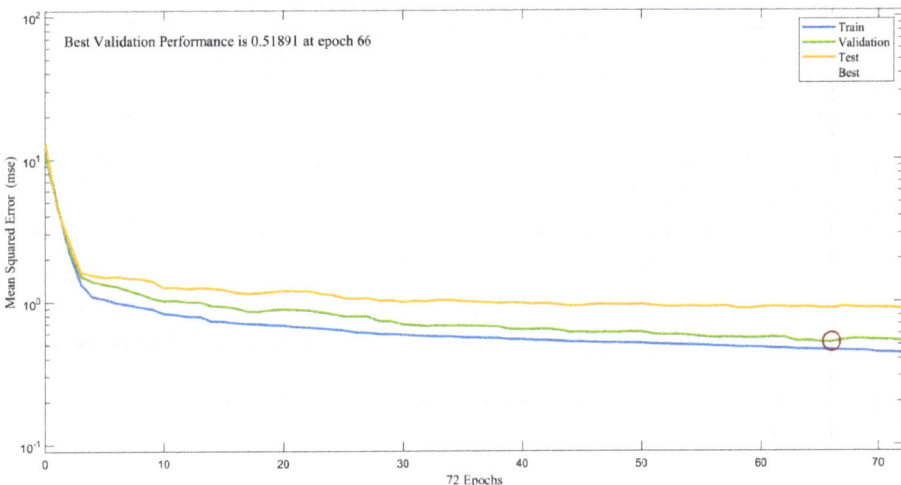

Figure 12. SCG model performance.

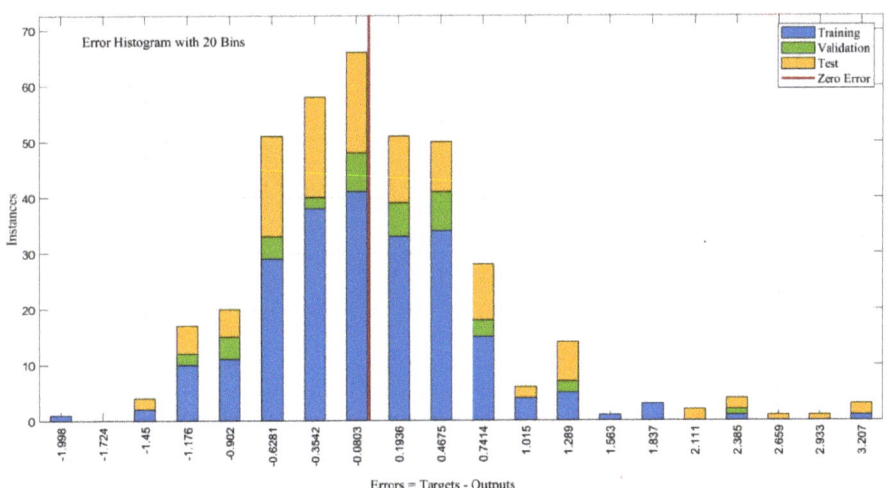

Figure 13. BR model error histogram.

Finally, all the performance parameters results, i.e., the R-value and MSE of the overall model with training, validation, and testing, are summarized in Table 6. These results indicate that Scaled Conjugate Gradient Backpropagation is rated as a below-par algorithm compared with LM and BR for predicting the splitting tensile strength of self-compacting recycled aggregate concrete.

Table 6. Summary of different model evaluation parameters of SCGB algorithm.

Step	Function	MSE	R
Training	trainscg	0.4588	0.6920
Validation	trainscg	0.5189	0.6616
Testing	trainscg	0.8925	0.5425
Overall	trainscg	0.6234	0.6368

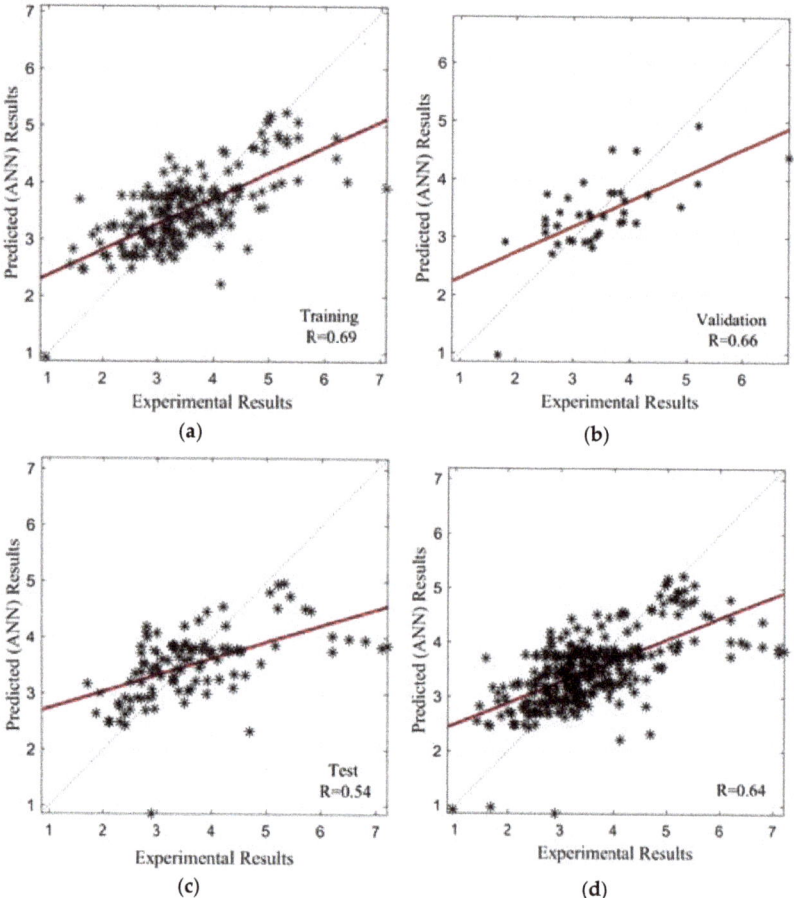

Figure 14. SCG algorithm regression graphs between the experimental and predicted tensile strength: (**a**) training; (**b**) validation; (**c**) testing, and (**d**) overall dataset.

5.4. Comparison of LM and SCG Approaches

The comparison between all three algorithms was performed on the basis of the experimental results and predicted results by ANN. Figure 15a–c shows the comparison between the experimental and predicted values of a model trained by LM, BR, and SCG approaches, respectively. On the y-axis, the blue line indicates the predicted values, and the red line shows the experimental values of tensile strength of SCC with recycled aggregates. On the x-axis, the data set of 381 samples is given.

All graphs indicate that values predicted from the three algorithms correlated well with the experimental values. The more significant difference between the two lines indicates a high error between the two parameters. The overall R-value and mean squared error of all three algorithms are summarized in graphical format, as shown in Figure 16.

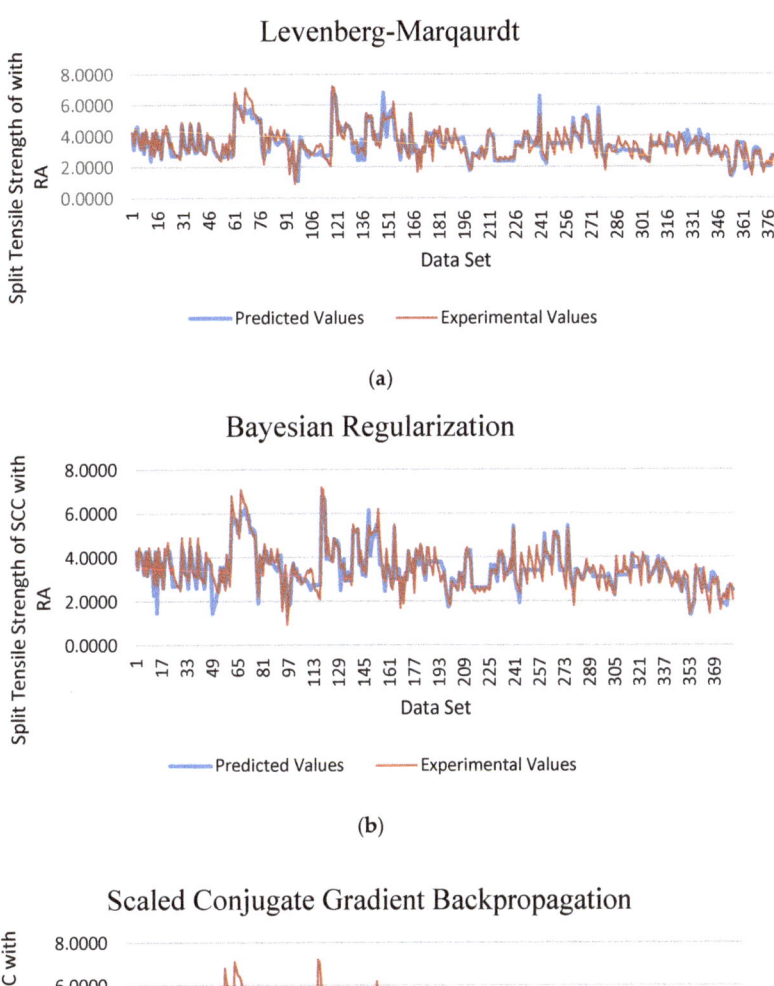

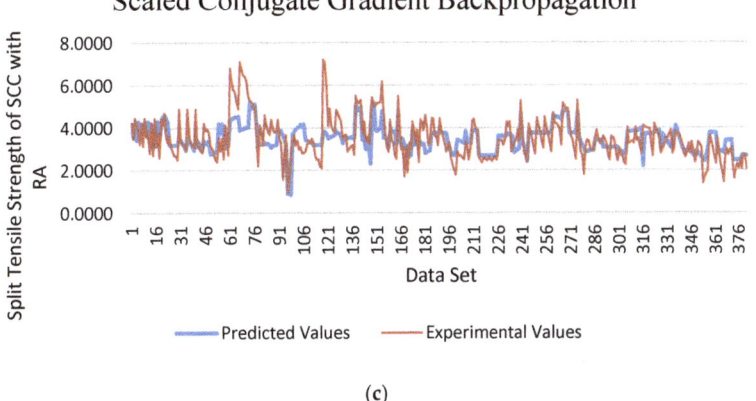

Figure 15. Comparison of experimental and predicted values by ANN of (**a**) LM, (**b**) BR, and (**c**) SCGB algorithms.

Thus, Figures 15a–c and 16 confirm that the best fitting graph is that of Bayesian regularization (Figure 15b), which has a more significant R-value and minimum MSE. The BR approach performed better because of the heterogeneity of the data, as it can provide strong generalization for complex datasets [98]. It was concluded that among all three algorithms, i.e., Levenberg–Marquardt, Bayesian regularization, and Scaled Conjugate Gradient Backpropagation, Bayesian regularization had the highest accuracy (>90%) and could accurately predict the splitting tensile strength of self-compacting concrete with recycled aggregates.

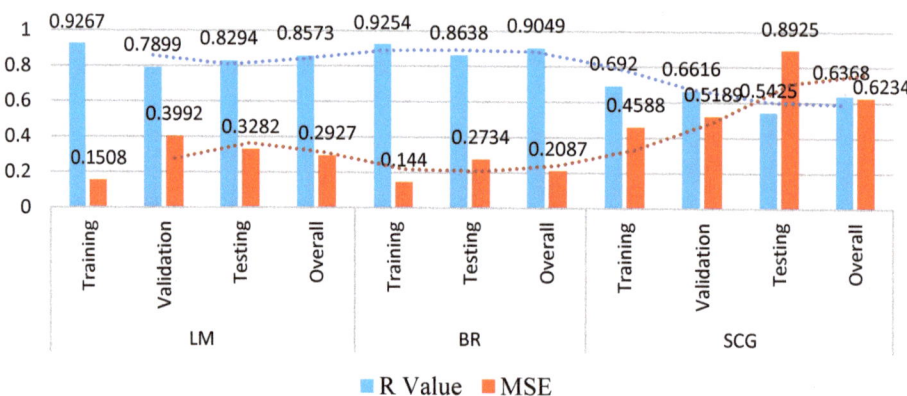

Figure 16. R-value and MSE of LM, BR, and SCGB algorithms.

5.5. Sensitivity Analysis

The sensitivity analysis allows us to see how each input variable affects the output variable. The more significant the influence of the input variables on the output variable, the higher the sensitivity values. As per Shang et al. [99], the variables of input have a significant influence on the prediction of the output variable. Sensitivity analysis was used to examine the impact of each input variable—fine-aggregate cement, coarse-aggregate superplasticizer, water, and superplasticizers—on the variability of splitting tensile strength of self-compacting concrete with recycled aggregates. Equations (2) and (3) were used to determine the sensitivity analysis:

$$S_i = \frac{N_i}{\sum_{i=1}^{n} N_i} \times 100 \quad (2)$$

$$N_i = f_{max}(x_i) - f_{min}(x_i), \ i = 1, \ldots, n \quad (3)$$

where $f_{max}(x_i)$ and $f_{min}(x_i)$ are the input variables projected highest and lowest splitting tensile strength.

As indicated in the graph (Figure 17), each of the variables of input—coarse-aggregate cement, water, superplasticizers, water, fine aggregate, and mineral admixture—had a considerable impact in forecasting the splitting tensile strength of self-compacting concrete with recycled aggregates. The most significant contributions to the estimate of splitting tensile strength of self-compacting concrete with recycled aggregates were cement (30.07%), fine aggregate (22.83%), and mineral admixture (22.08%). According to Shang et al. [99], cement is a factor that significantly impacts the prediction of the tensile strength of SCC with RA. The input variables of coarse aggregate and superplasticizer had contributions of 13.02% and 9.61%, respectively. On the other hand, water was the least efficient variable in predicting the tensile strength of SCC with RA (2.39%); these findings are consistent with prior studies [98].

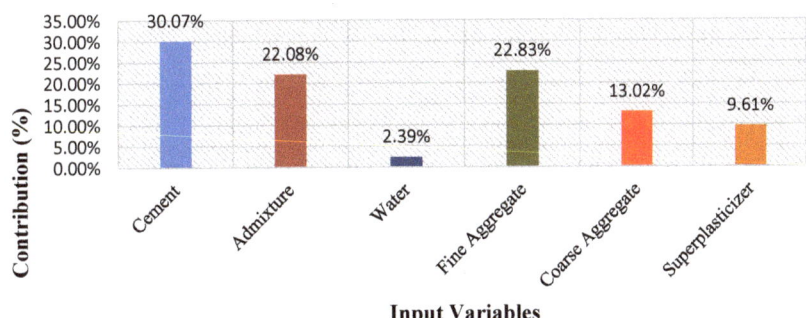

Figure 17. Contribution of input variables to split tensile strength of SSSC with RA in BR approach.

6. Conclusions

This study aimed to predict and compare the results of predicting the tensile strength of SCC modified with RA using different algorithms of artificial neural networks, namely LM, BR, and SCG. The model was trained with six input parameters: cement, water, admixtures, coarse and fine aggregates, and superplasticizer. For evaluation, two metrics were used: R-value and MSE. From this study, the following conclusions were drawn.

1. A dataset of 381 samples was collected through journals and randomly divided into 60%, 10%, and 30% for training (267), validation (38), and testing (114), respectively, for the development of the LM, BR, and SCG models. However, in the case of BR, the ratio was 70% for training and 30% for testing due to the built-in validation function in the training step.
2. Different algorithms, namely LM, BR, and SCG, were trained and tested for this study and gave an overall accuracy of 85%, 91%, and 64% with MSEs of 0.2927, 0.2087, and 0.6234.
3. It is evident that out of all three, the SCG algorithm was a poor model for predicting the tensile strength of SCC, with RA having the lowest R-value and the highest MSE.
4. Bayesian regularization gave the best performance with a high coefficient of correlation ($R > 90\%$) and a minimal MSE (0.2087) concerning LM and SCG.
5. The results showed that the BR algorithm is a good model and can be adopted for the prediction of the 28-day tensile strength of self-compacting concrete modified with recycled aggregates
6. According to the sensitivity analysis, cement is the essential input variable in predicting the 28-day tensile strength of SCC with RA (30.07%). On the other hand, water had the smallest influence on the 28-day tensile strength of SCC with RA (2.39%).

There are some limitations in this research regarding the collection of data. As there were not enough experimental data, we could not gather large datasets for this research. As a result, more datasets must be collected for future research on this topic to avoid this limitation and make a more accurate prediction model. With more data, various inputs and outputs can be further examined.

Author Contributions: Conceptualization, J.d.-P.-G.; investigation, J.d.-P.-G., O.Z. and R.M.-G.; writing—original draft preparation, J.d.-P.-G., O.Z. and R.M.-G.; writing—review and editing, J.d.-P.-G., C.P., O.Z. and R.M.-G.; supervision, C.P. and R.M.-G. All authors have read and agreed to the published version of the manuscript.

Funding: This research received no external funding.

Institutional Review Board Statement: Not applicable.

Informed Consent Statement: Not applicable.

Data Availability Statement: Data is accessible from the corresponding author on reasonable request.

Conflicts of Interest: The authors declare no conflict of interest.

References

1. Bilim, C.; Atiş, C.; Tanyildizi, H.; Karahan, O. Predicting the compressive strength of ground granulated blast furnace slag concrete using artificial neural network. *Adv. Eng. Softw.* **2009**, *40*, 334–340. [CrossRef]
2. Li, Z. *Advanced Concrete Technology*; John Willey & Sons: Toronto, ON, Canada, 2011.
3. Saidova, Z.; Yakovlev, G.; Smirnova, O.; Gordina, A.; Kuzmina, N. Modification of cement matrix with complex additive based on chrysotyl nanofibers and carbon black. *Appl. Sci.* **2021**, *11*, 6943. [CrossRef]
4. Okamura, H.; Ouchi, M. Self-compacting concrete. *J. Adv. Concr. Technol.* **2003**, *1*, 5–15. [CrossRef]
5. Zaid, O.; Hashmi, S.R.Z.; Aslam, F.; Abedin, Z.U.; Ullah, A. Experimental study on the properties improvement of hybrid graphene oxide fiber-reinforced composite concrete. *Diam. Relat. Mater.* **2022**, *124*, 108883. [CrossRef]
6. Zaid, O.; Ahmad, J.; Siddique, M.S.; Aslam, F.; Alabduljabbar, H.; Khedher, K.M. A step towards sustainable glass fiber reinforced concrete utilizing silica fume and waste coconut shell aggregate. *Sci. Rep.* **2021**, *11*, 1–14. Available online: https://www.nature.com/articles/s41598-021-92228-6 (accessed on 22 June 2022).
7. Zaid, O.; Mukhtar, F.M.; M-García, R.; El Sherbiny, M.G.; Mohamed, A.M. Characteristics of high-performance steel fiber reinforced recycled aggregate concrete utilizing mineral filler. *Case Stud. Constr. Mater.* **2022**, *16*, e00939. [CrossRef]
8. Yakovlev, G.; Polyanskikh, I.; Gordina, A.; Pudov, I.; Černý, V.; Gumenyuk, A.; Smirnova, O. Influence of sulphate attack on properties of modified cement composites. *Appl. Sci.* **2021**, *11*, 8509. [CrossRef]
9. Smirnova, O.M.; de Navascués, I.M.P.; Mikhailevskii, V.R.; Kolosov, O.I.; Skolota, N.S. Sound-absorbing composites with rubber crumb from used tires. *Appl. Sci.* **2021**, *11*, 7347. [CrossRef]
10. Shi, C.; Wu, Z.; Lv, K.; Wu, L. A review on mixture design methods for self-compacting concrete. *Constr. Build. Mater.* **2015**, *84*, 387–398. [CrossRef]
11. Smirnova, O.; Kazanskaya, L.; Koplík, J.; Tan, H.; Gu, X. Sustainability, and undefined 2020, Concrete based on clinker-free cement: Selecting the functional unit for environmental assessment. *Sustainability* **2021**, *13*, 135. [CrossRef]
12. Smirnova, O. Development of classification of rheologically active microfillers for disperse systems with Portland cement and superplasticizer. *Int. J. Civ. Eng. Technol.* **2018**, *9*, 1966–1973.
13. Nikbin, I.M.; Beygi, M.H.A.; Kazemi, M.T.; Vaseghi Amiri, J.; Rabbanifar, S.; Rahmani, E.; Rahimi, S. A comprehensive investigation into the effect of water to cement ratio and powder content on mechanical properties of self-compacting concrete. *Constr. Build. Mater.* **2014**, *57*, 69–80. [CrossRef]
14. Althoey, F.; Zaid, O.; De-Prado-Gil, J.; Palencia, C.; Ali, E.; Hakeem, I.; Martínez-García, R. Impact of sulfate activation of rice husk ash on the performance of high strength steel fiber reinforced recycled aggregate concrete. *J. Build. Eng.* **2022**, *54*, 104610. [CrossRef]
15. Zaid, O.; Ahmad, J.; Siddique, M.S.; Aslam, F. Effect of Incorporation of Rice Husk Ash Instead of Cement on the Performance of Steel Fibers Reinforced Concrete. *Front. Mater.* **2021**, *8*, 151. [CrossRef]
16. Tam, V.W.Y.; Shen, L.Y.; Fung, I.W.H.; Wang, J.Y. Controlling construction waste by implementing governmental ordinances in Hong Kong. *Constr. Innov.* **2007**, *7*, 149–166. [CrossRef]
17. Borrero, E.L.S.; Farhangi, V.; Jadidi, K.; Karakouzian, M. An Experimental Study on Concrete's Durability and Mechanical Characteristics Subjected to Different Curing Regimes. *Civ. Eng. J.* **2021**, *7*, 676–689. [CrossRef]
18. Huang, X.; Ge, J.; Kaewunruen, S.; Su, Q. The self-sealing capacity of environmentally friendly, highly damped, fibre-reinforced concrete. *Materials* **2020**, *13*, 298. [CrossRef]
19. Daungwilailuk, T.; Cao, T.; Pansuk, W.; Pheinsusom, P. Evaluating damaged concrete depth in reinforced concrete structures under different fire exposure times by means of NDT and DT techniques. *Mod. Eng. Technol.* **2017**, *21*, 233–249. [CrossRef]
20. Jiradilok, P.; Wang, Y.; Nagai, K.; Matsumoto, K. Development of discrete meso-scale bond model for corrosion damage at steel-concrete interface based on tests with/without concrete damage. *Constr. Build. Mater.* **2020**, *263*, 117615. [CrossRef]
21. Aslam, F.; Zaid, O.; Althoey, F.; Alyami, S.H.; Qaidi, S.; Gil, J.D.P.; Martínez-García, R. Evaluating the influence of fly ash and waste glass on the characteristics of coconut fibers reinforced concrete. *Struct. Concr.* **2022**. [CrossRef]
22. Ahmad, J.; Zaid, O.; Aslam, F.; Shahzaib, M.; Ullah, R.; Alabduljabbar, H.; Khedher, K.M. A study on the mechanical characteristics of glass and nylon fiber reinforced peach shell lightweight concrete. *Materials* **2021**, *14*, 4488. [CrossRef] [PubMed]
23. Smirnova, O.M.; Pidal, I.M.; Alekseev, A.V.; Petrov, D.N.; Popov, M.G. Strain Hardening of Polypropylene Microfiber Reinforced Composite Based on Alkali-Activated Slag Matrix. *Materials* **2022**, *15*, 1607. [CrossRef] [PubMed]
24. Carvalho, F.P. Mining industry and sustainable development: Time for change. *Food Energy Secur.* **2017**, *6*, 61–77. [CrossRef]
25. Zaid, O.; Martínez-García, R.; Abadel, A.A.; Fraile-Fernández, F.J.; Alshaikh, I.M.H.; Palencia-Coto, C. To determine the performance of metakaolin-based fiber-reinforced geopolymer concrete with recycled aggregates. *Arch. Civ. Mech. Eng.* **2022**, *22*, 1–14. [CrossRef]
26. Zaid, O.; Hashmi, S.R.Z.; Aslam, F.; Alabduljabbar, H. Experimental Study on Mechanical Performance of Recycled Fine Aggregate Concrete Reinforced With Discarded Carbon Fibers. *Front. Mater.* **2021**, *8*, 771423. [CrossRef]
27. Kaewunruen, S.; Meesit, R. Eco-friendly High-Strength Concrete Engineering by Micro Crumb Rubber from Recycled Tires and Plastic Components. *Adv. Civ. Eng.* **2020**, *9*, 210–226. [CrossRef]
28. Smirnova, O.M. Low-clinker cements with low water demand. *J. Mater. Civ. Eng.* **2020**, *32*, 06020008. [CrossRef]

29. Smirnova, O.J. Compatibility of shungisite microfillers with polycarboxylate admixtures in cement compositions. *Eng. Appl. Sci.* **2019**, *14*, 600–610. Available online: http://www.arpnjournals.org/jeas/research_papers/rp_2019/jeas_0219_7595.pdf (accessed on 22 June 2022).
30. Nguyen, H.Y.T.; Pansuk, W.; Sancharoen, P. The Effects of Electro-Chemical Chloride Extraction on the Migration of Ions and the Corrosion State of Embedded Steel in Reinforced Concrete. *KSCE J. Civ. Eng.* **2018**, *22*, 2942–2950. [CrossRef]
31. Berndt, M.L. Properties of sustainable concrete containing fly ash, slag and recycled concrete aggregate. *Constr. Build. Mater.* **2009**, *23*, 2606–2613. [CrossRef]
32. Nikoo, M.; Torabian Moghadam, F.; Sadowski, Ł. Prediction of concrete compressive strength by evolutionary artificial neural networks. *Adv. Mater. Sci. Eng.* **2015**, *2015*, 849126. [CrossRef]
33. Dabiri, H.; Farhangi, V.; Moradi, M.J.; Zadehmohamad, M.; Karakouzian, M. Applications of Decision Tree and Random Forest as Tree-Based Machine Learning Techniques for Analyzing the Ultimate Strain of Spliced and Non-Spliced Reinforcement Bars. *Appl. Sci.* **2022**, *12*, 4851. [CrossRef]
34. Du, X.; Cai, Y.; Wang, S.; Zhang, L. Overview of deep learning. In Proceedings of the 2016 31st Youth Academic Annual Conference of Chinese Association of Automation (YAC), Wuhan, China, 11–13 November 2016; pp. 159–164.
35. Schmidhuber, J. Deep learning in neural networks: An overview. *Neural Netw.* **2015**, *61*, 85–117. [CrossRef]
36. Levenberg, K. A method for the solution of certain non-linear problems in least squares. *Q. Appl. Math.* **1944**, *2*, 164–168. [CrossRef]
37. Marquardt, D.W. An algorithm for least-squares estimation of nonlinear parameters. *J. Soc. Ind. Appl. Math.* **1963**, *11*, 431–441. [CrossRef]
38. Mittelmann, H.D. The Least Squares Problem. 2004. Available online: http://plato.asu.edu/topics/problems/nlolsq (accessed on 22 June 2022).
39. Madsen, K.; Nielsen, H.B.; Tingleff, O. *Methods for Non-Linear Least Squares Problems*, 2nd ed.; Elsevier: Aalborg, Denmark, 2008.
40. MacKay, D.J.C. Bayesian Interpolation. *Neural Comput.* **1992**, *4*, 415–447. [CrossRef]
41. Winkler, D.A.; Burden, F.R. Robust QSAR models from novel descriptors and bayesian regularised neural networks. *Mol. Simul.* **2000**, *24*, 243–258. [CrossRef]
42. Hawkins, D.M.; Basak, S.C.; Mills, D. Assessing Model Fit by Cross-Validation. *J. Chem. Inf. Comput. Sci.* **2003**, *43*, 579–586. [CrossRef]
43. Lucic, B.; Amic, D.; Trinajstic, N. Nonlinear multivariate regression outperforms several concisely designed neural networks on three QSPR data sets. *J. Chem. Inf. Comput. Sci.* **2000**, *40*, 403–413. [CrossRef]
44. Hagan, M.T.; Demuth, H.B.; de Jesús, O. An introduction to the use of neural networks in control systems. *Int. J. Robust Nonlinear Control.* **2002**, *12*, 959–985. [CrossRef]
45. Kişi, Ö.; Uncuoğlu, E. Comparison of three back-propagation training algorithms for two case studies. *Indian J. Eng. Mater. Sci.* **2005**, *12*, 434–442.
46. Demuth, H.; Beale, M.; Hagan, M. *Neural Network Toolbox 6. User's Guide*; The MathWorks: Natick, MA, USA, 2010.
47. Møller, M.F. A scaled conjugate gradient algorithm for fast supervised learning. *Neural Netw.* **1993**, *6*, 525–533. [CrossRef]
48. Ali, E.; Al-Tersawy, S.H. Recycled glass as a partial replacement for fine aggregate in self compacting concrete. *Constr. Build. Mater.* **2012**, *35*, 785–791. [CrossRef]
49. Nieto, D.; Dapena, E.; Alaejos, P.; Olmedo, J.; Pérez, D. Properties of Self-Compacting Concrete Prepared with Coarse Recycled Concrete Aggregates and Different Water: Cement Ratios. *J. Mater. Civ. Eng.* **2018**, *31*, 04018376. [CrossRef]
50. Aslani, F.; Ma, G.; Yim Wan, D.L.; Muselin, G. Development of high-performance self-compacting concrete using waste recycled concrete aggregates and rubber granules. *J. Clean. Prod.* **2018**, *182*, 553–556. [CrossRef]
51. Nili, M.; Sasanipour, H.; Aslani, F. The Effect of Fine and Coarse Recycled Aggregates on Fresh and Mechanical Properties of Self-Compacting Concrete. *Materials* **2019**, *12*, 1120. [CrossRef]
52. Babalola, E.; Awoyera, P.O.; Tran, M.T.; Le, D.-H.; Olalusi, O.B.; Vilaria, A.; Ovallos-Gazabon, D. Mechanical and durability properties of recycled aggregate concrete with ternary binder system and optimized mix proportion. *J. Mater. Res. Technol.* **2020**, *9*, 6521–6532. [CrossRef]
53. Pan, Z.; Zhou, J.; Jiang, X.; Xu, Y.; Jin, R.; Mas, J.; Zhuang, Y.; Diao, Z.; Zhang, S.; Si, Q.; et al. Investigating the effects of steel slag powder on the properties of self-compacting concrete with recycled aggregates. *Constr. Build. Mater.* **2019**, *200*, 570–577. [CrossRef]
54. Bahrami, N.; Zohrabi, M.; Mahmoudy, S.A.; Akbari, M. Optimum recycled concrete aggregate and micro-silica content in self-compacting concrete: Rheological, mechanical and microstructural properties. *J. Build. Eng.* **2021**, *31*, 101361. [CrossRef]
55. Revathi, P.; Selvi, R.; Velin, S.S. Investigations on Fresh and Hardened Properties of Recycled Aggregate Self Compacting Concrete. *J. Inst. Eng. (India) Ser. A* **2013**, *94*, 179–185. [CrossRef]
56. Behera, M.; Minocha, A.K.; Bhattacharyya, S.K. Flow behavior, microstructure, strength and shrinkage properties of self-compacting concrete incorporating recycled fine aggregate. *Constr. Build. Mater.* **2019**, *228*, 116819. [CrossRef]
57. Revilla-Cuesta, V.; Ortega-López, V.; Skaf, M.; Manso, J.M. Effect of fine recycled concrete aggregate on the mechanical behavior of self-compacting concrete. *Constr. Build. Mater.* **2020**, *263*, 120671. [CrossRef]
58. Chakkamalayath, J.; Joseph, A.; Al-Baghli, H.; Hamadah, O.; Dashti, D.; Abdulmalek, N. Performance evaluation of self-compacting concrete containing volcanic ash and recycled coarse aggregates. *Asian J. Civ. Eng.* **2020**, *21*, 815–827. [CrossRef]

59. Sadeghi-Nik, A.; Berenjian, J.; Alimohammadi, S.; Lotfi-Omran, O.; Sadeghi-Nik, A.; Karimaei, M. The Effect of Recycled Concrete Aggregates and Metakaolin on the Mechanical Properties of Self-Compacting Concrete Containing Nanoparticles. *Iran. J. Sci. Technol. Trans. Civ. Eng.* **2018**, *43*, 503–515. [CrossRef]
60. Duan, Z.; Singh, A.; Xiao, J.; Hou, S. Combined use of recycled powder and recycled coarse aggregate derived from construction and demolition waste in self-compacting concrete. *Constr. Build. Mater.* **2020**, *254*, 119323. [CrossRef]
61. Señas, L.; Priano, C.; Marfil, S. Influence of recycled aggregates on properties of self-consolidating concretes. *Constr. Build. Mater.* **2016**, *113*, 498–505. [CrossRef]
62. Fiol, F.; Thomas, C.; Muñoz, C.; Ortega-López, V.; Manso, J.M. The influence of recycled aggregates from precast elements on the mechanical properties of structural self-compacting concrete. *Constr. Build. Mater.* **2018**, *182*, 309–323. [CrossRef]
63. Sharafi, Y.; Houshiar, M.; Aghebati, B. Recycled glass replacement as fine aggregate in self-compacting concrete. *Front. Struct. Civ. Eng.* **2013**, *7*, 419–428. [CrossRef]
64. Martínez-García, R.; Guerra-Romero, I.M.; Morán-del Pozo, J.M.; de Brito, J.; Juan-Valdés, A. Recycling Aggregates for Self-Compacting Concrete Production: A Feasible Option. *Materials* **2020**, *13*, 868. [CrossRef]
65. Khafaga, S.A. Production of high strength self compacting concrete using recycled concrete as fine and/or coarse aggregates. *World Appl. Sci. J.* **2014**, *29*, 465–474. Available online: https://www.idosi.org/wasj/wasj2914/1.pdf (accessed on 22 June 2022).
66. Gesoglu, M.; Güneyisi, E.; Öz, H.Ö.; Taha, I.; Yasemin, M.T. Failure characteristics of self-compacting concretes made with recycled aggregates. *Constr. Build. Mater.* **2015**, *98*, 334–344. [CrossRef]
67. Silva, Y.F.; Robayo, R.A.; Mattey, P.; Delvasto, S. Properties of self-compacting concrete on fresh and hardened with residue of masonry and recycled concrete. *Constr. Build. Mater.* **2016**, *124*, 639–644. [CrossRef]
68. Grdic, D.; Ristic, N.; Toplicic-Curcic, G.; Krstic, D. Potential of usage of self-compacting concrete with addition of recycled CRT glass for production of precast concrete elements. *Facta Univ.-Ser. Archit. Civ. Eng.* **2018**, *16*, 57–66. [CrossRef]
69. Singh, A.; Duan, Z.; Xiao, J.; Liu, Q. Incorporating recycled aggregates in self-compacting concrete: A review. *J. Sustain. Cem.-Based Mater.* **2019**, *9*, 165–189. [CrossRef]
70. Güneyisi, E.; Gesoğlu, M.; Algin, Z.; Yazici, H. Effect of surface treatment methods on the properties of self-compacting concrete with recycled aggregates. *Constr. Build. Mater.* **2014**, *64*, 172–183. [CrossRef]
71. Sun, C.; Chen, Q.; Xiao, J.; Liu, W. Utilization of waste concrete recycling materials in self-compacting concrete. *Resour. Conserv. Recycl.* **2020**, *161*, 104930. [CrossRef]
72. Guo, Z.; Jiang, T.; Zhang, J.; Kong, X.; Chen, C.; Lehman, D. E Mechanical and durability properties of sustainable self-compacting concrete with recycled concrete aggregate and fly ash, slag and silica fume. *Constr. Build. Mater.* **2020**, *231*, 117115. [CrossRef]
73. Surendar, M.; Gnana Ananthi, G.; Sharaniya, M.; Deepak, M.S.; Soundarya, T.V. Mechanical properties of concrete with recycled aggregate and M−sand. *Mater. Today Proc.* **2021**, *44*, 1723–1730. [CrossRef]
74. Katar, I.; Ibrahim, Y.; Abdul Malik, M.; Khahro, S.H. Mechanical Properties of Concrete with Recycled Concrete Aggregate and Fly Ash. *Recycling* **2021**, *6*, 23. [CrossRef]
75. Tang, W.C.; Ryan, P.C.; Cui, H.; Liao, W. Properties of Self-Compacting Concrete with Recycled Coarse Aggregate. *Adv. Mater. Sci. Eng.* **2016**, *2016*, 1–11. [CrossRef]
76. Khodair, Y.; Luqman. Self-compacting concrete using recycled asphalt pavement and recycled concrete aggregate. *J. Build. Eng.* **2017**, *12*, 282–287. [CrossRef]
77. Thienpont, T.; de Corte, W.; Seitl, S. Self-compacting Concrete, Protecting Steel Reinforcement under Cyclic Load: Evaluation of Fatigue Crack Behavior. *Procedia Eng.* **2016**, *160*, 207–213. [CrossRef]
78. Kou, S.C.; Poon, C.S. Properties of self-compacting concrete prepared with recycled glass aggregate. *Cem. Concr. Compos.* **2009**, *31*, 107–113. [CrossRef]
79. Tuyan, M.; Mardani-Aghabaglou, A.; Ramyar, K. Freeze–thaw resistance, mechanical and transport properties of self-consolidating concrete incorporating coarse recycled concrete aggregate. *Mater. Des.* **2014**, *53*, 983–991. [CrossRef]
80. Siva, S.; Krishna, R.; Sowjanya Vani, V.; Khader, S.; Baba, V. Studies on Mechanical Properties of Ternary Blended Self-Compacting Concrete Using Different Percentages of Recycled Aggregate. *Int. J. Civ. Eng. Technol. (IJCIET)* **2018**, *9*, 1672–1680. [CrossRef]
81. Uygunoılu, T.; Topçu, I.B.; Çelik, A.G. Use of waste marble and recycled aggregates in self-compacting concrete for environmental sustainability. *J. Clean. Prod.* **2014**, *84*, 691–700. [CrossRef]
82. Vinay Kumar, B.M.; Ananthan, H.; Balaji, K.V.A. Experimental studies on utilization of coarse and finer fractions of recycled concrete aggregates in self compacting concrete mixes. *J. Build. Eng.* **2017**, *9*, 100–108. [CrossRef]
83. Wang, J.; Dai, Q.; Si, R.; Ma, Y.; Guo, S. Fresh and mechanical performance and freeze-thaw durability of steel fiber-reinforced rubber self-compacting concrete (SRSCC). *J. Clean. Prod.* **2020**, *277*, 123180. [CrossRef]
84. Long, W.; Shi, J.; Wang, W.; Fang, X. Shrinkage of Hybrid Fiber Reinforced Self-Consolidating Concrete with Recycled Aggregate. In *Flowing Towards Sustainability, Proceedings of the SCC-2016 8th International RILEM Symposium on Self-Compacting Concrete, Washington, DC, USA, 15–18 May 2016*; Khayat, K.H., Ed.; RILEM: Paris, France, 2016; pp. 751–762.
85. Yu, T.; Fang, L.; Teng, J.G. FRP-Confined Self-Compacting Concrete under Axial Compression. *J. Mater. Civ. Eng.* **2014**, *26*, 04014082. [CrossRef]
86. Mahakavi, P.; Chithra, R. Effect of recycled coarse aggregate and manufactured sand in self compacting concrete. *Aust. J. Struct. Eng.* **2019**, *21*, 33–43. [CrossRef]

87. Chen, X.; Wu, S.; Zhou, J. Quantification of dynamic tensile behavior of cement-based materials. *Constr. Build. Mater.* **2014**, *51*, 15–23. [CrossRef]
88. Manzi, S.; Mazzotti, C.; Bignozzi, M.C. Self-compacting concrete with recycled concrete aggregate: Study of the long-term properties. *Constr. Build. Mater.* **2017**, *157*, 582–590. [CrossRef]
89. Rathakrishnan, V.; Beddu, S.; Ahmed, A. Comparison studies between machine learning optimisation technique on predicting concrete compressive strength. *Res. Square* **2021**. [CrossRef]
90. Hassan, A.N.; El-Hag, A. Two-Layer Ensemble-Based Soft Voting Classifier for Transformer Oil Interfacial Tension Prediction. *Energies* **2020**, *13*, 1735. [CrossRef]
91. Koya, B.P. Comparison of Different Machine Learning Algorithms to Predict Mechanical Properties of Concrete. Master's Thesis, University of Victoria, Victoria, Canada, 2021. Available online: http://hdl.handle.net/1828/12574 (accessed on 29 May 2022).
92. Khademi, F.; Jamal, S.; Deshpande, N.; Londhe, S. Predicting strength of recycled aggregate concrete using artificial neural network, adaptive neuro-fuzzy inference system and multiple linear regression. *Int. J. Sustain. Built Environ.* **2016**, *5*, 355–369. [CrossRef]
93. Uysal, M.; Tanyildizi, H. Predicting the core compressive strength of self-compacting concrete (SCC) mixtures with mineral additives using artificial neural network. *Constr. Build. Mater.* **2011**, *25*, 4105–4111. [CrossRef]
94. Hanbay, D.; Turkoglu, I.; Demir, Y. Prediction of wastewater treatment plant performance based on wavelet packet decomposition and neural networks. *Expert Syst. Appl.* **2008**, *34*, 1038–1043. [CrossRef]
95. Baghirli, O. Comparison of Lavenberg-Marquardt, Scaled Conjugate Gradient and Bayesian Regularization Backpropagation Algorithms for Multistep Ahead Wind Speed Forecasting Using Multilayer Perceptron Feedforward Neural Network. Master's Thesis, Uppsala University, Uppsala, Sweden, 2015. Available online: https://www.diva-portal.org/smash/record.jsf?pid=diva2%3A828170&dswid=6956 (accessed on 29 May 2022).
96. Babajanzadeh, M.; Azizifar, V. Compressive strength prediction of self-compacting concrete incorporating silica fume using artificial intelligence methods. *Civ. Eng. J.* **2018**, *4*, 1542.
97. Olu-Ajayi, R.; Alaka, H.; Sulaimon, I.; Sunmola, F.; Ajayi, S. Building energy consumption prediction for residential buildings using deep learning and other machine learning techniques. *J. Build. Eng.* **2022**, *45*, 103406. [CrossRef]
98. Suescum-Morales, D.; Salas-Morera, L.; Ramón Jiménez, J.; García-Hernández, L. A Novel Artificial Neural Network to Predict Compressive Strength of Recycled Aggregate Concrete. *Appl. Sci.* **2021**, *11*, 11077. [CrossRef]
99. Shang, M.; Li, H.; Ahmad, A.; Ahmad, W.; Ostrowski, K.; Aslam, F.; Joyklad, P.; Majka, T.M. Predicting the Mechanical Properties of RCA-Based Concrete Using Supervised Machine Learning Algorithms. *Materials* **2022**, *15*, 647. [CrossRef] [PubMed]

MDPI
St. Alban-Anlage 66
4052 Basel
Switzerland
Tel. +41 61 683 77 34
Fax +41 61 302 89 18
www.mdpi.com

Mathematics Editorial Office
E-mail: mathematics@mdpi.com
www.mdpi.com/journal/mathematics